D1716891

Cognition and Consciousness

The Dorsey Series in Psychology

Advisory Editors
Wendell E. Jeffrey
University of California, Los Angeles

Salvatore R. Maddi
The University of Chicago

Cognition
and
Consciousness

Colin Martindale, Ph.D.
University of Maine

 1981

THE DORSEY PRESS   Homewood, Illinois   60430
Irwin-Dorsey Limited   Georgetown, Ontario   L7G 4B3

ISBN 0-256-02408-1
Library of Congress Catalog Card No. 81–65112

Printed in the United States of America

1 2 3 4 5 6 7 8 9 0 MP 8 7 6 5 4 3 2 1

Preface

Scientific psychology began its existence a little over a century ago with the aim of explaining how the mind works. Early psychologists made some progress toward this goal but encountered many obstacles. Some of these obstacles—such as the difficulties inherent in direct or introspective observation of mental activity—led psychologists to abandon their original goal. Throughout much of the 20th century there was a consensus among psychologists that the proper subject matter of psychology should be observable behavior rather than unobservable mental events. These behavioral psychologists argued that behavior should not even be explained in terms of mental activity. In other words, the behaviorists said that psychology should have nothing to do with answering the question of how the mind works. It should be a science of behavior, not a science of the mind. In retrospect, it would seem that this behaviorist "retreat" from the historical subject matter of psychology was both unwise and unnecessary.

In increasing numbers psychologists have recently been concluding that a purely behavioral psychology is neither possible nor desirable. Human behavior simply cannot be plausibly explained without recourse to cognitive or mental processes. If this is the case, then we must develop methods for studying these processes. Cognitive psychologists argue that psychology should reorient itself toward its original goal of explaining mental activity. They hold that this goal can in fact be approached at least indirectly by observing overt behavior. Their confidence is supported by the steady accumulation of knowledge concerning cognitive processes.

The basic aim of this book is to present the most important findings of cognitive psychology in the context of a general theory of how the mind works. Early cognitive psychologists worked within the framework of what has been called a structural or stage model of mind. In this view, mental activity was seen as being analogous to the passage of information from one place to another in a computer. Perception, attention, and memory were seen as different stages in the transformation of information. As we shall see, there are grave difficulties with this model. More recently, psychologists have begun to converge on a "process" model of cognition. In this view, mental activity is seen as corresponding to the activation of preexisting cognitive units which are arranged in hierarchical fashion in various "analyzers" or systems. These cognitive units and associations among them code our long-term knowledge of the world. Depending upon how cognitive units are activated, we may speak of perception, attention, imagination, short-term memory, or consciousness. In the first half of this book, I have elaborated on one version of the process model of cognition and used it as a framework for presenting what we know about cognition.

A subsidiary aim in writing this book has been to apply cognitive psychology to many phenomena to which it has not generally been applied. It is self-evident to me that a viable science of cognition cannot restrict itself to explaining the mental activities of waking, rational subjects in psychological laboratories. If we are to have a complete understanding of mind, we need to study mental activity in all of its forms. We need to explore altered states of consciousness as well as normal, waking consciousness. We need to understand the "irrational" thought of the poet as well as the rational thought of the subject solving a logical problem. We need to study how one remembers the plot of a novel as well as how one remembers a list of nonsense syllables. We need to investigate the historical evolution of ideas in the real world as well as how concepts are formed in laboratory situations. Finally, since people are not computers, we must ask how emotional and motivational factors affect cognition. In the second half of the book, I have attempted to apply the general model of cognition to such traditionally "noncognitive" phenomena. I hope that the reader will agree that this attempt does shed new light on these phenomena and that, in so doing, the model itself is enriched and expanded.

In writing this book I have assumed no specialized background beyond an introductory course in psychology on the part of the reader. A more extensive background in psychology would, however, certainly be no hindrance. The first nine chapters cover the basic topics of cognitive psychology. They should be read in order, as later chapters build upon the foundations laid in earlier ones. For those in a hurry, Chapters 2 and 5 may be omitted. Chapter 2 is essentially an extended attempt to disabuse the reader of the commonsense notion that perception yields veridical images of the external world. It can be omitted by those few who do not hold to this notion. Chapter 5 treats the topic of word recognition in depth, as an example of how perception and recognition of other classes of stimuli hypothetically occur. It can be omitted by those willing to accept the general model of perception and recognition presented in Chapter 4 without extensive supporting evidence. Chapter 10 provides a bridge between the more purely cognitive topics of the first half of the book and the applications of these topics dealt with in the second half of the book. Chapters 11–16 need not be read in order, but they should be read after Chapters 1–10 since they build upon the principles laid down in these earlier chapters.

A number of colleagues and reviewers have provided helpful comments on portions of this book. I would especially like to thank Bruce L. Brown, James I. Chumbley, Gerald C. Davison, Diana Deutsch, Michel Grimaud, Michael Hartman, Ravenna Helson, Edmund S. Howe, Wendell Jeffrey, Anne Uemura, Robert E. Warren, and Alan West. I owe a special debt of gratitude to Roger Frey, Chairman of the Department of Psychology at the University of Maine, for provision of clerical assistance and of a pleasant milieu in which to think and work. Finally, I wish to thank Eva Benson, Lori Miller, Marian Perry, and Anne Theriault, who patiently typed and retyped successive drafts of the manuscript of this book.

COLIN MARTINDALE

Contents

tention. The capacity of attention: *Kahneman's model. What operations re-quire attention? Ability for divided attention.*

The subjective lexicon. Semantic feature theory. The semantic analyzer. Net-work models of semantic memory: *The hierarchical nature of semantic memory. Type nodes versus token nodes. Stored versus inferred knowledge. Spreading activation. False statements.* The strength of relations in semantic memory: *Production of category instances. Typicality. Similarity judgments.* Context effects: *Clustering. Typicality and memory. Category cues.* Masking: *Rate of production of category instances. Part-list cues. Inhibition by coor-dinate priming. Inhibition by category priming.* Semantic satiation. Concept formation: *Artificial categories. Natural categories. The Whorfian hypothesis.*

Types of memory: *Structural memory. Primary memory. Episodic memory.* Structure of the episodic analyzer: *Is there really an episodic analyzer? Episodic chunking. Propositions. Episode units. Functions. Lateral inhibition among episodic units.* Acquisition of episodic memories: *Reinforcement. Repetition. Attention. Depth of processing.* What is remembered? *Abstract-ness of episodic memories. Memory for sentences. Mediation. Sensory-motor memories. Visual memories. Reconstruction versus veridical memo-ries.* Retrieval: *Accessing episodic units. Assessing episodic units. Necessity of episodic chunking units. Encoding specificity.* Forgetting: *Decay. Interfer-ence. Conclusions.*

Arousal and cognition. Measurement: *Psychophysiological indexes. Self-reports.* Components of arousal. Determinants of arousal: *Arousal potential. Habituation. Cognitive units and arousal. Cycles. Drugs. Self-control. In-dividual differences.* The Yerkes-Dodson law: *Task complexity. Rate of information input. Hullian theory and the Yerkes-Dodson law.* Arousal, stimulation, and reinforcement: *Pleasure centers in the brain. Sensory deprivation. Reinforcing properties of stimulation.* Hedonic tone: *The Wundt curve. Neural basis of the Wundt curve. Psychophysical variables. Collative variables. Ecological variables. Adaptation level.*

Type of cognition and locus of neural activity. The triune brain: *Evolution of the brain. The R-complex. The limbic system. The neomammalian brain.* The cerebral hemispheres: *Methods of study. Left-hemisphere functions. Right-hemisphere functions. Hemispheric division of labor.*

1

Introduction

WHAT IS COGNITIVE PSYCHOLOGY?

Cognition refers to the process of knowing. Therefore, cognitive psychology deals with the questions of how an organism gathers, processes, stores, and uses information about its world. Cognitive psychologists use the term *knowledge* to include not only specialized knowledge, such as how to fix a car or how to play chess, but also knowledge in the broadest sense of the term. How does a person understand the meaning of words? How does a person recognize a friend's face? How does a person remember past events? All of these activities involve knowledge of one sort or another and are of interest to cognitive psychology. A moment's thought should reveal to you that any individual has a vast store of knowledge. The questions of interest to cognitive psychology include how the person came to have this information, how it is stored, and how it is used.

Cognitive psychologists hold that knowledge is stored in the form of internal or mental representations that stand for or symbolize external realities. These representations are ultimately derived from external reality; that is, they are based upon perception. However, perception does not give direct knowledge of the world. Perception is an active process involving the construction of a model of the world rather than a mere passive reception of external reality. Our perceptions are determined as much by our organs of perception as by what is really out there. Chapters 1–5 of this book are devoted to convincing you that this is the case and to describing how perception works. Chapters 6–9 deal with the organization of the mental representations that are derived from perception. In these chapters, we shall discuss the structure of memory for everything from *concepts* to what happened to a person the day before yesterday. Chapters 10–12 are devoted to the use of cognitive structures in thought and attention. Finally, in Chapters 13–16, the cognitive model is applied to questions concerning such topics as states of consciousness, creativity, and the understanding of complex narratives.

PARADIGMS IN PSYCHOLOGY

Introspectionism

The three dominant paradigms or approaches in 20th-century American psychology are introspectionism, behaviorism, and cognitive psychology. At the beginning of the century, psychology was dominated by the introspectionist approach. Introspectionists, exemplified by E. B. Titchener (1923), held that the proper subject matter of psychology is the study of consciousness or mental processes. Many of the methods employed by the introspectionists were subjective. Introspection involves an attempt to observe one's own mental activities as they occur. Of course, we observe our mental activities all the time. Because introspectionists felt that such casual observation is of little value, they held that observers must be trained in introspective methods in order to obtain useful data. Such training, however, opened the possibility that observers were in reality being trained only to observe whatever a given theorist expected that they should find. There was no real way to correct this problem, since no one can look into another person's mind. Because it was subjective, introspection was inherently unreliable.

Behaviorism

The behaviorists, led by J. B. Watson (1913), objected to the subjective and unreliable nature of introspection. They argued that overt behavior can be measured objectively by any observer who cares to do so. Unlike mental events, which are private, behavior is public. Hence, there is no problem in obtaining reliable observations. Two observers can both observe the same behavior—for example, a rat turning right or left at a given point in a maze—and agree on what they have seen. The behaviorist critique of introspection went even further. Watson (1913) argued that the proper subject matter of psychology is behavior rather than mental events and that there is no evidence that mental events are of any use in predicting behavior. He did not deny that mental events occur, but he did deny that they could be studied or that there was any value in studying them. The behaviorist idea was that mental events are just epiphenomena or by-products. Whatever causes behavior may also incidentally cause mental events (Skinner, 1975). Behaviorism was initially successful at explaining the behavior of lower animals, but it ran into grave difficulties when confronted with the problem of explaining complex human abilities, such as language. Its failure to offer adequate explanations for such phenomena opened the way for cognitive psychology.

Cognitive psychology

Cognitive psychology represents something of a return to the historical subject matter of psychology, since it asks questions concerning the nature of consciousness and of mind. The cognitive psychologist is in full agreement with the introspectionists that the proper subject matter of psychology is mind rather than behavior. As Paivio (1975) points out, however, cognitive psychology uses objective rather than subjective methods. Overt behavior is observed in order to infer mental events.

Cognitivism versus behaviorism

Behavioristic psychology was interested in what goes on within the organism only as a sort of last resort. The behaviorist psychologists postulated intervening variables or hypothetical constructs only when it became impossible to explain responses solely in terms of stimuli. Where a response was perfectly predictable from a stimulus, the behaviorist felt no necessity to discuss intervening psychological processes. In such a case, the cognitive psychologist would still maintain an interest in the internal processes that link stimulus and response. The real interest of behaviorism was in overt and observable behavior. Cognitive psychology, on the other hand, is primarily focused on what goes on inside the organism. Behavior is of interest only to the extent that it sheds light on internal processes rather than vice versa.

Cognitive psychology has also come to mean a particular information-processing approach to questions concerning mental activity. This approach involves a computer model of the mind. That is, cognitive psychology often tries to understand the mental workings of people by analogy with the operations of computers. A computer takes input (for example, cards with holes punched into them), transforms this input into a qualitatively different internal representation (a pattern of electrical charges), performs operations on this internal representation, and finally transforms it into output (for example, a pattern on a cathode ray tube) that is in a qualitatively different code from either the input or the internal representation. One quite real impetus for the development of cognitive psychology was that it seemed rather strained to maintain that computers can perform operations on internal representations and produce obviously useful results while denying—as behaviorism insisted upon doing—that human beings have this capacity.

The model of man at any given time often seems to be based ultimately upon the dominant technology of the age. Early views of man, such as *vitalism*, mirrored the agrarian economy of the times. Man was seen as following predetermined patterns of growth, just as plants seem to do. With the advent of mechanical technology, mechanistic models of man soon followed. In the steam age, hydraulic models came into fashion. Freud's view of man as a thermodynamically regulated machine is the clearest example of such a model. Perhaps the early 20th century telephone switchboard model of man was not so much a consequence of failures of earlier models as of a fascination with the analogies between organismic action and electrical switching circuits. Finally, the new computer models reillustrate the power of humanity's inventions in shaping our view of ourselves.

Talking about inputs, central processing, and outputs may at first seem to be little different than talking about stimuli, intervening variables, and responses. But there are really differences on several levels. Behavioral or stimulus-response psychology was prone to see internal events in terms of associationistic connections. According to Bolles (1975), behaviorist psychology rested upon a correspondence assumption. This was the assumption that there is an *isomorphism* or similarity between observable external events and unobservable internal events. A change in the strength of a response to a given stimulus was attributed to the strengthening of a bond or link between the neural event representing the stimulus and the neural event representing the response. Thus, the only internal processes were seen as being series of covert stimulus-response bonds. This left no place at all for constructs such as goals, purposes, or intentions let alone such constructs as ideas or images. These constructs cannot easily be construed as being simple stimulus-response associations.

On the other hand, the information-processing approach—because of its implicit computer analogy—is more prone to think of internal events in terms of programs and transformations that are not easily visualized as simple associations, wires, or connections running between two points. As Paivio (1975) points out, the basic atoms of mental activity are seen by cognitive psychologists as being qualitatively different from covert stimuli, covert responses, or covert stimulus-response bonds (just as the atoms of a computer's internal activity are qualitatively different from both its inputs and its outputs). A second difference is perhaps more important. A central telephone switchboard is a linking or gating device, which does nothing but connect two callers. Behavioral psychologists were prone, then, to try to think as little as possible about what went on between the two callers (that is, between stimulus and response). The cognitive approach inverts this approach. The focus is more on central mechanisms, such as thought and consciousness, and on looking at behavior in order to infer laws of central processing rather than being satisfied with formulating laws of behavior per se.

MODELS OF PERCEPTION

The copy theory

Before considering how the mind works, we must consider that on which it works. What is the nature of the inputs or percepts that are known by the mind? Historically, there have been two opposite approaches to the question of the nature of perception. What might be called the copy theory of perception holds that our subjective perceptual impressions are veridical copies or images of external reality. This is also the commonsense view of perception—that it is a passive reception of reality. The theory was first proposed by the Greek philosopher Democritus, who held that everything is composed of atoms of various types. Any object hypothetically emanates some of its atoms; that is, it throws off an image composed of atoms that are exactly like the atoms that compose it. This image enters the body of the perceiver and constitutes the percept. Objects seem rough or smooth, for example, because they are composed of rough or smooth atoms and some of these atoms penetrate the pores of the skin of the person who touches them. Vision consists of an actual image of the object which enters the perceiver's eyes.

Versions of this theory remained popular until the 17th century. By then, it became clear that the stimulus itself could not enter the body. However, a modified copy theory was proposed by Descartes (1662). Descartes's modified theory was that perception is not of the physical stimulus itself but of something bearing an exact, one-to-one relationship to it. Descartes's basic idea was that stimuli impinge upon sensory receptors and form an impression, such as a seal would form if it were pressed into wax. This impression excites motion of fluids that hypothetically fill the nerves. The result is that a copy of the impression is transmitted to the brain where it is perceived by the mind. How the mind goes about perceiving this image was not explained.

There are all sorts of problems with the copy theory, as we shall see. Several are rather immediately apparent. First, the theory does not really explain any-thing. If one holds that a copy of external reality is sent to the brain or to the mind, this merely complicates the issue. It is still necessary to explain how this copy is perceived. Second, we now know that the physical stimulus that produces a perception and the subjective perception are qualitatively dissimilar. For exam-ple, you hear sounds, but the physical stimulus that produced these sounds was vibration of air molecules. The mental event of hearing and the physical event of vibrating air are completely different. Hearing is not, in any sense, a copy of vi-brating air molecules. By the same token, odors are produced by certain mole-cules. The mental experience of smelling is in no sense a copy of these molecules. The same considerations apply to all of the other senses.

The solipsistic theory

The solipsistic or idealistic approach to perception is based on the inverse argument that sensory impressions are pure constructions of the senses. This theory was proposed by Bishop George Berkeley (1710). The copy theory implies a passive reception of impressions while the solipsistic view sees perception as an active process of construction. In regard to vision, the copy theorist would argue that what we see is an exact copy of what exists in reality. The solipsist would argue that there is no reality at all and that our eyes create everything we see. The two types of theorists would put forth similar arguments in regard to all of the other senses as well.

While the solipsistic viewpoint may seem silly at first, it is difficult to refute. The only evidence we have for the existence of reality comes through our senses. We know that our perceptual impressions exist, but that is all we know or can know. It requires an act of faith to suppose that these impressions are, in fact, caused by some external reality. What sense does it make to say that perception gives a copy of reality if there is no way of testing this assertion? There is no way of finding out what reality is except by perception. Thus, we could never find out if perception gives a veridical copy of it or not.

Well, you might argue, one can simply ask other people if their perceptions agree with one's own. This objection misses the point of the solipsistic argument. What evidence does one have for the existence of these other people? Of course, one can see, hear, and touch them, but this is all perceptual evidence. There is no other nonperceptual evidence for the existence of these other people. Thus, their reality is just as questionable as the reality of everything else. Although the solipsistic view is the philosophically more tenable theory, from a practical point of view, we lead our lives—usually with some success—as if the copy theory were true. This incongruity is resolved by what we shall call the relational theory of perception.

The relational theory

The relational theory holds that perceptual impressions are a joint function of both reality and our organs of perception. That is, what we perceive is not an exact copy of external reality but neither is it created wholly by our senses. Rather, what we see looks the way it does partly because of the way our eyes and brains are built and partly because of what the external stimulus is really like. William James (1890) compared perception to a statue. The statue is carved by the sculptor (the organs of perception) out of a block of marble (reality). Many statues could be carved from any block of marble. The stone puts only very general constraints on the final product. On the other hand, the sculptor certainly could not have created the statue out of thin air. The marble (reality) had to be there to give the sculptor something to work on.

If we take this view of perception seriously—and you will see as we go along that we *must* take it seriously—it has some far-reaching consequences for our view of the world. Let us look first at a philosophical aspect of the problem: How is it that we perceive objects in space? The English empiricists, such as John Locke (1690), argued that we learn to do this. The infant comes into the world as a *tabula rasa*. By watching the movement of objects, it gradually infers or learns the concept of space. This property of the world is thus hypothetically acquired from experience by means that are not radically different from those processes whereby we learn our names or the multiplication tables. Immanuel Kant (1781) pointed out some grave logical difficulties with this analysis. One could not perceive objects in the first place unless one already had the capacity to perceive in spatial terms. The concept of object *presupposes* the concept of space. Unless one could perceive space in the first place, objects could not be perceived. If you could not apprehend things or objects as existing in space, how could you apprehend them at all? An object has some volume or extension in space. An object with no length or breadth or width is an impossibility, since an object is something that takes up some space. Note that the very definition of an object thus presupposes the notion of space. How could our hypothetical infant see the movement of objects if not in space? It is logically impossible that things could work the way Locke said they did. The infant would have to have the ability for spatial perception before it could perceive objects. Thus, it is illogical to say that the infant learned the ability for spatial perception by observing objects. On the contrary, Kant argued, space must be an a priori or given preexisting property of mind or perception and not of the world. Reality may or may not be organized in terms of space. There is no way of knowing this, Kant argued. All we can know is that the mind organizes percepts in terms of space.

The same considerations apply to the question of why we perceive events as occurring in a temporal sequence. Locke argued that we learn the concept of time by observing that one event follows another. Kant points out that this argument is illogical. The ability to observe that one event follows another presupposes the concept of time. If perception were not already organized in terms of time, a temporal sequence of events could not be perceived in the first place. Kant went on to give similar analyses of a number of categories of knowing such as causality and plurality. All of these, he showed, must be properties of the mind rather than properties of the world. For Kant, the perceived world is, then, a joint product of unknowable things in themselves and a priori categories of understanding. The implications of this formulation are mind boggling.

Some analogies may help in understanding Kant's point. First, let us consider what he did not mean. For all we know, reality may exist in 16 dimensions rather than in the 3 we know. In this case, we would never be able to know what reality is really like. But this is not what Kant meant. The situation is even worse than this. Things may not exist in space and time at all. That is merely the way our organs of perception organize them. There is no way of knowing how things are really structured. For example, consider the organizational chart of a business firm (see Figure 1–1A).

FIGURE 1–1   Examples of schematic charts that do not have one-to-one relationships with physical reality

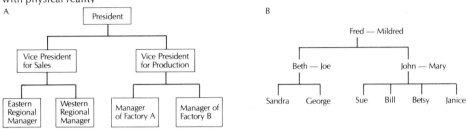

The president is at the top and is connected with the vice presidents on the next line, and so on. A family tree is also organized in this way (see Figure 1–1B). What do these diagrams have to do with the actual realities? They represent in a very abstract way a certain conceptual set of relationships. Certainly they do not mirror concrete reality. The business firm does not exist on the piece of paper or even in a pyramidal building with the president on the top floor, the vice presidents on the next floor, and so on. Your grandfather is above you in only a completely metaphorical sense. Certainly no sort of wire, cord, or line links the two of you. These things seem obvious because we realize that the diagrams are mere schematic abstractions. We can easily see, hear, and think about these phenomena from other perspectives, so we know that the diagrams do not set forth the whole of reality. But these other perspectives are not ultimate reality. Reality, for Kant, bears the same relationship to our perceptions as the physical layout of a factory bears to its organizational chart. Unfortunately, we have only one perspective on reality. We cannot know how it is really organized. A person who had never perceived factories or people other than via charts or organizational hierarchies, family trees, and the like might think that these things were reality. Kant says that this is exactly our situation. Our perceptions are to reality just as these charts are to the things they represent.

EVIDENCE THAT PERCEPTION IS NOT A COPY OF REALITY

If you distrust philosophical arguments, let us see if empirical considerations also lead us to the conclusion that perception is not a copy of reality. In the next several sections we shall consider several lines of research that lead us to exactly this conclusion. Each of these lines of research demonstrates that the organs of perception, as well as reality, determine what we perceive.

The question of interest is how a stimulus is related to the mental events of sensation and perception. By a stimulus we mean a pattern of physical energy, such as electromagnetic waves or vibrations of air molecules. A sensation refers to the activity of sensory receptors that are excited by physical stimuli. Examples would be the sensations of redness, roughness, or coldness. A perception is more organized than its component sensations. Generally, we speak of perceiving meaningful objects, such as trees, circles, or books. The copy theory would lead us to believe that there should be a fairly direct or one-to-one correspondence between stimuli and sensations and between sensations and perceptions. The result would be that perceptions could be seen as copies of physical reality. On the other hand, the relational theory holds that sensations are jointly produced by physical stimuli and sensory receptors and that perceptions are jointly produced by sensations and the perceptual apparatus. The result would be that perceptions are not simply copies of physical reality.

Sensory phenomena

SENSORY SELECTIVITY

Common sense tells us that our senses are windows on the world that serve to bring as much information as possible into consciousness. But it turns out that it is more profitable to take just the opposite viewpoint. Our sensory receptors really serve to reduce, filter, and exclude as much data as possible. This becomes clear if we look at the very limited range of stimuli to which our receptors respond. Let us consider vision. The electromagnetic spectrum ranges in wavelength from a billionth of a meter up to more than a thousand meters (see Figure 1–2). Of this spectrum we only see the tiny portion between 400 and 700 billionths of

FIGURE 1–2   The electromagnetic spectrum

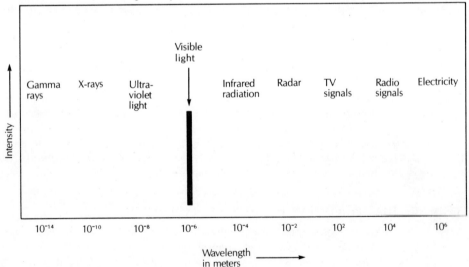

a meter. Our eyes are completely insensitive to everything else. It is beyond our conception as to what an x-ray would look like or what color it would be. There is a similar selectivity for all of the senses. We can hear only a small segment of the frequency range of vibrations, we can smell only a few of the molecules that exist, and so on.

An extreme in sensory selectivity is perhaps reached by the wood tick. The female of this species, once mated, climbs onto a branch or twig and stays there, oblivious to all stimuli, until she detects the smell of butyric acid, a component of sweat. This smell causes her to release her grip. She hopefully lands on the animal passing underneath and deposits her eggs. The biologist von Uexküll (1934) was able to keep a dormant tick in his laboratory for 17 years. When, after all this time, she was exposed to the odor of butyric acid, she came to life. It was not so much that the tick was dormant as that—for it—no stimuli had occurred for 17 years.

SENSORY THRESHOLDS

Just as we are sensitive only to a limited qualitative range of stimuli, we can only perceive stimuli within a limited range of quantity or magnitude. A stimulus must be above a certain *threshold* if it is to be perceived (see Figure 1–2). It must also be below an upper limit if it is not to destroy the sense organ in question. Thus, our senses are really like walls to the world into which are punched very tiny windows or pinholes. If the small black space in Figure 1–2 represents the window, you can see that the white area of the wall is much greater.

Research on signal detection has shown that sensory thresholds are not absolute (Tanner and Swets, 1954). It is not the case that a stimulus below a certain intensity will never be detected while a stimulus above a certain intensity will always be detected. Rather, detection of weak stimuli is probabalistic. In testing a person's hearing, tones of varying intensities are presented and the person is asked to say if the tone is heard. A very loud tone will, of course, be heard unless the person has a hearing loss. However, around the threshold of hearing, things are not so simple. On some trials, a tone will be heard; while on other trials, the very same tone will be missed or not heard. Furthermore, the person may have false alarms. He or she may "hear" something when a tone was not presented. Psychological factors are crucial in such a signal detection task. For example, if it is very important for the person to detect tones, actual sensory acuity may not change but the rate of false alarms may increase. This is because the person has changed the criterion for deciding that something has been heard. Something analogous happens when you decide to take a bath while waiting for an important phone call. You may hear the phone ringing over the running water even though it is not, in fact, ringing. Psychological factors—not just the presence or absence of a physical stimulus—can determine whether a signal will result in a sensation.

PHYSICAL INTENSITY VERSUS SENSED INTENSITY

But what of the metaphorical pinhole on reality with which our senses provide us? Does it invert our perceptions like looking through a real pinhole would, or is there a one-to-one correspondence between sensation and reality at least here? The answer would seem to be neither. Let us consider the question of how intense stimuli seem to be. The question of the relationship between the physical intensity of a stimulus and its psychic or sensed intensity was first investigated by Gustav Fechner over 100 years ago. It was he who founded the science of psychophysics, which deals with the question of the relationship between the physical and mental world. Fechner's partially correct intuition of this relationship is incorporated in Stevens's power law (1966): Subjective intensity, J, is a function of physical intensity, I, raised to a power, p, which is different for different sensory modalities. In symbols:

$$J = kI^p$$

where k is a mathematical constant. Figure 1–3 gives illustrations of this rela-

FIGURE 1–3   The relationship between perceived intensity and physical intensity

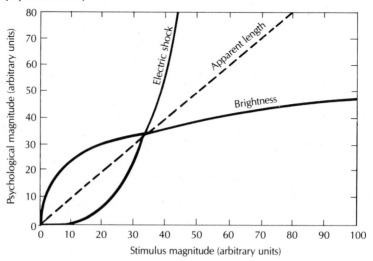

Source: S. S. Stevens, "The Psychophysics of Sensory Function," in *Sensory Communication*, ed. W. A. Rosenblith (Cambridge, Mass.: MIT Press, 1961), p. 11

tionship for selected sensory modalities. If $p = 1$, as it is for judgments of length, then there is indeed a one-to-one relationship between the physical and the mental world. But modalities for which $p = 1$ are the exception rather than the rule. If p is less than 1, then we have a negatively accelerated curve. What does this mean? Imagine a machine that produces flashes of light. Every flash of light is twice as bright as the previous one. Let's start the machine at an imaginary subject's threshold and ask the person to tell us how bright the flashes are. For a few trials, the subject will say something to the effect that each flash is twice as bright as the one before. But soon our subject will be saying that successive flashes seem to be just a bit brighter than previous ones, but not much. In fact, we have built the machine to double intensity in physical units each time, but that is not what the subject sees. Our experience of brightness does not bear a one-to-one relationship to the physical intensity of light. As the physical intensity of a light increases, so does the psychic or sensed intensity, but at a slower rate. Now assume that we rewire our machine to deliver electric shocks. Figure 1–3 illustrates that we will get very different responses from our subjects. Let us say we deliver a series of shocks each double the intensity of the previous one starting at our subject's threshold. The first few shocks will indeed seem to double. But then the subject will report—no doubt in less polite and precise terminology —that the next shock is 4 times as great as the previous one, the next 16 times as great, and so on. Thus, there is a lawful or regular relation between physical stimulation and subjective sensation, but it does not have one-to-one fidelity.

AFTEREFFECTS

Brief stimulation results in a sensation that persists for a fraction of a second after the actual physical stimulus is no longer present. This is called a *positive aftereffect*. There is an easy way of seeing visual positive aftereffects. Look straight ahead in a dark room and slowly move a lighted cigarette from side to side at arm's length. You will see a trail of light following the light produced by the glow of the cigarette. This trail of light, called *Bidwell's ghost,* is a positive aftereffect. The cigarette does not, of course, really leave a trail of light behind it. You are seeing a sensory memory from the past. We are not normally aware of positive aftereffects because they fade during the time it takes to move the eyes from one fixation point to another.

Prolonged stimulation results in a sensation that is precisely the opposite from the original sensation. This is called a *negative aftereffect*. If you stare fixedly at the black cross in Figure 1–4 for a few moments and then move your eyes to the center of the gray square, you will see a negative aftereffect: a white cross. A

FIGURE 1–4　Demonstration of a negative afterimage. Stare fixedly at the black cross for about a minute and then look at the gray field.

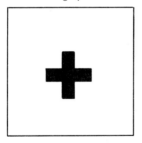 

similar phenomenon can be demonstrated with colors. If you stare fixedly at a red patch of color for a few seconds and then look away at a white surface, you will see a green patch of color. If you had stared first at a green patch of color, the aftereffect would have been red.

Positive aftereffects always occur before negative ones. Theoretically, a positive aftereffect is brief persistence of activity in the sensory receptor that detected the stimulus. It takes longer for the receptor to be deactivated than for the brief stimulus to disappear. Prolonged stimulation of a receptor leads it to become fatigued or adapted. This produces the negative aftereffect. Normally, when you look at a white surface, the red receptors and the green receptors cancel out each other's activity. However, if one set of receptors has been fatigued, this does not happen and you see the complementary color. With both positive and negative aftereffects, you see something that is not produced by the presence of a physical stimulus. On the contrary, the sensation is produced by your sensory receptors.

CONTRAST EFFECTS

Contrast effects are related to sensory aftereffects in that they demonstrate sensations produced by the sensory receptors rather than by physical reality. Look at the two patches of gray in Figure 1–5. Both are exactly the same shade of gray.

FIGURE 1–5   Demonstration of simultaneous contrast.
Both patches of gray are exactly the same shade; however,
the surrounding context makes them appear different.

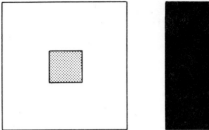

However, the one surrounded by the white field appears distinctly darker. This effect is called *simultaneous contrast;* the surrounding context of a stimulus influences the sensation that it induces.

Successive contrast refers to the case where an earlier sensation influences a later one. John Locke (1690) introduced the classic demonstration of this phenomenon. Take three glasses of water. Fill one with hot water, one with ice water, and the third with lukewarm water. Put your right hand in the hot water and your left hand in the cold water. After a few seconds you will note that the hot water seems less hot and the cold water seems less cold. This is because of the adaptation of the temperature receptors in your skin. Now, plunge both hands into the lukewarm water. It will feel cold to your right hand and hot to your left hand. The very same stimulus (the lukewarm water) is producing opposite sensations. It is difficult to argue in favor of the copy theory of perception while your hands are immersed in this contradictory water.

Perceptual corrections

We have produced evidence that our sensations do not have an exact or one-to-one correspondence with physical stimuli. In this section, we shall consider whether our perceptions have any exact correspondence with our sensations. As you will see, several profound perceptual corrections automatically lead us to perceive what we know we should be perceiving rather than something corresponding to our raw sensations. Our perception of external reality is hypothetically determined not only by reality but also by our organs of perception. Over the long course of evolution, we have evolved adaptive perceptual rules that, given our average expected environment, will give us useful information. But since evolution cannot provide for adaptation to all possible environments, our perceptual rules will only work over a certain range. It should be possible to construct perceptual tricks or illusions that lie outside this range. This is one of the ways psychologists have sought to investigate perception. The effect that such tricks produce sheds light on what the perceptual rules are.

STABILITY OF THE VISUAL WORLD

One of the most basic and easy ways to demonstrate perceptual corrections concerns the stability of our visual world. Why is it that we can see objects moving in the world, but we can move our heads or eyes without the world seeming to move? In both cases—objects actually moving and moving one's head—patterns of light move across the retina in exactly the same way. Obviously, only real movement is sensed as such, but why is this? The differentiation is accomplished by means of a feedback network that allows us to compensate automatically for head and eye movements. When the motor system operates, the visual system knows this and compensates for the exact degree of movement. We see what we know is supposed to be there, not anything with a one-to-one correspondence with patterns of light on the retina. Some animals do not have such a compensation mechanism. The housefly's world moves every time that its head moves. It has no way of discriminating this sort of movement from actual movement of objects in its visual field. This is why its movements are so jumpy and erratic. You can get a fly's eye view of the world by mechanically moving your own eye. Just press lightly on the outside of your eye. You will see the object in front of you jump in an opposite direction to that you have mechanically moved your eye. In the course of evolution, it was adaptive to develop a compensation system for voluntary eye movements. Since organisms other than children and experimental psychologists do not tend to move their eyes with their fingers, there was no evolutionary necessity to correct for this possibility. We can use such an evolutionary programming oversight to get some idea of how the program works.

THE BLIND SPOT ON THE RETINA

Another sort of compensation we make is for the blind spot on our retinas where the axons of the nerve cells collect to form the optic nerve. At this collection point, there are no receptor cells. Thus, any stimulus falling on this point of the retina cannot be seen. Focus your left eye on the X in Figure 1–6A. Now gradually move the book closer to your eyes. At some point, the dot to left of the X will vanish. It is now on the blind spot of your retina where there are no receptor cells. Without this sort of special effort, you cannot see this hole in your visual world. Since you know it is there, you compensate for it. Now focus on the X in Figure 1–6B and move the book toward and away from your eyes. There will be no point at which a gap appears in the bar to the left of the X. This is because the gap is being automatically closed up. Since most of the image of the bar falls onto visual receptors, this information is used to fill in the small gap. This is why you are not aware of the blind spot in everyday life.

FIGURE 1–6   Demonstration of the blind spot on the retina

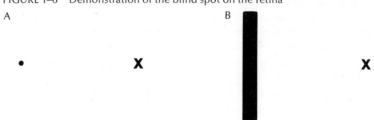

A   B

EXPERIMENTS WITH DISTORTING LENSES

Studies of the effects of wearing distorting lenses contribute to the view of perception that we are building. Stratton (1897) designed glasses that reversed the visual field from right to left and from top to bottom. As might be imagined, when he put on these glasses, tasks involving vision became tremendously difficult. Pouring a glass of water became a major operation, since the water seemed to flow upwards. Also, the world lost its stability. Head and eye movements made the world swing violently about. Since the glasses inverted right and left, the built-in corrections we described earlier malfunctioned: They now exacerbated rather than corrected for the effects of head and eye movements. The thing that is really surprising is that Stratton adapted to his new world rather quickly. After a week, he was able to get around fairly well, and his visual world no longer seemed strange. This adaptation would be difficult to explain if the brain were receiving anything remotely resembling copies of the images that fall on the retina.

An even more striking experiment involving distorting lenses was done by Ivo Kohler (1962). He designed glasses with lenses that were blue on the left half and yellow on the right half of each lens. Whenever subjects put on these glasses, leftward eye movements would cause the world to appear bluish, while with rightward eye movements, it would assume a yellow tinge. Kohler wanted to see exactly how blue or yellow the world looked after subjects had worn these glasses for a long time. To do this, he designed an apparatus that presented a uniform gray visual field to the subjects, whose task was to adjust a knob that optically added blue or yellow to the field until is appeared gray. On the first day of the experiment, without the goggles, subjects made no adjustment, since the field was gray to start with. With goggles, when they looked left while viewing the field, it appeared blue. So they had to add yellow to bring it to a neutral gray color. When they looked right, they had to add blue to bring it to the desired neutral gray color. Kohler had his subjects wear the glasses continually for 60 days.

At the end of this time, subjects said that they did not really even notice the glasses, which had at first been disorienting and rather annoying. What bothered them was taking off the glasses! Tests with the visual-field apparatus revealed an amazing finding. Subjects without glasses no longer saw the gray field as gray. When they looked left, it looked yellow to them, and when they looked right, it looked blue. Tested with the glasses, the field looked gray no matter which way they looked. Clearly, the subjects had somehow compensated for the glasses. Whenever they looked to the left through the blue glass, they subjectively added yellow to cancel the effects of the blue lens. On the other hand, an opposite strategy was used when they glanced to the right. The result was that the world looked quite normal with the glasses. Proprioceptive cues from moving the eyes had become a stimulus in a learned feedback loop involving color perception. This loop must be similar to the one that keeps our world from jumping when we move our eyes. The surprising thing is that such a basic biological process as color vision could be affected by experience or learning. To be learned or conditioned, something must be a response. If we can condition it, perception must be an active response rather than just a passive input.

CONDITIONING PERCEPTUAL RESPONSES

An experiment by Hefferline and Perera (1963) illustrates a more direct conditioning of perception. In this experiment, a small involuntary muscle twitch on the part of the subject was detected with an electromyograph. Whenever such a twitch was detected, a tone came on. The subject's task was to press a key whenever the tone was heard. Gradually, the tone was made fainter and fainter and, eventually, it was omitted altogether. Subjects not only continued to press the key at the appropriate times, but they also reported that they still heard the tone. The subjects knew that a faint tone followed each muscle twitch. Accordingly, they "heard" what they knew they were supposed to hear even after the experimenter had tricked them by turning off the tone altogether. Obviously the copy theory cannot explain this, since there was no reality to be perceived.

PERCEPTUAL CONSTANCIES

Perceptual constancies enable us to perceive what we know we should be seeing rather than anything resembling the pattern of light falling on the retina. That is, the percept resembles our idea of what reality must be more closely than it resembles the sensation that reality has engendered. We see a thing as maintaining its proper size, shape, and color regardless of the angle or distance from which we view it. The perceptual constancies allow this. As with the other mechanisms we have been discussing, the constancies can also be brought into play by various perceptual illusions. In the case of such illusions, we are correcting sensory impressions that should not be corrected.

Size constancy. The size of the retinal image of an object varies directly with the distance of the object. As shown in Figure 1–7, the more distant any given object is, the smaller its size on the retina will be. A six-foot-high man standing 50 feet away subtends a smaller retinal angle than your thumb held a few inches

FIGURE 1–7   The relationship between distance and retinal size. The further away something is, the smaller its retinal size will be.

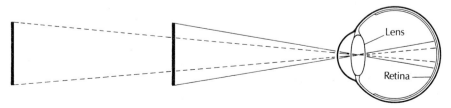

Lens

Retina

in front of your eye. However, the man is perceived as being his true height. In this case, we know quite well that a man cannot be an inch high. So, we do not see him that way. It never occurs to us that we are being confronted by a person only one inch tall. I think that you will agree that your perception of distant objects is automatic. We do not consciously compute a correction equation. The correction is "wired into" our perceptual apparatus. Correct perception of the size of distant objects does not even depend upon prior knowledge of exactly how large the object really is. A number of experiments show this. Let's say that we show a subject a 36-inch rod 24 inches in front of his eyes. The person's task is to pick out of a set of rods 12 feet away the one that is exactly the same size as the 24-inch rod. Normal subjects can perform this sort of task with virtually no errors. If they were choosing on the basis of retinal size, they would choose an 18-foot rod! How do they do this? Apparently they do it by an unconscious estimate of distance based on cues or hints regarding linear perspective (the convergence of parallel lines), aerial perspective (distant objects are hazy), interposition (an object apparently obscured by another object is perceived as more distant), and so on. Removing these cues by having the subject match luminous rods in a completely dark room destroys size constancy. With environmental cues, the subject in our hypothetical experiment will correctly pick a 36-inch rod, while with no such cues, the 18-foot one will probably be picked!

Other constancies. When you see a half-open door, you perceive it as being rectangular. It never occurs to you that someone has invented a rhomboidal door, even though the pattern on your retina is not at all rectangular. This represents the operation of shape constancy: the tendency to perceive objects as being the shape we know them to be regardless of the perspective from which we view them. A related phenomenon is seen with brightness constancy. The pages of this book look white to you even if you happen to be reading it in deep shade. Unless all context is cut off and you do not know that what you are seeing is white paper, it is very difficult for you to see the page as being its true brightness. Color constancy is similar. It is very difficult to see the leaves of a tree as any other color than some shade of green even though local conditions of light may make their actual color blue or yellow or purple.

Illusions involving constancy. The constancies are very basic and automatic, but they develop gradually in children and thus seem to be based upon some degree of learning. Turnbull (1961) reports on what happened when pygmies who had spent their whole lives in dense forest were first taken into an area consisting of open grasslands. A herd of buffalo was seen in the distance. The pygmies took them to be insects because of their small size. They refused to believe that such tiny creatures could be buffalo. As the herd was approached, the retinal size of the buffalo, of course, increased. The pygmies could only attribute this to witchcraft. They had never had any experience in seeing distant objects, since the forest restricted the line of sight to a few feet. As a consequence, they had not developed size constancy. Just the opposite experience can also occur. Edgar Allan Poe's short story, "The Sphinx" concerns a man looking out of a window and seeing a horrible creature of monstrous size crawling slowly along the distant horizon. Suddenly, he realizes that he is in reality observing a tiny insect crawling along the window pane a few inches in front of his eyes. The apocalypse is transformed into a mistake in size constancy. Castaneda (1971) reports a similar encounter with the "guardian of the other world." The guardian was perceived as a huge and grotesque animal seen approaching him from a distance. It really turned out to be a gnat a few inches in front of his eyes. With a little effort and imagination, we can achieve this sort of effect consciously. The same is true of shape constancy. We can almost see the door as being really rhomboidal. Other constancies, such as those involving brightness or color, are much more difficult to overcome.

The history of art as a disintegration of constancies. Psychoanalyst Anton Ehrenzweig (1953) has argued that we can interpret the history of Western painting as a series of successive abrogations of the perceptual constancies. Interestingly, the historical order of abrogation corresponds to the order of ease of abrogation for normal subjects. Medieval paintings—like the drawings of children—are in reality rather abstract. They depict what the artists knew was out there rather than what was actually seen. For example, distant people were depicted as being the same size as people in the foreground of a painting. This is because medieval artists were trying to represent their perceptions rather than their raw sensations. Similarly, roads and buildings look all wrong in this sort of art. Artists painted roads as being of equal width both nearby and at a distance. In fact, roads are of equal width, and this fact overrode the actual image on the retina of the artist. In the retinal image, parallel lines converge in the distance. What seems simple and obvious to us, in fact, took painters several thousand years to discover. The tricks of depicting perspective were finally discovered in the Renaissance. This involved an overcoming of size and shape constancies. Rather than painting their perceptions—what they knew they were seeing—Rennaissance painters moved toward depicting their sensations. For example, they painted people in the foreground of their paintings larger than people in the background.

Baroque painting of the 17th century represented another advance—the discovery of chiaroscuro techniques. Up to this time, shadows were handled with difficulty. White objects in shadow, for example, were painted as white. Earlier artists depicted faces as being one uniform color even if part of the face was in shadow. Baroque painters learned to ignore *brightness constancy.* They painted the part of an object upon which shadows fell as being darker than the lighted part. This abrogation of brightness constancy actually provoked some horror at first since, unless one has some sort of disease, a person's face is really pretty much the same color all over. As you can see, artists were moving away from painting perceptions and toward a depiction of raw sensations. This becomes clear in the next major revolution in painting, which Ehrenzweig sees as coming with the French impressionists. We automatically see things as being the color we "know" them to be. It takes a good deal of effort to see that any given leaf on a tree may, in fact, be blue or yellow or even purple rather than green. This is *color constancy.* In painting the exact sensed color of things, the impressionists violated this constancy. Again, this initially produced a good deal of horror. Potential customers actually wondered if the impressionist painters might not have defective vision.

With the cubists, we see a disintegration of what Ehrenzweig terms *localization constancy.* The cubist painters often depicted objects as viewed from several simultaneous perspectives. It is as if they did not combine momentary views of the world into one final integration from one stable viewing point. In normal vision, we sample pieces of the visual world with momentary eye fixations and then automatically integrate them into a total picture. Cubist objects arise from omitting the final integration. When you look at a visual scene, you seem to see it all at once. This is not really the case. Figure 1–8 shows a record of the eye fixa-

FIGURE 1–8   Eye movements during examination of a picture. Right picture shows the pattern of successive fixations of a subject examining the picture shown on left side.

 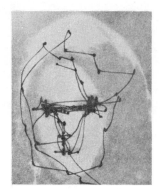

Source: A. L. Yarbus, *Eye Movements and Vision* (New York: Plenum, 1967), p. 179.

tions of a subject looking at a picture. This person's subjective experience would have been one of seeing the picture in a single glance. During any one fixation, however, only a small area around the fixation point would be clear. The rest of the picture would be in the peripheral field of vision and would actually be blurred. The fact that the picture seems subjectively to be seen all at once cannot be attributed to mere persistence of the clear sensations arising from each fixation. This would actually result in a completely blurred image because the persisting images would be superimposed on one another in a chaotic fashion (Hochberg, 1972). What is perceived is thus, in fact, a reconstructed theory in the brain rather than an image based directly on retinal sensations.

The paintings of the abstract expressionists do resemble the chaotic series of retinal sensations upon which perception is ultimately based. Ehrenzweig says that these paintings represent a complete disintegration of the "thing facade" that we impose on the world. Objects disappear, and we are left with only the sort of patternless chaos that is produced by splashing paint on a canvas more or less at random. In a certain sense, we could argue that the paintings of the abstract expressionists represent the chaos of sensation as it exists on our retinas at any second in time. From this chaotic *prima materia,* we construct the perceived world of objects much as James's sculptor constructed his statue.

Perceptual structuring

GESTALT PRINCIPLES

In the 1920s and 1930s, the gestalt psychologists (Koffka, 1935; Wertheimer, 1923) devised a number of experiments which demonstrate that we have built-in ways of structuring or organizing our perceptions. One of the most basic laws governing perception is that we automatically structure any input into figure and ground. Although we use environmental cues to do this, figure and ground are something we impose on the world rather than vice versa. For example, if you stare at Figure 1–9, you will see that it looks like two faces for awhile, then sud-

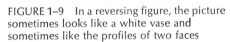

FIGURE 1–9 In a reversing figure, the picture sometimes looks like a white vase and sometimes like the profiles of two faces

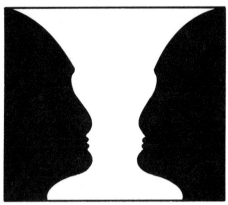

denly shifts to looking like a vase, than back to two faces, and so on. Obviously reality (the picture) is not changing. The only thing left to explain the variance in perception is your visual system. It automatically and quite unconsciously structures its input into figure and ground. Since in this case the environmental cues are ambiguous, figure and ground are not constant. Because the world does not come to us automatically structured into figure and ground or objects and backgrounds, there must be a set of implicit rules that our perceptual organs follow to so divide it. The gestalt psychologists were interested in determining these rules. One of them is the principle of *closure*. In Figure 1–10A, you see a square. In so doing, you are closing up small gaps between each dot and also

FIGURE 1–10 Illustrations of the gestalt principles of closure (A), similarity (B), and proximity (C)

the larger gap on the left. If someone asked you what you had seen in a day or so, you would probably remember having seen just a square unless you had made a special effort to do otherwise. Another perceptual rule is the principle of *similarity*. In Figure 1–10B, you are likely to see columns of circles and squares rather than rows of alternating circles and squares. This is because similar percepts tend to be perceived as groups. In Figure 1–10C, you perceive three sets of circles rather than just a number of unrelated circles. This is a demonstration of the principle of *proximity*. Stimuli that are close together are perceived as being grouped.

OBJECTIFICATION

It might be argued that our senses give us a limited and distorted view of reality but that they do, after all, give us some idea of the external objects that compose reality. It can be said, however, that things or objects are created as much by our mind as by reality. The theorist Ernest Schachtel (1959) has dealt with what he calls *objectification,* the tendency to perceive the world as structured into independent objects. We take it for granted that the environment is, in fact, so structured and forget that our organs of perception contribute as much if not more than the world to this view. Schachtel points out that structuring reality in terms of objects is only one of the modes of perception. He calls it *allocentric* or object-centered perception. With this type of perception, the organs of perception structure the world into objects. Schachtel terms the other mode of perception *autocentric* or subject centered. Here there is little or no objectification. In the adult, the higher senses—vision and hearing—operate allocentrically, while the lower senses—taste, smell, body awareness—operate autocentrically. According to Schachtel, the human infant originally apprehends the world autocentrically through all of its senses. Only gradually, over the course of time, does the child begin to structure its world in an allocentric way.

Perception in the autocentric mode is objectless. Think of taste. You do not taste an object in the sense that you see an object. Rather, there is just the taste. Of course, you may later consciously *infer* that the taste came from this or that source. But the point is that this inference is carried out automatically and unconsciously with an allocentric sense such as vision. A second difference between allocentric and autocentric modes is that the latter is more closely related to feelings of pleasure or pain and to reflexlike responses. Compare, for example, seeing a rotten object as compared to smelling or tasting it. In the latter case, there is an immediate feeling of unpleasantness and a reflexive withdrawal. Vision and hearing are thus more neutral and abstract. Another example would be touching a hot stove as opposed to merely hearing about it. In the latter case, you have to imagine the pain, since it is not an immediate consequence of the sensation.

Another difference between the two modes concerns what Schachtel calls *felt-organ localization*. In the allocentric senses, such as seeing or hearing, we project the object outwards. We hear or see something where we *know* it is, not where it is sensed. We do not see things on our retinas or feel sounds in our ears unless the sensations are extremely intense. But we do feel touches, smells, and tastes right at the receptors. All of our sensory receptors receive some sort of stimulation, translate this into firing of nerve cells, and finally set up a pattern of nervous activity in the brain. With the allocentric senses we automatically construct a model of what we know is causing the sensations and locate it where we know it is coming from. This is the basis for Schachtel's idea of objectification.

There is a built-in inferential leap that leads us to postulate objects and to structure sensory patterns into objects.

PERCEPTION AS CATEGORIZATION

We have been arguing that to perceive is actually to structure or objectify raw sensory input. Another way of putting this is to say that it involves categorization. This can go to rather striking extremes. Schachtel calls this tendency secondary autocentricity. He says that people—especially adults—tend not really to look at things in their own right but merely to classify them in terms of a label or a use. In other words, we do not see the world in the fresh, vivid way that a child does. We tend to name or label things and file them away without really looking at them or enjoying them. The remark attributed to Ronald Reagan that "When you've seen one tree, you've seen them all" is a good example of this tendency in all of us. The idea that perception is categorization is supported by an experiment conducted by Bruner and Postman (1949). Subjects were briefly shown playing cards, such as those illustrated in Figure 1–11. They merely had to report what card they saw. Look at the cards in the figure. Do you see any reason why

FIGURE 1–11   Cards of this type are used to illustrate the idea that perception is categorization

  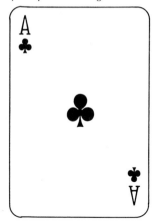

this might be an interesting experiment? Chances are that it took you some time to notice—if you noticed at all—that one of the cards is anomalous. It is a black six of hearts. As you might predict from your own experience, subjects, even with very long exposure times, "saw" a six of spades when they were shown this card. Unless they were specifically warned beforehand that some of the cards might not be exactly what they seemed to be, nobody saw the black heart for what it really was. In seeing something, we sample just a little bit of the available information, make our categorization, and let it go at that.

Everyone has had the experience of seeing something in the twilight that upon closer examination turned out to be something totally different than what it initially seemed to be. Several experiments have brought this phenomenon into the laboratory (Bruner and Potter, 1964; Wyatt and Campbell, 1951). Subjects were tachistoscopically shown unfocused pictures. The picture was brought into clearer focus on each successive presentation. After each presentation, the subject was encouraged to guess what the picture was. It turned out that if subjects made early incorrect guesses, this prevented them from correctly recognizing the picture even when it was focused enough so that nonguessing subjects had no difficulty at all in recognizing it. The early hypothesis or structure imposed on the picture actually prevented or delayed correct recognition.

This sort of effect can be explained with Jean Piaget's notion of the schema (1950). For Piaget, perception of the world involves an *assimilation* of stimuli to internal schemas, models, or categories. We assimilate inputs to preexisting schemas if at all possible and then pay relatively little attention to them. In other words, an input somehow activates a preexisting internal representation. This means in a very real sense that perceiving is remembering. Only if an input is quite different from our expectation do we have to *accommodate* our schema to the world. Then we really attend to or focus on the input and build a new schema to accommodate or fit it.

SUMMARY AND CONCLUSIONS

Cognitive psychology is the study of how knowledge is gathered, stored, and used. It involves the assertion that knowledge exists in the form of internal or mental representations. The most basic internal representations are sensations and perceptions. We argued that these must not be thought of as veridical copies of external stimuli. On the philosophical level, this makes no sense because sensations and perceptions are subjective mental events while stimuli are patterns of physical energy. Thus, reality and mental representations of it are qualitatively completely different. Furthermore, there are philosophical reasons to argue that many qualities—such as space and time—must be properties of mind and perception, while there is no way to know whether or not they are properties of physical reality.

On the empirical level, much evidence is inconsistent with the copy theory but is consistent with the idea that sensations and perceptions are joint products of reality and our perceptual apparatus. Sensory phenomena, such as aftereffects and contrast effects, and perceptual phenomena, such as the constancies and the gestalt principles, are examples of such evidence. We ended with the arguments that objects are not given in reality but created or structured by perception and that perception is ultimately an active process of categorization. Another way of putting these assertions is to say that to perceive is to remember or to activate a preexisting internal representation. What this means and how it is accomplished will be explained in the next several chapters.

2

Internal representations in brains and robots

In Chapter 1 it was argued that the inputs to the mind are in no sense copies or images of external objects. It was asserted that perception involves the activation of preexisting internal schemas or categories rather than the passive reception of veridical images. Are our perceptions not in some sense copies of reality? Perhaps it can be argued that they are just poor, incomplete, and systematically distorted copies. In this chapter we shall consider the "hardware" of cognition in brains and in robots that can respond in a meaningful way to stimuli. It will become clear as we do so that in neither case could internal representations be anything remotely resembling copies that are qualitatively similar to the reality that they symbolize.

INTERNAL REPRESENTATIONS IN ROBOTS

In this section, we shall consider how we might go about constructing robots that would be able to recognize and respond to stimuli. Why should we take up such a question? The reason is that it will shed light on the real question of interest—the way in which human beings perceive reality. Some principles are more easily grasped if they are first considered in a simple form. It will be easier to understand human internal representations if we first describe the much simpler internal representations of robots. Our discussion of robots has three basic purposes. First, we shall show that some possible ways of constructing a robot—based on the copy theory of perception and on behaviorist or stimulus-response theory —do not work. If these theories will not even help us to construct a simple automaton, they hold little promise of explaining human perception and cognition. Second, we shall show that an internal representation of a stimulus has to be qualitatively different from the stimulus. It cannot be a copy or an image of the stimulus if it is to be of any use. Third, our discussion of cognitive and computerized robots will introduce several concepts that are necessary to an understanding of how human cognition must work.

The world of a robot

Let us assume that our robot lives in a completely dark environment populated by several other types of creatures. The most important of these are its prey. We will assume that these are large, noisy creatures that glow in the dark. On the other hand, there are predators. They are equally luminous but completely silent. We would like to have our robot flee from predators or, at the very least, not to attack them. On the other hand, we do want the robot to attack its prey. Let's assume that we are building a motorized killer mosquito. Its mission in life is to run into large, noisy objects and suck vital fluids from them. So as not to become excessively gory, we could assume that the prey are actually mobile batteries and that the vital fluids are merely electricity needed to recharge our robot's batteries.

Our robot needs a motor system, since it has to move toward some things and away from others. To accomplish this, we could install two electric motors—one powering the left rear wheel and the other powering the right rear wheel. The robot would also need some means of plugging itself into its prey and of unplugging itself. To keep things simple, let's just assume that the robot has two sharp prongs that will pierce whatever it runs into. We shall further assume that the prey will eventually become aware of a plugged-in robot, shake it off, and flee. On the other hand, a predator will quickly destroy and dismantle a plugged-in robot. So, again, there is no need for it to be able to unplug itself. Now all we need to do is connect stimuli (light and noise) with responses (turning on motors).

A Cartesian robot

If we were to build our robot according to Descartes's copy theory of perception, the first thing we would need to do would be to pass an image of reality into the robot. In Figure 2–1, a Cartesian robot is illustrated. Light enters through two windows and is reflected by the prisms onto the rear-projection screen. This gets an exact image of the outside world into the robot. Now what? How do we connect the image on the screen with the motors? What is going to see the image? Perhaps it would help to pass the image further into the robot. In Figure 2–2 is a Hyper-Cartesian robot. The prisms focus the image onto the mirror at point A. This mirror reflects the image to the mirrors at points B and C and so on. Eventually the image is projected directly onto both the left and the right motors. But we are, of course, no closer to getting the motors turned on than we were before.

Clearly, there is no value at all in passing the image of external reality around inside the robot. At some point, the external world must be perceived or known, and this has to consist of extracting some critical features, making a response to them, and disregarding everything else. Because the more we pass the image around from mirror to mirror, the more degraded and fuzzy it will become and the more useless parts we will have, it makes sense that this feature extraction would occur as soon as possible. Nature would not be likely to build organisms like our Cartesian robots. B. F. Skinner's discussion of perception as an active response is relevant here. In explaining what happens when we see a rainbow, he says:

FIGURE 2–1   Schematic for a Cartesian robot in which an image of external reality is available inside the robot

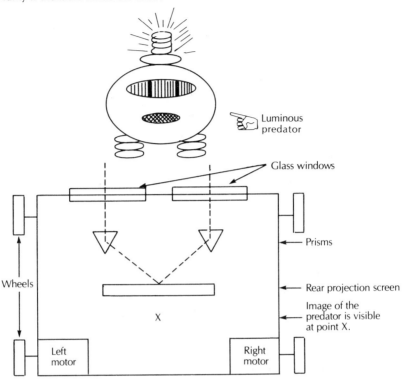

Seeing is a *response* to a stimulus rather than a mere camera-like registering. In carrying the pattern of the rainbow into the organism, almost no progress is made toward understanding the behavior of *seeing* the rainbow. It is of little moment whether the individual sees the actual rainbow or the sensation of a rainbow or some terminal neural pattern in the brain. At some point he must *see,* and this is more than recording a similar pattern. . . . If we say that the rainbow (either as an objective event in the environment or as a corresponding pattern within the organism) is not "what is seen" but simply the commonest variable which controls the behavior of seeing, we are much less likely to be surprised when the behavior occurs as a function of other variables (1953, p. 281).

Providing the robot with internal representations

If we are willing to deprive our robot of its veridical images of external stimuli, there is no great difficulty in getting it to make a response to them. For the windows of the Cartesian robot, we can substitute photocells, which are light-sensitive electrical devices. If light strikes them, they develop an electrical potential. The more light that strikes them, the greater this potential. In order to sense noise, we would employ a sound-activated device, which develops an electrical potential in response to sound waves. The louder the noise, the greater the electrical potential. The photocells and the sound-activated device are examples of analogue

FIGURE 2–2   Schematic for a Hyper-Cartesian robot in which the image
of external reality is passed around inside the robot

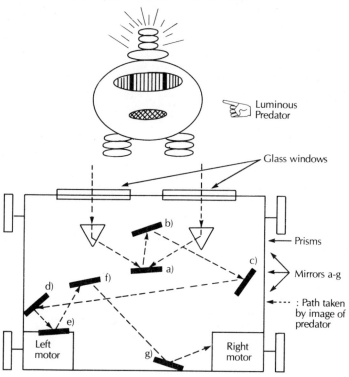

computing devices. They compute or represent light and sound by means of a
continuously variable electrical potential. This electrical potential is, of course,
qualitatively different from the things—light or sound—that it represents. It is in
no sense an image of these things.

Assume that the robot's prey is directly in front of it. The light that it emits will
cause both of the photocells to develop an electrical potential, while the noise that
it emits will cause the sound-activated device to develop an electrical potential.
Thus, the robot will sense the presence of the prey. By transducing the light and
noise to internal representations (electrical potentials), we are a lot closer to giving
the robot useful knowledge about its world. We could consider connecting the
sensing devices directly to the motors. A difficulty with this idea is that the further
away the prey was, the weaker the electrical response of the sensing devices would
be. Hence, the more distant the prey, the slower the motors would run. This is
the reverse of what we would prefer.

This problem could be solved by running the output of the sensing devices
to digital or bistable devices. This possibility is shown in Figure 2–3. Output of
the analogue sensing devices goes to level sensors. These are simply gadgets that
are on if their input voltage is above some predetermined level and off if their
input voltage is below this threshold level. On and off can be defined as we please.

FIGURE 2–3   Sensory transduction in a robot

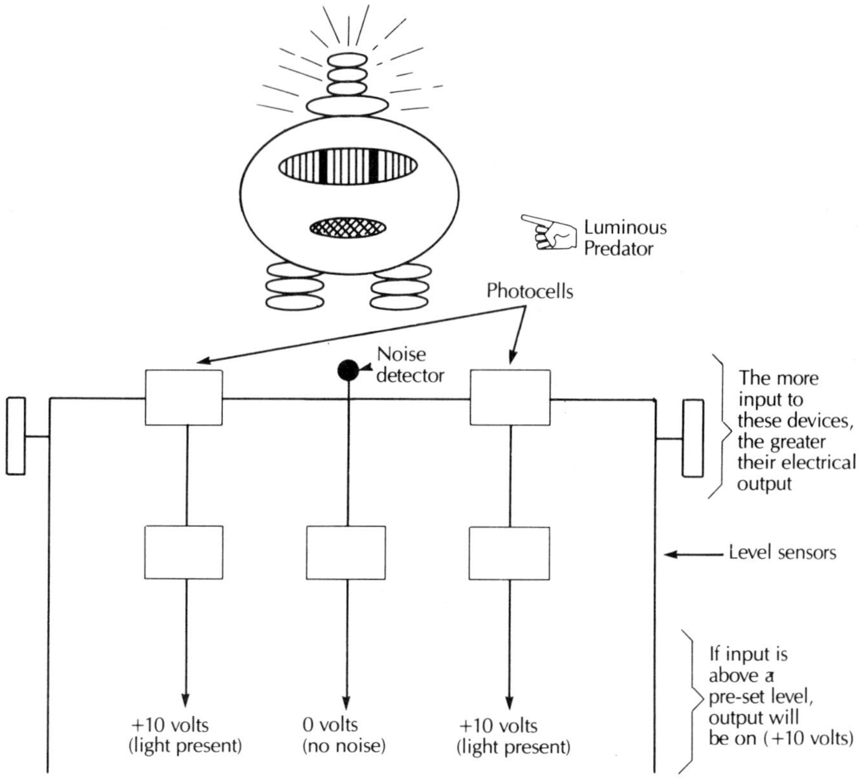

The more input to these devices, the greater their electrical output

Luminous Predator

Photocells

Noise detector

Level sensors

If input is above a pre-set level, output will be on (+10 volts)

+10 volts (light present)

0 volts (no noise)

+10 volts (light present)

For example, on could mean that the level sensor emits a direct-current voltage of +10 volts, and off could mean that it has an electrical potential of 0 volts. This is arbitrary, however. We could just as well have picked any other voltages. The important point is that these devices have two states: on and off. We could also call these states *yes* and *no* or 1 and 0. In the following discussion, we shall use 1 to mean that a digital device is on, and 0 to mean that it is off. The output of such digital devices can be used to turn other devices on and off. Both the 0 and the 1 states can be so used. If the device is on, we can use its output to turn on another device. However, we can also invert its output, so that it turns some other device on if it is off.

The three level sensors constitute our robot's sensory register. This register constitutes the robot's knowledge of the world: object in front of left eye? object in front of right eye? and noise? In comparison to the robot, your sensory registers can hold a good deal more information about your immediate environment. But the nature of this information must be analogous to the pattern of ons and offs in the robot's sensory register, as we shall see later. Be this as it may, we now need to connect the output of the sensory register to the robot's motors. We shall consider several ways of doing this.

A reflex robot

If we were dedicated behaviorists, we would insist upon making direct connections between the sensory registers and the motors. Recall what Bolles (1975)
called the correspondence assumption of behaviorism: All internal connections
should be simple S-R (stimulus-response) links. Let us see how much progress we
can make with such an assumption. A reflex robot is shown in Figure 2–4. Let's

FIGURE 2–4   Partial schematic for a reflex robot

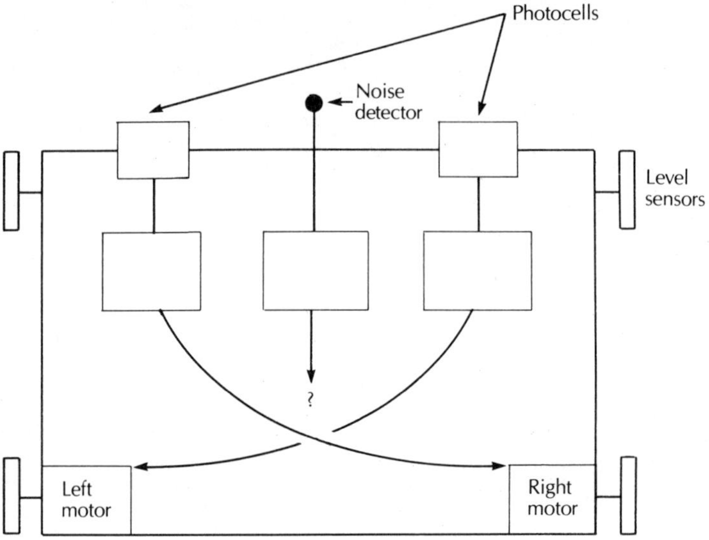

consider the visual system first. Note that output from the left eye controls the
right motor while output from the right eye controls the left motor. An object in
front of the left eye will thus cause the robot to turn toward the left (because
the right wheel will operate). This should get the robot pointed straight at the
object. Then, both eyes will be on. Hence, both motors will be on, and the robot
will move straight toward the object. Conversely, an object in front of only the
right eye will cause a turn toward the right and so on. In Chapter 11, we shall see
that the sensory input tracts of animals and humans exhibit this sort of crossing.
The evolutionary cause of this was probably the same considerations that led me
to cross the robot's sensory tracts.

Recall that we want the robot to approach only noisy objects and to avoid
silent objects. Thus, we want approach behavior when all three units in the
sensory register are on but we want avoidance behavior when two of them
(those sensing light) are on and one of them (the one sensing sound) is off. This
is where we begin to run into difficulties. The reason for the difficulties is that
direct S-R wiring gives us no way to represent even such a simple concept as *and*.
We want the robot to go forward if there is light *and* sound. However, we want it
to do just the reverse—back up—if there is light *and* no sound.

In the study of animal learning, this sort of task is called *configural conditioning:* One tries to teach an animal to make a response if A *and* B are present

but not to make the response if only one or the other is present. It turns out that birds and mammals can learn to do this, but more primitive organisms, such as fish or amphibians, cannot. Wickelgren (1979a) argues that this is because primitive organisms are "wired" in a direct or reflex manner, while more advanced organisms are "wired" in a way that allows them to learn the task. The difference is illustrated in Figure 2–5. Reflex wiring is shown in A. Output from the light

FIGURE 2–5   Methods of associating sensations with a motor response. Reflex connections are shown in A: either light or noise will initiate the motor response. Connections via a chunking unit are shown in B: only light and noise will initiate the motor response.

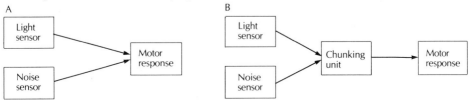

sensor goes to the motor as does output from the noise sensor. The problem is that the motor will be turned on by three things: noise alone, light alone, or noise and light. Higher organisms have what Wickelgren calls *chunking units* as shown in B. Output from the light sensor and the noise sensor goes to the chunking unit. The chunking unit is on only if both the light sensor and the noise sensor are on. As shown in the figure, output from the chunking unit turns on the motor. This gives us what we want. The response will be given if and only if light and noise are simultaneously present. However, if we provide the robot with chunking units, we would no longer have a reflex creature. Thus, we shall leave the output from the noise sensor dangling and go on to a better design.

A cognitive robot

Several types of logic gates are used in computers and computer-like devices that can be used to allow our robot to combine information and decide upon a course of action. These are digital or binary devices that are either on or off, like level sensors. However, the difference is that they perform logical operations. Several of the more common types of logic gates are illustrated in Figure 2–6,

FIGURE 2–6   Examples of logic gates

along with the logical function that they perform. An AND gate is on if and only if both (or all) of its inputs are on. Otherwise, it is off. As shown in the diagram, an AND gate can be used to make a logical deduction. If A (input A is on) and B (input B is on), then C (the output of the AND gate is on). An AND gate can be used to perform some function—such as turning on a motor—if certain preconditions—such as the presence of both light and sound—are met. The chunking unit shown in Figure 2–5 is, of course, nothing more than an AND gate. There are several other types of logic gates that are used in computing devices. Something similar to them must also be used in at least some biological organisms, since they perform functions that can easily be performed by humans and other higher organisms. An OR gate is on if either one or the other (or both) of its inputs are on. These and other types of logic gates can be hooked together so as to perform logical deductions.

How can such logic gates be incorporated into our robot? The schematic is shown in Figure 2–7. As you can see, some cognitive units in the form of logic

FIGURE 2–7   Schematic for a cognitive robot illustrating sensory transduction, internal representations, and chunking units (logic gates)

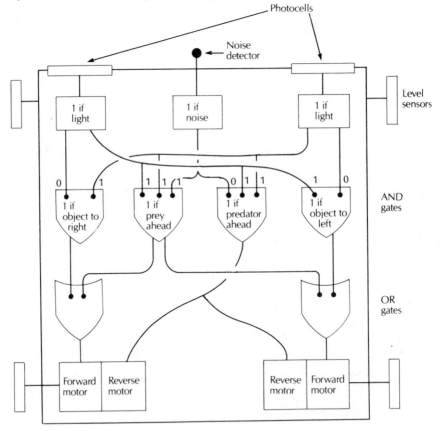

gates have been interposed between the sensory registers and the motor apparatus of the robot. The robot can now "recognize" four things by means of the AND gates. In Figure 2–7 the little 0s and 1s over the logic gates indicate whether a particular input is direct (1) or inverted (0). *Direct input* means that the gate receives input when the sensor is on, while *inverted input* means that the gate receives input when the sensor is off. The four states of affairs that the robot's AND gates code are (1) unknown object to the right (right visual field is on while left visual field is off), (2) prey (both visual fields are on and noise is present), (3) predator (both visual fields are on but noise is not present), and (4) unknown object to the left (left visual field is on while right visual field is off). Each of these four percepts results in a specific action: (1) an unknown object to the right leads to right turning, (2) prey elicits forward movement, (3) a predator elicits reverse movement, and (4) an unknown object to the left results in left turning. The OR gates allow control of the forward motors by either of two mutually exclusive percepts.

Knowledge of the outside world for the cognitive robot consists of a pattern of 0s and 1s in its sensory registers and cognitive units. For example, perception or recognition of a predator is activation of the AND gate that symbolizes or represents a predator. No isomorphic image is involved. Rather, a preexisting internal representation has been turned on. The form of this representation (an electrical potential of +10 volts) is completely unlike the form of the thing it represents (a silent, luminous object). In the following chapters, we shall argue that human perception, recognition, and knowledge ultimately consists of something similar to what we built into the robot. That is, human knowledge of the world consists of a pattern of cognitive units each of which is either on or off.

There are several "bugs" in our robot. For example, if it encountered a small object that was not large enough to activate both photocells simultaneously it would be fascinated or bewitched. It would move first one way and then the other until its batteries ran down. The robot was built to turn in order to bring an object into full view and then attack it or flee from it. It was built for an environment with no such small objects. An experimenter who stumbled on the idea of showing the robot such an object could figure out how it was wired by observing its behavior in response to this sort of stimulus. Another difficulty is that the robot has no memory. You may have wondered why it was built so that it would orient itself toward a predator before backing up. It could have been wired to "know" that any light in the absence of noise meant danger. Why not, then, have it turn away from rather than toward any noiseless object that stimulated only one visual field? The reason is that if the robot turned away, the object would no longer be visible. Since the robot has no memory, it would stop moving and the predator could easily destroy it. Because the robot has no memory, it has to have the stimulus in its line of sight if it is to respond to it.

A computerized cognitive robot

We could easily improve our robot by adding more logic gates, but let's take the drastic step of computerizing it. This will give it the memory that it requires to behave in a more intelligent manner. Assume that we want our computerized robot not only to search out and attack large noisy objects but also to flee from large or small quiet objects. Given that silent objects either attack or bewitch robots, we cannot have our robot merely turning away from such objects. Rather, it has to turn away and leave the area. This type of object has to lead not only to one action but to a sequence of actions. The ability to emit a sequence of actions— especially in the absence of the stimulus that evoked them—requires a memory of some sort. Without memory, the robot obviously could not remember what actions composed the sequence. Figure 2–8 presents a schematic for the computerized robot. Its basic components are a sensory register, an output register, and a memory.

FIGURE 2–8   Schematic for a computerized robot is shown in A. An expanded view of the robot's memory is shown in B.

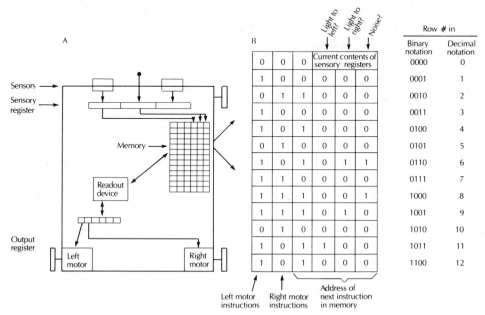

SENSORY REGISTERS AND THE REPRESENTATION OF REALITY

First, let us consider the possible contents of the sensory register, their meaning, and the action they are to elicit (0 indicates that the sensory register is off; 1 indicates that it is on). The eight possibilities are listed in Table 2–1. Note that if we take the three columns of the sensory register as numbers, we have the numbers from 0 to 7 in binary notation—that is, 000 is 0, 001 is 1, 010 is 2, 011 is 3, and so on.

OUTPUT REGISTERS

In the output register, the leftmost cell controls the left motor and the next cell controls the right motor. When the leftmost cell is on (1), the left motor will be turned on; when the next cell is on, the right motor will be on. The next four cells contain the memory address of the next statement to be read into the output register. We will not worry about how this reading-in process works. If these cells were on, off, off, and on (1001), the next statement to be read into the output register would be the one in row 9 (1001 is the number 9 in binary notation). A black box has also been provided that performs the task of delivering things from memory to the output register. Let's say that it is controlled by a clock so that every one fourth of a second the current statement in the output register

TABLE 2–1 Possible contents of the computerized robot's sensory registers along with their meanings and the appropriate action to be taken

Left eye	Right eye	Noise	Meaning	Action
0	0	0	Nirvana	Do nothing
0	0	1	Prey present but invisible	Search
0	1	0	Predator or distractor to right	Turn left and flee
0	1	1	Prey to right	Turn right
1	0	0	Predator or distractor to left	Turn right and flee
1	0	1	Prey to left	Turn left
1	1	0	Predator straight ahead	Full turn and flee
1	1	1	Prey straight ahead	Move forward and attack

is replaced by the one indicated by the last four digits. (In a real computer, this cycle time would, of course, be a great deal faster.)

MEMORY

The computerized robot has been equipped with a memory. The memory has 12 rows and 6 columns of units or 72 units in all. Each of these units is bistable: it can be either on (1) or off (0). This memory can thus code 72 bits of information. Such a memory can be constructed in several ways. One way would be to use a core memory. This might consist of 72 doughnut-shaped pieces of ferrite that can be magnetized in one of two directions representing 1 and 0. Note that our robot actually has several types of memory. The sensory registers are read into the last three columns of row 0000 of memory. The contents of these columns and of the sensory register change from moment to moment according to the stimuli that are present. As will be seen later, the contents of these columns are occasionally read into the last columns of the output register, where they stay for one fourth of a second. The output register, then, also functions as a short-term memory concerning the recent past. This information may, of course, be quite different from the information in the sensory register. The rest of the memory is static since it contains the permanent programs that govern the robot's behavior. It could thus be called long-term memory. However, it is long-term memory of a particular sort. It consists of knowledge about how to perform particular actions. You will note that the robot retains no permanent record of what has happened to it. This type of memory is called episodic memory. While this is what we usually think of when we hear the term *memory*, it is important to note that it is only one particular subtype of memory.

PROGRAMS FOR ACTION

Now, let's see how all of this works. Whenever row 0000 is read into the output register, no behavior is emitted: both left and right motor controls are 0. But the last four digits contain the row number that corresponds to whatever is in the sensory register at the moment. Let's say that the current state of affairs is 0011 (no object to left, object to right, noise—that is, prey to right). Note that the contents of row 0011 in memory is 100000. That is: run left motor, then fetch row 0000; or, just as listed in table 2–1: turn to the right. Fetching statement 0000 brings the current contents of the sensory register back into the output register as the last four digits. Let's say that the state of sensory affairs is now 0111 (prey straight ahead), so the output register now is 000111. Sure enough, row 0111 contains 110000: both motors on for one fourth of a second, then fetch the current contents of row 0000 again to see how things are going.

Each of the possible sensory input configurations defines its place in memory. This is called a *content addressable memory*. The general principle is to let an input by its attributes define where information about it is stored in memory, rather than putting the information in a random place and then having to search through memory for it. This type of system will be of great interest when we get to human memory storage, since it provides for extremely fast access. If you will inspect the program statements in each row of memory in Figure 2–8, you will see that each row does in fact correspond with the desired action for that row listed in Table 2–1. In most cases, only one action is called for. However, let's examine the most complex case: Danger straight ahead, make full turn and flee. In this case (0110), row 0110 contains 001011: run left motor and fetch row 1011. The latter row contains the first statement of what might be called the full turn program: 101100 (run left motor and fetch row 1100). Row 1100 in turn says 101000 (run left motor again and fetch row 1000). Row 1000 contains the first statement of the three-statement fleeing program: 111001 (run both motors and fetch row 1001, which says to run both motors again and fetch row 1010, which says to run the right motor and then go to row 0000 to check the current contents of the sensory register). So, confronted with a dangerous object, our robot turns right (arbitrarily) for three fourths of a second, then moves away in a straight line for one half of a second, and finally turns left a bit (to see if the object is coming after it).

Unless you have developed some empathy for our robot, you may wonder what the point of this is. The point is that by means of binary logic units that can only be on or off, we can program the robot to exhibit a good deal of meaningful behavior. It can sense or know things about the external world and take appropriate sequential action. It does this by means of the very abstract patterns of ons or offs that have no isomorphism at all with the objects it is fleeing from or pursuing. Your mind must work something like that of the robot, although obviously the range of things you can sense and do is much more complex.

COGNITION AND COMPUTER PROGRAMS

In real computers, the numbers or words on data and program input cards are transformed into the sort of binary notation our robot uses. There is no essential difference between program and data as far as the computer is concerned. Real computers have vastly larger memory registers than the robot. Rather than running motors, they usually perform logical operations, such as adding, comparing, and so on. But the principle is essentially the same. Programs for computers are usually written in quasi-English languages, such as Fortran or PL/I. A sample statement written in PL/I might read

$$\text{IF AX GT AY THEN SUM} = \text{SUM} + 1$$

which means that if variable AX is greater than variable AY, then add 1 to the variable SUM. Before such a program can be run, it has to be compiled into machine language, which is made up only of 0s and 1s. Thus, 011000110 might be the machine's code for addition. As you probably discovered with the computerized robot example, it is particularly noxious for humans to think in terms of strings of binary numbers. That is why higher level programming languages have been developed.

This is what is so exciting, though: Higher level programming languages obviously can be compiled into machine language. This is done whenever a program is run on a computer. Is English, then, compiled into binary neuronal language in any sort of similar fashion? When I tell you to hand me a pencil, is this statement compiled into some neural pattern of 0s and 1s that lead to the appropriate response? The answer to this question literally has to be yes. The other exciting thing is this: Since computers and brains seem to share the property of operating in a binary machine language and since higher level language programs are obviously translatable into such language, such programs can *in principle* be seen as things that could be compiled into a neural machine language. This is why there has been such interest in computer programs that simulate some property of human thought or behavior.

INTERNAL REPRESENTATIONS IN THE NERVOUS SYSTEM

Structure of the nervous system

The human nervous system is composed of a variety of types of cells. The most important of these types are sensory receptor cells and neurons. As the name implies, receptor cells are devices that are specialized to detect stimuli. All of them are transducers. They transduce or translate physical energy into an electrical potential just as the sensory receptors used in the robots described in the previous section of this chapter. Information from these sensory receptors is relayed to the brain by neurons bundled into afferent tracts. The brain is composed of at least 12 billion neurons, each connected with from 1,000 to 6,000 other neurons. Some neurons leave the brain in efferent tracts. Signals from these efferent neurons control the action of muscles and glands. Hypothetically, perception of any given object corresponds to a specific pattern of activity in the brain. That is, it corresponds to a specific set of neurons being active. Your consciousness at any given moment is presumably the result of the pattern of neural activity occurring at that moment. If this assertion is true, then it is important to know something about how neurons work.

The neuron

STRUCTURE

A typical neuron is illustrated in Figure 2–9. It is composed of a cell body or soma, dendrites, and an axon. Inputs from other neurons reach a given neuron via

FIGURE 2–9   A typical neuron

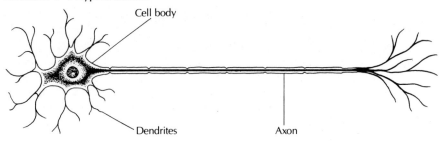

the dendrites or cell body and are passed on via the axon. A neuron is literally covered with *synapses,* or connections with the axons of other neurons. There are many kinds of neurons in the brain. Two basic types are Golgi Type 1 and Type 2 neurons. Golgi Type 1 neurons are large as neurons go. The cell body can be 50 to 100 μm (1 μm = 1/1,000,000 of a meter) in diameter. Something of this size is almost but not quite visible to the naked eye. The axons of this type of neuron may be up to 20 μm in diameter and up to a meter in length. These neurons connect regions of the nervous system fairly distant from each other. Their axons are usually covered by a sheath of *myelin,* a sort of insulating material. Golgi Type 2 neurons, or interneurons, are much smaller. The cell body is on the order of four or five μm in diameter and their nonmyelinated axons are short and no more than one or two μm in diameter. There are many other types of neurons, but this should give some idea of the range of variation.

THE ACTION POTENTIAL

Most neurons, like binary logic devices, have two states: on and off. As is the case with logic devices, we could just as well call these states 0 and 1 or yes and no. We can speak of the neuron as being on when it exhibits what is called an action potential. The action potential is an electrical "spike" of constant amplitude that moves along the cell membrane at a speed of up to 70 meters per second. The action potential lasts from one to two milliseconds (1 millisecond = 1/1000 of a second). Any given neuron can thus fire no more than about 500 times per second. In general, the more inputs a neuron receives, the more frequent the rate of production of action potentials. The action potential follows what is called the *all-or-none law.* That is, the spike is either present at its full amplitude or it is not present at all.

The mechanism behind the action potential was investigated by Hodgkin (1964) and by Huxley (1964). In their research, they used the giant neuron of the squid. Since its axon is about the diameter of a pencil, it is easy to study. In the resting state, there is a difference in electrical potential of −70 mV (1 mV =

1/1000 of a volt) between the inside and the outside of the cell membrane at the cell body. The reason for the difference is that more positive sodium and chloride ions are on the outside and more negative potassium ions are on the inside of the membrane. The action potential consists of a momentary depolarization. When a neuron is stimulated, the cell membrane becomes more permeable and the sodium ions rush in. The more a neuron is stimulated, the more permeable its cell membrane becomes and the more sodium ions that cross it. Once this depolarization reaches −60 mV, a critical threshold is crossed and an action potential is propagated. When the spike itself is present, the difference in electrical potential is +40 mV. The action potential consists of the depolarization traveling along the cell membrane of the neuron. Note that your perceptions, which seem to be such a rich collection of images of reality, are ultimately a complex pattern of sodium and potassium ions.

THE FUNCTIONING OF NEURONS

Neurons serve to transmit information. This information is coded in electrical pulses. We know that not only the presence or absence of a pulse is important. The rate at which pulses are produced also conveys information. In this, neurons are more complex than the logic devices we discussed in the first section. Given that any one neuron is connected to many other neurons and that it needs inputs from a fair number of them before it is turned on, it seems reasonable to suppose that neurons are logic gates of some sort. No doubt they are not simply AND gates or OR gates but devices of considerably more complexity. Nonetheless, the analogy to logic gates is probably a good one.

Neurons are analogue as well as digital devices. In deciding whether to fire, a neuron computes the activity of surrounding neurons in an analogue fashion. It adds up excitatory influences on it and subtracts inhibitory influences. If the total amounts to a depolarization of −60 mV, an action potential is produced. Some neurons are entirely analogue in their operation. That is, they exhibit no action potentials at all but only modulate the activity of surrounding neurons by exciting (depolarizing) or inhibiting (hyperpolarizing) them.

How neurons communicate

THE SYNAPSE

One neuron is stimulated by another neuron at a *synapse*. This is not an actual connection at all but, rather, a tiny gap. One type of synapse involves the axon of one neuron terminating on the dendrite of a second neuron. In another type of synapse, the axon terminates on the cell body of the second neuron. There is some evidence that synapses of the first type are excitatory and that those of the second type are inhibitory (Thompson, 1973). That is, stimulation across Type 1 synapses makes the next neuron more likely to fire while stimulation across Type 2 synapses makes it less likely to fire. Most axons branch into *telodendria* before they come into contact with other cells. Each of these branches terminates in a presynaptic terminal knob. In Figure 2–10, this knob is shown synapsing with a dendritic postsynaptic membrane.

FIGURE 2–10   Schematic illustration of a synapse. One neuron communicates with another neuron by releasing neurotransmitters that fit specific receptors.

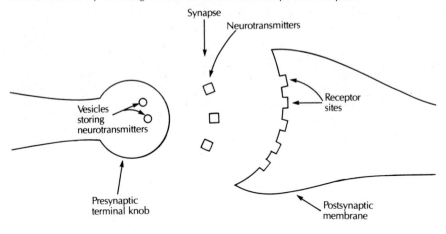

NEUROTRANSMITTER SUBSTANCES

In all higher animals, synaptic transmission involves chemicals rather than a simple electric connection. There are no sparks jumping across the synaptic gap. When an action potential has traveled along the axon and reached the terminal knob, it causes the release of a chemical transmitter substance from vesicles in the terminal knob. The brain uses several transmitter substances, including the monoamines, dopamine, norepinephrine, and serotonin. The transmitter substance is released into the synaptic gap and then attaches to receptor sites on the postsynaptic membrane (see Figure 2–10). The process seems to work in a lock-and-key fashion with the receptor site being the lock and the molecules of the transmitter substance the key. As with a lock and key, only the correct transmitter will fit into the receptor site. This unlocking induces an electrical response in the next neuron. Once the transmitter substance reaches the receptor site, it is decomposed or broken down into its chemical components so that it loses its excitatory capability. Otherwise, it would continue to excite the neuron.

DRUGS AND NEUROTRANSMITTERS

Schizophrenia is the most common form of psychosis. Its major symptoms are disordered thinking, delusions, and hallucinations. Hallucinations involve seeing or hearing something that is not really present in the environment. Seeing something in the environment occurs when a certain set of neurons are activated. In normal people, the only way for this to happen is for the stimulus actually to be present in the environment. In the schizophrenic, something else can activate these neurons. This something else is apparently the presence of too much of certain neurotransmitters. Drugs that improve schizophrenia deplete the amount of monoamine transmitter substances in one way or another. The phenothiazines block postsynaptic dopamine and norepinephrine receptors. Reserpine seems to destroy monoamines outright. The net effect is decreased amounts of neurotransmitter substances. On the other hand, giving L-dopa (a chemical precursor of dopamine) to schizophrenics makes them worse.

Hallucinogenic drugs, such as LSD, mescaline, psilocybin, and marijuana, seem to act as fake neurotransmitters. Their chemical structures are similar to the chemical structures of neurotransmitters. Thus, they will fit the receptor sites of the transmitters and produce an effect comparable to an excess of transmitter substance. Thus they tend to mimic the effects of psychosis and induce disordered thought and perception comparable to schizophrenia. Since the brain has no enzymes designed to decompose these agents, they continue to occupy postsynaptic receptor sites, leading to continual stimulation. Since not all receptor sites are so occupied, normal neurotransmission also continues but the resultant thoughts and percepts appear distorted and strange.

What no neuron can do

It should be made explicit at this point that we have given an exhaustive survey of the main things that neurons can do. They can produce all-or-none electrical spikes. They can exude and take up chemical transmitter substances. There is no earthly way they can pass images back and forth. All of your sensations, perceptions, and thoughts are ultimately due to some pattern of electrical and chemical activity in the neurons that make up your brain. When you see a green tree in front of you, this is a complex pattern of electrical activity inside your skull. The "seeing" is inside your brain, not out in the world. If you have the misfortune to develop schizophrenia or the poor judgment to ingest hallucinogenic drugs, you can readily demonstrate this, since you will see many things that are not present in the world at all.

THE PROBLEM OF RECOGNITION

Perception is an active response process. Rather than involving the movement of a copy or image into the brain, it involves the activation of preexisting internal schemas. In this way, we can see perception as involving the active construction or synthesis of a model of the world rather than the passive reception of pictures of the world. This model is based on samples of some of the information that is potentially available from the sensory receptors. To see how this system works, let us consider the problem of recognition, or how information concerning an external stimulus makes contact with the correct schema or memory trace. This was no particular problem for the robots discussed earlier in this chapter, since they had to recognize only very simple stimuli. What about the problem of recognizing more complex patterns? How, for example, does one recognize and know the meaning of the letter B, the word DOG, or a friend's face? In our view, to perceive is to activate a schema or category in memory. Given a stimulus, how do we connect it with the correct schema. Why does one pattern of light or, more correctly, a whole family of patterns of light on the retina yield the response, "That's my dog," while another family of patterns yields the response, "That's my grandmother." Once we have agreed that perception is the activation of schemas, it is a small step to speculating that these schemas are localized in grandmother cells or cell assemblies in the brain. A grandmother unit would be the neuron or set of neurons that is activated when you recognize your grandmother. Activation of this unit would unleash a set of grandmother-recognizing behaviors. Among these might be hugging; a lot of verbalizations about having been meaning to write, her health, and the weather; and subjective feelings to the effect that this is indeed your grandmother and none other. Before we consider the question of how you recognize your grandmother, we shall need to have a bit of information about how you see in the first place.

Anatomy of the visual system

A basic flowchart for human visual perception is given in Figure 2–11. The physical stimulus for vision consists of electromagnetic waves, which fall on the

FIGURE 2–11   Schematic flowchart of the human visual system

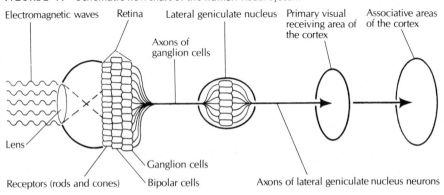

lens of the eye and are focused onto the retina. The lens focuses the stimulus image and projects it in inverted form onto the retina. The retina is a cortical structure, in that it consists of several discrete layers of neural tissue as is illustrated in Figure 2–11. The actual receptor cells are the rods and cones. The rods are specialized for reception of dim light while the cones are specialized for bright light and color perception. Rods occur more frequently around the periphery of the retina while cones are concentrated in the fovea or center of the visual field. There are about 130 million rods and 4 million cones in the human retina. The rods and cones contain light-sensitive chemicals. These are chemicals that react in a specific way to light. In general, the more light they receive, the greater the chemical reaction that is brought about. Now, this chemical reaction causes a change in the electrical potential of the receptor cell. In other words, rods and cones are transducers. They translate light into a direct-current voltage by means of an intermediate chemical reaction. These changes in voltage are in turn sensed by the bipolar cells, which in turn excite the ganglion cells. Both receptor cells and bipolar cells operate in an analogue fashion. It is not until we get to the ganglion cells that action potentials are produced. If its electrical potential crosses a certain threshold, the ganglion cell will fire or produce an action potential. This is a brief electrical pulse. Other things being equal, then, the more activity in the receptors, the more electrical pulses the ganglion cells will produce. (I should warn you that other things are not equal. Several of the crucial components of the retina will not be described until Chapter 3.) The pulses travel along the axons of the ganglion cells. These axons are bundled together to form the optic nerve, which goes to the lateral geniculate body, a part of the midbrain. Here, the axons connect with other neurons whose axons run to the occipital cortex of the brain. This is the primary receiving area of the visual system. Immediately surrounding the primary visual receiving area are association areas that apparently have to do with elaboration or understanding of visual inputs and with integrating inputs from different sensory modes, such as vision and hearing. Damage to the primary visual receiving area leads to blindness, while damage to the visual association areas leads to agnosia. This means that the person can still see but is quite unable to recognize or understand what is seen. Depending upon the area damaged, one may lose the ability to recognize faces, written words, or objects.

It is apparent that the mental event of seeing is the end result of a number of translations. We go from electromagnetic waves to a chemical reaction to a change in direct-current voltage to an alternating-current signal (the action potential). After all of these translations, we have only gotten to an impulse traveling along the axon of a ganglion cell. When this electrical impulse gets to the end of the ganglion cell's axon in the lateral geniculate nucleus, it has to produce another action potential in the next neuron in the series. As we have seen, neurons excite one another not by a direct electrical contact but via an intermediate chemical reaction. To get from receptors in the retina to the primary receiving area of the cortex requires traversal of three neurons. To get to the association areas—where we presumably recognize or understand what is seen—will require traversal of a good many more neurons. Interposed between each of these neurons is a chemical reaction. Thus, there is a long series of translations and retranslations between chemical and electrical codes between the initial reception of the stimulus and its final recognition. It seems awfully likely that all this translation and retranslation serves some useful function. If it did not, it certainly would have been simpler for nature to have made the axons of the ganglion cells longer, so that they could be attached directly to the neurons in the association areas where recognition ultimately takes place.

Descartes's experiment with a dead man's eye

Descartes thought that there was a direct connection from the eye to the brain. In fact, he thought that each receptor cell in the retina was the end of a tiny filament that ended up in the pineal gland, which he took to be the dwelling place of mind. As explained in Chapter 1, the theory was that light falling on any one retinal cell would produce an excitation at the other end of the filament in the pineal gland. Descartes performed an interesting experiment that provided support for his ideas concerning the initial stage of visual processing. He scraped off the back covering of the eye of a man who had recently died and looked through it. What he saw was an image of the part of space the eye was pointed at. The image was inverted by the eye's lens to be sure, but it was a little copy of the external world. It thus seemed reasonable to postulate that the image falling on the back of the eye could be sent through the optic nerve to the brain much as bills used to be sent through pneumatic tubes in department stores. Unfortunately for this theory, it turned out that nerves are not hollow tubes but solid neuronal tissue that can transmit electrical impulses but, alas, not images.

We could certainly modernize Descartes's theory. The modern version would be that the 268 million receptors in the two eyes converge on 134 million neurons somewhere in the brain. Descartes proposed this sort of convergence to explain why there are two retinal images—one in each eye—but only one object is perceived. This system eventuates in a one-to-one correspondence between patterns of retinal activity and patterns of neuronal activity. In other words, a copy or image of the retinal pattern is transmitted. Now, on to the question of how objects are recognized. As you may recall, Descartes is a bit vague on this point. The mind, he says, recognizes the image. This will hardly do. You can see that we have the same problem here as we did with the Cartesian robot. Passage of an image or copy of the stimulus does no good. The whole point of recognition is to get information from a very large set of receptor cells converging onto one neuron. The Cartesian copy theory overshoots this goal by a factor of 100 million or so.

Template matching

One possible solution to the question of recognition involves template matching. This goes back to an idea first put forth by the gestalt psychologists. If recognition has to do with a stimulus making contact with a memory trace, there are various ways of effecting this contact. The simplest way would involve connection of a set of retinal cells to form a template or pattern. The latter would be an exact copy of the pattern on the retina as shown in Figure 2–12. Whenever a pattern of excitation on the retina exactly fitted the template, the recognizing neuron or neurons in the brain would be activated.

FIGURE 2–12   A retinal template for recognizing one's grandmother

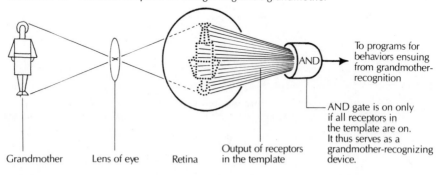

Grandmother   Lens of eye   Retina   Output of receptors in the template

To programs for behaviors ensuing from grandmother-recognition

AND gate is on only if all receptors in the template are on. It thus serves as a grandmother-recognizing device.

PROBLEMS WITH TEMPLATE MATCHING

Now this approach immediately runs into problems. You can recognize your grandmother from a variety of perspectives and distances. A template of this sort would only work if she were standing, say, exactly four feet away. If she were any closer, her size on your retina would be too large. If she were standing further away, her size would be too small. If she were lying down, you would be at a total loss. This problem could conceivably be solved by having a whole family of grandmother templates—one for grandmother standing four feet away, another for grandmother standing three feet away, and so on. All of these would be connected to the same grandmother neuron in your brain. The problem with this solution is that literally an infinite number of templates would be necessary just to enable you to recognize your grandmother from all possible distances and in all possible orientations. The same would be true of every other object you are capable of recognizing. We would run out of neurons before enough templates had been constructed to account for all of the things you can recognize.

Well, you might argue, perhaps we cannot recognize objects in nearly as many orientations or from as many distances as I am assuming. Perhaps one cannot, in fact, recognize objects that are tilted or upside down. This argument, though, will not hold up. Even rotation has surprisingly little effect on recognition of many stimuli. Kolers, Eden, and Boyer (1964) studied the effect of rotations of letters on reading speed. For example, 180° rotations wherein letters are upside down and backwards are surprisingly easy to read. It seems awfully unlikely that people would have reversed and upside-down letter-recognizing templates, since they almost never have occasion to recognize such stimuli. When they begin to write, children often reverse letters. Sometimes, they look at pictures without bothering to turn them right side up. Gibson, Gibson, Pick, and Osser (1962) did a study that illustrates the tendency of children to ignore rotations of visual stimuli. The children's task was to match one of several geometric stimuli to a standard they had just seen. In this experiment, preschool children had great difficulty discriminating rotations from the standard. This difficulty decreased with the age of the child. It was not that children were simply bad at the matching task in general. They did not confuse stimuli that differed from the standard in terms of closures or breaks. They were specifically insensitive to rotations.

A similar phenomenon can be seen on the Bender-Gestalt test, in which the subject has to draw copies of several fairly simple geometric shapes. One of the most common mistakes on this test that is made by children (and also by people suffering from certain types of brain damage and psychosis) is rotation. That is, the subject reproduces the stimulus figure adequately except that the reproduction is rotated from the correct orientation. This mistake, too, decreases with age. In both the Gibson et al. study and in copying designs, children seem to be reacting in terms of critical features rather than templates. A template theory cannot easily explain why children would be insensitive to rotations. However, if children were classifying designs on the basis of critical features, such as presence versus absence of right angles, their performance would be understandable.

COMPUTER TEMPLATE MATCHING SYSTEMS

The gestalt psychologists recognized these problems with template matching but offered no real solution to them. Their answer was that somehow stimuli must merely be similar to, rather than exactly like, the neural template to which they are fitted. This does make some intuitive sense, but the question now arises as to how the correlation between stimulus and template is computed. Some possible answers have been suggested as a by-product of attempts to construct computer programs that will recognize patterns. There has been much work on this because of its obvious utility. One of the bottlenecks to full usage of the processing capacity of computers is getting information into them rapidly. If we could construct computers that could recognize patterns, such as spoken or handwritten words directly without having these first coded and keypunched, much time and money could be saved. An example of such a pattern recognition system is the one used by banks to read the account numbers on checks (Evey, 1959). This system uses a template-matching system. Checks are exactly positioned over a grid of light-sensitive sensors. The sensors are connected together such that if all the sensors connected together are off and all others are on, a switch is set indicating the presence of the number for which the template is searching. The logic of this is the same as that shown in Figure 2–12.

PREPROCESSING

This system is a good one—for reading the numbers on checks. What if one wanted a system that would also read the amount that a check was written for or the name of the person to whom it was written? These are not printed clearly. Rather, they are scrawled out in a style that is a little bit different for each individual check writer. One solution to this sort of problem involves what is called preprocessing (Selfridge and Neisser, 1960). Let's say we want to build a system that recognizes the number 8 no matter how it is written. Assume that our machine's input consists of a matrix of light-sensitive devices as shown in Figure 2–13 and that the original input to be recognized is as shown in Figure 2–13A.

FIGURE 2–13   Local preprocessing for an input figure (A). Preprocessing closes up gaps (B), moves the figure to the center of the field (C), rotates the figure to a standard orientation (D), and expands it to a standard size (E).

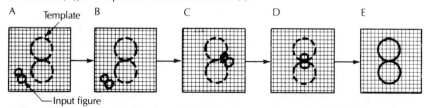

One of the first things that can be done would involve local processing. Our program could scan the rows and columns of its input matrix and close up small gaps and irregularities. This gets us from Figure 2–13A (the original input) to Figure 2–13B. Second, the program could normalize the input by moving it to the exact center of the input grid (C), rotate it so that its longest axis was vertical (D), and expand or contract it so that its height and width conformed to some preselected standard (E). Now, if it is an 8, it should match our template. There would of course be no reason to require that it overlap 100 percent of our template cells. We could allow some leeway, but not too much lest our machine confront a *B* and confuse it with the number 8.

These preprocessing techniques are rather similar to the sorts of things humans do when they fixate on a stimulus. When you pick up this book, you turn it right side up, move it to some optimal distance from your eyes, and place it conveniently in front of your eyes. In spite of this surface similarity, template-matching systems do not work very well as models for human recognition. They are too stimulus bound. If we try to fix them so as to read wide varieties of type faces, they make too many mistakes. If we try to cut down on their rate of mistakes, we are back where we started with a machine like that for reading checks, which recognizes only a special typeface. Somehow, human beings, are able to equate a much wider range of stimuli without making mistakes than are template-matching computers.

SUMMARY AND CONCLUSIONS

In order to understand what is involved in perception and recognition, we considered how robots might be constructed. Passing a veridical copy of the external world into a robot served no purpose. Passing the copy around inside the robot resulted in an absurd hall of mirrors. On the other hand, transducing or translating physical signals from the environment into electrical internal representations resulted in useful and usable perceptions. It quickly became apparent, however, that attempting to connect these perceptions to responses in a reflex-like way according to behavioristic principles did not allow intelligent behavior. Incorporating some simple logic devices did allow us to construct a cognitive robot capable of recognizing and responding to complex stimuli.

We then saw that the nervous system operates in ways that are analogous to our cognitive robot. It, too, transduces physical signals into electrical ones. It, too, performs logical operations on these electrical signals. We described some of the details of the chemical basis of these electrical signals. The point of this description was not to convince you that you do not see what you quite obviously do see. Rather, it was to convince you that what you see is an internal representation that is no more isomorphic to reality than the pattern of electrical potentials that a robot sees. Seeing is not the registration of a copy of reality. Rather, it is a pattern of electrical and chemical activity in the brain.

Finally, we turned to the question of how we recognize what we see. If perception is the activation of preexisting schemas or cognitive units, then it is necessary to explain how a variety of patterns of physical energy all lead to activation of the appropriate or correct cognitive unit. We saw that the copy theory of perception is no help at all in answering this question. We then considered the template-matching theory of recognition. While this theory offers an intuitively plausible explanation of recognition, a number of problems suggest that this is not the correct explanation. In Chapter 3, we shall present the more robust feature analytic theory of recognition.

3

Feature analysis

We have argued that to perceive or recognize something is to activate a pre-existing schema or cognitive unit. In Chapter 1 we discussed a number of lines of evidence that support this view. In Chapter 2 we presented some more arguments for it and showed how some simple stimuli—such as the mere presence of light—could be recognized and acted upon. However, human beings recognize, understand, and act upon some extremely complex stimuli—such as grandmothers. Such stimuli engender many different sensations. For example, the sensations induced by your grandmother will vary according to how far away she is, the angle from which she is viewed, the color of the dress she is wearing, and so on. The problem is how all of these sensations converge upon or activate the same cognitive unit—the one coding your grandmother. The template-matching theory represents an attempt to answer this question. We saw, however, that the attempt fails. Virtually an infinite number of templates would be necessary in order to enable you to recognize your grandmother. The same is, of course, true for each of the other complex objects that you are able to recognize.

In this chapter, we shall describe an opposite—and more successful—answer to the question of recognition. This answer involves the idea that recognition is based upon the detection of invariant or distinctive features. A distinctive feature is an attribute that characterizes an object and can be detected throughout a wide range of circumstances. For example, it remains invariant at varying distances. The idea is that any given object is defined by a unique set of distinctive features. When they are all present, the object is recognized as being present. After explaining the general theory of feature analysis, we shall consider some evidence based on research with frogs, cats, and crabs. This evidence suggests that organisms are sensitive to distinctive features and that the detectors of these features are wired together so as to permit recognition of complex patterns. We shall also investigate how distinctive features are detected in the first place. Just as our consideration of simple robots helped us to understand some complex principles, so our consideration of how simple organisms recognize objects will set the stage for our discussion of the analogous but much more complex principles of human recognition and understanding.

WHAT IS A DISTINCTIVE FEATURE?

A distinctive feature is a relatively invariant cue or signal. The robots described in Chapter 2 were actually sensitive to distinctive features. The mere presence of light was the cue that alerted them to the presence of an object. Note that this cue was quite abstract. The robots' sensory receptors ignored the color of the light and the form of the object emitting the light. The robots also used presence of noise as a cue. The type of noise was immaterial. It could have been human speech or an artificial pure tone. In the robots' world, all of the extra information was superfluous. The robots were built to respond to abstract distinctive features or cues.

Could such an approach be used as a basis for recognition? Exactly such an approach is used by certain lower animals. The male stickleback fish stakes out a bit of territory which he considers to be uniquely his own. If another male stickleback fish enters this territory, he does so at his own considerable risk, for the original owner will attack him. On the other hand, the owner is unconcerned if other species of fish pass through his territory. Quite evidently, then, one male stickleback can recognize another one. By what means does he do so? Evidently, recognition is based upon a single distinctive feature: the presense of a red underbelly. Tinbergen (1951) prepared several models, as shown in Figure 3–1. The one on the top left looks exactly like a male stickleback fish except that it is not red

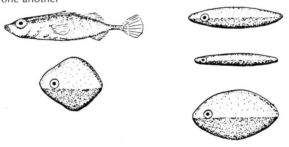

FIGURE 3–1 Stickleback models used by Tinbergen to demonstrate that the presence of a red underbelly is the distinctive feature whereby stickleback fish recognize one another

Source: N. Tinbergen, The Study of Instinct (Oxford: Clarenden Press, 1951), p. 28.

on its underside. The others are red underneath but do not look much like fish, let alone those of the stickleback variety. Tinbergen floated these models through stickleback territory. It turned out that virtually anything with a red underside elicited attack, while anything lacking it (including the otherwise realistic model) was ignored. It would seem then, that male sticklebacks define one another by the presence or absence of a single distinctive feature—a red underside. Tinbergen also describes a number of other species that respond to the presence of simple distinctive features in this manner.

Could recognition in higher organisms work in a similar way? Perhaps recognition is based not upon a complete analysis of a pattern of sensations but upon the detection of a feature that uniquely defines an object. Suppose that your grandmother were Hester Prynne, the heroine of Hawthorne's *The Scarlet Letter*. You will recall that Hester Prynne was compelled always to wear a scarlet letter *A* on the bosom of her dress. While Hester Prynne did not wear a scarlet letter in order to help people recognize her (it was a punishment for adultery), you will agree that the presence of such a scarlet letter would be a tremendous aid in recognition. In order to recognize Hester Prynne, all one would need to do would be to detect the presence of this single attribute. The problem with this idea concerns how one would recognize the scarlet letter in the first place. How would you differentiate among the true Hester, (*A*), a red cross nurse (+), and a lazy wolf who thought you would fall for any scarlet letter at all (for example, *R*)? For that matter, how would you tell the difference between any of these and one of Tinbergen's fake stickleback fish? Even a letter of the alphabet is a complex pattern defined by the simultaneous presence of several distinctive features. Perhaps lower organisms recognize things on the basis of individual distinctive features, while higher organisms recognize them on the basis of combinations of distinctive features.

PANDEMONIUM

Hierarchical feature analysis

Pandemonium is the name that the poet John Milton gave to the capital of hell. This was certainly the ultimate destination of Hester Prynne in the eyes of her puritan judges. The demon who came to fetch her there would be up against the same problem we are facing—how to recognize her. Selfridge (1959) has offered a general feature-detection model for pattern recognition. He, in fact, calls the model *Pandemonium* in reference to the demons that make the model go. Let us consider a pandemonium system for recognition of letters of the alphabet. A pandemonium system is organized into several hierarchical layers or levels. Figure 3–2 shows a depiction of a pandemonium system for recognizing letters of the alphabet. You will note that Hester is not providing the stimulation. The demons have got the wolf instead. At the lowest level is the image demon. Its task is to record an image of the incoming stimulus so that it can be examined by demons on the level above. The latter are the feature demons. All of them simultaneously examine the image for their own particular feature. One of them might be interested in right angles, another in acute angles, another in continuous curves, and so on. Whenever one of these demons sees its feature, it begins yelling. On the next tier are the cognitive demons—one for each of the things to be recognized. We would want 26 of them: one for each letter of the alphabet. These demons listen for cries from the feature demons. The A demon, for example, would be listening for very loud and excited yells from the obtuse angle demon, since As contain two obtuse angles. It would also be listening for some vociferous yelling on the part of the acute angle demon, since As also have three acute angles. When the A demon hears what it is listening for, it too begins to yell. The more it hears the relevant feature demons yelling, the louder it yells. In Figure 3–2, the A demon does not have much to shout about. However, several of the other demons—most notably the R demon—are yelling. On the final level lives the decision demon. It is needed because a lot of voices are rising from

FIGURE 3–2   A pandemonium system for recognizing letters of the alphabet

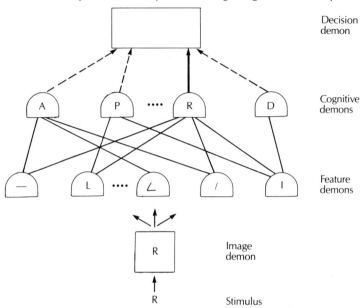

the pandemonium below. Whenever an R is put in, the R demon should be yelling the loudest, but anything that excites it will also set the P, B, and F demons to yelling as well. However, they would not be yelling quite as loudly, since they would have detected less of the features that they were looking for.

Implications of the pandemonium model

The important thing to note about the pandemonium system is its efficiency. First, it is what is called a parallel-processing system: all of the demons work simultaneously. Second, it is economical. There need only be a few feature demons. Certainly, there can be fewer feature demons than letter demons. Third, it ignores the sorts of minor differences that should be ignored, such as the size, orientation, and minor details of the input letters. An another level, note that when the system recognizes a letter, this means yelling or activation of one of the cognitive demons. In no sense does the image itself move up through the system. This internal representation (the yelling of a cognitive demon) has no qualitative similarity at all to the physical or other characteristics of the input stimulus.

Substituting logic gates or neurons for demons

If we were building a pandemonium, we would find that we could economize in the long run if we employed electrical circuits rather than demons. In Figure 3–2, we used AND gates rather than demons. Rather than listening for yelling, these logic gates simply detect inputs from the feature detectors. A given AND gate will go on if and only if all of its inputs are simultaneously on. Of course, we would have to be careful that each different letter of the alphabet was, in fact, defined by a unique combination of distinctive features. We shall talk later about how the features would be detected in the first place.

It is certainly possible that a set of neurons could operate as a pandemonium system. The system would look at it does in Figure 3–2. The basic difference would be that it would be constructed of neurons (rather than logic gates) and their axons (rather than wires). Recall that neurons communicate in terms of rate of firing rather than by yelling or simply producing a steady voltage level. In our example, the neural pandemonium would know than an *R* was being presented because the *R*-detecting neuron was firing most rapidly. We shall see later in this chapter that there is a good deal of evidence for the existence of neural feature-detection systems.

How people recognize letters

There is fairly wide agreement that human beings recognize letters (and others things as well) in a fashion similar to that proposed by Selfridge. We shall discuss the process of recognition in detail in the next several chapters, but it may help to give a concrete example of what is thought to go on in letter recognition before we go any further. Massaro and Schmuller (1975) have developed a model of letter recognition that operates in a pandemoniumlike way. The model is illustrated in Figure 3–3. Following sensory transduction, a preperceptual visual image is hypothetically formed. This is the analogue of Selfridge's image demon. It is essentially a brief persistence of the sensation induced by the stimulus. Its function is to maintain the sensation while feature analysis occurs. Primary recognition involves determining which letter of the alphabet the extracted features define. This is done by reference to the master chart shown at the top of the figure. In this chart, each letter of the alphabet is uniquely defined by a set of distinctive features. The chart illustrates the system developed by Gibson (1969). Several other feature systems have been formulated. This one is merely used as an example. In reading, each letter is hypothetically recognized in this way. Finally, recognized letters are strung together to form words—the synthesized visual percept in the figure.

In the case of recognizing Hester Prynne, the synthesized visual percept would be constructed from input from a number of hierarchical pandemonium systems, not just the one for letters of the alphabet. The thing seen—a woman wearing a scarlet letter—would be a mental event synthesized from many visual features. As we shall see in later chapters, much evidence exists that people do seem to recognize letters—and all sorts of other things as well—by means of pandemoniumlike feature-detection systems. Are these systems constructed from sets of neurons? Presumably they are, but it would be extremely difficulty to find out the details of the wiring arrangements. To do so, we would have to record the responses of individual neurons. The only way to do this is to insert recording electrodes directly into the neurons, and that would require brain surgery. This is a far too dangerous procedure to undertake for research purposes even if we could get anyone to volunteer in the first place. Thus, we have to turn to studies of lower animals for our evidence.

FIGURE 3–3   Sample flowchart for human letter recognition

Feature description	A	B	C	D	E	F	G	H	I	J	K	L	M	N	O	P	Q	R	S	T	U	V	W	X	Y	Z
Straight																										
1 horizontal	+				+	+	+	+				+					+									+
2 vertical		+			+	+	+		+	+	+	+	+	+		+		+		+				+		
3 diagonal (/)	+							+	+													+	+	+	+	+
4 diagonal (\)	+							+		+	+			+	+								+	+	+	+
Curve																										
5 closed		+		+											+	+	+	+								
6 open, vertical							+											+								
7 open, horizontal			+			+	+									+										
8 intersection	+	+			+	+		+		+						+	+	+	+				+			
Redundancy																										
9 cyclic change			+			+						+					+		+							
10 symmetry	+	+	+	+	+			+	+		+		+		+					+	+	+	+	+	+	
Discontinuity																										
11 vertical	+	+		+		+	+		+				+			+		+		+				+		+
12 horizontal						+	+					+								+						+

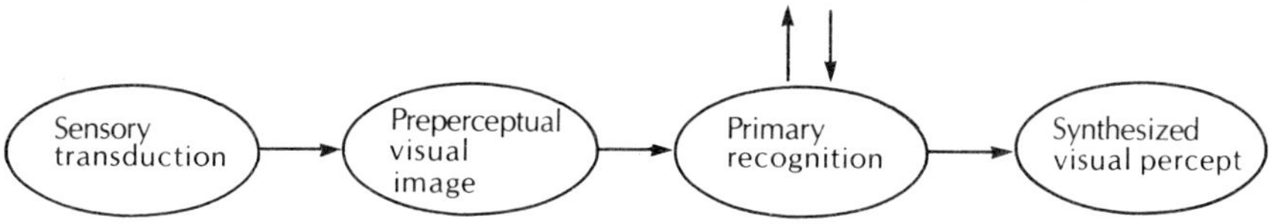

Source: Eleanor J. Gibson, *Principles of Perceptual Learning and Development,* © 1969, p. 88. Reprinted by permission of Prentice-Hall, Inc., Englewood Cliffs, N.J. Also, D. Massaro and J. Schmuller, "Visual Features, Perceptual Storage, and Processing Time in Reading" in *Understanding Language,* ed. D. Massaro (New York: Academic Press, 1975), p. 208.

WHAT THE FROG'S EYE TELLS THE FROG'S BRAIN

Several hundred years after Descartes' experiment with a dead man's eye, Lettvin, Maturana, McCulloch, and Pitts (1959) conducted a similar experiment with a living frog's eye. However, they used 20th-century techniques. To their question, "What does the frog's eye tell the frog's brain?" we might give the brief answer: not much. However, the details of this brief answer have revolutionized our view of perception.

A schematic diagram of the frog's visual system is shown in Figure 3–4. The frog's retina is composed of light-sensitive receptor cells. Ganglion cells receive inputs from several receptor cells in a roughly circular area. This is the receptive field of the ganglion cell. The receptive fields of neighboring ganglion cells overlap somewhat. That is, a given receptor may send information to more than one ganglion cell. The axons of the ganglion cells are collected into optic tracts that run to the tectum. The tectum is the analogue of the lateral geniculate nucleus in humans. Note that the optic tracts of the frog are completely crossed. All of the fibers from the right eye go to the left part of the tectum and all of the fibers from the left eye go to the right part of the tectum.

FIGURE 3–4   The visual system of the frog

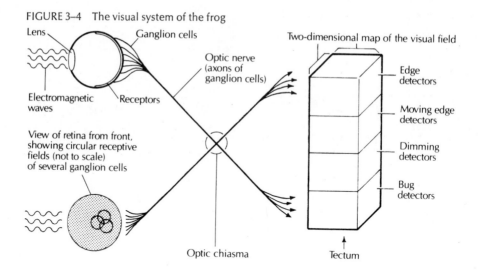

Feature detection in the retina

In Lettvin's et al.'s experiment, the frog's eye was fixed at one point in a metal sphere. By means of magnets, a variety of objects could be presented and moved around in the frog's visual field. With this system all sorts of natural and artificial objects could be presented. Meanwhile, the experimenters were recording the impulses from a single ganglion cell. This was done by inserting a recording electrode into the axon of the ganglion cell. The logic of the experiment was to find out what would make a ganglion cell fire at its maximal rate. This would be the thing that the ganglion cell was constructed to detect. Of course, if a stimulus were not falling upon a given ganglion cell's receptive field, there would be nothing for it to detect, so it would remain silent.

The results that Lettvin and his coworkers obtained were little short of astounding. They found that the frog's eye sends only four types of message back to its brain. That is, there are four types of ganglion cells sending information: edge detectors, which respond to any border between light and dark regions; moving contrast detectors, which respond to moving edges; dimming detectors, which respond to an overall decrease in illumination; and convex edge detectors, which respond only to small, dark, moving objects. It takes little imagination to dub the last as bug detectors. These four types of ganglion cells have overlapping receptive fields. That is, in a given small region of the frog's retina, one ganglion cell will be searching for edges, another for bugs, and so on.

Three things can be noted about the results of this experiment. First, the ganglion cells are responsive to abstract features rather than to specific attributes or nuances. For example, edge detectors respond to any edge at all to about the same degree. It is completely immaterial whether it is the edge of a leaf, the edge caused by the shadow of our friend, Hester Prynne, or an artificial edge created by an abrupt change in light intensity. Any edge will do. The same is true of bug-detecting ganglion cells. They exhibit the same response to moving dark spots as to real bugs. The ganglion cells, then, are very abstract or general with respect to what they detect. Second, although the detectors do not care what caused the thing they detect, they are tuned so as to respond only if it is unambiguously present. For example, an edge detector will fail to respond if an edge is too fuzzy—that is, if the transition from light to dark is too gradual. A bug detector will not respond if the small, dark spot is not moving. Thus, a frog will starve to death in the presence of a generous supply of freshly killed bugs. Since they are not moving, it cannot see them. Third, each of the four types of ganglion cells are specialized. That is, each ignores the features that the others detect. An edge detector, for example, is unresponsive to a general dimming of its receptive field.

Organization of the tectum

The axons of each of the four types of ganglion cells end up in a separate layer of the tectum (Arbib, 1972). All of the axons from edge detectors go to one layer, those from bug detectors to another layer, and so on. Interestingly enough, they remain in registration. That is, information about any receptive field on the retina ends up in the same column of the tectum. As shown in Figure 3–4, the tectum is not so much a map of the visual field as a three-dimensional data matrix. For any region in the visual field, the frog knows four things: Is an edge there? Is it moving? Is the area dim? Is a bug there? The answers to each of these questions can be coded in a binary or yes-no fashion: The frog has four bits of information about each region of its visual field. Lettvin et al. also found what seem to be "newness" neurons in the tectum. These are not quite so neatly organized into layers. They seem to code in binary fashion an answer to the question: Is the information in this region the same as it was previously or is it new? Is something changing here?

A frog is essentially a biological machine for killing bugs and avoiding moving shadows. There are outputs from the tectum to the frog's motor regions. They code two basic programs: (1) Move away from moving shadows (possible predators) toward dim regions while taking care not to run into things such as rocks and trees (indicated by unmoving edges) and (2) place your (sticky) tongue in the spatial coordinates occupied by a bug. The reader is referred to Arbib (1972) for a fascinating and plausible description of how this circuitry must operate. Note that the frog's eyes send the frog's brain only the information needed to execute its basic programs.

Somatotopic mapping

The frog has information about spatial localization. However, since space is the organizing principle of the tectum, it is not coded explicitly. Wherever it is relevant, the brain tends to operate in this sort of somatotopic fashion. That is, it stores information about location not explicitly but by preserving the relative relationships of data cells to one another. This is true of all organisms, not just of frogs. In humans, too, there is a point-for-point correspondence between points in the visual field and points in the visual cortex. An experiment by Dobelle, Mladejovsky, and Girvin (1974) illustrates this. They placed an 8 × 8 array of 64 electrodes on the exposed cortex of their subject who was, incidentally, blind.

With these electrodes, they were able to stimulate the cortex in various patterns. Stimulation with any one electrode led the subject to experience a phosphene or flash of light that appeared to be about the size of a quarter held at arm's length. Stimulation with various combinations of electrodes resulted in the person seeing circles, squares, and other geometric figures. A circular array of electrode stimulation points did not necessarily produce a circle, but each electrode did correspond with some retinal point, so by trial and error a pattern of electrodes could be found that would produce a circle.

The somatotopic principle of storage gives us a handle on what Kant was talking about when he said that space is an a priori category. The frog is built so as to organize its information about the world in spatial terms. It is prewired so that it has to perceive in this way. That is, a given column of the tectum contains all of the information about a given region of space, and the columns are rationally arranged so as to constitute a spatial map. If the axons of ganglion cells all went to random places in the tectum, the frog could not perceive the world in spatial terms. Information about the same point in space would not be in registration. There would be no way to tell what was occupying a given place. Worse, information about neighboring points in space would be randomly scattered. There would be no way to know what was next to what. No matter how much learning does or does not influence the development of the frog's visual abilities, if these develop at all, they will develop such that objects are seen in a spatial framework. To say that the frog learned to see in spatial terms is almost as implausible as saying that it learned its tectum.

Implications

The frog's visual world consists of bugs and shadows. It is at least a little better off than the creatures in Plato's cave, who could see only shadows! As we shall find in a few pages, other investigators have shown that similar feature detection systems exist in higher animals. Before getting to that, though, let us consider the broader implications of Lettvin et al.'s study. First, the frog—if it could conceive at all—could not conceive of our world. Color, for example, is excluded by the nature of its feature detection system. This raises the possibility that we too are limited by our feature detection systems. It could not be otherwise if perception is the activation of preexisting schemas or feature detectors. Second, the brain gets only a few bits of information. It reconstructs a model of the world with this information. This has to be true, because it is information about abstract features that are transmitted to it, not whole images. Third, even the idea that the brain reconstructs an image is a bit misleading. In vision, patterns of electromagnetic waves falling on the retina are transduced not into patterns of neural firing that track the intensities of the impinging light but into patterns of firing that represent the presence or absence of specific features, such as edges. The transformation is not merely quantitative but qualitative. The world you see is a pattern of neural activity inside your brain. You seem to see objects out there in the world. It would be better to say that you *construct* an idea of the world based on hints given by light patterns on the retina. If you are not willing to agree with Schopenhauer (1818) that "The world is my idea" perhaps you will agree that "The world is my hypothesis." Your sight, just as that of the frog, is in your brain, not out in the world where you seem to see it in three-dimensional depth.

LATERAL INHIBITION AND FEATURE DETECTION

Mechanics of lateral inhibition

How are features such as edges extracted by ganglion cells from the activity of retinal receptors? There are four types of feature detectors in the frog's eye, but exactly how does each find the feature that it detects? If receptor cells are simply light-sensitive devices and if ganglion cells simply receive input from a set of receptor cells, how could ganglion cells detect anything other than the presence or absence of light? They could not. (Recall that in Chapter 2 I warned you that I was withholding some crucial details about the structure of the retina.)

Figure 3–5 shows a schematic cross section of the human retina. The retinas

FIGURE 3–5   Schematic cross section of the human retina

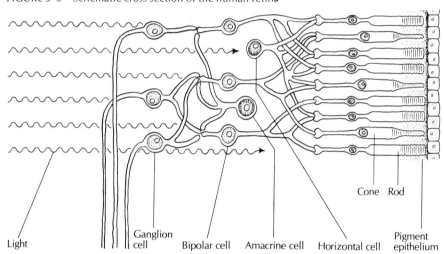

Cone   Rod

Light   Ganglion   Bipolar cell   Amacrine cell   Horizontal cell   Pigment
           cell   epithelium

Source: Coren, Porac, and Ward, (1979), p. 71.

of other vertebrates are similar in structure. Note that the retina has a latticelike structure. We have already talked about the vertical connections from receptors to bipolar cells to ganglion cells. Perpendicular to this pathway are cells—the amacrine and horizontal cells—which have horizontal rather than vertical connections. It turns out that the vertical connections are excitatory, while the horizontal connections are inhibitory (Werblin and Dowling, 1969). Thus, activating a receptor will activate a bipolar cell which will, in turn, activate a ganglion cell. However, activating a horizontal cell will cause it to inhibit neighboring cells. The result of the structural arrangement is that activation of a receptor cell will activate both bipolar cells and horizontal cells. The bipolar cells will pass the activation on to ganglion cells while the horizontal cell will inhibit neighboring receptors. The closer they are, the more it will inhibit them. The ultimate consequence is that neighboring receptive fields exercise a lateral inhibitory effect on each other (because of the inhibitory horizontal cells). The closer two receptive fields are, the more inhibition there is. On the other hand, the vertical connections of receptors to ganglion cells are excitatory. We have a situation where the lateral connections are inhibitory and the vertical ones are excitatory. This turns out to be a very general feature of nervous tissue that is organized in layers. We find just this arrangement not only in the retina but also in the skin, the chochlea, the cerebellum, and the neocortical and paleocortical areas of the brain.

Edge detection

EDGE DETECTION IN A LATERAL INHIBITORY NETWORK

The latticework arrangement of the retina must somehow function to extract features. Consider the problem of detecting edges. First, consider a case where the horizontal inhibitory connections are not present. One receptor is connected to one ganglion cell. As pointed out earlier, this sort of 1:1 arrangement is of no real value. As shown in Figure 3–6, the output of such a system is isomorphic with the input. Here, we show a spot of light—represented by the numbers at the top of the figure—being shined onto the receptor cells. Let us assume that the vertical connections are excitatory and, further, that for every unit of stimulus brightness we get a proportional number of spike potentials out of the ganglion cells. Thus, when 5 units of brightness arrive at a receptor, the ganglion cell to which it is connected produces 5 spikes per unit of time. This system cannot detect edges. The ganglion cells can only code whether or not light is present in the region of the retina that they monitor.

Lindsay and Norman (1977) and others have discussed how we might modify such a system by adding lateral inhibition to construct feature detectors. For example, in Figure 3–7, we show Lindsay and Norman's hypothetical design for an edge detector. They assume that the lateral inhibitory connections inhibit neighboring ganglion cells to a degree proportional to one half of their own input. The basic wiring scheme is shown on the left side of Figure 3–7. For the typical connection shown there, if each of the three receptors at the top were receiving 1 unit of input, the output of the ganglion cell would be zero. Why? It gets 1 unit of input from its receptor, but from this we must subtract ½ unit because of the inhibitory input coming from the receptor on one side and another ½ unit from the receptor on the other side. Clearly, $1 - \frac{1}{2} - \frac{1}{2} = 0$. On the right-hand side of the Figure 3–7 is shown what happens when a whole array of ganglion cells are connected to one another in this fashion. Note that the input is the same as it was in Figure 3–6. However, the output is quite different.

If we compute the output from the ganglion cells, we find that, in fact, it is zero except for the cells at the edges of the light. This circuit will serve to detect edges. The output of a ganglion cell will be 0 if no edge is present over the receptor that it monitors. Note that the output will be 0 regardless of whether its region is bright or dim. On the other hand, the output of a ganglion cell will not be 0 if there is in fact an edge near its receptor. If it is on the bright side of the edge, its output will be $+ 2\frac{1}{2}$ spikes per unit of time; if it is on the dim side of an edge, its output will be $- 2\frac{1}{2}$ spikes per unit of time. Thus, we have an array of detectors that ignores brightness and respond only to edges. One minor problem is that two of our outputs are $- 2\frac{1}{2}$. Since it does not make sense for a ganglion cell to be emitting a negative number of spikes, something is amiss. This could not be the way the real circuit in an eye works. But this problem is easy enough to fix. Let's assume that the ganglion cells fire continually at a spon-

FIGURE 3–6   Retinal input (top) and output (bottom) in a system with no lateral inhibition

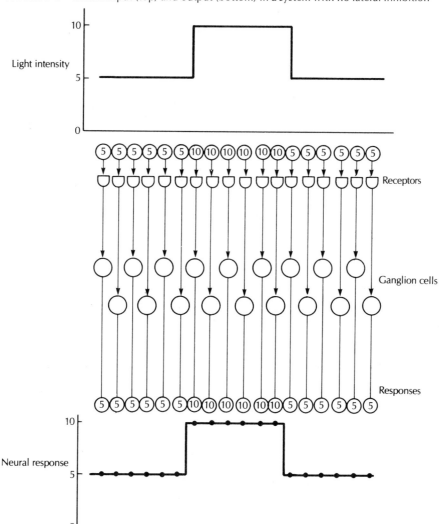

Source: P. H. Lindsay and D. A. Norman, *Human Information Processing: An Introduction to Psychology* (New York: Academic Press, 1977), p. 206.

taneous rate of, say, 20 spikes per unit of time. This would eliminate the problem of negative rates of firing. Nature seems to have solved this problem in a similar way, since neurons do, in fact, exhibit this sort of spontaneous firing.

EDGE DETECTORS IN THE EYE OF THE HORSESHOE CRAB

We have seen how we could construct an edge detector. If we were engineers building a machine, we could stop here. But our question now must be whether

FIGURE 3–7   Retinal input (top) and output (bottom) in a system with lateral inhibition (note that this system is capable of detecting edges)

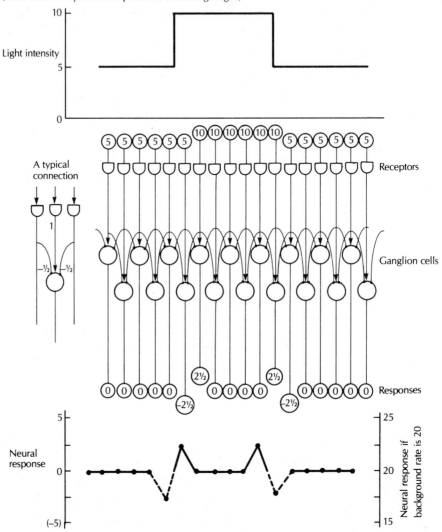

Source: P. H. Lindsay and D. A. Norman, *Human Information Processing: An Introduction to Psychology* (New York: Academic Press, 1977), p. 209.

this is in fact the way that edge detectors work in real organisms. Ratliff's work (1965) with the visual system of *limulus,* the horseshoe crab, sheds light on this question. Limulus is an ideal organism for the study of vision because of the construction of its eye. It has a large compound eye constructed of individual receptors or omatidia. The omatidia are interconnected in a lateral inhibitory network. Stimulating only one omatidium inhibits neighboring ones. If one removes the lens and other biological matter covering the eye, exactly one receptor can be stimulated. By recording the spikes emanating from the ganglion cell collecting information from the omatidium in question, one can observe the effect of stimuli on the receptor. Ratliff observed the effect of an edge of light on the output of ganglion cells. The results of Ratliff's experiment are shown in Figure 3–8. Although this is not exactly what Ratliff did, the logic of the experiment was to

FIGURE 3–8   Results of Ratliff's experiment with the eye of the horseshoe crab. The ganglion cells detect both brightness and edges.

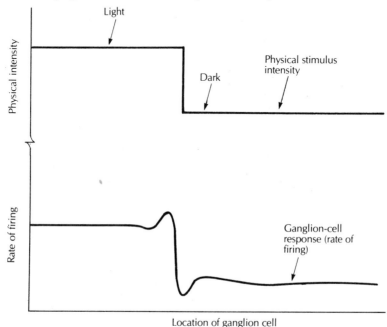

Location of ganglion cell

record the output of a number of ganglion cells while some were exposed to light and others to dark. As shown in the Figure 3–8, the physical stimulus exhibited an abrupt transition from light to dark—that is, an edge. As may be seen in Figure 3–8, the ganglion cells were responsive to the edge. Those on the bright side of the edge exhibited the highest rate of firing while those on the dark side of the edge exhibited the lowest rate of firing. However, the ganglion cells were also responsive to brightness per se. Those exposed to light fired at a higher rate than those exposed to darkness. Thus, the ganglion cells detect both edges and brightness. As Lindsay and Norman (1977) point out, if the inhibitory coefficients in Figure 3–7 are reduced from $\frac{1}{2}$ to $\frac{1}{5}$, the system shown in the figure will mimic the response of the eye of the horseshoe crab rather closely. You can verify this by working out the arithmetic.

MACH BANDS AND EDGE ENHANCEMENT

The human eye seems to function in a similar way to that of the horseshoe crab; that is, it, too, is sensitive to both brightness and edges. In the 19th century,

Ernst Mach (1865) first described what have come to be called *Mach bands* (see Figure 3–9A). Note that the bands of gray seem to be separated by slightly darker strips. The actual physical changes in brightness are as illustrated in Figure 3–9B while your subjective impression is illustrated in Figure 3–9C. The reason for this difference between the physical input and the resultant sensation would seem to be that human feature detectors also function to detect both brightness and edges.

FIGURE 3–9   Illustration of Mach bands. The bands of gray shown in A are of uniform brightness, as shown in B. However, they seem to be separated by dark bands as shown in C.

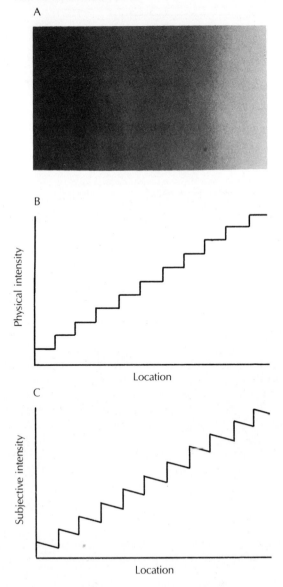

One of the results of this is that our eyes tend to enhance or intensify the edges of things. Most of the stimuli that we see—for example, human faces—have much fuzzier edges than we perceive them as having. Consider how realistic line drawings seem to be. If you are asked to draw a human face, it is extremely likely that your drawing will consist wholly of lines or edges rather than of shadings. The Italian painter Botticelli actually painted thin black lines around his figures in order to accentuate their edges. Presumably, he outlined because he wanted to be realistic. He knew and saw that objects have edges, so he outlined the objects in his paintings. Part of the reason for this sensitivity to edges is presumably due to the edge enhancement brought about by the lateral inhibitory network in the retina.

Motion detection

MOTION DETECTION IN A LATERAL INHIBITORY NETWORK

Quite feasible designs for other sorts of feature detectors can be constructed on the basis of what we know about the construction of neural networks. For example, Lindsay and Norman (1977) have suggested a design similar to the one shown in Figure 3–10 for a detector that would be sensitive to motion from left to right. Here, the inhibitory connections are all biased in one direction. As you can see in Figure 3–10, inputs to the motion detector come from light-sensitive receptors. We have to assume that whenever a given receptor is stimulated, it immediately activates the intermediate cell to which it is connected. Furthermore, after a delay comparable to the speed of the motion the system is supposed to detect, the receptor laterally inhibits the intermediate cell to the left of it. Finally, we assume that the ganglion cell functions as an OR gate: It fires whenever it gets input from any of the intermediate cells.

FIGURE 3–10   Hypothetical design for a motion detector sensitive to an edge of light moving from right to left

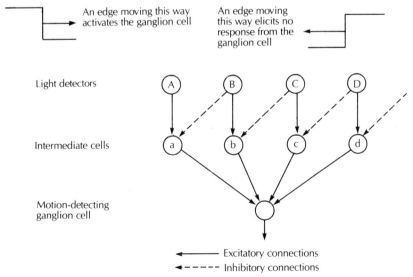

An edge moving this way activates the ganglion cell

An edge moving this way elicits no response from the ganglion cell

Light detectors

Intermediate cells

Motion-detecting ganglion cell

Excitatory connections
Inhibitory connections

A light moving from left to right would elicit continuous firing of the ganglion cell. When the light was over A, A would activate intermediate cell a, and it would in turn activate the ganglion cell. By the time the light was over B, it would begin activating the ganglion cell, and so on. On the other hand, a light moving from right to left would elicit no activity in the ganglion cell. When the moving light was over C, C would activate intermediate cell c, but at the very same time the delayed inhibitory signal from D would deactivate c. Thus, the activation and inhibition would cancel each other. By the time the light was over B, the delayed inhibition from C would be arriving at intermediate cell b just in time to cancel the excitatory input from B.

ILLUSIONS OF MOTION

This system could malfunction under certain circumstances. Consider what would happen if a small spot of light were shined steadily only onto receptor B. It should elicit activity in the motion-detecting ganglion cell since no inhibitory input would be arriving from receptor C. Actually, if you fixate on a small spot of light in a completely dark room, it will appear to move about erratically. This is called the *autokinetic* effect. If two lights are quickly flashed in an alternating fashion, one will perceive a single light moving back and forth between the two points. This is called the *phi phenomenon* (Wertheimer, 1912). Our hypothetical motion detector would certainly be susceptible to this illusion as well if the spots of light were small enough to stimulate only one receptor.

Note that a light moving very quickly from right to left would be able to outrace the inhibition in the system and activate the ganglion cell. Such a light would, however, lead the ganglion cell to detect a slower left-to-right motion. This is because the meaning of the ganglion cell's firing is that a left-to-right motion is present. Such an illusion is analogous to what you see in a motion picture when the spokes of a stagecoach wheel seem to be slowly rotating in the wrong direction. Thus, Lindsay and Norman's hypothetical motion detector would be susceptible to many of the perceptual illusions of motion that are actually found in human beings. This is actually a point in its favor, since the point was to suggest a model of how organisms perceive motion rather than a build a foolproof motion detector. However, the fact that people show some of the same illusions of motion as the hypothetical motion detector does not necessarily mean that the causes of the illusions are the same in both cases.

HIERARCHICAL FEATURE DETECTION IN THE CAT'S BRAIN
Structure of the cat's visual system

We could easily use lateral inhibitory networks to design plausible analyzers to detect other features, but hopefully the principle is now clear. Let us return to empirical realities. In the frog and crab, a lot of feature analysis goes on right in the eye itself. Lower animals, in fact, often possess more complex retinas than do higher animals. The higher up the phylogenetic scale we go, the more feature analysis seems to be deferred to higher centers. Hubel and Wiesel (1965) have investigated visual processing in cats. The cat's visual information-processing system is similar to that of humans. Ganglion cells collect information from roughly circular fields of receptors. There are two basic types of ganglion cells (Robson, 1975). One type has what is called an on-center off-surround receptive field. This type of ganglion cell is maximally activated if there is a spot of light in the center of its receptive field which is surrounded by darkness on the fringes of its receptive field. The other type of ganglion cell has an off-center on-surround receptive field. It is maximally activated by a spot of darkness surrounded by light in its receptive field. Thus, one type of ganglion cell detects spots of light and the other type detects dark spots.

Signals from retinal ganglion cells are relayed to the lateral geniculate nucleus of the cat's thalamus. Here, they synapse with neurons that send their axons to the occipital cortex. The cat's cortex is composed of five layers. Axons from the lateral geniculate nucleus neurons end up in level 4 of the cortex. (Cortical layers are numbered from the outside inwards.) The cat's visual cortex is somatotopically arranged. That is, it is a map of the visual field. Input from the two eyes is collated at the cortical level so that a given point in the cortex contains information about a given point in space rather than information specific to one or the other eye.

Pandemonium in the cat's brain

HUBEL AND WIESEL'S EXPERIMENT

Hubel and Wiesel (1965) presented visual stimuli to cats and recorded the activity of individual neurons on different layers of the cat's cortexes. The idea was to find out what each neuron was specialized to detect. Hubel and Wiesel found evidence that supports the hypothesis that the cat's visual cortex operates as a hierarchical feature detection system. Neurons on lower levels seem to detect simple features while neurons in successively higher layers of the cortex detect more and more complex features. Hypothetically, the more complex feature detectors receive input from the lower level detectors, just as is the case in Selfridge's pandemonium model.

The feature-detecting neurons on all levels share several properties. Each exhibits a maximal response to a specific visual feature but will respond somewhat to similar features. The closer the fit of a stimulus with the feature the neuron detects, the faster the rate of firing. Each of the neurons can be fatigued by prolonged exposure to the thing that it detects. That is, prolonged stimulation will lessen the sensitivity of the detector. The neurons on each layer of the cortex constitute a lateral inhibitory network (Nelson and Frost, 1978; Sillito, 1979). When a neuron is activated by the feature it detects, it laterally inhibits surrounding neurons. These surrounding neurons hypothetically code similar features in nearby areas of visual space. Presumably, the lateral inhibitory arrangement is useful in feature extraction in somewhat the same ways as explained in previous sections.

SIMPLE CELLS

In layer 4 of the occipital cortex, Hubel and Wiesel discovered what they called *simple cells*. These cells seem to be detectors for visual features, such as edges, slits, and lines. Hubel and Wiesel also found motion-detecting cells at this and other levels of the cortex. However, to simplify our discussion, we will not deal with them. Whereas retinal ganglion cells have small circular receptive fields, simple cortical cells have larger, more oblong receptive fields. As shown in Figure 3–11, firing in a given edge-detecting neuron can be elicited by shining a light anywhere along a specific area on the retina. Usually, right next to this line was a line that, if light was shined on it, would depress the spontaneous rate of firing of the cell. Light shined anywhere else on the retina would have no effect. The situation is shown in Figure 3–11. The +s indicate points that in-

FIGURE 3–11   Retinal receptive fields of edge detectors, slit detectors, and line detectors

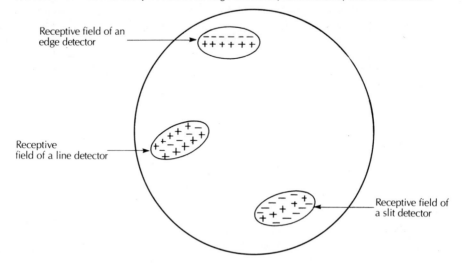

Receptive field of an edge detector

Receptive field of a line detector

Receptive field of a slit detector

crease the firing rate of simple cortical cells, while the −s indicate points that decrease the firing rate. The maximum rate of firing of this type of cell is elicited by positioning an edge of light over the receptive field such that the + line is in light and the − line in darkness. On the other hand, overall illumination of both the + and − fields would elicit no change in the spontaneous firing rate: In this case the inhibition from the − field and the excitation from the + field would cancel each other out.

The reason for this is illustrated in Figure 3–12. Here we show an array of receptors connected to a ganglion cell. These receptors form the + field of the ganglion cell. Next to them is an array of receptors that form the − field. Note that these receptors are not directly connected to the ganglion cell. Rather, they laterally inhibit the receptors in the + field. Figure 3–12 illustrates what happens under four possible conditions: (A) light over both + and − fields, (B) darkness over both + and − fields, (C) light over + field and darkness over − field, and (D) darkness over + field and light over − field. As you can see, the ganglion cell output is zero when no edge is present. However, one sort of edge brings about negative output while the opposite sort of edge brings about positive output. Of course, in a real neural circuit, the cells would have a spontaneous firing rate so as to avoid negative rates of firing. The figure also shows that the system would be able to detect a fuzzy edge—as shown Figure 3–12E—but would respond somewhat less strongly to it than to an abrupt edge.

FIGURE 3–12   Lateral inhibition can be used to detect edges

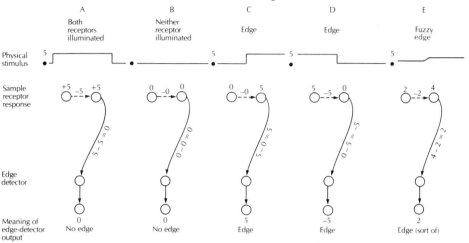

Closely related to edge detectors are the slit detectors. These cells have a central excitatory fields surrounded by an inhibitory field on both sides (see Figure 3–11). They respond maximally only if a bright slit surrounded by darkness on both sides is positioned over their receptive field. They respond minimally —that is, their spontaneous firing rate is maximally depressed—if a dark line surrounded on both sides by a bright field is presented to the receptive field. Line detectors are just the opposite. They respond maximally to a line of darkness surrounded by brightness (see Figure 3–11). Slit and line detectors are constructed in a similar way to edge detectors, but the wiring is a bit more complex.

Hubel and Wiesel reasoned that simple cells must receive input from a number of retinal ganglion cells. For example, if we wanted to build a line detector in the cat's cortex, it would make sense to connect together the output of a string of off-center on-surround ganglion cells to one simple cortical cell, as shown in Figure 3–13. The simple cell would be thought of as a sort of AND gate. Each ganglion cell would be on if there were darkness in the center of its own field and brightness on the periphery. All of them would be on only if a line of darkness were correctly positioned over the whole series. The simple cell would be on only if all of the ganglion cells were on. Thus, it would be on only if a line were present.

COMPLEX CELLS

The simple cells are general or abstract in what they detect but they are still specific in that they are only responsive to patterns in a specific location and in a specific orientation. In level 3 of cat cortex, Hubel and Wiesel found neurons, which they called *complex cells*, that extract more general information. Here again were edge, slit, and line detectors, but they could be turned on by a wider variety of stimuli. Furthermore, the complex cells showed a strong preference for

FIGURE 3–13   Hypothetical connections of ganglion cells (spot detectors), simple cells (specific-line detectors), complex cells (general-line detectors), and hypercomplex cells (general-angle detectors)

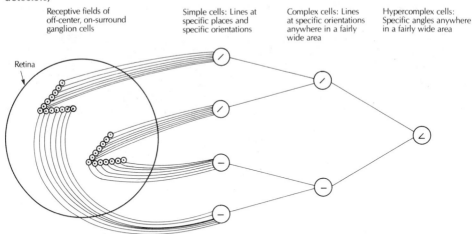

moving slits, lines, and edges. The specific location of a slit, line, or edge was not very crucial. However, orientation was still crucial. Thus a complex line detector might be specialized for the detection of 45° lines of a certain width at any place over a fairly wide area of the visual field. A moment's thought will show that there is an obvious way to build this sort of cell: merely connect together the outputs of a number of simple cells as the input to the complex cell. In this case, we might think of the complex cell as an OR gate (see Figure 3–13).

HYPERCOMPLEX CELLS

The story does not end here. Moving higher in the cortex to level 2, Hubel and Wiesel found what they labeled *hypercomplex cells.* One type of hypercomplex cell actually showed more specificity than simple and complex cells. It is sensitive to lines and edges of a specific length. A simple or complex cell that detects lines exhibits the same response if the line continues beyond its receptive field as if it exactly fills its receptive field. On the other hand, a line must be a specific length in order to excite a hypercomplex line detector. However, its exact position on the retina is not crucial. This led Hubel and Wiesel to speculate that this sort of cell must receive inputs from complex cells rather than from simple cells. Hypercomplex line-segment dectectors could conceivably receive excitatory input from some complex line-detectors (indicating the presence of the line) and inhibitory input from others (indicating the end of the line).

Another type of hypercomplex cell, the angle detectors, are still more general than the complex cells. As the name implies, these cells are actually sensitive to angles. Also, they have rather wide receptive fields. Hubel and Wiesel argue that the logical principle of construction would be to connect outputs from lower-level orientation-specific line or segment detecting hypercomplex cells to the angle-detecting cells at this level, as is illustrated schematically in Figure 3–13.

Early experience and feature detection networks

One question of interest concerns whether the cat's feature analysis system is learned or is already present at birth. The traditional answer among psychologists to this sort of question has been—at least for the last half century or so—that the brain begins as a randomly connected set of neurons and that experience leads to learned systems being built up in some sort of self-organizing manner (for example, Hebb, 1949). This traditional answer is now going rapidly out of fashion. Only in a rather desperately environmentalistic culture could it seem even remotely plausible that an organ so obviously complex as the brain could be wired up randomly. The reason for suggesting the possibility has always been the tremendous plasticity of behavior. That is, organisms seem to exhibit a lot of learning. Certainly a large computer can learn or remember a lot more than a desk calculator, but no one has suggested that this is because its connections are arranged in a more random fashion. Be all that as it may, Hubel and Wiesel (1963) offer us a clear answer in this particular case. Newborn kittens have the same feature detection systems as adult cats. Sensory deprivation of kittens—such as rearing them in the dark—does cause degeneration of these systems. Prolonged exposure of kittens to gratings of a given orientation causes them to develop more detectors tuned to that orientation (Hirsch and Spinelli, 1970). These results, however, only show that learning and experience can have some influence on the feature detection system that kittens already possess at birth.

Conclusions about cats

The process involved in the feature detection system in the cat's brain is clearly quite similar to what happens in Selfridge's pandemonium model. Animal perception does appear to be carried out by a hierarchical feature analysis network involving parallel processing. Clearly, too, the system is a content addressable one. The act of perceiving is a lookup in memory. When the cat sees an angle in some part of its visual field, this means that the angle cell for that region has been activated. Perceiving and activating the long-term memory trace are the same thing. The feature analysis system in the cat's brain is now known to be a lot more complicated and much less rigidly hierarchical than Hubel and Wiesel originally thought (Blakemore, 1975). For example, some complex cells begin to respond to a stimulus before the simple cells that hypothetically send them input. Thus, at the very least, complex cells get some early hints from a source other than the simple cells.

ARE THERE COMPLEX OBJECT DETECTORS?

It does not take much imagination to speculate that the output of hypercomplex cells could be used as input to other neurons that would detect even more complex patterns. For example, output from angle detectors could be used to construct detectors for squares, triangles, and so on. Eventually, mouse detectors and even grandmother detectors could be constructed. This would solve the problem of recognition; that is, it would explain how a mouse or a grandmother is recognized regardless of where it is in the visual field. Gross (1973) has come closer than anyone to discovering object-detecting neurons. Monkeys have a hierarchy of feature detectors in their visual cortex that is quite similar to the hierarchy found in the cat (Hubel and Wiesel, 1965). In other areas of monkey cortex, however, Gross found neurons that seemed to be detectors for much more complex patterns. One type of neuron seemed to be a monkey-paw detector. It exhibited a maximal response only to a monkey paw in a certain orientation! It responded a bit to a human hand and to other things resembling monkey paws and not at all to other stimuli. Other neurons exhibited maximal responses to such things as a bottle brush and a hemostat. Presumably, these were not the optimal trigger stimuli for these neurons. It was just that they were the things nearest at hand that resembled whatever the neurons were really looking for.

Is it possible that outputs from detectors for monkey paws, monkey feet, and so on converge on neurons that serve as general monkey detectors? It is certainly possible, but most investigators deem this to be a rather unlikely possibility. What seems much more likely is that a whole ensemble or set of neurons would serve as the ultimate monkey, mouse, or grandmother detector. If this were the case, then finding the exact set of neurons would be extremely difficult given that there are billions of neurons in the brain. As psychologists, though, our real concern is whether there are *cognitive units* coding unitary percepts such as monkeys, mice, and grandmothers. We can leave to neuroscientists the task of figuring out exactly how these cognitive units are constructed from neurons.

HUMAN FEATURE ANALYSIS

Is there any reason to believe that human visual processing involves the sort of hierarchical feature analysis that is found in cats and monkeys? In the next several chapters, we shall discuss a great deal of indirect evidence supportive of the contention that human perception of all types involves hierarchical feature analysis. This section describes several lines of research concerning the lower levels of visual feature analysis.

The basic problem in getting evidence that human beings have neurons that function as line, edge, or motion detectors is that we cannot poke electrodes through peoples' skulls and record the activity of single neurons. However, certain types of visual illusions and aftereffects can be used to study the activity of hypothetical cortical feature detectors in an indirect way. Some visual illusions are peripheral while others are central. The surest way to find the locus is to see if the illusion or aftereffect transfers from one eye to the other. If it does, then we know that the phenomenon must be occurring centrally, after inputs from the two eyes have been combined. If it does not, then we know that the phenomenon is due to a peripheral process in the retina. For example, color aftereffects do not transfer from one eye to the other. Close your left eye and stare at a red patch of color. Now if you look away at a white surface you will seen a green afterimage. However, if you now close your right eye and open your left eye, you will not see the afterimage. This suggests that the afterimage is due to processes confined to the retina of your right eye. Other sorts of phenomena—such as motion and figural aftereffects—do transfer interocularly. These phenomena can help us in our quest for cortical feature analyzers.

Adaptation effects

Recall that Hubel and Wiesel (1965) found that all of their feature detecting neurons showed adaptation effects. That is, prolonged stimulation led to a diminution of response. Some investigators have argued that selective adaptation effects can be taken as evidence for the existence of a feature detector. The logic is that for adaptation to occur, something must be adapted, and this something is a feature detector. Several effects connected with the perception of motion are supportive of this line of reasoning.

Sekuler and Ganz (1963) exposed subjects to black and white gratings moving from either right to left or from left to right. Then, they tested their subjects' luminance thresholds for moving gratings (that is, how much black-white contrast was needed before the gratings could be seen). If the test gratings were moving in the same direction as the adapting gratings, large increases in threshold were observed. However, there was no effect if the test gratings were moving in the opposite direction. This suggests that direction-specific motion detectors had been fatigued in the first part of the experiment. A simpler movement adaptation effect is the fact that prolonged viewing of a stimulus moving at a constant speed leads to the perception that its speed is slowing down (Goldstein, 1957). Sekuler (1975) argues that these and a number of similar findings support the contention that human beings have motion detectors that can be fatigued or adapted.

Inhibition and disinhibition effects

MOTION AFTEREFFECTS

A motion aftereffect can be demonstrated by staring at something in motion— such as a waterfall—for a period of time. If you then look away at a stationary object, it seems to be moving in an opposite direction. This could be explained by arguing that a cortical motion detector has been fatigued or adapted so that it can no longer laterally inhibit a neighboring detector for motion in the opposite direction (Sekuler, 1975). Recall that cortical feature detectors hypothetically exist in a lateral inhibitory network.

TILT ILLUSIONS AND AFTEREFFECTS

Look at Figure 3–14A. Is line a vertical? It is, in fact, quite vertical, but it probably seems to tilt a bit in a counterclockwise direction. The presence of line b causes this effect. This is called a tilt illusion or orientation contrast. A similar effect is obtained if one is first exposed to line b and is then presented with line a alone. This is called a *tilt aftereffect*. Both effects were described several decades ago by Gibson and Radner (1937). The discovery of orientation-specific line detectors in lower animals caused a renewal of interest in tilt effects. The basic explanation would be this: Human beings have cortical orientation-specific line detectors which exist in a lateral inhibitory network. The detector activated by line b laterally inhibits the detector for line a. This causes it to respond at a less than maximal rate. Thus, people see line a as being not quite vertical. (Of course, the detector for a would have a similar inhibitory effect on the detector for b. It

FIGURE 3–14   The tilt illusion (A) and disinhibition of
the tilt illusion (B)

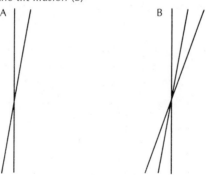

is merely more convenient to have subjects judge whether a line is vertical rather than asking them to judge whether a line is tilted 10° from verticality.) This is a plausible explanation, but there are other equally plausible ones. Fortunately, the case can be made much stronger. Look at Figure 3–14B. The vertical line appears less tilted than the vertical line in Figure 3–14A. Why? Hypothetically, the detector that responds to line c is now inhibiting the detector that responds to line b. As a result, the detector that responds to line a is *disinhibited*; that is, since the b-detector is itself inhibited, it can no longer inhibit the a-detector as much. Carpenter and Blakemore (1973) first demonstrated this disinhibition effect for the tilt illusion, while Magnussen and Kurtenbach (1980) showed that it also occurs with the tilt aftereffect. The disinhibition effect can be readily explained by the feature detector theory, while it is difficult to think of any other plausible explanation for it. Thus, it can be taken as good, although indirect, evidence for the existence of orientation-specific line detectors in humans. A lot of other indirect evidence of this sort supports the contention that human beings also have feature detectors for curvature, directional motion, and so on.

SUMMARY AND CONCLUSIONS

We began this chapter still faced with the problem of recognition. How does a vast array of different sensations lead to activation of the same cognitive unit or memory trace? We saw that some lower organisms solve the task of recognition by detecting simple invariant distinctive features. We then considered Selfridge's pandemonium model of recognition. The basic idea behind this model is that complex stimuli can be defined in terms of the simultaneous presence of unique sets or bundles of distinctive features. Recognition, in this view, consists of hierarchical extraction and combination of these features.

The classic experiment of Lettvin et al. on the eye of the frog showed that frogs are indeed sensitive to distinctive features. We saw that the latticelike structure of the retina could serve to extract distinctive visual features, such as edges. A variety of evidence ranging from Ratliff's studies of the eye of the horseshoe

crab to Mach's demonstration of edge enhancement in human perception suggests that the retina not only could but does, in fact, extract such features. The
experiments of Hubel and Wiesel on cats and monkeys were then considered.
These studies suggest that these animals do seem to process visual stimuli with
a hierarchical feature analytic system similar to that proposed by Selfridge. Indirect evidence suggests that human beings must possess feature analysis systems
similar to those found in lower animals. In the following chapters, we shall explore
in detail the evidence for this assertion and its implications for human cognition
and information processing.

4

A model of human cognition

In previous chapters, we considered the question of how a stimulus impinging upon a sensory receptor activates the appropriate cognitive units or mental representations so that perception and recognition occur. We dealt with this question in a general way and described some research on crabs, cats, and frogs. Our investigations led to the conclusion that perception involves hierarchical feature analysis. Indeed, the generally held view is that human perception is an automatic an effortless phenomenon that is carried out by parallel-processing feature analysis networks (Shiffrin and Schneider, 1977). These networks are hypothetically similar to the ones Hubel and Wiesel (1965) found in cats. When we are confronted by a stimulus, it elicits analysis at a series of successively more and more abstract levels. Parallel processing occurs on any given level. However, the successive analyses are performed in a roughly serial fashion. Each depends upon the previous one.

In this chapter, we shall describe the systems that are hypothetically involved in perception of the various classes of objects that people can recognize. Then, a preview will be given of the systems that come into play once perception has occurred. The systems we shall deal with are sensory systems, gnostic or perceptual systems, the semantic system, the episodic system, and the action system. After describing what is involved at each of these stages of information processing, we shall describe some evidence that information is actually processed in the theoretically specified order. Hypothetically, each of the cognitive systems has the same latticelike structure. We shall describe this structure and the general consequences it has for perception, understanding, memory, and action. Then we shall discuss some subjective phenomena—sensations, percepts, ideas, mental images, and hallucinations—in terms of different types of activity in the cognitive systems. In later chapters, we shall discuss in much greater detail each of the systems and processes described in this chapter.

An example will help to illustrate the stages of information processing to be described. Suppose that a friend hands you a note that reads, "Meet me tonight at six o'clock on the library steps." Hypothetically, this note will elicit successive analyses at the sensory level (you sense bright and dark patches on the sheet of paper), the perceptual level (you recognize individual letters and words), and the semantic level (you understand what the words mean). The analyses must proceed in this order. You cannot very well understand what a word means until you know what the word is. The successive analyses proceed in a roughly serial manner because it is almost certainly the case that higher-level analyses begin before lower-level analyses are completely finished. Because of this, higher-level analyses can influence the lower-level ones to some extent. If you are actually going to meet your friend, some further processing will be necessary. The analyzed message must be stored in episodic memory, so that you do not forget it. At the appointed hour, you need to get from wherever you are to the library steps. Hypothetically, this involves two more systems. The action system contains general programs or scripts such as those for walking, opening car doors, driving, and so on. It controls the motor system, which contains memories for the specific muscle movements necessary to execute the actions generated by the action system.

KONORSKI'S THEORY OF COGNITION

Many cognitive psychologists have recently developed theories based upon the concept of hierarchical feature analysis. These often seem to be independent reinventions of a theory advanced by Konorski (1967). Since the reinvented theories are generally not as complete or robust as the original, it seems reasonable to turn our attention to Konorski's theory. His general idea was that the mind may be seen as being composed of a number of analyzers each of which is structurally similar to Selfridge's pandemonium system. Konorski holds that human beings have a number of different gnostic or perceptual analyzers. There is a different analyzer for each class of stimuli that we can recognize. The analyzers are all constructed in a similar fashion. Each analyzer has several layers or strata (from four to six, corresponding to the number of layers in the cortex) and each layer has a large number of *cognitive units*. The vertical connections among units on different layers are generally excitatory, whereas the lateral connections are generally inhibitory.

Input to units on the lowest level of a gnostic analyzer is from a sensory system. This input may come either directly from the sensory receptor or from a cortical sensory receiving area. For gnostic analyzers dealing with the more primitive senses—such as touch or taste—input hypothetically comes directly from sensory receptors. Both sensory and perceptual analysis are carried out by the same analyzer. For the higher senses—such as vision and hearing—input from receptors goes first to purely sensory analyzers located in the primary receiving areas of the cortex. The output from these sensory analyzers serves as the input to the gnostic or perceptual analyzers.

At the highest level of each gnostic analyzer are cognitive units that code what Konorski calls *unitary percepts*. A unitary percept might be the sound pattern of a particular word for the speech analyzer or the face of a friend for the analyzer concerned with the recognition of faces. Konorski calls these units at the highest level of each analyzer *gnostic units*. The highest stratum of each analyzer is called a *gnostic area.* (The word *gnostic* derives from a Greek word meaning to know.) Thus, all of the various things that we can recognize are hypothetically coded by gnostic units which are located in gnostic areas at the top level of the gnostic analyzers.

Between the highest and the lowest level of an analyzer are a series of levels. As we move upward, units on each level are seen as coding or detecting more specific aspects of the class of stimuli appropriate for that analyzer. As Konorski puts it, the higher level, "the more complex and refined the adequate stimuli." The adequate stimulus for any unit is the thing that fully activates it. The hierarchy of simple, complex, and hypercomplex visual units investigated by Hubel and Wiesel is an example of this. The higher the level, the more complex the feature detected by the units at that level. Higher-level units are formed by convergence of inputs from lower-level units. For example, in the visual analyzer, units coding angles are formed by convergence of outputs from units coding straight lines. An example of a gnostic analyzer for printed words is shown in Figure 4–1. Hypothetically there would be a gnostic unit for each printed word

FIGURE 4–1   Gnostic analyzer for printed words. Only a few cognitive units are shown on each level

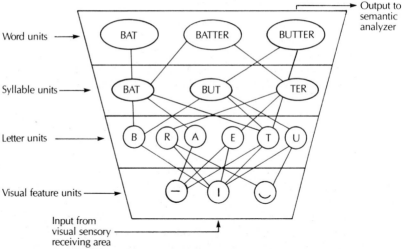

a person could recognize at the highest level of this analyzer. In general, the higher we go in a gnostic analyzer, the larger the number of units. Thus, many units at the highest level of a gnostic analyzer are detected by a relatively smaller number of units at lower levels. We found the same principle in Selfridge's pandemonium model.

SENSORY ANALYSIS

Sensory analyzers lie in the primary sensory reception areas of the cortex. Presumably, there is at least one of them for each of the senses. Activation of cognitive units in these analyzers eventuates in raw sensations rather than in the perception of meaningful objects. For example, in the case of vision, the sensory analyzers deal with brightness, color, and—perhaps—spatial location. In the case of audition, sensory analysis deals with loudness and pitch. Lesions in the primary projection areas (sensory analyzers) tend to eventuate in specific sensory deficits. For example, damage to the occipital area could result in a blank "hole" in the visual field, or damage to the primary auditory receiving area could result in deafness or inability to hear sounds in a certain frequency range. Output from sensory analyzers goes to what Konorski calls *gnostic analyzers*.

GNOSTIC ANALYSIS

Gnostic analyzers are hypothetically located in the association areas of the cortex that surround the sensory analyzers. They deal with unitary *perceptions*. Lesions in the associative areas (gnostic analyzers) lead to very specific—and often bizarre—difficulties in *recognition* of various objects. With this type of brain damage, the person may still see perfectly well but may be unable to recognize a specific category of stimuli, such as printed words or the faces of other people. Konorski used data from the effects of brain lesions to get an idea of the variety and location of gnostic analyzers. These data show some very interesting things. They suggest the independent existence of several different types of analyzers that we would probably never guess at on the basis of common sense or even on the basis of purely psychological experimentation. Let's consider a few of the analyzers that Konorski postulates. We shall begin with the visual system.

Visual analyzers

Konorski postulates the existence of separate gnostic analyzers for the following types of things:

1. Small manipulable objects.
2. Large nonmanipulable objects.
3. Human faces.
4. Expressions of human faces.
5. Animate objects (human figures and animals).
6. Signs (for example, printed words).
7. Handwriting.
8. The postures of one's own limbs.

The independent existence of each of these analyzers is suggested on the basis of brain lesions that destroy just the ability to recognize the class of objects in question and leave all other visual perception and recognition undisturbed. Let's consider a few of these analyzers.

PRINTED-WORD ANALYZER

As an example of what types of units occur on each level of an analyzer, let's consider the perception of printed words. There is supposedly a gnostic analyzer devoted to just this sort of perception. This is hypothetically a vertically layered structure as shown in Figure 4–1. Input to units at the lowest level is from the purely sensory visual analyzers. The lowest level of the analyzer for printed words hypothetically is composed of units coding distinctive visual features of letters, such as curves, vertical lines, right angles, and so on. At the next higher level would be units coding the 26 letters of the alphabet. The next higher level contains units coding printed syllables. Hypothetically, output from syllable units goes to units at the highest level coding individual printed words. There is fairly general agreement that the perception of printed words must work in this sort of hierarchical fashion (for example, LaBerge and Samuels, 1974; Smith and Spoehr, 1974).

Alexic agnosia is a disorder involving the inability to recognize printed letters and words. Alajouanine, Lhermitte, and de Ribacourt-Ducarne (1960) described six patients suffering from this syndrome. These patients could not read, although they had previously been able to do so. Either they could not read printed words at all or they responded with completely incorrect words. Most could recognize a few isolated letters but confused letters with similar shapes, such as *P* and *R*. Frequently occurring letters, such as *A* or *B*, were recognized better than infrequent ones, such as *Q* or *Z*. On the other hand, the patients could write down a dictated text and had no trouble reading familiar handwriting! They could all speak and understand spoken language. These very selective losses suggest that completely separate gnostic analyzers must be involved in the three different tasks of reading printed text, understanding spoken language, and reading handwritten text. Patients with alexic agnosia must have brain damage restricted to the area containing the analyzer for printed words.

VISUAL OBJECT ANALYZER

Another analyzer deals with small, manipulable objects. Examples would be eyeglasses, knives, forks, keys, clocks, and so on. Konorski points out that these all tend to share several attributes: They have sharply defined contours or edges; they can be moved; and they are routinely seen from various angles, so they must be represented by a number of different mental images. In many cases of brain damage, one finds that visual recognition of just such objects is impaired in the absence of other visual deficits. This disorder is called *visual object agnosia*. For example, Hécaen and Ajuriaguerra (1956) had a patient who could not recognize such objects when shown them. While he could not recognize an ashtray visually, he could immediately recognize it when he took it in his hand. On the other hand, he could recognize pictures of animals with little difficulty.

FACIAL ANALYZER

Another type of agnosia is called *prosopagnosia,* or *facial agnosia.* Patients with this disorder have lost the ability to recognize even familiar human faces but have no other visual deficit! Cole and Perez-Cruet (1964) describe one such patient as follows:

> He stated that he first looked at the chin, and mouth, then carefully inspected the sides of the face, nose, eyes, and forehead but according to his own statement "could not put it all together." . . . This disability prevented visual recognition of those who were familiar to him including his wife. . . . When he looked into the mirror he stated that his own face appeared blurred and strange to him. . . . There was no difficulty in pointing to objects . . . when the examiner named them: nor was there any difficulty in naming the objects or pictures when the examiner pointed to them.

This patient, like many others suffering from prosopagnosia, had no difficulty in recognition of facial expressions of emotions, such as anger or surprise. This strange fact led Konorski to postulate the existence of a completely separate analyzer for facial expressions.

Auditory analyzers

Konorski postulates the existence of at least four separate gnostic analyzers for auditory inputs. These are concerned with:

1. Known sounds such as those of bells, whistles, and different musical instruments.
2. Voice quality.
3. Speech.
4. Musical melodies.

Again, the reason for saying that these different categories are processed by different analyzers is that we can find people with localized brain damage in whom perception of just one of the categories is defective.

The most important of the auditory analyzers is the one that deals with speech sounds. Konorski holds that the unitary percepts of speech are the sound patterns of individual words. That is, the cognitive units at the highest level of the speech analyzer code the sound patterns of individual words. In *audioverbal agnosia,* the patient has lost the ability to recognize speech sounds but has no hearing loss and no problem in recognizing other sorts of sounds. These patients hear an indistinct murmuring rather than speech. In less severe cases, the patient may be able to recognize some words, but has a lot of trouble discriminating similar words from each other. The patient may, for example, hear *bat* when *pat* should be heard. Remarkably, these patients can copy a written or printed text with no problems. In this, the syndrome is just the reverse of alexic agnosia.

The problem in speech recognition is to make a connection between a complex pattern of sound waves impinging upon the ear and cognitive units that encode meanings, concepts, or ideas. Almost everyone agrees that this involves a hierarchical series of analyses (for example, Lamb, 1966; Liberman, 1970; Pisoni, 1978). As shown in Figure 4–2, the speech analyzer is structurally similar to the analyzer for printed words. The difference, of course, is that it is devoted to the decoding of auditory rather than of visual inputs. At the top level of the speech analyzer are hypothetically cognitive units coding the sound patterns of individual spoken words. These sound patterns are called *morphemes.* There would have to be at least 50,000 or more of these units. Morphemes are composed of syllables, which are encoded at the next lower level. There are about 10,000 syllables in the English language, so there would have to be at least this many syllable units. At the next lower level are phoneme units. A *phoneme* is the smallest unit of sound that makes a difference in the meaning of a word. For example, if we change the phoneme /a/ in TAP to /i/, we have a completely different morpheme, TIP. There are about 30 to 40 phonemes in any language. A phoneme is signaled by the simultaneous presence of a "bundle" of distinctive features, each of which may be signaled by much more easily detectable acoustic cues. An example of a distinctive feature is the property of voicing. All phonemes are either voiced or

FIGURE 4–2   Gnostic analyzer for speech sounds, with examples of units on each level

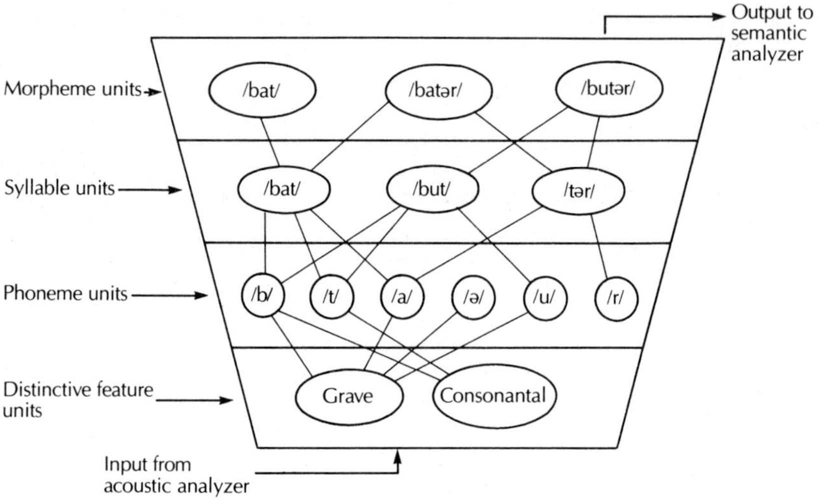

unvoiced. In a voiced phoneme, the vocal chords vibrate during production, while in an unvoiced phoneme they do not. This results in a detectable difference in the resultant sound wave. Only about 8 to 10 distinctive features are needed to specify the properties of all of the phonemes in any given language. (Table 5–1 in the next chapter lists these features.)

Emotional analyzer

Konorski says that there is also a gnostic analyzer for emotions. This system receives inputs from two sources. First, it gets inputs from the other analyzers. This is reflected in the fact that, for example, a loud noise or a particular combination of words is capable of evoking an emotion. Second, it gets inputs from internal receptors. These are receptors that sense or transduce various chemicals and hormones present in the blood and other body fluids. In Konorski's view, emotion ultimately involves activation of gnostic units coding unitary emotions— anger, fear, and so on. Thus, we perceive our own emotions in more or less the same way that we perceive visual objects or words. The main difference is that with emotions, many of the relevant stimuli are internal rather than external. Some psychologists argue that there is a type of emotional agnosia, called *alexithymia* (Nemiah and Sifneos, 1970). Alexithymia refers to an inability to recognize one's own emotions and the emotions of others.

Other gnostic analyzers

Konorski postulates the existence of several other gnostic analyzers. The more important of these are as follows:

1.   Olfactory, dealing with smells.
2.   Vestibular, dealing with sense of balance.

3. Somesthetic, dealing with touch.
4. Gustatory, dealing with taste.
5. Kinesthetic, dealing with feedback from self-produced movements.

CONCEPTUAL ANALYSIS

Levels of processing

Craik and Lockhart (1972) introduced the concept of *level of processing*. The idea is that stimuli can be analyzed to varying depths. Shallow processing corresponds to activation of only sensory analyzers. Even at the shallow level of processing, we could envision several degrees of depth according to how many levels of a sensory analyzer were activated by the stimulus. A medium level of processing corresponds to activation of units in gnostic analyzers. In this case, we not only sense the stimulus but also perceive it as a recognized object. Again, several degrees of depth are possible according to how many levels of a gnostic analyzer were activated. For example, when you listen to a foreign language you do not know, no morpheme units will be activated but units on the featural, phonemic, and syllabic levels will be activated. On the other hand, when you listen to your native language, units on all of these levels as well as units on the morphemic level will be activated. Thus, processing will be slightly deeper. Deep processing involves understanding or interpreting the stimulus. Konorski does not deal with how deep processing is carried out. I would contend that another type of analyzer must be postulated to account for the deeper levels of processing. We shall refer to this sort of analyzer as a conceptual analyzer.

Characteristics of conceptual analyzers

Conceptual analyzers receive input from the highest levels of gnostic analyzers. This input hypothetically goes to units on the top level of the conceptual analyzer rather than to units on the bottom level, as was the case with the gnostic analyzers. Perception, which is carried out by gnostic analyzers, consists of recognizing many objects on the basis of a few distinctive features. Understanding, which is carried out by the conceptual analyzers, consists of abstracting a few basic conceptual features from many concepts or ideas. Consider what happens when you read a novel. A few distinctive perceptual features ultimately activate a very large number of printed-word units. These, in turn, activate many conceptual units. But these conceptual units ultimately activate only a few conceptual features, such as the typical-love-story unit or the hero-is-deceived-by-villain unit.

Semantic analyzer

Postulation of a separate semantic analyzer is consistent with most current cognitive theories. The semantic analyzer stores our knowledge of the meanings of concepts and percepts. We could see the semantic analyzer as being a multilayered system like the gnostic analyzers. The units at the highest level— semantic units—would receive inputs from gnostic units at the highest levels of gnostic analyzers. Semantic units hypothetically code abstract concepts rather than unitary percepts. The semantic units could serve to collate units in many different gnostic analyzers. Thus, for example, the semantic unit coding the concept, APPLE would receive inputs from units in the speech analyzer (the unit coding the sound of the word APPLE), the visual analyzer for small manipulable objects (the unit coding the visual image of an apple), and so on. A crucial difference between gnostic analyzers and the semantic analyzer would be that the semantic analyzer has no direct input from sensory systems to the units at its lowest level. What would the multilevel structure be good for then? Presumably, the units at each lower level would code successively more and more abstract concepts or semantic features. Thus, units at the highest level would code elementary concepts or ideas, such as the concept of a BAT or a DOG. Units at the next lower level might code superordinate concepts, such as the general concept of MAMMAL. Units at the next lower level might code even more abstract concepts, such as ANIMAL. Presumably, as with the other analyzers, the lower the level, the fewer the number of units. Figure 4–3 presents a diagram of the semantic analyzer.

FIGURE 4–3   The semantic analyzer, with examples of units on each level. Note that input is to units on the top level of the analyzer. Only a few sample units are shown.

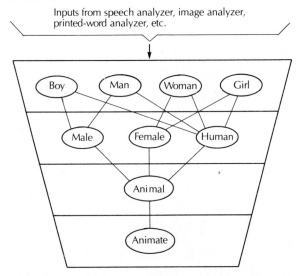

Musical-interval analyzer

Why should there be a separate conceptual analyzer devoted to the understanding of music? I don't know, but there seems to be one. Evidence based on localized brain lesions makes this pretty clear. Damage to certain regions of the brain can destroy the ability to process music without having much of any other effect. Deutsch (1969) has proposed an interesting theory of the structural organization of this analyzer. Let's consider what we have to explain. The basic unit of the Western musical scale is the semitone. Each successive key on a piano differs by one semitone from the previous one. Thus, C-sharp is a semitone higher than C. Each of the keys on a piano produces a sound that is different from that produced by any of the other keys. This sound is a complex sound wave, but it is characterized by one dominant frequency, which defines the pitch of the note. For example, the A in the middle of the keyboard produces a sound wave with a dominant frequency of 440 Hz (cycles per second). We can perceive an identity among, say, the A produced by a piano, a violin, and the human voice, although the timbre or quality of each of these sounds is quite different. The reason for this may be that inputs from auditory sensory or gnostic analyzers converge on cognitive units coding musical notes as shown in Figure 4–4.

FIGURE 4–4   Conceptual analyzer for musical intervals. Note that input is to units on the top level of the analyzer. Only a few sample units are shown.

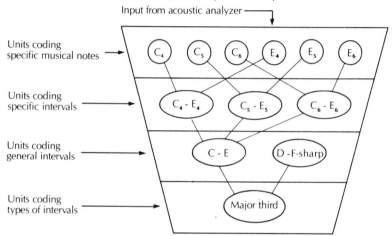

The musical scale is organized by octaves. The A in the middle of the piano and the A an octave higher differ by 12 semitones. In terms of frequency, the two notes are in a 1:2 ratio. The lower A is 440 Hz while the higher one is 880 Hz. Why do we use the same names for notes separated by an octave? Why do we call both of these notes A rather than calling one A and the other H? The ultimate reason must be that notes an octave apart sound similar to each other. Subjectively, they certainly do. This is not just due to our musical training. They also sound alike to rats. That is if a rat is conditioned to make some response to a given tone, it will also tend to make that response to a tone an octave higher or lower (Blackwell and Schlosberg, 1943). The same result is found with human subjects (Humphreys, 1939).

A model of music recognition has to account for why we equate notes an octave apart. My rather slight modification of Deutsch's explanation is that pitch-sensitive units on the top layer of the musical analyzer are connected to cognitive units on the next lower level that code specific octaves. Each of these units receives input from two units on the top level of the analyzer. For example, the output from middle C and high C converge on an octave unit that is on if and only if both of the higher-level units are on. Thus, the unit is an AND gate coding this specific simultaneous octave. There is hypothetically one octave unit for each possible combination of notes an octave apart. An octave is only one musical interval. An interval is any combination of two musical notes. Examples of other intervals are as follows: A minor third consists of notes three semitones apart (for example, C to E-flat or C-sharp to E) in a frequency ratio of 5:6. A major third consists of notes four semitones apart in a frequency ratio of 4:5 (for example, C to E). A fifth consists of notes seven semitones apart in a frequency ratio of 2:3 (for example, C to G). There are two things to note about all musical intervals. First, each specific one has a unique sound. Thus, the minor thirds C to E-flat and C-sharp to E can be distinguished. They do not sound exactly alike. Second, the sounds are not completely unique. They do not sound completely different either. Anyone with some musical training can recognize a given interval—an octave, a minor third, and so on—irrespective of what the component notes are. Present a musician with any two notes three semitones apart and the person will say, "Why, that's a minor third." Nonmusicians are sensitive to these similarities, too. They often just do not know how to label them.

Perception of all specific intervals can be accounted for in the same way octaves were explained. That is, we can postulate that there are units at the second lowest level of the music analyzer for each specific interval. As shown in Figure 4–4, these could converge on yet more abstract units on the next lower level. For example, such a unit might be activated by any C to E combination. Finally, output from these units descends to the lowest level. Here are units that code not specific intervals but general ones. Output from all of the specific octave units converges on a general octave unit. This unit would function as an OR gate. Whenever any specific octave unit was on, it would be on. The same principle applies to the other intervals.

Episodic analyzer

According to Tulving (1972), there are two quite distinct types of long-term memory. Semantic memory contains our general store of knowledge. On the other hand, episodic memory is time tagged and contains memories of events that have occurred to us or that we have heard about. Recall the example—the note about meeting on the library steps—with which we began this chapter. Once it has been processed by the relevant sensory and gnostic analyzers, the meaning of each word is hypothetically looked up in semantic memory. However, in order to understand the message, you have to know more than the meaning of each individual word. You have to know where and when who is supposed to meet whom. Theoretically this is done by combining the meanings into an abstract proposition (Fillmore, 1968). A proposition describes an action or event in terms of cases such as agent, object, time, location, and so on. The note in question might be represented in propositional form as MEET (SELF, FRIEND, SIX O'CLOCK, LIBRARY STEPS, IMPERATIVE). Hypothetically, the cognitive units on the highest level of the episodic system code such propositions. Any one unit would receive labeled inputs from semantic memory units. Thus, these units perform a grammatical analysis of a message. They also serve to establish a long-term memory of what the message was. Propositions are very abstract or conceptual; that is, they are not tied to any one gnostic system. Thus, the proposition in our example could be realized about equally well by a spoken sentence, a written sentence, or a series of mental images.

As shown in Figure 4–5, the episodic analyzer is also a multilayered structure. The idea is that each lower level is more general or abstract. Suppose that you

FIGURE 4–5   The episodic analyzer, with examples of units on each level

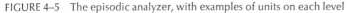
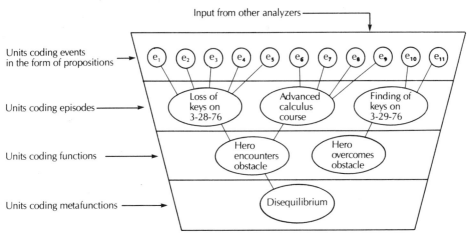

meet your friend on the library steps and the two of you go to a party. This will be an episode in your life. Hypothetically, an episodic unit will be established to code it. The episodic unit will be connected to several proposition units which code its component events. At the next lower level are units coding *functions*. These are very general plot units (for example, HERO ENCOUNTERS OBSTACLE). Vladimir Propp (1928), the Russian folklorist, suggested that all stories or narratives are ultimately constructed from only 20 to 30 functions, just as all the words in a language are composed from only 20 to 30 phonemes. At the lowest level of the episodic analyzer are hypothetically metafunction units. We might envision 10 or so of them—one for each of the small number of basic components that a story (including the story of a person's life) can be composed from.

The action system

We have gotten ahead of ourselves by a good bit. You cannot get to a party before getting to the library steps in the first place. Shallice (1972, 1978) has postulated the existence of what he calls the action system. In our adaptation of Shallice's action system, as illustrated in Figure 4–6, we have placed what he calls action units on the top layer of the action system. Hypothetically, there is an action unit for every molar act that a person can perform. At a minimum, Shallice argues that there would be one of them for every action that can be described by a transitive verb. These units code molar actions, such as WALKING, EATING, STANDING, KISSING, and so on. Output from action units goes to the motor system. The basic reason for postulating such units is that once we decide upon a given act, it is executed in an automatic fashion. You can decide to EAT, but you cannot control or even be conscious of all the specific muscle movements involved in eating.

At lower levels of the action system are cognitive units controlling more and more general types of action. At the second level are units coding what Schank and Abelson (1977) call scripts. A script codes a sequence of actions, such as GOING TO A RESTAURANT or BUILDING A HOUSE. Lower yet, we have placed

FIGURE 4–6   The action system, with examples of units on each level

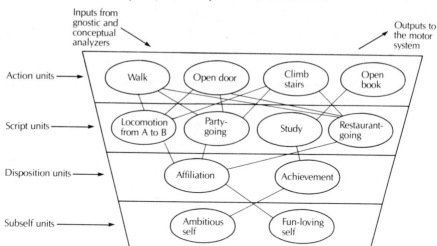

units coding dispositions. These are connected to many script units. An achievement disposition, for example, would be connected to scripts having to do with achievement, such as SEWING A DRESS, REPAIRING A MOTOR, and so on. At the bottom level of the action system, we have placed units coding what are called *subselves* for want of a better term. These units hypothetically exert an executive control over behavior. Whichever one is regnant or currently activated inhibits competing subselves and activates disposition, script, and action units to which it is vertically connected. Among other things, subselves are useful in explaining how we remember to act in quite different ways in different situations.

In our example of getting to the library steps, all levels of the action system will be involved to some degree. If all the currently active subself and disposition units had to do with achievement, you might not go at all. Given that you did have a disposition to go, a script unit coding the plan for something such as LOCOMOTION FROM ONE POINT TO ANOTHER would take over. This unit would serially activate action units coding such things as opening doors, starting cars, driving, parking, walking, and so on. Each of these will take care of the details of the required motor movements. Eventually, you will arrive at the steps of the library. At that point, you will be confronted with the problem of recognition once more. The facial analyzer will be of help here. Then the whole process will begin again. Your friend will say something, you will have to understand the message, and so on.

OVERVIEW OF HUMAN COGNITION

It may help to step back and get an overview of the analyzers that we have discussed. Figure 4–7 presents a schematic diagram of some of the more important analyzers. There is fairly general agreement that discrete systems such as those shown in Figure 4–7 must be postulated in order to account for human information processing and action. There is also agreement that the flow of information must be as shown in the diagram. Thus, for example, one cannot under-

FIGURE 4–7   Flowchart of human-information processing, illustrated by the stages of
processing involved in responding to a spoken message

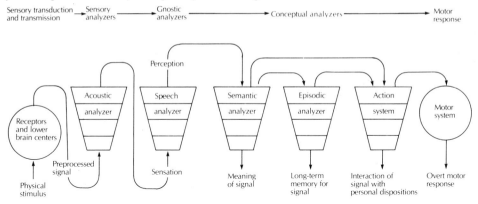

stand a stimulus before it has been sensed and perceived. The further to the right
we go in the diagram, the less consensus there is as to the structure of the
systems. Most cognitive psychologists would probably agree that the gnostic and
semantic analyzers must have a hierarchical structure such as that shown. The
hierarchical structures of the episodic and action systems are much more
speculative.

MENTAL CHRONOMETRY

Posner and Rogers (1978) define *mental chronometry* as "the study of the time
course of information flow in the nervous system." Mental chronometry is often
used to help us gather evidence supportive of the hypothesis that the different
levels of processing that we have just described actually occur in the hypothesized order. Is there any evidence that, when we understand a spoken word,
the stimulus goes through successive levels of acoustic, phonological, morphemic,
and semantic processing? Is there any evidence that, when we understand a
printed word, the stimulus goes through successive levels of visual, featural, lexical,
and semantic processing? If these successive stages of processing occur, then each
must take some finite amount of time. Thus, a decision that calls only for a
lower level of processing should be faster than one that calls for more complete
processing. On the other hand, if understanding does not involve the sequential
series of stages we have postulated, no such time differences should be found.

Posner (1969) introduced a letter-matching technique to get at this question.
In this procedure, subjects are simply shown two letters of the alphabet and asked
whether or not they are identical. The letters can be physically identical (for example, *AA* or *bb*), phonetically identical (for example, *Aa* or *bB*), or semantically
identical (for example, both vowels or both consonants). Posner found that
subjects could make correct same judgments in an average of 549 milliseconds
when they had to judge physical identity and 623 milliseconds when they had to
judge phonetic identity. Semantic judgments took even longer—699 milliseconds
for vowels and 905 milliseconds for consonants. Cole, Coltheart, and Allard
(1974) got similar results using auditory stimuli. Physically identical speech
sounds (same pitch) were identified as being the same in an average of 575 milli-

seconds. Phonemically identical stimuli (same phoneme but different pitches) took 610 milliseconds to identify as the same. Wood (1975) simultaneously varied the pitch and the distinctive feature of place of articulation (/b/ versus /g/) of speech sounds. Pitch discriminations took an average of 413 milliseconds whereas place-of-articulation discriminations took an average of 467 milliseconds.

Other experiments have compared deeper levels of processing. Steinheiser and Barroas (1973) used a task in which two spoken syllables separated by a two-second interval were presented. Subjects had to respond whether the two syllables were physically identical (both sounded the same) on some trials and whether they were lexically identical (both were real words or both were nonsense syllables) on other trials. Reaction time was about 200 milliseconds faster for the physical match than for the lexical match. Craik (1973) compared three levels of processing. Subjects had to make three different types of judgments in regard to words: physical (Was the word printed in upper- or lower-case type?), lexical (Did the word rhyme with another word?), and semantic (Did the word make sense when inserted into a given sentence?). Reaction times were longest for semantic judgments and shortest for physical judgments.

PROPERTIES OF COGNITIVE UNITS

Cognitive units as logic gates

Units at any level of any analyzer have several properties in common. Konorski thinks of cognitive units as being individual neurons. Thus, the properties of cognitive units are the properties of neurons. Konorski's theory makes sense whether or not we want to identify cognitive units with neurons. Conceptually, cognitive units are like the AND gates and OR gates that we described in Chapter 2. The cognitive unit coding the letter A, for example, may be seen as an AND gate. It will be on only if all of the units coding its component features are on. The cognitive unit coding the concept HUMAN BEING functions as an OR gate. It will be on if any one of its component units—for example, WOMAN, BOY, GIRL—is on. Although, in our examples, we have shown the thing that a cognitive unit codes inside of it, actual cognitive units do not contain a little picture of the thing they code. They do not contain anything. Perception of the letter A is simply a state where a specific set of cognitive units are simultaneously on.

Operating characteristics

If cognitive units are like logic devices, it makes some sense to ask about their operating characteristics. What is their rise time? That is, how long does it take to fully activate one of them? Do they have a minimum dwell time? That is, once a cognitive unit has been activated, does it stay in the on state for some minimum length of time? Some studies which we shall consider in later chapters give us some information about rise times. Cognitive units in episodic memory, for example, seem to take a second or so to become fully activated. Units in analyzers devoted to shallower levels of processing seem to have somewhat faster rise times. As we shall see in Chapter 6, there is some evidence that cognitive units in sensory analyzers may have a dwell time of 100 milliseconds or so. Even if the stimulus does not last this long, the unit stays on at least this long. There is no real evidence about the dwell times of cognitive units in analyzers devoted to deeper levels of processing, but it would make sense that they might have longer dwell times. The activation of cognitive units seems to decay at a rather leisurely pace. This accounts for some of the short-term memory effects discussed in Chapter 6. As we shall see, there is reason to suspect that the fall time of units in analyzers devoted to deeper processing is on the order of at least several seconds, while the fall time of units at shallower levels is somewhat faster than this.

All-or-none activity

Hypothetically, each cognitive unit has a threshold. If its inputs cause its activation to exceed this threshold, it goes on. Actually, cognitive units are a bit more complex than logic gates in that they can hypothetically exhibit states intermediate between being completely on or completely off. That is, they can be partially activated. Nonetheless, cognitive units are enough like logic gates (that is, generally, they are either on or off) to lead us to expect that there should be something of an all-or-none or discrete quality to perception. If perceiving something corresponds to activation of units that are either on or off, then this conclusion is inescapable.

One line of evidence for the discrete activity of cognitive units concerns stopped visual images. The human eye exhibits what is called *physiological nystagmus*. This refers to fast (30 to 70 per second) oscillatory eye movements. These are so slight that we are unaware of them. Riggs, Ratliff, Cornsweet, and Cornsweet (1953) and Pritchard, Heron, and Hebb (1960) designed special apparatus to compensate for these movements. By means of tiny mirrors mounted on the eye, an absolutely stable image could be presented. Every eye movement moved the image exactly the same distance and direction so that the stimulus remained over the same receptors. When this was done, an amazing thing occurred. The visual image disappeared! Even more amazingly, it did so in meaningful chunks. Examples are shown in Figure 4–8. If subjects were shown a

FIGURE 4–8 Stopped visual images disappear in meaningful chunks

face, it did not just gradually fade away, but, rather, first the eyebrows went, then the nose, and so on. Shown the word BEER, the diagonal of the R might disappear so that the subject now saw BEEP. Finally, the stimulus would end up as B, then P, and so on. An explanation for these findings would be that human perception depends upon a feature detection process. The oscillations of the eye function to avoid the fatiguing of the detectors at any given point. Canceling this movement leads to a fatiguing of the receptors, which stop driving the feature detectors. If the process only involved fatiguing of the receptor cells, the image would fade gradually rather than disappearing in chunks.

Ease of activation

STRENGTH OF COGNITIVE UNITS

One problem with Konorski's theory might occur to you. If one neuron codes one percept, what would happen if that neuron was damaged or destroyed? Konorski gets around that problem by saying that percepts are coded redundantly. That is, a lot of neurons—rather than just one—redundantly code each percept or feature. If a lot of cognitive units code each percept, then it makes sense to ask whether some percepts are coded by more units than others. Assume that each word we know is coded by at least one gnostic unit. Are some words coded by a lot of units and others by just a few? Yes, says Konorski. Words that are more frequently encountered are coded by more units. Also, words that were learned earlier in a person's life are redundantly coded by more units than those learned later. If you prefer not to think in terms of neurons, you could think of some cognitive units as merely being stronger than others. If this were true, then it should be the case that whatever they code should be recognized more easily or more quickly. As we will see in Chapter 5, there is a lot of evidence that this is indeed the case.

THRESHOLD EFFECTS

Each cognitive unit has a threshold. So long as input to the unit is below this threshold, the unit is off. As soon as the amount of input to the unit rises above this threshold, the unit is on. Do these units differ in their thresholds? There is reason to postulate that activation of a cognitive unit leads to a temporary lowering of its threshold. Thus, it should be possible to activate it more easily at a subsequent time. This would lead to *repetition effects*. It should be easier to recognize a stimulus if the stimulus has been presented recently. In Chapter 5, we shall see that there is a lot of evidence for such effects. On the other hand, repeated or continuous activation of a cognitive unit should fatigue the unit. Its threshold would be temporarily raised. This would lead to *adaptation effects*. We shall see in Chapter 5 that there is also evidence for this type of effect. Of course, there are other ways to account for these sorts of effects. Their existence does not prove that cognitive units exist.

CONNECTIONS AMONG COGNITIVE UNITS

Cognitive units in any analyzer—whether it be a sensory, gnostic, or conceptual one—are hypothetically arranged in a latticelike structure. The general principle is that vertical connections joining units on different levels of the same analyzer are excitatory, whereas lateral connections joining units on the same level of an analyzer are inhibitory. In either case, the effect of one unit on another would decline with the number of intervening units. At least some units also are connected with lower brain centers—the arousal system, the emotional system, and the hippocampus. Also, units at the highest level of an analyzer (and, possibly, units on lower levels as well) are connected with units in some other analyzers. Figure 4–9 illustrates the types of inputs and outputs that a cognitive unit can have. For practical purposes, all of the connections tend to be two-way ones, though often a connection in one direction may be stronger than a connection in the opposite direction.

FIGURE 4–9   Possible connections of a cognitive unit. Solid lines indicate excitatory connections, and dashed lines, inhibitory connections.

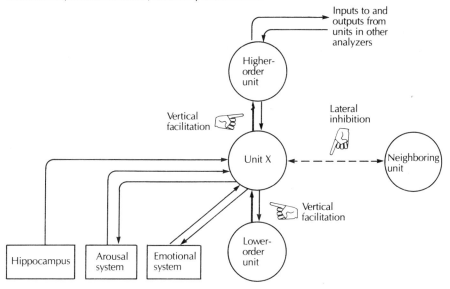

Vertical excitation

Vertical connections—those between units on different levels—are hypothetically excitatory. If we stimulate units on the lowest level of the analyzer, they will activate units on the next higher level. These units will, in turn, activate units on the next level, and so on. This is what happens when a stimulus causes activation of the cognitive unit that codes it. It might be called data-driven or bottom-up activation (Norman and Bobrow, 1976). There are also descending vertical connections among the units in a given analyzer. In general, the ascending connections are hypothetically stronger than the descending ones. The ascending connections account for perception and recognition—how we connect sensations with unitary perceptions. The descending connections account for various influences of higher-order understanding on lower levels of perception. For example, they allow us to explain why expectation and context sometimes cause us to see or hear what we know the stimulus should be rather than what it actually is. The descending connections also allow us to explain such self-generated phenomena as mental images and hallucinations. Such cases where higher-level cognitive units activate lower-level ones might be called instances of conceptually driven or top-down activation (Norman and Bobrow, 1976).

Actually, perception involves both bottom-up and top-down activation of cognitive units. Consider the letter strings RWDO and WORD. Presumably, WORD has captured at least one gnostic unit but RWDO probably has not. If this is the case, then it should be easier to perceive or recognize the word WORD. In fact, it is easier if the letter strings are presented for a very brief duration. Presumably, the reason is that RWDO activates cognitive units (letter detectors) only at fairly shallow levels. On the other hand, WORD also activates lower-level letter detectors, but these, in turn, activate higher-level gnostic units coding the unitary percept WORD: these higher-level units, in turn, reactivate the shallower-level letter detectors. The result is more activation of the relevant cognitive units and, hence, better recognition. In stopped-image experiments, a consistent finding has been that the more meaningful features are, the longer they last. An experiment by McKinney (1966) involved two groups of subjects. Both groups were exposed to the same stimuli: geometric shapes, some of which were letters of the alphabet. One group was told that some of the things they would see would be letters. The other group was not given this expectation. It turned out that the letters lasted longer for the first group than for the second. Presumably, they perceived or coded them as meaningful letters rather than as meaningless shapes.

Lateral inhibition

Konorski hypothesizes that cognitive units are also subject to lateral inhibition. At any level, adjacent units laterally inhibit each other. Konorski further hypothesizes that the higher the level the greater the extent of lateral inhibition. At the highest level of an analyzer, the units coding unitary percepts are extremely antagonistic to each other. Thus, it is very difficult simultaneously to activate two units coding similar unitary percepts. For example, it is very hard to hear two words at the same time. It is certainly more difficult than hearing a word and recognizing a face at the same time. In their elaboration of Konorski's model, Walley and Weiden (1973) argue that—within any analyzer—the principle of arrangement is one of similarity. The more similar two percepts, the closer together are the gnostic units coding them. As a consequence, we should expect greater similarity between two percepts to lead to greater antagonism between the gnostic units coding them. This is because lateral inhibition would be greater the closer together the two units are. If such lateral inhibition exists, we should expect activation of a cognitive unit to interfere with or inhibit activation of neighboring cognitive units. On the level of perception, this is called *masking*. On the level of memory, it is called *interference*. It seems to account for why we forget the things we do. We shall also see that lateral inhibition seems to be important in both voluntary and involuntary focusing of attention. The following chapters will contain evidence concerning all of these effects.

There is not general agreement among psychologists that lateral inhibition occurs among cognitive units—whether or not these units are identified with neurons. In fact, many psychologists actually postulate a mechanism of lateral facilitation. However, there is increasing usage of the concept of lateral inhibition on the part of cognitive theorists (for example, Crowder, 1978; Grossberg, 1980; Hoffman and Ison, 1980). Why is lateral inhibition so important? Consider the models of networks with only excitatory connections discussed by Beurle (1956) and Ashby, von Foerster, and Walker (1962). These models deal with nodes representing neurons or cognitive units and relations among these nodes. In such systems, input to the system eventuates in only two possible outcomes: Activation decays gradually until all of the nodes in the network are off, or it increases explosively until all of the nodes are on and continue to be on. Since neither of these outcomes even remotely corresponds to the reaction of the brain or the mind to stimuli or to the spontaneous, sustained activity of the mind or brain in the absence of stimuli, such networks have generally been rejected in favor of models incorporating both excitatory and inhibitory bonds (Griffith, 1963; Wilson and Cowan, 1972). Such networks exhibit a much closer fit with actual cognition and brain activity.

The ultimate reason that neural models incorporating only positive bonds do not adequately model brain activity is that both excitatory and inhibitory connections exist throughout the brain: "Never does excitatory synaptic action have the unchallenged power to cause discharge of impulses that, in turn, have an unchallenged excitatory action upon the next neuronal relay" (Eccles, 1969). That inhibitory connections are crucial in normal neural processing is demonstrated by the effects of drugs such as strychnine that selectively block such inhibitory connections. Strychnine produces convulsions and death. In the absence of inhibitory synaptic action, the brain literally electrocutes itself. Therefore, any neuropsychological model must somehow take account of both inhibition and excitation. It is not really a question of *whether* inhibitory connections must be incorporated into a neuropsychological model of cognition but only of how and where they may best be incorporated.

Connections to lower brain centers

Cognitive units also receive nonspecific inputs from the arousal system centered in the midbrain reticular activating system. Thus, they can be activated at least to some extent by the arousal system as well as by the specific features that they code. Arousal occurs when we orient toward or attend to a stimulus (see Chapter 6). Inputs to the cortex from the arousal system are diffuse rather than specific. Thus, arousal or attention would lead to indiscriminate or wholesale activation of cognitive units on a given level. There must also be outputs from some units *to* the arousal system, since specific stimuli, such as the word FIRE!, can lead to arousal. At least some cognitive units must also be connected with emotional centers in the lower brain. Wickelgren (1979a) has suggested that cognitive units may also have connections with the hippocampus. As will be explained later, these connections may have to do with how cognitive units are captured or bound so that they come to code a given perceptual feature.

Connections between analyzers

Units at the highest level of an analyzer have excitatory connections with some units at the highest levels of some other analyzers. Such connections allow us, for example, to associate the face of a friend with the friend's name or to associate the word DOG with the visual image of a dog. It seems likely that there must also be connections among units at lower levels of different analyzers. Thus we can, for example, associate the sound of an individual phoneme with an individual printed letter of the alphabet. There is no general agreement as to the details of how cognitive units in different analyzers are connected. Assume that we have separate cognitive units coding the printed word DOG, the sound pattern of the word DOG, the visual image of a dog, and the meaning of a dog. Everyone knows that all of these units refer to the same thing. In order for us to know that, the units must be connected. But how? Paivio's dual-coding theory (1978) holds that image units and units coding the sound patterns of words are directly connected to one another. Konorski (1967) makes the same hypothesis (see Figure 4–10A). On the other hand, many theorists (for example, Norman and Rumelhart, 1975) argue that the two types of units are connected only indirectly, via semantic units (see Figure 4–10B). A similar controversy surrounds the connections among semantic units and units coding spoken and printed words. Some theorists (for example, Rubenstein, Lewis, and Rubenstein, 1971) argue that printed-word units are connected to semantic units only via spoken-word units

FIGURE 4–10 Possible ways in which cognitive units in different analyzers are interconnected. Some theorists propose that image units and morpheme units are directly connected (A), while other theorists hold that they are indirectly connected via semantic units (B). Some theorists hold that printed word units are connected to semantic units only via morpheme units (C), while others say that there are direct connections (D).

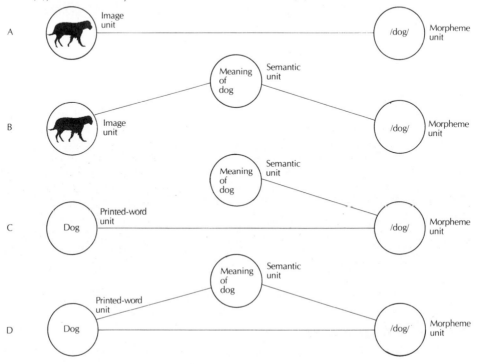

(see Figure 4–10C). Others (for example, Baron, 1973) argue that there are also direct connections from both printed-word and spoken-word units to semantic units (see Figure 4–10D). Because the evidence is not compelling on either side, it makes some sense to assume that all possible connections probably exist among these units.

BINDING OF COGNITIVE UNITS

Bound versus free cognitive units

There are two types of cognitive units. Bound or occupied units already code some feature or percept. Free or unoccupied units do not yet code anything. The process of learning consists of transforming free units into bound ones. Once a unit is occupied—once it codes a given percept or feature—it cannot be occupied by any other percept or feature. Konorski does not explain what would happen if all cognitive units were bound. Evidently, there are enough free units to last for a lifetime of learning. A little bit later, we will discuss how units get captured by perceptual features. When we are born, Konorski says that units are free. As we learn about the world, more and more units become bound. Percepts encountered early thus have a better chance of occupying larger numbers of units—since there are more free units early in life than late. Every time we encounter a feature or percept, it has a chance to occupy more cognitive units. Thus, the more frequently a thing is encountered, the more units that should redundantly code it. It makes some sense to argue that many cognitive units are preordained or destined to code certain features. The results of Hubel and Weisel (1963) with young kittens are certainly supportive of such a contention. Weimer (1973) makes a compelling case for the argument that higher-level units could also be prewired to code certain concepts. His arguments are similar to those advanced by Kant (1781) for the a priori nature of some concepts (see Chapter 1).

Konorski's theory

How are cognitive units formed? That is, how does a given cognitive unit come to code or represent a given stimulus feature or unitary percept? Konorski holds that the brain comes prewired. An infant has multilayered analyzers with the units already interconnected. However, most of these are only potential connections. Some of these potential connections are transformed into actual connections with experience. Konorski ventures the guess that, in order for this transformation to occur, the units to be connected must simultaneously be activated by the nonspecific inputs from the arousal system. This would occur when the organism was attending (since attention accompanies arousal) or when it was rewarded (the drive centers in the brain are connected with the arousal centers). Presentation of a stimulus hypothetically activates lower-level feature units. These are prewired to higher-level units. Thus, the stimulus will activate a given set of higher-level units. If this is done in the presence of arousal, these potential connections will be actualized. Now the higher level units will code the stimulus in question. Konorski assumes that once this occurs, the units cannot be attacked and captured by any other stimulus pattern. Thus, a new stimulus would have to occupy other unoccupied units. He also assumes that the various levels of an analyzer are very richly interconnected, so that a lot of higher-level units could be used to encode any given unitary percept.

Wickelgren's theory

Wickelgren (1979a) has proposed another theory aimed at explaining how free units become bound. The essential idea is that at birth all cognitive units receive excitatory inputs from both the hippocampus and the arousal system. When a unit becomes bound, the hippocampal input is disconnected from that unit. This prevents it from being occupied by any other stimulus pattern. Thus, when new stimulus patterns are encountered, only the free units receive hippocampal input. This excitation makes it more likely that one of them will be captured by the new pattern. Once such a free unit is captured, some process of *memory consolidation* begins. This process consists of disconnecting the hippocampal input to the unit.

Why propose such a theory? The reason has to do with the effects of hippocampal damage. Milner (1966) has reported on the case of H. M., a patient whose hippocampus was completely removed for treatment of epilepsy. The operation had a profound and unfortunate effect on H. M. He cannot learn anything new at all! His long-term memory stops on the day of his operation. Since that time, he has apparently been able to transfer no information at all into memory. Any new information is forgotten within a matter of seconds. On the other hand, old knowledge has not been forgotten. H. M.'s speech, perception, and intelligence are all normal. According to Wickelgren's theory, the problem is that no free cognitive units can be bound to new stimulus patterns. Thus, nothing new can be learned. The reason is that the free units do not receive the necessary excitatory input from the hippocampus—because in H. M.'s case, there is no hippocampus to provide the input.

A lateral inhibition theory

While these theories seem reasonable, I think that they need to be modified. The processes outlined would not serve to get cognitive units coding similar percepts next to each other. Rather, cognitive units would be located at random. Here is what I think happens. Once a given cognitive unit has been captured, it exerts lateral inhibition on neighboring units. The closer these units are to it, the more it inhibits them. Thus, once a unit is occupied, it should prevent surrounding units from being occupied. However, if a new percept were very similar to an old one, units coding its features would inhibit the units coding the features of the old one at the lower level. Then, the old unit on the higher level would be deactivated and the new percept could occupy one of the surrounding units since it would no longer be inhibited. Consider this example. In Figure 4–11 we show cognitive units coding morphemes (the upper level) and cognitive units coding phonemes (the lower level). Assume that the PAT unit is already in place, as illustrated. What if we present the name, BETH? Now, /b/ inhibits /p/, /e/ inhibits /a/, and /th/ inhibits /t/. Thus the PAT unit is deactivated, and its neighboring unit becomes the unit coding the word BETH.

FIGURE 4–11   How a cognitive unit is captured. Solid arrows indicate previously existing connections, wavy arrows indicate new connections, dashed arrows indicate inhibitory connections, and hatch marks indicate inhibited units.

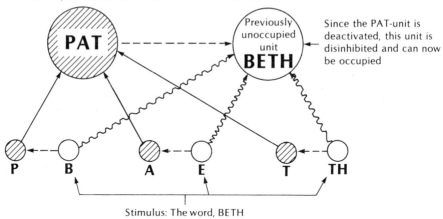

Stimulus: The word, BETH

PERCEPTS, IMAGES, IDEAS, AND HALLUCINATIONS

Bottom-up versus top-down activation

A cognitive unit in a gnostic analyzer can be activated in at least two different ways. First, it can be activated by sensory input or bottom-up activation, which corresponds to perception of the stimulus object coded by the unit. Second, it can be activated via connections with units in conceptual analyzers or top-down activation. This corresponds to having a mental image of the stimulus object.

Konorski argues that perceiving involves activation of units in a gnostic analyzer along with concomitant activation of units in the corresponding primary sensory receiving area. This is most likely to occur in the presence of an external stimulus. We *hear* speech when both the primary auditory receiving area and the speech analyzer are active. We *see* objects when both the primary visual receiving area and one of the visual gnostic analyzers are active. On the other hand, Konorski says a mental image corresponds to activation of units in a gnostic analyzer in the absence of activity in sensory analyzers. This is most likely when the activation has originated from inputs from a conceptual analyzer or from another gnostic analyzer. We have an image of speech when the speech analyzer is active in the absence of activity in the primary auditory receiving area. We have a visual mental image when one of the visual gnostic analyzers is active, but the primary visual receiving area is inactive. A more general way of putting the distinction between a mental image and a percept would be this. A percept is the result of a bottom-up pattern of activation; that is, it consists of the activation of a gnostic unit by—and along with—all of its lower-level component sensory units. On the other hand, a mental image is the result of a top-down pattern of activation. It consists of the activation of a gnostic unit along with some—but not all—of its lower-level component units by an internal rather than an external source of stimulation.

It is common in psychology to differentiate between a sensation and a perception. In line with what we said in the previous paragraph, we could say that a sensation corresponds to activity in a sensory analyzer in the absence of activity in a gnostic analyzer, while a perception is activity in both a sensory analyzer and a gnostic analyzer. Because of the close connections between the two types of analyzer, sensations are likely to be accompanied by perceptions.

Another common differentiation is that between a mental image and an abstract idea or an imageless thought. It would seem that we could define an abstract idea as corresponding to activation of units in a conceptual analyzer in the absence of activity in gnostic or sensory analyzers. When we think, there are apt to be bits and pieces of inner speech, visual images, and so on thrown into the stream of consciousness. Presumably these are not the basic components of thought. Rather, thought consists of a sequence of activity in conceptual analyzers. Since the units in these analyzers are strongly connected to gnostic units, the activation tends to overflow into gnostic areas.

Similarity of percepts and mental images

PRIMITIVE ANALYZERS

The distinction between percepts and images is especially poor for the more primitive analyzers. Examples of more primitive analyzers would be those for what Schachtel called the autocentric senses—touch, taste, and smell. These analyzers have rather few different unitary perceptions to detect. The average person may know 50,000 or so different words that must each be coded by a cognitive unit. In contrast, we can discriminate rather few tastes, smells, or types of touch. The emotional analyzer would also be classified as a rather primitive one. We certainly cannot discriminate anywhere near 50,000 different emotions. With all of the primitive analyzers, Konorski argues that all of the feature analysis goes on right in the primary sensory receiving area. As a consequence, the sensory units and the gnostic units are either the same units or very closely connected units. Thus, the very same unit may be activated by sensory input and by associative input from other gnostic areas. Thus, there is no subjective difference between images and perceptions for these analyzers.

Consider seeing someone else's finger being cut. Most of us have an empathic, queasy sense of real pain. Seeing someone else being cut leads to an image that is very much like the perceived pain we would actually experience. Ribot (1911) cites an interesting example: "A butcher remained hanging by one arm from a hook, he uttered frightful cries, and complained that he was suffering cruelly, while all the time the hook had only penetrated his clothes, and the arm was uninjured." It is very difficult to form images of touch, taste, or smell. But when they are formed, they seem to be percepts rather than images. The same is true of emotions. Can you form an emotional image? I suspect that, if you succeed in doing so, you will actually be feeling the emotion itself. As Sully-Prudhomme put it, "I am almost inclined to ask myself if every recollection of feeling does not take on the character of a hallucination" (quoted by Ribot, 1911).

VISUAL IMAGES

In the case of vision, perceiving a thing and forming a mental image of that thing hypothetically involve activation of the same gnostic units. What differs is only the manner in which these units have been activated. Lots of operations on visual mental images resemble perceptual processes rather than conceptual ones. Shepard and Metzler (1971) showed their subjects two-dimensional drawings of three-dimensional objects, such as those shown in Figure 4–12. The subjects' task in this experiment was to say whether the two drawings were of the

FIGURE 4–12 In this experiment, the subjects were to say whether the two members of the pair were identical except for spatial orientation. The stimuli in A and B are the same but rotated; the stimuli in C are different.

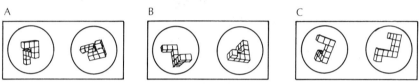

Source: R. N. Shepard, and J. Metzler, "Mental Rotation of Three-Dimensional Objects," *Science* 171 (1971):702. Copyright 1971 by the American Association for the Advancement of Science.

same object in different spatial orientations. When they were the same, the difference in orientation varied from 0° to 180°. Reaction time to say that the two members of a pair were the same was a linear function of the degree of difference in orientation. To answer the question, subjects seemed to be mentally rotating mental images at a constant speed. That is, it must be that they formed images of the members of the pair and then mentally rotated one of these images to see if it could be made to correspond with the other member of the pair. The more rotation that was necessary, the longer it took them to do this. Hence, the longer it took them to answer the question. This suggests that the subjects were operating on images very much like percepts rather than on the more abstract propositional representations that hypothetically were used to generate these images.

Several other lines of evidence suggest that people can form mental images that resemble percepts and then look at them in order to make decisions. Moyer (1973) presented subjects with pairs of animal names. The task was to say which member of the pair was larger in size. The greater the difference in size, the quicker was reaction time. For example, the decision could be made more quickly for FLY versus ELEPHANT than for FLY versus DUCK. This makes sense if subjects formed images in order to answer the questions. On the other hand, such differences in reaction time would not be expected if more abstract semantic units were used in answering the questions.

Podgorny and Shepard (1978) used a 5 × 5 square grid such as the one shown in Figure 4–13. On each trial, subjects had to indicate whether a probe dot in one of the squares fell on a stimulus figure (a letter of the alphabet, such as the F shown in Figure 4–13) or outside of it. There were three conditions. In the perceptual condition, the stimulus figure was actually shown. In the memory condition, it was shown before the trial, so subjects had to remember where it was. In the mental imagery conditions, subjects were given a verbal description of what and where the stimulus figure was supposed to be. Then, they had to project a mental image of it onto the grid. Reaction times to say whether the dot was on

FIGURE 4–13   Example of pattern used in the experiment using a probe dot

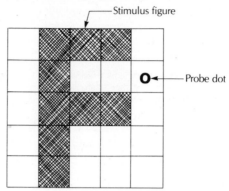

Source: P. Podgorny and R. N. Shepard, "Functional Representations Common to Visual Perception and Imagination," *Journal of Experimental Psychology: Human Perception and Performance* 4 (1978):25.

or off the stimulus figure were practically identical in all three conditions. Furthermore, other details of responding were essentially the same in all three conditions. For example, reaction times for on-figure dots were always faster; and for off-figure dots, reaction time was faster the further the dot was from the figure. In summary, there were no differences in the pattern of responses to percepts and to mental images. This suggests that the same cognitive units were involved in both cases.

Questions about salient attributes (for example, CATS HAVE CLAWS) can generally be answered more quickly than questions about less salient attributes (for example, CATS HAVE HEADS). However, this should not always be the case if one were answering questions by looking at mental images. If you were to form an image of a cat, the claws would probably be small in comparison to the large and prominent head, if they were even represented at all. If you were answering questions by looking at mental images, you should be faster if the questions concerned parts of the image that were large (for example, CATS HAVE HEADS) than if they concerned parts that were small (for example, CATS HAVE CLAWS). This is exactly what Kosslyn (1976) found. In his experiment, half of the subjects were told to answer questions by reference to mental images and half were given no such instructions. The questions concerned attributes of objects that are salient but small and attributes that are nonsalient but large. Reaction times for the imagery group were a function of attribute size. Reaction times for the nonimagery group were a function of attribute salience.

Hallucinations

Hallucinations involve nonsensory activation of gnostic units that are experienced as perceptions rather than images. To explain hallucinations, we have to assume that vertical connections in an analyzer can go from higher to lower units as well as vice versa and from gnostic areas to sensory receiving areas as well as vice versa. If such connections exist, why do we not hallucinate all of the time? Associative activation of higher-level gnostic units should activate lower-level units, and we should have continual hallucinations. One reason that this does not happen probably has to do with the strength of downward vertical connections. As compared with the upward vertical connections, they are relatively weak. However, if arousal were very high, such downward activation would be easier. Indeed—as in the case of the butcher mentioned by Ribot—hallucinations do tend to occur in high-arousal states.

Another reason we do not have more hallucinations is probably due to lateral inhibition. Sensory input activates gnostic units corresponding to external sensory patterns and these laterally inhibit other units that are associatively activated. If this were the case, then shutting off external sensory inputs should lead to hallucinations. This certainly should be a consequence. And it is. The most common example occurs with dreaming. During sleep, sensory inputs are systematically reduced. Dreaming meets the basic criterion for being an hallucination rather than a series of mental images. Hallucinations are often confused with perceptions, whereas images are not. While dreaming, the dream images have a perceptual reality. That is, we are not generally aware that we are just dreaming while the dream is going on. A more clearcut case of hallucinations arising from reduced sensory input involves sensory deprivation. In a sensory deprivation experiment, the amount of stimulation reaching a subject is cut down as much as possible. The result is startling. Perfectly normal people tend to have hallucinations after spending a few hours in such a situation.

Why do hallucinations not begin immediately when stimulation stops reaching an analyzer? Konorski argues that there are a number of units—called *off-units*—in each analyzer that respond to the absence of whatever it is the analyzer detects. Electrophysiological studies have shown that many such units do exist in the brain. Such units are turned off by stimulation and fire maximally in the absence of stimulation. Whether such units exist in all analyzers is an open question. Konorski argues that in the absence of stimulation, such units become active and laterally inhibit units that would otherwise be activated by associative connections. Only when such off-units are fatigued—by the continued absence of stimulation—can the activation via associative connections activate units to the extent that hallucinations are produced.

SUMMARY AND CONCLUSIONS

A response to a stimulus hypothetically involves sequential activity in a number of different systems or analyzers. These are the sensory, perceptual, semantic, episodic, action, and motor systems. Reaction-time studies support the contention that processing does occur in this order. We have argued that each of the systems may be seen as an hierarchical latticelike structure consisting of cognitive units and connections among these units. The higher the level of an analyzer, the more units that occupy it and the more specific the things that they code. Conversely, the lower the level of an analyzer, the fewer units that occupy it and the more abstract the things that they code. Hypothetically, all cognitive units function more or less as logic gates. They vary, however, in their strengths and in their thresholds.

Presumably, all cognitive units also show repetition effects. A few repetitions of the thing they detect sensitizes them, while a lot of repetitions adapts or fatigues them. The wiring diagram for all of the analyzers is hypothetically the same: vertical connections among units tend to be excitatory while lateral connections among units tend to be inhibitory. These structural similarities lead us to expect that we should find analogous effects in all of the analyzers.

We have argued that to perceive something is to activate a set of preexisting cognitive units. In the case of actual perception, this is accomplished by hierarchical feature analysis. It became apparent, though, that these cognitive units must be connected to units in other analyzers. For example, the gnostic unit coding the unitary perception of the printed word DOG must be connected to a cognitive unit in the semantic analyzer coding the meaning of this word. This raises the possibility that the gnostic unit could be activated from the top down (that is, it could be activated via its connection with the unit in the semantic analyzer) as well as from the bottom up. A brief review of some studies of mental imagery showed that mental images do, in fact, behave remarkably like percepts. This supports the notion that at least some of the same cognitive units must be involved in imagination and in perception.

5

Word recognition

According to the model presented in Chapter 4, perception involves the activation of cognitive units in hierarchically organized gnostic analyzers. In this chapter, we shall discuss evidence for this assertion as it pertains to the perception of spoken and printed words. There are two reasons for concentrating on this topic. First, word recognition is very important for cognition; that is, we get a lot of our information about the world from spoken and written words. Second, more research is available on this topic than on many others. Hypothetically, similar processes are involved in the perception of everything from faces to musical melodies. However, our knowledge about word recognition is more complete than our knowledge about the recognition of other classes of stimuli. Thus, as well as being interesting in its own right, learning about word recognition will give us a model for understanding how other things are perceived and recognized.

A spoken word is made up of a string of phonemes or speech sounds. A printed word is, of course, composed of a string of letters. In the last chapter, we discussed the successive levels of analysis that are hypothetically involved in recognizing both spoken and printed words. In this chapter, we shall see that, besides being reasonable, the model makes predictions that are confirmed by experimental research. First, we shall deal with the perception of letters of the alphabet. Then, we shall discuss the recognition of speech sounds. Finally, we shall look at the research on how whole words—both spoken and written—are recognized. We shall save for later chapters the questions of how we understand and remember words once we have recognized them.

LETTER RECOGNITION

Structure of the printed-word analyzer

The constituent units of printed words are the 26 letters of the alphabet. Are these letters recognized by a feature analysis network as has been asserted in the last two chapters? In Chapter 3, we discussed some of the extensive research on visual perception. We ended up arguing that all visual perception and recognition involves feature analysis. So, it is certainly reasonable that reading would, too. We may envision several levels of analysis in reading. At the lowest level would be purely sensory analysis. Here the cognitive units involved in reading would be the same as those involved in any other visual perception. Output from some of the detectors in visual sensory analyzers hypothetically goes to the gnostic analyzer for printed words. Detectors on the lowest level of this analyzer would search for distinctive features of letters. Output from these detectors hypothetically goes to cognitive units coding individual letters of the alphabet. In turn, output from these letter detectors would go to units coding syllables. For example, Smith and Spoehr (1974) propose units coding "vocalic center groups"—that is, spelling patterns composed of a vowel and from zero to three consonants preceding and/or following it. In Chapter 4, we proposed that output from the syllable units goes to cognitive units coding entire printed words. (The hypothesized hierarchical arrangement was diagrammed in Figure 4–1.)

In this section, we shall confine our interest to the two lowest strata of the printed-word analyzer and concentrate on two basic questions: First, is there evidence that printed letters of the alphabet are recognized on the basis of feature analysis? Second, is there evidence that letter recognition is carried out by the sort of latticelike analyzer postulated in Chapter 4. If it is, there should be evidence for vertical facilitation (top-down or context effects) and for lateral inhibition (masking effects).

Distinctive features of letters

Several suggestions have been made as to exactly which distinctive features are searched for in the perception of individual letters of the alphabet. Gibson (1969) proposed a set of features for the recognition of capital letters (see Figure 3–4). The system involved only 12 distinctive features. Each of the 26 letters of the alphabet is uniquely determined by the presence versus absence of each of these features. Several other distinctive feature systems have been proposed. At present, there is no compelling reason to favor any one system over the others. They are all rather similar, and they all work pretty well. There is no question that letters can be described in terms of distinctive features. The question is whether there is any evidence to support the hypothesis that these features are, in fact, involved in perception and that there are cognitive units sensitive to them.

Psychological reality of letter features

If distinctive features are relevant to perception of letters, then it follows that the more features shared by two letters, the more confusion there should be between the two and the more similar the two should be judged. Gibson, Osser, Schiff, and Smith (1963) showed letter pairs to both adults and children. The subjects were asked to judge quickly whether the two letters were the same or different. Both errors and reaction times for making such judgments increased as a function of number of features shared by the two letters. That is, the more visual features two letters shared, the more likely it was that subjects would erroneously say that they were the same and the longer it took subjects to correctly say that they were different. Clement and Carpenter (1970) wondered if the results of Gibson et al. might not really be due to acoustic similarity rather than to visual similarity between letters. Thus, some letters (for example, B and P) not only look similar; they also sound similar. However, their results were clear. With visual presentations, errors were a function only of the number of visual features shared by two letters. They had nothing to do with the number of phonetic features in common. This, as we shall see, contrasts with the findings of Miller and Nicely (1955) and others: in the case of spoken speech, confusions among phonemes are a function of number of shared phonetic features and have nothing to do with the number of shared visual features.

Townsend (1971) and Rumelhart and Siple (1974) used a tachistoscope to present individual letters of the alphabet. Subjects simply had to identify which letter was shown. When mistakes were made, they tended to involve seeing a letter sharing a number of visual features with the stimulus. The more features shared, the more likely a letter would be incorrectly substituted for the correct one. Using an opposite approach, Dunn-Rankin (1968) and Kuennapas and Janson (1969) simply asked subjects to judge how visually similar pairs of letters were. Results were in conformity with the expectation that judged similarity should increase with number of shared visual features.

Neisser (1964) presented subjects with long lists of letters. Their task was to search for a given letter. The task took longer to the extent that the target letter (the one searched for) shared features with the distractor letters (the ones not being searched for). For example, it took less time to search for the letter Z in a list of curved letters (for example, C, G, and O) than in a list of uncurved letters (for example N, V, and X). This result may seem obvious but note that it tells us something very important. If people had templates that were sensitive only to whole letters, the characteristics of the distractor letters should not make any difference. Only if we have detectors sensitive to specific features, such as curves and angles, should these characteristics have an effect on the rate of visual search.

Context effects

MISREADING

You will probably find a few typographical errors in this book. Rest assured that various copy editors and I have proofread it ad nauseum. Why, then, did we not find all of the mistakes? The reason is that proofreading is extremely difficult. Especially if the material is familiar, one tends to see what one knows is there rather than what is actually printed. A long time age, Pillsbury (1897) showed that this expectation effect is found with tachistoscopic presentations. If FOY-EVER is briefly presented, subjects are likely to report that they have seen the word FOREVER.

One way to explain this effect would be to argue that the cognitive unit coding the word FOREVER receives input from the letter detectors coding F, O, R, E, and V. Presentation of FOYEVER activates most of the relevant letters detectors. These, in turn, activate the cognitive unit coding the word, FOREVER. This word-unit does not, of course, get quite enough input. The R detector should be more activated than it is. Evidently, cognitive units are not terribly picky, since they are used to operating under less than perfect conditions. So, especially if no other units at the same level are activated, a cognitive unit may become activated even when all of the lower-level units feeding into it are not fully activated. Presumably the higher-level unit, in turn, *reactivates* its component lower-level units to some extent. Thus, in this case, people actually see the third letter in the stimulus as being R rather than Y.

THE WORD SUPERIORITY EFFECT

If this line of reasoning is correct, then it should be the case that we should recognize individual letters better when they are presented in a word than when they are presented alone. When a letter is presented alone, the relevant letter-unit has only the bottom-up stimulus input to activate it (see Figure 5–1A). On the other hand, when a letter is presented in a word, the letter detector should be

FIGURE 5–1   Recognition of a letter of the alphabet corresponds to activation of the relevant cognitive unit. (A) When a letter is presented in isolation, the unit can only be activated by a bottom-up process. (B) When the letter is embedded in a word, top-down activation of the relevant unit is also present.

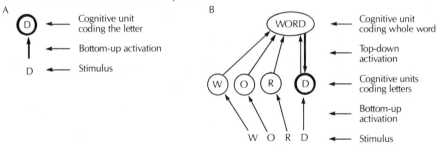

activated not only by the stimulus but also by the top-down reactivation from higher-level syllable and word detectors (see Figure 5–1B). In fact, individual letters are recognized better when they are embedded in words than when they are not. This is called the *word superiority effect*. Reicher (1969) and Wheeler (1970) have both provided recent demonstrations of this effect. Reicher tachisto-scopically presented either a four-letter word (for example, WORD), an anagram of this word which did not itself spell a word (for example, OWRD), or a single letter. Then, subjects had to say which of two letters (for example, D or K) had just been shown. Performance was better when the letter was embedded in the real word than when it was embedded in either the nonword or presented alone. The experiment included lots of controls to make sure that the results were not just artifactual. Note that either of the possible letters (D or K) would spell a word (WORD or WORK). This eliminates the possibility that subjects may have just seen the first several letters of the word and then guessed at what the last letter must have been. The letter to be recognized could occur in any of the four positions of the word, so it was not the case that subjects could always just concentrate on one letter position. Strong evidence that the word-superiority effect is due to reactivation of letter detectors by higher-level detectors is provided by an experiment conducted by Johnston and McClelland (1974). They instructed their subjects to attend either to the whole word being presented or to the specific location of the letter to be recognized. Surprisingly enough, the word superiority effect almost totally disappeared in the latter condition. Telling subjects exactly where to look for the letter to be recognized led them to do worse than if they focused on the whole word! When they looked just at one letter, the top-down reactivation was removed since the word unit was never activated.

The word-superiority effect is also found when letters are embedded in pronounceable nonwords as opposed to nonpronounceable ones (Aderman and Smith, 1971) or in nonwords that follow the spelling patterns of English as opposed to those that do not (Baron and Thurston, 1973). Thus, words that could be—but happen not to be—English words also provide this effect. This suggests that the relevant higher-order units providing the facilitation may actually be syllable units. The pseudo-English words would activate such syllable units which could, in turn, reactivate the lower-level units coding individual letters.

Masking

The cognitive model presented in Chapter 4 would lead us to expect interference or masking effects in letter recognition arising from lateral inhibition. On the level of distinctive features, the more similar two features are, the closer together the cognitive units coding them should be. Activation of one unit should inhibit the other. On the level of individual letters, the more similar two letters are, the closer together the cognitive units coding them should be. Again, activation of one letter unit should laterally inhibit neighboring letter units. Most theorists agree that perception of letters is carried out by an hierarchical feature-detection system. Thus, there is fairly general agreement as to the vertical structure of the printed-word analyzer. However, there is disagreement as to the horizontal structure. Several theorists (for example, Gardner, 1973; Shiffrin and Geisler, 1973; Eriksen and Eriksen, 1974) hold that the feature detectors on any level are completely independent. In the view of these models, any inhibitory effects are ascribed either to masking at the purely sensory level or to confusion at a later level of decision making. Closer to the view proposed in Chapter 4 are the models developed by Estes (1972b) and by Bjork and Murray (1977). Both models propose inhibitory relationships among feature detectors for letters.

Several studies have provided evidence for masking effects in letter perception. For example, Bouma (1970) tachistoscopically presented letters of the alphabet either alone or between two Xs. At an exposure duration when there was virtually perfect recognition of single letters, recognition of the same letters fell to 60 percent when presented between the two Xs. The presence of the Xs thus makes the to-be-recognized letter more difficult to see. This could be due to lateral inhibition among neighboring receptive fields in the retina: the Xs activate receptors that laterally inhibit the receptors activated by the to-be-recognized letter. Such retinal masking does occur with all sorts of visual stimuli. However, Flom, Heath, and Takahashi (1963) showed that masking effects, such as those found by Bouma, are also found when the target letter is presented to one eye and the masking letters are presented to the other eye. This strongly suggests that the locus of the effect occurs not in the retina but at some later level of processing after inputs from the two eyes have been merged. A comprehensive series of 19 experiments conducted by Turvey (1973) leaves no doubt that visually presented letters are subject to masking at both peripheral and central levels.

These and several other similar studies have clearly demonstrated masking effects in the perception of letters. The problem is that these effects can be attributed to lateral inhibition of units in the visual sensory analyzer. Similar results can be obtained with any sort of visual stimulus. The studies cannot really be taken as providing evidence that higher-level cognitive units for letter features or letters in the gnostic analyzer for printed words exist in a lateral inhibitory network. In all of the studies cited so far, amount of masking was dependent upon how close together the letters were. Spatial location is hypothetically kept track of at the sensory level. It should not be so crucial for the gnostic analyzer for printed words. Thus, it would be nice to find evidence of masking where the stimuli were not in immediate spatial contiguity.

Let us consider another line of research. It is a well-established finding that, if subjects are given the task of saying whether or not a target letter is in a briefly presented display of letters, performance declines as the number of distractor items in the display increases (for example, Estes and Taylor, 1964). Gardner (1973) argued that this might be due not to the number of items that have to be scanned before finding the target letter but to the fact that, as the number of items increases, more of the distractor items will be confusable with the target item. If letter detection involves a parallel-processing set of feature detectors, then the number of stimuli should be irrelevant. Only if letter detection involved serial processing should the number of items slow down detection. Gardner's idea was that the number of items per se is irrelevant. The crucial factor is the presence of confusable items (that is, items sharing distinctive features with the target letter). To test this idea, he designed a simple experiment. Subjects' task was to say whether an F or T was presented in a visual display. Distractor items were either dissimilar from either target (0) or highly similar to both targets (the artificial letter, ⊢). The items were distant enough from one another so that sensory-level masking would not be a factor (Flom, Heath, and Takahashi, 1963). The results were clear. Performance was not affected at all by display size when the distracting items were not confusable with the targets. It took no longer to recognize an F in the presence of two or three 0s than in the presence of only one 0. On the other hand, performance declined as display size increased when the distracting items were similar to the target items. One way of explaining this would be to postulate that cognitive units coding the features of the distractor items inhibited the cognitive unit coding features of the target item. Further, the cognitive units coding the distractors should laterally inhibit the unit coding the target. In either case, the more distractors, the more inhibition there would be.

An important experiment along the same lines by Shiffrin and Gardner (1972) provided several very interesting results. Again, subjects' task was to decide whether one of the target letters F or T had been presented. There were two conditions. In one condition, one of the target letters and three distractor items were presented simultaneously at the corners of an imaginary square for 40 milliseconds. The distractors were again the dissimilar 0 and the similar ⊢. The targets could occur in any of the four positions. Figure 5–2 gives examples of the dis-

FIGURE 5–2   Examples of the displays used by Shiffrin and Gardner

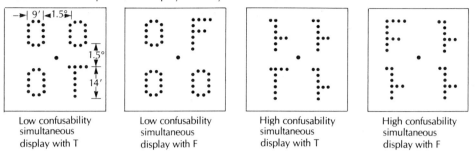

| Low confusability simultaneous display with T | Low confusability simultaneous display with F | High confusability simultaneous display with T | High confusability simultaneous display with F |

Source: R. M. Shiffrin and G. T. Gardner, "Visual Processing Capacity and Attentional Control," *Journal of Experimental Psychology* 93 (1972):74. Copyright 1972 by the American Psychological Association. Reprinted by permission.

plays in this condition. In the other condition, the four items—one target and three distractors—were presented one at a time for 40 milliseconds each with a brief interval between each presentation. They were always presented in the same clockwise direction.

The surprising result was that detection accuracy was the same in both conditions, even though subjects had four times as much time in the second condition. The results provide clear evidence for parallel processing: It is just as easy to detect four letters simultaneously as to detect only one. Shiffrin and Gardner conclude from these results that perception and feature analysis at least up to the stage of letter recognition is effortless, parallel, and of unlimited capacity. Four is certainly not a very large number, but they argue that severe capacity limitations emerge later in processing—at the level of memory and attention.

But what about the effects of confusability? In both simultaneous and sequential displays, performance was worse—by about the same amount—for confusable arrays. Shiffrin and Garner's stimuli were far enough apart so that masking at the sensory level could not have occurred. Here again we must have evidence for lateral inhibition at a higher level of analysis where stimulus location is no longer relevant. The results can certainly be interpreted in this way, but Shiffrin and Gardner suggest a different interpretation. They attribute the interference caused by the presence of similar distractors to the decision-making stage. Their argument is essentially that, at the end of each trial, four cognitive units are activated—those coding the target and the three distractors. Subjects must then search through these units to decide whether an F or a T was presented. This will take longer if the activated units are confusable with each other. This does seem reasonable. An experiment is needed that will shed light on whether the interference effect is due to such a problem in decision making or to actual inhibitory effects at the feature analysis level. Fortunately, just such an experiment has been done.

An experiment conducted by Bjork and Murray (1977) produced evidence that inhibitory effects in letter recognition are perceptual rather than being due to confusion during decision making. They did this by changing the procedure in Shiffrin and Gardner's experiment so that no decision was necessary. Following a prestimulus display (see Figure 5–3A), target letters—either B or R—were pre-

FIGURE 5–3   Example of the sequence of displays used in
trials by Bjork and Murray

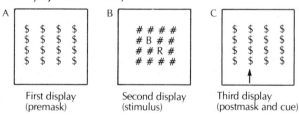

A	B	C
First display (premask)	Second display (stimulus)	Third display (postmask and cue)

Source: E. L. Bjork and J. T. Murray, "On the Nature of Input
Channels in Visual Processing," *Psychological Review* 84 (1977):
474. Copyright 1977 by the American Psychological Association.
Reprinted by permission.

sented in any of the positions of an array presented for from 25 to 50 milliseconds
(see Figure 5–3B). It was followed by a masking stimulus designed to blot out all
of the letters and prevent further sensory processing (see Figure 5–3C). As shown,
an arrow also occurred simultaneously with the masking stimulus. It indicated
which column the target had occurred in. This column always contained a target
letter and never contained a distractor item. Thus, all of the other columns
could be ignored. The crucial question was whether subjects *could* ignore the
other columns.

On some trials, the target letter occurred alone. On other trials, distractor
stimuli were present in one of the columns other than the one the target was
in. These distractor stimuli were of three types: The distractor item was the same
letter as the target (for example, both target and distractor were Bs); the distractor item was the alternative target (for example, the target was B and distractor
was R); or the distractor item was a nontarget letter (for example, the target was
B and distractor was K). The nontarget distractor items—P and K—were chosen
so as to be more similar to R than to B.

The experiment yielded several interesting results. The target letter was correctly recognized most often with single target displays and least often when the
distractor letter was the same as the target letter. Intermediate performance was
obtained when the distractor was the alternate target or a nontarget item. The
nontarget distractors—P and K—interfered more with recognition of the more
similar target (R) than with recognition of the less similar target (B). Finally, the
closer the distractor item was to the target item, the greater was the interference.
We can conclude several things from these results. First, they do not support theories that ascribe the interference effect to the decision-making stage. In this
experiment, there was no decision to be made other than whether the target
letter was a B or an R, since the column containing the target never contained
a distractor item. Subjects were made well aware of this before the experiment
began. They did not have to process the distractor letters at all. Apparently, they
could not help processing them. We know that they did process them because
they interfered with recognition of the target letters. These interference effects
must thus have arisen during the automatic perceptual processing of the stimuli.
The finding that spatial separation had some effect on masking suggests that at
least part of the interference occurred at a fairly low level of processing—that

is, at the level of location-specific feature detection. Had the effect arisen at the level of units detecting presence or absence of individual letters regardless of location, we would not expect spatial separation of target and noise items to be important. Further, at this higher level we might expect facilitation rather than inhibition when the distractor was the same as the target item since both would activate the same cognitive unit. I expect that we might find both of these effects had there been a longer delay between termination of the display and the subject's response. With a longer delay, we would expect the activity of units in the lower-level sensory analyzer to have faded away and the activity of units in the higher-level gnostic analyzer to have become stronger. Unfortunately, though, the relevant experiment has not been done, so we do not know what would happen.

PHONEME RECOGNITION

Structure of the speech analyzer

The structure of the speech analyzer is similar to that of the printed-word analyzer. The basic difference, of course, is that the speech analyzer processes auditory rather than visual inputs. (Figure 4–2 diagrams the levels of analysis carried out in hearing speech.) As you will recall, the idea is that the cognitive units on the highest level of the speech analyzer code the sound patterns of spoken words or morphemes. There is one cognitive unit for each morpheme that you can recognize. Morpheme units receive input from syllable units. These receive input from phoneme units, which in turn receive input from distinctive-feature units. Hypothetically, distinctive-feature units are activated by specific acoustic cues which are detected by units in the auditory sensory analyzer.

In this section, we will be interested in the two lowest strata of the speech analyzer—those devoted to distinctive features and phonemes. The questions of interest will be the same as in the last section. First, is there evidence for the existence of such cognitive units? Second, is there evidence that they exist in a latticelike analyzer as described in Chapter 4? To answer the second question, we shall again be looking for vertical facilitation and lateral inhibition effects.

Distinctive features of phonemes

THE LOGIC OF DISTINCTIVE FEATURES

Phonemes, like letters of the alphabet, are complex stimuli. We need to find a small number of simpler features that could be combined to form phonemes. Let's consider a few of the phonemes that occur in English. Specifically, let's consider the phonemes [b], [p], [d], [t], [g], and [k]. Table 5–1 indicates how each of these speech sounds is pronounced. Note that these phonemes all seem rather similar. Actually, there are several reasons that they seem similar. All of them are called stop consonants. This is because all of them involve a complete stoppage of the air stream at some place in the mouth. The exact place of articulation differs. Two of these phonemes—[b] and [p]—are bilabial: The breath is stopped at the lips. Two—[d] and [t]—are alveolar: There is stoppage at the alveolar ridge, which is just behind the teeth. Finally, two—[g] and [k]—are velar: The air stream is stopped at the velum or back of the mouth.

TABLE 5–1 A distinctive feature system for phonemes

	o	a	e	u	ə	i	l	ŋ	ʃ	ʃ̂	k	ʒ	ʒ̂	g	m	f	p	v	b	n	s	θ	t	z	ð	d	h	#
1. Vocalic/Nonvocalic	+	+	+	+	+	+	+	−	−	−	−	−	−	−	−	−	−	−	−	−	−	−	−	−	−	−	−	−
2. Consonantal/Nonconsonantal	−	−	−	−	−	−	+	+	+	+	+	+	+	+	+	+	+	+	+	+	+	+	+	+	+	+	+	−
3. Compact/Diffuse	+	+	+	−	−	−		+	+	+	+	+	+	+	−	−	−	−	−	−	−	−	−	−	−	−		
4. Grave/Acute	+	+	−	+	+	−									+	+	+	+	+	−	−	−	−	−	−	−		
5. Flat/Plain	+	−		+	−																							
6. Nasal/Oral								+	−	−	−	−	−	−	+	−	−	−	−	+								
7. Tense/Lax									+	+	+	−	−	−		+	+	−	−		+	+	+	−	−	−	+	−
8. Continuant/Interrupted									+	−	−	+	−	−		+	−	+	−		+	+	−	+	+	−		
9. Strident/Mellow									+	−		+	−								+	−		+	−			

Key to phonemic transcriptions: /o/ -pot, /a/ -pat, /e/ -pet, /u/ -put, /ə/ -putt, /i/ -pit, /l/ -lull, /ŋ/ -lung, /ʃ/ -ship, /ʃ̂/ -chip, /k/ -kip, /ʒ/ -azure, /ʒ̂/ -juice, /g/ -goose, /m/ -mill, /f/ -fill, /p/ -pill, /v/ -vim, /b/ -bill, /n/ -nil, /s/ -sill, /θ/ -thill, /t/ -till, /z/ -zip, /ð/ -this, /d/ -dill, /h/ -hill, /#/ -ill. The prosodic opposition stressed versus unstressed, splits each of the vowel phonemes into two.

Source: R. Jakobson, G. Fant, and M. Halle, *Preliminaries to Speech Analysis* (Cambridge, Mass.: MIT Press, 1963), p. 43. Reprinted by permission of The MIT Press, Cambridge, Massachusetts. © 1965 MIT Press.

We have now isolated one possible feature that differentiates these six phonemes. It is *place of articulation*. But what differentiates [b] from [p], [d] from [t], and [g] from [k]? Well, the same thing differentiates the first and the second members of each of these pairs. It has to do with what is called *voicing*. With [b], [d], and [g], the vocal cords begin to vibrate immediately after the stopped air is released. On the other hand, with [p], [t], and [k], there is a delay in *voice onset time;* that is, the vibration of the vocal cords does not begin immediately. Rather, there is a slight delay of about 40 milliseconds. Put your fingers on your larynx (Adam's apple) and repeat the syllables *ba, pa, da, ta, ga,* and *ka.* You will be able to feel a clear difference. The vibrations begin immediately for *ba, da,* and *ga,* but there is a delay when you say *pa, ta,* or *ka.* We can summarize the system as in Figure 5–4. To detect the six phonemes in question, we would need to detect only two features: voicing and place of articulation.

FIGURE 5–4 A distinctive feature system for describing stop consonants

		Voicing	
		Yes: Early voice onset time	No: Late voice onset time
Place of articulation	Front (bilabial)	b	p
	Middle (alveolar)	d	t
	Back (velar)	g	k

BINARY DISTINCTIVE FEATURES

Suppose that we wanted to apply such a system to all of the phonemes in the English language. Several such systems have actually been proposed. I prefer one that involves the use of binary features; that is, features that are either present or absent—such as voicing—rather than having several possible values—as does place of articulation in our example. Depending upon which theorist you listen to, English or American speech is composed of from 38 to 45 different phonemes. For purposes of illustration, let's assume that there are 40 phonemes. Suppose the 40 phonemes could be divided into two groups on the basis of the presence or absence of some distinctive feature. That is, 20 in one group would have the feature while the other 20 would not. Then suppose we could find another feature that would divide, say, 10 phonemes in each group into one category and the other 10 into another category. If we kept doing this we would need only 6 distinctive features to recognize all of the phonemes (since $2^6 = 64$, but $2^5 = 32$ is not quite enough).

This is exactly the line of reasoning that Jakobson, Fant, and Halle (1963) followed. They argue that a phoneme is a bundle of simultaneous distinctive features. Each of the distinctive features they propose is binary: it is either present or absent. They proposed that only 10 distinctive features are needed to characterize all English phonemes. This, of course, is a few more than would theoretically be necessary in a perfectly logical system. But who would argue that English is a perfectly logical system? The basis for Jakobson, Fant, and Halle's distinctive features has to do with how speech sounds are produced (see Table 5–1). To understand its logic, we need to consider how this is done. Essentially, the vocal tract is a tube through which air can be forced. Different sounds can be produced depending upon how the air goes through. For one thing, we can vary the degree to which the vocal tract is open or closed. If we leave the vocal tract completely open, we will produce a vowel. If we constrict it, we will produce a consonant. We can constrict the vocal tract by raising the tongue, closing the lips, and so on. Another possibility is that we can connect the nasal tract into the system by lowering the velum or soft palate. In English, this is done only to produce the nasal sounds, /m/ or /n/. For all other phonemes, the velum is kept in the raised position. Another binary possibility is to allow the glottis (the vocal cords) to vibrate or not to vibrate. When they vibrate, we produce a voiced phoneme. When they do not vibrate, we produce a voiceless or unvoiced phoneme.

ACOUSTIC CUES FOR DISTINCTIVE FEATURES

Just because we are able to formulate a set of distinctive features on the basis of how phonemes are articulated or produced does not mean that these features have anything to do with how speech sounds are recognized. We need evidence that there are aspects of the acoustic stimulus that could serve as signals that a given distinctive feature is present or absent. One way of studying the nature of an auditory stimulus is to look at its spectrum. The spectrum tells us how much energy is present at any given frequency. Since auditory stimuli are composed of sound waves or oscillations at different frequencies, each unique auditory stimulus has a unique spectrum. A pure tone consists of an oscillation at just one frequency. Its spectrum consists of a single line at this frequency. A more complex sound is composed of many different frequencies. For example, a musical note has not only one dominant frequency but also several overtones (having less energy) of this fundamental frequency. The spectrum of the vowel /u/ is shown in Figure 5–5. As you can see, there is some energy at all frequency levels measured. Thus, a vowel sound is characterized by an "envelope" of frequencies. Speech sounds have several *formants* or energy peaks. It is conventional to number these as F_1 (the first formant, corresponding to the lowest frequency peak), F_2 (the next higher frequency peak), F_3, and so on. Generally only the first three formants are of importance. Each vowel sound has a different envelope and a different set of formants. Thus, each vowel is characterized by a unique set of acoustic cues.

FIGURE 5–5   The spectrum of the phoneme /u/

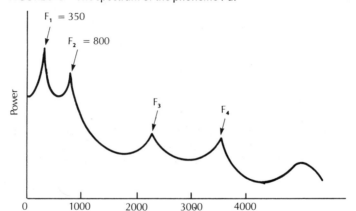

For vowels, the formants are relatively constant over the whole time the vowel is being pronounced. In this, vowels are rather like musical notes. On the other hand, the formants change over time when consonants are pronounced. Thus, we would need a three-dimensional spectrum (frequency × intensity × time) in order to depict the acoustic pattern of a consonant. Of course, a three-dimensional graph cannot be drawn on a two-dimensional piece of paper. The best that can be done is to construct what is called a sound spectrogram. An example is shown in Figure 5–6. A sound spectrogram shows the amount of energy (symbolized by degree of darkness) at various frequencies (on the ordinate) over time (on the abscissa). The case may look rather hopeless at first glance, since Figure 5–6 looks like a messy set of smudges. Rest assured that if we reversed the process with a pattern playback device—something that synthesizes sounds at the various frequencies rather than recording them—we could roughly reproduce the original speech sounds.

In order to detect the distinctive features of consonants, it would be necessary to detect not merely the presence of certain formants, but also their rate of

FIGURE 5–6   Sound spectrogram of the word *cognitive*

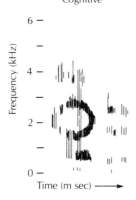

Source: D. B. Pisoni, "Speech Perception," in *Handbook of Learning and Cognitive Processes,* vol. 6, ed. W. K. Estes (Hillsdale, N.J.: Erlbaum, 1978), p. 179.

change. Fant (1973) and Stevens (1975) say that there are indeed context-free or invariant acoustic cues for each distinctive feature. For example, they hold that certain rapid spectral changes in the first 10 to 30 milliseconds after release of air act as cues for the place of articulation feature. However, some theorists (for example, Dorman, Studdert-Kennedy, and Raphael, 1977) dispute the claim that there are invariant acoustic cues that signal the presence of distinctive features. These theorists say that detection of distinctive features is a good deal more complicated than merely detecting an invariant cue.

DETECTION OF ACOUSTIC CUES

Work with animals has produced evidence for the existence of fairly complex feature detectors at the sensory level. For example, Evans and Whitfield (1964) found neurons in the auditory cortex of the cat that were responsive to rate of change in loudness of auditory stimuli. Nelson, Erulkar, and Bryan (1966) found neurons in the brain of the cat that were sensitive to frequency change in a given direction. Some of the units responded to rising frequencies but not to falling transitions while others showed a reverse pattern of response. Abbs and Sussman (1971) suggest that sensory feature detectors responsive to acoustic properties, such as rate of frequency change, bandwidth, and intensity change, could serve as the basic building blocks for distinctive feature units in what we have called the speech analyzer. They hold that these acoustic detectors exist in lateral inhibitory relationships. For example, a given detector might be tuned to a given rate of frequency change. Neighboring detectors would be responsive to higher and lower rates of change. Whenever one detector was activated, it would laterally inhibit neighboring detectors. The basic idea is that output from a set of these sensory detectors would serve as input to cognitive units coding the distinctive features of speech sounds.

Psychological reality of distinctive features

Phonemes can be defined in terms of a relatively small number of distinctive features, and there is at least some evidence that each distinctive feature is signaled by relatively invariant acoustic properties. There is also some evidence that the sensory analyzer for auditory inputs may have units that can detect these properties. All of this evidence merely shows that speech could be perceived by detection of distinctive features. In this section, we shall examine several lines of evidence that are more directly supportive of the hypothesis that there are cognitive units in the speech analyzer that code distinctive features and phonemes.

SIMILARITY JUDGMENTS AND CONFUSION ERRORS

Distinctive feature analysis allows us to group phonemes in terms of how similar they are to one another. Thus, in Jacobson, Fant, and Halle's system (1963), /p/ and /b/ differ in terms of only one distinctive feature: /p/ is tense while /b/ is lax. On the other hand, /p/ and /v/ differ by two distinctive features: /p/ is both tense and interrupted while /v/ is lax and continuant. For any pair of phonemes, we can determine the degree of similarity based upon the number of shared features. If distinctive features are psychologically relevant, degree of similarity in terms of number of shared distinctive features allows us to make predictions about what phonemes will be confused with each other. The more similar two phonemes are in terms of distinctive features, the more confusable they should be—if distinctive features really are psychologically important.

Miller and Nicely (1955) tested this hypothesis with 16 English consonants. Subjects listened to the consonants buried in different levels of white noise. Each consonant was spoken in a consonant-vowel context with the vowel always being /a/. Confusion errors were predictable from the number of distinctive features shared by any pair of consonants. The more distinctive features shared by two consonants, the more likely it was that one would be heard when the other was actually spoken. Klein, Plomp, and Pols (1970) also obtained similar results using vowels rather than consonants. An even more straightforward way of investigating the psychological relevance of distinctive features would be simply to ask subjects for subjective judgments of similarity among pairs of phonemes. This is what Greenberg and Jenkins (1964) did. Judged similarity of phonemes correlated quite well with similarities based on number of shared distinctive features.

CATEGORICAL PERCEPTION

For most types of stimuli, people can discriminate a lot more stimuli than they can identify (Miller, 1956). For example, if I present you with two tones that differ in loudness or pitch, you might be able to tell them apart fairly readily. However, if I presented a tone an hour or so later and asked you if it was one of these two, you might then have great difficulty telling me. Or consider colors. You can discriminate many shades of yellow, but you would be hard put to name or identify more than a few of them. Thus, with most stimulus dimensions we are much better at discriminating differences than at making absolute identifications. Just the reverse seems to be true with speech sounds. Here, we tend to be better at absolute identification than at discrimination.

Liberman, Harris, Hoffman, and Griffith (1957) constructed artificial speech-spectrogram stimuli that varied in small steps. Some of their stimuli are shown in Figure 5–7. Subjects had two different tasks. First they were asked to categorize

FIGURE 5–7   Artificial spectrograms identified as /b/, /d/, and /g/. Only the first half of each stimulus (except for stimulus 14) is shown.

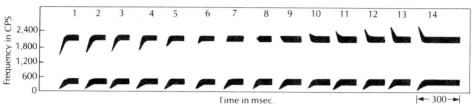

Source: A. M. Liberman, K. S. Harris, H. S. Hoffman, and B. C. Griffith, "The Discrimination of Speech Sounds within and across Phoneme Boundaries," *Journal of Experimental Psychology* 54 (1957): 359. Copyright 1957 by the American Psychological Association. Reprinted by permission.

the stimuli. They showed good agreement on this task. Results are shown in the left panel of Figure 5–8. As you can see, subjects divided the continuum into three consonants—/b/, /d/, and /g/. Second, subjects were given discrimination tests; that is, they were presented with pairs of sounds and asked whether they were the same or different. Here is where the interesting results were found. As shown in the right panel of Figure 5–8, subjects were very good at discriminating between stimuli classified as belonging to different phonemes. However, they were very poor at discriminating between stimuli classified as belonging to the same phoneme. In fact, they performed at almost the level of chance.

This finding has come to be known as *categorical perception:* If a speech sound is classified as being a given phoneme, people cannot discriminate it from other

FIGURE 5–8   Identification (left) and discrimination (right) of the stimuli shown in Figure 5–7. Note that discrimination is very poor between stimuli classified as belonging to the same category.

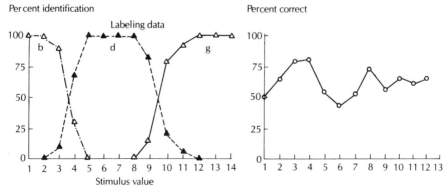

Source: A. M. Liberman, K. S. Harris, H. S. Hoffman, and B. C. Griffth, "The Discrimination of Speech Sounds within and across Phoneme Boundaries," *Journal of Experimental Psychology* 54 (1957):361. Copyright 1957 by the American Psychological Association. Reprinted by permission.

sounds also classified as that phoneme. The finding is consistent with the idea that there are detectors for distinctive features and phonemes that operate in an all-or-none fashion. If one of these detectors is activated, we hear the phoneme in question and ignore the subleties of the sound pattern that activated the detector. Subsequent studies have replicated the findings of Liberman et al. for various consonants. On the other hand, the general finding has been that vowels are not perceived categorically (Fry, Abramson, Eimas, and Liberman, 1962). Subjects can, of course, categorize sounds as belonging to one or another vowel. However, they can discriminate just as well within vowel categories as across them. The reason for this apparent anomaly seems simply to be that vowels as they are usually articulated last for a very long time as compared to consonants. Thus, subjects have lots of time to make a discrimination. Both Fujisaka and Kawashima (1970) and Pisoni (1975) found that vowels also tend to be perceived categorically when they are of short duration (40–50 milliseconds). Stevens (1968) found greater categorical perception of vowels when their duration was reduced by presenting them in a consonant-vowel-consonant context. Lane (1965) found categorical perception of vowels when they were presented against a noisy background. Finally, Pisoni (1973) presented pairs of vowels and asked his subjects to indicate whether they were the same or different. He varied the length of time between presentation of the two stimuli. The longer the interstimulus interval, the more the vowels were perceived categorically. Between-category discrimination stayed high with long interstimulus intervals, but within-category discrimination declined. Thus, it would seem that vowels are also perceived categorically in situations where their long duration and high energy content is controlled.

ADAPTATION OF FEATURE DETECTORS

If there are feature detectors for distinctive features, then it should be possible to fatigue or adapt them by repeatedly presenting the feature that they detect. If a word is repeated over and over, it seems to transmute itself into a series of different words. This is called the *verbal transformation effect* (Warren and Warren, 1970). For example, if a person is exposed to the word DRESS over and over, what will happen? Of course, it will first be heard as DRESS. Fairly soon, though, it may be heard as TRESS, then STRESS, and so on. Warren and Warren (1970) found that when a word is repeated for three minutes at a rate of two times per second, the average person hears it as changing form about 30 times. These changes involve hearing about six different words. All the while, of course, exactly the same stimulus is being presented. As the earlier example suggests, the changes tend to involve hearing a closely related phoneme (that is, one differing by only one or two distinctive features) rather than the correct one (Abbs and Sussman, 1971). These findings suggest that the repeated presentations of the word may fatigue the feature detectors involved in hearing its component phonemes.

Distinctive feature detectors seem to respond to a range of stimuli. When people are asked to discriminate speech sounds, they tend to be very good at the boundaries between two phonemes, but they are not perfect. Detectors must be set to respond to a range of stimuli, but two neighboring detectors must show a little bit of overlap (see Figure 5–8). For example, assume that there is a detector for the voiced feature ($+V$) and another detector for the unvoiced feature (−V). The crucial difference between these two features has to do with voice onset time. A certain range of voice onset times activates the voiced detector, while another range of times activates the unvoiced detector. But what of the gray area in between? Presumably, there is a little bit of overlap here.

Eimas and Corbit (1973) followed this line of reasoning. They further assumed that if one feature detector was fatigued by repeated presentation of the feature it detected, then this should lead to a shift in the category border between two detectors. Stimuli formerly categorized as belonging to the fatigued detector should now be categorized as belonging to the unfatigued one. This should be especially noticeable near the border between the two detectors. For example, suppose the voiced detector were fatigued by repeated presentation of a voiced phoneme. This detector would now be more difficult to activate. On the other hand, the detector for the unvoiced property should be unaffected or even disinhibited. As a consequence, stimuli in the region of overlap that were formerly heard as a voiced phoneme should now be heard as an unvoiced phoneme.

Eimas and Corbit (1973) studied a range of synthetic speech stimuli that are categorized as being either [da] or [ta]. Thus, the stimuli differed in being voiced (/d/) versus unvoiced (/t/). First, Eimas and Corbit repeatedly presented [da]. Then they asked their subjects to categorize stimuli from along the whole range of stimuli. The results are shown in the left panel of Figure 5–9. As compared with judgments in a control condition, the category border shifted toward [da]. Stimuli formerly heard as [da] were now heard as [ta]. Just the reverse happened when the unvoiced detector was fatigued with repeated presentations of [ta].

In another part of the experiment, Eimas and Corbit demonstrated that the effects were not due to fatiguing of phoneme detectors. If the category shift were due to fatiguing of phoneme detectors, then it should be specific to a given phoneme. On the other hand, if it were due to distinctive feature detectors, then

FIGURE 5–9   Identification functions before adaptation (solid lines) and after adaptation (broken lines). The symbols in brackets indicate the adapting stimulus.

Percent of voiced identification responses

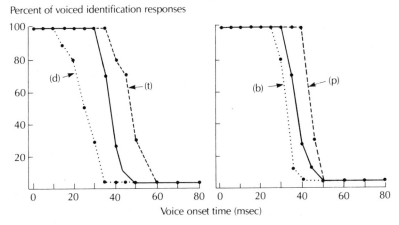

Voice onset time (msec)

Source: P. D. Eimas and J. D. Corbit, "Selective Adaptation of Linguistic Feature Detectors," *Cognitive Psychology* 4 (1973):104.

fatiguing with any phoneme possesing a given feature should have the same effect on any other phoneme possessing this feature. This was what Eimas and Corbit found. The phonemes /d/ and /t/ are alveolar stops that differ in the voiced versus unvoiced feature. The phonemes /b/ and /p/ are bilabial stops that also differ on the voiced versus unvoiced feature. As may be seen in the right panel of Figure 5–9 adapting with [ba] and [pa] had almost as much effect on the [da] to [ta] continuum as did adapting with [da] or [ta]. Thus, it must be the detectors for the voiced versus unvoiced features—rather than detectors for phonemes (/d/ or /t/)—that are responsible for the effect.

These effects, which have been replicated in subsequent studies, seem to be specific to speech sounds. Eimas, Cooper, and Corbit (1973) got these results only when subjects perceived the stimuli as sounding like speech. When only the first 50 milliseconds of the sounds were presented, subjects did not perceive them as being speech sounds and did not show the category-shift effect following repeated presentations. In a later study, Eimas, Cooper, and Corbit (1973) presented strong evidence that the category shift effect is due to detectors located in the brain rather than in peripheral auditory tracts. They showed that the effect could be obtained by presenting the adapting stimuli to one ear and the test stimuli to the other ear. It is only in the brain that the inputs from the two ears are combined. Thus, if the effect were a peripheral one, it would not transfer between ears.

Rudnicky and Cole (1977) showed that adaptation could be produced using connected speech—a passage containing many phonemes with a given feature—as well as by synthetic speech stimuli. Rudnicky and Cole (1977) also found differences in the amount of adaptation for different classes of phonemes. That is, less adaptation was found using voiced stop consonants than for others, such as unvoiced stop consonants or nasal consonants. Similar results for voiced versus unvoiced detectors were also found by Eimas, Cooper, and Corbit (1973). Cooper (1975) hypothesizes that the detectors for voiced stop consonants are stronger or more resistant to adaptation, perhaps because they are more frequently used in speech (Lisker and Abramson, 1964) and are learned earlier by children (Preston, 1971).

Context effects

We saw that, for visually presented letters, there is a word superiority effect. A letter is recognized more quickly and more accurately if it is presented in the context of a word than if it is presented alone. This effect was attributed to descending reactivation from higher-level syllable and word units. The word superiority effect is also found with speech (for example, Stevens and House, 1972). Individual phonemes are extremely difficult to hear in isolation. In fact, consonants in isolation with no preceding or following vowel hardly sound like speech at all. This is why, in all of the experiments discussed earlier, consonants were presented in the context of a vowel. Even in this context, performance is not perfect, as the studies on confusion errors show. It is interesting just how unintelligible isolated speech sounds are. Pollack and Pickett (1964) surreptitiously tape-recorded conversations. Then they presented isolated single words from these conversations to their subjects. Only 47 percent of these isolated words were correctly recognized. This is quite surprising. In another part of their experiment, Pollack and Pickett had people read prose passages at a normal rate. Again, individual words were isolated from the tape recordings and presented to other subjects. Only 55 percent of these words were correctly recognized! Shockey and Reddy (1974) had phonetically trained listeners make phonetic transcriptions of speech in a language unknown to them. Only 56 percent of the phonetic segments in the original were correctly identified. If we assume that we correctly hear almost 100 percent of words spoken in a normal conversation, these findings imply that about half of this correct hearing is due not to the stimulus but to our understanding of what is being said—that is, to top-down or descending facilitation from higher-level morphemic, syntactic, and semantic analyses.

Warren (1970) conducted an experiment showing that subjects actually hear speech sounds that have been completely deleted from meaningful sentences. He cut out the first [s] in the word, LEGISLATURES in the sentence, "The state governors met with their respective legislatures convening in the capitol city." The [s] was replaced by either a cough or a tone. Subjects in the experiment "heard" the [s] even though it was not there. They continued to hear it even when specifically warned that a sound was missing. Presumably, descending facilitatory inputs from higher level units sensitive to the meaning of the sentence to the [s]-unit had activated it.

Masking

If there are distinctive feature detectors, then our model would lead us to expect to find masking effects due to lateral inhibition. Pisoni and McNabb (1974) found evidence for backward masking with dichotically presented phonemes. In a backward-masking paradigm, the subject has to report the first stimulus and ignore the second one. What we are looking for is whether the second stimulus makes the first one more difficult to recognize. Pisoni and McNabb used as targets either voiced (for example, /b/) or unvoiced (for example, /p/) phonemes. All of the targets were followed by the phoneme /a/. As masking stimuli, they used either a voiced—/g/—or unvoiced—/k/—phoneme. Masking stimuli were followed by /a/, /ae/, or /e/. Responses were scored as correct if they had the correct feature. Thus, if a subject heard [ba] but the stimulus was really [da], this was scored as correct because both /b/ and /d/ are voiced. If the mask and the target shared the same feature, there was no real effect. We would not expect there to be one. In fact, we might even expect some facilitation. For example, if [da] is masked by [ga], the voiced feature detector has been stimulated twice— and remember that any response with the voiced feature is scored as correct. Be this as it may, there was a masking effect when a voiced phoneme was masked by an unvoiced one or vice versa. This is what we would expect if voiced and unvoiced feature detectors laterally inhibit one another.

Pisoni and McNabb also found differential masking as a function of vowel context. Most masking was found if both target and mask shared the same vowel —for example, [da] versus [ka]. Somewhat less was found if they shared a similar vowel—for example, [da] versus [kae]. Still less was found if they shared less similar vowels—for example, [da] versus [ke]. This suggests that the masking is at least partially due to effects at the acoustic as opposed to the phonetic level. At the phonetic level, the vowel context should not make any difference because we would be dealing with units coding /d/ and /k/ irrespective of slight differences in their pronunciation. The same conclusion is suggested by the fact that backward masking—if the target and the mask differed on the voicing feature—was a function of intensity of the masking stimulus. The louder it was relative to the target, the more masking. We might expect the phonetic distinctive feature analyzers to be either on or off. Intensity of the masking stimulus should not have as much effect on them as on units in the acoustic analyzer.

RECOGNITION OF WHOLE WORDS

Morton's logogen model

Morton (1969) has proposed an influential model of how words are recognized. The model is shown in diagramatic form in Figure 5–10A. The model holds that words are recognized by a system composed of units that Morton calls *logogens*. Each logogen codes, stands for, or symbolizes a single word. When the logogen

FIGURE 5–10   Morton's logogen model. Morton's diagramatic representation is shown in A. A reformulation in terms of activation of cognitive units in morpheme, printed-word, and semantic analyzers is shown in B.

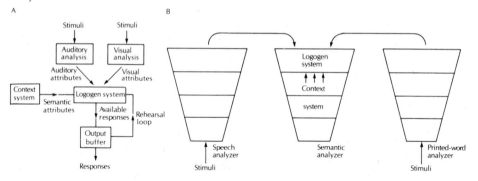

Source for A: J. Morton, "Interaction of Information in Word Recognition," *Psychological Review* 76 (1969):166. Copyright 1969 by the American Psychological Association. Reprinted by permission.

is fully activated, that word is made available to consciousness—the output buffer in the diagram. Logogens receive inputs from several sources. First, they receive auditory inputs from lower-level speech analyzers. Morton does not deal with what these lower-level units are, but we may assume that logogens receive inputs from morpheme units which, in turn, receive input from syllable, phoneme, and distinctive feature units. Second, logogens receive inputs originating from analyzers detecting visual inputs. Thus, they stand at the end of a hierarchy ranging from purely visual analyzers through feature detectors for letter features, letters, syllable groups, and printed words. Logogens also receive inputs from the context system. These inputs from the context system correspond to expectations based upon prior inputs. In terms of the model presented in Chapter 4, a logogen corresponds to a cognitive unit at the top level of the semantic analyzer. Such units receive inputs from morpheme units, printed word units, and from units on deeper levels of the semantic analyzer that code the meaning of prior inputs (see Figure 5–10B). The only real difference between our model and Morton's is that he holds that logogens operate independently of one another. On the other hand, we would predict that they should inhibit each other in proportion to their similarity.

Each logogen hypothetically accumulates a count of how much input it is receiving from each of its three possible sources of input. Morton holds that the count in a logogen decays very rapidly. Four things can serve to keep the count high. Obviously, continued auditory or visual presence of a stimulus are two ways of doing this. A third way is continued inputs from the context system. A fourth way involves rehearsal. One can overtly or covertly repeat the word over and over by cycling it through the output buffer and rehearsal loop (see Figure 5–10A).

Each logogen also has a threshold. If the count in a given logogen exceeds this threshold, the logogen is activated or becomes available as a response. The subjective aspect of this activation would be that the word coded by the logogen is recognized. Morton postulates that there are differences among logogens in their thresholds. One important difference has to do with word frequency. Logogens corresponding to words of higher frequency of usage hypothetically have permanently lower thresholds; that is, less input is required to activate them than is the case for logogens corresponding to words with lower frequencies of occurrence. On the other hand, the thresholds of logogens can be lowered temporarily. Morton theorizes that there are at least two ways of doing this. First, he holds that once a logogen has been activated, its threshold is temporarily lowered. The threshold very gradually returns to the original level. However, if a word is repeated, it should be easier to recognize than the first time it appeared. Morton does not consider what would happen if we tried to adapt the unit by presenting it over and over. Based on what happens at other levels, we might assume that this would eventually raise the threshold. A second way of temporarily lowering the threshold of a logogen involves a more voluntary process. Hypothetically, informing people which stimuli will be presented to them leads to a temporary lowering of the thresholds of the logogens coding these stimuli. The reason for this could be that telling subjects which stimuli will be presented leads to activation of the logogens coding these stimuli. This activation lowers the thresholds of these logogens. Thus, if the range of possibilities is restricted, it should be easier to recognize stimuli.

Threshold effects

A lot of studies support the contention that words that occur more frequently in the language are recognized more easily or more quickly than less frequent words. Howes and Solomon (1951) found evidence for such an effect with visual tachistoscopic presentations of words. Brown and Rubenstein (1961) got similar results when subjects were asked to recognize spoken words presented in noise. The same result has been found with lexical decision tasks (Scarborough, Cortese, and Scarborough, 1977). A lexical decision task is one where a letter string is presented to the subject and the task is simply to say whether or not the letter string is a real word. The critical variable is reaction time—how long it takes the subject to make this decision. The decision is made more quckly for high frequency words than for words of lower frequency. Presumably, this is because the cognitive units coding more frequent words have lower thresholds.

There is also a lot of evidence that a word is recognized more quickly on later presentations than on its first presentation. Using a lexical decision task, Scarborough, Cortese, and Scarborough (1977) found that lexical decisions were made much faster on the second presentation of a word than on the first presentation. This repetition effect declined a bit as a function of time between the first and second presentations of the word, but it was still there two days later! They also noticed that repetition had a larger facilitatory effect on low-frequency words than on high-frequency words. Scarborough, Cortese, and Scarborough argue that the word frequency effect may, in large part, simply be a repetition effect; that is, before coming to the laboratory, a subject will have heard more high frequency words over the prior several days. Because of this, their thresholds will be lower purely as a consequence of the repetition effect.

Several studies have also confirmed Morton's prediction (1969) that restricting the size of the set of words to be recognized has a beneficial effect on recognition; that is, the fewer the alternatives the better recognition is. One of the most extensive studies was carried out by Miller, Heise, and Lichten (1951). They presented their subjects with spoken syllables in the context of varying amounts of background noise. Subjects were told beforehand that the words to be recognized would come from a specific list of words. These lists varied in size from two words all the way up to 1,000 words. At all noise levels, the fewer the alternatives the better recognition was.

Context effects

We saw that there is a word-superiority effect for individual letters and phonemes: They are perceived better when they are embedded in a word than when they are presented alone. It turns out that there is an analogous *sentence-superiority effect* for words: Words are identified more easily when they are embedded in a sentence than when they are presented in isolation (Miller, Heise, and Lichten, 1951). This effect can be ascribed to Morton's context system or to ascending facilitation from deeper-level syntactic and semantic analyses. In a subsequent study, Miller and Isard (1963) found that words in syntactically correct sentences are more intelligible than those in ungrammatical sentences. Furthermore, words in grammatical sentences that are meaningful are recognized better than those in sentences that are syntactically correct but not meaningful. An example of the latter type of sentence would be A JEWELER EXPOSED THE ANNUAL FIRE-BREATHING DOCUMENT. Words in a sentence such as this are not recognized as well as words in a sentence that is both semantically meaningful and grammatical, such as, A JEWELER APPRAISED THE GLITTERING DIAMOND EARRINGS.

Tulving and Gold (1963) showed their subjects from one to eight words of context and then briefly presented the word to be recognized. The prior context was either relevant or misleading. For example, the context, MORE MONEY BUYS FEWER PRODUCTS DURING TIMES OF _____ might be followed by the word INFLATION or the word RASPBERRY. Compared to the case when there was no prior context, the more relevant context that was presented, the more quickly the test word was recognized. On the other hand, just the opposite was found for misleading context. The more misleading context, the longer it took for correct recognition. The results are shown in Figure 5–11. Presumably, the prior context activated deeper-level semantic units which in turn activated a

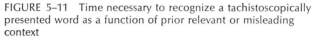

FIGURE 5–11   Time necessary to recognize a tachistoscopically presented word as a function of prior relevant or misleading context

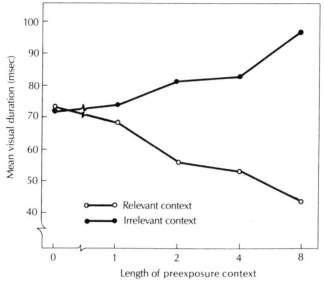

Source: E. Tulving and C. Gold, "Stimulus Information and Contextual Information as Determinants of Tachistoscopic Recognition of Words," *Journal of Experimental Psychology* 66 (1963):322. Copyright 1963 by the American Psychological Association. Reprinted by permission.

set of logogens. In this example, the logogen coding INFLATION would already have been partially activated as a result of the prior context. Thus, less stimulus information would be needed to bring total activation of the logogen above its threshold. Schuberth and Eimas (1977) used a lexical decision task and found results similar to those of Tulving and Gold. Subjects could decide that a word was, in fact, a word more quickly if it was preceded by relevant context. On the other hand, it took them longer to make this decision if the prior context was misleading. Thus, the effects are not restricted to the specific procedures used by Tulving and Gold.

Masking

Why should misleading prior context actually interfere with recognition? One possibility, of course, would be that the units partially activated by prior context laterally inhibit other units. Another possibility would involve a sort of hydraulic model. One could postulate that the total amount of activation in the logogen system is constant. If this were the case, then activating some units would automatically deactivate others. Schuberth and Eimas (1977) and Loftus (1975) have suggested just such an explanation. Actually, this is not incompatable with the lateral inhibition model. The lateral inhibition model just suggests a mechanism that would explain how this automatic deactivation would occur. However, we cannot rule out other less interesting possibilities. One of these possibilities would be that the interference is due to problems at the decision-making level. It might be that when subjects are presented with a word that does not fit the prior context—such as RASPBERRY in the earlier example—they wait until they have more stimulus information before making their response. That is, they change their criterion for reporting. This is the explanation preferred by Morton.

SUMMARY AND CONCLUSIONS

Hypothetically the gnostic analyzers for printed words and for speech are structurally similar. Each is a lattice composed of cognitive units and the connections among them. Units at the highest level of each analyzer code unitary percepts—printed words or morphemes. Units at successively lower levels code syllables, letters or phonemes, and distinctive features. The vertical connections are held to be excitatory, while the lateral connections are held to be inhibitory.

Distinctive feature systems have been formulated for both spoken and written language. In these systems, a letter of the alphabet is seen as being defined by a simultaneous bundle of visual features, while a phoneme is defined by the simultaneous presence of a set of acoustic features. Visual features of letters obviously can be detected since they are things such as angles and curved lines. However, it is less obvious that the distinctive features of speech are signaled by invariant acoustic cues, but there is some evidence for this contention. Evidence for the existence of cognitive units sensitive to such features is provided by similarity judgments, confusion errors, categorical perception, and adaptation effects.

There is very good evidence for vertical facilitation in the case of both speech sounds and printed letters. Letters of the alphabet and phonemes are easier to recognize when they are presented in a word than when they are presented in isolation. This is called the word superiority effect. It is especially strong for speech. Phonemes, syllables, and even whole words are surprisingly difficult to recognize when they are presented without context. While there is a good deal of evidence for masking effects with both speech sounds and printed letters, it is difficult to attribute these effects solely to lateral inhibition of cognitive units in gnostic analyzers. They seem to be at least partially due to inhibitory interactions in the relevant sensory analyzers.

We considered Morton's influential model of how whole words are recognized. It was pointed out that the model is essentially the same as our theory of how cognitive units at the highest level of the semantic analyzer are activated. The only important difference is that Morton does not postulate that these units exist in a lateral inhibitory field. Evidence that these units differ in threshold as a function of frequency of usage, recency of activation, and expectation of presentation was considered. As was the case with units in other analyzers, there is evidence for vertical facilitation or context effects. Just as there is a word superiority effect, there seems to be a sentence superiority effect in that words presented in meaningful sentences are more easily recognized.

6

Primary memory

MEMORY

The term *memory* is used to describe two quite distinct phenomena. William James (1890) referred to our permanent store of memories as *secondary memory*. Others have called this type of memory *long-term memory*. James distinguished a different type of memory which he called *primary memory*. Primary memory consists of whatever is in consciousness at any given moment. This is a fundamental distinction. Elements stored in secondary memory may or may not be present in consciousness at any moment in time. However, we only speak of such secondary-memory elements as being forgotten if it has become impossible to retrieve them or to make them conscious. On the other hand, in James' view, the contents of primary memory are simply the contents of consciousness itself. Elements in primary memory only stay conscious for a few moments. Then they are replaced by others. Thus, loss from primary memory is a very different sort of forgetting than loss from long-term memory. In the case of primary memory, forgetting or loss merely refers to the item's passing out of consciousness.

In terms of the model developed in the preceding chapters, secondary memory is the inventory of cognitive units that a person possesses. Regardless of whether these units reside in sensory, gnostic, semantic, or episodic analyzers, they could be seen as constituting the contents of long-term memory. Therefore, primary memory refers to the subset of these cognitive units that is activated at any given moment in time. Given this definition, you can understand that there is no real difference between perceiving and remembering. To perceive is to activate a set of cognitive units; primary memory refers to this set of activated units.

In order to avoid any possible confusion, it might be best to use terms such as perception and recognition to refer to the process of activating cognitive units by means of external stimuli. In contrast, we shall use the term *primary memory* to refer to cognitive units that have already been activated. In the case of perception and recognition, the basic questions concern how and why a given set of cognitive units becomes activated. In the case of primary memory, the basic questions concern what happens once these units are activated. How long will they stay activated? What deactivates them? How many of them can be active at any one time? What functions does their continued activation serve?

Sensory memory versus short-term memory

Today, most theorists divide James' primary memory into two components. The first of these is *sensory memory*. After a stimulus is presented, a primary memory that is rather similar to a positive sensory aftereffect persists. This memory is extremely short lived; in fact, most estimates put the duration of a sensory memory at well under one second. Almost everyone agrees that sensory memory is modality specific (the memory has the same form as the original sensation), that it is preattentive and automatic (no active attention or effort is required to maintain it), and that loss is due to decay or masking caused by subsequent stimuli. There is some controversy as to whether sensory memories are maintained by persistence of activity in the peripheral receptor organs themselves, by persistence of activity in cognitive units in sensory analyzers, or by both types of persistence.

A second and later component of primary memory is what is commonly called *short-term memory*. We might see short-term memory as referring to persistence of activation of cognitive units in gnostic analyzers. This type of memory is somewhat less modality specific than sensory memory. Thus, some theorists argue that people have a tendency to translate or transfer information to the speech analyzer in order to maintain it in short-term memory regardless of which analyzer originally processed the information. Short-term memory is commonly believed to have a natural duration of 15–30 seconds at most. In contrast to information in sensory memory, information in short-term memory can be maintained for longer periods of time by exertion of attention and effort.

A good example of short-term memory is remembering a telephone number you have just looked up. As you have probably noticed, it is very easy to forget such a number. To counter this tendency, you may *rehearse* the number: that is, you may repeat it (either aloud or covertly), over and over to yourself. Somehow, this helps to keep you from forgetting the number. Note that the telephone number has been recoded from visual to phonetic form before rehearsal. You perceived a visual stimulus (the number printed in the telephone book), but you are rehearsing the digits in overtly or covertly spoken form. You may also have noticed that the capacity of short-term memory is severely limited. When a telephone number is unfamiliar, can you remember both the area code and the seven-digit number? Most people cannot. Another interesting thing about short-term memory is that items somehow get from it into long-term memory. When you first need to use a new telephone number, you have to look it up every time you want to use it. But after a few times, you can retrieve the number from your long-term memory rather than from the telephone book.

MODELS OF PRIMARY MEMORY

Structural models

How do the different types of memory fit together? By the end of the 1960s, there was general agreement that the situation is as diagrammed in Figure 6–1.

FIGURE 6–1   Model of primary memory (sensory register and short-term store)

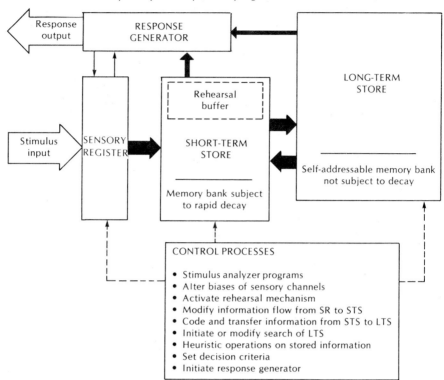

Source: R. M. Shiffrin and R. C. Atkinson, "Storage and Retrieval Processing in Long-Term Memory," *Psychological Review* 76 (1969):180. Copyright 1969 by the American Psychological Association. Reprinted by permission.

This model of memory, suggested by Shiffrin and Atkinson (1969), was based on earlier models proposed by Broadbent (1958) and Waugh and Norman (1965). The idea was essentially this. Stimuli excite activity in sensory registers. There is a different sensory register or analyzer for each of the senses. Some of the information in the sensory registers is read into short-term memory. This "reading-in" process was seen as involving a recoding of information into phonetic or acoustic form. Short-term memory was seen as being provided with about seven "slots" to hold chunks of phonetically coded information. If these slots were filled, old items were theoretically displaced when new ones entered. Items in short-term memory were seen as being subject to rapid decay unless they were rehearsed. This process was hypothetically carried out by the rehearsal buffer. The purpose of short-term memory was seen as being to keep items available for immediate use. Items in short-term memory could be transferred into long-term memory. The longer they stayed in short-term memory, the more likely they were to get into long-term memory. In fact, information was seen as having to go through short-term memory before it can reach long-term memory. There was no way for information to get into long-term memory if it had not first passed through the short-term store. On the other hand, retrieval of information from long-term memory was seen as consisting of placing it into short-term memory. Incidentally, we would ascribe to the action system a number of the processes listed in Shiffrin and Atkinson's "Control Processes" box shown in Figure 6–1.

In this view of memory, short-term memory is a place or structure that is different from long-term memory. The early models also tended to see this as a place with a few slots or boxes that hold information. This view of memory does not make much sense in terms of how we have explained recognition. Let's say that I read you the following list of words: DOG, BOX, and RAT. We have said that recognition of these words involves activation of preexisting cognitive units in long-term memory. It is not just activation of three morphemic units. It is activation of three columns or sets of units on the featural, phonemic, syllabic, and morphemic levels. These units are solidly fixed in a complex network of other units. Konorski would say that they are actually neurons. In what possible way could we move these units or neurons into slots in short-term memory? It makes sense to say that short-term memory is the temporary activation of pre-existing units in long-term memory. It does not make any sense to say that it consists of movement of these units—or copies of them—into a separate area of storage. Even if it did consist of such a transfer, the movement would have to occur after—rather than before—activation of the relevant units in long-term memory. Thus, if one wished to think in terms of the sort of place metaphor shown in Figure 6–1, the short-term store should logically come after rather than before the long-term store.

Process models

LEVELS OF PROCESSING

Craik and Lockhart (1972) have put forth an influential model of memory. It has to do with what they call *levels of processing*. They argue that stimuli are analyzed or processed by the sort of hierarchical analysis that we discussed in the last several chapters. Primary memory, they say, is a by-product of this analysis. It consists of whatever analyses are being carried out at the present moment. Thus, sensory memory consists of activities at the lower levels of feature analysis. Short-term memory consists of current activities at deeper (that is, less sensory and more semantic) levels of processing. Both types of primary memory consist of temporary activation of cognitive units in long-term memory. Craik and Lockhart say that long-term memories of any sort can be established as a result of primary memory processing. Such new long-term memories might involve construction of new units or of new associations among preexisting units. They also argue that this is more likely to occur the deeper a stimulus has been processed. Thus, analyzing a stimulus at the semantic level is more likely to leave a new long-term memory than just analyzing it at a shallower—more sensory—level.

The idea that short-term memory consists of temporary activation of pre-existing units in long-term memory has become more or less standard. That is, almost everyone has come round to this or a similar view of how memory works (see Shiffrin and Schneider, 1977). The reason for this is that—as we saw in previous chapters—the hierarchical feature analysis theory allows us to explain how stimuli are perceived and recognized in the first place. This theory equates perception and recognition with activation of preexisting units in long-term memory. If this is the case, it is contradictory to say that short-term memory is a separate system that comes into play before units in long-term memory are activated. That would mean that primary memory would occur before perception. By definition, primary memory is supposed to occur after perception. To summarize, the idea is that primary memory is not a separate memory store. Rather, it is equivalent to temporary activation of units in long-term memory. Sensory memory is transient activation of cognitive units at lower (more sensory or less deep) levels of analysis. Short-term memory is transient activation at deeper or more semantic levels of analysis.

It would seem that the shallower the level of analysis, the less persistent this temporary activity is. Thus, sensory memory does not last as long as short-term memory. This does make sense. Consider what happens when you watch a television program or read a book. I suppose that inputs are automatically decoded to the deepest level possible. Given the nature of the gnostic analyzers, the more sensory the level, the fewer the number of different units. Thus, for speech, there are about 8 or 10 distinctive features, 30 phonemes, 10,000 syllables, 50,000 words, and who knows how many semantic units. The view from the top in this: a semantic unit, or an episodic unit coding a proposition, has to accumulate information for quite a while before it is fully activated. This may take several sentences of input. By this time, the eight or ten distinctive feature units will have been used (activated) and reused many times over. The deeper the level of processing, the slower the decay time of units would have to be. Most accounts of short-term memory say that it lasts only 15–30 seconds. I really doubt that this could be true for short-term activity at deep levels of the semantic and episodic systems. If it were, how would we be able to understand the plot of a half-hour television program? Eysenck (1977) points out that the reason deeper processing is more likely to lead to formation of permanent long-term memories may have to do merely with the fact that there are more units at deeper levels of processing. Because of this, there is less possibility for interference. As we shall see later, the less interference there is, the more likely we are to remember something.

DOMAINS OF PROCESSING

Baddeley (1978) has criticized the levels of processing theory on several grounds. Craik and Lockhart's original idea is that there is a continuum of processing levels from shallow to deep. The deeper the processing, the better the chances of a new long-term memory being established. However, several experiments suggest that this is only roughly true. For example, Craik and Tulving (1975) attempted to constrain subjects to different depths of linguistic (for example, phonemic versus morphemic) processing. No differences in long-term memory for the stimulus material were found. Similarly, no differences were found when they attempted to constrain their subjects to use different depths of semantic processing. While semantic processing generally leads to better long-term memory than linguistic processing, there is no evidence that different depths of processing within either domain leads to differences in long-term memory. Such results led Baddeley to suggest that we should speak of processing domains (for example, sensory, phonetic, semantic) rather than processing levels.

This view is consistent with our postulation of separate sensory, gnostic, and semantic analyzers. Given the strong vertical excitatory bonds in each analyzer, it is difficult to stop activation once it has begun. For example, once a set of phoneme units have been activated by a spoken word, there is no way to keep them from activating the relevant syllabic and morphemic units to which they are connected. Baddeley makes the same point using different terms. The idea that there are domains of processing allows us to reconcile the old and new views of memory. Leaving aside details, we could equate Shiffrin and Atkinson's sensory registers with our sensory analyzers, their short-term store with our gnostic analyzers, and their long-term store with our semantic and episodic analyzers. From this perspective, it makes sense that the deeper the domain of processing, the more likely it will be that a new (episodic) memory will be established. In fairness, it should be pointed out that the earlier theorists tended to use the term *long-term memory* to refer more or less exclusively to what is now called semantic and episodic memory.

SENSORY MEMORY

Iconic memory

PARTIAL-REPORT STUDIES

Visual sensory memory is usually called *iconic memory*. The existence of iconic memory is demonstrated by experiments done by Sperling (1960) and by Averbach and Coriell (1961). The procedure in both studies was to present an array of letters, such as the one shown in Figure 6–2 for 50 milliseconds on a

FIGURE 6–2   Example of stimulus array used in studies of iconic memory

X   C   N

T   R   F

Z   B   Y

tachistoscope. With such a short exposure duration, no matter how many letters are shown, only four or five can be read when the whole-report method is used. When using the whole-report procedure, one simply tells subjects to read as many letters as they can. Sperling (1960), however, devised a partial report procedure. By means of a prearranged tone signal, he indicated which row of the array his subjects were to read. A high-pitched tone might indicate the top row; a medium-pitched tone, the middle row; and a low-pitched tone, the bottom row. When the onset of the tone coincided with the offset of the visual display, subjects could read off any row with virtually 100 percent accuracy. Thus, immediately after its termination, all nine letters of the display were "visible" to the subject. Then why can only four or five letters be seen when the whole-report procedure is used? Sperling reasoned that there is a briefly persisting icon or sensory memory. With the whole-report method, this icon has faded by the time four or five letters have been read. As we shall see, four or five items seems to be the capacity of short-term memory. Even though all nine items are present in sensory memory, only four or five can be transferred and retained in short-term memory. The partial-report procedure allows the subject to read any row of the icon before it has faded. If this is the case, then sounding the tone after the display was terminated should still be helpful. Indeed it was, even when the lag was as long as 300 milliseconds. Furthermore, at short lags the subjects experienced the tone and the visual display as being simultaneous. However, when the tone was delayed for 500 milliseconds, it no longer helped. Apparently the icon had faded completely by this time.

Averbach and Coriell (1961) used a similar display. First, an array of letters was exposed for 50 milliseconds. A bar marker appeared from 50 to 200 milliseconds after termination of the display over the letter the subject was supposed to read. Of course, the letter was no longer physically present. Again, subjects performed with very high accuracy even with displays containing many letters and saw the marker superimposed over the letter. Since the letter was not there, we must assume that the bar was imposed on a memory image rather than on a perceptual one. Incidentally, the reason iconic memory does not interfere when you move your eyes is that the iconic memory images fade in the time (about 250 milliseconds) it takes to move your eyes between two fixation points.

BACKWARD MASKING

Averbach and Coriell (1961) tried what seemed to be a minor variation on their procedure, but it had a major effect. In one of their experiments, they substituted a circle for the bar marker. The idea was that the subject was supposed to read the circled letter. The problem was that the circle erased the letter! That is, it made it difficult or impossible to read. This effect is called *backward masking* or *metacontrast*. In order to obtain backward masking, the second stimulus must follow the first one by less than 100 milliseconds (Turvey, 1973). The most common explanation of the phenomenon is that the second stimulus disrupts, destroys, or interferes with the icon of the first stimulus. The more visually similar the mask is to the target stimulus, the more masking there is. This suggests that lateral inhibition among units in the sensory analyzer may be involved in masking. (We know from Turvey's studies that backward masking can occur centrally since the target can be presented to one eye and the mask to the other.) Evidently, perception is not instantaneous. We might see the visual icon as the analogue of Selfridge's image demon. It holds a brief memory of the original sensation while the process of feature extraction occurs. If a second stimulus disrupts this memory, feature analysis cannot be done and recognition fails.

STIMULUS DURATION AND ICON DURATION

Haber and Standing (1970) devised an ingenious procedure to determine how long visual icons last. Subjects were presented with periodic light flashes. Their task was to align an auditory click with onset and offset of the flashes by means of a manually controlled dial. At all flash durations, the subjects were quite accurate at aligning the clicks with the onset of the flashes. They were also accurate at aligning the click with the offset of flashes that lasted a second or more. However, when the flashes lasted less than a second, they overestimated their duration. Based upon where they put the clicks, they seemed to perceive all flashes from 10 to 200 milliseconds as lasting for about 200 milliseconds. Stimuli lasting from 200 milliseconds to 1 second were also overestimated but not to such a large extent. In this range, the longer the stimulus was on, the less it was overestimated.

In general, then, the shorter a stimulus is, the more its duration is overestimated. Presumably, this overestimation is based upon iconic persistence. This finding is consistent with the hypothesis that the fall time or decay time of the cognitive units involved in iconic memory is related to how long the units have been on: The longer they have been on, the faster the decay time. Thus, the longer a stimulus is, the shorter the icon it leaves. The fact that stimuli lasting from 10 to 200 milliseconds all seem to have a duration of about 200 milliseconds suggests that these cognitive units also have a minimum dwell time. Once they are activated, they stay activated for some standard length of time. Studies we will consider in the next chapter suggest that this dwell time may be on the order of 100 milliseconds. Thus, a sensory unit activated by a 10 millisecond light flash may stay fully activated for about 100 milliseconds and then begin a decay process consuming another 100 milliseconds or so. Its total duration, then, seems to be about 200 milliseconds.

LOCUS OF ICONIC MEMORY

There is no theoretical consensus as to the locus of iconic memory. Sakitt (1976) argues that it is due to persistence of activity in the rod receptors of the retina. Others, such as Di Lollo (1977), say that it is due to persistence of activity of cognitive units in what we would call the *visual sensory analyzer*. Some phenomena—such as backward masking—classified as involving iconic memory are central, since they transfer between the eyes (Turvey, 1973). Both Sakitt and Di Lollo could be right. From the levels-of-processing perspective, memory is a by-product of activity of units at any level. Activity in all cognitive units presumably takes some time to decay. Processing at the next higher level will always have begun before activity at lower levels has completely disappeared (McClelland, 1979). Given this, it is reasonable that iconic memory would not necessarily reflect persistence of activity at only the peripheral or only the central level.

Echoic memory

DURATION

Just as there is a sensory memory connected with the visual system, there is another type of sensory memory connected with the auditory system. Neisser (1967) called this type of memory *echoic memory*. Several methods have been used to estimate the duration of echoic memory. For example, Massaro (1970) used a backward-masking procedure to estimate the duration of echoic memory. A 20-millisecond target tone was presented. Then, after a variable delay, a second masking tone was presented. The second tone did not interfere with perception of the first one if the delay was greater than 250 milliseconds. However, interference occurred if the delay was less than this. This led Massaro to postulate that 250 milliseconds is the duration of echoic memory. Incidentally, Massaro's results suggest a central locus for echoic memory. The same results were obtained regardless of whether target and mask were presented to the same ear or to different ears. Other estimates of the duration of echoic memory are longer than Massaro's and range up to 2 seconds (Crowder and Morton, 1969). Most theorists argue that echoic memory does last longer than iconic memory. The function of this longer lasting sensory trace may be to help in speech perception (Crowder and Morton, 1969). While a long-lasting visual memory would be a hindrance, a long-lasting auditory memory could definitely be helpful. Pronunciation of a given consonant may depend upon what vowels follow it. Thus, identification of speech sounds may sometimes be dependent upon identification of other speech sounds that follow them.

THE STIMULUS-SUFFIX EFFECT

Crowder (1978) used a variant of the masking procedure known as the *stimulus-suffix effect* to study echoic memory. This effect was first observed by Dallett (1965). It has to do with what is basically a short-term memory task. The experimenter reads a list of items (words, letters of the alphabet, or digits). The subject has to repeat back the list. The average person can repeat back a list of from four to seven unrelated items. To obtain the stimulus-suffix effect, an extra or redundant item is added at the end of the list. This item does not have to be recalled and the subject is told this. The extra item just signals that the list is complete. However, the presence of this redundant suffix item impairs memory for the list. It is as if the suffix item automatically takes up space in memory even though it does not need to be remembered. The suffix item especially interferes with memory for the last item on the list. This is a striking effect, since in control conditions where there is no redundant suffix, memory for the last item on the list is virtually perfect! In the control condition, a tone or just the experimenter's ceasing to read items signals the end of the list.

The degree to which the suffix item interferes with memory has nothing at all to do with its semantic similarity to the list items. On the other hand, it is related to physical similarity (Crowder, 1978). Thus, a suffix spoken by a voice different from the one that read the list has less effect. Also, there is less effect if the list comes from one direction in space and the suffix from another even if both are spoken by the same voice. The fact that sensory but not semantic similarity is important suggests that the suffix effect occurs at a low level of processing and could be due to some type of interference in echoic memory. Crowder (1978) found that a suffix exerts maximal interference when it follows the last item by about 500 milliseconds. It has very little effect if it occurs simultaneously with the last item. Increasing delay of the suffix leads to increasing interference until the delay reaches 500 milliseconds. Further delays beyond 500 milliseconds lessen the amount of interference. After a two-second delay, there is essentially no interference. This suggests that echoic memory has decayed after two seconds at most.

Crowder (1978) has proposed a lateral inhibition theory of echoic memory. The idea is that the cognitive unit coding the suffix item laterally inhibits the cognitive units coding the last list items. Crowder's theory is that echoic memory consists of activity in an array of units that code information about the physical characteristics of auditory stimuli. We would say that these are units in the acoustic sensory analyzer. Simplifying a bit, the idea is that these units are arranged according to time of arrival and channel (for example, spatial location) as shown in Figure 6–3. Thus, stimuli that arrive via the same channel and are close together in time should inhibit each other.

FIGURE 6–3   Crowder's lateral inhibition theory of the suffix effect

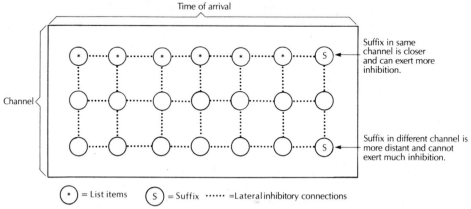

When a list of items is read, a lot of units are activated. All of them laterally inhibit each other. However, the last item (the suffix) has a special advantage. Since no item follows it, it is inhibited by only one other item (the previous one). All of the other units (except the first) are inhibited by both preceding and following units. Thus, the unit coding the suffix is strongly activated and can mask the unit coding the last list-item. If this line of reasoning is correct, then two suffixes should do less damage than only one. Since the first suffix would itself be partially inhibited by the second suffix, it could not inhibit the last list-item as much. In other words, the unit coding the last list-item should be disinhibited. This prediction is diagrammed in Figure 6–4. Crowder (1978) tested this predic-

FIGURE 6–4   Why two suffixes exert less inhibition than one suffix

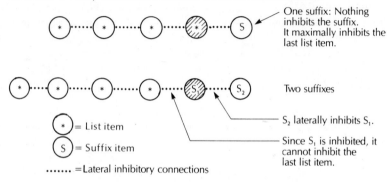

tion and found strong support for it. Two suffixes in fact have a less detrimental effect than does a single suffix.

SHORT-TERM MEMORY
Form of short-term memory codes

When short-term memory was viewed as a place or store separate from long-term memory, it made sense to ask what sort of code is used in this separate place. The initial answer to this question was that short-term memory operates with an acoustic or phonetic code while long-term memory operates with a semantic code. Short-term memory confusions among letters and words tend to be based on phonetic rather than visual similarity regardless of whether presentation is auditory or visual (Conrad, 1963, 1964). Of course, this contrasts with what is found with immediate recognition: Recognition errors for letters are based on similarity of visual features if presentation is visual and on phonetic similarity if presentation is auditory (see Chapter 5). As noted earlier in our example of looking up a telephone number, people certainly seem to have a tendency to translate visual material into a phonetic code when they have to remember it for a short interval.

The early view, then, was that there is but one short-term memory and its code is phonetic. Later research has cast doubt on this view. The results of Peterson, Rawlings, and Cohen (1977) concerning short-term memory for visual images suggest that there are separate short-term memories for images and for words. Simultaneous retention of the two types of material was just about as good as retention of one or the other alone. Deutsch (1970) found similar effects for pitches and verbal stimuli; that is, simultaneous short-term retention of the two types of material has no interfering effect. Thus, there also seems to be a separate short-term memory for pitch.

Finally, consider the study by Kroll, Parks, Parkinson, Bieber, and Johnson (1970). Following the presentation of a single letter, either visually or auditorily, the subjects had to repeat auditory material aloud for a few seconds. Recall of the letter was 70 percent for visual presentations and only 40 percent for auditory presentations. There must, then, also be a separate visual short-term memory for verbal material.

Looking at the other side of the coin, is there any evidence that there is long-term memory for phonetic material? A moment's thought reveals that we obviously have a long-term memory for phonetic properties. The entire speech analyzer is a long-term memory for such properties. To say that the form of long-term memory is only semantic would be to say that we cannot remember the speech sounds that make up the English language or that we cannot remember the sounds of any of the words in the language. That is ridiculous. I think the problem is a matter of definition. If we define *short-term memory* as objectively consisting of temporary activation of units in long-term memory or as subjectively consisting of the contents of consciousness, then the question of coding form becomes meaningless. Clearly, the contents of consciousness can be visual, verbal, semantic, and so on. Units at any level of long-term memory can be temporarily activated. We have seen that there are many independent short-term memory stores. There must be one for each gnostic analyzer. To ask whether the code of short-term memory is phonetic is really to ask whether the code of phonetic short-term memory is phonetic.

Capacity

THE SPAN OF IMMEDIATE APPREHENSION

Historically, one of the first questions to be asked about what is now called short-term memory concerned its capacity. How many items can it hold? In the 19th century, Sir William Hamilton (1859) introduced the concept of the "span of immediate apprehension." This is the number of things we can apprehend in a single moment of time. Hamilton noted that we can say how many objects we see in a brief glance so long as there are not more than about six objects to be seen. Jevons (1871) devised a method of testing Hamilton's assertion. Using himself as a subject, Jevons threw beans into a tray and glanced at an area of the tray that he had previously marked off. Then, he made a quick judgment of the number of beans in that area. With three or four beans, he made no errors. When there were actually ten beans in the area, he was wrong 50 percent of the time. When there were 15 beans, he was wrong 82 percent of the time. Erdmann and Dodge (1898) used a tachistoscope so that the length of subjects' glances could be more precisely controlled. When stimuli were presented for 100 milliseconds, they found that only four or five unrelated letters could be reported. Note that all of these early studies used the whole-report method. Thus, they give us an idea of the capacity of short-term memory rather than of sensory memory.

CHUNKS AS THE CONTENTS OF SHORT-TERM MEMORY

In an influential review, Miller (1956) concluded that the span of immediate apprehension is 7 ± 2 items. He noted that the basic unit seems to be what he called the *chunk*. Let's say that a person can remember seven unrelated letters. Chances are that the person will also be able to remember seven unrelated three-letter words. But these seven words will be composed of 21 letters. Why does the unit change when the material to be remembered changes? Miller argued that the reason is that the unit of short-term memory is not the individual letter but the meaningful chunk. Short-term memory can hold seven chunks. These may be letters, words, or sentences. This view is consistent with the idea that short-term memory is the momentary activation of cognitive units. We can translate Miller's hypothesis into the contention that—on any level of a gnostic analyzer—about seven cognitive units can be active at once. If we are talking about the phonemic or graphemic levels, this would mean seven different sounds or letters. If we were talking about the morphemic level, this would mean different words.

Subsequent work suggests that the number seven is not as magical as Miller had thought. First, it has become clear that the capacity of short-term memory is not constant. Generally, the deeper (more semantic) the level of processing, the smaller the capacity; that is, short-term memory can actually hold more shallow-level units than deeper-level units. For example, Simon (1974) used himself as a subject. He found that he could use short-term memory to recall seven one- or two-syllable words, six three-syllable words, four meaningful two-word phrases, and three meaningful longer phrases (for example, "All's fair in love and war"). These estimates are probably a bit generous. Simon recently won the Nobel prize. We might expect that the average person might not do quite as well.

PROBLEMS IN MEASURING CAPACITY

A second problem with Miller's idea is that his estimate of seven items for the span of immediate apprehension may be right, but the capacity of short-term memory is probably more like four or five items. What we can recall at any given moment does not depend only on what is in short-term memory. We can also draw on sensory memory and long-term memory. If I present you with a string of seven words and you can repeat them back, that does not necessarily mean that you held them all in short-term memory. How do I know that you did not put some in long-term memory and then retrieve them from there when I asked you to repeat them back? We just saw in the previous section that you can also draw on sensory memory for some of the items. This is a real problem in determining the capacity of short-term memory. We shall consider it in the next section.

Serial-position effects

SHAPE OF THE SERIAL-POSITION CURVE

Suppose we present a person with a list of from 15 to 30 unrelated words. The person's task is to repeat back as many of the words as possible in any order once the whole list has been presented. This standard experimental task yields very stable and predictable results. These results concern serial-position effects. The probability that a word will be recalled is a function of its sequential order in the list. The primacy effect refers to the finding that the first few items on the list are fairly well recalled. However, the probability of recall decreases from the first to the second word, from the second to the third, and so on. Words in the middle of the list are poorly recalled. The recency effect refers to the finding that the last few words on the list are also well recalled. Typical serial position curves are shown in Figure 6-5.

Why do we get these effects? In a free-recall experiment of this sort, subjects are given several lists. After each one, they have to recall as many of the words as they can from it. On the first few trials, people often attempt to recall the words in the order that they were presented on the list (Craik and Levy, 1970). Then, they see the utter folly of this strategy, so they change their tactics. Now, they quickly recall the last few words from the list and only then report the earlier ones. It seems a reasonable conjecture that only the last few words are retrieved from short-term memory. (Recall of the very last word may be helped by persistence of sensory memory, especially with auditory presentations.) This would account for the recency effect. On the other hand, items occurring earlier on the list have to be retrieved from long-term memory. If the capacity of short-term memory is only seven items at most, all of the list items could not very well be in short-term memory.

FIGURE 6–5   Serial position curves for lists composed of 10 words, 15 words, 20 words, 30 words, and 40 words. Recall is best for words at the ends of the lists (recency effect) and at the beginnings of the list (primacy effect).

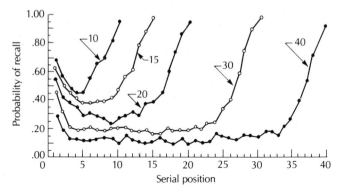

Source: B. B. Murdock, "The Serial Position Effect of Free Recall," *Journal of Experimental Psychology* 64 (1962):482. Copyright 1962 by the American Psychological Association. Reprinted by permission.

THE PRIMACY EFFECT

If the recency effect is due to retrieval from short-term memory, what accounts for the primacy effect? There is general agreement that it is due to retrieval from long-term memory. There is more time for the earliest items to be transferred to long-term memory. Presumably, this transfer takes place because of rehearsal. Clearly, the first word in the list can be rehearsed the most, the second word can be rehearsed next most, and so on. To test this idea, Murdock (1962) devised an experiment where he varied the presentation rate of the list to be remembered. The idea was that a faster presentation rate should leave less time for rehearsal. Thus, it should lead to worse performance on the first and middle items since these items are retrieved from long-term memory. On the other hand, it should have no effect on the recency effect: short-term memory presumably holds the last few items irrespective of the rate at which these items were presented. Murdock found evidence for both predictions. Faster rate of presentation had no effect on the recency effect. On the other hand, it led to worse recall of items earlier in the list.

THE RECENCY EFFECT

If the recency effect is due to retrieval of items from short-term memory, then it should disappear if recall were delayed. If short-term memory does not last very long, then we should get the recency effect only if recall begins immediately after the list is presented. Glanzer and Cunitz (1966) tested this idea by presenting lists of words to be recalled. Subjects were asked to recall the words immediately or after a delay of 10 seconds or 30 seconds. During the delay, subjects had to do mental arithmetic in order to prevent them from rehearsing the words on the list. The results are shown in Figure 6–6. As you can see, a clear recency effect can be seen with immediate recall. There is less of an effect

FIGURE 6–6   Results of Glanzer and Cunitz's (1966) experiment showing recall of a list after 0, 10, and 30 seconds. The recency effect disappears quickly if there is a delay between presentation of the list and recall.

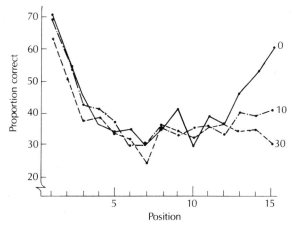

Source: M. Glanzer and A. R. Cunitz, "Two Storage Mechanisms in Free Recall," *Journal of Verbal Learning and Verbal Behavior* 5 (1966):358.

with just a 10-second delay, and the recency effect is completely wiped out by a 30-second delay.

If amount of rehearsal determines how well an item is transferred to long-term memory, then the final items on a list—the ones retrieved from short-term memory—should be poorly recalled after a long interval. This is because, as compared with any of the earlier items on a list, they were rehearsed less often. Craik (1970) gave his subjects a number of lists to remember. After each list, they had to recall as many words as they could. Then, at the end of the whole experiment, he asked them to recall all of the words on all of the lists. The subjects had not been led to expect such a test. Craik found clear evidence for *negative recency* in this final free recall task; that is, words from the ends of the lists were less likely to be recalled than those at the beginning or in the middle of the lists.

These experiments all suggest that the recency effect is due to retrieving the last few words on a list from short-term memory. If the capacity of short-term memory were about seven items, we would expect the recency effect to cover the last seven items on a list. However, it usually covers only the last four or five. This suggests that the real capacity of short-term memory is four or five items rather than the seven items that were earlier hypothesized.

Loss from short-term memory

PASSIVE DECAY

What causes loss of information from short-term memory? Early experiments by Brown (1958) and Peterson and Peterson (1959) suggested that a passive process of decay might account for forgetting in short-term memory. The idea was that—if rehearsal is prevented—information held in short-term memory will simply fade away in a few seconds. The design of Peterson and Peterson's experiment was quite simple. On each trial, a subject was given three consonants to remember. The task was simply to remember these consonants for from 3 to 18 seconds. The retention interval was filled by having subjects do mental arithmetic. Their task was to count backwards by threes from a specified three-digit number. To make sure that everyone did this at the same rate, the counting had to be done in synchrony with the beats of a metronome. The whole point of the mental arithmetic was to prevent rehearsal. The ideal study would consist of having the subjects do absolutely nothing during the retention interval. However, this is impossible. Mental activity—including rehearsal—cannot be brought to a halt at will. Thus, the subjects had to be given something to do in order to prevent them from rehearsing.

Peterson and Peterson's results were quite surprising. They are shown in Figure 6–7. As you can see, retention was about 60 percent after three seconds,

FIGURE 6–7   According to Peterson and Peterson, the probability of correct recall of consonant trigrams declines rapidly with lengthening retention intervals during which rehearsal is prevented.

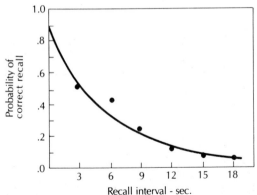

Source: L. R. Peterson and M. J. Peterson, "Short-term Retention of Individual Verbal Items," *Journal of Experimental Psychology* 58 (1959):195. Copyright 1959 by the American Psychological Association. Reprinted by permission.

but it dropped to only about 10 percent after only 15 seconds! Unrehearsed information in short-term memory fades away after about 15 seconds. This is amazing. It does not seem quite right that we cannot remember the simplest things for even 15 seconds! But remember that rehearsal has been prevented. In everyday life this is not the case, so perhaps we do not notice the transience of the contents of short-term memory. There is no question that this is a real effect. Brown (1958) had gotten essentially the same results, as have many experimenters since then. Murdock (1961) showed that the effect applies to other things besides consonants. He got the same decay curves for three unrelated words as for three-consonant trigrams. He also found that there is a relationship between decay rate and amount of material held in short-term memory: the more items being held, the faster the decay rate.

INTERFERENCE

What accounts for these findings? One view would be that the strength of short-term memory traces simply decays with time. This was the view favored by Peterson and Peterson (1959). The alternative view is that the forgetting is due to interference. The reason that this alternative view was suggested is that in long-term memory there is not much evidence that passive decay causes forgetting and a lot of evidence that interference causes forgetting (see Chapter 9). There are two types of interference. *Proactive inhibition* occurs when something already learned interferes with learning something new. In studies of long-term memory, we shall see that proactive inhibition can be demonstrated by having subjects learn one list of words (list A) and then having them learn a second list (list B). The more similar the two lists, the harder it will be to learn and remember list B. *Retroactive inhibition* refers to the finding that learning something new interferes with retention of something already learned. In the example we just gave, once subjects finally do learn list B, they will recall list A less well. The inhibition works in both directions.

With both retroactive and proactive inhibition, the amount of interference is a function of similarity. It does not seem unreasonable to ascribe the interference to lateral inhibition among the units coding similar items. If short-term memory consists of momentary activation of units in gnostic or conceptual analyzers and if these units tend to laterally inhibit each other in proportion to the similarity of the stimulus pattern that they code, then we would certainly expect to find interference effects in short-term memory. Whether these interference effects would account for all forgetting from short-term memory is an empirical question.

Proactive inhibition. The question at hand is how we might explain Peterson and Peterson's (1959) results with either retroactive or proactive inhibition. Let's consider their experimental procedure in more detail. Their subjects received 2 practice trials and then 48 regular trials, 8 at each of the 6 different retention intervals. The results shown in Figure 6–7 are averages based upon all of these trials. On each trial, of course, subjects were shown three consonants. One possibility would be that proactive inhibition accounts for the forgetting. On all trials but the first, the consonants presented on prior trials could interfere with retention of the consonants presented on that trial. If this were the case, then the "decay" phenomenon should build up gradually. The more prior trials, the worse performance should be. This is, in fact, the case. Keppel and Underwood (1962) repeated Peterson and Peterson's experiment, but they looked at trial-by-trial performance. Some of their results are shown in Figure 6–8. They are clear and unambiguous. On the first trial, retention is very good at all retention intervals. Subjects can remember the consonants just about as well after 18 seconds as after 3 seconds. There is no decline in performance at all. On the second trial, there is a little bit of decay. On the third there is more, and so on. In other words, the decay does in fact build up gradually over trials. This is consistent with the idea that it is due to proactive inhibition. The pure decay hypothesis cannot explain why decay should build up over trials.

FIGURE 6–8   According to Keppel and Underwood,
short-term memory "decay" is not present on the first trial
(test), but it builds up gradually over trials

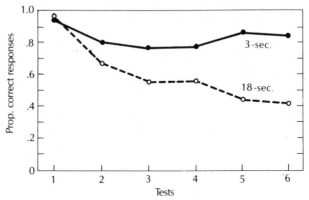

Source: G. Keppel and B. J. Underwood, "Proactive Inhibition
in Short-Term Retention of Single Items," *Journal of Verbal
Learning and Verbal Behavior* 1 (1962):158.

Release from proactive inhibition.   Wickens (1973) produced further evidence that proactive inhibition is behind loss of information from short-term
memory in the Peterson and Peterson paradigm. On each of the first three trials
of his experiment, subjects were given the names of three fruits to remember. As
shown in Figure 6–9, performance got worse on each successive trial. On the
crucial fourth trial, some subjects (the group labeled control) were given the
names of three more fruits to remember again. Their performance deteriorated
even further. Other subjects were given three words from other categories. Their
performance improved. Thus, shifting from one category to another leads to a
release from proactive inhibition. Figure 6–9 shows the performance of subjects
shifted to various other categories. Note that the more distant the category, the
more release from proactive inhibition. Shifting to the category of vegetables leads
to a small improvement in retention; shifting to the category of flowers leads to
even more; and so on. If we assume that the cognitive units coding instances of
a given category are spatially near each other in the semantic analyzer, then
shifting to a new category would involve a shift to a region where less lateral
inhibition had built up. Thus, recall should improve. The further away from the
region of inhibition we move, the better performance should be.
   Retroactive inhibition.   What about retroactive inhibition in the Peterson and
Peterson paradigm? The only possibility for retroactive inhibition would be if the
mental arithmetic task interfered with the verbal items to be recalled. Peterson
and Peterson originally chose the mental arithmetic task so that it would involve
something—digits—that should be distinct enough from the consonants to be
remembered that there should be no interference. Early critics seem to have
agreed, since they did not raise the possibility of such retroactive inhibition. However, Reitman (1971) substituted an auditory signal detection task for the mental
arithmetic task. It was supposed to be difficult enough so as to leave subjects with
no time for rehearsal. In one condition, the task was to detect a pure tone of a

FIGURE 6–9 Release from proactive inhibition. Subjects are given names of fruits to remember on the first three trials. Experimental groups receive names from another category on the fourth trial. The further removed this category is from the category of fruits, the greater the release from proactive inhibition.

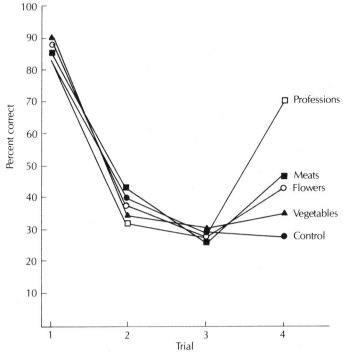

Source: D. D. Wickens, "Some Characteristics of Word Encoding," *Memory and Cognition* 1 (1973):490.

given pitch. In this condition, there was no evidence at all for decay even at the longest retention intervals. In a second condition, subjects' task was to detect the spoken syllable TOH in a series of syllables most of which were DOH. Otherwise, this task was similar to the signal detection task in the first condition of the experiment. This task did cause decrements in recall. These results make it look as if the decay occurs only if the interpolated task is a verbal one. Some interference apparently occurs even if the interpolated task is as different from the material to be recalled as Peterson and Peterson's original mental arithmetic task or Reitman's syllable detection task.

Waugh and Norman's experiment. If retroactive inhibition is a cause of loss from short-term memory, then the reason that performance in the Peterson and Peterson paradigm is worse at 18 seconds than at 3 seconds would be that more interfering material has been interpolated in the longer retention interval. The decay theory holds that loss from short-term memory occurs purely as a function of the passage of time. In the Peterson and Peterson paradigm, the original purpose of the interpolated task was to allow the passage of time without rehearsal. On the other hand, the interference theory says that it is the amount of interpolated material rather than the mere passage of time that is crucial. At first glance, it seems hard to decide between these alternatives. If we interpolate more material between presentation and recall, interference theory predicts that recall will be worse. But this is the same prediction that is made by decay theory, since to interpolate more material should require the passage of more time and the passage of more time will allow more decay.

Waugh and Norman (1965) disentangled the two variables—passage of time and number of interfering items—by varying rate of presentation. They designed the following experiment. Their subjects heard a series of 16 digits. The last digit was a probe. When it was heard, the subject had to say which digit had followed it in the original series. In this way, each of the digits in the series could be probed. Consider the situation if the fifth digit were the probed one. Time has passed since its presentation, so decay theory says that its memory trace should have decayed. On the other hand, 11 digits have been presented after it, and interference theory says that each should interfere with its retention. Now consider what the predictions would be if the digits were presented twice as fast. Decay theory predicts that memory for the probed digit should be better than in the first condition since only half as much time would have elapsed. On the other hand, interference theory predicts that there should be no difference between the two conditions since, in both cases, 11 interfering digits would have been presented. In either condition, the same number of intervening digits have been heard, and it is the number of interfering items that is crucial. Thus, there is a clear differential prediction. Decay theory says that performance should be better at the faster rate, while interference theory says that there should be no difference in recall. Since there was no appreciable difference in recall between the two rates of presentation, decay theory loses again.

LATERAL INHIBITION IN MEMORY FOR PITCH

A series of experiments by Deutsch have provided evidence for her lateral inhibition theory of music memory. These experiments also shed light on how short-term memory in general must work. In most of Deutsch's experiments, the same paradigm has been used. A tone of a given pitch is presented. Then there is an interval of a few seconds. During this interval, the subject has to do various things. Then a second test tone is presented. The subject has to say whether this second tone is the same or different from the first tone. In order to answer correctly, the subject must, of course, have held the first stimulus in short-term memory so that it can be compared with the second stimulus.

Interference effects. Deutsch (1970) selected subjects who had perfect performance in comparing two musical notes separated by a five-second blank retention interval. The first note and the test note were either the same or differed by one semitone. Subjects were then given three other memory tasks in which the retention interval was filled with distracting material. Some were given six interpolated musical notes which they were told to ignore. Their error rate rose to 32.3 percent. This is not much better than the 50 percent error rate we would expect purely by chance. Hypothetically, activation of the units coding the interpolated notes laterally inhibited the unit coding the to-be-remembered note. Other subjects were given six spoken digits which they were also told to ignore.

Their error rate was only 2.4 percent. The third group of subjects were also given digits, but they also had to recall them after they had made the pitch judgment. Their error rate was 5.6 percent. (I would not make much of the difference between 2.4 percent and 5.6 percent.) The clear finding is that interpolated musical notes caused a lot of forgetting, while interpolated digits did not cause very much forgetting regardless of whether they, too, had to be recalled or not. These results suggest that loss from short-term memory for pitch is due to interference caused by similar (musical notes) but not by dissimilar (digits) stimuli. Hypothetically, short-term memory for musical notes and for spoken digits involves activity in two separate gnostic analyzers.

In later experiments, Deutsch showed that the amount of interference is a lawful function of the exact degree of similarity between the to-be-remembered note and the interpolated notes. Deutsch (1972) used a five-second retention interval with six interpolated notes. Of these interpolated tones, all but the second were at least one and a half full tones removed from the to-be-remembered tone. The second tone was systematically varied from being the same as the first tone to a whole tone different. Results of the experiment are plotted in Figure 6–10 as a function of what this crucial interpolated tone was. The line marked "null" indicates the number of errors in a baseline condition when this crucial note was also at least one and a half tones distant from the to-be-remem-

FIGURE 6–10   Errors in pitch recognition as a function of the distance between the to-be-remembered note and a critical interpolated note. The line marked "null" indicates performance of a control group.

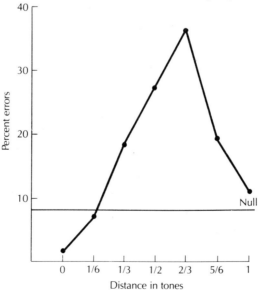

Source: D. Deutsch, "Mapping of Interactions in the Pitch Memory Store," *Science* 168 (1972):1021. Copyright 1972 by the American Association for the Advancement of Science.

bered note. The results show that there was a facilitation effect—performance was better than in the baseline condition—when the crucial note was identical to the first one. There was more and more interference with more difference between the test note and second intepolated note until interference was maximal when the crucial note was two thirds of a tone different from the to-be-remembered note. From that point, interference declined almost to the baseline level if the interpolated note was a whole tone different.

These results are consistent with the theory of Deutsch (1969) that was described in Chapter 4. The analyzer for pitch is hypothetically an array of cognitive units subject to recurrent lateral inhibition. Amount of separation between units in this array is proportional to the difference in the frequency coded by the units. Neighboring units must code frequencies about two thirds of a tone different from each other. This model accounts for all of the findings described so far. The reason that we get the interference effects found by Deutsch is hypothetically as follows: The to-be-remembered note activates the unit in the array that codes it, as do each of the interpolated notes. If these interpolated notes are close in frequency to the to-be-remembered note, the units coding them will laterally inhibit the unit coding the to-be-remembered note. The amount of inhibition will be a function of how similar the frequencies are. If one of the interpolated notes is two thirds of a tone different, there will be maximal inhibition because the two units will be immediately contiguous. If the interpolated note differs by more than two thirds of a tone, there will be less inhibition because the unit coding it will be further away. If it differs by less than two thirds of a tone, there will also be less inhibition because this note will fall between the frequency coded by the unit activated by the to-be-remembered note and its immediate neighbor. Presumably, when the test note occurs, the subject responds "same" if activation of the unit coding the to-be-remembered note is above some threshold level. If the unit coding the first note has been inhibited, this is less likely and a mistake will be made.

Disinhibition effects. The lateral inhibition model allows us to make a further prediction. We said that the crucial interpolated note laterally inhibits the to-be-remembered note and that this causes forgetting. What if we inhibited this inhibiting note? We should be able to eliminate its damaging effect! This was Deutsch and Feroe's (1975) reasoning. Consider their design. The to-be-remembered note is presented. This activates the relevant unit in the pitch analyzer. Then the interpolated sequence begins. The second note is two thirds of a tone distant from the to-be-remembered tone. Its presentation activates the unit next to the one activated by the to-be-remembered tone. This unit inhibits the unit coding the to-be-remembered tone. The fourth note in the interpolated sequence was systematically varied from being identical to the second note to being a whole tone removed from it. Let's consider what should happen when the fourth note is two thirds of a tone distant from the second note (that is, one and one third tones distant from the original note to be remembered). The fourth note activates a unit that inhibits the unit coding the second note. This, in turn, disinhibits the unit coding the to-be-remembered note. Presentation of the fourth note should get us back to where we started. Memory for the to-be-remembered note should be as good as under baseline conditions where the interpolated notes are all well removed from the test notes. On the other hand, consider what should happen if the fourth note were the same as the second note. This should intensify the interference, since the inhibiting unit has been activated twice. The hypothetical sequence of events is illustrated in Figure 6–11.

FIGURE 6–11   In their experiment, Deutsch and Feroe were interested in two predictions: (A) What happens when the second and fourth interpolated notes are the same? (B) What happens when the fourth interpolated note inhibits the second one?

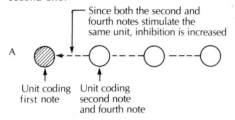

Since both the second and
fourth notes stimulate the
same unit, inhibition is increased

A

Unit coding   Unit coding
first note   second note
                    and fourth note

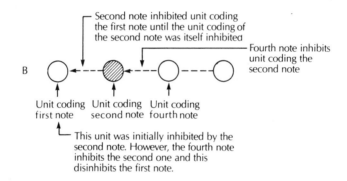

Second note inhibited unit coding
the first note until the unit coding of
the second note was itself inhibited

Fourth note inhibits
unit coding the
second note

B

Unit coding   Unit coding   Unit coding
first note   second note   fourth note

This unit was initially inhibited by the
second note. However, the fourth note
inhibits the second one and this
disinhibits the first note.

If these predictions were verified, they would constitute very strong evidence for lateral inhibition in the pitch analyzer. The results are shown in Figure 6–12. Errors are graphed as a function of distance between the second and fourth interpolated note. Performance is even better than under baseline conditions when the fourth note is two thirds tone removed from the second note. The results are just as predicted. I do not see how this result could be easily explained without postulating some sort of lateral inhibitory mechanism. Note that exactly the same sorts of results should be gotten in short-term verbal retention. The problem in that case would, of course, be to figure out the exact principle of organization. In the case of pitch, it makes sense that the relevant units would be organized according to frequency. Further, it is possible to vary the frequency of musical notes in a very precise fashion. In the case of verbal memory, the principle of organization must be sound similarity, but it is hard to say exactly how this would work. What unit would be next to the unit coding PAT? Would it be the unit coding BAT? Or perhaps the unit coding BETH? There are not a huge number of possibilities, but there are enough to make it difficult to do the extremely precise sort of work that Deutsch has been able to do with short-term memory for pitch.

FIGURE 6–12   In the results of Deutsch and Feroe's experiment, triangles show errors for a condition where only the second interpolated note was varied: Maximal forgetting was found when this note was ⅔ tone removed from the to-be-remembered note. Circles show errors when the fourth interpolated note was also varied. Maximal forgetting was found when both the second and fourth interpolated notes were ⅔ tone distant from the to-be-remembered note, and memory was best when the fourth note was ⅔ tone distant from the second note.

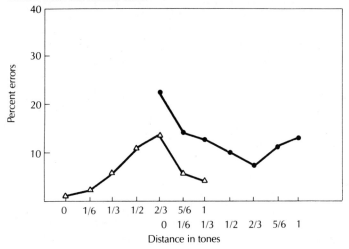

Source: D. Deutsch and J. Feroe, "Disinhibition in Pitch Memory," *Perception and Psychophysics* 17 (1975):322.

Rehearsal

We have seen that unrehearsed material in short-term memory disappears in a matter of seconds. Rehearsal supposedly has two functions: (1) to maintain information in short-term memory and (2) to transfer this information to long-term memory. Preventing rehearsal leads to quick loss of information from short-term memory. But what about the other side of the coin? Does more rehearsal lead to better short-term retention? Hellyer (1962) carried out a variation of the Peterson and Peterson paradigm. Rather than preventing rehearsal during the retention interval, he had subjects rehearse aloud the words to be recalled from one to eight times. As you might imagine, the more rehearsals, the better the recall for the rehearsed items.

What about transfer to long-term memory? Rundus (1971) gave subjects a list of words to be recalled and asked them to rehearse aloud. They could rehearse any items they wanted to. On an immediate recall task, the more rehearsals a word had received, the better it was recalled. This was true except for the last few words on the list, and presumably these were retrieved from short-term memory. Rundus's experiment also sheds light on what is rehearsed. A new word was more likely to get rehearsed if it fit in with words already being rehearsed. If a person happened to be rehearsing names of cities, a newly presented city name was more likely to be added to the rehearsal set than, say, the name of a plant. As this finding implies, people tend to rehearse a set of things that are congruent—belong to the same category, are associated, and so on. Of course, if the list of things to be remembered does not allow this, it cannot very well be done. That implies that long-term memory for such an unclusterable list will be worse. This is indeed the case.

Craik and Lockhart (1972) argue that there are really two different types of rehearsal. *Maintenance rehearsal* consists of just mindlessly repeating items without thinking about them. They say that such rehearsal serves to keep material in short-term memory but does nothing to transfer it to long-term memory. *Elaborative rehearsal* consists of doing something with the new material. This would involve processing it to a deeper level. An example would be picking out items that belong to the same category or engaging in some other mnemonic trick. As the experiment by Rundus suggests, people have a natural tendency to do this sort of thing. That—it seems to me—may be the problem with Craik and Lockhart's idea. Our vertical excitation model of the mind suggests that stimuli will automatically be processed to the deepest possible level. Activation of units on any one level automatically activates units on the next higher level. Activation of units on the highest level of a gnostic analyzer activates semantic units, and so on. My point is that maintenance rehearsal may be a rather artificial process. Left to their own devices, people would seldom do it and, more important, could not do it. The reason is the automatic vertical excitation which more or less corresponds to elaborative rehearsal. Be that as it may, we could certainly induce maintenance rehearsal by trying to prevent deeper processing. We could do this by making the task difficult or by presenting stimuli at a fast rate. What happens when we do so?

Craik and Watkins (1973) presented subjects with a long list of words. Subjects were told that when the whole list ended they would have to report the last word that began with a particular letter, for example, S. Subjects did not know how many words would begin with this letter or when the list would end. Clearly, they had to keep the last word beginning with the letter S in mind until the next word beginning with that letter occurred. The list was arranged so that some words would not have to be rehearsed (the very next word also began with S) while others would have to be rehearsed up to 12 times. After several such lists, a free-recall task was unexpectedly given. The person had to recall as many of the words from all of the lists as was possible. There was no relationship between amount of rehearsal and recall. Glenberg, Smith, and Green (1977), however, showed that such maintenance rehearsal does have an effect on recognition memory. The more times a word was rehearsed, the more easily it was recognized as having been on one of the lists. Some experiments (for example, Nelson, 1977) have even found that—contrary to Craik and Watkins' results—maintenance rehearsal has some effect on recall. Thus, maintenance rehearsal seems to leave some trace, but the trace may not always be strong enough to show up on a task requiring recall. Certainly, however, elaborative rehearsal leads to much better recall than does maintenance rehearsal.

Semantic effects in short-term memory

We have been talking about short-term memory as if it consisted more or less entirely of activity of units in gnostic analyzers. We should expect to find semantic effects on short-term memory. I say this because there are clear semantic effects in recognition. In the previous chapter, we ascribed these effects to the connections between units in the semantic analyzer and those in the gnostic analyzers. It does not make any sense to suppose that these connections get decoupled after recognition takes place. However, early research suggested an absence of semantic effects in short-term memory. For example, Baddeley (1966a, 1966b) presented subjects with lists of words that were either phonetically similar (for example, MAN, MAD, and MAT) or semantically similar (for example, BIG, HUGE, and LARGE). For immediate recall, involving short-term memory, phonetic similarity hurt performance. Recall of phonetically similar lists was worse than recall of phonetically dissimilar lists. On the other hand, semantic similarity had no effect. Just the reverse was found when recall was delayed so that retrieval from long-term memory was necessary. With delayed recall, semantically dissimilar lists were remembered better than semantically similar lists, but there was no difference between phonetically similar and phonetically dissimilar lists. Thus, for short-term memory, phonetic similarity interfered with retention, but for long-term memory, semantic similarity interfered with retention.

Later studies, however, have demonstrated that meaning does have some effect on retention in short-term memory. The phenomenon of release from proactive inhibition clearly shows that the meaning or category membership of items in the Peterson and Peterson paradigm is important. Short-term recall gets worse and worse if members of the same category are presented. However, a shift to a new category leads to a dramatic improvement in recall. We explained that this was due to a buildup of lateral inhibition in the field containing the relevant deeper-level semantic units. This effect has to be ascribed to interactions of units in a field in the semantic analyzer rather than the speech analyzer. Why? The principle of organization in the speech analyzer should be sound similarity: Units coding words with similar sounds should inhibit each other. Since words with similar meanings do not have similar sounds, the inhibition must occur in the semantic analyzer.

There is other evidence for the influence of meaning in short-term retention. In an experiment by Shulman (1972), subjects saw a ten-word list followed by a test word. They had to indicate whether the test word was on the list. A lot of mistakes were semantically based; that is, subjects were apt mistakenly to say "yes" if the test word was a synonym of one of the list words. Presumably, the words on the list activated higher-order semantic category units. These, in turn, reactivated the units coding their subordinate instances. Among these would be synonyms of the list words. In a recognition test of this sort, it must be that a person says "yes" if the activation of the test word is above a criterion level, and this leads to false recognitions. The only way that synonyms of list words could become activated would be via semantic processing of the list words.

Memory scanning

STERNBERG'S EXPERIMENT

Short-term memory consists of momentary activation of some of the cognitive units composing long-term memory. Once items are in short-term memory, how do we know what is there? While this may not be a good question, there is certainly a good answer for it. This answer is provided by a classic experiment conducted by Sternberg (1966). On each trial of this experiment, a subject was shown a string of from one to six digits. This was called the *memory set*. Then the subject was shown a single digit—the test item—and had to respond by pressing one of two keys as to whether or not the test item was part of the memory set. All of this occurred so quickly that it seems reasonable that the memory set was being held in short-term memory. The crucial question of interest was how long it would take subjects to make their responses.

Sternberg (1966) analyzed this task from an additive factors point of view: Once the test digit has been presented, at least four things occur. The subject must (1) perceive the test digit, (2) search short-term memory to see if the test digit is in the memory set, (3) decide whether it is or not, and (4) make a motor response indicating this decision. Each of these stages must take some amount of time. Sternberg was interested in the second stage—the time it takes to search short-term memory. To find the answer, he systematically varied the size of the memory set. Consider what effect this should have. There is no reason to expect it to have any effect on the first or last stages; that is, the time for these stages should be more or less constant no matter how many items were being held in short-term memory. There is no reason to expect that it would affect the time necessary to perceive the test digit, make a decision, or to press a key once a decision had been made. The size of the memory set could have several different effects on the time necessary to search short-term memory depending upon exactly how the contents of short-term memory are searched.

TYPES OF MEMORY SEARCH

A list of items can be searched in several ways. In a parallel or content-addressable search, all of the items are searched simultaneously. Thus, search time should be constant no matter how many items have to be searched. This seems to be exactly what happens in perception and recognition. At any one level of perceptual analysis, all of the units are searched simultaneously, and the stimulus automatically activates the unit that codes it. It is certainly reasonable to expect that search of short-term memory might be in parallel. If it were, then the size of the memory set should have no effect on reaction time. No matter how many items were in short-term memory, it would take the same amount of time to search them. Presumably, time to decide if the test item was contained in the memory set would also be unaffected by the size of the memory set.

Another possibility would be that search through short-term memory is serial. If this were the case, then the more items in short-term memory, the longer the search should take. There are actually two sorts of serial search procedures that could be used. In an *exhaustive search*, the test item would be compared with each item in short-term memory and then a decision would be made as to whether the test item was in the memory set. That seems rather implausible, though. What if the memory set were 967 and the test item were 9? Since this would be the very first item of the memory set, one should be able to decide immediately that the test item was indeed in the memory set. There would be no point in checking through the rest of the contents of short-term memory. This would be called a *self-terminating search*. As soon as the item being searched for is found, the search is terminated. Note that a self-terminating search could be differentiated from an exhaustive search only if the test item was actually in the memory set. If the test item were *not* in the memory set, a subject would always have to search all of the memory set in order to find this out. However, for items that are in the memory set, a differential prediction emerges. Sometimes the test item will match the first item in the memory set, and other times it will match the last item. However, on the average, we would expect that "yes" responses should be faster than "no" responses if a self-terminating search were being employed because the search can terminate more quickly on some trials. Given that the location of the test item in the memory set was random, we would expect that on the average trial only half of the memory set would need to be searched for "yes" responses. Therefore, search time for "yes" responses should be only half that for "no" responses.

EVIDENCE FOR SERIAL SEARCH OF SHORT-TERM MEMORY

That search of short-term memory should be self-terminating certainly sounds reasonable, but that is not what Sternberg found. His results are shown in Figure 6–13. Reaction time was dependent upon the number of items held in short-term memory. The more items in short-term memory, the longer it took to make a response. Thus, short-term memory seems to be searched in a serial rather than a parallel manner. Further, reaction times for "yes" and "no" responses were

FIGURE 6–13   Reaction time (reaction latency) as a function of number of symbols in a memory set. Filled circles show "yes" responses, and open circles show "no" responses.

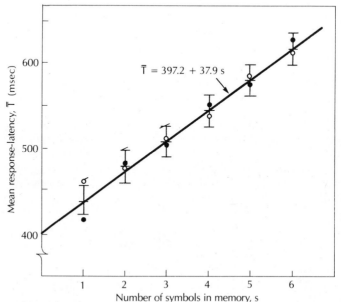

$$\bar{T} = 397.2 + 37.9\, s$$

Source: S. Sternberg, "High-Speed Scanning in Human Memory," *Science* 153 (1966):653. Copyright 1966 by the American Association for Advancement of Science.

about the same. This suggests that the search is an exhaustive rather than a self-terminating one. Why should this be? One possible explanation would be that the decision process takes a relatively long time. In a self-terminating search, a decision would have to be made after each item in memory was compared with the test item. It might be more efficient to search all the way through memory and only then ask whether there had been a match.

Sternberg's results can be described by the following equation

$$RT = 38M + 397$$

Reaction time in milliseconds was equal to 38 times M (the number of items in the memory set) plus a constant time of 397 milliseconds. In the additive-factors model, this constant time would be attributed to the time for perceiving the test item, making the decision as to whether the test item was in the memory set, and actually executing the motor response. Comparison of the test item with each item in short-term memory hypothetically took 38 milliseconds. If there was only one item in the memory set, reaction time was about $397 + 38 = 435$ milliseconds. If there were two items, reaction time was about $397 + 76 = 473$ milliseconds, and so on.

EVIDENCE FOR DIRECT ACCESS OF SHORT-TERM MEMORY

Perhaps the elegance of Sternberg's results has misled us. The idea of a serial search makes sense if short-term memory is a place with locations to be searched through. But does it really make sense if short-term memory is the momentary activation of units in long-term memory? Consider what happens in the Sternberg experiment. The memory set—say, 5, 9, 3—is presented. Perception of it consists of activating the cognitive units coding 5, 9, and 3. Then the test digit—say, 9—is presented. Perception of it consists of activating the unit coding 9. But this is the very same unit that was just activated by the 9 in the memory set. In what sense, then, is a serial search supposed to take place? To say that the subject compares the test digit with the memory set is to say that the (preexisting) unit coding 9 is compared with other (preexisting) units—including itself. That makes no sense at all.

What might happen is this: Presentation of the memory set activates some units in memory. The more items there are in the memory set, the less activated any one cognitive unit will be. This is because there seems to be a limited amount of activation available on any level of an analyzer. There is only enough to allow a few cognitive units to be simultaneously active. This is what accounts for the severe capacity limitations on short-term memory. A positive test digit (a digit in the memory set) further activates one of these units. A negative test digit (a digit not in the memory set) activates some other unit. The subject responds "yes" if one unit in memory is above some level of activation as compared with all of the others. Otherwise, the subject responds "no." The more items in the memory set, the more difficult this discrimination will be. Why should this be? One reason might be that the most activated unit (the one coding the positive test digit) laterally inhibits other units until it is much more active than any other unit. At this point, it captures attention and the subject responds "yes." Exactly how this process of capturing attention works will be explained in the next chapter. The crucial point is that this process will take longer if there are more items in the memory set because the units coding any one of them will be less fully activated. What I am saying is that there is no serial search. Rather, there is a parallel discrimination of amount of activation in a set of cognitive units. This discrimination is slower and more difficult the more units that are simultaneously activated. This direct-access theory is based on the theory of recognition suggested by Wickelgren and Norman (1966). It has been applied in various ways to the Sternberg task by Townsend (1972), Cavanaugh (1976), Wickelgren (1977), and others.

If the direct-access theory is true, there should be several consequences: Consider this memory set: 9,2,2,6. The serial search model predicts that a "yes" response to the test digit 2 should be no faster than a "yes" response to 9 or 6 and no faster than a "no" response to any digit not in the memory set. On the other hand, the direct-access theory predicts that a subject should be able to respond positively more quickly if the test digit is 2 than if it is 9 or 6. The reason is that the unit coding 2 should be especially strongly activated. Baddeley and Ecob (1973) found that there is, in fact, a difference. Presenting a digit more than once in the memory set decreases the reaction time for a positive decision concerning that digit.

Another consequence of the direct-access theory is that there should be serial position effects. For example, items toward the end of the memory set are more recent. Therefore, activation of the units coding them should be stronger. If the test item corresponds to one of them, reaction time for a positive decision should be faster. Sternberg and others using his procedure have not found this. Reaction time is related only to list length, not to serial position of the test digit in the memory set. Sternberg presented the digits in the memory set at a rate of one per second followed by a two-second delay. Then the test digit was presented. This presentation rate allows rehearsal of the memory set digits, and the two-second pause allows some time for the recency effect to disappear. What would happen if we presented the memory set at a faster rate and then immediately presented the test digit? We should get a clear recency effect; that is, positive decisions should be faster for items occurring later in the memory set. Wickelgren (1977) and Monsell (1978) cite a number of studies finding exactly this effect. The serial search model cannot explain this effect. If the entire contents of short-term memory are searched before a decision is made, there should be no such recency effect. Evidently, the specific details of Sternberg's original procedure allowed rehearsal to get all of the items in the memory set to about equal levels of activation. This wiped out any recency effect. With some minor changes in the procedure, we get results that are no longer consistent with the theory that an exhaustive serial search is carried out.

SUMMARY AND CONCLUSIONS

Perception consists of the activation of preexisting cognitive units in sensory and gnostic analyzers. Once activated, these units remain active for a period of time. This persistence of activity is referred to as primary memory. We may subdivide primary memory into sensory memory (persistence of activity of units in sensory analyzers) and short-term memory (persistence of activity of units in gnostic analyzers). Presumably, the function of this continued activity is to allow analysis at deeper levels of processing. If sensory memory is disrupted, gnostic analyzers cannot carry out the tasks of perception and recognition. If short-term memory in gnostic analyzers is disrupted, the semantic and episodic analyzers cannot carry out the tasks of understanding and formation of long-term memory traces.

There is hypothetically a separate sensory memory system for each sensory analyzer. By the same token, there appears to be a separate short-term memory system for each gnostic analyzer. However, people often have a tendency to maintain short-term memories in the speech analyzer regardless of the origin of the stimuli giving rise to these memories. The capacity of sensory memory appears to be rather large, while the capacity of short-term memory is restricted to four or five items or "chunks." On the other hand, the duration of sensory memories is much shorter (less than a second) than that of short-term memories (around 15 seconds). Loss from sensory memory may involve passive decay, but there is evidence from studies of backward masking and of the stimulus-suffix effect that loss can also be caused by interference. Loss from short-term memory appears to be due purely to interference. Crowder and Deutsch have proposed lateral-inhibition theories to account for loss of information from sensory memory and short-term memory, respectively. These theories are consistent with the latticework model of the analyzers presented in earlier chapters. A clear difference between sensory memory and short-term memory is that the contents of the latter can be preserved indefinitely by rehearsal. No comparable process exists for the preservation of sensory memories.

Experiments by Sternberg and others have produced evidence supportive of the contention that the contents of short-term memory are searched in a serial fashion. Thus, the more items being held in short-term memory, the longer it takes people to say whether or not a test item is identical to one of these items. The idea of a serial search through a short-term memory does not make much sense if short-term memory is merely the momentary activation of units in long-term memory. Who or what would do the searching? We suggested that Sternberg's results could be explained in terms of the length of time necessary for one cognitive unit to seize attention by laterally inhibiting competing units. In order to see if this explanation makes sense, we shall need to consider what attention is and how it works. This will be our task in the next chapter.

7

Attention

THE STREAM OF CONSCIOUSNESS AND THE ATTENTION WAVE

In the last chapter it was argued that the contents of primary memory are the contents of consciousness. There is general agreement that consciousness can, as Titchener (1923) put it, be "arranged into focus and margin, foreground and background, centre and periphery." Attention is the focus or foreground, and the other contents of primary memory become the background. The mental representation upon which attention is fixed is somehow more conscious than the other contents of consciousness. It is, the introspectionists argued, clearer than the other things of which we are less focally aware. Titchener (1923) compared attention to a wave, as illustrated in Figure 7–1A. Consciousness is represented

FIGURE 7–1 The attention wave. (A) Titchener argued that there is only one degree of attentional focus; (B) other introspectionists said that there are two degrees of attentional focus; and (C) still others said that degree of focus is continuously variable.

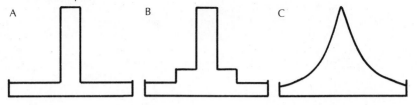

as a stream moving toward the reader. The focus of attention is the raised wave, while the fringe of consciousness is the lower part. Titchener argued strongly that Figure 7–1A best represents attention: A conscious mental representation is either attended to or it is not. However, other introspectionists felt that there are several degrees of focus (as shown in Figure 7–1B), and still others thought that there is a continuous gradient (as shown in Figure 7–1C).

Introspectionism could never provide an answer to the controversy of how attention can best be depicted, but the diagrams are helpful so long as we do not get too fussy about their details, because they give us a way of representing some interesting questions about attention that psychologists are still trying to answer. Perhaps the most obvious question concerns the width of the attention wave: How many items can be attended to at once? William James (1890) gave the answer to this question that is still generally held today: "not easily more than one, unless the processes are very habitual; but then two, or even three." Another question concerns the height of the attention wave. Height deals with the intensive aspect of attention. A higher wave would represent more intense attention, whereas a lower one would represent a less intent state. How many heights can the wave have? How can height be measured? Another crucial question concerns the length of the attention wave. In other words, how long can attention to one thing be maintained? We could take height, width, and length together to construct the notion of the volume or capacity of attention. Is this capacity in any sense a constant? That is, can we, for example, reduce height in order to gain width?

ATTENTION, ANALYZERS, AND COGNITIVE UNITS

In terms of our model, primary memory consists of the set of currently activated cognitive units. Attention may be seen as the subset of these units that are most strongly activated. In this view, Titchener's attention wave could be better depicted as illustrated in Figure 7–2. Here, the focus and fringe of consciousness are shown distributed across the surface of a gnostic field. If we look at attention in this way, the introspectionists' questions can be rephrased to refer to questions about the activation of cognitive units. How many degrees of activation can a cognitive unit have? How many cognitive units can be maximally activated (attended to) at once? How long can a cognitive unit remain maximally activated? We can also ask the question of volume or capacity: Is there any set

FIGURE 7–2   Attention depicted as a pattern of activation and lateral inhibition of cognitive units

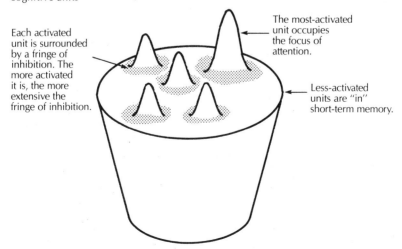

Each activated unit is surrounded by a fringe of inhibition. The more activated it is, the more extensive the fringe of inhibition.

The most-activated unit occupies the focus of attention.

Less-activated units are "in" short-term memory.

limit to the amount of activation available to the units in an analyzer? Is there a pool of activation that must be divided among all of the analyzers?

We cannot focally attend to all of the things of which we are aware at any moment in time. This limitation is implicit in our definition of attention as a subset of currently activated cognitive units. Most theorists have held that we can focally attend to only one or two things at once. Thus, attention can be seen as imposing a severe bottleneck on human cognition. The selectivity of attention can be of two types. It is either automatic and involuntary, as when a sudden and unexpected noise seizes our attention, or effortful and voluntary, as when we attend to a distasteful and uninteresting task. In either case, the basic question to be answered is how the selection is made. How is one mental event selected to occupy the focus of attention while others are relegated to the fringes of awareness? Two opposite answers have been offered to this question. Filter theories involve the contention that all but the selected event are filtered, attenuated, or inhibited. What might be called amplification theories hold that the most activated cognitive unit or units automatically come to occupy the focus of attention. Adherents of both theories have devoted a lot of effort to determining where filtering or amplification occurs. Although they have generally used other terms, the question of interest has been whether these processes operate in sensory analyzers, gnostic analyzers, or in the semantic analyzer.

VOLUNTARY SELECTIVE ATTENTION

Shadowing

Have you ever noticed that when you are at a noisy party you can focus your attention on a conversation across the room and ignore all of the other voices. Imagine that one group of people is discussing the relative merits of different types of cabbage while another group somewhere in the room is gossiping about a friend. With remarkable facility you can tune out the cabbage conversation and tune in the more interesting conversation. With just as much ease, you could also do the reverse. That is, you could attend to the cabbage conversation and ignore the gossip. This ability for selective attention has been called the *cocktail-party phenomenon*. How does it work? Colin Cherry (1953) was the first to study it in any detail. Rather than doing his research at parties, Cherry devised another procedure that was not as much fun for his subjects but allowed him to be more systematic in his investigations. What he did was simple. He tape-recorded two different messages. Then, using headphones, he played both messages at once, one to each ear of his subjects. Their task was to *shadow* or repeat back one of the messages.

This task turned out to be fairly easy to do. Cherry's subjects could repeat one or the other of the messages virtually without error. It was very easy for them to switch their attention from one ear to the other as directed. Cherry's experiments seem to show that the basis for attention might have to do with selection on a very basic level: People can direct their attention to one ear or the other. Perhaps the mechanism underlying attention is simply an ability to select on this basis. If selection of one or the other ear were the only basis for selective attention, people should not be able to disentangle two messages presented to the same ear. Cherry tried simultaneously playing two messages recorded by the same speaker to the same ear. His subjects could not disentangle these and correctly repeat one of them back on first hearing.

Spieth, Curtis, and Webster (1954) tried the same thing, but first they put one of the messages through a band-pass filter. This process filtered out some of the frequencies in that message so that the two messages differed in their voice quality. Subjects could now shadow one or the other message with ease. Spieth, Curtis, and Webster also found that subjects could shadow on the basis of the location of the messages in space. In this experiment, different messages spoken by the same voice emanated from two separate loudspeakers. Egan, Carterette, and Thwing (1934) demonstrated that subjects can also shadow on the basis of loudness. People can repeat either the louder or the softer message as directed, at least so long as the louder one does not completely drown out the softer one. Thus, people can use ear-of-arrival as a basis for selective attention, but when both messages go to the same ear, they can use some other cues. All of the cues used for shadowing are sensory or physical as opposed to semantic. Perhaps subjects can focus attention on the basis of such sensory cues.

Cherry's subjects had relatively little comprehension of or memory for the message that they had repeated. But the really interesting finding concerned their memory for the rejected message (the one they did not shadow). They remembered virtually nothing from the rejected message—not a single word or phrase. Moray (1959) showed that even if the same word is repeated up to 35 times in the rejected message, it is not remembered. Subjects apparently have no long-term memory for any of the words in the rejected message. Does this mean that they do not notice anything at all about it? To find out, Cherry (1953) varied what was in the rejected message. First, he tried playing the message to the rejected ear backwards. The rejected message started and ended with normal English but the midsection was entirely reversed. When questioned afterwards, a few subjects said that there was something funny about the rejected message, but they could not say what! Most noticed nothing at all. Next, Cherry tried changing the speaker of the rejected message from male to female in the middle of the tape. Subjects did notice and remember this. They also noticed if a 400-cycle-per-second tone was substituted for the voice in the rejected channel. These results are consistent with the hypothesis that subjects were filtering out the rejected message on the basis of purely sensory cues.

Early selection models of attention

BROADBENT'S MODEL

In order to make sense of these findings, Broadbent (1958) offered a filter model of attention (see Figure 7–3). According to Broadbent, the organism has only a limited capacity to process the information that impinges upon it. This information arrives via the various sensory channels (for example, vision, hearing, or touch) and is retained for a very short time in what is now called sensory memory. During that time, it decays and is lost unless it is selected for further processing. The selective filter in the model picks out one type of information and passes it on. According to Broadbent, this filter operates by selection on the

FIGURE 7–3   Early selection or filter model of attention in schematic form

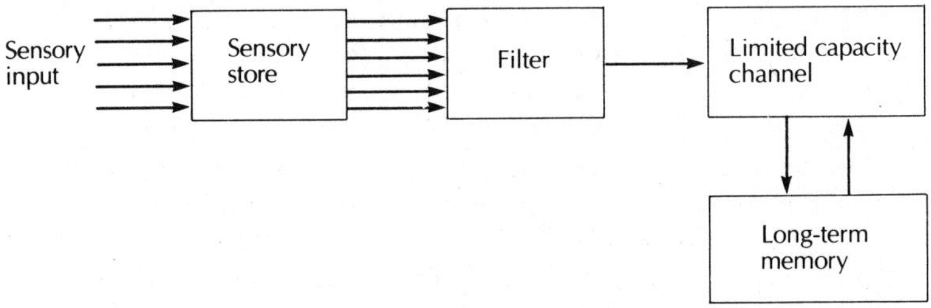

Source: D. E. Broadbent, *Perception and Communication* (New York: Pergamon, 1958), p. 299.

basis of sensory or physical attributes, such as intensity, frequency, sensory modality, or location. Thus, it can select high-pitched signals, low-pitched signals, messages to the left ear, and so on.

According to Broadbent's model, only information that has reached the limited capacity channel (the equivalent of short-term memory) is remembered for any length of time. Thus, only items that have occupied the focus of attention can be stored in long-term memory. The model incorporates the observation of William James (1890) that, unless something is specifically attended to, it is not remembered. In a shadowing experiment, some of the shadowed message gets into long-term memory, but none of the rejected message should, since none of it ever gets through the filter. In the Broadbent model, understanding or comprehension of a message requires that it be looked up in long-term memory. For example, in order for you to understand spoken English, you need to attend to it and recall what each of the words means. From the perspective of the model we have developed in the last several chapters, Broadbent is essentially saying that attentional selection takes place in purely sensory analyzers. Thus, for verbal material, the theory comes down to saying that we can select one or another input for attention only in the auditory analyzer, not in the speech analyzer or the semantic analyzer. For this reason, Broadbent's model has been called an *early-selection* model of attention.

PROBLEMS WITH BROADBENT'S MODEL

According to Broadbent's model, unattended inputs are filtered out at the level of sensory analysis. Thus, not even gnostic or perceptual analysis of the rejected message is done. However, this seems to be incorrect. The rejected message does, in fact, make its way to short-term memory. Moray and Cherry had asked their subjects if they remembered anything from the rejected channel at the end of the whole experiment. Norman (1969) tried another approach. He simply stopped the tape in the middle of the experiment and asked his subjects what they had just heard. They were all able to report the previous few words in *both* the rejected and the shadowed message! The subjects could recall more words than could have been retrieved from sensory memory. Thus, information from the rejected channel was present in short-term memory. If we view short-term memory as consisting of momentary activity in the gnostic analyzer for speech, this finding is contrary to Broadbent's model. The rejected message was supposed to have been completely filtered out in the sensory analyzer. Also consistent with the idea that the rejected message reaches the speech analyzer is Moray's finding (1959) that if a subject's name is mentioned in the rejected message, the subject recalls this at the end of the experiment. Thus, at least this item in the rejected channel has gotten to long-term episodic memory. This may sound trivial, but recognition of one's name has to do with morphemic rather than with purely acoustic analysis of the message. It would not be very elegant to revise the model so as to have the selective filter select on the basis of pitch, intensity, and . . . one's own name.

Subsequent experiments demonstrated that information from the rejected channel was also reaching the semantic analyzer. McKay (1973) had subjects shadow ambiguous messages, such as HE IS THROWING STONES AT THE BANK. At the time, the word BANK occurred in the attended channel, either the word SAVINGS or RIVER might occur in the unattended one. Later, subjects tended to interpret the shadowed message in accord with whichever word they had heard in the unattended channel. Lewis (1970) demonstrated that the meaning of words in the unattended channel has an effect with a somewhat more complicated method. He recorded shadowing latency—that is, the time between the occurrence of a word and the subject's repetition of it. Shadowing latency was longer when the word in the unattended channel was a synonym of the shadowed word than when it was unrelated.

Corteen and Wood (1972) used the method of galvanic skin response (GSR) conditioning to demonstrate that the meaning of words in the unattended channel is, in fact, detected. The GSR, a brief change in the resistance of the skin to electrical current, is probably caused by increased activity of the sweat glands. Subjects tend to exhibit GSRs when they are presented with emotional stimuli. Corteen and Wood used this effect as follows. Before their subjects performed a shadowing task, they listened to a list of 12 words. Three of these words were names of cities. Every time that a person heard one of these names, an electric shock was given. After a few trials, when one of these words was heard, a shock was expected and this expectation was accompanied by a galvanic skin response. This kind of effect tends to generalize. That is, the expectation of shock will tend to arise when the name of any city is heard, not just when the specific cities on the list are heard. Corteen and Wood had their subjects shadow a message presented to one ear. This message contained none of the words from the pretest list. However, the unattended channel contained not only names of cities previously paired with shock but also some names of new cities as well as completely new words not on the list that the subjects had heard. GSRs were elicited by 8.7 percent of the new words but by 37.7 percent of the city names previously paired with shock and by 22.8 percent of the names of cities not previously paired with shock. Now, the fact that 37.7 percent of names of cities previously paired with shock elicited GSRs does not prove that subjects were responding to the meanings of the words. They could have just been responding to the sound patterns of the words. However, the fact that they generalized their fear response along the semantic dimension does suggest that the stimuli in the unattended channel had been processed at the level of meaning. In other words, stimuli in the unattended channel were activating units in the semantic analyzer.

Late-selection models of attention

Several theorists have advanced models of attention that differ radically from the filter model of attention proposed by Broadbent. These models differ in four basic respects. (1) They deny the existence of an attentional filter operating on sensory characteristics. (2) They involve the denial that short-term memory is a place or bin where partially analyzed representations reside prior to lookup in long-term memory. Rather, they argue that short-term memory is the temporary activation of cognitive units in long-term memory. (3) They hold that all incoming stimuli make contact with their cognitive units in long-term memory but that only the most strongly activated units are attended to. (4) They thus argue that the limited-capacity attentional channel essentially comes after, rather than before, long-term memory.

NORMAN'S MODEL

Early examples of such models are those of Blum (1961) and Deutsch and Deutsch (1963). However, we shall describe the later model proposed by Norman (1968). A diagram of the major features in this model is given in Figure 7–4. As you can see, attention comes after rather than before lookup of incoming signals in long-term memory. According to Norman, initial analysis of sensory signals is automatic. He ascribes to the sort of initial feature analyses we described in previous chapters. External stimuli give rise to some sort of physiological representation from which features are extracted. These features determine the address

FIGURE 7–4   Late selection model of attention

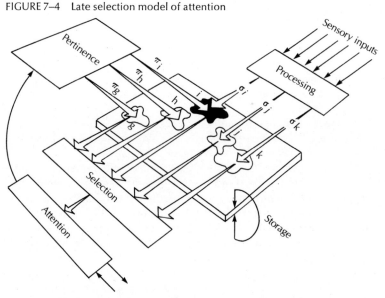

Source: D. A. Norman, "Toward a Theory of Memory and Attention," *Psychological Review* 75 (1968):526. Copyright 1968 by the American Psychological Association. Reprinted by permission.

of the signal in long-term memory. That is, to sense or perceive something means that the cognitive units coding that thing have been activated in long-term memory. This temporary activation of traces in long-term memory is short-term memory according to Norman. Norman's long-term memory is equivalent to what we have called semantic memory. He compares it with Morton's logogen system (1969).

Unless something else happens, the temporary activation of units in semantic memory will decay in a matter of seconds, and one will have no episodic memory that the semantic memory unit was activated. Recall from Chapter 6 that unrehearsed items in short-term memory disappear in a matter of seconds having left no long-term memory trace. This something else is being attended to. As to how the unit to be attended to is chosen, Norman elaborates upon a suggestion made by Deutsch and Deutsch (1963). The most strongly activated unit is the one upon which attention is focused. According to Norman's model, sensory inputs activate units in long-term memory, but these units can also be activated by a pertinence mechanism. This mechanism—which resembles Morton's context system—is meant to account for several features of attention. In general, we switch our attention rapidly if pertinent or important information arrives in an unattended channel. Norman's pertinence mechanism really corresponds to two phenomena: (1) some cognitive units have lower thresholds than others and (2) expectation can prime cognitive units, thus making them easier to activate. Subjects tend to hear their own names in the unshadowed channel during shadowing experiments. There is evidence that the unit coding a person's own name has a lower threshold than comparable units. For example, Howarth and Ellis (1961) presented subjects with names that were difficult to hear because they were buried in white noise. These subjects correctly recognized their own names more often than the names of other people. Sometimes activation via the pertinence mechanism can overwhelm activation via sensory input. In reading, we have seen that our expectations can led us to see the word we expect rather than the word that is actually printed—as in the case of the misspelled word in this sentence. In the case of attention, Norman argued that the pertinence mechanism can be used to explain shadowing. The idea would be that it could be used to prime or partially activate units corresponding to the message to be shadowed.

Norman's model has several advantages. First, it has no difficulty in explaining why some of the words in the rejected channel are recalled or why words in the rejected channel can interfere with shadowing on the basis of their meaning. Everything in both channels hypothetically reaches semantic memory. Second, the model is consistent with the view of mind as a multileveled feature analysis system. In our terms, Norman's model comes down to saying that we can select an input for attention only in the semantic analyzer, not in the auditory or the speech analyzer. The model implies that all stimuli are processed to the deepest possible level. For this reason, Norman's model has been called a *late-selection* model of attention.

PROBLEMS WITH LATE-SELECTION MODELS

Both Treisman and Riley (1969) and Broadbent (1971) argue against late-selection models of attention. They point out that late-selection models imply that people should be able to shadow just as well on the basis of meaning as on the basis of physical cues. This, however, is clearly not the case. Shadowing in the absence of any physical cues is extremely difficult. Cherry's original experiments showed that it is hard to shadow one of two messages presented to the same ear and spoken by the same voice even though the content of the two messages differs. A related problem is that the effects of content or meaning are quite small when physical differences between messages are present. Several studies were cited earlier that showed that the meaning of the nonshadowed message has a disruptive effect on shadowing. But in all cases, this disruption was relatively slight. In any event, it is certainly much easier to shadow on the basis of physical cues than on the basis of only semantic cues.

Treisman's attenuation model

Broadbent's early-selection model of attention (1958) cannot account for the effects of meaning on shadowing performance. On the other hand, late-selection models of attention cannot account for why the effects of meaning are relatively slight. Nor can they explain why it is so easy to shadow on the basis of sensory cues and so difficult to shadow on the basis of semantic cues. Treisman (1969) has proposed a compromise model of attention that resolves these difficulties. First, she argued that the selective filter attenuates signals rather than working on an all-or-none basis. This explains why some items in the rejected channel—such as a subject's name—do manage to get through the filter. Second, she proposed that there are a series of filters or analyzers: (1) sensory analyzers, (2) analyzers for specific sounds and words, and (3) analyzers for grammatical structure and meaning. The function of these analyzers is similar to that of the sensory, gnostic, and semantic analyzers that we have postulated. Filtering is done at the lowest level on which the shadowed message can be discriminated from the rejected message. If two messages cannot be discriminated on the sensory level or the gnostic level, then filtering is done in the semantic analyzer. This revised model will account for all of the findings fairly well, but the filter has become quite complex. If it makes such complex analyses, then it seems to have become indistinguishable from the activity of long-term memory itself; that is, there is no attentional filter per se. Rather, attention must consist of filtering or attenuating operations in sensory, gnostic, and semantic analyzers. After all of these operations, one set of cognitive units will be left. These units will occupy the focus of attention.

Treisman's model of attention fits well with the view of mind that we have been developing. Essentially, Broadbent's early-selection model said that the basis for selective attention was filtering or selection that could occur only in sensory analyzers. The late-selection theorists said that such filtering or selection could be done only in semantic analyzers. Treisman, however, says that attenuation can occur in any analyzer—sensory, gnostic, or semantic. This certainly seems reasonable. Given that the structure of all three types of analyzers is basically the same, there is no a priori reason to expect that attentional selection should be confined to only one type of analyzer as both early-selection and late-selection theories say it is. As we shall see later, the lateral inhibitory structure of the analyzers lends itself to the task of attenuating certain signals.

INVOLUNTARY SELECTIVE ATTENTION
What normally attracts attention?

Research on voluntary selective attention really tells us nothing about which events are normally attended to. Subjects in a shadowing experiment are told what to attend to and they dutifully try to do so. It is not really clear what everyday circumstances—other than eavesdropping at a cocktail party or studying while a radio is on—a shadowing experiment simulates. We attend to both environmental and internal events throughout the whole day. What sorts of things do we single out for attention? It might really be better to ask, what sorts of events seize our attention? This is the question of involuntary selective attention. Interestingly enough, most of the answers to this question have come from studies of cats and other animals, but these answers are quite relevant to human attention.

In 1958, when Broadbent proposed his theory of attention, a quite different line of inquiry had been going on for almost ten years. This research culminated in a theory of attention that was quite compatible with Broadbent's theory—and therefore quite susceptible to the same criticisms. It concerned involuntary attention, the orienting reflex, and the reticular activating system. The reticular activating system has its origin in the midbrain and sends projections to virtually every part of the cortex. It is roughly equivalent to what we have called the arousal system. The anatomical existence of this system had been known for some time. But no one knew what it was good for until 1949, when it became clear that it is intimately connected with attention and what is called the *orienting reflex.*

The orienting reflex

Animals—including humans—show a characteristic pattern of responses when they attend to something. Pavlov (1927) called this pattern the orienting reflex. He noticed that, when his dogs were confronted with something novel, they oriented toward the stimulus, and ongoing behavior was arrested as they did a sort of double take. Subhuman animals often prick up their ears and sniff when they display the orienting reflex. Going along with gross motor orientation toward the source of stimulation are actual increases in sensory sensitivity. The pupil of the eye dilates, and there is a drop in the threshold for detection of light. The auditory threshold drops by as much as 10 dB (Gershuni et al., 1960). Psychophysiological indexes exhibit a characteristic pattern. The EEG shows an arousal response. This consists of high-frequency, low-voltage brain wave activity. On the other hand, there is a pause and then a decrease in respiration rate, while heart rate actually decreases (Lynn, 1966). Blood flow shows an interesting pattern. The blood vessels to the limbs constrict while those to the brain dilate. Presumably, this functions to facilitate cortical processing of the new stimulus (Sokolov, 1963). The orienting reflex seems to occur whenever attention is automatically or involuntarily drawn to a stimulus. While humans tend not to exhibit the gross behavioral signs of the orienting reflex when they attend to something, they do exhibit the more subtle psychophysiological signs described earlier.

According to Berlyne (1971), three aspects of stimuli are likely to elicit an orienting reflex in both humans and animals:

1. *Psychophysical properties* are sensory characteristics of a stimulus, such as brightness or loudness. Generally, the more intense a stimulus, the more likely that it will draw attention.
2. *Ecological properties* refer to the meaning or signal value of a stimulus. In general, the more meaningful a stimulus, the more likely it is to elicit an orienting reflex.
3. *Collative properties* refer to collation or comparison processes. Novelty and surprise refers to collating expectation and reality; incongruity refers to a collation of conflicting percepts; conflict refers to collation of incompatible response tendencies. All of the collative properties are potent elicitors of the orienting reflex.

Habituation

What happens if we repeat the same stimulus over and over? Since novel stimuli elicit the orienting reflex, we would expect some change in the orientation reaction as the novelty of a stimulus decreases. Sokolov (1963) argues that a systematic series of events called *habituation* occurs. The orienting reflex is elicited by the first 10 to 15 repetitions of a stimulus but with gradually decreasing intensity until is vanishes altogether. By this time, only the localized orientation response remains. This consists of an EEG arousal response to the stimulus restricted to the cortical receiving area appropriate to the stimulus. (On the other hand, the generalized orientation response is accompanied by EEG arousal over the whole cortex.) This localized reaction also disappears over the course of 25–30 further stimulations. At this point, the organism often becomes drowsy and the EEG gives evidence of low arousal. Repetitive stimulation does seem to induce sleep rather quickly. For example, Gastaut and Bert (1961) did an experiment with adult human subjects in which repetitive stimulation was presented. After only eight minutes, almost half of their subjects showed the low-arousal EEG waves characteristic of sleep and many were clearly asleep.

The arousal system

In a classic paper, Moruzzi and Magoun (1949) reported that electrical stimulation of the reticular system in cats had several startling effects. On the level of behavior, such stimulation led to awakening (if the cats were asleep) and to an orienting reflex (if the cats were awake). When the cats' brain waves were recorded, it was seen that stimulation of the reticular activating system elicited an arousal or alerting response. The usual slow alpha rhythm was blocked, and the brain waves resembled those seen when a cat attends to a stimulus. These results were amazing. Stimulation of a small region in the brain stem aroused the whole cortex! The reticular activating system seemed to be the control site for attention. This conclusion was strengthened by the finding of Lindsley, Bowden, and Magoun (1949) that surgical destruction of the reticular system leads to coma and a sleeplike pattern of EEG waves.

Each of the senses is connected to a specific receiving or processing area in the cortex. Each also sends collateral neural fibers to the reticular activating system. What happens if these collateral fibers are severed surgically? The animal remains awake, and stimuli still excite activity in the cortical receiving areas via the direct pathways, but the animal pays absolutely no attention to them (Lindsley, 1957). It appeared that for a stimulus to be attended to, it must also arrive at the reticular centers in the midbrain. Unless these are activated by it, it cannot hope for attention.

Hernández-Péon, Scherrer, and Jouvet (1956) conducted a classic study of the orienting reflex in cats. The cats were presented with a series of clicking noises. Hernández-Péon and his colleagues recorded the evoked potentials (amount of neural activity) that these clicks elicited in the cochleas of the cats. Each click elicited a distinct evoked potential. Then, while the clicks were still being presented, the cats were shown a mouse in a glass jar. As might be expected, the cats found this mouse quite interesting. At least, they rather obviously oriented toward it. When they did so, the auditory evoked potentials being recorded from the cochlea diminished in amplitude. This was—wrongly, it turned out—interpreted to mean that—as well as activating the cortex—the reticular activating system could selectively shut down or attenuate sensory signals at the periphery.

The classical theory of the reticular activating system

What has been called the classical theory of the reticular system emerged from these experiments. This view was quite similar to the filter theory proposed by Broadbent. It held that the reticular system has two functions. First, it alerts the cortex to attend to incoming stimuli. Second, it acts as a selective filter by attenuating unattended inputs at the periphery of the organism. In this view, any incoming stimulus is processed by the reticular system. If it is of interest, the cortex is activated and other sensory input channels are shut down. Focused attention results. If it is not of interest, the cortex is not activated and the stimulus is ignored. Habituation was explained by postulating that the reticular activating system gradually raises the threshold of the sensory input channel along which the repeated stimulus travels. After enough repetitions, the threshold will be so high that the stimulus will be filtered out and no more attention will be paid to it.

Problems with the classical theory

The classical view of the reticular activating system is quite consistent with Broadbent's theory of attention. Thus, it is not surprising that it is subject to the same problems. First, research on the orienting reflex and its habituation strongly suggests that the meaning of stimuli is important even though the classical filter theory says it should not be. For example, Sharpless and Jasper (1956) showed that cats habituate not only to tones of specific frequencies but also to rhythms. In order to handle this finding with the classical theory, one would have to postulate that the reticular system filter has a sense of rhythm. The studies cited earlier, which showed that unattended signals reach the semantic analyzer, also present just as much of a problem for the classical theory as for Broadbent's theory.

Sokolov (1960) presented cats with a series of 600 Hz tones at regular intervals. As had been found many times before, the cats gradually habituated to the tones. Then, after habituation was complete, one of the tones was omitted. The cats showed an orienting response to the omission of the tone! This is completely contrary to the classical view that habituation consists of gradually shutting off input at the periphery by raising sensory thresholds. If this were the case, omission of one of the tones should never be noticed. In order for an omission to be noticed, one must postulate that expectations are important; that is, the cats were habituating to the regular, expected tones and orienting toward any stimulus (or lack of stimulus) that violated this expectation. To accommodate this finding, we would have to build a mechanism for expectation into the reticular system. This could be done, but we would wind up with the reticular system doing the work of the cortex. The point of the filter theory is that the filter is simple and works on purely sensory dimensions of stimuli. The more complex the work assigned to the filter, the less intellectually satisfying the theory becomes.

Finally, the results of Hernández-Péon, Scherrer, and Jouvet (1956) have been called into question (Hugelin, Dumont, and Paillas, 1960; Worden, 1967). First, the attenuation of evoked potentials in the cochlea is slight and inconsistent. Second, the attenuation seems to be artifactual anyway; that is, it is not a real attenuation but is caused by irrelevant things, such as muscle contractions of the animals' ears and the orientation of the ears toward the source of the sounds being listened to. It now appears that there is, in fact, no peripheral habituation of evoked potentials at all.

Sokolov's theory of attention

CORTICAL MODELING

While the findings concerning habituation present great difficulties for the classical view of the functioning of the reticular system, the evoked potential findings present insurmountable difficulties. The theory is just not right. Sokolov (1960) presented a radically different theory that provides an explanation of all of the facts. The theory is presented in diagrammatic form in Figure 7–5. According to Sokolov's theory, the cortex compares all incoming stimuli with models or expectations. If the incoming stimulus matches a preexisting cortical model, the cortex blocks the reticular system and nothing happens: the reticular system does not activate the cortex, and no attention is paid to the stimulus. On the other hand, if the stimulus is novel—that is, if it does not exactly match any cortical model—then the cortex does not block the reticular system. In this case, the stimulus input activates the reticular system, the latter activates the cortex, and the cortical activation leads to attention.

You may have noted that this model involves the assumption that the cortical modeling system can check to see whether the incoming stimulus matches one of its models *before* the stimulus has activated the reticular system via the collateral fibers that connect all sensory input channels to the reticular system. On the other hand, the classical view had been based upon the assumption that the collaterals activate the reticular system *before* the direct input fibers activate the cortical receiving areas. It turns out that the facts are once more on Sokolov's side. The collaterals to the reticular system are rather circuitous. The cortex is, in fact, the first to receive the message.

FIGURE 7–5 In Sokolov's (1960) model of
attention, sensory input goes to both the cortex
(system for formation of model) and the arousal
system (amplifying system). If inputs to the cortex
match a preexisting model, inputs to the arousal
system are inhibited via pathway A. If there is a
mismatch, the arousal system is informed via
pathway B and it activates the cortex via
pathway C.

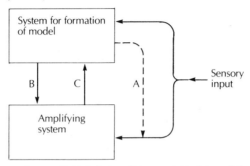

Source: E. N. Sokolov, "Neuronal Models and the
Orienting Reflex," in *The Central Nervous System and
Behaviour,* ed. M. A. Brazier (New York: J. Macy,
1960), p. 216.

THE MATCH-MISMATCH RULE

In Sokolov's view, habituation—or the waning of attention—has to do with
the gradual building of a cortical model to predict the new stimulus situation.
When the cats in Sokolov's experiment first hear the 600 Hz tone, it is a new
stimulus. They are surprised and orient toward the novel stimulus. After a few
repetitions, a cortical model or expectation to the effect that "a 600 Hz tone
will occur every two seconds" is developed. The cats pay less and less attention
the more times this model has been matched. Now, anything that fails to fit this
model will elicit attention whether that anything is a 900 Hz tone, a 300 Hz tone,
or silence when a tone was expected.

Several things can be noted about Sokolov's model. First, although Sokolov
did not go into detail as to how the cortex matches stimuli with models, it is easy
enough to see this as involving the sort of feature analysis system that we discussed in previous chapters. The basic principle that Sokolov adds is a match-
mismatch rule: If a percept exactly matches a set of cognitive units, nothing happens other than passive perception. If a percept mismatches the best-fitting set
of cognitive units, then the arousal system activates the cortex. This arousal response is accompanied by an orienting reflex, attention, and the construction
of a new cortical model (that is, a set of cognitive units that matches the percept).

Second, think a moment about the implications of Sokolov's model. It provides
an elegant theory of attention and its relationship to the arousal system. However,
it has larger implications than this. What Sokolov is really saying is that the brain
is basically a machine for detecting novelty! How much this contrasts with the
emphasis of earlier behavioristic psychology on drives, such as hunger, thirst, and

sex. To be sure, the brain has centers that deal with these functions. It is certainly reasonable to suppose that the brain is so sensitive to novelty because of evolutionary reasons, since novel stimuli include those that are dangerous on the one hand and those that are biologically desirable on the other. But the interesting point is that attention tends to get allocated to novelty in general, not just to stimuli that are, say, both dangerous and novel. In Chapter 10, we shall describe a good deal of evidence that novelty and disruption of expectation govern not only attention but also hedonic tone or feelings of pleasure and pain as well.

EXPLANATION OF VOLUNTARY ATTENTION

While the classical view of the reticular system is clearly analogous to Broadbent's early-selection model, Sokolov's theory of the reticular system seems to be analogous to the late-selection models of Norman and others. However, nothing in Sokolov's model explicitly says that all stimuli need to be fully and completely analyzed. Presumably, unchanging aspects of the environment may so fully match cortical models at sensory and gnostic levels that semantic analysis is never carried out. In other words, Sokolov's model is not really inconsistent with Treisman's attenuation model of attention. However, it is not immediately apparent how Sokolov could explain voluntary selective attention. In this case, there is no mismatch of inputs with expectations. It should be noted for the sake of completeness that Sokolov acknowledges that a perfect match between some stimuli and some cortical models can elicit attention. This occurs when the stimuli are meaningful signals—for example, the word FIRE. The mechanism would be a direct connection from the relevant cognitive units to the arousal system. Since any cognitive unit can at least potentially become a meaningful signal, it would be necessary to postulate that all cognitive units have at least latent connections to the arousal system. This mechanism could be invoked to explain shadowing. In this case, the message to be shadowed gains temporary pertinence, or meaningfulness. Thus, the relevant cognitive units are temporarily connected to the arousal system.

THE MECHANISMS OF SELECTIVE ATTENTION

Lateral inhibition and the seizure of attention

Perception consists of the activation of columns of cognitive units in sensory, gnostic, and semantic analyzers. Short-term memory or consciousness corresponds to the four or five most highly activated columns of units, while attention hypothetically corresponds to the one or two most activated of these currently active columns of units. We have seen that attention can operate in either sensory or gnostic or semantic analyzers according to Treisman's attenuation model. The models considered here do not give a very clear explanation of exactly how the most activated column of cognitive units is selected for attention. Broadbent's filter model suggests that unattended inputs are filtered out, but it does not specify how this filtering process is accomplished. Late-selection models suggest that the most activated cognitive unit is selected for attention. But how is this unit located? What does the selecting? Certainly, we cannot have the mind's eye looking over the cognitive units to find the most excited one. Deutsch and Deutsch (1963) in considering this problem suggest the analogy of trying to determine the tallest person in a room. One method would be to measure the height of each person, write down each person's height, and then serially search through this list for the largest number. More efficient would be to line everyone up and then lower a board until it touched the head of one of them. This would, of course, be the tallest one. This is a nice metaphor, but it is hard to see how it would fit into the mind; that is, what cognitive mechanism would serve the function of the board?

Walley and Weiden (1973) have proposed a view of attention that goes a long way toward illuminating how the most strongly activated unit could become the focus of attention. The appropriate analogy for their proposal is not Deutsch and Deutsch's board but rather the strongest person in the room knocking down all of the others. Walley and Weiden's proposals are based upon Konorski's model of the brain (1967). Attention, they argue, is due to the fact that excitation of a given unit inhibits surrounding units by means of lateral inhibition. The more activated a unit is, the more it will inhibit surrounding units. Walley and Weiden's argument is essentially that there is no problem of having to search for the most strongly activated unit from among many activated units. The most strongly activated unit will automatically inhibit other units. In this view, attention is not really an operation of selection but a completely automatic affair.

So long as one cognitive unit at a given level of an analyzer is appreciably more activated than others, it seems reasonable that it might be able to more or less completely laterally inhibit activity of neighboring units. In the case of involuntary attention, a very intense or a very meaningful stimulus will almost invariably seize attention. Presumably, this is because the cognitive units coding such stimuli become very strongly activated when these stimuli are present. In the case of voluntary selective attention, it is possible to speculate that instructions—for example, the instruction to shadow the message to the left ear and disregard the one to the right ear—could lead to priming or partial activation of units in the sensory analyzer dealing with inputs from the left ear. When actual inputs from the two ears arrive, the units coding those coming from the left ear will thus be more activated than those coding inputs from the right ear. The result would be that the left-ear units could attenuate or laterally inhibit the right-ear units. So far so good, but how are we to explain attention in cases where several cognitive units are about equally activated? Each unit should laterally inhibit the other and there would be no attention paid to either. However, this is not correct. Novelty, conflict, and any mismatch between expectation (a primed cognitive unit) and perception (a cognitive unit activated by an external stimulus) are all cases where several cognitive units would be activated. As we have seen, novelty, conflict, and mismatch are, in fact, very potent elicitors of attention. How are we to explain this? The answer seems to have to do with nonspecific inputs from the arousal system.

The arousal system and attention

We proposed in Chapter 4 that cognitive units receive nonspecific input from the arousal system. Hypothetically, this input is crucial in focusing attention. Empirically, attention seems always to be accompanied by increased arousal. This is the case whether or not the attention is brought about by novelty. Involuntary attention—regardless of whether it is elicited by psychophysical, ecological, or collative variables—is, as we have seen, invariably accompanied by arousal. Kahneman (1973) notes that voluntary attention is always accompanied by a sense of effort. He has conducted several studies showing that this sense of effort is the subjective aspect of increases in arousal. We might argue that, in order for attention to occur, a cognitive unit must receive both informational input from other cognitive units and nonspecific input from the arousal system (see also Shallice, 1978).

At first glance, it might not seem that indiscriminately adding activation to all of the cognitive units in an analyzer via nonspecific inputs from the arousal system would be of any use. However, Walley and Weiden (1973) hold that inputs from the arousal system actually serve only to increase lateral inhibition. The consequence of increased lateral inhibition is that more activated units exert more inhibition on less activated units. The ultimate consequence of this is to magnify the difference between the most activated cognitive unit and other units on the same level of an analyzer. Eventually, one unit will be much more activated than other units. This unit will occupy attention—not because it was selected but because all of the competing cognitive units have been inhibited.

An equally plausible explanation would be that inputs from the arousal system do increase the activation of cognitive units themselves but in a multiplicative rather than in an additive way. This would, of course, serve to exacerbate the difference between the most activated cognitive unit and other less activated cognitive units. In turn, the most activated unit would now exert even more lateral inhibition over neighboring units and the difference in activation would be further amplified. In fact, although he used quite different terms, Hull (1943) made the "behavioral law" that arousal multiplies rather than adds to the activation of cognitive units the cornerstone of his entire theory of behavior. Later in this book, we shall consider some of the evidence for this behavioral law. The important point, however, is that—somehow or other—input from the arousal system allows one or perhaps two cognitive units to become dominant over other neighboring units.

If this line of reasoning is correct, then an arousal reaction should be most likely when several cognitive units are nearly equally activated. The reason is that this is the case where an exacerbation of differences in activation would be most necessary. In a mismatch between perception and expectation, one cognitive unit is activated because of expectations while an altogether different one is activated by perceptual inputs. In the case of voluntary attention, more effort (and, hence, more arousal) is necessary to the extent that it is difficult to discriminate the stimulus to be attended to from other stimuli. A necessary consequence of attentional hyperactivation will be that the cognitive units so activated will produce more vertical excitation. In other words, the stimuli that they represent will be subjected to deeper processing. A consequence of this deeper processing is likely to be the formation of new associative connections. Some of these may be connections to episodic memory. Things attended to tend to be remembered. Presumably, the reason that novelty and disruption of expectation elicit arousal and attention is so that deeper processing can occur—so the mind can see what went wrong and construct a better cortical model. Once the new model has been constructed, inputs exactly match existing cognitive units and attention is no longer necessary.

Arousal and the range of cue utilization

In an important article, Easterbrook (1959) reviewed several studies of incidental learning and came to the conclusion that increases in arousal cause decreases in what he called the range of cue utilization. His idea was essentially that the focus of attention is narrowed with increases in arousal. This is consistent with the idea that more arousal will cause more amplification of the already most activated cognitive unit and that this will result in more inhibition of other units. Easterbrook hypothesized that if there are a lot of irrelevant cues or stimuli in a situation, then an increase in arousal will improve performance because attention will be more focused and the irrelevant cues will not be attended to. On the other hand, if there are lots of relevant cues in the environment, then an increase in arousal will cause a decrement in performance. The reason is that, since attention will be more focused, some of the relevant cues will not be attended to.

An example of this effect comes from a study by Mendelsohn and Griswold (1967). Their subjects differed in level of anxiety or arousal. When they arrived for the experiment, they were taken to a waiting room. A seemingly irrelevant list of words was being played over a tape recorder in the next room. Later, the subjects were asked to solve some anagrams. The solutions to the anagrams had all been played on the tape recording. A control group of subjects did not hear the tape recording. As would be predicted from Easterbrook's theory, the low-arousal subjects benefited from the irrelevant stimuli whereas the high-arousal subjects did not. Presumably, the difference was due to differences in focus of attention.

A series of experiments by Callaway and his associates (Callaway, 1959; Callaway and Dembo, 1958; Callaway and Thompson, 1953) also support the idea that arousal tends to focus attention. Recall that size constancy seems to be due to the fact that we automatically estimate the distance of an object by attending to intervening stimuli. Any constriction of attention should decrease awareness of these distance cues and increase awareness of the retinal image. The result should be that the estimated size of the object should be more proportional to retinal size and less proportional to true size. Simply put, one should underestimate the size (since the size of the image on the retina will generally be smaller than true size). This was the effect obtained whether arousal was induced by the cold pressor test (this is a fancy name for a simple procedure: plunging the subject's foot in a bucket of ice water) or by stimulant drugs.

Another type of task which suggests that arousal focuses attention involves the use of a basic tracking task and a secondary task involving detection of peripheral stimuli. The subject's main task is to keep a pointer on top of a moving spot of light by means of moving a lever. The spot of light moves around on an oscilloscope screen in an unpredictable way. The secondary task is to detect faint flashes of light that also appear occasionally on the screen. Increasing arousal by offering a large reward (Bahrick, Fitts, and Rankin, 1952), by increasing ambient temperature (Bursill, 1958), or by playing loud noise (Hockey, 1970) facilitates performance on the basic task while making performance on the peripheral task worse. This is consistent with the idea that increases in arousal serve to focus attention. It is important to note that these effects are not visual but attentive; that is, arousal does not lessen sensitivity to stimuli in the periphery of the visual field. Rather, it lessens sensitivity to stimuli in the periphery of the attentional field regardless of whether these are in the periphery or in the center of the visual field.

Cortical scanning and attention

THE FUNCTION OF ALPHA WAVES

There is some reason to believe that inputs from the arousal system to cognitive units do not arrive continuously but rather in bursts or quanta. In a resting state, the human brain is characterized by alpha waves. These are regular, sinusoidal fluctuations in electrical potential with an average frequency of 10 cycles per second. The cortical scanning hypothesis of the alpha rhythm (Harter, 1967) is that this rhythm is due to a synchronized vertical sweeping of activation up and down the layers of the cortex at a rate of 10 times per second. The idea is that —just as a beam of electrons sweeps across a cathode ray tube—the arousal system sweeps the layers of cortical analyzers with a "beam" of activation. The purpose is presumably similar in both cases—enhancement and refreshment of activity. This idea fits well with the models of recognition and attention we have developed. Stimuli excite activity in certain cognitive units. This activity is enhanced by inputs from the arousal system. All cognitive units on a layer may receive the same amount of input from the arousal system on each sweep. However, this input multiplies with the activation already induced by stimulation so that the more activated a unit is, the more it benefits from the arousal input. Finally, the more activated a unit becomes, the more it inhibits neighboring units and, thus, the more it dominates attention. The hypothetical function of the alpha rhythm is, then, regularly (10 times per second) to provide the arousal input to all cognitive units so as to allow one of them to enter the focus of attention.

When an organism is actively attending to something, the EEG shows an arousal pattern. This means that alpha waves are replaced by beta waves. These waves are of higher frequency (14 to 30 cycles per second) than alpha waves. It is not unreasonable to suggest that at least part of the function of these waves is to provide a faster scan rate so that the focus of attention may be shifted more quickly. As explained earlier, the increased arousal indicated by the presence of such waves would serve to exacerbate small differences in the activation of cognitive units more quickly than the lower dosages of arousal indicated by alpha waves.

STROBOSCOPIC HALLUCINATIONS

Alpha waves can be entrained by a light flashing at a rate of about 10 flashes per second; that is, the alpha waves become exactly synchronized with the flashing light. *Stroboscopic hallucinations* can be induced when such flashes illuminate a uniform blank field into which the subject stares (Smythies, 1959). These hallucinations generally consist of fairly complex geometric figures, but they can also be images of natural scenes. It makes sense to speculate that the entrained alpha waves exacerbate the activity of cognitive units in visual analyzers to the extent that the patterns they code seize attention and are actually "seen." A given unit might be slightly more activated than other units for no other reason than random moment-to-moment fluctuations. Each successive scan amplifies its activation further and further. Since alpha waves do not occur exactly every 100 milliseconds under normal circumstances, this sort of recursive amplification of the same cognitive unit does not occur in the absence of stroboscopic stimulation.

RAPID ATTENTIONAL INTEGRATIONS

The psychological present. Blumenthal (1977) argues that the temporal length of a single attentional fixation is about 100 milliseconds. This would allow a maximum of 10 fixations per second. It could hardly be irrelevant that the hypothetical length of an attentional fixation is equal to the average period of the alpha rhythm. Hypothetically, each cortical scan by the arousal system results in a single attentional fixation much as a strobe light illuminating a moving object produces a series of frozen scenes of that object. The basic idea is that anything occurring within a 100-millisecond unit of time is perceived as happening at the same time: The psychological present comes in 100-millisecond chunks. Further, stimuli arriving within this time span are integrated with each other into one attentional gestalt; that is, they interact with each other by fusing together, masking each other, and so on. On the other hand, stimuli separated by more than 100 milliseconds are dealt with as discrete entities since they fall into separate attentional integrations.

Sensory interactions. Blumenthal (1977) cites several phenomena to support this contention. Stimuli in the same sensory modality that occur within 100 milliseconds tend to interact with each other. One stimulus can mask another if it occurs within 100 milliseconds, but if more than 100 milliseconds intervenes, masking is generally not found. At other times, stimuli separated by less than 100 milliseconds may fuse and be processed as one stimulus. Thus, two flashes separated by less than this amount of time may be perceived as only one flash. Generally two events tend to be perceived as simultaneous when they occur within 100 milliseconds of each other (Harter, 1967; White, 1963). Bloch's law (Bloch, 1885) states that for judgments of the brightness of light flashes lasting 100 milliseconds or less, time $\times$ intensity = constant. For example, a light flash lasting 30 milliseconds is perceived as being of the same brightness as a less intense flash lasting 60 milliseconds. Both are perceived as being of equal duration—about 100 milliseconds.

The law of prior entry. A different effect is found for stimuli in different sensory modalities. The astronomer Bessel (1823) was confronted with a vexing problem. In order to ascertain the exact time at which a star was in a given place, the following method was devised. The observer would glance at a clock, observe the time, and then count the beats of a metronome while watching for the star to cross a grid line. By counting the beats, the exact time of crossing would be determined. The problem was that the method did not work. Different observers reported different estimates of when the star crossed the grid line. The differences ranged from 70 milliseconds too early to 250 milliseconds too late in one experiment that Bessel devised.

The phenomenon was the subject of the first psychological experiment done by Wundt in 1862 (Blumenthal, 1977). Wundt's complication experiment involved having subjects watch a hand sweeping around a clock face. Their task was to report the position of the hand when they heard a tone. Wundt found that reports of where the hand was when the tone sounded ranged from 100 milliseconds too early to 100 milliseconds too late. The direction of error was dependent upon whether subjects were instructed to attend primarily to the tone or to the clock. When the tone was the focus of attention, it was experienced as occurring earlier than it had. When the clock was focused upon, the tone was experienced as occurring later than it had, in fact, occurred. These results, which have been replicated over and over during the last century, suggest that only one thing can be attended to at any one moment. Thus, if two stimuli in different sensory modalities arrive simultaneously, processing of one or the other—depending upon the direction of attention—is delayed for 100 milliseconds; that is, one of the stimuli is displaced into the subsequent attentional integration.

THE CAPACITY OF ATTENTION

Early in this chapter, Titchener's wave model of attention was mentioned. Attention can be likened to a wave in a stream. This wave can be characterized by its width (number of items in the focus of attention), height (intensity of attention), and length (temporal duration of an attentional fixation). The analogy also suggests some hydraulic questions. Does the stream have a constant volume? If so, then width, height, and length of the attention wave must interact with each other. Thus, for example, height could only be increased by decreasing width and/or length. This is consistent with the findings of some of the studies of the effects of arousal on attention. In the tracking studies described earlier, it would seem that the more attention is focused on the basic task, the less attention there is left over for the secondary task. The wave analogy also fits with Walley and Weiden's model of attention. In this model, attention has to do with the density and pattern of neural activity in a sensory, gnostic, or semantic analyzer. Here, attention is identified with a high degree of activation of cognitive units. Again, we can ask how many units can be so activated, how intensely activated they are, and for how long they can remain activated. We can also ask whether the total amount of activation in an analyzer is constant. If it is, then interactions would be expected like those suggested for Titchener's attention wave.

Kahneman's model

Kahneman (1973) argues that the total amount of capacity for mental work is limited. At any given time, several different cognitive units can be activated. Some of these cognitive units correspond to perceptions, ideas, and other mental contents. Others correspond to mental operations (for example, rehearsal, decision processes). In order to activate any one cognitive unit, some of the limited capacity will be required. Some cognitive units, such as those corresponding to perceptions, hypothetically require no capacity or very little. Other cognitive units, such as those corresponding to mental operations, require a good deal of capacity. Mental operations also vary in how much capacity they consume. The more difficult they are, the more capacity they consume.

Kahneman identifies capacity with cortical arousal. In order to perform any mental act, other than passive perception, two types of input to a cognitive unit are required: (1) information input from other cognitive units (for example, vertical excitatory input) and (2) input from the arousal system. Convergence of these two types of input leads to attention; that is, a cognitive unit is in focal attention when it receives enough of both types of input. Amount of arousal input corresponds to the intensity of attention. Subjectively, arousal corresponds to the sense of effort in the case of voluntary attention and to feelings, such as surprise, interest, fear, and so on, in the case of involuntary attention.

At any given moment, there is a fixed amount of arousal available. It is distributed among cognitive units according to an *allocation policy*. The relationships among arousal, allocation policy, and mental activities are illustrated in Figure 7–6. Four basic types of rules hypothetically govern the allocation of arousal.

FIGURE 7–6   Kahneman's (1973) capacity model of attention. The allocation policy determines how much arousal will be allotted to an activity. Various influences on allocation policy are indicated.

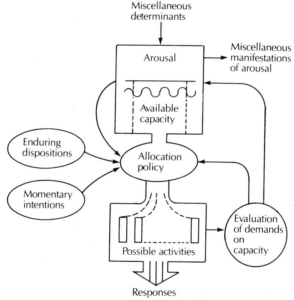

Source: Daniel Kahneman, *Attention and Effort,* © 1973, p. 10. Reprinted by permission of Prentice-Hall, Inc., Englewood Cliffs, N.J.

1. Enduring dispositions. There are the built-in policies governing involuntary attention. In general, capacity seems to be automatically allocated to a stimulus in accord with its collative, psychophysical, and ecological properties. Thus, for example, the more novel, intense, or meaningful a stimulus, the more capacity it is allocated.
2. Momentary intentions. These are the temporary policies governing voluntary attention. An example would be the intention to direct attention to the left-ear message in a shadowing experiment.
3. Evaluation of demands. In general, we allocate to a task only as much capacity as it requires, even if that leaves some capacity unconsumed. On the other hand, if total task demands exceed total capacity, more arousal can be

created. Within certain limits, we can increase our arousal or force ourselves to exert more effort.

4. Effects of arousal. The amount of available capacity or arousal also influences allocation policy. For example, if arousal cannot be increased any more, this will have to be taken into account. Kahneman suggests that, if task demands completely and clearly exceed capacity, a person tends to do one or another task and to omit other tasks altogether.

Level of arousal fluctuates from moment to moment. As Kahneman's third rule suggests, the need or demand for arousal can even, within limits, create the supply. Given these considerations, it is clear that the attention wave does not have one fixed and unchanging volume or capacity. The reason is that this volume corresponds to arousal and amount of arousal is not constant. In spite of this, it still makes some sense to ask some questions about the allocation of the volume of attention.

What operations require attention?

PERCEPTION IS EFFORTLESS AND PREATTENTIVE

Hypothetically, simple perception or recognition requires no effort, capacity, or arousal; that is, no inputs from the arousal system are necessary for us to see or hear. Only activation via inputs from other cognitive units is necessary. We are aware of such passive perception, but such activity quickly fades, leaving no memory of its occurrence. Late-selection models of attention argue that all inputs are processed rather deeply. Exactly how deeply is not clear. However, at some rather indeterminate point, processing presumably ceases unless inputs from the arousal system are present. When such inputs are present, deeper processing ensues. The units benefiting from such inputs are in consciousness or short-term memory. The most activated unit is in the focus of attention.

In previous chapters, we presented some evidence for the effortless quality of perception. Let's review some of it briefly. Reicher (1969) used a tachistoscope to show his subjects a single letter or a four-letter word. Then, two letters were exposed, and the subject's task was to say which of these had just occurred. Performance was better following the four-letter word than the single letter. If recognition of each letter had required attentional capacity, this would not be possible. Shiffrin and Gardner (1972) carried out a similar study. Four characters were presented, and subjects had to say whether the letter *T* or the letter *F* had been shown. (One or the other was always shown.) There were two different experimental conditions. In the sequential condition, each of the four characters was shown successively, and in the simultaneous condition, all were shown at once. The length of time any one character was exposed was the same in both conditions. The surprising result was that performance in both conditions was about the same. This suggests that no more capacity is required to recognize four things at once than to recognize one.

EVIDENCE FROM DIVIDED ATTENTION TASKS

A different approach to the question of capacity was taken by Posner and Boies (1971). Their experiment involved having subjects perform two tasks at once. The primary task involved letter matching. Two letters were shown, one after the other, and subjects had to say whether they were the same or different. While this task is very simple, it does involve several cognitive operations, as indicated by the following list:

Task	Cognitive operation
1. Wait	None
2. Warning signal	Alerting
3. First letter presented	Retrieval from long-term memory
4. Delay	Rehearsal of first letter
5. Second letter presented	Retrieval from long-term memory
	Matching of memory traces
	Selection of response
	Motor response (saying "same" or "different")

Each of the cognitive operations might require some of limited capacity. The problem is to find out how much each one takes. Posner and Boies did this by an indirect means. At various points throughout the task, a noise was presented. Subjects were instructed to press a key as quickly as possible whenever they heard this noise. The reaction time for each key press was recorded. Posner and Boies reasoned that the more attention or capacity was taken up by the letter-matching task, the less would be left over for the noise-detection task. The less attention devoted to noise detection, the longer the reaction time should be for the key presses. Of course, this line of reasoning only holds so long as subjects devoted all necessary attention to the letter-matching task. This is what they were instructed to do, and evidence was presented that the noises did not disrupt performance on this primary task.

Very clear differences in reaction times to the tones were found at different points in the Posner and Boies experiment. These are graphed in Figure 7–7. As

FIGURE 7–7   Reaction times for detection of probes in letter-matching experiment

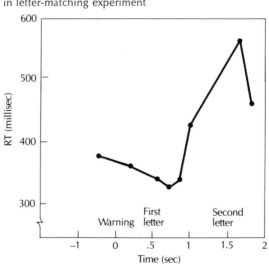

Source: M. I. Posner and S. J. Boies, "Components of Attention," *Psychological Review* 78 (1971):403. Copyright 1971 by the American Psychological Association. Reprinted by permission.

can be seen in the figure, reaction time improved following the warning signal. Apparently, the alertness brought about by the warning signal, although it involved waiting for the first letter, also improved detection of the tone. The crucial finding was that reaction time to the tone did not increase in the 300-millisecond period following presentation of the first letter. Other studies make clear that, during this time, perception or encoding of the letter would be taking place. The implication is that this encoding is effortless, that it requires no attention. About 500 milliseconds after onset of the first letter, reaction time began to increase. Presumably the letter had now been encoded and rehearsal had begun. Rehearsal —in contrast to encoding or recognition—does require attention. Thus, reaction time to the tone was lengthened and continued to increase after presentation of the second letter. Hypothetically, even more attention was now being consumed by the decision-making process and selection of the correct response.

Ability for divided attention

Note that Posner and Boies' results demonstrate that people can attend to more than one thing at a time and can perform both the letter-comparison task and the noise-detection task at the same time. Although when the first task demands more attention, the second one gets a bit less attention. It certainly seems reasonable to me that people can attend to more than one thing at a time. Unless we could attend to at least two things at once, it is difficult to see how we could perform such simple operations as comparison and discrimination. How would we be able to say if two things (for example, the two letters in the letter-comparison task) were similar or dissimilar if we could only attend to one of them at a time?

Walley and Weiden (1973) point out that, if their lateral inhibition model of attention is correct, then attention should be able to be sustained in several analyzers simultaneously. The reason is that cognitive units only laterally inhibit other units in the same analyzer. Consider what happens when you are talking with someone. It does not seem unreasonable to say that you can simultaneously attend to the person's facial expression, the person's tone of voice, and the meaning of whatever the person is saying. Presumably, these three acts of attention involve three spatially separated analyzers. Perhaps an even better example would be what happens when you watch a television program. In general, one certainly does not have the impression of having to switch attention back and forth between what one is hearing and what one is seeing. This seems to be the case even when both channels are filled with novel or meaningful material which would be expected to seize attention.

SUMMARY AND CONCLUSIONS

We began this chapter with a brief description of the introspectionists' metaphors of the stream of consciousness and the wave of attention, but we saw that these metaphors are not really alien from the model we have developed. We defined consciousness as the set of currently activated cognitive units and attention as the subset of these units that are most strongly activated. In any given analyzer, consciousness would generally contain only four or five units and attention no more than one or two. Thus, attention is extremely selective. This selectivity can be either voluntary or involuntary.

Voluntary attention has been studied primarily by means of shadowing tasks wherein subjects are asked to repeat one message and ignore another one. We saw that this is fairly easy to do, especially if the messages differ in sensory quality. This fact led Broadbent to propose a filter model of attention in which attentional selection was held only to occur in sensory analyzers. However, the clear finding that unattended messages activate units in semantic memory led Norman and others to propose that attentional selection only occurs in the semantic analyzer. We argued that this was a bit of an overreaction and settled on Treisman's attenuation model—which says that attentional selection can occur in any analyzer—as the one most able to account for the findings of shadowing studies.

Involuntary attention is determined by what Berlyne called the psychophysical (for example, intensity), ecological (for example, meaningfulness), and collative (for example, novelty) properties of stimuli. It seems to be invariably accompanied by arousal. The original theory of the arousal system was similar to Broadbent's filter theory, and it was rejected for similar reasons. Sokolov's theory of attention is compatible with our model of cognition in that he holds that all incoming stimuli are compared with or analyzed by preexisting cortical models. However, Sokolov adds an important match-mismatch rule. If stimuli match existing models, nothing other than passive perception results. If a mismatch occurs, the arousal system is disinhibited, it arouses the cortex, orientation and attention result, and a new cortical model is constructed.

Walley and Weiden argue that cognitive units select themselves for attention by laterally inhibiting surrounding units. Cognitive units are aided in this by nonspecific inputs from the arousal system. While Walley and Weiden hold that these inputs exacerbate lateral inhibition directly, we argued that they may do so indirectly by multiplying with rather than adding to the activation of cognitive units. Regardless of exactly how the arousal system affects cognitive units, several studies suggest that arousal does narrow the focus of attention. Some evidence indicates that inputs from the arousal system to cognitive units arrive periodically rather than continuously. This evidence is consistent with the seeming tendency of the psychological present to come in 100-millisecond chunks.

Kahneman's capacity model of attention involves the contention that there is a fairly fixed amount of arousal that must be drawn upon in order to perform psychological work. Some activities, such as perception, appear to require little or no arousal. Others, such as rehearsal and decision making, require a good bit of arousal. So long as the pool of available arousal is not exhausted, it appears that attention can be divided among more than one task. We speculated that this should be especially true when tasks are carried out by different analyzers.

8

Semantic memory

THE SUBJECTIVE LEXICON

By now, we have some idea of how things are recognized, remembered, and attended to. Once something is recognized, there is still the question of how it is understood or of how we know what it means. For example, if I show you a foreign word, you can certainly see it. You can pronounce it—or at least attempt to do so. On the other hand, consider what happens when you see the English word MALLARD. You can recognize and pronounce this word, too, but there is something more to your experience. This something more is that you understand the meaning of the word. You know what a MALLARD is. You could give a description of a mallard. You could answer such questions as the following: Is a mallard a duck? Does a mallard have eyes? Can a mallard write? (The answers are "yes," "we hope so," and "of course not.") The study of semantic memory is concerned with how all of the knowledge that allows you to answer such questions is stored or represented.

All of us carry in our minds a vast mental dictionary or subjective lexicon. The meanings of all of the concepts that we know are stored in this subjective lexicon. In earlier chapters we have called this mental dictionary the *semantic analyzer*. Let's refer to the cognitive units on the highest level of the semantic analyzer as *semantic units*. A semantic unit is a purely conceptual unit. Its activation does not correspond to experiencing the sound of a word. That is what happens when we activate a morpheme unit. The activation of a semantic unit corresponds to experiencing at least some aspect of the meaning of a concept. Presumably, semantic units are connected to morpheme units, but they are also connected to image units and to printed-word units. These connections need not be thought of as simple, one-to-one affairs. There are concepts that cannot be expressed or realized by a single word or single image, for example, the concept realized as THE MIDDLE AGES.

Just saying that there are semantic units does not explain how we know the meaning of things. To do this, we have to consider how the semantic units are connected to or defined by other cognitive units. Just as the words in a dictionary are all defined in terms of one another, so semantic units are in large part defined by other units in semantic memory. There is some circularity in both cases. Did you ever try looking up a word in a dictionary, looking up all of the words in the definition, looking up all of the words in the definitions of the definitions, and so on? Eventually, you may end up right back where you started. Somehow this sort of fairly closed system (where any one element is defined in terms of other elements) works. Whether the system is a subjective lexicon or a real dictionary, it works in the sense of allowing us to answer questions about meanings and in giving us a subjective sense of understanding. Psychologists have made some headway in discovering how the subjective lexicon must be arranged in order to allow us to store knowledge and to answer questions about meanings. We simply do not know much about why accessing this knowledge is often accompanied by a subjective sense of understanding.

SEMANTIC FEATURE THEORY

One of the first theories of semantic memory was proposed by Katz and Fodor (1963). Their basic idea was that concepts are defined by what they call semantic features. Just as a phoneme is a bundle of distinctive features, so perhaps the meaning of a concept is a bundle of semantic features. Thus, the concept MAN would be defined by the semantic features /animate/, /human/, /adult/, /male/. On the other hand, the concept WOMAN would be defined by the semantic features /animate/, /human/, /adult/, /female/. As you can see, the two differ by one distinctive semantic feature. Katz and Fodor were not explicitly thinking in terms of cognitive units arranged in a hierarchy. If they had been, though, it is fair to say that most people have construed their theory in terms of a two-level system with the semantic units on one level and the semantic features on another. This two-level idea does not work very well; the whole point of distinctive features is that there are supposed to be fewer of them than of things at the next higher level. A moment's thought, though, suggests that there would have to be a great many semantic features. We already used five of them in defining MAN and WOMAN. We still have to define TRUCKS, MOUNTAINS, CIVIL WARS, and thousands of other concepts. In a two-level system, it is not at all clear that there would be fewer semantic features than semantic units.

THE SEMANTIC ANALYZER

Perhaps we would make better progress if we thought in terms of a system with four or five levels rather than just two. This would make the structure of the semantic analyzer similar to that of the other analyzers. At the highest level of the semantic analyzer would be the semantic units we have just postulated. They would receive inputs from the morpheme units at the highest level of the speech analyzer as well as from units at the highest levels of the other gnostic analyzers. A diagram of the hypothetical structure of the semantic analyzer is given in Figure 8–1. The basic idea is that semantic units are connected to and defined by superordinate units. These are, in turn, connected to and defined by meta-

FIGURE 8–1   The semantic analyzer, with examples of units on each level

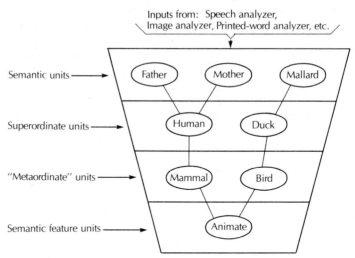

ordinate units. Finally, the latter would be connected to semantic feature units. There would be a fairly small number of semantic feature units, just as there is a fairly small number of distinctive feature units in the speech analyzer or the printed-word analyzer. Ultimately, the semantic features would define many semantic units or concepts. We do not know the identity of these semantic features, but it makes sense to postulate their existence.

The vertical connections in the semantic analyzer may be seen as defining cognitive units on any one level by units on the next lower level. If we are to follow the model we have been developing, we might expect that units on any one level should relate to one another primarily in a lateral inhibitory fashion. Such lateral inhibitory bonds would certainly be of use in coding what a semantic unit *does not* mean. Thus, the lattice structure of the semantic analyzer would provide a way of coding what a concept is (for example, a MOTHER is a HUMAN is a MAMMAL) and what it is not (for example, a MOTHER is not a FATHER or a DAUGHTER). However, this only provides us with a bare skeleton for defining the meanings of things. We certainly know more about a concept than can be provided by knowledge about what it is and what it is not.

NETWORK MODELS OF SEMANTIC MEMORY

The hierarchical nature of semantic memory

Hierarchical network models of semantic memory allow us to flesh out our skeletal theory. The most influential of these models was proposed by Collins and Quillian (1969). In their theory, semantic memory is seen as being composed of a hierarchy of cognitive units and relations among these units. The units code or represent concepts. The relations among these units are of different types. This means that they are *labeled*. One type of labeled relation codes superordinate relationships. Following Rumelhart, Lindsay, and Norman (1972), we shall call these *isa* relations (for *is a*, as in "a CANARY is a BIRD"). The *isa* connections are what we have been calling vertical excitatory relations. Other types of relations code attributes. Such relations are labeled as *has, can, is,* and so on. An example of a hypothetical portion of semantic memory is shown in Figure 8–2.

FIGURE 8–2   Hypothetical portion of semantic memory

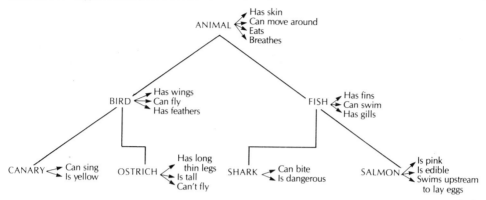

Source: A. M. Collins and M. R. Quillian, "Retrieval Time from Semantic Memory," *Journal of Verbal Learning and Verbal Behavior* 8 (1969):241.

Collins and Quillian (1972) note that semantic memory seems to be rather shallow. That is, the *isa* or superordinate chains tend to be only three or four steps long. At the very most, they are only five or six steps as in the example, MALLARD isa DUCK isa BIRD isa ANIMAL isa LIVING THING isa OBJECT. Thus, semantic memory will fit quite nicely into the four- or five-layer structure that we have available for it in our model. It should be noted that Collins and Quillian do not claim that semantic memory is rigidly hierarchical or rigidly logical. In fact, all sorts of short-cut paths can and probably do exist. In the semantic memory of a given person, there may well be a direct *isa* relation between DUCK and ANIMAL as well as or even instead of the more taxonomically correct indirect connections, DUCK isa BIRD isa ANIMAL.

Type nodes versus token nodes

The idea that the connections among cognitive units can be labeled raises several questions. The obvious question concerns how many different types of labeled relations there are. The unfortunate answer is that there would seem to be many possibilities. Virtually any verb could potentially serve as a label. For example, it is not only true that a BIRD can FLY but also that a BIRD eats WORMS, a BIRD lays EGGS, and so on. Thus, we have the problem of coding the meaning of the labeled relations. The way around this problem is to postulate that relations are not really labeled as shown in Figure 3–3A. Rather, semantic units are connected via chunking nodes as illustrated in Figure 8–3B (Wickelgren, 1979b). Connection of more than one pair of cognitive units via the same chunking node— as shown in Figure 8–3C—could potentially cause problems. The arrangement shown in Figure 8–3C does not allow us to keep straight what eats what. It would lead us to believe that cats eat worms as well as birds. In order to get around

FIGURE 8–3   Hypothetically relations in semantic memory are not really labeled as shown in A. Rather, semantic units are indirectly connected via chunking units as shown in B. In order to avoid the sort of confusion illustrated in C, it is necessary to postulate the existence of type and token nodes as shown in D.

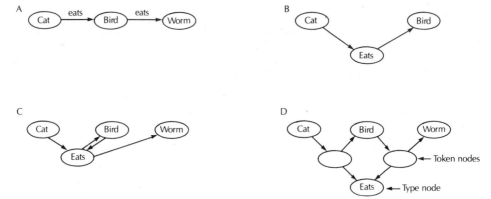

this problem, it is necessary to differentiate between *type nodes* and *token nodes,* as shown in Figure 8–3D. A type node is a semantic unit which defines a concept, while a token node is defined by its connection to the type node. Use of token nodes allows the same concept to be used in defining many other concepts without leading to confusion. As we shall see in the next chapter, cognitive units can be interconnected to form much more complex propositions than those illustrated in Figure 8–3. Thus, although we speak of labeled relations in this chapter, keep in mind that this is a simplified and metaphorical usage. Labeled relations are better thought of as indirect associations via token nodes.

Stored versus inferred knowledge

One very interesting attribute of the semantic memory system postulated by Collins and Quillian (1969) is its cognitive economy. Consider the question of whether a canary has wings. Well, of course, it does, but how do you know that? Have you stored the knowledge directly via the linkage CANARY has WINGS? If so, this is not terribly efficient, since you would have to have such a link between the cognitive unit coding every bird and the cognitive units for WINGS. Or consider whether a canary has weight. Again, it clearly does. But, then, every object that exists has weight. Would it not make more sense to store this fact only once— with the concept of OBJECT—rather than to store it for each of the thousands of objects that exist? That is what Collins and Quillian argue actually is the case. You do not *know* that a canary has wings. Rather, you *know* that A CANARY isa BIRD and that A BIRD has WINGS. From this information, you *infer* that A CANARY HAS WINGS. The same line of reasoning applies as well to superset relations. You do not *know* that a canary is an animal. Rather you have the stored information CANARY isa BIRD and BIRD isa ANIMAL. Thus, when I ask you if a canary is an animal, you can reply that it certainly is, even though that knowledge may not be represented in your semantic memory by a direct link between the two concepts.

There is a clear consequence of this model. If you have to infer some pieces of knowledge (for example, A CANARY HAS WINGS) while some other bits of knowledge are stored directly (for example, A CANARY IS YELLOW), then the inferred knowledge should take longer to retrieve. Certainly, the inference process could not be instantaneous. It may be very fast, but it is not reasonable to assume that it is so fast that careful measurements would not reveal it. What Collins and Quillian argue, then, is that questions where the relevant knowledge would have to be stored directly (for example, A CANARY IS YELLOW) should be answered more quickly than questions that have to be answered after some inference (for example, A CANARY HAS WINGS). Further, the longer the inferential chain, the longer it should take to answer the question. Thus, it should take longer to answer true to the statement, A CANARY HAS BLOOD, than to the statement A CANARY HAS WINGS. To respond to the first question you have to traverse the links, CANARY isa BIRD and BIRD has WINGS. But to answer the second question, you have to traverse more links: CANARY isa BIRD, BIRD isa ANIMAL, and ANIMAL has BLOOD.

In a classic experiment, Collins and Quillian (1969) found evidence for these predictions. Subjects were shown many statements like the types we have been discussing. They had to respond "true" or "false" as soon as possible to each statement. The results are shown in Figure 8–4. As you can see, the length of time to respond correctly to statements was as predicted by Collins and Quillian. When the relevant information was hypothetically directly accessible from a semantic unit (level 0 sentences), reaction time was quickest. When one intervening cognitive unit had to be traversed to find the information (level 1 sentences), reaction time was longer. It was longer still for level 2 sentences, where two

FIGURE 8–4   Mean reaction times for correct responses to questions of various types

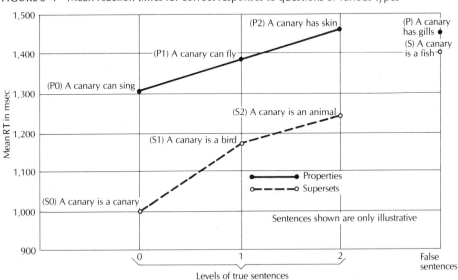

Source: A. M. Collins and M. R. Quillian, "Retrieval Time from Semantic Memory," *Journal of Verbal Learning and Verbal Behavior* 8 (1969):244.

intervening cognitive units had to be traversed. Questions involving properties always took longer to answer than questions involving superset relationships. It is possible to speculate that this is because knowledge about superset relations may be represented by direct vertical linkages while knowledge about attributes is always represented by indirect linkages via chunking units.

I should reiterate that Collins and Quillian do not claim that their model is completely general. For one thing, they do not claim that redundant or unnecessary knowledge is erased if it happens to be learned. It is certainly possible that you might at some time have directly learned that a canary has blood. If this knowledge is stored in a direct CANARY has BLOOD link, then you would be able to verify the statement, A CANARY HAS BLOOD just as quickly as a statement such as A CANARY IS YELLOW. Another claim that Collins and Quillian do *not* make is that semantic memory is rigidly hierarchical. Just because you classify a canary as a bird does not prevent you from cross-classifying it as a pet. Furthermore, while semantic memory is hierarchically arranged, the hierarchy represents the person's own conception of the world rather than being a perfectly logical one. For example, it actually takes longer for most people to confirm that A DOG IS A MAMMAL than to confirm that A DOG IS AN ANIMAL (Rips, Shoben, and Smith, 1973). For most people, ANIMAL rather than MAMMAL is the relevant superordinate. This merely shows that most people organize their knowledge in a way that does not conform to standard biological taxonomy or that there are shortcut direct paths from some concepts to higher-order superordinates. It must be the case that there are individual differences in the structure of semantic memory. If so, we could use reaction times to various types of questions to get some idea of what they are.

Spreading activation

In their revision of the original Collins and Quillian theory, Collins and Loftus (1975) put forth a spreading activation theory of semantic memory. The original Collins and Quillian model was based on attempts to provide computers with semantic knowledge. If one wants to program a computer to understand language, the computer has to be given the same sort of semantic knowledge that real people have. This is what Quillian (1962, 1967) was originally interested in doing. It occurred to Collins and Quillian (1969) that perhaps people might store semantic knowledge in the same way that Quillian had programmed his computer to store it. Then, Collins and Loftus (1975) attempted to further transform the theory "from computer terms to quasi-neurological terms a la Pavlov." In their model, processing a concept is seen as involving activation of the cognitive unit representing that concept. Activation spreads from the cognitive unit along relational paths in a decreasing gradient so long as the unit remains activated. It is further assumed that activation of a cognitive unit decays gradually with the passage of time, that activation impinging upon a cognitive unit from various directions summates, and that units have thresholds that must be exceeded for full activation to occur. The more similar two concepts, the more relations that presumably join the cognitive units encoding them. As in the model we have developed, the names of concepts are hypothetically stored in a separate lexical network organized according to phonetic, as opposed to semantic, similarity. Collins and Loftus' basic idea is that when a cognitive unit in semantic memory is activated, this activation spreads along all of the paths or relations connecting this unit with other units. They do not consider the possibility of any lateral inhibition in the system. We will discuss this later. Subjectively, the spread of activation corresponds to understanding the meaning of a concept. Objectively, the spreading activation explains performance in question-answering experiments. When a statement such as A CANARY HAS WINGS is presented to a person, activation hypothetically spreads from the activated units—CANARY and WINGS —in all directions. In the case of a true sentence, this activation will converge or summate. The activation from CANARY will reach WINGS and vice versa. When the activation passes some threshold value, the person will respond that the statement is true. The further apart the two nodes, the longer this will take. In the case of a false sentence, such as A CANARY HAS WHEELS, no convergence will occur. Hypothetically, if activation has not passed some threshold value after a given amount of time, the person will respond that the statement is false. This is consistent with the fact that false sentences almost always take longer to respond to than true sentences. We shall consider how false sentences are answered in more detail later in this chapter.

If activation spreads in semantic memory, then various sorts of priming effects should be observed. Activating a superordinate unit—for example, BIRD— should automatically activate subordinate units, such as CANARY, CHICKEN, and so on. Thus, if we asked about a canary on a given trial, people should be able to answer the question more quickly if they had answered a question about a bird on a prior trial than if they had not. The reverse should also be the case; that is, activation of any subordinate should automatically activate the relevant superordinate. In general, this tends to be the case. Rosch (1975) has done several experiments that provide clear evidence for this sort of "vertical" facilitation. However, a little later we shall discuss some other experiments conducted by Rosch (1975) that show some very interesting exceptions to this generalization.

Another implication of the Collins and Loftus spreading activation model is that semantic memory searches use parallel processing; that is, activation spreads out simultaneously in all directions from an activated node. The model is explicit in holding that semantic memory is not searched in a serial or item-by-item manner. An experiment by Freedman and Loftus (1971) provides some evidence for this contention. Their method was to ask subjects to produce an instance of a category beginning with a given letter of the alphabet. If semantic memory searches were performed serially, this task should take longer the larger the category to be searched. For example to name a season of the year beginning with S, one only would have to scan through four seasons. On the other hand, to name a month of the year beginning with S, one would have to scan through 12 months. However, Freedman and Loftus found that category size had no effect. It took subjects no longer to produce a correct instance from a large category than from a small category. This finding constitutes evidence that searches of semantic memory are carried out in a parallel rather than a serial manner.

False statements

Is a duck a toasted cheese sandwich? Is it a dog? Is it a goose? How do you know? It hardly seems reasonable to think that you know that a duck is not a toasted cheese sandwich by reference to directly stored knowledge; that is, it does not seem likely that there is a *not* relation between the semantic units coding DUCK and TOASTED CHEESE SANDWICH. We would have to have a *not* relationship between DUCK and virtually every other entry in semantic memory. There are very few things that a duck *is* or *has,* but there are thousands of things that a duck *is not* and *does not have.* The same would be true for all of the other entries in semantic memory. It hardly seems reasonable or even remotely likely that every semantic unit would be connected with virtually every other semantic unit by *not* relationships. Some sort of inference process must be used to disconfirm false sentences. But what sort of inference process?

CONTRADICTIONS

Glass and Holyoak (1975) have considered this question in some detail. Their basic idea is that false statements involve contradictions. We can respond false as soon as we find such a contradiction. Consider the statement ALL DUCKS ARE GEESE. Presumably, both DUCK and GOOSE are connected by *isa* relations to the superordinate node BIRD. According to the Glass and Holyoak theory, two nodes connected by the same relation to the same superordinate node are different things. Thus, Duck isa BIRD and GOOSE isa BIRD implies that DUCK and GOOSE are *not* equivalent. (This is diagrammed in Figure 8–5). Hence the statement is contradictory, and we can assert that it is false. Now consider the statement, ALL DUCKS ARE DOGS. This is not true, but the contradiction occurs at a deeper level. DUCK isa BIRD does not contradict DOG isa MAMMAL, but BIRD isa ANIMAL contradicts MAMMAL isa ANIMAL (see Figure 8–5). Since the contradiction is deeper, it should take longer for spreading activation to converge on the contradictory link. Glass and Holyoak (1975) found just this sort of thing— not just for the sentences we used as examples, but for the two types of sentence in general.

FIGURE 8–5   Illustration of Glass and Holyoak's contradiction theory for determining the falsehood of statements

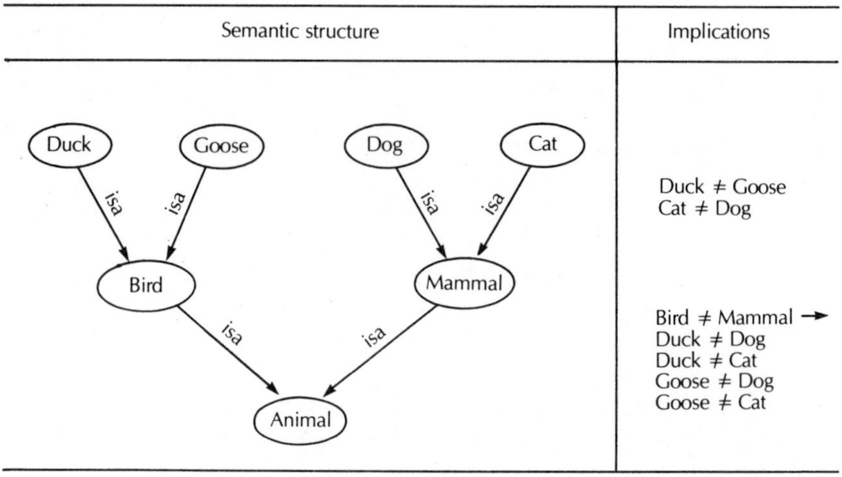

RESPONDING TO RIDICULOUS ASSERTIONS

What about ridiculous false sentences, such as A DUCK IS A TRICYCLE? Does it take even longer to disconfirm these? No. Actually such sentences are disconfirmed even more quickly than highly contradictory statements, such as A DUCK IS A GOOSE (Glass, Holyoak, and O'Dell, 1974). Perhaps the strategy is this: We wait a decent—but very short—interval for activation to spread. If there is no convergence or summation at all, then we respond "false." Thus, we can reject ridiculous assertions very quickly. On the other hand, if there is some convergence or summation of activation, then an evaluation must take place to determine if the summation is contradictory. Because of this need for evaluation, more overtly contradictory statements take longer to evaluate than do ridiculous statements.

SALIENT COUNTEREXAMPLES

Glass and Holyoak (1975) also discuss some other rules for discovering falsehood. Consider the statement, ALL BIRDS ARE CHICKENS. This can be disconfirmed by finding a *salient counterexample*—for example, our friend the duck. Activating the BIRD unit leads to a spread of activation to units connected with it. One of these would certainly be the DUCK unit. In the preceding paragraphs, we have established that a duck is not a goose. It is my hope that you can pursue the same line of reasoning to establish that a duck is not a chicken either. Well, if a duck *is* a bird and it *is not* a chicken, then it cannot very well be the case that *all* birds are chickens. The idea is not that such ratiocination actually occurs. Rather, a salient counterexample leaps into the focus of attention—because the unit coding the superordinate activates the unit coding the counterexample—and one automatically responds that the statement is false.

Using various sorts of sentences, Holyoak and Glass (1975) found evidence for the hypothesis that the longer it is likely to take to find a salient counterexample, the longer it will take to disconfirm a false statement. For example, it should take less time to disconfirm the statement, ALL GENERALS ARE SIAMESE CATS, than to disconfirm the statement, ALL GENERALS ARE AMERICANS. When I think of generals, I think first of General Patton. Some other generals who come to mind are Eisenhower and MacArthur. When the GENERAL node in my subjective lexicon is activated, activation automatically spreads to the nodes coding these individuals. As soon as I have thought of General Patton, I can disconfirm the first statement since General Patton was not a Siamese cat. But, so far, nothing has come to mind that will allow me to disconfirm the second statement. That takes a tiny bit more time, but by the time that instant has passed, I have thought of Rommel, Napoleon, and a host of others. As soon as the semantic unit coding one of these non-American generals has been activated, I can disconfirm the second sentence. The point is that the first example that crossed my mind allowed me to disconfirm the first statement, but more time was required for a counterexample to occur for the second statement. Of course, there are other ways to explain these results, but the Glass and Holyoak (1975) theory probably provides the most parsimonious explanation.

THE STRENGTH OF RELATIONS IN SEMANTIC MEMORY
Production of category instances

Let's think a little more about generals. Why, when I think of generals, do I think of some before others? When the GENERAL node in my brain gets activated, is this activation not supposed to flow outward at an equal speed along all possible channels? Surely it should activate all of the specific nodes categorized under it at about the same time. If so, why do some generals become available to consciousness before others? One possible answer would be that the bonds between the superordinate node, GENERAL, and the subordinate units are not all of equal strength. Perhaps more of the activation gets through along the stronger bonds. Thus, I think of Patton and Eisenhower at once. Only after continued activation of the superordinate unit does enough activation spread to the nodes coding Rommel or Napoleon to make them available to consciousness. Think of the superordinate node as a large reservoir and each of the subordinate nodes as smaller ones. Imagine that ditches of varying capacity connect the large reservoir with each of the smaller ones. Some of these ditches are wide and deep while others are shallow and narrow. Clearly, the reservoirs connected by wide and deep channels will be filled first. Of course, things are not likely to be quite so neatly arranged in semantic memory. The category, AMERICAN GENERALS may be cross-classified under several categories, such as GENERALS-IN-GENERAL, AMERICAN OFFICERS, and so on. For this reason, it is a good idea to study categories where there is likely to be fairly wide agreement that items belong only to this single category.

On a piece of blank paper, list the names of all of the different pieces of furniture that you can think of. Sixty or so will be sufficient for the purposes of my demonstration.

Whether you were able to think of 60 pieces of furniture or not, I can make a few predictions about what you wrote on the paper. Fairly early, you probably thought of such items as CHAIR, COUCH, TABLE, and EASY CHAIR. These items came to mind easily. If you compare your list with those of others in your class, you will probably find that almost everyone else thought of these items also. After awhile, I expect that you started to "scrape the bottom of the barrel." By that time, you would be down to items such as LAMP, and HASSOCK. You probably tried priming yourself by trying to think of specific types of furniture, such as living-room or bedroom furniture. You may have tried forming images of various rooms and scanning them for likely candidates. In the end, if you persisted, you may have gotten to some rather questionable pieces of furniture. You may have been saying to yourself things such as "technically speaking, a rug is furniture," or "in the broad sense of the term, an ashtray is a piece of furniture," or "loosely speaking, a telephone could be furniture."

Typicality

When people are asked to list items that belong to a category, some items are produced by almost everyone, others by many people, and some by just a handful of people. In other words, items differ in the probability that the category name will elicit them (Battig and Montague, 1969). Rosch (1975) asked subjects to rate items drawn from various categories on 7-point scales as to the degree that the item represented their idea of the category. This kind of rating is called a *typicality rating*. For 60 items from the furniture category, CHAIR and SOFA were tied for first place as being of highest typicality. Both got average ratings of 1.04. Of the items Rosch used, TELEPHONE got the lowest mean typicality rating—6.68. The typicality ratings in Rosch's experiment were very highly correlated with the probability that an item was produced as an instance of the category by Battig and Montague's subjects.

What happens if we ask people to respond as to the truth or falsity of statements such as A CHAIR IS FURNITURE or A TABLE IS FURNITURE? It turns out that the higher the typicality of the subordinate, the more quickly the question can be answered (Rips, Shoben, and Smith, 1973; Rosch, 1973b). This is a very strong and well-replicated finding. The easiest way to account for it would be to postulate that the bonds between a superordinate category and its subordinate instances vary in strength. The higher the typicality of a subordinate, the stronger the bond between it and the superordinate category unit. Thus, according to spreading activation theory, more activation spreads along these stronger bonds. This accounts for why we think of some—more typical—instances before others. It also accounts for why we can verify that these more typical instances are indeed category members more quickly.

Differences in the strength of relations in semantic memory may actually have accounted for some of Collins and Quillian's (1969) original findings. Recall their cognitive economy hypothesis: the cognitive units coding BIRD and FEATHERS are hypothetically directly connected, whereas BIRD and EAT are hypothetically bonded only indirectly via the connections, BIRD isa ANIMAL and ANIMAL can EAT. Hence, people should and do respond more quickly to the statement, A BIRD HAS FEATHERS, than to the statement A BIRD CAN EAT. An alternative view would be that BIRD is bonded directly to both FEATHERS and EAT but the BIRD has FEATHERS bond is stronger than the BIRD can EAT bond. Experiments by both Conrad (1972) and Smith, Shoben, and Rips (1974) suggest that it may be the strength of the bond rather than the number of links in the hierarchy that is the crucial factor. Collins and Loftus (1975) disagree with this contention but agree that bonds certainly must differ in their strength.

Similarity judgments

One question of interest has been whether typicality of category instances reflects something structural or is due merely to frequency of pairing of the instance with the category. Typicality could be seen as referring to the similarity between a prototype representing a category and an instance of that category. The question is whether typicality has to do with the formal resemblance of an instance with the prototype represented by the category or if it is just due to learning because of contiguity. Rosch, Simpson, and Miller (1976) got the same sorts of effects with artificial categories and instances as Rosch (1975) had gotten with natural-language categories and instances. Rosch et al. taught their subjects artificial categories. Some instances of these categories were shown a lot of times, and others, just a few times. The instances also varied in typicality—the degree to which they resembled the prototype representing the category. Reaction times for judgments that an instance was a category member were a function of typicality. They were unrelated to how often the instance and the prototype had been shown in contiguity. This suggests that mere frequency of co-occurrence is not the crucial variable. Further, in a large sample of American English, Rosch (1975) found that category names are actually more likely to occur in the same sentence with instances of *low* typicality. Again, this argues against frequency of co-occurrence as the basis for typicality. The conclusion would seem to be that typicality is not due to frequency of co-occurrence. Rather, it reflects degree of resemblance to the ideal prototype that the category unit stands for. Thus, the strength of bonds between semantic units coding subordinate instances and superordinate units coding categories is hypothetically not determined by learning per se. Rather, it is determined by how similar the instance is to the category prototype.

CONTEXT EFFECTS

Vertical associations in the semantic analyzer are hypothetically excitatory. These associations code category membership. We have just seen that they vary in their strength. The higher the typicality of an instance, the stronger the vertical association between the semantic unit that codes it and the unit that codes the category to which it belongs. We have already mentioned several findings that are supportive of the hypothesis that vertical associations in semantic memory are excitatory. Almost all of the studies supportive of spreading activation theory involve a vertical spreading of activation. Several effects found in long-term memory studies are also supportive of the hypothesis that vertical connections in semantic memory are excitatory.

Clustering

In a free-recall task, a person is shown a list of words and then has to recall the items on the list in any order at all. To the extent that order of recall deviates from the order in which the items occurred in the list, we may get some hints concerning the organization of memory. Bousfield (1953) gave his subjects a 60-word list for free recall. The random-ordered list consisted of 15 instances each from four categories: animals, names, professions, and vegetables. When the list was recalled, however, the subjects tended to cluster the words; that is, they tended to recall items from the same category together regardless of the order in which they had been presented. This effect has been replicated in a lot of subsequent studies and is a very robust finding. As might be expected, clustering at the time of recall is stronger if all of the instances of each category are presented together in the first place (Cofer, Bruce, and Reicher, 1966).

Typicality and memory

Lists composed of high typicality instances are recalled better than those composed of low typicality instances (Bousfield, Cohen, and Whitmarsh, 1958). However, this difference is not found if memory is tested by the recognition method—presenting items and asking whether or not they were on the list

(Kintsch, 1968). How can we explain these findings? We have argued that semantic memory contains cognitive units coding instances. These units occupy
the top layer of the semantic analyzer. The principle of arrangement is according
to similarity of meaning. Each unit is connected by a vertical association to a
deeper-level superordinate unit. The vertical associations vary in strength. Instances of higher typicality are more strongly connected to the superordinate unit.
When a list of words is presented, the semantic units corresponding to each
word are activated or marked. This activation automatically activates the superordinate unit. At the time of recall, subjects can hypothetically access the superordinate unit and then read out the most activated instances. Clustering at input
causes more or quicker activation of the superordinate unit and more reactivation of the relevant subordinate instance units. Therefore, recall is better. On a
recall test, activating the superordinate activates all subordinates to some extent.
Low-typicality list items may actually be laterally inhibited by high typicality
nonlist items. On a recognition test, this lateral inhibition is overcome because
the units coding the low-typicality list items are directly activated by perceptual
input. Figure 8–6 diagrams this explanation.

FIGURE 8–6   Effects of typicality on recall and recognition tests. Units coding list items are
marked with an asterisk; stronger excitatory connections are indicated by heavier lines; dashed
lines indicate inhibitory connections; and hatch marks indicate inhibited units. A. In a recall test
the superordinate unit is accessed. This unit activates subordinate units. High typicality
subordinates (those connected to the superordinate by a heavier line) can laterally inhibit units
coding list items, thus preventing their recall. B. In a recognition test, subordinate items are
directly activated. This prevents low typicality items from being masked or inhibited.

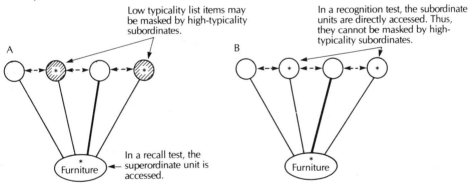

Category cues

If the explanation of clustering and typicality effects presented earlier is
correct, then there are several consequences. First, if we told subjects what the
categories were at the time of recall, it should be helpful. This would directly
activate the units coding the superordinates. Tulving and Pearlstone (1966) did
just this. They gave their subjects 48 items (4 each from 12 categories) to be recalled. When they were asked to recall the lists, half of the subjects were given
the names of the 12 categories and half were not. A subject not given the category
cues recalled words from an average of 7 categories. On the other hand, almost all
subjects given category cues recalled words from all 12 categories. The group

given category cues recalled more words. It is interesting, though, that both groups recalled about 2.6 items per category accessed. Cueing did not help the subjects to recall any more words from a category. It just reminded them of what all of the categories were.

MASKING

Is there any evidence for lateral inhibition in the semantic analyzer? According to our general theory, we would expect vertical bonds—for example, semantic unit to superordinate unit—to be excitatory. This is the same view presented by the spreading activation theory. On the other hand, we would expect units on the same level to laterally inhibit each other in proportion to their similarity. The hypothetical inhibitory bonds may be seen as more or less contentless. Their function is not so much to store information explicitly but to sharpen discrimination. The model does not rule out indirect excitatory bonds between co-ordinate units (units on the same level) but it does hold that direct connections among units on the same level are inhibitory. Logically, it is unclear why excitatory lateral bonds were explicitly postulated and emphasized by Collins and Loftus (1975) in the first place. What are the postulated direct relationships among say, ELK, DEER, and MOOSE that cannot be handled by the indirect excitatory loops such as, for example, ELK isa ANIMAL isa MOOSE? In general, it would seem that the extent of our knowledge about most coordinates is that they are similar (connected to the same superordinate) or occur together but are not identical. It could be argued that this nonidentity is the relation coded by lateral inhibitory connections.

Rate of production of category instances

When subjects are asked to produce category instances, the instances are produced in bursts or scallops (Bousfield and Barclay, 1950) at a negatively accelerated rate (Christensen, Guilford, and Wilson, 1957). For example, a number of instances are produced, then there is a pause, then another bunch of instances is produced, and so on. Over time, the rate at which this is done slows down. The scalloping is consistent with the oscillatory pattern of activation in networks with inhibition (Wilson and Cowan, 1972). The negatively accelerated rate of production is consistent with a gradual buildup of lateral inhibition. The pure spreading activation model cannot account for such scalloping, because networks with no inhibition cannot produce oscillations. Further, the spreading activation hypothesis would predict that retrieval rate should actually be positively accelerated, since each instance retrieved should add to rather than subtract from activation of other category instances.

Part-list cues

The units coding instances of a given category are supposed to laterally inhibit each other. What if we used category instances rather than category names as the cues in a recall task? This should inhibit recall rather than facilitating it because the cues should activate cognitive units that would laterally inhibit the cognitive units coding the words to be recalled. This is exactly what Slamecka (1968, 1969) and several other subsequent experimenters have found. The basic procedure in these studies was this: Subjects were given a list of category instances which came from several different categories. The subject's task was to remember the list. At the time of recall, subjects were given an instance of each category as a retrieval cue. The basic finding has been that recall is worse in this case than if no such cues are given. About the same amount of inhibition is found if the category instance used as a cue is one that appeared on the list that was learned or if it is an instance that was not on the list (Watkins, 1975). The more instances that are given as cues, the worse performance becomes (Roediger, 1973). Hypothetically, giving more instances as cues leads to more lateral inhibition and, therefore, to worse recall. A category instance should laterally inhibit other category instances. However, it should also vertically activate the superordinate unit. If such activation reminds a subject of a category that would otherwise not have been recalled, then an instance cue should actually aid in recall. In fact, the inhibition effect is only found when a few categories are used (Roediger, Stellon, and Tulving, 1977). In this case, it is unlikely that any of the categories will be forgotten. Since all of the superordinate category units are activated anyway, any further activation of them by the instance cues does not aid recall.

Inhibition by coordinate priming

There is some more direct evidence that similar coordinates produce interference effects consistent with the lateral inhibition hypothesis. Collins and Quillian (1973) found relatively weak interference effects on reaction times to the second statements of sequentially presented pairs of statements concerning semantically similar coordinates. It tends to take longer to answer a question about a DUCK, say, if one has just answered a question about a GOOSE. The weakness of these effects could be due to the use in this study of coordinates of relatively high category typicality. With such coordinates, indirect activation via the superordinate unit is possible. Coordinate inhibition should be inversely proportional to the strength of the relevant subordinate-superordinate bonds.

Inhibition by category priming

Perhaps the most clearly damaging evidence against the spreading activation model comes from a series of studies by Rosch (1975). The crucial finding was that category priming facilitates reaction times for decisions concerning high typicality category instances but inhibits reaction times for decisions concerning low typicality category instances. Subjects first saw a category prime (that is, the name of the category was presented) and then had to judge whether two words were the same (physically identical) or different. If the words were of high typicality, the category prime facilitated reaction time, while if they were of low typicality, the category prime had an inhibitory effect. This is clearly impossible to explain with an unmodified spreading activation model with only excitatory bonds. Since all connections are supposed to be excitatory, no matter how weakly a subordinate unit is connected with a superordinate unit, a superordinate prime should activate the unit and make reaction time quicker.

The lateral inhibition explanation of the effect found by Rosch treats it as an analog of visual Mach bands. If a light is shined onto an ommatidium in the eye of the horseshoe crab, the result is that the ommatidium is activated while surrounding ommatidia are inhibited (Ratliff, 1965). The ommatidia are interconnected in a lateral inhibitory network and the activation of a unit is the net product of the excitation and inhibition impinging upon it. If very small amounts of light are allowed to shine on the surrounding ommatidia, they will still be inhibited by the strongly illuminated ommatidium because their excitation will be overwhelmed by lateral inhibition (see Figure 8–7). By the same token, activation of a superordinate unit in semantic memory will activate both high- and low-typicality instance units. However, the latter may be laterally inhibited by the former. Thus the explanation of Rosch's results rests upon the idea that category primes activate cognitive units coding superordinate categories. These units, in turn, excite units coding subordinate instances in proportion to their typicality. The greater the typicality of an instance, the stronger the bond should be between it and the superordinate. Hence, activation of a superordinate unit should activate high typicality instances more than low typicality instances. The activated instance units hypothetically laterally inhibit each other. The more activated a unit, the more it should inhibit neighboring units. Since high typicality units will be more activated, they should tend to inhibit low typicality units more than they are inhibited by low typicality units. The net effect on weakly activated units coding low typicality instances may be some degree of inhibition. If so, reaction times to questions involving these instances will be retarded.

The Collins and Loftus model, with only excitatory bonds, can explain interference or inhibition effects only in terms of decision processes or some version of response competition wherein many units are excited and then the correct

FIGURE 8–7   The Rosch category-priming inhibitory effect (A) is similar to the reaction of a horseshoe crab's eye to a fuzzy patch of light (B). In both cases, weakly activated units are laterally inhibited by more strongly activated units.

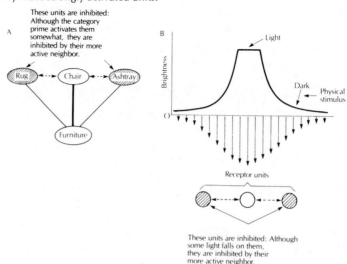

one must be found by a search through the activated alternatives. Since such explanations are not always very compelling, Loftus (1975) has added a hydraulic assumption to the spreading activation model in order to account for the Rosch effect: The net amount of activation in semantic memory is constant. Because a category unit is differently connected to subordinates, when it is activated, the spread of activation to high-typicality instances somehow draws away the ongoing or background-level activation of low-typicality instances. Realization of this hydraulic model would involve introducing at least temporarily inhibitory bonds into the spreading activation model. It would seem preferable to explain such inhibitory bonds not in terms of hydraulic dynamics but in terms of structural lateral inhibition.

SEMANTIC SATIATION

If there are semantic units coding the meaning of words and other objects, then it should be possible to fatigue them just as it seems to be possible to fatigue other types of cognitive units. If a word is repeated over and over, it should lose its meaning. Severance and Washburn (1907) had their subjects stare at words for three minutes and report any changes in their subjective experience. The subjects first reported experiencing the verbal transformation effect. They also reported that the words lost their meanings. This effect has come to be called *semantic satiation*. Most subsequent studies have induced it by having subjects repeat the words aloud over and over. You can demonstrate the effect to yourself by picking a word—any word will do—and repeating it to yourself or writing it down and staring at it.

A lot of subsequent studies have attempted to demonstrate this effect in a way that does not rely purely on the self-reports of subjects. For example, Gampel (1966) had subjects search for instances of a target word in a long list of words. This was done after having repeated the target word for 5, 10, 15, 30, 60, or 120 seconds. Search time was actually shortest after having repeated the word for 15 seconds. This suggests that some amount of repetition was actually beneficial in fully activating the relevant semantic and/or morphemic units. Search time was slowest after 60 seconds of repeating the word. In a second experiment, target words were always repeated for 60 seconds, but the interval between repeating the word and beginning the search was varied. Searching was slowest after a 5-second delay but was actually faster after a 15-second delay than after no delay at all. This suggests some sort of rebound effect.

Esposito and Pelton (1971) in reviewing research on semantic satiation have pointed out several methodological problems. One difficulty involves the verbal transformation effect. If the stimulus word is transformed into something else, then it is not really the same stimulus any more. If the stimulus word is MITTEN, but it has been transformed into MY TEN or something of the sort, then we cannot very well say we are still fatiguing a unit dealing with the meaning of MITTEN. Esposito and Pelton also point out that in many of the studies of semantic satiation, subjects have been told to repeat a word "until it loses its meaning," or something to that effect. They say that this biases the subject toward experiencing such a loss of meaning. This may well be the case, but if one tells subjects to look at words until they turn green, that will not make them see the words turn green. In semantic satiation studies, subjects are instructed, they repeat the word a few times, and then they cheerfully reply that they are ready—the word has lost its meaning. Whether or not we have been able to show its effects on experimental tasks, people do indeed seem to experience a loss of meaning when a word is repeated a number of times. Try it. You will see that it is an odd sensation.

CONCEPT FORMATION

Semantic memory contains our knowledge about the meaning of concepts. How do we come to have this knowledge? As has been mentioned in previous chapters, one can make a strong philosophical case that at least some concepts must be unlearned or a priori in nature (Kant, 1781; Weimer, 1973). The reason for saying this is that, unless one postulated that these concepts come "pre-wired," it would be impossible to explain how any other concepts could be learned. Be this as it may, few theorists dispute the notion that most of the concepts that we have are based upon experience or learning. The question of interest has concerned exactly what sort of learning process is involved.

Artificial categories

Bruner, Goodnow, and Austin (1956) argue that concept formation is an active process of framing and testing hypotheses. In order to test this idea, they used the set of 81 stimuli shown in Figure 8–8. These stimuli differ along four independent dimensions, each of which can have one of three values:

FIGURE 8–8   The stimuli used in experiment on artificial categories

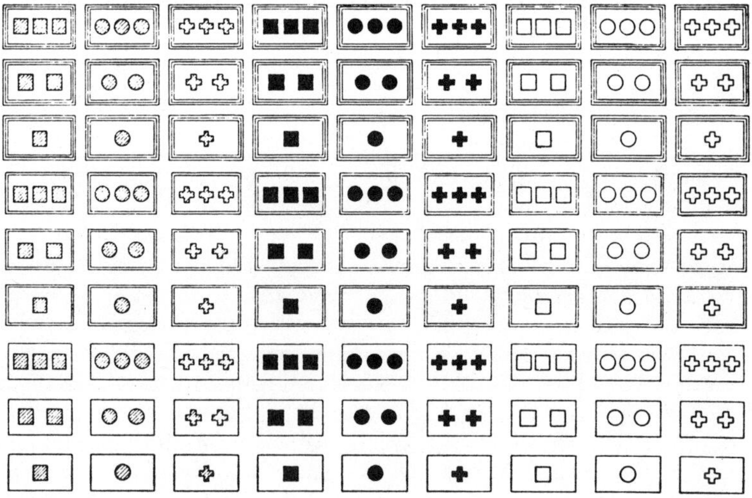

Source: J. S. Bruner, J. J. Goodnow, and G. A. Austin, *A Study of Thinking* (New York: Wiley, 1956), p. 42.

shape of objects (circle, cross, or square), color (black, red, or green), number of objects (one, two, or three), and number of borders (one, two, or three). Bruner and his colleagues did several experiments with these stimuli, but we will describe only one of them. In this experiment, the experimenter thought of a concept (for example, green circles) and showed the subject one example of this concept (for example, a card showing three green circles and having two borders). Then, the subject picked up other cards and asked whether each was an example of the concept. The point was for the subject to guess what the concept was. In our example, the subject would have to find out that number of objects and number of borders were irrelevant, while shape of objects and color were relevant.

Presumably, subjects confronted with such a task develop a hypothesis and then test it by selecting a card and noting the experimenter's response. Several different strategies of hypothesis testing are possible. One common strategy called *focusing* consists of varying one factor at a time. Consider our hypothetical subject who has been shown a card with two green circles and two borders. The subject might select a card with two green circles with three borders. The information that this card belonged to the category would suggest that number of borders was irrelevant. This hypothesis could be tested by selecting a card with two green circles and one border. This would confirm the hypothesis. Then a card with two red circles might be selected to test whether color was crucial.

Less efficient is the strategy known as *scanning*. In this case, hypotheses are tested one at a time. For example, a person might first test the hypothesis that two borders are crucial. With the scanning strategy, this hypothesis might be tested by choosing any card with one or three borders. The subject in this case does not take care to keep the other features constant from trial to trial. Say that the card with one border and three red crosses is selected and that this turns out not to be a member of the category. However, this only tells the subject that number of borders or color or shape or number of objects is crucial. In other words, it does not yield any information at all other than the fact that this specific card is not a member of the category.

Natural categories

CATEGORY MEMBERS SHARE FEW ATTRIBUTES

Does the experiment by Bruner, Goodnow, and Austin tell us how concepts are learned in everyday life? For a long time, psychologists thought that it did. However, Rosch (1973b) argues that it does not, since the artificial categories used in the experiment do not resemble real concepts. It turns out that natural concepts, such as FURNITURE, are not defined by a restricted set of features. A CHAIR, a TABLE, and an ASHTRAY are all examples of pieces of furniture. What features do they all share? Not very many. Rosch and Mervis (1975) argue that members of a category have a family resemblance to one another. The term *family resemblance* is used to mean that each possesses some attributes belonging to some but not all of the other category members. No one set of attributes is absolutely necessary in order to belong to a natural category. Rosch and Mervis studied 20 items from each of six superordinate categories, such as FURNITURE. Subjects were given 50 seconds to list all of the attributes possessed by each given instance. Then Rosch and Mervis tabulated how many other items in the category shared each attribute. Figure 8–9 illustrates the frequency with which attributes were applied to differing numbers of items in a category. Note that most attributes applied to only one item in the category. Almost none of the attributes applied to all 20 items. Thus, it could not very well be that category membership is defined by possession of a specific set of features or attributes. Hypothetically, the

FIGURE 8–9   Number of items per category sharing attributes

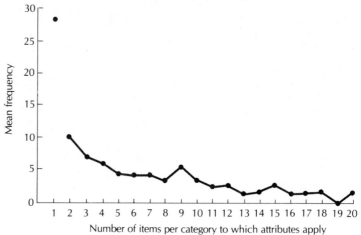

Source: E. Rosch and C. B. Mervis, "Family Resemblance: Studies in the Internal Structure of Categories," *Cognitive Psychology* 7 (1975):581.

greater the family resemblance (sharing of attributes with other category members), the greater the typicality of an item should be. Rosch and Mervis also found strong support for this hypothesis by correlating typicality ratings with the number of shared or common attributes that a category member had.

CATEGORIES DEFINED BY PROTOTYPES

Rosch's idea is that natural categories are prototypes and that category instances vary in their typicality (the degree to which they resemble this prototype). This is consistent with the model we have developed: Categories are coded by cognitive units at a deep level of the semantic analyzer. Their instances are coded by cognitive units at a shallower level of the semantic analyzer. Each of the instance units is connected to the category unit, but the strength of these connections varies as a function of typicality. The higher the typicality, the stronger the connection. Units on any level can also be connected to other units that code their attributes or features. These features or attributes, however, do not define category membership. There is no requirement that all category members be connected to the same feature units. The only requirement for category membership is that the instance-unit be connected to the unit coding the category.

One way that categories could be learned is as follows. Every time a stimulus is presented, the semantic unit coding it is activated. This activation may spread vertically, leading deeper-level units to be activated. A number of such deeper-level units will be activated by any one stimulus. However, one such unit will tend to be activated to the extent that different stimuli resemble each other. Exactly how they resemble each other is immaterial. This deeper-level unit will eventually come to code the superordinate category. Galton (1907) advanced a similar idea. He compared the process of concept formation to making a composite photograph—that is, to using the same frame of film to take pictures of a number of different things. If these things bear a family resemblance to one another—as would, for example, the faces of people belonging to the same family—a photograph that is a sort of average of all the individual things photographed will emerge. This corresponds to the formation of a new concept. Galton actually took composite photographs of faces of people belonging to the same family to illustrate that such a procedure does lead to a sort of prototype—at least in the realm of photography. If, on the other hand, there is no family resemblance, a meaningless blur will result. This could happen if one took pictures of a heterogeneous or randomly selected set of things, such as faces, airplanes, dandelions, and so on. In this case, no concept would be formed.

In forming categories, we may do more than simply average together instances. We may improve upon the average. Posner and Keele (1968) used the prototypes shown in Figure 8–10. They produced distorted variants by

FIGURE 8–10   Prototypes used in experiment on formation of categories

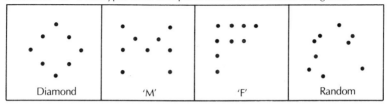

Source: M. I. Posner, R. Goldsmith, and K. E. Welton, "Perceived Distance and the Classification of Distorted Patterns," *Journal of Experimental Psychology* 73 (1967): 30. Copyright 1967 by the American Psychological Association. Reprinted by permission.

randomly displacing some of the dots. Subjects were shown a series of these variants (but not including the original prototypes) and had to learn that they belonged to four different categories. Once they had learned which category each instance belonged to, they were tested. The test materials consisted of the prototypes, the variants subjects had just been shown, and a new set of variants. Subjects could correctly classify the new variants though this took them longer than to classify the variants they had orginally been shown. Interestingly enough, they could classify the original prototypes as quickly as the stimuli they had been shown during the original training session even though they had never seen these original prototypes before. This suggests that the prototype that subjects learned was idealized or regularized rather than simply being an average of all of the instances they had been shown. Thus, the previously unseen original prototypes matched the idealized prototypes that subjects had developed on the basis of their experience with distorted instances.

The Whorfian hypothesis

LINGUISTIC RELATIVITY

Perhaps, you may argue, the subjects in Posner and Keele's experiment had already assimilated the variants to named categories. Maybe they just said to themselves something to the effect that THESE LOOK LIKE DIAMONDS, THESE LOOK LIKE M'S, and so on. Does having a name for a category make it easier to learn or use? Whorf (1956) advanced what has been called the linguistic relativity hypothesis. The hypothesis is that the language one learns determines in large part what categories one will have, and these categories in turn determine what will be perceived and thought about. The idea is that language shapes our thinking rather than merely giving us a way of expressing it.

The Eskimos have 32 different words for types of snow, while we have just one word—SNOW. Whorf's hypothesis was that having these category names means that Eskimos have 32 different concepts for types of snow and that this leads Eskimos to be able to perceive all the different types of snow. On the other hand, since we have only one category name, all snow looks pretty much alike to us. I have always thought that this was a particularly silly idea, so I am glad to say that it has been put to rest. The reason I think it is silly is that Whorf implied that unless a concept can be described by one single word, it does not exist. But even in introducing his hypothesis, Whorf himself presented evidence against this assumption:

> We have the same word for falling snow, snow on the ground, snow packed hard like ice, slushy snow, wind-driven flying snow. . . . To an Eskimo, this all inclusive word would be almost unthinkable; he would say that falling snow, slushy snow, and so on, are sensuously and operationally different (Whorf, 1956, p. 216).

But what are falling snow, snow on the ground, and so on if they are not completely adequate descriptions of concepts?

I do not take issue with the idea that assimilation to concepts per se influences how we think about and remember events. Several experiments have shown this influence. Carmichael, Hogan, and Walter (1932) showed their subjects the ambiguous figures shown in Figure 8–11. Later, the subjects had to reproduce the figures from memory. As each figure was presented, the experimenter remarked that "The next figure resembles a _____." The blank was filled in by the description in Word List 1 for some subjects and by the description in Word List 2 for other subjects. When the subjects drew the figures, the label had a large effect. The figure was distorted so as to resemble the label. This experiment is often cited to show that language has an effect on memory. It does not really show that at all. It shows that assimilation to conceptual categories (described in this case by either single words or whole strings of words) has an influence on memory.

EVIDENCE CONCERNING COLOR NAMES

Different languages have different words for colors. They cut up the spectrum in different ways. For example, the Dani of New Guinea have only two words for all hues, MILI (dark) and MOLA (bright). To describe even such seemingly basic colors as RED or BLUE, they have to use long phrases. According to the Whorfian hypothesis, the Dani should not be able to distinguish colors as well as Americans. We, after all, have many more words for colors. Rosch (1973a) argues that all people have pretty much the same color concepts and that these are represented by the same prototypical hues. The presence or absence of color names in a language is irrelevant, she says, because the categories come more or less neurologically wired in. Under her former name, Eleanor Heider, she published two experiments that strongly supported her view and offered no support at all for the Whorfian hypothesis. Heider and Olivier (1972) studied

FIGURE 8–11 Stimuli and word lists used in experiment designed to illustrate effects of labels on subjects' reproductions

Reproduced figure	Word list I	Stimulus figures	Word list II	Reproduced figure
	Curtains in a window		Diamond in a rectangle	
	Bottle		Stirrup	
	Crescent moon		Letter "C"	
	Bee hive		Hat	
	Eye glasses		Dumbbells	
	Seven		Four	
	Ship's wheel		Sun	
	Hour glass		Table	
	Kidney bean		Canoe	
	Pine tree		Trowel	
	Gun		Broom	
	Two		Eight	

Source: L. Carmichael, H. P. Hogan, and A. A. Walter, "An Experimental Study of the Effect of Language on the Reproduction of Visually Perceived Forms," *Journal of Experimental Psychology* 15 (1932):80.

memory for colors among the Dani and among Americans. Subjects were shown a color chip for five seconds. Then, after a 30-second wait, they had to select the chip they had been shown from a set of 40 color chips. The Americans should have done better at this task, since they could name the color chip they were shown, remember the name, and then retrieve the correct chip. Actually, there were no differences between American and Dani subjects. Having a single-word name made no difference at all.

Some hues have higher typicality than others; that is, some reds, for example, are better examples of RED than others. American subjects show good agreement as to what is a good example of the color RED and what is a poor or off-color example. Heider (1972) had American subjects choose high-typicality and low-typicality examples of various colors. Then she taught color concepts to Dani subjects using either high-typicality or low-typicality colors (as determined by American subjects) as prototypes. That is, she showed them prototypes of various colors and gave each color a different name. Then she tested her subjects' ability to name color chips of varying hues. This procedure was repeated for a number of days. As shown in Figure 8–12, performance was much better with high-

FIGURE 8–12   Number of errors on successive days when Dani subjects were given color categories to learn in which prototypical colors were either of high or low typicality

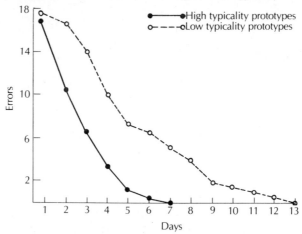

Source: E. Rosch, "Natural Categories," *Cognitive Psychology* 4 (1973):338.

typicality colors. When high-typicality colors were used as prototypes, it took about a week until no errors were made in classification. On the other hand, when low-typicality colors were used, it took almost twice as long until no errors were made. In both cases, a correct response was one where the color chip was assigned to the category whose prototype it matched most closely in wavelength. In the case of high-typicality colors, this essentially came down to teaching the subjects the American system for naming colors. This system must have fit better with already existing but simply unnamed natural categories. Americans and the Dani must see colors the same.

Another line of evidence against the Whorfian hypothesis of linguistic relativity also concerns color names. Languages differ in how many color terms they have, but the colors these terms refer to are always the same (Berlin and Kay, 1969). That is, if a language has only two color terms, these always refer to BRIGHT or WHITE and DARK or BLACK. If a language has three color terms, these invariably are WHITE, BLACK, and RED. Berlin and Kay say that there is an invariant evolutionary sequence in which color terms are added. The full progression is: (1) BLACK and WHITE; (2) RED; (3) GREEN or YELLOW; (4) GREEN and YELLOW; (5) BLUE; (6) BROWN; (7) PURPLE, PINK, ORANGE, or GRAY. Thus, for example, a language with eight color terms will always have names for all of the colors in sets 1–6 and for one of the colors in set 7. It would seem that the principle is one of differentiation. More inclusive colors are subdivided at each stage in the progression. The fact that the evolutionary progression is universal suggests that color categories must be based upon some neural predisposition rather than upon cultural or linguistic factors. If language determined color concepts rather than vice versa, there should not be one invariant order in which color names are added to all languages.

SUMMARY AND CONCLUSIONS

Semantic memory contains our knowledge concerning the meaning of concepts. According to Collins and Quillian's cognitive economy hypothesis, knowledge in semantic memory is stored in a nonredundant fashion. For example, we hypothetically store the knowledge that all objects have weight only with the general concept of OBJECT, not with each of the objects about which we have knowledge. Thus, a lot of our knowledge is not explicit but must be inferred. Reaction-time studies have tended to support this hypothesis. It takes longer to answer questions involving inferred knowledge (for example, A CANARY HAS BLOOD) than to answer questions involving specific knowledge (for example, A CANARY IS YELLOW).

The semantic analyzer is hypothetically structurally similar to other analyzers. Semantic units at the highest level of the semantic analyzer are connected to or defined by deeper-level units coding superordinate categories. Units on deeper levels code even more abstract concepts. Much evidence is consistent with the hypothesis that vertical connections in semantic memory are excitatory: Priming with category names generally shortens reaction times for responses to subsequent questions concerning category instances. On memory tasks where subjects have to remember lists of words, they tend to cluster these words together by category at the time of recall. Giving category names as recall cues improves performance on such memory tasks. Rosch has presented a lot of evidence that concepts vary in their typicality (that is, the degree to which they are typical of the category to which they belong). We hypothesized that typicality is coded by the strength of the vertical bond between the cognitive unit representing a category and the semantic unit representing a category instance. This is consistent with several findings. High typicality instances are produced first when people are asked to list category instances. In reaction-time studies, the higher the typicality of an instance, the more quickly people can say that it does in fact belong to a category.

Some evidence supports the contention that units on any one level of semantic memory exert a lateral inhibitory effect upon one other. In memory experiments, using category instances as cues hurts rather than helps performance. In reaction-time studies, priming with category instances exerts a mildly inhibitory effect on reaction time for questions concerning other category instances. Rosch's finding that category priming inhibits reaction times in responding to low typicality instances can be interpreted in terms of indirect masking. The category prime strongly activates high-typicality instances, and these laterally inhibit low-typicality instances. There is also some evidence that units in semantic memory can be fatigued or satiated; repeating a word over and over leads to the subjective feeling that the word has lost its meaning.

Rosch has been responsible for doing away with two rather venerable theories of concept formation. Bruner, Goodnow, and Austin asserted that concepts are formed by a process of hypothesis testing whereby the defining features of a concept are discovered. Rosch and Mervis, however, showed that natural categories do not have a set of defining features. All that category instances seem to share is a family resemblance to the prototype that hypothetically defines a concept. Rosch and others have produced evidence that it is this similarity to the prototype rather than amount of learning that seems to be crucial in defining category membership. Whorf asserted that concepts are created by language. If the language one speaks has a word for a concept, one will have the concept. In her work with color concepts among the Dani of New Guinea—who have only two color names—Rosch produced evidence that more or less destroyed the Whorfian hypothesis. It would seem that color concepts may be neurologically prewired rather than being dependent upon language or learning. One wonders whether this is the case only for color concepts or whether it may not be true of other basic concepts as well.

9

Episodic memory

TYPES OF MEMORY

Structural memory

We have already discussed two types of memory. The multileveled analyzers described in the previous chapters can be seen as being long-term memory stores as much as being sensory, gnostic, or semantic analyzers or systems. In the last chapter, we used the terms *semantic memory* and *semantic analyzer* interchangeably. We could just as well have called the speech analyzer morphemic memory or called the printed-word analyzer printed-word memory. Let's use the term *structural memory* to refer to all of these analyzers or long-term memory systems. Structural memory is composed of permanent cognitive units not subject to forgetting in the usual sense of the term. Unless you are the unfortunate victim of brain damage, you will not wake up one morning and discover that you have forgotten the speech sounds of the English language or the meaning of the word CAT. You certainly will not forget how to hear music or see cats, dogs, or anything else. Another characteristic of cognitive units in structural memory is that they are not time tagged; that is, you do not remember *when* you learned the phoneme, /b/, or the meaning of the word, ELEPHANT.

Primary memory

Primary memory consists of whatever cognitive units are currently activated. Given this, it is perfectly consistent to say that to sense, to perceive, to recognize, or to understand are all to remember. I say this because all of these processes involve the activation of preexisting cognitive units in structural memory. This idea is hardly an original one. Plato made more or less the same assertion. You will recall that we agreed to use terms such as *sensation* and *perception* to refer to the initial activation of cognitive units by external stimuli and to use the term *primary memory* to refer to persistence of activity in these units. This is a rather artificial distinction, but we made it in order to make our use of terms as consistent as possible with the way other psychologists use these terms.

Episodic memory

Neither primary memory nor structural memory are consistent with the everyday notion of memory. Actually another type of long-term memory corresponds with everyday usage of the term *memory*. It is fundamentally different from structural memory. Tulving (1972) calls it *episodic memory*. According to Tulving's distinction, episodic memory contains information such as what you did last weekend, what words were on the previous page of this book, and so on. In large part—but not wholly—episodic memory concerns what has happened to *you*. As we shall see, it would be the perfect place to put not only the story of your life but other stories as well, such as the plots of novels, jokes, gossip about friends, and so on. Episodic memory is hypothetically coded in the language of structural memory, but it is distinct from structural memory in that it keeps track of the temporal order of events. Structural memory contains the basic building blocks of knowledge, and episodic memory is made up from these elements. Structural memory is like a vast dictionary. It lists the words in a language along with their pronunciations. It lists the unitary percepts or images you can have along with the rules for how to see, hear, or feel them. Beyond that, it lists the meanings of all of these words and images. In short, it consists of the sensory, gnostic, and semantic analyzers we have discussed in preceding chapters. Episodic memory is like a novel or a movie. It puts these words, images, and concepts together in particular ways. This is a good analogy, but it does nothing to help locate the exact dividing line between the two types of memory. A fact such as how the word DOG, is pronounced is clearly in structural memory, as is the meaning of the word. On the other hand, a fact such as when you got up this morning is clearly in episodic memory. What about something such as the knowledge that Napoleon was exiled to St. Helena after being defeated at Waterloo? Is that general knowledge, or does it belong with episodic memory? I do not have any very good answers to this question, but I am in good company on that count, since no one else does either.

STRUCTURE OF THE EPISODIC ANALYZER

Is there really an episodic analyzer?

One view is that structural and episodic memory are in the same place. In this view, episodic memory consists of associations among units in structural memory. These associations are no different from the associations that code, say, semantic knowledge. On the other hand, others have argued that episodic memory traces are in a separate place. In this view, we could see this memory as being composed of seriated sets of propositions: one for every event that has occurred to you. Rather than cluttering up semantic memory or gnostic analyzers, these propositional units might be somewhere else in the brain. Aside from keeping the mind neat, there are some far more compelling reasons to think that episodic memory might be a separate store. People who go into fugue states or suffer amnesia forget who they are and cannot recall what has happened to them, but usually they do not forget the meanings or sounds of words. On the other hand, various types of aphasia and agnosia can destroy knowledge of word sounds and meanings while leaving memory for one's personal history intact. Later in this chapter, we shall discuss experimental evidence on what is called *encoding specificity* that is also supportive of the idea that episodic memory is a separate memory store.

Episodic chunking

Let's assume that all episodic memories are stored in an analyzer that is separate from those containing structural memories. As I said earlier, it is not completely clear whether this is the case or not. It does not really make a lot of difference whether episodic memory is in a different place than structural memory. Everything that we shall say would make just as much sense—with minor modifications—if the two memories were in the same place. We shall assume that the cognitive units at the highest level of the episodic memory system are connected to units at the highest level of other analyzers. These connections define the episodic units and can also be used to realize or express them. Presumably, cognitive units in the episodic analyzer can be connected to units in any of the other analyzers. However, they seem to have a particular affinity for units in the semantic analyzer and—as we shall see later—for units in visual gnostic analyzers. On the other hand, the episodic analyzer seems to be poorly connected to the speech analyzer and to the printed-word analyzer. Hypothetically, an episodic unit is set up at least temporarily for each event that occurs to us. What good does this do? Episodic memory is useful for remembering associations among cognitive units. Structural memory contains the basic units. If we had to learn a completely new word or concept, that would involve constructing a new entry in structural memory. Thus, all we have to worry about with episodic memory is associations among preexisting units. It makes sense to argue that episodic memory stores associations between cognitive units and that it does this by what Wickelgren (1979a) calls indirect or vertical associations. Elements in other analyzers are associated by connecting them via chunking nodes in episodic memory.

Let's consider a few of the things that people can remember. First, let's discuss some simple tasks used in laboratory experiments. About the simplest thing we can do would seem to be to ask someone to remember a list of words—for example, VIOLET, ROSE, DAISY, LILY, and IRIS. In Figure 9–1A, we show how this might be accomplished. The units in semantic memory coding these words are all connected to a unit in episodic memory. The episodic-memory unit codes the concept, WORDS ON THE LIST I JUST LEARNED. In a paired-associate task, we give a subject a list of word pairs. The task is to remember which word goes with which. In Figure 9–1B, I show how this might be done. This time, chunking nodes representing the pairs are set up on the top layer of episodic memory and the list unit is on the next lower level.

You may be wondering why in the world we have a separate analyzer devoted to remembering sets of unrelated words. This is a good question. The answer is that we probably do not have such an analyzer. We can use episodic memory to perform such a task, but that could hardly be what it was designed for. In

FIGURE 9–1   Use of the episodic analyzer for simple memory tasks: (A) In a simple list-learning task, units coding each list item are hypothetically connected to an episodic chunking unit. (B) In a paired-associate list-learning task, each pair is hypothetically connected to an episodic chunking unit. Then, each of these chunking units is connected to a deeper-level chunking unit coding the fact that the pair was on the list.

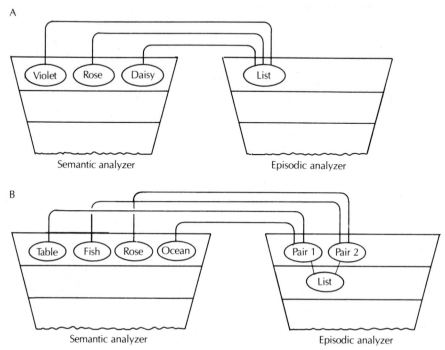

real life, we seldom have to remember lists of unrelated words. If we do, we simply write them down. It must be that episodic memory was designed to remember something quite different, namely, meaningful events.

Propositions

Several theorists (for example, Anderson and Bower, 1973; Kintsch, 1972; Rumelhart, Lindsay, and Norman, 1972) have argued that the proposition is the basic unit of what we are calling episodic memory. A *proposition* is an abstract structure that codes an event in terms of its basic components. Since episodic memory is memory for events, and since propositions code events, it makes sense that they might be the basic units of episodic memory. The basic notion of the proposition can be traced to Fillmore's case grammar (1968, 1969). Fillmore's idea was that a spoken or written sentence is an expression or realization of an abstract proposition. A proposition has a fairly limited number of cases or components. The more important of these are as follows:

Action: The action defining an event. Usually it is described by a verb (for example, The man *sold* the book).

Agent: The person or thing that performs the action in question (for example, *The man* sold the book).

Object: The person or thing that is affected by the action (for example, The man sold *the book*).

Recipient: The person or thing that bears the brunt or receives the effect of the action (for example, The man sold the book to *the customer*).

Instrument: The thing by means of which the action is brought about (for example, The man sold the book *through persuasiveness*).

Location: Where the action takes place (for example, The man sold the book in *the bookstore*).

Time: When the action takes place (for example, The man sold the book *this morning*).

We could combine the information given in the earlier examples as follows: SELL (MAN, BOOK, CUSTOMER, PERSUASION, BOOKSTORE, THIS MORNING). All I have done has been to put the components of the action together in a specific order: ACTION (AGENT, OBJECT, RECIPIENT, INSTRUMENT, LOCATION, TIME). Note that this proposition could be expressed in a variety of ways. Here are two of many possibilities: (1) THE MAN PERSUADED THE CUSTOMER TO BUY THE BOOK THIS MORNING IN THE BOOKSTORE (2) IN THE BOOKSTORE THIS MORNING, THE MAN SOLD THE CUSTOMER A BOOK BY MEANS OF PERSUASION. We could go on and on. The point is that a proposition does not have a one-to-one relationship with a given spoken or written sentence. For that matter, propositions do not have to be realized as sentences at all. You could also realize the proposition as a series of visual images. Thus, a proposition is an abstract structure that can be expressed in a variety of ways.

A proposition could be coded or remembered as shown in Figure 9–2. Here I show a propositional unit at the highest level of the episodic analyzer connected by labeled associations to units in semantic memory. The episodic unit is essentially a chunking node that codes the proposition we have been using as an example. There could be one such propositional unit for each event that one can remember. Reality must certainly be much more complex than the situation shown in Figure 9–2. When you hear a sentence, for example, syntactic analysis must occur before you know the agent, object, and so on. This analysis

FIGURE 9–2   How propositions describing events could be coded by units in episodic memory

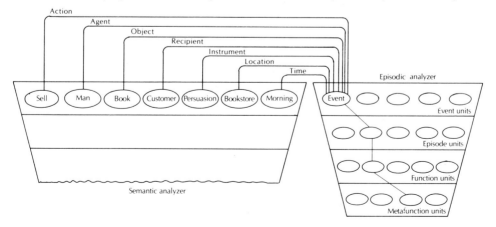

could be seen as occurring in a syntactic analyzer interposed between episodic and semantic memory. This analyzer would attach the labels to the associations between semantic and episodic memory.

Episode units

So far we have only accounted for one level of the episodic analyzer. What units are on deeper levels? It is not unreasonable to think that there could be deeper-level units that chunk together sets of propositional units. We might call these episodic units. An episode consists of a whole series of events. For example, what you did last weekend might be seen as an episode in your life. No matter how boring your weekend was, you must have engaged in more than one action. If so, memory for what you did would have to be coded by more than one proposition, since one proposition can code only one action. Episode units could code whole episodes in a person's life if they were connected to the propositional units coding the component events of these episodes (see Figure 9–2).

Functions

What units can be found on still deeper levels of the episodic analyzer? One possibility would be that units on deeper levels chunk together episode units. Recall of events from episodic memory seems to cue off other memories. These other memories are often related to the initial memory in terms of similarity rather than in terms of time. If you doubt this, sit down next to a grandmotherly type on a bus and ask about her last operation. Prepare for a long story. Chances are that you will get to hear about *every* operation she has ever had. You can get the same result if you ask a football player about his last/best/first game or if you are incautious enough to utter the word FISH within hearing of a fisherman. What I am getting at is this. A lot of people spend a lot of time reading out the contents of episodic memory. I do not know of any studies on this, but I would bet that this is what most people do most of the time that they are talking. Furthermore, these readouts are usually not indiscriminant core dumps beginning at a given time. Rather, they seem to be retrievals of memories that fit deeper-level schemas such as "funny things happening while waiting in lines," "episodes concerning loss of keys," "fish that got away after struggles," "fish that would not respond to bait," "embarrassing events occurring on dates," and so on.

Perhaps all the episodes that are similar in some abstract way are connected to a deeper-level unit. This possibility is illustrated in Figure 9–2. The Russian folklorist Vladimir Propp (1928) argued that about 30 or so *functions* can subsume all of the specific episodes that can occur in any narrative. A function might be something such as HERO ENCOUNTERS OBSTACLE. Such a function might chunk together all episodes concerning this theme regardless of whether the obstacle was loss of keys or an insoluble math problem. At the deepest level of the episodic analyzer, we might expect to find only a few "distinctive-feature" units. We shall discuss the deeper levels of the episodic analyzer in Chapter 14, but for now, we shall stick to the surface. We cannot very well ask profound questions before we know more about simple things.

Lateral inhibition among episodic units

If the episodic memory system is constructed like the sensory, gnostic, and semantic analyzers, then we should expect units on the same level to laterally inhibit each other. But what units would be next to what other ones? What is the principle of organization on any given level? One possibility would be that the principle of organization is similarity. Proposition-, episode-, and function-units coding similar things might be close together. As we shall see later, much evidence supports this contention. We forget a lot of the information entered into episodic memory quite quickly. This forgetting is not due to simple decay. Rather, it seems to be due to an active process of inhibition. The more similar two episodic memories are, the more each causes forgetting of the other. We shall argue that this is due to extremely antagonistic lateral inhibitory relations among units in episodic memory.

Units in episodic memory could also be arranged according to temporal order in at least one dimension. Units coding events close in time would be close to each other. One of the things that we have to remember is the serial order of events. Estes (1972a) has proposed an explicit lateral inhibition theory of memory for serial order. The basic idea is that asymmetrical lateral inhibitory bonds could allow us to code the temporal relations among events. As illustrated in Figure 9–3, a deeper-level chunking node in episodic memory is connected in an excita-

FIGURE 9–3   Estes' (1972a) asymmetrical inhibition model of memory for serial order applied to episodic memory

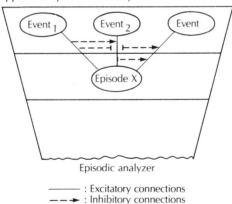

Episodic analyzer

——— : Excitatory connections
– – → : Inhibitory connections

tory fashion with a set of units coding events. Suppose that it is necessary to recall the events in a specific order, as it would be if they were components of an episode or story. Activating the chunking node would activate all of the component event units. However, the unit coding each event could laterally inhibit units coding all later events. Thus, when the chunking node was activated, the unit coding event$_1$ would be activated and would also inhibit the units coding events $_{2-4}$. The result would be that only event$_1$ would be available to consciousness. If we asume that the activation of the unit coding event$_1$ was automatically squelched after a period of activity allowing the recall of event$_1$, this would disinhibit the unit coding event$_2$. Event$_2$ would then be recalled, the unit coding it would be deactivated, allowing the recall of event$_3$, and so on. It makes some sense to speculate that units in episodic memory could be organized along both the temporal dimension and the dimension of similarity. This would mean that propositional units, for example, might be organized as strings of units (with serial position in the string coding temporal order).

ACQUISITION OF EPISODIC MEMORIES
Reinforcement

How does information get into episodic memory? Research on animal learning and conditioning suggests that events are more likely to be remembered if reward or reinforcement is connected with them. There is no doubt that this is also true for people. However, there is also what is called incidental learning. *Incidental learning* refers to the fact that things not accompanied by reward can be learned. Incidental learning so clearly occurs that it led behaviorists as diverse as Tolman (1932) and Spence (1956) to argue that reward affects only performance, not acquistion or learning. Their idea was that learning (acquiring an episodic memory) is a consequence only of such factors as repetition. Reward only influences whether or not the organism will bother to demonstrate that the memory is present. For example, suppose that we allow a rat to wander about in a maze that contains no food. The rat will show no particular tendency to enter any alley of the maze. Now suppose that we introduce food at some particular place in the maze. Given that our rat is hungry, it will very quickly learn how to run from the starting box to this food (Haney, 1931). Something was learned just by wandering around in the maze.

Repetition

It is completely clear from a variety of experiments and everyday observations that more repetitions of an event lead to better episodic memory for that event. Thus, if I show you a list of items 20 times you are certainly more likely to remember what items are on that list better than if I show it to you only once or twice. However, suppose that this is the list: THEODORE ROOSEVELT, MARTIN VAN BUREN, ABRAHAM LINCOLN, JOHN KENNEDY, GRETA GARBO, CALVIN COOLIDGE, LYNDON JOHNSON. Which name is least likely to be forgotten? Why, that of Greta Garbo, of course. This is the von Restorff (1933) effect. Not that Greta Garbo is hard to forget. The effect is more general than that. It refers to the tendency for something that is striking or stands out to be better remembered. You may have a more vivid memory of what you saw on a trip to Europe, say, than of things you see regularly, such as the buildings you pass on the way to your classes. In this case, uniqueness rather than repetition leads to better memory.

Attention

William James (1890) argued that only events that at least for a moment occupy the focus of attention find their way to what we are calling episodic memory. As we have seen, attention and arousal are intimately connected. Thus, when

Konorski says that nothing is learned except in the presence of arousal, he is really saying the same thing as William James with different words. The same is true of those theorists who say that events have to be rehearsed in short-term memory before they can get into episodic memory, since rehearsal requires attention. Again, it is perfectly clear that the memorability of events is enhanced when we attend to these events. However, it is not clear that attention is absolutely necessary to establish an episodic memory trace.

Depth of processing

Craik and Lockhart (1972) argue that depth of processing is a prime determinant of retention in episodic memory. Shallow processing occurs when a stimulus activates only sensory cognitive units. A medium level of processing is said to occur when gnostic units are activated. Deep processing occurs when semantic units are activated. Thus, depth of processing refers to how semantic the analysis of a stimulus is. The deeper the level to which a given stimulus is processed, the more likely that a long-term episodic memory will be formed, according to Craik and Lockhart. To demonstrate the effect of depth of processing, Craik (1973) asked subjects to make three types of judgments concerning each item on a list of words. These were a shallow physical judgment (whether the word was printed in upper or lower case type), a medium-depth lexical judgment (whether the word rhymed with another word), or a deep semantic judgment (whether the word made sense when inserted into a given sentence). The subjects were not warned that they would be asked to recall the words at the end of the experiment. The deeper the initial level of processing had been, the better a word was recalled in a subsequent test. Thus, depth of processing seems to facilitate entry into episodic memory. However, subjects could remember some words that had been processed only at a shallow level.

We have seen that reward, repetition, strikingness, attention, and depth of processing all influence the probability that an event will be recorded in episodic memory. All of these factors have a big effect on the probability that something will be remembered. However, there does seem to be some purely incidental learning. That is, an event may be remembered even if all of these factors are absent. The probability of this happening, though, seems not to be very great.

WHAT IS REMEMBERED?

Abstractness of episodic memories

If depth of processing influences entry into episodic memory in the way that Craik and Lockhart say that it does, then this has implications not only for how well something is remembered but also for what is remembered. Deeper processing is less sensory and more semantic. This implies that what is remembered should not be concrete, sensory details but the abstract gist of an event. This conclusion is reinforced when we remember that the proposition is supposed to be the basic unit of episodic memory. A proposition is abstract. Furthermore, it is dependent upon semantic analysis. Without prior semantic analysis, one could not very well form a proposition. This is because to form a proposition one needs semantic information about an event: one needs to know what the action was, who the agent of this action was, and so on. The idea that episodic memory is abstract is hardly a novel conclusion. Everyday experience teaches us that this must be the case. Think of the last book that you read. Suppose that I were willing to pay you ten dollars for each sentence in that book that you could recall verbatim. I think you will agree that you would not make very much money. In the diagram of episodic memory shown in Figure 9–1, I connected the episodic units with semantic units. This assumes that it is meanings that are stored in episodic memory. While I did not mean to imply that these are the only possible connections, I did mean to imply that these are the most likely or most common connections.

Memory for sentences

Several experiments confirm and extend this contention. Sachs (1967) presented her subjects with sentences. She warned the subjects that they would be tested for verbatim memory of these sentences. The tests occurred at three points in time: Immediately after the sentence had been shown, 80 syllables afterwards, or 160 syllables afterwards. The test consisted of presenting three types of sentences and asking if the test sentence was exactly the same as the original. The test sentences were of three types: (1) exactly the same as the original, (2) the same in meaning except that grammatical form was changed from active to passive or vice versa, and (3) similar in grammatical form but with meaning changed from the original. When the test was immediate, changes in either form or meaning (type-2 or type-3 sentences) were almost always detected. When the test came either 80 or 160 syllables later, detection of changes in form (type-2 sentences) were hardly better than would be expected purely from guessing. On the other hand, changes in meaning (type-3 sentences) were easily recognized What this suggests is that people retain the meaning of events rather than their detailed form.

Wanner (1968) conducted a similar experiment. His subjects reported for an experiment and were presented with instructions on what to do. Then, when they were ready to begin, Wanner surprised them. Rather than doing what they had been instructed to do, they were tested for their recognition of sentences in the instructions they had just read. Test items were of three types: (1) sentences that were exactly the same as the original, (2) sentences with different word order but exactly the same meaning, and (3) sentences with different word order which also changed the meaning. All three sentences contained exactly the same words but in different arrangements. Subjects showed poor ability to discriminate the second type of test sentence from the original sentences, but they were very good at recognizing that they had not seen the third type of sentence before. Again, verbatim memory was poor but memory for meaning was good.

Bransford and Franks (1971) carried out an experiment that extended these findings in an important direction. Their subjects were shown sentences each of which expressed some elements of a proposition. Here is an example of the basic elements for one of the propositions.

1.   THE ROCK ROLLED DOWN THE MOUNTAIN.
2.   THE ROCK CRUSHED THE HUT.

3. THE HUT IS AT THE RIVER.
4. THE HUT IS TINY.

These basic elements could be combined to form two-element sentences. These would combine two of the one-element sentences shown earlier. An example: THE TINY HUT IS AT THE RIVER. This sentence combines all of the information in the third and fourth sentences. Three-element sentences could also be formed. An example would be: THE ROCK CRUSHED THE TINY HUT AT THE RIVER. Finally, a four-element sentence would combine all four of the simple sentences: THE ROCK THAT ROLLED DOWN THE MOUNTAIN CRUSHED THE TINY HUT AT THE RIVER. The four-element sentence could be described in terms of a complete proposition. The one-, two-, and three-element sentences give only parts of this proposition.

Now for the experiment. Subjects were shown a series of sentences. Some were one-element, two-element, or three-element sentences of the type described earlier. Others were altogether unrelated filler sentences. No four-element sentences were ever shown to the subjects. After each sentence was shown, subjects had to answer a question about it. Five minutes after all the sentences had been responded to, subjects were shown another series of sentences. Their task was to indicate whether or not they had previously seen each sentence. They were also asked to say how sure they were of their judgments. The test sentences included one-, two-, and three-element sentences as well as some of the four-element sentences that subjects had never seen before. Figure 9–4 shows the results. The more elements the test sentence contained, the more confident subjects were

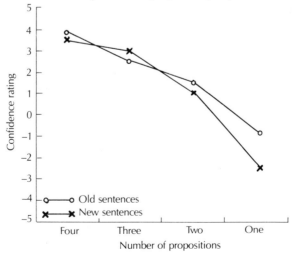

FIGURE 9–4   Results of Bransford and Franks (1971) experiment. Confidence ratings of old and new sentences. Confidence ratings are primarily a function of number of propositions in the sentence rather than of whether the sentence had really been seen (old) or not (new).

Source: J. D. Bransford and J. J. Franks, "The Abstraction of Linguistic Ideas," *Cognitive Psychology* 2 (1971):341.

that they had seen it. The subjects were most confident that they had seen the four-element sentences—which, of course, they had never seen at all. They were more confident that they had seen four-element sentences than that they had seen three-element sentences which they had, in fact, been shown.

What does the Bransford and Franks experiment tell us? It suggests that people tend to assimilate inputs to propositions. Given several sentences that can be combined into a single proposition, this combination tends to be made. Furthermore, the components that were combined to form the proposition are then thrown away or discarded. Only the abstract proposition is retained. In other words, we remember the gist of what is said rather than the individual sentences. Moreover, if the speaker has not put all of the components together, we do it ourselves.

Mediation

When Ebbinghaus (1885) began the scientific study of memory, he invented the *nonsense syllable*—a short string of letters that does not form a word (for example, DAX, XJZ). Ebbinghaus studied how well he could learn lists of nonsense syllables. He had begun his study of memory by learning meaningful material, such as passages from Shakespeare. Very soon, it became clear that the meanings and prior associations of the words in such passages had large effects on memory. Ebbinghaus hoped to circumvent these effects by using nonsense syllables. The idea was to control the effects of meaning and prior memory associations so that other factors could be studied. Subsequent researchers had the same idea. If we were correct in arguing that the basic unit of episodic memory is the proposition, then the whole enterprise of studying the acquisition of lists of nonsense syllables was rather misguided. If human memory is designed to store the gist of meaningful material, then lists of unrelated meaningless syllables are not really the best material to use. For that matter, lists of unrelated meaningful words are not very appropriate either.

ASSIMILATION TO PROPOSITIONS

Subjects in memory experiments designed to study rote memorization tend rather regularly to circumvent the experimenter's aims. For a long time, this was regarded as a terrible nuisance. More recently, researchers have taken a different approach. Perhaps, rather than maliciously trying to destroy experimenters' theories, the subjects are trying to tell them something about how episodic memory works. Consider someone given a list of unrelated words to remember. One strategy is to weave the words into a meaningful sentence. Bower and Clark (1969) gave their subjects a serial learning task. In such a task, one has to recall a list of unrelated words in the correct order. The subjects got 12 lists of 10 words each. There were two conditions. In the control condition, subjects were told just to memorize the words. In the experimental condition, subjects were explicitly told to weave the list words into a meaningful story. Immediately after each list was presented, subjects in both groups were tested for recall of just that one list. At this point, no differences in recall were found between the two groups. About 20 minutes after the last list had been learned, recall of all 12 lists was tested. As a cue, subjects were given the first word on each list and had to recall all of the rest of the words on that list. The differences were spectacular. The control group could recall only 13 percent of the words, but the experimental group could recall 93 percent of them! Why the difference? One explanation would be that the experimental condition allowed memory to function in its natural manner—by forming propositional units.

Paired-associate learning involves giving subjects a list of word pairs (A–B) for memorization. To test recall, A is presented and the subject must recall B. This sort of learning fits nicely into a behaviorist or stimulus-response viewpoint. From this viewpoint, the task consists of forming a direct or horizontal association between A (the stimulus) and B (the response). The trouble is that subjects do not seem to see the task in this way. One common strategy they use is called *mediation*. Rather than learning A–B, they learn A–X–B, where X is some mediating unit that is connected with both A and B. For example, if subjects are given the task of learning paired associates such as DOG–OSTRICH, they may actually use a mediation strategy and learn something such as DOG RIDES OSTRICH. In propositional form, this sentence could be expressed as RIDES (DOG, OSTRICH). Rohwer (1966) and others have shown that memory for lists of paired associates is greatly improved if subjects are instructed to commit them to memory by embedding each pair in a meaningful sentence. The implication is that it is easier to remember a meaningful sentence than a pair of unrelated words. This is not at all paradoxical if the natural unit of episodic memory is the proposition. It should be much easier to activate a proposition unit when the component elements of a proposition are present (as they are with a meaningful sentence) than when they are not (as with a pair of unrelated words).

DIFFICULTY OF ROTE MEMORIZATION

These and similar experiments suggest that items are remembered by forming a higher-order unit in episodic memory that chunks, mediates, or codes the items to be remembered. Lists of words are remembered by activating a chunking unit in episodic memory coding a proposition that contains all of the words. Lists of simple propositions are remembered by collecting units coding them into a more complex proposition. People may be able to commit lists of words and sentences to memory in a purely rote fashion. If so, ability to do so is extremely poor. When it comes to learning lists of pairs of items, a similar picture emerges. We seem to remember such pairs by connecting both of them to an episodic chunking unit. We may be able to form direct or horizontal associations between pairs of words or sentences. Again, if we can do so at all, our ability to do so is extremely limited.

Sensory-motor memories

Our argument is that what is learned and remembered tends to be an abstract proposition rather than the concrete sensory details of experience. How general is this conclusion? Most of the experiments cited involve language comprehension. Perhaps there is something special about language. However, this conclusion also clearly applies to many motor habits. Try writing something with your non-preferred hand. For that matter, try putting the pen between your teeth and writing that way. Or hold it with your toes. Although you may not be terribly skillful at these tasks, you can certainly do them. If your memories for how to write were specific, you should be completely unable to write in any of these ways. It would seem that you have learned an abstract schema. This schema can be *realized* in a variety of ways. This seems to be generally true of motor habits, whether they are learned by humans or by animals.

What does a rat in a maze learn? It seems to learn an abstract proposition (about getting to the goal box). It seems not to learn specific motor responses. Let's say we train a rat to run through a T-maze to get to a food reward. What would happen if we flooded the maze with water? If the rat had learned a specific set of motor responses connected with running, it would be at a complete loss. If it had learned the general idea of how to get to the goal box, it could realize this idea just as well by swimming as by running. What does the rat in fact do? It swims (MacFarlane, 1930). Gleitman (1955) and McNamara, Long, and Wike (1956) carried this line of research to its logical conclusion. They put their rats in little vehicles and carried them through mazes. At the goal box, the rats were given a food reward. The rats thus made no overt responses at all. What did they do when placed in the maze with no vehicle? They walked to the goal box.

Visual memories

We have seen that verbatim memory for sentences is quite poor even after rather short delays. People remember the gist or meaning of a sentence and promptly forget the exact words that composed it. A similar phenomenon seems to occur with memory for actions. We remember the gist or point of an action, not its specific details. These facts reinforce the contention that episodic memory is coded in terms of abstract propositions. Research on episodic memory for visual scenes complicates things. It turns out that people seem to have extremely good memories for pictures. For example, Shepard (1967) showed his subjects 612 pictures. Later, when some of these pictures and some other new ones were shown, the task was to say which ones had been seen previously. Accuracy was virtually perfect after a delay of a week and was still very good after a delay of four months. Standing (1973) carried out a similar experiment with 10,000 pictures and got similar results.

The subjects in Shepard's and Standing's experiments did little more than glance at the pictures. Yet, they had very good recognition memory for them after long delays. What are we to make of this? There are several possible explanations. The one I prefer is this: The episodic analyzer does code memories in terms of abstract propositions. However, propositional units in the episodic analyzer are very strongly connected to units in the visual image system while they are only weakly and indirectly connected to units in the speech analyzer or the printed word analyzer. This explains why episodic memory is poor for the details of verbal material but good for the details of visual material. It is also consistent with the introspective observation that the episodic memory system prefers to express itself via visual images; that is, we tend to remember our past experiences by forming visual images rather than by forming auditory images.

Reconstruction versus veridical memories

It might seem more parsimonious just to propose that we have an episodic memory resembling an archive of visual pictures or snapshots. Some theorists would argue just this. Penfield and Roberts (1959), in the course of operating on people's brains, had occasion to stimulate various areas of the cortex with a mild electric current. When certain areas were stimulated, subjects seemed to relive episodes in their lives. They felt that they were actually in the past, hearing and seeing things that they had previously experienced. After the experience was over, they said that this was an exact reexperiencing of the event. These *experiential responses* led Penfield and Roberts to the rather incautious conclusion that we retain veridical memories of every second of our lives. I say that this conclusion was incautious for two reasons. First, no one checked on whether what Penfield and Roberts' subjects experienced were, in fact, actual memories or new constructions that seemed realistic; that is, was every detail exactly as the patient remembered it? Indeed, it would be very difficult to make this determination. Second, even if we were to grant that these were veridical memories, the presence of one or two such memories certainly does not warrant the conclusion that we have such memories for every event we have ever experienced. If I say two Japanese words to you, are you likely to conclude that I know all Japanese words? If so, you would be quite wide of the mark, for, in fact, these are the only Japanese words that I know. There is no more reason to conclude that I have a snapshot memory of everything that has ever happened to me than to conclude that I am fluent in Japanese.

Can you remember your high school graduation? I'll bet that with a bit of effort, you can recall seeing your friends receiving diplomas. Can you see yourself getting your diploma? If so, the memory must be a reconstructed one. You could not very well have seen yourself going up to the stage and being handed a diploma because that would have required stepping out of your body. If memory images were veridical, we should see remembered scenes from the perspective we originally viewed them from. However, we are able to see ourselves in the scene in many of our memories. This strongly suggests that the image we conjure up is a reconstruction rather than an actual memory. Hypothetically, when any sort of event occurs, we code or remember it as an abstract proposition. We do this whether the event consists of hearing a sentence, brushing our teeth, going out on a date, or whatever. When we have to recall the event, we retrieve this abstract schema. Then we *reconstruct* the memory on the basis of the proposition. Often, this reconstruction takes a visual form. However, that does not mean that the memory was stored in this form. It may be that the abstract proposition coding the memory is merely realized or expressed in visual form.

RETRIEVAL

Once an item or an association is in episodic memory, how is it retrieved or remembered? Let's assume that retrieval means activation of the cognitive unit or units coding the item in question. If this is the case, then asking how retrieval works is the same as asking how cognitive units are activated. We have already considered this question in some detail. A cognitive unit can be activated via any of the input paths to it. For example, we can retrieve the cognitive unit coding the word BAT in several ways. Hearing the word BAT will activate the unit. We could also activate the unit indirectly by asking a person to tell us the names of flying mammals. The unit might also be spontaneously activated if a person got to thinking about werewolves, vampires, witches, and the like.

Accessing episodic units

Presumably, episodic memory traces are retrieved in a similar fashion. Some sort of retrieval cue will always be necessary; that is, something must activate the units to be retrieved. There are two ways of testing memory. A *recognition test* uses the item to be remembered as the retrieval cue. For example, suppose that we gave a person a list of words to remember. We could test memory for the list by showing the person a set of words and asking whether each was on the list or not. In a *recall test,* the person has got to activate the relevant units himself. In this case, the retrieval cue is indirect. It might consist of saying to the person, "What were the words on the list I just taught you?" This question should activate an episodic chunking node coding the concept, WORDS-ON-THE-LIST-I-JUST-LEARNED. Activation of this unit should activate each of the words connected to it. Recognition tests guarantee that all of the relevant cognitive units will be activated, but recall tests do not. Thus, recognition memory should generally be better than recall. It usually is (Postman, Jenkins, and Postman, 1948), but there is an interesting exception.

Assessing episodic units

Just activating or accessing cognitive units does not explain memory. For example, suppose that a person is shown the word BAT in a recognition test. Presenting the word should fully activate the BAT unit whether or not it was on the list of words that was learned. We need to explain how the person is able to respond correctly as to whether or not BAT was on the to-be-remembered list. There are several possibilities. First, activation should be easier or faster if the unit had been recently activated. This should be the case regardless of whether activation is direct (as in a recognition test) or indirect (as in a recall test). Thus, ease of activation would be a clue that could be used. Second, presence and/or strength of an association between the unit and the episodic chunking node could be assessed. In a recognition test, the word is presented and one waits to see whether the chunking node is activated. If it is, one concludes that the word was on the list. In a recall test, the episodic chunking node is activated, and one waits to see what word-units are activated.

This theory of retrieval is similar to the dual-process theory proposed by Anderson and Bower (1972). The basic idea of their theory is that list items are "marked"—for example, by a decrease in threshold or an increase in activation —upon presentation. In a recognition test, the experimenter activates the relevant units and a decision is made as to whether a "mark" is present or not. This is similar to the suggestion that the decision is made on the basis of ease-of-activation of the unit. In a recall test, Anderson and Bower hold that the subject must select a set of candidate units and then perform a recognition test (search for a "mark") on each. This is similar to my suggestion that a higher-order chunking node activates a set of lower-order units.

Necessity of episodic chunking units

It may not be immediately apparent to you that it is necessary to postulate episodic chunking nodes to explain how people remember a list of words. Why not just say that the cognitive units corresponding to the list words are marked or activated and that, at the time of recall, the subject articulates the words corresponding to the most activated cognitive units. The difficulty with this idea is that it does not account for the obvious fact that the subject can differentiate the list words from other words that happen to be spoken or seen. At the time of recall, the cognitive units corresponding to list words may, in fact, not be the most activated ones.

Suppose the experimenter says, "Okay, now repeat the words on the list I just taught you." The cognitive units corresponding to the words in the experimenter's instructions will be the most activated ones. Why does not the subject cheerfully repeat back the instructions in the mistaken belief that these are the list words? This should happen if the set of currently most activated words were taken to be the ones constituting the list. Of course, this is not what happens. In order to explain why not, we have to postulate that the list words are marked in some special way. Connecting all of them to an episodic chunking unit is one way of accomplishing this special marking.

Encoding specificity

Do you recall the example of remembering a list of women's names that I used a few pages ago? If not, you may be a victim of encoding specificity. If so, a different retrieval cue will be helpful: Do you recall the example of remembering a list of flowers? The list I have in mind was composed of VIOLET, ROSE, DAISY, LILY, and IRIS. If you took these to be the names of flowers, you hypothetically set up an episodic chunking node connected to the semantic units coding these flowers. This episodic unit was hypothetically not connected to semantic units coding VIOLET, ROSE, and so on as women's names. This is illustrated in Figure 9–5. Because of this, the retrieval cue—a list of women's names—would be of no help in recall.

The encoding specificity principle states that what is perceived or understood at the time of input is what is stored in episodic memory (Tulving and Thomson, 1973). In other words, "A retrieval cue can provide access to information avail-

FIGURE 9–5 Example of the encoding specificity principle. The retrieval cue "women's names" will be ineffective if a subject thought of the list words as names of flowers during learning.

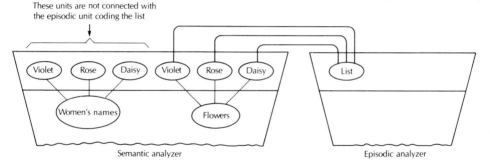

These units are not connected with the episodic unit coding the list

Semantic analyzer   Episodic analyzer

able about an event in the memory store if and only if it has been stored as part of the specific memory trace of the event" (Tulving and Thomson, 1973: 16). Tulving has argued that encoding specificity is supportive of his contention that episodic memory consists of a store separate and distinct from structural memory (Tulving and Watkins, 1975; Watkins and Tulving, 1975). The reason for saying this is that if episodic memory merely consisted of marking or associating units in structural memory, then retrieval cues not present—or not thought of— at the time of learning should be effective. However, they seem not to be.

Let's consider an experiment by Thomson and Tulving (1970). They taught subjects several word lists under three conditions: strong cues (highly associated words) accompanied each list word during learning (for example, dark–LIGHT), weak cues (weakly associated words) accompanied each list word (for example, head–LIGHT), or no cues accompanied each list word. Whichever type of cue was present at input was also present at the time of recall. The point of the initial trials was to get subjects used to encoding or remembering words in terms of strong cues, weak cues, or no cues. Without this initial practice, subjects might have spontaneously generated strong word associates at the time of learning in order to help themselves remember the words. Finally, on a crucial trial, subjects were given a different set of cues at the time of recall than they had been given at the time of learning. The results were clearcut. Giving strong cues at the time of recall did not help at all if weak cues were present during learning; that is, recall in this condition was no better than in a control condition where no cues were given at the time of recall.

Figure 9–6 shows how encoding specificity might work in this situation. Learning the pair head–LIGHT consists of establishing the directed association shown in the figure. Only presentation of the word "head" allows retrieval of the node marked Pair$_1$. Presentation of the word "dark" should activate the cognitive unit coding LIGHT because of their preexisting association. Perhaps it does, but it is evidently Pair$_1$ (head–LIGHT) that was entered into episodic memory. The encoding specificity principle says that it is not just the list words that are entered in episodic memory but the list-words-in-the-experimental-context. Thus, for example, it is not LIGHT that is entered in episodic memory, but LIGHT-in-the-context-of-head. Because of this, LIGHT-in-the-context-of-dark is not recognized as being on the list. If this line of reasoning is correct, then we could even show the subject the pair dark–LIGHT and LIGHT should not be recognized as being

FIGURE 9–6   Encoding specificity in paired-associate learning. Only "head" is an effective retrieval cue for Pair$_1$ even though "dark" is strongly associated with LIGHT because of prior learning.

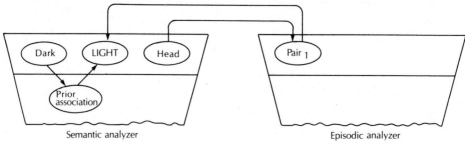

Semantic analyzer   Episodic analyzer

on the list. That seems a bit farfetched. Maybe so, but it is exactly what happens.

Tulving and Thomson (1973) report an experiment that demonstrates this phenomenon. Subjects first learned a list of paired associates (for example, HEAD–LIGHT). Then they were given a free-association test with words that were quite likely to elicit the response words on the paired-associate list. For example, the stimulus, DARK, might be expected to elicit the response, LIGHT. Once subjects had written down all of their associations, they were asked to go through them and circle the ones that they recognized as being on the original list. Only 25 percent of the list words that subjects produced were recognized! Thus, LIGHT might actually be produced as a word association to DARK but not recognized as being on the original list. Finally, a free-recall test was given. The first member of each of the pairs on the original list was given and the subject had to respond with the correct second member. Now, 60 percent of the list words were recalled. This included many of the same words that people had just failed to recognize!

This is a very odd finding indeed. As Flexner and Tulving (1978) put it, "Why should a perfectly normal and intelligent person not be able to recognize a familiar word that he has studied only a short time before and about whose presence in the list he is perfectly well aware as judged by his ability to produce it in response to the list cue?" The finding is not just a bizarre fluke. Flexner and Tulving cite 21 subsequent experiments that have found the same thing. It is not necessary to have the subjects produce the word associations themselves. The same results are found if they are just shown sets of words and asked to circle the ones they recognize. They still fail to recognize many of the list words they are able to recall when provided with the correct retrieval cue. It would be difficult to explain these findings with the theory that episodic memory consists merely of marking units in structural memory. If this were the case, then subjects should instantly recognize list words when they were shown to them.

FORGETTING

Once we have entered something in episodic memory, it becomes harder and harder to retrieve it the longer we wait. The probability that we will be able to retrieve an item falls off extremely rapidly at first. Then the rate of decline slows down. As far as we know, though, the probability of correct recall keeps on going down with the passage of time. You can demonstrate this to yourself. Get a blank piece of paper. Write down what you had for dinner last night. Rate how confident you are of this answer. Now do the same for the night before last, and so on. Chances are that your memory (and your confidence in it) for the immediately preceding few days is fairly good. But the further back in time you go, the worse your memory will become.

Decay

What causes this? The simplest explanation would be that the strength of episodic memory traces decays as time passes. This is the commonsense view. That does not necessarily mean that it is wrong. As McGeoch (1932) pointed out, though, the logic of a simple decay theory is somewhat faulty. The passage of time alone certainly cannot cause forgetting. It must be that, as time passes, processes in the nervous system act to bring about decay. The point is that if time could pass with nothing happening in the nervous system, then there should be no loss of memory. This is certainly true. However, decay theory can be re-formulated to handle this criticism. A decay theorist might well argue that decay is indeed a gradual process in the nervous system, but it occurs independently of other activities. Perhaps it is like the gradual loss of radioactivity in radium. This decay process goes on irrespective of what is happening to the radium—whether it is buried in the earth, lying on the ground, or being carried about in someone's pocket.

If forgetting is indeed this sort of autonomous decay process, then it should occur at the same rate no matter what is going on in a person's mind. In a classic experiment, Jenkins and Dallenbach (1924) taught their subjects lists of nonsense syllables. Then the subjects either slept or carried out their normal activities for one, two, four, or eight hours. As you can see in Figure 9–7, recall was better at all intervals after sleep than after normal waking activities. Presumably, less is going on in the nervous system during sleep than during waking. It must be that other activities in the mind, not a passive process of decay, cause forgetting. If so, then why did the subjects who slept through Jenkins and Dallenbach's

FIGURE 9–7   Amount of recall of newly learned material after various periods of sleeping and of waking. Results for two subjects—H and Mc—are shown.

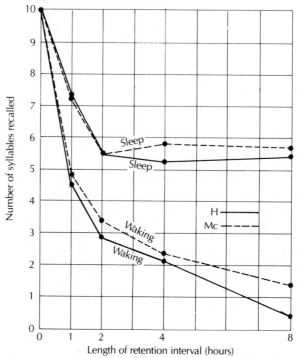

Source: J. G. Jenkins and K. M. Dallenbach, "Oblivescence During Sleep and Waking," *American Journal of Psychology* 35 (1924):610.

experiment forget anything at all? Well, there is not a complete cessation of all mental activity during sleep. For example, we do dream. Perhaps even this causes forgetting. It does seem to do so. Yaroush, Sullivan, and Ekstrand (1971) showed that retention of newly learned material is worse after sleep filled with dreams than after dreamless sleep.

Interference

The Jenkins and Dallenbach experiment led to an almost universal abandonment of decay theories of forgetting. If decay does not cause us to forget, then what does? Subsequent theories have suggested that some form of interference causes forgetting. The essential idea in all of these theories is that once something is entered in episodic memory, other episodic memory traces somehow interfere with its retrieval. How this happens is explained in different ways by the different theories. There have been four main theories, each suggesting a different mechanism: response competition, unlearning, response inhibition, and blocking. We can easily reformulate the last three in terms of lateral inhibition theory. The first theory is not true, so we don't need to reformulate it.

THE BASIC DATA

Before we reformulate anything, let's see what it is that we have to explain. One of the easiest ways to study memory is with paired-associate learning. One gives subjects a list of paired items in the form A–B. The items are generally either words (for example, CAT–MOUNTAIN) or nonsense syllables (for example, DIX–FUG). Although the specifics vary, the basic idea is for the subject to learn all of the pairs on the list. Memory can be tested by presenting each A-item and having the subject respond with the correct B-item. Given that one wants to study newly formed memories, one would want to take care to form the list with pairs that are not already associated in subjects' minds. A list formed of pairs such as CAT–DOG, BLACK–WHITE, and so on would be of little use for this purpose. Just teaching a subject a list of paired associates will not help us study interference. Here is the most common way of studying interference: First, subjects are taught an A–B list. Then they are taught an A–C list. By an A–C list, I mean one where all of the A-items have been repaired with new (C) items. Let's say that this is the A–B list: CAT–MOUNTAIN, PAPER–GREEN, STOVE–DOOR, RUG–EAR, and so on. This might be the A–C list: CAT–FLOOR, PAPER–TRUCK, STOVE–RED, RUG–HILL, and so on.

Now what? There are two basic paradigms for studying interference in memory. The more intuitively obvious one is called the *retroactive inhibition* paradigm. Here, we teach subjects A–B. Then we teach them A–C. Finally, we test them for memory of the original A–B list. Before we can make any sense of what we find, we need a control group. This group learns A–B. Then, while the experimental group learns A–C, this group does something equal in difficulty to. learning the A–C list but otherwise as irrelevant as possible. Finally, this group too is tested on A–B. The reasoning behind this design is that there should be minimal interference for the A–B list in the control group. On the other hand, learning A–C should interfere with retention of the A–B list in the experimental group. The basic finding is well established. The experimental group recalls the A–B list worse than the control group. Furthermore, the more similar B-items and C-items are, the worse is recall in the experimental group (Friedman and Reynolds, 1967). Thus, the basic principle of retroactive inhibition is that the more similar new material is to previously learned material, the more forgetting of the previously learned material it will cause.

The other type of interference effect is called *proactive inhibition*. Here, it is prior memories that interfere with subsequent memories. To study proactive inhibition, we would first teach subjects the A–B list and then the A–C list, just as in a retroactive inhibition experiment. The difference is that we then test them for their memory of the A–C list. The proper control group would be one that engaged in a control task while the experimental group learned the A–B list. Then, the control group would also learn the A–C list and be tested on it. The basic finding is that the experimental group recalls the A–C list less well than the control group. Retention is again a function of similarity between B- and C–items. The more similar they are, the more interference there is. Thus, the basic principle of proactive inhibition is that the more similar previously learned material is to new material, the more forgetting of new material there will be.

Proactive inhibition implies that what we have learned before hinders new learning. It is a very strong effect. The German psychologist Ebbinghaus began the scientific study of memory in the 19th century. His method was to use himself as a subject. He learned lists of nonsense syllables and then tested himself after various delays in order to study forgetting. On a typical list, Ebbinghaus (1885) could recall only 35 percent of the nonsense syllables after one day's delay. Later on, Underwood (1949) noted something very interesting. When he brought naive undergraduate students into his laboratory and gave them the same task, they could recall about 80 percent of the nonsense syllables after the same delay. Why should this be? Ebbinghaus should have been much better at this task since he had done it hundreds of times. Maybe that was the problem. Perhaps proactive inhibition due to learning all of the previous lists actually interfered with retention of new lists. This does seem to have been the case. Underwood (1957) repeatedly taught subjects lists of nonsense syllables and tested memory 24 hours later. On the first list a person was exposed to, 80 percent of the items were correctly recalled. By the time a person had learned 20 lists, only 20 percent of the items on the 20th list were correctly recalled. The effects of such proactive inhibition are graphed in Figure 9–8.

RESPONSE COMPETITION

The earliest and most obvious theory of interference (McGeoch 1942) had to do with *response competition*. Consider learning in an A–B, A–C paradigm. If we test for memory of the A–B list, we will find retroactive inhibition. If we test for memory of the A–C list, we will find proactive inhibition. Perhaps the reason is this. A-words become associated with both B-words and C-words. In order to test memory, A-words are presented. Perhaps the A-words lead subjects to recall *both* the B-word and the C-word, and they cannot remember which one is correct. In other words, the subject does not forget the A–B or A–C associations. Rather, what is forgotten is simply which list the association goes with.

This is a reasonable possibility, which has one very clear implication. Errors

FIGURE 9–8   Illustration of proactive inhibition. Recall of a list declines
as a function of number of previous lists learned.

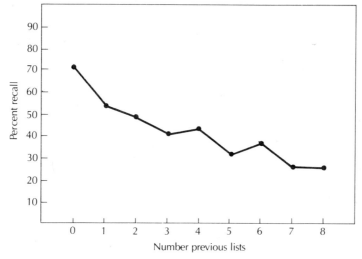

Source: B. J. Underwood, "Interference and Forgetting," *Psychological
Review* 64 (1957):52. Copyright 1957 by the American Psychological Association. Reprinted by permission.

should be intrusions from the interfering list. Suppose we present the A-items and
ask our subjects to respond with the correct B-items. When mistakes are made,
they should consist of giving the A–C association rather than the A–B association.
Melton and Irwin (1940) performed just such an experiment. Their results are
shown in Figure 9–9. As you can see, there were some intrusion errors. However,

FIGURE 9–9   Results of Melton and Irwin's (1940) experiment. Most retroactive
inhibition (RI) is not due to response competition.

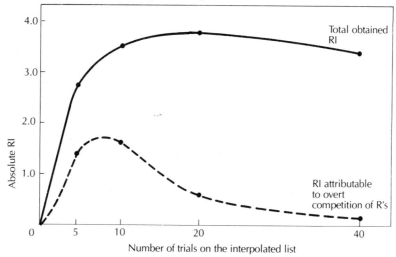

Source: A. W. Melton and J. M. Irwin, "The Influence of Degrees of Interpolated
Learning on Retroactive Inhibition and Overt Transfer of Specific Responses,"
American Journal of Psychology 53 (1940):198.

no matter when memory for the A–B list was tested, intrusion errors did not account for all of the retroactive inhibition. Further, the longer the memory test was delayed (that is, the more A–C trials there have been), the *fewer* intrusion errors there were, but the *more* forgetting there was. The response competition theory simply cannot account for these facts.

UNLEARNING

Melton and Irwin (1940) suggested an alternative theory of forgetting. Their idea is that forgetting is like extinction in Pavlovian conditioning. In extinction, an association is actively inhibited. In this view, learning the A–C association causes the A–B association to be actively suppressed or inhibited. I would interpret this to mean that the episodic memory unit that chunks A and C laterally inhibits the unit that chunks A and B. When a conditioned response is extinguished, there is some spontaneous recovery if a period of time elapses (Pavlov, 1927). Presumably, this is because the old association is still present, but the process of extinction has inhibited it. With the passage of time, some of this inhibition will dissipate.

The same effect is found in paired-associate learning. In an A–B, A–C paradigm, with longer retention intervals, the original A–B associations spontaneously recover in strength (Underwood, 1948a, 1948b). That is, the longer one waits before testing a subject's memory, the more proactive inhibition there is (that is, the less good the retention of A–C) and the less retroactive inhibition there is (that is, the better the memory for A–B items). Briggs (1954) devised a technique called modified free recall for use in the A–B, A–C paradigm. With this procedure, subjects are given A-items and asked for the first response that comes to mind regardless of whether it is a B-item or a C-item. This allows us to get some idea of the relative strength of A–B versus A–C associations. Given an A-item, three types of responses are possible: The subject can give a response not on either list (a preexperimental response), a B-item, or a C-item. Briggs tested memory using the modified free recall technique at various points during learning of the A–B list (left-hand panel of Figure 9–10), during learning of the A–C list (middle panel of Figure 9–10), and after learning of both lists (right-hand panel of Figure 9–10). Before the experiment begins, 100 percent of the responses are, of course, preexperimental ones. As the first (A–B) list is learned, preexperimental responses decline and B-responses increase. Then the second (A–C) list is learned. Now, C-responses increase and B-responses decrease. Note that the second list is a bit harder to learn; that is, at the end of the same number of trials, C-responses are not as common as B-responses had been at the end of learning the first list. Presumably, the A–B associations make the A–C associations harder to acquire. After both lists had been learned, retention was tested at intervals ranging from 4 minutes to 72 hours. As you can see in Figure 9–10, C-responses declined in frequency with time. On the other hand, both B-responses and preexperimental responses increased in frequency as time passed. Hypothetically, these associations were released from inhibition with the passage of time.

One difficulty with Briggs' modified free recall technique is this: Since subjects are allowed to give only one response, when B is given we do not know if C could also be given and vice versa; that is, we do not know if the

FIGURE 9–10   Results of Briggs (1954) experiment. As list 1 is learned, preexperimental responses decline. As list 2 is learned, list 1 responses and preexperimental responses decline. Later, both list 1 responses and preexperimental responses recover in strength, while list 2 responses decline in strength.

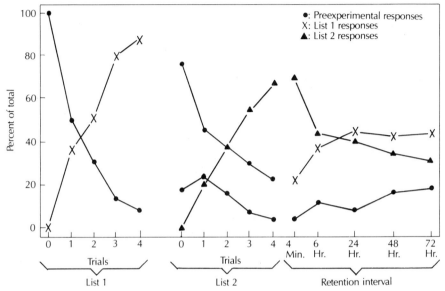

Source: G. E. Briggs, "Acquisition, Extinction, and Recovery Functions in Retroactive Inhibition," *Journal of Experimental Psychology* 47 (1954):288. Copyright 1954 by the American Psychological Association. Reprinted by permission.

response not given has actually been forgotten. To get around this difficulty, Barnes and Underwood (1959) introduced the technique of modified-modified free recall. The technique is simple enough. You just present A to your subjects and ask them to recall both B and C. Barnes and Underwood first taught their subjects an A–B list. Then an A–C list was taught. Recall was tested with modified-modified free recall after from 1 to 20 trials of the A–C list. The results were straightforward. The more A–C trials, the fewer B responses. The A–B associations evidently become genuinely unavailable. Note that both the Briggs experiment and the Barnes and Underwood experiment provide further evidence against the response competition theory. The supposedly competing responses are simply not present. We can reject the response competition theory of forgetting. But can we accept the unlearning theory?

RESPONSE INHIBITION

The unlearning theory holds that it is the association between two items that is inhibited or forgotten. This could be construed as involving lateral inhibition between chunking units in episodic memory: The chunking unit coding A–B and the chunking unit coding A–C inhibit each other. The more similar B and C are, the closer together these chunking units are and, therefore, the more interference there is. But wait a minute! Maybe it is the B-units and C-units themselves that cause the problem. The more similar B and C are, the closer together the units coding them should be and, therefore, the more lateral inhibition there should be. Maybe we do not even need the chunking units to explain forgetting. Perhaps we could explain it simply by reference to inhibitory relations among the component units. Take a look at Figure 9–11. The idea is that—no matter what happens with chunking units—the B and C units should inhibit each other in proportion to their similarity. Postman, Stark, and Fraser (1968) propose that, during A–C learning following A–B learning, the B-items are selectively inhibited while the C-items are primed. This can be called the response inhibition hypothesis of forgetting.

FIGURE 9–11   Possible loci of forgetting: unlearning is lateral inhibition of chunking units; response inhibition is lateral inhibition of component response units.

Semantic or gnostic analyzer

Episodic analyzer

Response inhibition: The component response units inhibit each other

Unlearning: The chunking units inhibit each other

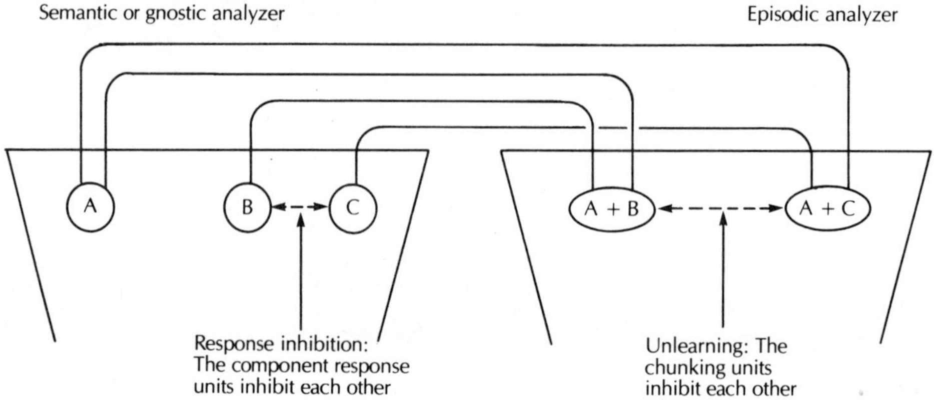

How can we tell if it is the association units or the item units that are inhibited? Here is one possibility. We could use the A–B, A–C paradigm. Then, we could give subjects all of the A-items and all of the B-items. Their task would simply be to match the A-items and B-items. If it were the A–B association (or the chunking unit coding it) that was inhibited, then providing the B-items should not help all that much because the chunking unit tells which B-item goes with which A-item. On the other hand, if inhibition of the B-units themselves was behind forgetting, then this procedure should be quite helpful. Postman and Stark (1969) used an A–B, A–C paradigm. Then, they tested memory for the A–B list in the manner just suggested. Subjects were given all of the A-items and B-items and simply had to match them. The results were quite striking. Subjects did very well indeed on this task as compared with tasks where the B-items have to be recalled. There was no statistically significant evidence for retroactive inhibition. However, results did show a trend toward some forgetting of the association itself.

Other studies using the same procedure have clarified the issue, and virtually all have found evidence that suggests some unlearning or inhibition of the association itself. Wickelgren (1976) cites 21 other studies showing this effect and only two failing to find it. Here is what the studies have found: Performance is better with the matching task than with a recall task. Three possible explanations come to mind: (1) Matching or recognition is in general simply easier than recall, not only in this task but in most memory tasks. (2) Some forgetting is in fact due to inhibition of the response items themselves, as the response inhibition theory claims. (3) Presenting both the A and B units more strongly activates the episodic units coding the A–B association. One could certainly argue that it is in fact these episodic units that are actually responsible for forgetting, but presentation of both A and B is sufficient to release them from inhibition. It is unclear which of these explanations are correct. A second consistent finding of these studies has been that there is in fact some evidence for unlearning the associations themselves. Even with the recognition matching task, performance is not perfect. Thus, it is well established that some forgetting is due to inhibition of associations or of the episodic chunking units coding these associations.

BLOCKING

Wickelgren (1976) has suggested a variant of the response inhibition hypothesis called the blocking hypothesis. (Although he discusses it as a possible source of interference, Wickelgren argues against the blocking hypothesis.) The idea is that the act of recalling one item inhibits recall of another one. Consider a modified-modified free recall test of memory in an A–B, A–C paradigm. The blocking hypothesis holds that recall of B inhibits the C-unit. Of course, if C were recalled first, it would be expected to inhibit the B-unit. Whereas Postman's response inhibition theory says that the inhibition occurs during acquisition, the blocking theory says that it occurs during recall. Of course, both theories could be true. There is relatively little evidence for blocking. Postman, Stark, and Fraser (1968) used what might be called modified-modified-modified free recall to study retention of B items in an A–B, A–C paradigm. On the recall test, both the stimulus, A, and the correct C-item were presented. Subjects' task was to recall B. According to the blocking theory, the mere presence of C-items should inhibit retrieval of the B-items. It did, but only at a very short retention interval (two minutes). At a longer interval, the C-items had no inhibitory effect. A study by Houston (1967) did find inhibitory effects at longer intervals, but they were not statistically significant. The studies of part-list cueing which we described in the last chapter are also supportive of the blocking hypothesis.

Conclusions

Simple decay or response competition cannot explain forgetting. Rather, inhibition of one cognitive unit by another seems to be the culprit. What remains unclear is which cognitive units are inhibiting each other. The unlearning theory can be interpreted as saying that episodic chunking units coding associations inhibit each other. The response inhibition and blocking theories can be interpreted as saying that the inhibition occurs between units in semantic memory or in one of the gnostic analyzers coding the items that are associated. Present evidence does not allow us to reject any of these theories. Our lateral-inhibition model would lead us to expect inhibition on all levels of the episodic analyzer and other analyzers as well. Thus, it would suggest that all of the theories are partially true.

SUMMARY AND CONCLUSIONS

Structural memory contains our general knowledge about sensations, perceptions, and concepts. This knowledge is hypothetically stored in sensory, gnostic, and semantic analyzers. In contrast, episodic memory contains knowledge about specific events that a person has been involved in, has heard about, or has thought about. In large part, it is composed of one's personal memories. Hypothetically, these memories are stored in a separate episodic analyzer. We argued that the basic unit of episodic memory is a chunking node that associates cognitive units in other analyzers. Such chunking nodes are theoretically designed to receive inputs from a number of remote units so as to code a proposition. A proposition is a schema that describes an event; each of the inputs to a proposition hypothetically defines one component of an event (such as the action involved, the agent, the object, and so on).

Some evidence is available for the abstract nature of propositions. Verbatim memory for verbal material is very poor. We tend to remember the gist or meaning of sentences rather than the specific words that composed them. Another way of putting this is to say that we remember the abstract proposition conveyed by a sentence rather than the sentence itself. Memory for unrelated lists of words or syllables is also poor but improves spectacularly when such lists are remembered by assimilating them to abstract propositions. Motor habits also seem to be remembered in terms of propositions rather than in terms of specific motor responses. In contrast to these findings, episodic memory for visual material is quite good. We interpreted this in terms of a special affinity between episodic memory and the visual analyzers. The idea was that remembering an event consists of retrieving an abstract proposition and then realizing or expressing this proposition in mental images. The usual medium of expression is a series of visual mental images.

Retrieval of episodic memories always requires some sort of retrieval cue. In a recall task, this cue is rather vague. An example would be asking you to recall everything that happened to you in the fourth grade. Hypothetically, the retrieval cue in this case activates a chunking unit in episodic memory, and this unit, in turn, activates component units coding the relevant memories. In a recognition task, items are presented, and one is asked if they are familiar. In this case, the retrieval cue activates units coding relevant memories, and the task is to see whether these units in turn activate a chunking unit in episodic memory. Tulving's encoding specificity principle states that a retrieval cue will be effective in eliciting an episodic memory only if it was specifically associated with a to-be-remembered item at the time of learning. A lot of evidence supports this rather surprising principle. Even if retrieval cues are strongly associated with an item in structural memory, they are useless as cues for retrieving episodic memories involving that item unless they were encoded with the item at the time the episodic memory was established.

Theoretically, the structure of the episodic analyzer is similar to that of other analyzers. Units at successively deeper levels of episodic memory are hypothetically more and more abstract. Presumably, vertical connections among episodic units are excitatory. This accounts for the effectiveness of certain retrieval cues and explains why recall of one type of episode often brings to mind similar episodes. Hypothetically, neighboring episodic units on any one level are inter-connected to form a lateral inhibitory network. It is possible that lateral inhibition is important in preserving information about the temporal order of events. Much evidence has been found for the hypothesis that lateral inhibition is responsible for forgetting. Episodic memories do not merely decay with the passage of time. Rather, forgetting can be attributed to a process of interference or inhibition. The more similar two memories are, the more they inhibit one another. This interference can be attributed to lateral inhibition among chunking units in episodic memory (the unlearning hypothesis) or to lateral inhibition among component units in structural memory (the response inhibition hypothesis and the blocking hypothesis).

10

Arousal

AROUSAL AND COGNITION

We have talked about a number of cognitive processes in the preceding chapters. From time to time, we have had occasion to mention the notion that there are nonspecific inputs from the arousal system to cognitive units. It was hypothesized in Chapter 7 that these inputs are necessary in order to focus attention. Later, in Chapters 12 and 13, we shall argue that the arousal system is also crucial in determining what type of thinking a person engages in and what one's overall state of consciousness is. It turns out that *arousal* is a unifying concept that offers answers to questions even more basic than those concerning attention, thought, and state of consciousness.

A task can either be done well or poorly. Cognitive tasks are no exception to this rule. Up to now, though, we have devoted most of our efforts to understanding how cognitive processes work in the first place. The arousal system governs how well or how efficiently these cognitive processes are carried out. In this chapter, we shall describe the Yerkes-Dodson law, which specifies the relationship between arousal and efficiency of learning and performance. The concept of arousal offers an answer to an even more basic question than that of efficiency. Why are cognitive processes carried out at all? We have been so busy describing *how* these processes are carried out that we have not stopped to confront this question of *why* they are carried out. Even if we grant that sensation and perception are relatively effortless and automatic, it is certainly reasonable to ask why people bother to attend to, understand, and remember what they have perceived. Ultimately, the answer to this question must be that it is somehow rewarding or pleasurable to do so. The concept of arousal allows us to explain why it is pleasurable. In so doing, it also allows us to make predictions about what sorts of events will be attended to, thought about, and remembered.

By arousal, we mean how active the arousal system is and, by extension, how much nonspecific input it is sending to the cognitive analyzers. Although the situation is somewhat more complicated than this, we may think of the cognitive analyzers as residing in the cortex of the brain and the arousal system being centered in the reticular activating system of the midbrain. As mentioned in Chapter 7, the reticular activating system sends diffuse, nonspecific projections to all areas of the cortex. Subjectively, arousal corresponds to the general degree to which an organism as a whole is excited, stirred up, tense, or activated. Arousal is a continuum running from sleep, coma, drowsiness on the low end through wakeful attentiveness to states of agitation and panic on the high end. In this chapter, we shall consider five major topics: how arousal is measured, exactly what is meant by arousal, what factors influence or elicit arousal, how arousal governs the efficiency of cognition, and how arousal determines hedonic tone (feelings of pleasure and displeasure).

MEASUREMENT

Psychophysiological indexes

If arousal is a diffuse and general activation of the nervous system, then anything that measures an aspect of such activity should measure arousal. Certainly, the electroencephalogram (EEG), which measures degree of cortical activation, should be useful. It seems that there is, in fact, at least a rough correspondence between the type of brain waves observed and level of arousal. Generally speaking, the higher the level of arousal, the faster the frequency and the lower the amplitude of brain waves. During sleep, delta waves (1–3 Hz) are observed. In the drowsy state just before falling asleep, we find somewhat faster theta waves (4–7 Hz). When a person is awake but relaxed, alpha waves (8–13 Hz) are present. In states of higher arousal, alpha waves are blocked and replaced by beta waves (14–30 Hz). Thus, the higher the level of arousal, the faster the frequency of brain waves. In general, at any one time, one finds pretty much the same type of EEG waves no matter where on the scalp the recording electrodes are placed. It is extremely unlikely that one set of electrodes would yield delta waves while another set a few centimeters away would yield beta waves. This supports the idea that level of arousal is general rather than specific to different regions of the brain. (In Chapter 11, we shall see that there are some differences in the activation of different regions of the brain. While these differences are very small, they are quite instructive in regard to localization of different cognitive processes in different parts of the brain.) EEG evoked potentials also have been used to measure the degree of arousal induced by a stimulus. Generally, the more arousal a stimulus induces, the larger the evoked potential.

Many other psychophysiological measures have been used to measure arousal. One of the most commonly used is galvanic skin conductance. This is measured by passing an imperceptible electrical current between two electrodes. Conductance—the ease with which the current flows—rises with increases in arousal. This is probably because of a slight increase in the activity of the sweat glands. A related measure is skin potential, which is an index of the spontaneous electrical activity of the skin. The electromyogram (EMG) measures the degree of muscular tension, which increases with arousal. Other common measures include heart rate, blood pressure, and respiration rate. As you might imagine, increased arousal is generally accompanied by a faster heart rate, heightened blood pressure, and faster rate of respiration. There are some other less obvious measures as well. Hess (1975) has done several studies that suggest that the dilation of the pupil is a sensitive index of arousal; that is, the more aroused the person is, the more dilated the pupil. Others have suggested that skin temperature can be used as an index of arousal.

Self-reports

Another method of measuring arousal is deceptively simple. One can just ask people. Thayer (1967) developed an Activation-Deactivation Adjective Check List. This is a list of adjectives on which a person is asked to check off those that most apply at the moment. Thayer gave this scale to 221 college students and then factor analyzed the results. The results indicated four separate dimensions that have to do with arousal: general activation (for example, lively, active, energetic), high activation (for example, jittery, stirred up, intense) general de-activation (for example, calm, placid, quiescent), and deactivation-sleep (for example, tired, sleepy, drowsy). Thayer found that these factors correlated in the expected direction with heart rate and skin conductance. Even simpler is the method used by Dermer and Berscheid (1972), who merely had their subjects rate their current state of arousal on a continuum ranging from − 10 to + 10.

COMPONENTS OF AROUSAL

Earlier theorists treated arousal as one unitary dimension that could be measured in a variety of ways. However, the various indexes mentioned earlier do not correlate perfectly with each other. For example, if one were to take all of these measurements while subjects were simply doing nothing in a relaxed state, the measures would show fairly low positive correlations. Somewhat better correlations have been found if a state of arousal is induced. Berlyne (1965) reviewed several studies on the effect of mental effort. In general, these studies indicate that, with increased mental effort, all of the measures move in the expected direction. Thus, average EEG frequency increases, as do muscle tension, heart rate, and skin conductance. Further, the more difficult (and, hence, the more arousing) the task, the greater the change. The studies reviewed by Berlyne did not measure all of the indexes concurrently. When this is done, similar results tend to emerge. For example, Eason and Dudley (1971) measured EEG evoked potentials, heart rate, skin resistance, and muscle tension. Under conditions of induced arousal, all of the measures acted together. However, the correlations were still not perfect.

In some cases, the indexes that hypothetically measure arousal actually move in different directions. For example, Lacey (1967) has shown that, during tasks requiring intake of information, heart rate decreases while skin conductance rises. On the other hand, with tasks requiring internal processing or thinking, a reverse pattern is found: heart rate increases while skin conductance falls. This sort of result suggests that there may not be one unitary arousal system. Rather, the nervous system may have several systems than can, under some circumstances, operate independently. On the anatomical level, the arousal system clearly is not one completely unified structure. Several different brain structures seem to have arousal functions. Most researchers now agree that there are at least two general types of physiological arousal—cortical and visceral (Berlyne, 1971; Eysenck, 1967; Lacey, 1967). Cortical arousal is under the control of the reticular activating system and related brain structures. Most directly measured by the EEG, it is elicited by fairly mild stimuli, goes along with interest or attention, and can occur without visceral arousal. Visceral or autonomic arousal is elicited by strong stimuli. It goes along with fear and other intense emotions and occurs only when high levels of cortical arousal are also present. In this chapter, we will concentrate on cortical arousal. In the next chapter, we shall have more to say about visceral arousal. Unless otherwise noted, when we speak of the arousal system, we mean only the one regulating cortical arousal.

DETERMINANTS OF AROUSAL

At any moment, a person's level of arousal is determined by several different factors. The most important of these factors are amount and type of stimulation, natural rhythms or cycles, and internal factors ranging from self-induced effort to specific drives such as hunger or thirst. All of these various causes are added up to determine level of arousal. Just as you can get to a given location via several routes, you can arrive at a given level of arousal by means of various combinations of the determinants of arousal.

Arousal potential

Any stimulus has two aspects. First, it has some meaning or significance. It bears some information that is processed in the ways we have discussed in previous chapters; that is, it activates some set of cognitive units. Second, it induces arousal; that is, it activates the arousal system. This is true whether the stimulus is a flash of light, your grandmother, your own ideas about cognition, or the total configuration of events converging on you at any given moment. Any stimulus, thus, has *arousal potential* or *impact value*. This is the ability of the stimulus to induce arousal. Stimuli vary in their arousal potential. Some, such as a speck of dust or the *u* in the word DUST, have very little arousal potential. Others, such as being in a car wreck, have the capability of inducing quite a bit of arousal. What determines the arousal potential of a stimulus? Berlyne (1971) argues that three basic things determine arousal potential: psychophysical properties, ecological properties, and collative properties of stimuli. Note that these are exactly the same properties that are relevant in eliciting involuntary attention and the orienting reflex.

PSYCHOPHYSICAL PROPERTIES

The psychophysical properties of a stimulus refer to its physical characteristics, such as loudness and pitch for auditory stimuli or brightness and hue for visual stimuli. In general, the more intense a stimulus is, the more arousal it induces. A faint tap induces less arousal than a pistol shot, a dim light induces less arousal than a bright one, and so on. This can be and has been demonstrated with the indexes of arousal already described. Other physical attributes of stimuli besides intensity have a lawful effect on arousal. For example, long wave (red) light induces more arousal than short wave (blue) light (Berlyne, 1971). High and low pitched tones induce more arousal than those of medium pitch (Berlyne et al., 1967). Internal stimuli are also important in determining arousal. One important class of internal stimuli is biological needs or drives, such as hunger, thirst, and sex. Deprivation of food, water, or sex will increase the intensity of these needs. Because of this, arousal will be increased. Thus, the more intense a stimulus— whether external or internal—the more arousal that it produces.

ECOLOGICAL PROPERTIES

Ecological properties of stimuli refer to their signal value or meaning. If you hear someone yelling FIRE, this is apt to induce more arousal than if you hear someone yelling FREE FLOWERS. If you are alone on a dark night, the slightest footfall may cause a massive arousal reaction whereas a loud airplane passing overhead may elicit virtually no reaction at all. Berlyne (1971) argues that the signal value or meaningfulness of a stimulus can arise from either instinctual sources or from learning. Biological rewards have genetically predetermined meaningfulness whereas the importance or significance of other sorts of stimuli is rather clearly learned. Irrespective of intensity and other psychophysical properties, stimuli differ in their impact value. This is because they differ in their meaning or significance for the organism. However, virtually every stimulus pattern presumably has some degree of meaningfulness. If it did not, we probably would not notice it at all.

COLLATIVE PROPERTIES

Collative properties of stimuli are things such as novelty, complexity, incongruity, surprisingness, ambiguity, and conflict. All of these are extremely potent elicitors of arousal. Berlyne uses the term *collative* to describe these things because all of them involve some collation or comparison. Novelty, surprise, and incongruity all involve comparison of a stimulus with an expectation. Thus, all have to do with a mismatch between a stimulus and a cognitive category or template. On the other hand, complexity, conflict, and ambiguity involve a different sort of mismatch. Here, the stimulus may match several templates at least partially. The important point is that all of the collative properties refer to deviation from the circumstance where the stimulus perfectly matches one and only one cognitive model. The greater the deviation from this perfect match, the greater the arousal potential of the stimulus. Such states as stress, guilt, loneliness, and so on are related to the collative properties. In the case of stress, what is demanded of you (the stimulus) does not fit with what you think that you can do or what you want to do (the cognitive model). In the case of guilt, what you have done does not fit with your idea of what you should have done. With loneliness, the stimulus (no one) and the cortical model (someone) are discrepant. In general, then, a discrepancy of any sort refers to the collative aspects of cognition.

Habituation

In Chapter 7 we discussed habituation. If a stimulus is presented over and over, it gradually loses its arousal potential. On each successive presentation, it elicits less arousal. Often this is true because a cognitive model is gradually constructed. The stimulus matches this model better and better as the model is built up. Because arousal is a consequence of the degree of mismatch between a stimulus and a cognitive model, the result is that the stimulus elicits less arousal on each successive presentation. However, while habituation seems to be quickest in regard to the collative properties, repeated presentation of an intense or meaningful stimulus also results in habituation.

Cognitive units and arousal

When we say that all stimuli, whether external or internal, elicit some degree of arousal we are really saying that every cognitive unit provides input to the arousal system. Why? The model we have developed holds that perception is activation of some set of preexisting cognitive units. Thus, to say that a stimulus elicits arousal is really the same thing as saying that activation of cognitive units elicits arousal. The question of the arousal potential of a stimulus is really the question of the degree to which a cognitive unit is connected in an excitatory fashion with the arousal system.

Berlyne's psychophysical, ecological, and collative properties may be seen as referring to three types of connections to the arousal system. Psychophysical effects may be seen as due to connections from units in sensory analyzers to the arousal system. The more these units are excited, the more they excite the arousal system. Ecological effects may be seen as connections from units in gnostic and semantic analyzers to the arousal system. The more significant or meaningful the stimulus or idea coded by a unit, the stronger its connection to the arousal system. Collative effects may be seen as due to a mismatching or contradictory set of units in any type of analyzer being simultaneously activated. The greater the mismatch, the greater the input to the arousal system. Figure 10–1 illustrates these three types of connections to the arousal system. The basic idea is that the more inputs from cognitive analyzers the arousal system receives, the more likely it is to become activated. When the arousal system is so activated, it sends nonspecific arousal inputs to the cortex. A weak, meaningless signal that exactly matches some set of cognitive units will not activate the arousal system. On the other hand, an intense signal that is either meaningful or does not exactly match any set of cognitive units is most likely to activate the arousal system.

A person's level of arousal will be determined by *all* of the cognitive units activated at any given moment. Your arousal now is determined not only by the words in this book, upon which your attention is focused. Other background stimuli are also quite important. Background noises, temperature, general level of illumination, hunger, thirst, and so on are also causing arousal. Thus, your level of arousal at this moment is the sum of the arousal potentials of all of the internal and external stimuli confronting you.

FIGURE 10–1   Types of connections between an analyzer and the arousal system.
Psychophysical inputs hypothetically arise only from sensory analyzers. Ecological inputs
hypothetically come only from gnostic or conceptual analyzers. Collative inputs can come
from any analyzer.

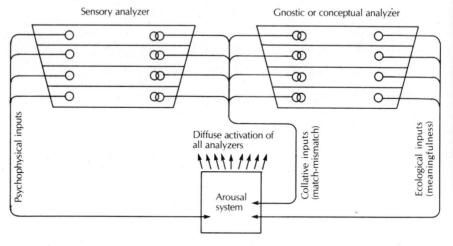

Cycles

CIRCADIAN RHYTHMS

Much evidence exists that arousal level fluctuates in a rhythmic or cyclic
fashion. Some scientists argue that there are natural or endogenous arousal
rhythms. Others argue that these rhythms are due to rhythms in the amount
and type of stimulation impinging upon us at different times. The most obvious
arousal rhythm is the circadian sleep-waking rhythm. Arousal is obviously higher
during waking than during sleeping. But there is evidence that arousal tends to
show a fairly clear cycle throughout the day; that is, arousal is low in the morning,
rises gradually to a peak in the mid-afternoon, and then declines. Dermer and
Berscheid (1972) had 51 subjects rate their own arousal at one-hour intervals on
a scale ranging from − 10 to + 10 (see Figure 10–2). Thayer (1967) used the
adjective checklist procedure described earlier in a similar study and obtained
similar results. Because arousal is related to efficiency of task performance, the
circadian arousal rhythm means that we are maximally efficient at different sorts
of tasks at different times of the day.

ULTRADIAN RHYTHMS

There is also evidence for an ultradian arousal rhythm of about 90 minutes.
This cycle was first noticed during sleep. When we go to sleep, our arousal drops
off to a low level. However, about every 90 minutes, arousal as measured by the
EEG increases so that the EEG actually resembles that seen when waking subjects
are actively aroused; that is, there are a lot of low-voltage, fast-frequency beta
waves. Rapid eye movements accompany this arousal. Although the eyes remain
closed, they move back and forth quickly. If subjects are awakened during these
periods they generally report that they have been dreaming.

FIGURE 10–2   Cyclical variation in arousal across the course of a day, based upon self-reports of waking subjects

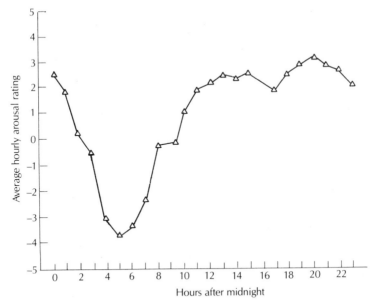

Source: M. Dermer and E. Berscheid, "Self-Report of Arousal as an Indicant of Activation Level," *Behavioral Science* 17 (1972):425.

Kripke and Sonnenschein (1978) found evidence that the 90-minute arousal cycle persists throughout the whole day, not just during sleep. Arousal increases and decreases in a 90-minute cycle throughout the entire day. Even more interesting, a 90-minute fantasy cycle coincides with this oscillation in arousal; that is, our thought oscillates from being logical, abstract, and reality oriented to being illogical, concrete, and dreamlike in a 90-minute cycle. Throughout the night, we lapse into dreams about every 90 minutes; throughout the day, we lapse into dream-like fantasy about every 90 minutes. This 90-minute arousal cycle is superimposed on the more extreme diurnal arousal rhythm.

SHORTER RHYTHMS

The EEG—the most important index of cortical arousal—is itself cyclic. For example, alpha waves constitute a rhythm with an average frequency of 10 cycles per second in the electrical potential of the brain. Several theorists have interpreted these fluctuations as minute variations in cortical excitability or arousal. There is some evidence for this idea. As we saw in Chapter 7, the cortical scanning hypothesis of the alpha rhythm holds that it arises from the arousal system's scanning layers of the cortex in order to focus attention.

Drugs

A number of drugs have an effect on arousal. Barbiturates, such as phenobarbital, decrease arousal, apparently because they decrease reticular activating system activity. On the other hand, stimulant drugs, such as amphetamine and benzedrine, increase reticular activating system activity and, hence, arousal. Most hallucinogenic drugs—such as LSD, psilocybin, and mescaline—increase arousal. Other common drugs also have an effect on level of arousal. Alcohol and many narcotics, such as opium, heroin, and morphine, act as central nervous system depressants. Both caffeine and nicotine are mild stimulants. In general, it seems to be the case that any drug that has effects on cognition or consciousness also has an effect on arousal level. On the other hand, drugs that do not affect arousal do not affect consciousness.

Self-control

We are able to exert some self-control over our own level of arousal. One way of doing this is to manipulate the amount and type of stimulation that is impinging upon us. Thus, if we want to lower our level of arousal, we can reduce the arousal potential of our environment. We can turn down the radio, read a less complicated book, choose to walk in the woods rather than go to an amusement park, and so on. Conversely, if we want to raise our level of arousal, we can go to a discotheque, seek out novel experiences, take up parachute jumping, and so on. If none of these things suffice, we can resort to drugs that raise or lower arousal to the desired level.

Other methods of varying level of arousal seem more genuinely to be instances of self-control. We can decide to exert mental effort on a difficult problem, for example. By means of willpower we can maintain mental effort—and concommitant heightened arousal—for considerable periods of time. Studies of biofeedback and relaxation techniques have shown that people can exert control over many of the indexes of arousal. Although I do not know, I expect that these instances of self-control do not really differ very much from instances where arousal is controlled by exposing oneself to (or withdrawing from) stimuli that increase (or decrease) arousal. Will and effort must correspond to cases where arousal is induced by cognitive units that have been activated from within (by internal stimuli or by other cognitive units) rather than from without (by external stimuli).

Individual differences

Some important individual differences are found in arousal. Indeed, some theorists have argued that the most important dimensions along which personality and temperament vary can be ascribed to variations in arousal. We might expect to find individual differences in arousal in several ways. People could differ in their basal arousal and in their reactive arousal. We might also expect differences in the rate of habituation. Finally, each of these differences could be manifest in terms of cortical arousal, visceral arousal, or both. The most studied individual difference has been reactivity. Some people seem to amplify stimuli, while others attenuate stimuli; that is, given exactly the same stimulus, some people react with a lot of arousal. They amplify or magnify its arousal potential. Other people react with much less arousal. They act is if they attenuate or damp down the arousal potential of the stimulus. Pavlov said that those who amplify stimulation have a weak nervous system (Gray, 1964). Eysenck (1967) says that this is the introverted personality type. On the other hand, Eysenck holds that extroverts damp down stimuli. Pavlov said that the extroverted type has a strong nervous system. Eysenck argues that the difference between introverts and extroverts is in cortical arousability. Since introverts amplify the arousal potential of all stimuli, the result is that the level of arousal of introverts at any point in time is higher than the level of arousal of extroverts. This is the reason that extroverts seek out other people—and strong stimuli in general—while introverts avoid them. Other theorists have related variations in arousal to phenomena as diverse as schizophrenia (Venables, 1964) and creativity (Martindale, 1977a). In Chapter 15 we shall investigate some of the ways that creativity and arousal are related.

THE YERKES-DODSON LAW

The distinctive feature of arousal theories is the postulation of an inverted-U relationship between level of arousal and efficiency of performance of any task (Freeman, 1948; Hebb, 1955; Lindsley, 1957; Malmo, 1959; Schlosberg, 1954). This is referred to as the Yerkes-Dodson law. Yerkes and Dodson (1908) originally formulated the law to refer only to learning. However, later theorists extended it to apply not only to the acquisition but also to the performance of virtually any overt or covert behavior. The law states that a medium level of arousal is optimal for performance of a task. As arousal increases or decreases from this medium level, efficiency of performance declines. It is further postulated that the simpler the task, the higher the optimal level of arousal; while the more complex or difficult the task, the lower the optimal level of arousal. Thus, each task has a different optimal level of arousal, and this optimal level is determined by the complexity of the task. Figure 10–3 illustrates curves that might be expected for a very simple task, a task of medium complexity, and a very complex task.

FIGURE 10–3   The Yerkes-Dodson law. Efficiency of performance is a curvilinear function of arousal. Simple tasks (A) are best done at fairly high arousal levels, tasks of medium complexity (B) are best done at medium levels of arousal, and tasks of high complexity (C) are best done at low levels of arousal.

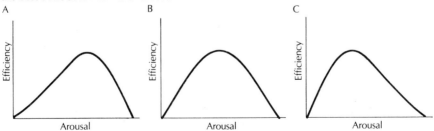

Task complexity

Simple tasks include such things as pounding nails into a board, hearing a clearly spoken word, or pressing a key every time a bright light appears. The Yerkes-Dodson law tells us that—up to some very high level of arousal—the more aroused a person is, the better the task will be performed. Beyond that point, however, further increases in arousal will lead to decrements in performance. Several studies have shown that this is the case for simple tasks. For example, Freeman (1940) and Schlosberg (1954) have shown that reaction time in fairly simple tasks varies curvilinearly with skin conductance. Stennett (1957) measured arousal by skin conductance and muscle tension. Arousal was manipulated by offering subjects different levels of incentive or reward (both to avoid electric shock and to earn money). Hypothetically, the bigger the incentive, the more arousal there will be. The task involved auditory tracking (that is, the subject had to rotate a knob in order to keep a randomly varying noise off). As expected, arousal did increase with increasing incentives and task performance was an inverted-U function of arousal. Complex tasks would include such things as writing an essay examination for a difficult course. In this case, the Yerkes-Dodson law suggests that the optimal level of arousal will be much lower than for the simple task. As you probably know from your own experience with essay examinations, it is generally the case that the more anxious you are the worse you do. But on the other hand, a little bit of anxiety or arousal is necessary. Imagine what your performance might be if it made absolutely no difference to your grade how well you did on the test—or, to take an extreme case, if your arousal was so low that you went to sleep while taking the examination.

Several studies have varied both task complexity and arousal in the same experiment. For example, Broadhurst (1959) conducted a study using rats which involved underwater brightness discrimination. The rats were placed under water, and a sheet of glass at the surface of the water prevented them from coming up for air. They were confronted with two doors that differed in brightness. One was locked and the other could be pushed open. If this door was opened, it allowed the rats to get out of the water. Arousal was varied by different lengths of air deprivation. Longer deprivation should result in higher arousal. Difficulty was varied by varying the difference in brightness between the two doors. As predicted, the more difficult the discrimination, the lower the optimum level of arousal for its performance.

Streufert (1969) studied two-person groups playing a complex war game. Subjects had to make decisions concerning movements of the troops they controlled. In turn, they received information from the experimenter concerning the outcome of these decisions. Streufert varied the noxiousness of information received by subjects by telling them that varying proportions of their moves had resulted in failure. Hypothetically, arousal should increase with increasing noxiousness. Several interesting findings are illustrated in Figure 10–4. Integrated decisions peaked at a moderate level of noxiousness. Integrated decisions were complex decisions taking into account all relevant information, including that gained on prior trials. On the other hand, simpler decisions—unintegrated decisions ignoring relevant information—peaked at a much higher level of noxiousness.

Rate of information input

Arousal should be proportional to the rate at which stimuli are presented. The faster the rate, the higher arousal should be. Many studies have shown that curves such as those predicted by the Yerkes-Dodson law are found when rate of

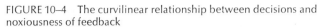

FIGURE 10–4   The curvilinear relationship between decisions and noxiousness of feedback

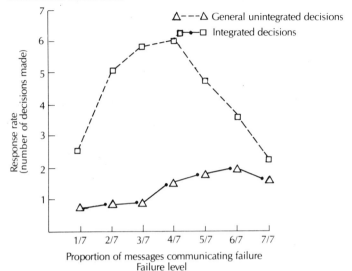

Source: S. Streufert, "Increasing Failure and Response Rate in Complex Decision Making," *Journal of Experimental Social Psychology* 5 (1969): 318.

information input to a cognitive system is varied; that is, as the rate of input rises, output rate also rises at first. However, beyond a critical point, output rate declines. Miller (1978) cites several studies showing that this effect is found even with single neurons. For example, DeValois (1958) varied the rate of light flashes to a cat's eye and measured rate of spike output from a single cell in the cat's lateral geniculate nucleus. Output rate was a curvilinear function of input rate. As the flash rate increased, spike output first rose and then declined so that a very fast flash rate elicited even less spikes than a very slow flash rate. The Yerkes-Dodson law seems to hold even down to the level of individual cognitive units!

Quastler and Wulff (1955) varied the rate of information input to skilled pianists and to skilled typists. Input was random sequences of musical notes in the first case and random sequences of letters in the second case. The response measure was the number of correct notes or letters reproduced. With increasing rates of input, the number of correct responses first rose and then declined. Klemmer and Muller (1969) used an apparatus consisting of five lights arranged in a semicircle. Beneath the lights was a set of five keys. The task was to depress the corresponding key when a light was illuminated. Number of correct responses was a curvilinear function of rate of light flashes, as predicted by the Yerkes-Dodson law. It is important to note that the rate of responding increased as input rate increased; that is, the more flashes, the more responses. The decrement in performance at high rates was not simply due to the inability of the fingers to depress the keys at these rates, since the rate of key pressing was proportional to the rate of light flashes. However, beyond a certain point, more and more of these responses were errors.

Hullian theory and the Yerkes-Dodson law

THE BEHAVIORAL LAW

A lot of experiments with a wide variety of tasks support the validity of the Yerkes-Dodson law. It seems to apply to virtually any behavior or cognitive activity. Thus, it is important to try to understand why it is true. We shall consider an explanation that is based on the behavioral theory originally proposed by Hull (1943), but we will state it in terms of the model of cognition developed in the previous chapters. So, keep in mind that this is a reinterpretation of the Hullian theory rather than the theory as originally stated. The basic explanation has to do with what Hull (1943) called the "behavioral law." This law states that increased arousal increases the probability of whatever response is already most probable. By definition, this means that the probabilities of other responses are decreased. Thus, increasing arousal makes the dominant response to any situation even more dominant. Conversely, decreasing arousal serves to decrease the probability of the dominant response relative to other possible responses. We might reformulate this into a "cognitive law": increases in arousal lead to increases in the activation of whatever cognitive unit is already most activated and to decreases in the activation of other less activated units. Thus, increasing arousal increases the activation of the most activated cognitive unit relative to the activation of other cognitive units in the same analyzer. You will recall that we used this cognitive law in Chapter 7 to explain how a cognitive unit comes to occupy the focus of attention.

EXCITATORY POTENTIAL

If the Yerkes-Dodson law is a consequence of Hull's behavioral law, then we have to ask why the latter is true. Hull's idea is that the excitatory potential ($_sE_r$) of any behavior is a multiplicative function of its habit strength (H) and of drive (D):

$$_sE_r = H \times D$$

Excitatory potential is the probability of a behavior actually being emitted. Hull's notion was that a given stimulus elicits habits that are stored in habit-family hierarchies; that is, any stimulus elicits a set of different habits or potential responses. These habits vary in their probability of being activated by the stimulus. The more probable a habit is, the greater its habit strength. In order to determine excitatory potential, Hull says that it is necessary to multiply habit strength by drive (level of arousal). The habit that is actually emitted in response to the stimulus is the one with the greatest excitatory potential.

In terms of our model of cognition, we could restate this as follows: Any stimulus configuration activates a number of cognitive units. This set of units is the habit-family hierarchy elicited by the stimulus. The degree of activation of each unit varies as a function of the strength of the association between the unit and the unit coding the stimulus and also as a function of the ease of activation of the unit in question. This is the equivalent of habit strength. Degree of activation is also influenced by input from the arousal system. This input corresponds to Hull's concept of drive. All cognitive units hypothetically receive the same amount of input from the arousal system. Excitatory potential corresponds to the degree to which a cognitive unit is activated by input from both the stimulus and the arousal system. In order to determine the net activation or excitatory potential of a cognitive unit, we multiply the activation supplied by the stimulus and the activation supplied by the arousal system.[1]

STEREOTYPED AND VARIABLE COGNITION

Hull's equation states that, to estimate the probability of a response, H and D are multiplied rather than added. So what? Figure 10–5 illustrates the difference.

FIGURE 10–5 The relationship between H and D is multiplicative. Consequently, increases in D steepen the slopes of associative hierarchies, as shown in A. If the relationship between H and D were additive, as shown in B, increases in drive would merely increase the excitatory potential of all habits to an equal degree.

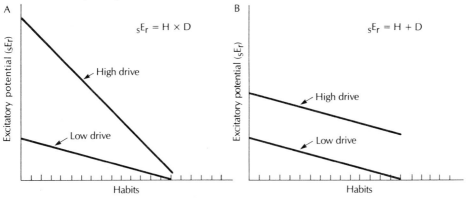

As you can see, if H and D are multiplied, the slope of the response-strength curve becomes steeper (see Figure 10–5A). On the other hand, if H and D are added, the whole curve is merely raised, but the slope does not change (see Figure 10–5B). Again, your own most probable response may once more be "so what?" The point is that according to Hull's formulation, increasing arousal increases the activation of the dominant or strongest unit relative to the activation of other units. We argued in Chapter 7 that the most activated unit is the one that captures attention. If we were dealing with behaviors rather than thoughts, it would seem to be a reasonable extension to say that the most activated action unit is the one that is emitted as a behavior. The more aroused a person is, then, the more likely it is that the strongest cognitive unit will be the most activated one. In other words, the more aroused a person is, the more stereotyped thought and behavior will be: Attention will always be fixed on the most salient or obvious aspect of a

---

[1] Actually, this is only an approximation. In order to determine the net activation of a cognitive unit, we really should have an equation that adds activation from the arousal system and subtracts activation because of recurrent lateral inhibition among neighboring units. The point is that the net effect of the increased activation and lateral inhibition arising from increased nonspecific arousal is essentially a multiplication of the activation of cognitive units by arousal-system inputs.

stimulus; the behaviors emitted will always be the most well-learned ones. On the other hand, the less aroused a person is, the more variable thought and behavior will be. Attention will wander from one aspect of a stimulus to another; low-probability behavior and thoughts will have a comparatively high probability of emission.

If the most activated cognitive unit is the one that captures attention or results in action, how can there be any variability in thought or action? Should not the strongest unit (the one with the highest habit strength) always capture attention? Not necessarily. Remember that we are talking about probabilities; that is, habit strength refers to the *probability* that a given cognitive unit will be the one that is most activated in response to a stimulus. A cognitive unit with low habit strength *may* become strongly activated. However, the probability of this is low. Moreover, Hull (1943) argued that habit strength oscillates somewhat from moment to moment in a more or less random fashion. This is a sort of fail-safe theoretical mechanism for guaranteeing some variability in behavior. Hull could not explain why such oscillation would occur. Actually, though, networks with lateral inhibition automatically oscillate in the manner suggested by Hull.

This clarifies the question of why arousal tends to improve performance of simple tasks and interferes with performance of complex tasks. In the terms we have been using, a simple task is one where the dominant response in the habit family hierarchy is the correct one. The cognitive unit most likely to be activated by a stimulus is the one that, in fact, needs to be activated in order to perform the task. Examples might be recognizing words spoken clearly at 90 dB in a quiet room or pressing a telegraph key whenever a very bright light comes on in a dark room. On the other hand, a difficult or complex task would be one where the stimulus elicits many potential habits at about equal strength and we must somehow pick the correct one. Or it could be one where we must make a whole array of responses—none well learned—to the stimulus. An example of such a task might be writing an essay summarizing current findings on semantic memory. Let's consider in more detail exactly how arousal helps or hinders performance.

AROUSAL AND ATTENTION

In Chapter 7 we discussed Easterbrook's theory of attention (1959). His basic idea is that—at least in a medium range of arousal—increases in arousal lead to increased focusing of attention. If we equate the degree to which attention is focused with the degree to which one cognitive unit in an analyzer is more activated than other cognitive units in an analyzer, this hypothesis follows directly from Hullian theory as Easterbrook himself pointed out. In Figure 10–6 we show the expected patterns of activation in an analyzer as arousal goes from very low to very high. The first column of the figure gives a graphic depiction of how activated each of a set of cognitive units should be; the second column shows the same thing in terms of a graph of the excitatory potentials of a habit family hierarchy; and the third column illustrates how wide the corresponding focus of attention is.

In a low-arousal state, all cognitive units are about equally activated (see Figure 10–6A). Another way of stating this is to say that the slope of the line depicting the activation of each unit is relatively flat. Still another way of putting

FIGURE 10–6   Effects of arousal on the activation of cognitive units and the implications for attention. As arousal goes from very low (A) to fairly high (C), the focus of attention is constricted. When arousal becomes very high (D), attention is fractionated. Note that the diagrams in the three columns are alternative representations of the same phenomenon.

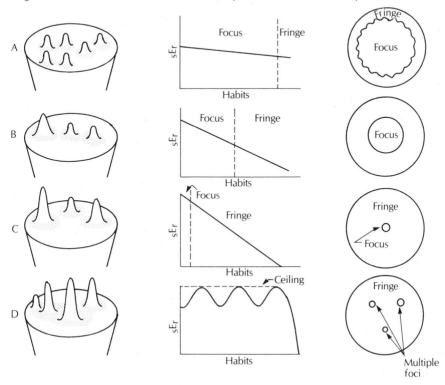

it is to say that attention is defocused. Such a state would be conducive to performance of a task requiring simultaneous attention to many things at once. As arousal increases, differences in the activation of cognitive units are increasingly exacerbated (Figures 10–6B and C). This corresponds to increased focusing of attention, because the strongest unit is becoming more and more activated relative to other units. So long as the degree of activation of each unit corresponds to the amount of attention that must be paid to whatever it codes, this should lead to more efficient performance. On the other hand, if this not the case, performance should deteriorate. Attention may become so focused that some relevant cues are not attended to. Since complex tasks require attending to many cues, increases in arousal and focusing of attention should quickly bring about deterioration in performance. On the other hand, simple tasks require attention to fewer cues. Thus, increases in arousal should facilitate their performance.

Too much arousal should cause a deterioration in the performance of even simple tasks (see Figure 10–6D). The reason is that several cognitive units will become maximally activated. Even worse, these units may not be the ones coding relevant cues. Because of fatiguing of units and lateral inhibition, attention may be fractionated or broken up. With very high levels of activation, fatiguing of units would be expected to occur quickly. Moreover, as soon as a cognitive unit fatigues at all, lateral inhibition from neighboring units will decrease its activation even more. But these units should themselves fatigue rapidly, thus disinhibiting neighboring units. The result should be that the pattern of activity in an analyzer would oscillate wildly. In simple terms, the person becomes confused and cannot perform any kind of task very efficiently.

AROUSAL, STIMULATION, AND REINFORCEMENT

The classic behaviorist view of reinforcement was that organisms are reinforced by the reduction of biological drives. Drives were viewed as ultimately resting upon tissue needs that make themselves felt as irritation or stimulation of internal or external receptors. Thus, hunger, thirst, or sex involve stimulation of internal receptors. Pain may involve stimulation of either internal or external sensory receptors. In this view, any reduction of stimulation or arousal is rewarding or reinforcing while any increase in stimulation or arousal is punishing. Going along with this view was the idea that behaviors, such as exploration or curiosity, are essentially things to be explained away; that is, such phenomena were held to be secondary drives or habits that are really due to pairing of certain activities with reduction of basic biological drives. This view was strongly espoused by Hull (1943) as well as by most other behaviorists. Psychoanalytic theory was essentially in complete accord with this viewpoint. This drive-reduction viewpoint had to be abandoned during the 1950s because of findings of three types. The first experiments reporting these findings were all published in 1954 but have been replicated and extended several times since then.

Pleasure centers in the brain

Olds and Milner (1954) discovered that stimulation of certain brain centers is extremely reinforcing and pleasurable. They implanted electrodes in what is now known as the primary reward system, a structure located in the midbrain. These electrodes were connected with a lever that their subjects—rats—could press. Whenever the lever was depressed, mild electrical stimulation was delivered via the implanted electrode. Once the rats discovered this, they pressed the lever repeatedly at a high rate for hours on end. Presumably, stimulation of the centers was rewarding, since rats have no propensity to press levers unless they are somehow rewarded for their efforts. When analogous centers have been stimulated in humans during the course of brain operations, the patients report intense feelings of pleasure. These brain centers must be the ones that are activated when natural rewards, such as food or sex, are given to an organism. This suggests that reward or reinforcement involves not decreased stimulation but increased stimulation or activation of these centers. Be this as it may, Olds and Milner's results clearly showed that at least some increases in stimulation are rewarding. This is directly contrary to the drive-reduction theory.

Sensory deprivation

The second crucial experiment was carried out by Bexton, Heron, and Scott (1954). It concerned the extreme reluctance of 22 college students to be paid

$20 per day to do absolutely nothing. The subjects' only task was to lie on a comfortable bed in a cubicle. The point of the experiment was to reduce sensory input to a minimum. Subjects wore translucent goggles that admitted only unpatterned light. Tactual stimulation was cut off by gloves with cardboard cuffs around the forearm. Auditory stimulation was cut off by sound proofing of the experimental chamber. Contrary to what drive-reduction theory would predict, subjects found this situation extremely unpleasant. After an initial nap, subjects woke up bored and eager for any sort of stimulation—of which there was none. Most of the subjects refused to continue the experiment for as long as two or three days.

Subsequent sensory deprivation experiments have been conducted. They are summarized in Schultz (1965), Solomon et al. (1961), and Zubek (1969). The results are fairly consistent. First, virtually no one finds the experience at all pleasant. For example, all 20 of the subjects in an experiment conducted by Smith and Lewty (1959) reported either anxiety or actual attacks of panic. Second, the perceptual and cognitive systems do not work properly under conditions of sensory deprivation. Normal subjects quite frequently hallucinate after a few hours of sensory deprivation. Performance on a wide variety of cognitive tasks is impaired. Third, subjects develop what might be called *stimulus hunger* when subjected to sensory deprivation; that is, they report a desire for stimulation of any kind. They tend to take an intense interest in any stimuli they can find, even if these would normally be of no interest.

Results concerning indexes of arousal during sensory deprivation are consistent but not altogether clear in their meaning. If arousal is a function of amount of stimulation impinging on an organism, then we might predict that arousal should fall during sensory deprivation. On the other hand, if there is a biological need for stimulation, then sensory deprivation would increase the level of this need. In this case, we should predict an increase in arousal, just as we would predict an increase in arousal consequent upon food or water deprivation. Actually, the results support both of these hypotheses. Cortical arousal (as measured by the EEG) decreases, while visceral arousal (as measured by skin conductance and biochemical indexes) increases. Findings concerning both cortical and visceral arousal have been replicated a number of times (Schultz, 1965). Perhaps, after all, both hypotheses are correct.

Reinforcing properties of stimulation

Butler and Harlow (1954) began a third line of research that yielded evidence contrary to the drive-reduction theory. Rhesus monkeys were confined in opaque boxes. Each box had two windows that could be covered by cards of two colors. On each trial, one of the windows was locked and the other could be opened if the monkey pushed it. The one that could be opened was always indicated by one of the colors. A food-deprived monkey can quickly learn such a color discrimination if it is rewarded by food. But the only reward in the Butler and Harlow experiment was that the monkey got to look out of the box into the laboratory for 30 seconds. In spite of this—or, rather, because of it—the monkeys learned the discrimination. They kept opening the correct window for two four-hour sessions. Apparently, just the opportunity for visual exploration was rewarding. In a later study, Butler (1957) showed that the amount of time rhesus

monkeys spent in visual exploration is a function of prior amount of visual deprivation. Other studies have shown that even rats will learn to run a maze when the
only reward is the opportunity to explore another maze (Montgomery, 1954) or
to explore novel stimulus objects (Berlyne and Slater, 1957).

I have emphasized studies of lower animals because these were most devastat-
ing to the drive-reduction viewpoint. If rats and monkeys are motivated to seek
out stimulation for its own sake, it would be difficult to deny that humans also
have such a motive. The net effect of the three lines of evidence discussed in this
section was a new view of the functioning of organisms that prepared the way
for cognitive psychology. The old view was that behavior can and should ultimately be explained in terms of reductions of basic drives, such as hunger and
thirst. The new view is not that such drives are unimportant. Rather, when they
are satisfied, organisms are motivated to increase arousal by seeking out stimulation, exploring, learning for its own sake, and so on. Cognitive units "want" to
be activated; the mind "wants" to work.

HEDONIC TONE

The Wundt curve

To say that organisms seek stimulation and arousal or that they like novelty is
too simple. We must ask how much is enough and how much is too much. Berlyne (1967, 1971) argues that the arousal potential of a stimulus determines its
pleasantness or reward value. Hedonic tone (feeling of pleasantness versus unpleasantness) is hypothetically an inverted-U function of arousal potential, as
shown in Figure 10–7. The function relating hedonic tone to arousal potential
is called the Wundt curve. This idea was first proposed by Wundt (1874) in regard
to stimulus intensity; that is, Wundt argued that we like stimuli of medium
intensity.

FIGURE 10–7   The Wundt curve

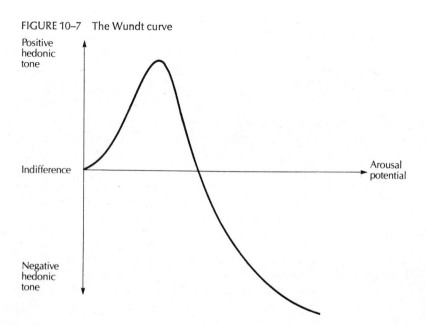

Neural basis of the Wundt curve

Berlyne (1971) hypothesizes that the Wundt curve arises from the action of two neural systems: a reward or pleasure system and an aversion or punishment system. These systems lie directly in the path of the projective tracts from the arousal system to the cortex. In the process of activating the cortex, the arousal system also activates these two systems. However, the two systems have different thresholds for activation. Mild stimulation activates only the pleasure centers. With increasing stimulation, they are increasingly activated and thus produce more and more pleasure up to a point. Slightly more intense stimulation activates the aversion system. At about this same point, the pleasure system reaches its asymptotic level of activity. With increasing stimulation, the aversion system, too, is increasingly activated. However, as shown in Figure 10–8, its asymptotic level of activation is more extreme than that of the pleasure system. Hedonic tone is obtained by subtracting pain from pleasure. The result is the Wundt curve.

FIGURE 10–8   Berlyne's explanation of the Wundt curve. Output from the aversion system (pain) is subtracted from output from the primary reward system (pleasure) to yield the Wundt curve.

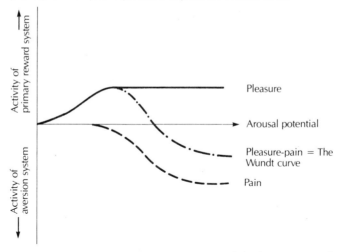

Source: D. E. Berlyne, *Aesthetics and Psychobiology* (New York: Appleton-Century-Crofts, 1971), p. 88.

In this view, changes in hedonic tone are necessary correlates of changes in attention, since the arousal system "adjusts" feelings of pleasure and displeasure in the process of "adjusting" the focus of attention. This could hardly be a coincidence. It must be that this particular wiring arrangement has some evolutionary significance. Its implication is that the more arousal potential a stimulus has, the more attention an organism will devote to it. Up to a certain point, this increasing attention will be accompanied by increasing pleasure. Presumably, this will lead the organism to approach the stimulus in question. Beyond this point, the increasing attention will be accompanied by increasing displeasure. This, presumably, will lead the organism to withdraw from the stimulus while keeping an attentive eye on it. When an organism is confronted by an environment with very low arousal potential, it will be motivated to seek out a more arousing (that is, a more intense, novel, or meaningful) environment. But if it comes upon an environment that is too arousing, it will withdraw to a safe distance.

Psychophysical variables

Much evidence supports Wundt's original contention about stimulus intensity. Engel (1928) had his subjects rate the pleasantness of the taste of water with varying concentrations of cane sugar, salt, tartaric acid (a sour substance), and quinine sulfate (a bitter substance). In each case, results were in conformity with the Wundt curve; that is, preference increased up to a medium concentration and then declined. Pfaffman (1960) found very similar preference curves when he allowed rats to choose among similar substances of varying concentrations. Vitz (1972) reports evidence for an inverted-U relationship between ratings of pleasantness and the loudness of tones. The Wundt curve also holds for a number of other psychophysical characteristics besides intensity. Thus, Martin (1906) found a curvilinear relationship between preference for circles and the size of these circles. The circles varied in diameter between 1 mm and 500 mm. Vitz (1972) found an inverted-U relationship between pitch and judged pleasantness. His stimuli varied between 60 Hz and 5,000 Hz. A peak in preference occurred at 750 Hz, with liking declining with either increases or decreases from this point.

Collative variables

Does the Wundt curve hold for arousal potential induced by collative properties as well as by psychophysical properties? There is a huge body of studies showing that people like novelty, complexity, and so on (Berlyne, 1971). However, most studies have dealt with a restricted range of stimuli. In order to see whether preference for collative properties follows the Wundt curve, we need to examine studies that have investigated stimuli varying across a wide range of values. When we do so, we find that much evidence shows that people prefer stimuli with medium degrees of collative properties. Quite a bit of research has been done on the relationship between complexity and preference. Vitz (1966) had subjects rate the pleasingness of tone sequences that varied in complexity. Complexity was manipulated by using more or less different frequencies, loudness levels, and durations in the sequences. The predicted inverted-U relationship between complexity and preference was found. Kamann (1963) obtained similar results when he had subjects rate the quality of poetry varying in complexity, as did Evans (1969) when he had subjects rate the pleasingness of prose varying in complexity. Munsinger and Kessen (1964) and Day (1967, 1968) asked subjects to rate the pleasingness of polygons varying in complexity. Again, inverted-U curves were obtained. Munsinger and Kessen's subjects tended to like very simple polygons as well as ones of intermediate complexity. However, this was apparently due to the meaningfulness of the simple figures. When rated meaningfulness of the polygons was controlled for, the expected inverted-U relationship was found.

One way of investigating preference for novelty is to present the same stimulus over and over and obtain ratings after each presentation. If a stimulus has high arousal potential to start with, we should expect that it should be disliked at first. With repeated presentations, liking should increase up to some point and then decrease again. This prediction is based on the assumption that a stimulus loses a quantum of arousal potential with each presentation. If the stimulus had only medium arousal potential to start with—because, for example, it was not very complex or not very intense—we would expect it would be liked immediately and that this liking should decline with repeated presentations. Skaife (1967) reviewed studies where music was presented to subjects over and over. The results of these studies are as predicted. Especially if the music is unfamiliar (for example, complicated contemporary music), there tend to be successive stages of disliking, liking, and indifference (for example, Alpert, 1953). On the other hand, popular music tends to be liked initially, but preference declines with repeated presentations. (Note that one way of increasing its arousal potential is to increase its intensity. Thus, at a rock concert or a discotheque, music is played at very high intensities.)

Ecological variables

It might be asked whether hedonic tone is also curvilinearly related to the ecological aspects of stimuli; that is, do we like stimuli of medium signal value or meaningfulness? There is very little experimental evidence that bears on this question. Several existential theorists argue that one of our fundamental needs is a need for meaning, but they seem to imply that the more meaning the better. Most of us would certainly agree that we like meaningful things better than meaningless ones. On the other hand, most people have probably had social relationships that were so meaningful as to be almost painful. Berlyne (1967) includes biological gratifications (reward) and punishments under the heading of ecological variables. He cites a study that suggests that at least very mild electric shock can reinforce or reward behavior and that its reward value increases with increases in voltage. Of course, if voltage were increased even further, the shock would certainly become painful and unrewarding. There is, of course, a vast body of studies showing that rewards of various sorts are both pleasurable and reinforcing. However, at least under some circumstances, rewards can be negative. Deci (1971) reports that people will work hard at some tasks that they seem to find intrinsically interesting but that their performance actually deteriorates when a reward is introduced. Perhaps the reward adds to the arousal potential already induced by the intrinsic interest. The result would be too high an arousal potential and consequent negative affect.

Adaptation level

Steck and Machotka (1975) investigated the relationship between hedonic tone and musical complexity. They found evidence supportive of the Wundt curve, but their experiment is more important in terms of what it tells us about adaptation levels. Assume that musical complexity can vary from 0 (very simple) to 100 (very complex). Steck and Machotka gave the same subjects pieces of music from different ranges on this scale. For example, a subject would be given pieces in the range from 0 to 50 on one occasion and pieces in the range from 50 to 100 on another occasion. On still another occasion, the subject would be given pieces from the whole 0 to 100 range. The interesting result was that Steck and Machotka found strong evidence that preferences followed the Wundt curve on all three occasions; that is, their subjects tended to prefer music of intermediate complexity relative to the range of possibilities. Thus, a given subject might most prefer 25 units of complexity when the range was 0–50, 75 units when the range was 50–100, and 50 units when the range was 0 to 100. There was virtually no evidence for absolute anchoring of the preference curves. Steck and Machotka found rather wide individual differences in preference for complexity. Some subjects preferred low complexity and others high complexity, but this preference was relative. A subject preferring low complexity might show a peak in preference at, say, 10 units when the range was over 0–50. However, rather than disliking all of the stimuli in the 50–100 range, such a subject would show a preference for stimuli around 60 units. At least across the range of stimuli studied by Steck and Machotka, it would seem that the arousal system adapts to the range of possibilities rather than operating in an absolute manner.

Berlyne (1971) argues that if we get used to or adapt to an environment full of stimuli of high arousal potential, the whole Wundt curve is shifted to the right (see Figure 10–9). Thus, if someone is used to a very novel environment, the zero

FIGURE 10–9   The Wundt curve is shifted to the right as one becomes used to a high arousal potential environment. Stimulus A is pleasant for one person but indifferent for the other; stimulus B is pleasant for the second person but unpleasant for the first person.

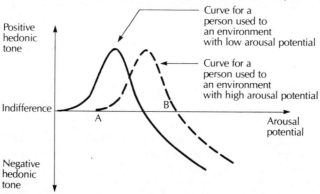

point of neutrality will eventually migrate to this point. Now, only stimuli that deviate from this adaptation level will produce pleasure. Note that this level could be one that induces displeasure in someone used to very low-arousal environment. For example, a stimulus that has only medium arousal potential for a city dweller may have very high arousal potential for someone used to a quiet, rural environment. However, if the city dweller moves to the country there should be a relatively quick movement to the new adaptation level. Berlyne (1971) uses this line of reasoning to explain why artistic products of more complex societies tend themselves to be more complex. A complex society provides its members with a relatively arousing environment. Thus, they will prefer art works that are more complex, since simple works will not have enough arousal potential to induce pleasure. On the other hand, the adaptation level in more primitive societies is lower. A complex work of art would have too high arousal potential and would thus induce displeasure.

SUMMARY AND CONCLUSIONS

Let us pause for a moment to put together what we have said in this chapter. The essential point is that the organism seeks an optimal or medium level of arousal. People clearly avoid and dislike very high arousal states, such as those that accompany panic, very intense stimulation, or high drive states. During the 1950s, it became clear that people also avoid low arousal states. Arousal is maintained by the net arousal potential of all of the stimuli composing a person's environment at a given time. If arousal is too low, a person will seek out stimuli of sufficient arousal potential to increase arousal. The correct amount of stimulation will be found naturally or automatically since pleasure will increase with arousal potential only up to a certain point. Beyond that point, more arousal potential will yield decreases in pleasure and, eventually, will lead to displeasure. I presume that people usually seek pleasure. If so, then they must necessarily seek an environment yielding—overall—medium arousal potential. If for some reason, a person winds up in a state of too high arousal, action will be taken to cut off some sources of stimulation so as to bring the overall arousal potential of the environment down to a medium level.

You may object that there is a flaw in this system. If pleasure consists of medium increments in arousal potential, does this not imply that people would very soon after birth end up at an extremely high level of arousal indeed since the only way to obtain pleasure is to seek more arousal? This objection overlooks the fact of habituation. Stimuli lose their arousal potential with repeated exposure. Thus, we have to keep running to stay in the same place; that is, after some exposure to a pleasant stimulus configuration, it will not be pleasant any more. The reason that it was pleasant to start with was because it elicited medium arousal. If we but stay staring at it, it will gradually elicit less and less arousal so that our hedonic tone will move toward neutrality. Thus, we must seek some change in stimulation, but this change will not get us into a higher arousal state than we were in when we were happy in the first place.

It may occur to you that I have explained my way out of one difficulty only by backing into a much greater one. The implication of the argument is that people must continually seek change, novelty, and complexity. If this is the case, then we would expect to find continual change and increasing complexity in the environments of people across their life times or even in the environments of people throughout the history of the human race. But this is no difficulty at all. In Chapter 16 of this book we shall argue that no other force need be postulated to explain the extremely regular trends found in the history of art forms and in the history of the organized cognitive endeavor known as science. On a more mundane level, the principle goes a long way towards explaining why people change anything from their interests to their spouses.

On the purely cognitive level, the perspective of arousal theory helps us to understand why attention is drawn to relatively novel stimuli and away from unchanging ones and why we seek out information to process in the first place. Beyond the light it sheds on the Yerkes-Dodson law and the mechanisms involved in focusing attention, arousal theory does not tell us anything terribly important about how cognition occurs, about what structures are involved. What it gives is a context for understanding cognition outside the laboratory. It ties attention and other cognitive processes to hedonic tone and reward value. More specifically, it tells us why we orient or attend to certain things—we do so because attending to these things is accompanied by pleasure. Arousal theory tells us why this is so.

Arousal theory also tells us a good deal about natural variations in attention and the efficiency of learning and performance at any given task. Everyone seeks to maintain an optimal level of arousal for hedonic reasons. Maintenance of this level of arousal, of course, functions to keep the machinery of cognition running smoothly. But the Yerkes-Dodson law states that every task has its own optimal level of arousal. Is there a problem here? Does this mean that a person will perform optimally only on a certain type of task and can get to the optimal levels for other simpler or more difficult tasks only at the cost of a change in arousal and, hence, a lessening of pleasure? It does mean this, but while this may pose problems for the person involved, it is hardly a problem for the theory. Rather, it would seem to be in complete conformity with our everyday experience. There are any number of tasks that we must perform either poorly or at the cost of considerable displeasure.

11

Brain and mind

TYPE OF COGNITION AND LOCUS OF NEURAL ACTIVITY

In the last chapter, we saw that the arousal system tends to activate the whole brain in a diffuse manner. The amount of arousal-system activation is systematically related to hedonic tone, focus of attention, and type of cognition. While arousal tends to affect the brain as a whole, different parts of the brain can be differentially active. Exactly which parts are most active at any given time hypothetically determines what type of mental activity will be going on at that time. In this chapter, we shall examine some of the evidence for this assertion. It is hardly a matter of idle curiosity to ask how cognitive activity is related to neural activity. Knowledge about the localization of different cognitive activities in the brain may shed light on how these activities are related to one another.

The cortex—where Konorski (1967) locates the cognitive analyzers—is only a thin rind covering evolutionarily older and more primitive brain systems. As well as taking care of several biological "housekeeping" tasks, these older systems send signals to the cortex. In many ways, these signals are more difficult to recognize and understand than signals coming from the external world. In the first part of this chapter we shall take a look at how the cognitive activity of the cortex is related to the activity of the more primitive brain systems. The brain is not only vertically stratified. It is also divided into right and left sides which are more or less mirror images of each other. Evidence suggests that different mental functions are segregated in different sides of the brain. For example, linguistic processing generally seems to go on in the left hemisphere while spatial processing usually goes on in the right hemisphere. In the second part of this chapter, we shall examine the evidence that these and other functions are lateralized. In the process, we shall have a chance to look at some cognitive functions—such as the recognition of emotion and the production of language—that we have not yet discussed in any detail.

THE TRIUNE BRAIN

Evolution of the brain

Paul MacLean (1958, 1979) argues that the human brain is really three brains in one, as shown in Figure 11–1. The process of evolution has essentially laid each one down on top of the other without always bothering completely to inter-

FIGURE 11–1   The triune brain

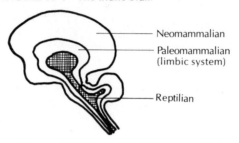

Source: P. MacLean, "Paul MacLean and the Triune Brain," *Science* 204 (1979):1066.

connect the later stratum with the earlier one. The oldest stratum is the ancient reptilian core of the brain. MacLean calls this the R-complex. It corresponds to the hindbrain and midbrain and is the most primitive part of the human brain. But it is all that a reptile has, and that is why MacLean refers to it as the reptilian brain. The next stratum is the paleomammalian brain. It corresponds to the limbic system. As shown schematically in Figure 11–1, the limbic system consists of a set of brain centers that is wrapped around the older portions of the brain. The paleomammalian brain first emerged when the earliest mammals evolved. The neomammalian brain corresponds to higher brain centers, especially the neocortex. It is found only in the highest mammals, including man. But why make these distinctions? The three strata correspond to three levels of evolution. Each of these evolutionary advances has brought with it significant additions to the behavioral repertoire. Furthermore, the three strata are anatomically separable. For example, limbic-system centers are intimately interconnected with one another, but connections from the limbic system to the neocortex are rather sparse in comparison. Moreover, the three strata tend to speak different neurochemical languages; that is, the neurotransmitters used in each tend to be different. Most important, each of the strata specializes in a different set of functions. The R-complex deals with basic, self-preserving behavior, the limbic system deals with emotions and biological drives, and the neocortex deals with cognition.

The R-complex

Centers in the R-complex, MacLean says, code the formats for specific instinctual behaviors. These turn out to be more complex than such obvious necessities as remembering to breathe, pump blood through one's veins, and digest one's food. The best way to get an idea of what the R-complex does is to look at what reptiles do, since the R-complex is completely responsible for their behavior. When we do this, we find that a reptile is ruled by what MacLean (1979) calls a "master routine." Every day, it does exactly the same things in exactly the same order: "It emerges cautiously from its dwelling place, basks awhile to get its temperature up . . . defecates, goes hunting, eats, has a siesta, does more errands, basks again, and returns home." This is really only the master routine governing warm weather behavior. The master routine for winter is often far simpler: sleep.

In order to carry out its master routine, a reptile can call upon subroutines. One class of these consists of the four basic displays. The signature display essentially says that "I am I." The reptile uses it for greeting others. Each species has its own type of signature. For one type of lizard, the signature involves puffing out the throat and bobbing the head from side to side. Other reptiles announce their presence in other ways. The territorial display is used to warn unwanted others to get off of a reptile's turf. Quite opposite is the submissive display. It usually consists of a lowering of the head in order to signify defeat. Also useful is the courtship display. As the name implies, it is used on reptilian dates. Each of these displays consists of a stereotyped set of behaviors that seem to be universally understood by other members of the same species.

MacLean argues that perseverative, ritualistic R-complex behaviors form the basis for similar but somewhat more variable behaviors in higher animals, including humans. For example, the R-complex is important for imitation and social conformity in a variety of species. Removing parts of it can lessen an animal's tendency to imitate other members of its species or even to take any special interest in them at all. This is true whether the animal happens to be a reptile or a more advanced species, such as one of the primates. MacLean (1979) even speculates that something may be wrong with the R-complex in highly creative human beings, since they show a lessened tendency to imitate the thought and behavior patterns of other members of their species.

The limbic system

The limbic system is composed of several brain centers, including the hypothalamus, the septum, and the amygdala. Since this system has to do with motivation and emotion, it corresponds to what we have called the emotional system. It contains the general pleasure and pain centers described in Chapter 10. Other centers in the limbic system control motivational activities, such as eating, drinking, and sex. Some centers, for example, cause an organism to begin or continue eating when they are stimulated. Other centers do just the opposite. When they are stimulated, the organism stops eating. If these centers are destroyed, the organism no longer knows when to stop eating. As a result, it becomes grossly obese (Thompson, 1973). Yet other centers in the limbic system control specific emotions, such as rage.

CORTICAL INHIBITION OF LIMBIC-SYSTEM ACTIVITY

Centers in the limbic system are interconnected in a rich and complex manner. MacLean (1958) says that once activity begins in the limbic system, it is likely to reverberate in a chain-reaction fashion because of this. Once we become emotionally aroused, it is often not an easy task to calm down even when we know there is no longer any reason for the emotion we are feeling. This is because we *know* in the neomammalian brain but we *feel* in the paleomammalian brain. The neocortex tends to damp down or inhibit limbic system activity, but it is not always completely successful at this. We know that the neocortex exerts such an inhibitory effect because of experiments with decorticated animals. These are animals where the neomammalian brain has been removed or all of its connections with lower brain centers have been severed. Some of the first experiments of this sort were done by Bard and Mountcastle (1948). They removed the forebrains of cats down to the level of the hypothalamus. When irritated, such cats exhibited "sham rage." They became extremely upset at the slightest affront. Thus, removing the higher centers seemed to disinhibit the lower ones. As a consequence, the animals showed strong, exaggerated emotional behavior. When the hypothalamus was also removed, this effect disappeared. This suggests that the hypothalamus was responsible for triggering the rage. In an intact animal, any irritation presumably provokes rage on the part of the hypothalamus. However, the cortex inhibits this rage—unless the irritation is extreme—and we see an emotion more appropriate to the situation, such as annoyance.

CORTICAL DECODING OF LIMBIC-SYSTEM MESSAGES

The neomammalian brain is also faced with the task of deciding what emotion the organism is feeling. This is not a completely straightforward task. Emotions are generated by the limbic system, but this system speaks a different language than does the neomammalian brain. Feeling an emotion and knowing exactly what it is are two quite different things. The limbic system does the feeling, but the cortex does the knowing. In a certain sense, recognizing our own emotions is like recognizing an external stimulus. According to Schachter (1964), any emotion consists of a state of visceral or limbic-system arousal plus a cognitive label. He argues that the same absolute level of visceral arousal can result in quite different emotions according to the way it is labeled. The label for a state of visceral arousal is inferred from the situation in which the arousal occurs. In many situations, the stimulus configuration that produces the arousal suggests an unambiguous label. Thus, if you find yourself in a state of high visceral arousal while confronted by a knife-bearing stranger in a dark alley, labels such as *terror* or *fear* readily suggest themselves.

Schachter and Singer (1962) injected subjects with epinephrine, a substance that increases arousal. A control group was given a placebo substance (saline solution) that has no effect at all on arousal. Then, subjects were taken to a room and asked to wait for the next part of the experiment to begin. They thought that they were waiting with another subject, but in reality the other person was a paid confederate of the experimenter. With half of the subjects, the confederate acted in a very euphoric manner and told jokes and engaged in various sorts of horseplay. With the other half of the subjects, he behaved in an angry fashion. He complained about the long wait and the incompetence of the experimenter and insulted a secretary who happened to enter the room. At the end of this charade, subjects were asked to rate their own emotional state. They had also been observed through a one-way mirror by judges who rated their actual behavior. On both measures, the results were clear cut. The high-arousal subjects became either euphoric or angry depending upon the behavior of the confederate. On the other hand, the saline-injected control group showed no such effect. Recall that the type and level of arousal of both euphoric and angry subjects was exactly the same. Only their environments differed. Evidently, they used environmental cues to label their visceral arousal. Since these cues differed, they came up with different labels.

In another study, Schachter and Wheeler (1962) showed subjects a comedy film. Some subjects were given a placebo (saline solution), some were given an arousal-increasing stimulant (epinephrine), and some were given an arousal-decreasing tranquilizer (chlorpromazine). The subjects given epinephrine found the film most amusing, and the subjects given chlorpromazine found it least amusing. Apparently, when people are in an aroused state, they cast about for an explanation of this state. They find this explanation in their environment and use environmental cues to label their arousal. This line of reasoning is supported by the fact that the effects found in these studies disappear if people are told beforehand that the arousal-inducing drug will make them tense and jittery. When told this, they attribute their arousal to the drug rather than to any emotion.

Each emotion and motive is probably a unique physiological signal. We know that stimulation of different subcortical centers produces quite different emotional and motivational reactions. However, these signals are difficult to discriminate. If they were unique and easy to recognize, we would not be talking about general visceral arousal in the first place but rather about specific types of visceral cues. Recognizing our emotions is rather like recognizing words buried in noise or flashed for a brief duration on a tachistoscope. In both cases, the stimulus is not very clear, so we depend a lot upon contextual cues and expectations. Another problem is that we may be receiving more than one emotional signal at the same time. There is no reason to expect emotions to come one at a time. Indeed, psychoanalytic theorists claim that we are always ambivalent toward important stimuli, such as other people; that is, we may have several—often conflicting—emotions at the same time.

In short, emotions are internal signals arising from subcortical, limbic-system centers. They resemble a confused babbling. First, the signals are not very clear. Second, they are sent over a noisy channel. Third, the signals may be contradictory. The task of the cortex is to decode this babbling and to recognize or label which signals it is receiving. As compared to the task of recognizing external stimuli, this tends to be rather more difficult. Thus, we seem to rely even more upon contextual cues than we do in the case of, say, recognition of spoken or printed words.

ALEXITHYMIA

People differ in the acuity with which they are able to recognize emotions. Nemiah and Sifneos (1970) have coined the term alexithymia to refer to an inability to recognize one's own emotions. They say that this inability is usually also accompanied by difficulty in recognizing other people's emotions from facial expressions and other cues. From your own experience, I am sure you can think of people who are particularly insensitive to how other people are feeling. It is probably the case that such people are just as insensitive to their own emotions. A person suffering from alexithymia once told me how her father had, after a violent argument, ordered her to move out of his house. I remarked that this must have made her feel rather bad. As I made the comment, I thought how inane it was since the answer should have been obvious. The young woman's reply was amazing: "I don't know," she replied, "You'd have to ask Diane." Diane was a friend who had witnessed the scene. Even with what should have been a clear-cut emotion, the woman could not recognize or label her own feelings. She assumed that an external observer of her behavior would be in a better position to recognize her emotions than she herself was. Whenever she was asked about what emotion she was feeling, this person either replied that she had no idea or tried to *infer* her feelings from her overt behavior or the situation she was in.

MISLABELING LIMBIC-SYSTEM ACTIVITY

Berscheid and Walster (1974) argue that romantic love can be explained in terms of Schachter's theory of emotion. It is, they say, essentially a mislabeling of a state of heightened visceral arousal. Consider the phenomenon of falling in love on the rebound. Someone is jilted by one person and almost immediately falls in love with another. Berscheid and Walster explain this as follows. The initial rejection leads to a stirred-up or aroused state. Rather than labeling this as depression or sorrow, one may—given the opportunity—mislabel it as romantic love directed at the second person. Another source of arousal would be frustrated sexual desire. Rather than labeling one's state of arousal as frustration, one may label it as romantic love. At least in literature, rather extreme cases of mislabeling can occur. Recall the method by which El Cid courted—and won—the heart of Diana Ximene. First, he killed her father. Then every day he killed one of her pet birds. Richard's method in Shakespeare's play, *Richard III*, was along the same lines. He killed both the father and the husband of his intended lover. She did end up in love with him. Such extreme measures are not recommended, but it does seem to be the case that someone in a state of high visceral arousal—whatever its cause—is more likely to fall in love with you than someone who is not so aroused.

Whoever wired up the emotional system seems to have done rather slipshod work. The wiring is not as well sorted out for the emotional system as it is with the visual or auditory analyzers. Although word recognition is often aided by contextual cues, the response of the emotional analyzer is often determined entirely by context. This is because emotions are extremely difficult to recognize or label. We are all rather agnosic in regard to emotions much of the time. Apparently, emotions are not sufficiently distinctive for different labels to be reliably attached to them. Let's move on to a region of the brain where things are a bit more reasonable.

The neomammalian brain

According to MacLean, the neomammalian brain performs the types of cognitive and perceptual operations we have described in the previous chapters. It takes care of higher levels of perception, recognition, memory, and attention and also deals with thought and the generation of planned action, two topics to be discussed in Chapter 12. Konorski (1967) says that the multilayered structure of the neocortex specifically suits it to carrying out these activities. It may be of interest to you to know where the various analyzers are thought to be located in the cortex.

WHERE ARE THE ANALYZERS?

Figure 11–2 shows a side view of the brain along with a stretched-out schematic diagram of it. The figure shows where Konorski (1967) believed the sensory and gnostic analyzers to be located. Since he did not discuss what we have called the conceptual analyzers, their locations are not shown. If I had to guess, I would locate the semantic analyzer in the parietal lobe, the episodic analyzer in the temporal lobe, and the action system in the frontal region of the brain; however, this is only a speculative guess. It could very well be that these analyzers are actually distributed over wide regions of the cortex rather than being localized in the way that the sensory and gnostic analyzers are.

The sensory input tract for each sense goes to a primary sensory receiving area of the cortex. There is also a cortical area controlling the generation of motor movements. Most of the sensory receiving areas and the motor area are organized in a somatotopic fashion; that is, there is a correspondence between the spatial location of an area of the cortex and the spatial location of whatever it keeps track of. This correspondence is shown in Figure 11–3 for both the motor and the somesthetic areas. As you can see, in each case, a point in the cortex corresponds to a point of the body. The distortions are due to the fact that the cortex devotes a lot of space to important body regions, such as the tongue, and less space to perhaps larger but less important regions, such as the back of the leg. Because of this point-for-point correspondence, the sensory receiving areas were discovered and mapped out quite early. It has been somewhat more difficult to identify the associative areas surrounding the sensory receiving areas. Thus, even the locations of the gnostic analyzers shown in Figure 11–2 are rather tentative. For the most part, our knowledge of where these analyzers are has come from cases of brain damage. When a person has a stroke, for example, a fairly limited area of the brain may be destroyed. A stroke is caused by the blockade of a cerebral artery by a blood clot. As a result of this, blood is cut off from the area served by that artery. This results in the destruction of the neurons in that area. By studying stroke victims, we can establish a correlation between the area in which damage was sustained and the type of deficit that has ensued.

LATERALIZATION OF ANALYZERS

The cerebrum is divided into two halves that are at first glance mirror images of each other. These are the right and left cerebral hemispheres. The two hemispheres are connected by a large band of fibers called the corpus callosum. The fibers of the corpus callosum serve to connect analogous regions in the two hemispheres. Presumably, they transmit information from one side of the brain to the other. However, at least some of the fibers seem to allow an area on one

FIGURE 11–2   Locations of sensory and gnostic analyzers

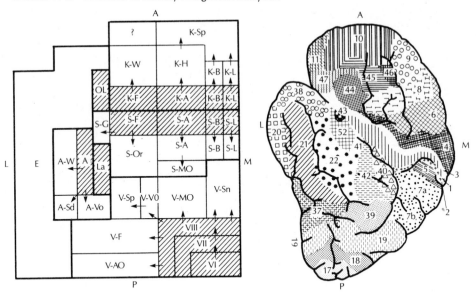

Conceptual map of the human cerebral cortex of left hemisphere (left) and the cytoarchitectonic map of that hemisphere according to Brodmann (right)

Symbols: A, P, L, M, outside the figure denote the anterior, posterior, lateral (and laterobasal), and medial sides of the cortex. Projective transit fields are hatched; gnostic (exit) fields are plain. The boundaries of particular analyzers are drawn by thick lines; the boundaries of particular fields by thin lines. Arrows denote connections between transit and gnostic fields.

The projective and gnostic fields of the conceptual chart are tentatively related to the cytoarchitectonic fields of the Brodmann chart.

Visual analyzer (V): VI VII, VIII, transit visual fields (areas 17, 18, 19 respectively); V–Sn, signivisual field (area 7b); V–MO, visual field for small manipulable objects (7b); V–VO, visual field for large purely visual objects (39); V–Sp, visual field for spatial relations (39, right hemisphere); V–F, visual field for faces (37); V–AO, visual field for animated objects (37).

Auditory analyzer (A): A, projective auditory field (41, 42); A–W, audioverbal field (22); A–Sd, auditory field for various sounds (22, right hemisphere); A–Vo, auditory field for human voices (21).

Somesthetic analyzer (S): S–F, S–A, S–B, S–L, projective somesthetic fields for face, arm, body and leg, respectively (3, 1, 2); S–Or, oralsomesthetic field (40); S–A, S–B, S–L, gnostic somesthetic fields for arm, body and leg, respectively (5, 7a); S–MO, somesthetic field for small manipulable objects (7a); S–G, gustatory field (43).

Kinesthetic analyzer (K): K–F, K–A, K–B, K–L, projective kinesthetic fields for face, arm, body and leg, respectively (4); K–W, wordkinesthetic field 44, 45); K–H, handkinesthetic field (6); K–B, K–L, gnostic kinesthetic fields for body and leg, respectively (6); K–Sp, kinesthetic field for spatial relations (9, right hemisphere); La, vestibular analyzer (not known); OI, olfactory analyzer (not seen on Brodmann's map); E, emotional analyzer not seen on Brodmann's map).

Note that for the sake of simplicity all the gnostic fields have been put in the left hemisphere, although in reality some of them are situated in the right hemisphere. Note also that our conceptual brain map is unfolded so as to show the latero-basal aspect of the cortex (not seen in Brodmann's map). The medial part of the emotive brain is not shown.

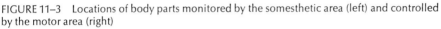
FIGURE 11–3   Locations of body parts monitored by the somesthetic area (left) and controlled by the motor area (right)

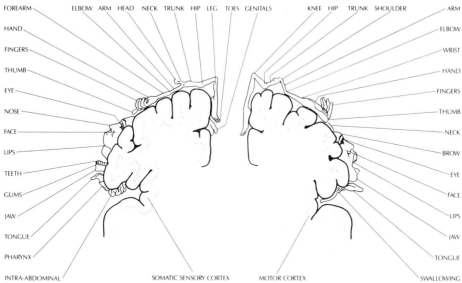

side of the brain to inhibit its mirror image on the other side of the brain. Each of the sensory receiving areas really consists of two analyzers, one in the right hemisphere and one in the left hemisphere. With one exception, an analyzer in one hemisphere receives information about the region of space contralateral to it. The exception is the olfactory system. In this case, input from the right nostril goes to the olfactory analyzer in the right hemisphere and input from the left nostril goes to the left hemisphere. For all of the other analyzers, things are not so straightforward.

The somesthetic analyzer in each hemisphere receives input from the side of the body opposite it. Similarly, the motor cortex of one hemisphere normally exerts control over the side of the body contralateral to it. Thus, a stroke that affects the region of the right-hemisphere motor area controlling the arm will lead to a paralysis of the left arm. However, the motor area in each hemisphere also has some control over unilateral motion as well. The cochlea in each ear sends fibers to the cortical auditory receiving areas of both ipsilateral and contralateral hemispheres. However, more fibers go to the contralateral hemisphere. In the case of vision, it is the visual fields rather than the eyes that are crossed. The situation is shown in Figure 11–4. Stimuli to the left of the central fixation point end up in the right hemisphere while those to the left of the fixation point end up in the left hemisphere.

The gnostic analyzers could not very well show somatotopic organization, if for no other reason than the fact that the information that they code is not usually location-specific. It also turns out that the gnostic analyzers seem not to be bilaterally represented; that is, some gnostic analyzers are in the right hemisphere

FIGURE 11–4   Visual pathways, illustrating that stimuli to one side of a central fixation point are directed to the contralateral hemisphere

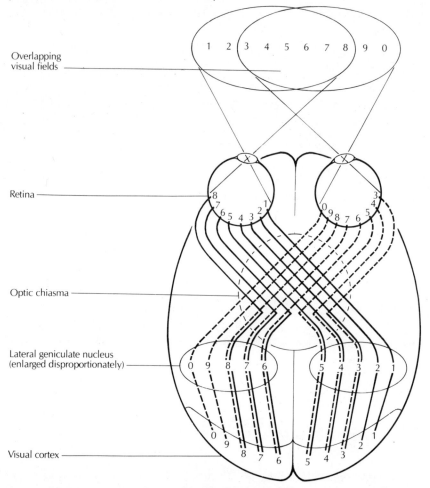

Source: P. H. Lindsay and D. A. Norman, *Human Information Processing: An Introduction to Psychology* (New York: Academic Press, 1977), p. 74.

and others are in the left hemisphere. Exactly why this should be no one really knows. However, I can tell you where various analyzers are thought to be and give you some of the evidence for this.

THE CEREBRAL HEMISPHERES

Methods of study

ABLATION

A variety of methods can be used to study the functioning of the two cerebral hemispheres. Several varieties of the method of ablation are appropriate. The oldest of these methods is the examination of the behavior of patients with localized brain lesions. For this method to shed any light on the question of what the two hemispheres do, one has, of course, to observe patients in whom there is damage to only one or the other side of the brain. Epilepsy is caused by runaway activation in some region of the brain. Often the temporal lobe is the focus of this activity. Usually, epilepsy can be controlled by medication. When it cannot, it is sometimes necessary surgically to remove the part of the brain containing the epileptic focus. Since epileptic foci are sometimes in the right hemisphere and sometimes in the left, patients who have had such operations constitute another population for study.

Another more drastic treatment of epilepsy involves severing the connection between the hemispheres, the *corpus callosum*. The reason for doing this is that an epileptic focus in one hemisphere sometimes sets up a mirror focus in the other hemisphere. It does so via the corpus callosum. The result can be that the epileptic activity sets up a sort of positive feedback loop. Each focus further excites the other. The result is that the patient may go into *status epilepticus,* a permanent epileptic seizure. Unless this can be stopped, the result is death. The cure may be bad, but it is certainly not worse than the disease. Nonetheless, this operation has been performed on only several dozen people. However, the cognitive behavior of these people is of great interest to psychologists. The reason is that they have two independently operating hemispheres that are in communication with each other only via quite indirect pathways. (The subcortical parts of the brain are not split in such operations.)

It is also possible to perform a sort of functional ablation of one or the other hemisphere. This is done by injecting the barbiturate, sodium amytal, into either the right or left intracarotid artery (Wada, 1949). Each artery carries blood only to the ipsilateral hemisphere. When this blood gets to the hemisphere, the sodium amytal anesthetizes that hemisphere more or less completely for a few seconds.

DIFFERENTIAL STIMULATION

A variety of methods involve differential stimulation of only one hemisphere. We can take advantage of the asymmetry of sensory input tracts to send a stimulus to one or the other hemisphere. In the split visual field technique, a visual stimulus is presented either to the right or to the left of a central fixation point. This stimulus excites activity in the contralateral hemisphere. Of course, unless we are dealing with split-brain patients, this information will also be available to the other hemisphere. The trick to the method is time. First, we have to present the stimulus very briefly. Since it takes about 250 milliseconds to change our visual fixation, we have to present it for less than 250 milliseconds. Thus, so long as a subject's eyes were fixated in the first place, we know that any stimulus presented for less that 250 milliseconds will end up in the hemisphere opposite to the visual field in which it was presented. What then? Let's say that we have asked our subjects to recognize or identify visual stimuli. Suppose that a certain class of stimuli is recognized more accurately or more quickly when it is presented in the right visual field than when it is presented in the left visual field. There are two basic ways to explain this. We might reason that the left hemisphere (the initial recipient of right visual field presentations) is better at recognizing this class of stimuli than is the right hemisphere. In this view, both hemispheres have analyzers for the class of stimuli in question, but the one on the left is better or quicker. This would explain the difference between left- and right-field presentations. Another equally reasonable view would be that only the left hemisphere has an analyzer for the class of stimuli. The difference in performance would in this case be attributed to transfer across the corpus callosum. This takes time, so stimuli initially sent to the right hemisphere will be recognized more slowly. Any transfer of information will tend to degrade that information, so the less accurate identification of stimuli initially sent to the right hemisphere would also be explained. It is often impossible to decide between these alternative theories in split visual field studies.

We can use a similar method with auditory stimuli. Since auditory input tracts tend to be crossed, we can see if different classes of stimuli are better recognized by one ear or the other (Fry, 1974). However, because the crossing is in this case far from complete, results with this method tend to be rather weak. Another method, which is similar to those used in shadowing tasks, can be used to overcome this difficulty. A different stimulus is presented to each ear and we see which one is heard (Kimura, 1961). What seems to happen in this case is that input from the contralateral ear inhibits the input from the ipsilateral ear. Which ear is dominant depends, as we shall see, on what class of auditory stimuli we are dealing with.

Several artificial methods of stimulation have also been used to study hemispheric specialization. Penfield and Roberts (1959) used very mild electrical stimulation of exposed cortex in the process of doing operations on the brain. Such stimulation may give a clue as to what a particular part of the brain does. This clue will not only advance scientific knowledge, but it may also prevent the neurosurgeon from cutting out the wrong part of the brain. More extreme electrical stimulation is involved in electroconvulsive therapy. As the name implies, a rather substantial shock is delivered to the brain. For reasons that are not altogether clear, this tends to alleviate depression. For reasons that are even less clear, delivering the electrical current to the right hemisphere is generally more effective than delivering it to the left hemisphere.

PHYSIOLOGICAL METHODS

After these esoteric and imaginative procedures, it seems mundane to mention that we can simply monitor the electrical activity of different regions of the brain by means of EEG. If a given region is involved in performing a given task, it should show more activation (more suppression of alpha-wave activity) than other regions. The method of evoked potentials can also be used. In this method, a stimulus is repeatedly presented and the average EEG response to it is recorded. The point is to get rid of or cancel out the ongoing background noise that is present if we look at the EEG response to just one presentation of the stimulus. If a given brain region is specialized for processing a certain type of stimulus, then that type of stimulus should elicit larger evoked potentials over this region than over other regions.

LATERAL EYE MOVEMENTS

Did you ever notice that when you ask people a question, they often move their eyes and head as if the answer to the question were written on the ceiling.

Classroom teachers have known this for centuries. Day (1964) was the first to notice that people tend to be consistent in the direction—right or left—that their eyes move when they are asked a question. Bakan (1971) pointed out that, since such lateral eye movements are triggered by the hemisphere opposite the direction of gaze, such movements could reflect differential degrees of activation of the hemispheres. When the right hemisphere is activated, the eyes should move leftward, but when the left hemisphere is activated they should deviate toward the right. It would seem as if we could ask people different sorts of questions, watch their eyes, and infer which hemisphere was activated in order to answer the question. Indeed, we can do this, and many scientists have done so.

Left-hemisphere functions

SPEECH AND LANGUAGE

With this imposing array of methods at their disposal, what have scientists found out about the two hemispheres of the brain? If nothing else, they have amply confirmed one fact that began to be suspected over 100 years ago: the left hemisphere is important for speech and language. Broca (1861) discovered that damage to one area of the left hemisphere consistently causes aphasia while damage to the analogous area of the right hemisphere does not. *Aphasia* is really a family of language disorders. They involve inability to speak and/or to understand language in the absence of specific difficulty in either hearing or making the motor movements of the mouth necessary for speech. In other words, there is damage to the speech and/or semantic analyzers in the absence of damage to the auditory analyzer or the motor system. We shall discuss the subtypes of aphasia presently. For the moment, it is only important to note that Wernicke (1874) discovered that another subtype of aphasia is connected with damage to another part of the left hemisphere but not with damage to the analogous region of the right hemisphere. Subsequent research has confirmed the initial findings of Broca and Wernicke. Well over 95 percent of cases of aphasia are caused by damage to the left hemisphere (Geschwind, 1979). Handedness has some effect. Almost all cases of aphasia in right-handed people arise from left-hemisphere damage, while only about two thirds of cases in left-handed people arise from left-hemisphere damage. This suggests—or we might even say compels—the hypothesis that language is localized in the left hemisphere, especially in right-handed people. This hypothesis has been confirmed by virtually all of the methods described earlier.

Rasmussen and Milner (1977) temporarily suppressed activity of right and left hemispheres with intracarotid sodium amytal injections in 296 patients awaiting brain surgery. Suppression of the left hemisphere rendered 96 percent of right-handed and 70 percent of left-handed people temporarily aphasic. On the other hand, suppression of the right hemisphere rendered only 4 percent of right-handed patients and 15 percent of left-handed patients temporarily aphasic. Finally, 15 percent of left-handed people seemed to have language bilaterally represented. Suppression of either the left or the right hemisphere made them temporarily aphasic.

Split-brain patients can name objects placed in their right hands. Tactual input from the right hand goes to the left hemisphere. On the other hand, they cannot name objects placed in the left hand, which sends tactual input to the right hemisphere (Gazzaniga, 1970). Similarly, such a patient can write with the right hand (controlled by the left hemisphere), but cannot write at all with the left hand (Bogen, 1969). Does this mean that the right hemisphere has no language capacity at all or simply that it has no access to motor pathways involved in speech and writing? It does not quite mean either.

Sperry and Gazzaniga (1967) used a split visual field technique with split-brain patients. Words were flashed in one or the other visual field. The patient's task was to pick up the object that the word represented. For example, a toy car would be picked up if the word CAR were shown. Using this technique, they found that the right hemisphere can, in fact, recognize many words, including fairly abstract ones. When words were shown in the left visual field, the patients would often verbally deny that they had seen anything while at the very same time picking up the correct object with the left hand. The left hemisphere had seen nothing since the word was shown in the left visual field. However, the right hemisphere had recognized the word. Since it had no access to the speech apparatus, it could only indicate this by picking up the object with the hand that it controlled.

The right hemisphere of split-brain patients can also understand some verbally presented words (Levy, 1979). Given an auditory presentation of a word to the right hemisphere, a split-brain patient can select its written form. However, the right hemisphere apparently cannot reverse this process; that is, it cannot generate the phonetic representation of a word if shown, for example, a picture of the thing the word represents. Levy (1974) used split-field tachistoscopic presentations with split-brain patients. Pictures of objects were shown, and the task was to pick up a picture showing something with a name rhyming with the name of the object shown. For example, if a picture of an EYE were shown, the subject should select a picture of a PIE. The results were quite clear. The patients could perform the task with right-field (left-hemisphere) presentations, but they could not do it at all with left-field (right-hemisphere) presentations.

Gazzaniga and Hillyard (1971) also used a split-field technique with split-brain patients. However, the stimuli were more complex. For example, in response to a stimulus such as CAR HITS HOUSE, the patient would be expected to provide a demonstration with the toy objects at his disposal. The right hemisphere could understand the meanings of the individual words, but it could not understand their meaning in the sentence. It recognized and understood CAR, HIT, and HOUSE, but it did not understand what was supposed to hit what. It could not tell singular from plural, active from passive, or present tense from future tense. In other words, the right hemisphere has no grammatical or propositional ability. It can recognize words but cannot understand how they are related to one another in a sentence or proposition. The left hemisphere had no difficulty at all with this task. It does possess grammatical understanding.

Split-field techniques have been used extensively with normal subjects. The consistent finding has been that words and letters are recognized more quickly and more accurately when they are presented in the right visual field than when they are presented in the left visual field (for example, Mishkin and Forgays, 1952; Rizzolatti, Umilta, and Berlucci, 1971). Kimura (1961) used a dichotic listening task with normal subjects. Different syllables were presented to each ear. The one presented to the right ear was the one that tended to be heard.

This effect, often called the right-ear advantage, is found only for speech sounds, and not for sounds in general. Hypothetically, the speech sound from the contra-lateral ear suppresses or inhibits the one from the ipsilateral ear. The right-ear advantage for speech sounds can also be demonstrated in a more straightforward way by presenting a stimulus to only one ear. When this is done, speech sounds presented to the right ear are better recognized than those presented to the left ear (Fry, 1974). Interestingly, the right-ear advantage is strongest for stop con-sonants and is absent for vowels (Studdert-Kennedy, 1975) This makes sense. Recall that the spectrum of a vowel is rather similar to that of a pure tone, while a complicated set of features defines a stop consonant. As we saw in Chapter 5, vowels often do not give us the same effects as consonants. This is especially true when they are presented at their normal long durations. In fact, when shortened vowels are used as stimuli in dichotic listening tasks, a right-ear ad-vantage is found (Godfrey, 1974).

Findings with EEG methods have also been consistent in assigning linguistic processing to the left hemisphere. Morgan, McDonald, and MacDonald (1971) and others have found more alpha suppression in the left hemisphere than in the right hemisphere during linguistic tasks than during nonlinguistic tasks. Galin and Ellis (1975) found larger evoked potentials in the left than in the right hemisphere with speech stimuli. Wood, Goff, and Day (1971) found larger left-hemisphere than right-hemisphere evoked potentials when subjects were asked to make pho-nemic discriminations. This asymmetry disappeared when subjects were asked to make pitch discriminations with the same stimuli. Presumably, the pitch judgment could be made in either hemisphere since it is a purely sensory one. However, the phonemic judgment could only be made in the left hemisphere. Kinsbourne (1972) used the lateral eye-movement technique and found the same thing: Questions that require linguistic processing induce rightward eye movements (indicative of left-hemisphere activation).

LANGUAGE CIRCUITS IN THE LEFT HEMISPHERE

Components of language. Speech, says Jakobson (1956), has three com-ponents: selection, combination, and realization. *Selection* refers to the necessity of selecting from semantic memory a specific set of meanings that is to be con-veyed and connecting these with certain morphemes. In order for selection to occur, we must have a subjective lexicon from which to select and a speech analyzer in which meanings are attached to morphemes. *Combination* refers to the necessity of arranging these morphemes into a syntactically correct string. In order to do this, we must have a knowledge (whether we are consciously aware of it or not) of the syntactic rules of the language we are speaking. *Realization* is the task of expressing the string of morphemes as spoken words. In order to perform this task, we must have control of the motor apparatus that controls our mouth, tongue, and vocal chords.

Evidence from aphasia. The type of aphasia discovered by Broca is what Jakobson (1956) calls a combination disorder. Patients suffering from this disorder have particular difficulty with syntax. They also have trouble with the function words, such as prepositions (for example, ON, IN), pronouns (for example, HE, SHE), and connectives (for example, AND, BUT) that are used to express syn-tactic intent. In contrast, they have little difficulty producing or understanding nouns. Here is an example (quoted by Geschwind, 1979) of such a patient's response to a question about a dental appointment: "Yes . . . Monday . . . Dad and Dick . . . Wednesday nine o'clock . . . 10 o'clock . . . doctor . . . and . . . teeth." This kind of speech is like a "word heap." The nouns are all there, but the syntax is missing. The nouns are not strung together by means of function words into a complete sentence. Such patients show the same problem when they try to write.

The type of aphasia discovered by Wernicke is what Jakobson (1956) calls a selection disorder. In some ways, it is just the opposite of Broca's aphasia. In a patient with Wernicke's aphasia, speech sounds normal so long as you do not listen to what is being said. There is no problem with grammar or intonation and inflection. The problem is that what is said makes little or no sense. The wrong words or even neologisms may be used. Geschwind (1979) quotes this speech sample from a patient asked to describe a picture of boys stealing cookies while their mother's back was turned: "Mother is away here working her work to get her better, but when she's looking the two boys looking in the other part. She's working another time." Jakobson (1956) describes such a patient who was reduced to only two made-up nouns, SERIAT and FERIAT. When asked his occupation (blacksmith) he responded, "I am a feriat. Work at a seriat." The examiner replied, "You mean an anvil?" "That's right," the patient said, "a seriat." When this patient read a printed text, he pronounced every word as "seriat."

Wernicke's theory. Broca's area is in the left frontal lobe, just beneath the motor area. Wernicke's area is in the left temporal lobe, just behind the primary auditory receiving area. Their positions are shown in Figure 11–5. As you can see, the two areas are connected by a bundle of fibers called the *arcuate fasciculus.*

FIGURE 11–5   The left hemisphere, showing regions important for language processing

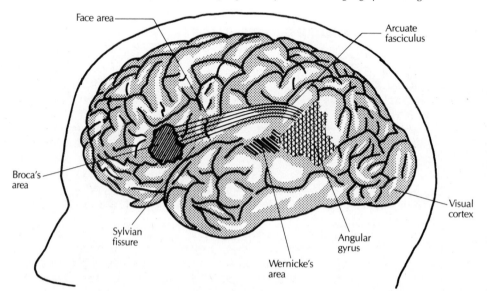

On the basis of the findings concerning damage to Wernicke's and Broca's area, Wernicke (1874) proposed a theory of speech that is still widely accepted. Geschwind (1972) presents a modernized version of the theory as follows. Wernicke's area contains what we have called the speech analyzer. When we speak, we first select a set of meanings from the semantic analyzer. Where the semantic analyzer is, the model does not say. Perhaps these meanings are coded in the form of a proposition—for example, SPEAK (JOHN, MARY, APHASIA, PAST). Of course, Wernicke did not put it in quite these terms, since case grammar had not yet been devised. This is my reinterpertation of his theory (Martindale, 1977b). The basic point is that the elements of the sentence are not yet arranged as words in a sequential string. Once the proposition has been selected, it is sent to Wernicke's area. Here, the meanings are associated with morpheme representations. From Wernicke's area, information about these elements is sent to Broca's area via the arcuate fasciculus. Broca's area arranges them into a sequential string of elements—for example, JOHN SPOKE TO MARY ABOUT APHASIA. When the proposition is arranged in this way, the different cases are expressed in various ways. The past tense is expressed by using SPOKE rather than SPEAK. On the other hand, the object and the recipient are expressed by the addition of the function words TO and ABOUT. Finally, all of the elements are arranged into a sequential string. However, it is not right to think about these elements as being words. They are not words until they are spoken. Broca's area passes information about the elements to the motor speech area, the part of the motor cortex controlling the mouth, tongue, and vocal cords. This area moves the speech apparatus and the elements are realized as words. If these words are heard by someone else, they will go first to the auditory receiving area. From there, they will be passed to Wernicke's area where they will be looked up. Then, they will excite activity in the semantic analyzer, where they will be understood.

This model allows us to explain what occurs in aphasia. In Broca's aphasia, Broca's area is damaged but Wernicke's area is intact. The patient can perform the task of selection. A semantically meaningful proposition can be generated and passed to Broca's area via the intact arcuate fasciculus. However, when it arrives, it cannot be correctly decoded and strung together because Broca's area is damaged. Because Wernicke's area is intact, the patient can still understand spoken and written words with almost no problem. Understanding a spoken word involves passing information from the auditory receiving area to the speech analyzer (Wernicke's area) to the semantic analyzer. In Wernicke's aphasia, we have an opposite state of affairs. Understanding of spoken or written words is poor. This is because information about the word cannot get from the auditory cortex to the semantic analyzer. The only way to do this is via Wernicke's area, which is damaged. Also, the patient's speech is semantically deviant. Presumably, the patient's semantic memory can generate the propositions, but once they get to the damaged Wernicke's area they get jumbled. The propositions sent to Broca's area are not right in the first place because they are formed by the damaged speech analyzer. Since Broca's area is working normally, it can string together what it receives. The problem is that it receives gibberish. Destruction of the arcuate fasciculus leads to speech that sounds like that of a patient suffering from Wernicke's aphasia (Geschwind, 1972). Regardless of whether it is Wernicke's area or the arcuate fasciculus that is damaged, the result is the same. Broca's area does not receive well-formed propositions. However, damage to the arcuate fasciculus leaves understanding of either spoken or written words untouched since Wernicke's area is not damaged (Geschwind, 1972). In contrast, the patient with Wernicke's aphasia has severe comprehension problems.

Destruction of the angular gyrus, a region directly behind Wernicke's area does not affect comprehension or production of spoken speech. However, the patient can no longer read, even though vision per se is normal. Hypothetically, the angular gyrus contains the analyzer for printed words. The person can see the words because the visual receiving area is intact. But these visual forms cannot be connected with meanings in the semantic analyzer because this connection is carried out via the printed-word analyzer, which has been destroyed. Wernicke argued that the printed word analyzer is almost always connected to what we call semantic memory via Wernicke's area. This is because of the way people are taught to read. This would explain why damage to Wernicke's area almost always destroys the ability to understand written as well as spoken language.

Geschwind (1972) studied a woman with a brain lesion that had completely isolated the speech regions from other cortical regions; that is, Broca's area and Wernicke's area were intact, as was the connection between them. The auditory tract and the motor speech tract were also undamaged. However, these regions were isolated from everything else. This means that they were cut off from semantic memory as well. This patient never uttered any spontaneous speech during the nine years she was studied. During this time, she seemed to show no comprehension at all of speech. This is consistent with the absence of a connection with semantic memory. This is where the propositions that finally end up as speech are originally generated. It is also where speech is ultimately understood. Interestingly, the woman could repeat words or sentences that she had just heard. This is consistent with the intact circuit from auditory receiving area to Wernicke's area to Broca's area to motor speech area. The woman could also complete stereotyped phrases. For example, if she heard ROSES ARE RED, she would respond with the rest of this familiar phrase—VIOLETS ARE BLUE, and so on. Hypothetically, the routines for such stereotyped phrases are stored in Broca's area. The woman could sing and could even learn to sing songs she had never heard before.

In Figure 11–6, Wernicke's theory is summarized. We show the circuits that must be completed in order to perform five different tasks: voluntary production of speech, understanding of speech, repetition of speech, reading aloud, and understanding what is read.

Right-hemisphere functions

The right hemisphere also has its share of duties. These, however, are not quite as well understood as those of the left hemisphere. One reason for this is that right-hemisphere brain damage generally leads to much subtler cognitive disorders than does left-hemisphere damage. Another reason is that localization in the right hemisphere seems to be more diffuse than in the left (Hécaen, 1967). That is, we do not find the same sort of fairly precise correlation between location of lesion and type of disorder as often found with left-hemisphere damage. This has suggested to some that the functions carried out by the right hemisphere are themselves more holistic and thus less subject to precise localization.

FIGURE 11–6   The brain circuits hypothetically involved in five linguistic tasks: (A) voluntary production of speech; (B) understanding speech; (C) repetition of speech; (D) reading a printed text aloud; and (E) understanding printed text.

SPATIAL ANALYSIS

The right hemisphere seems to be specialized to perform a variety of spatial analyses. Damage to the right hemisphere, especially to its posterior regions, impairs performance on a variety of spatial tasks. It often induces somatagnosia and apraxias of various sorts (Hécaen, 1967). *Somatagnosia* is a lack of awareness of one's own body. The patient loses awareness of where the parts of the body are in space and how they relate to one another. This can induce a variety of apraxias. These are difficulties in performing spatial tasks. For example, the patient may have great difficulty in getting dressed. *Constructional apraxias* are also caused by right-hemisphere lesions (Butler, 1971). These are difficulties in constructing spatial forms. Examples would be difficulty in putting together puzzles or in making designs with blocks.

Milner (1968) studied patients who had undergone ablation of the right temporal lobe for treatment of epilepsy. Such patients—as compared with patients who had left temporal lobe ablations—showed deficits on tactile maze learning and on a task involving estimation of how many dots were shown in a briefly presented stimulus. They also showed deficits in memory for complex, irregular designs. However, they showed no deficits in memory for simple shapes. This suggests that the right hemisphere may be specialized for dealing with complex spatial material but that either hemisphere can handle simple spatial tasks.

This hypothesis is confirmed by split visual field studies of normal subjects. Complex visual shapes are recognized better if they are presented in the left visual field (Fontenot, 1973), but no visual field differences are found for simple shapes (Fontenot, 1973; Kimura, 1966). The difference between the hemispheres seems to lie in the ability to code and remember complex shapes rather than in the ability to perceive them in the first place. Dee and Fontenot (1973) briefly presented complex shapes in either the right or left visual field. Then they presented a test stimulus and asked subjects if this was the same as the briefly presented stimulus. When the test stimulus immediately followed the first stimulus, no visual-field differences were found. However, visual-field differences did emerge when a delay between the first stimulus and the test stimulus was introduced. The longer this delay was, the greater was the advantage of left-field (right-hemisphere) presentations. Both hemispheres have sensory analyzers. With no delay, iconic sensory memory should preserve a representation of the first stimulus. This can be matched against the test stimulus. Hypothetically, only the right hemisphere has higher-level gnostic analyzers for complex spatial forms. Thus, as delay is increased, the iconic representation in the left hemisphere decays and performance deteriorates. However, the right hemisphere now has the first stimulus coded in a gnostic analyzer. Thus, it does better at the task. Both hemispheres can perceive complex shapes, but hypothetically only the right hemisphere can code and, thus, remember them.

Other methods of study have also been supportive of the idea that the right hemisphere is specialized for performing spatial analyses. Morgan, McDonald, and MacDonald (1971), Galin and Ornstein (1972) and Galin and Ellis (1975) found more right-hemisphere EEG activity than left-hemisphere activity while people were working on problems of a spatial nature. Vella, Butler, and Glass (1972) got similar results using the evoked potential technique. Kinsbourne (1972) found that people tend to show leftward head and eye movements (indicative of right-hemisphere activation) when they are asked questions that require them to think in terms of spatial relations.

FACE RECOGNITION

We saw in Chapter 4 that there seems to be a specialized analyzer that deals with the recognition of faces. As you will recall, certain types of brain damage do not affect vision per se, but they leave the patient unable to recognize faces. Such facial agnosia is almost always due to lesions in the right rather than in the left hemisphere (Hécaen, 1967). Patients whose right temporal lobe has been surgically removed show decreased ability for facial recognition (Milner, 1968). Such findings strongly suggest that the analyzer for facial recognition is located in the right hemisphere. Other methods of study have yielded results that support this notion. Rizzolatti, Umilta, and Berlucchi (1971) used a tachistoscope to present pictures of faces in either the right or the left visual field. Recognition was faster for faces presented in the left visual field. Dumas and Morgan (1975) recorded EEG activity while their subjects were engaged in a facial recognition test. As expected, there was more right-hemisphere activation while this task was being performed.

VISUAL IMAGERY

Are visual images produced by the right hemisphere? We have seen that the right hemisphere seems to be specialized for the perception and analysis of complex visual stimuli. It thus certainly seems reasonable that it might also be responsible for the production of mental images. Paivio (1978) hypothesizes that there are separate systems or analyzers for speech and for visual images and that these systems may be lateralized to the left and right hemispheres. Bogen (1969) reports that patients who have undergone split-brain operation say that they no longer dream. If the production of visual images—which is certainly involved in dreaming—is a right-hemisphere function, this makes sense. Presumably, such patients do still dream but, since the corpus callosum has been severed, the left hemisphere is unaware of the dreams. Since it controls the vocal apparatus, the patient says that he has no dreams. Goldstein, Stoltzfus, and Gardocki (1972) recorded EEG as their subjects slept. They found that during dreaming the right hemisphere became more activated than the left. Goldstein and Stoltzfus (1973) found that hallucinogenic drugs—which generally produce intense visual images—led to a similar pattern. Indeed, the same thing (greater right-hemisphere activation as indicated by EEG measures) is found when normal subjects are simply asked to form mental images (Morgan, McDonald, and MacDonald, 1971; Robbins and McAdam, 1974).

Penfield and Roberts' (1959) experiential responses were mentioned in Chapter 9. As you may recall, when certain areas of the exposed cortex were electrically stimulated, patients reported intensely vivid auditory and visual images. These experiential responses were almost never elicited when the left hemisphere was stimulated. They were elicited most frequently by stimulation of the right hemisphere, especially the part of the right temporal lobe analogous to Wernicke's area.

Seamon and Gazzaniga (1973) gave their subjects the task of remembering pairs of words. Half of the subjects were instructed to use only auditory rehearsal, while the other half were instructed to form an image in order to remember each pair. For example, given the pair TABLE–GIRAFFE, one group was supposed to form a visual mental image involving both members of the pair while the other group was supposed to avoid doing so. Subjects were tested by presenting the first word in each pair. Their task was to recall the second word. The testing involved presenting the test word tachistoscopically in either the right or the left visual field. The subjects instructed to form images performed better when the test word was presented in the left visual field. Just the opposite was the case for the subjects instructed to use verbal rehearsal. These findings make sense if we assume that the image was formed or stored in the right hemisphere. Left-field presentations would then make contact with this image more quickly.

MUSIC

Patients suffering from aphasia caused by damage to the left hemisphere often retain the ability to sing (Geschwind, 1979). A patient who cannot produce or understand any words at all may still be able to sing old songs and even to learn new ones. This is quite surprising. One would expect the speech system to be intimately involved in singing, since the lyrics of songs are, of course, made up of words. But this is not the case. A completely separate right-hemisphere system seems to be involved in singing. The earliest forms of singing did not involve words.[1] Rather, singing originally consisted of the production of mean-ingless nonsense syllables. Only late in the course of historical development did singing come to consist of the same words used in speech. This fact sheds some light on why the brain centers for speech and song are in different places: Orig-inally, speech and song had nothing to do with each other beyond the fact that they both used the vocal apparatus.

The analyzers involved in music recognition as well as the centers for the production of music are located in the right hemisphere. Milner, Branch, and Rasmussen (1966) found that surgical removal of the right temporal lobe impairs recognition of music and memory for music whereas removal of comparable areas of the left temporal lobe has no such effect. While there is a right-ear advantage for the recognition of speech, there is a left-ear advantage for recognition of music; that is, musical stimuli are recognized and recalled better if they are presented to the left ear than if they are presented to the right ear. This is the case for melodies (Kimura, 1967), musical tones (Goodglass and Calderon, 1977), and musical chords (Yund & Efron, 1976). This makes sense if the musical analyzer is in the right hemisphere: Stimuli presented to the left ear will get there faster. Other methods of study have yielded consistent results. Both evoked potential techniques (Shucard, Shucard, and Thomas, 1977) and EEG recordings (McKee, Humphrey, and McAdam, 1973) show greater right-hemisphere activation while subjects are listening to music. These findings are true of musically untrained people. In the case of professional musicians, music seems to elicit bilateral activity (Bever and Chiarello, 1974). Perhaps, this is because they have learned to attach verbal labels—for example, the names of notes, chords, and so on—to musical stimuli.

---

[1] A. Lomax, 1979: Personal communication.

EMOTION

Recognition of emotion.   We said earlier that the limbic system is the ultimate locus of emotion and that the cortex is confronted with the task of recognizing what emotion we are feeling. Another cortical task is recognizing what other people's emotions are. There is evidence that analyzers in the right hemisphere are devoted to these tasks. We often infer other people's emotions from their facial expressions. We know that the facial recognition analyzer is in the right hemisphere. Therefore . . . nothing. Patients with facial agnosia very often retain the ability to infer emotion from facial expressions. They cannot recognize who the face belongs to but they can recognize the emotion it is expressing! Odd as it may be, the emotional analyzer is apparently not directly dependent upon the analyzer for facial recognition.

Patients with brain lesions in the right hemisphere are less able to judge other people's emotions correctly than patients with left-hemisphere lesions (Heilman, Scholer, and Watson, 1975). A variety of studies with normal subjects suggests that the right hemisphere has a special role in the recognition of emotion. There is a left-ear advantage for judging the emotional tone of speech (Carmon and Nachson, 1973). The emotional tone of a voice is judged better if it is heard by the left ear (sent initially to the right hemisphere) than if it is heard by the right ear. Questions involving emotion induce leftward eye movements (Schwartz, Davidson, and Maer, 1975) and right-hemisphere EEG activation (Davidson and Schwartz, 1977).

Production of emotion.   Some other findings make the picture a bit more complicated but a lot more interesting. While the right hemisphere does seem to be the primary locus for emotional recognition, it seems that each hemisphere is specialized for the production of a different type of emotion. Gainotti (1972) studied the type of emotional reaction displayed by patients with unilateral brain lesions. Those with right-hemisphere lesions tended to have euphoric-maniacal reactions, while those with left-hemisphere lesions tended to have depressive-catastrophic reactions. It is odd that one should react to brain damage with euphoria, but this is indeed often the reaction when the damage is on the right side. The momentary suppression of a hemisphere with sodium amytal is often accompanied by a change in mood. Suppression of the left hemisphere tends to induce depression, while suppression of the right hemisphere often induces euphoria (Hommes and Panhuysen, 1971; Rossi and Rosadini, 1967). Electro-convulsive therapy is used to treat depression. It tends to work better when the electric current is delivered to the right hemisphere than when it is delivered to the left hemisphere (Cronin et al., 1970; Halliday et al., 1968). All of these studies are consistent in their findings. *Suppression* of right-hemisphere activity—whether by brain lesions, sodium amytal, or electroconculsive shock—moves one toward euphoria. Suppression of the left hemisphere, on other other hand, moves one toward depression. These results, therefore, suggest that *activation* of the right hemisphere goes with negative affect, while activation of the left hemisphere goes with positive affect. It would seem that the forces of evolution have wired our brains so as to make it more pleasant to use the left hemisphere than the right. Why should that be? I am not privy to the councils of these forces, but I am told that there is only one item on their agenda: survival. Let us step back and consider in broader perspective what functions the two hemispheres serve. Then, perhaps the answer to our question will become clear.

Hemispheric division of labor

LINGUISTIC VERSUS SPATIAL THEORIES

The earliest idea about the division of functions between the two hemispheres was that the left hemisphere is specialized for verbal processing and the right hemisphere for spatial processing. However, this view turned out to be too simple. The right hemisphere has not only spatial functions but also musical and emotional ones. The left hemisphere has several other specialties besides language. Although we did not review it in this chapter, there is evidence suggesting that the left hemisphere is also specialized for mathematical reasoning (Prohovnik, 1978) and perception of rhythm (Gordon, 1978), among other things. The right hemisphere has some linguistic capabilities and the left has some spatial capabilities. Thus, the right hemisphere can recognize and understand many individual words. What it lacks is the syntactic ability to put these words together into propositions. On the other hand, the left hemisphere can recognize and react to simple spatial stimuli. What it lacks is the spatial syntax necessary to combine these into complex shapes and forms.

TEMPORAL VERSUS SPATIAL THEORIES

One more general formulation is that the left hemisphere deals with temporal ordering and the right hemisphere deals with spatial ordering. Levy (1979) holds that "the left hemisphere seems to map sensory input into a temporal domain, the ordering of events in space being transformed into events in time, while the right hemisphere maps sensory input into a spatial domain, organizing sequential temporal events as a spatial pattern." This view accounts for most of the right-left differences. Language, rhythm, and arithmetic are sequential or temporal in nature. It could be argued that the left hemisphere processes the rhythmic aspects of music while the right hemisphere processes its tonal and chordal aspects in a spatial manner. However, it seems to be stretching things a bit to categorize emotion as being either spatial (as it should be since it seems to be a right-hemisphere function) or temporal. We need a more general formulation.

SECONDARY PROCESS VERSUS PRIMARY PROCESS THEORIES

A number of theorists have argued that the left hemisphere is specialized for analytic-sequential functions while the right hemisphere is specialized for synthetic-holistic functions (Bogen, 1969; Levy, Trevarthen, and Sperry, 1972; Ornstein, 1972). The basic idea is that the left-hemisphere analyzers are good for analyzing stimuli into their parts and processing these parts in a serial or sequential fashion. On the other hand, the right-hemisphere analyzers do more or less just the opposite. They serve to process stimuli as simultaneous wholes or gestalts. Clearly, this accounts for the linguistic versus spatial specialization of functions. It would also seem to account for the other lateralized functions. Emotion, which does not fit with the temporal versus spatial theory, does fit with the analytic versus holistic theory; that is, emotions are perceived in an amorphous or holistic way, just as the theory would predict, given that perception of emotion is a right-hemisphere function.

In Chapter 12, we shall argue that there are two polar types of cognition: Secondary process thought characterizes normal waking states. It is analytic, rational, reality oriented, and devoted to problem solving. On the other hand, primary process thought occurs in dreams, reveries, and altered states of consciousness as diverse as mystical experience and psychosis. It is synthetic, irrational, autistic (unrelated to reality), and devoted to wish fulfillment rather than to the planning of practical action. Several theorists have argued that the left hemisphere operates in a secondary process fashion, while the right hemisphere operates in a primary process fashion (Galin, 1974; Hoppe, 1977). This is essentially a restatement of the analytic versus holistic theory.

SUMMARY AND CONCLUSIONS

The process of evolution has led to a stratification of the brain with newer regions laid down on top of older ones. MacLean argues that there are three basic strata: the reptilian brain, the paleomammalian brain, and the neomammalian brain. Although higher strata tend to inhibit lower ones, each stratum has some autonomy. The reptilian brain controls basic functions in a reflexlike manner. The paleomammalian brain—or limbic system—contains a richly interconnected set of centers controlling drives and emotions. The neomammalian brain takes care of cognitive functioning. It is also faced with the task of decoding or recognizing limbic-system signals. Context effects are apparently quite strong in the recognition of such signals. They may even lead us to mislabel or misperceive our emotions and drives.

The brain is bilaterally symmetrical. This is especially apparent at higher levels, where the cerebrum is divided into the right and left hemispheres. In general, the portion of a sensory analyzer in one hemisphere processes information about the contralateral side of space or of the body. The same principle holds for the motor system. The portion of the motor system located in one hemisphere controls the contralateral side of the body. In contrast, gnostic analyzers seem to be lateralized according to a different principle. Analyzers dealing with spatial analysis, imagery, face recognition, music, and the recognition of emotion seem to be segregated in the right hemisphere. On the other hand, analyzers dealing with the production and recognition of language seem to be located in the left hemisphere. Those analyzers dealing with the component element of language—the sound patterns of spoken words and the visual patterns of printed words—are located in posterior portions of the left hemisphere. On the other hand, analyzers devoted to the combination and realization of these linguistic elements are located in the anterior portions of the left hemisphere. Evidence from various types of brain disorders tells us how these linguistic analyzers must be interconnected.

Several theorists have sought to describe the general principle according to which a cognitive process is localized in the right or the left hemisphere. One general formulation is that analyzers operating in a holistic or primary process manner are located in the right hemisphere while analyzers operating in an analytic or secondary process manner are located in the left hemisphere. Our consideration of hemispheric differences has led us to the notion that there are two radically different modes of cognition and thought. In the next two chapters, we shall examine the evidence for this contention. These two modes of cognition seem, in fact, to be the poles of a continuum defining a whole spectrum of types of thought and states of consciousness.

12

Thought and action

WHAT IS THINKING?

Berlyne (1965) defines *thought* as any process that involves a chain of symbolic responses. A *symbol* is anything that stands for or means something else. A *cognitive unit* is clearly one type of symbol. In the model we have developed, a *symbolic response* would be the activation of a cognitive unit. Thinking, then, would be sequential activation of cognitive units. The study of attention and primary memory or consciousness concerns the question of which cognitive units are activated at any one moment in time. The study of thinking concerns the question of which units are activated across a series of such moments. Thought, in other words, is attention or consciousness stretched out over time. In order to differentiate thinking from sensation, let's say that the cognitive units involved in thinking are at a deeper level than units in purely sensory analyzers. On the other hand, in order to differentiate thinking from behavior, let's say that the cognitive units involved in thinking are not in motor systems either. In this definition, *thinking* is a chain of activity in cognitive analyzers that deal with neither raw sensory input nor final motor output.

The locus of thinking suggests that it could serve to link sensory input with motor output. Indeed, many theorists assign it exactly this function. Klein (1967), for example, says, "By a train of thought, I mean a temporally extended series of events linked at the receptor end to stimulation, at the motor end to . . . effector processes, and to each other by facilitative and inhibitive signals in a patterned sequence." Lashley (1958) holds that the mechanisms of thought and of action are identical "save for the lack of facilitation of the final motor path" in the case of thought. If Lashley is correct in this assertion, then it would be a good idea for us to get some understanding of what the mechanisms of action are. We have an idea of how people perceive, attend to, and understand stimuli. By what mechanisms do these processes eventuate in behavior? If we can answer this question, then we should be able to back up and explain thinking.

THE STRUCTURE OF ACTION

As explained in Chapter 1, behaviorist psychology held that the basic building block of the nervous system is the reflex arc. A stimulus excites a sensory neuron and it, in turn, excites a motor neuron which causes a muscle to contract or relax. Complex processes were seen as involving a longer circuit—for example, a stimulus excites a sensory neuron, it excites neuron B, neuron B excites neuron C, and finally neuron C excites the motor neuron. This is a serial or left-to-right process. However, this theory of behavior can only explain reflexes and cannot cope very well with purposive behavior. Miller, Galanter, and Pribram (1960) suggest that a better building block for explaining action would be the feedback loop, since it would allow not only horizontal or left-to-right sequencing but also hierarchical sequencing and control. Miller, Galanter, and Pribram call the basic unit of action the TOTE (for Test-Operate-Test-Exit) unit (see Figure 12–1).

FIGURE 12–1   TOTE (Test-Operate-Test-Exit) Unit

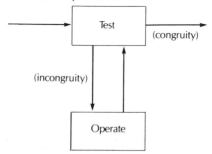

Source: G. A. Miller, E. Galanter, and K. H. Pribram,
Plans and the Structure of Behavior (New York: Holt, Rinehart & Winston, 1960), p. 26.

They hold that "Action is initiated by an 'incongruity' between the state of the organism and the state that is being tested for." The idea is that we test for the presence of some desired goal or state of affairs. If it is present (there is a congruity between percept and goal), then we exit from the test. If it is not present (there is an incongruity between the percept and the goal), then we operate (perform some action). After this operation is performed, control returns to the test unit. Why should control return to the test unit? So that we can see if the goal has been met; that is, there is another test for congruity between the desired goal and the present state of affairs. If there is now a state of congruity, control exits from the test unit. If there is not, the operation is performed again.

The operation of TOTE units may be illustrated with the simple action of hammering a nail into a board. First, we test for having the nail flush with the board. If the nail is flush, we can exit; that is, we can turn our attention to something else. If it is not flush, then we must perform the operation of hammering. After hitting the nail with the hammer, control passes back to the test unit. We check to see whether the nail is flush. If it is, we can exit. If it is not, we have to keep hammering. Note that the sequence in a TOTE unit involves feedback. We check the results of an action rather than merely emitting the action. Control passes back and forth between perceptual and operational units.

Miller, Galanter, and Pribram (1960) find the origin of action in incongruity between an internal goal and perceptual reality. Another way of saying this is that there is a mismatch between a cognitive model and perceptual input. Recall that this is exactly what Sokolov (1960) says causes cortical arousal and focused attention. It is what Berlyne (1971) says causes pleasure or displeasure, depending upon the degree of the mismatch. A mismatch between internally activated cognitive units (goals, expectations, or desires) and externally activated cognitive units (percepts) thus leads to arousal, affect, and attention. The result of such a state is some action aimed at reducing the mismatch. Sokolov talked about covert actions (building a new goal or model) in order to bring about a match. Miller, Galanter, and Pribram talk about overt actions undertaken in order to bring about a match.

THE ACTION SYSTEM

Propositional nature of action units

Are there cognitive units that correspond to general actions such as hammering? Shallice (1972, 1978) argues that there are. He says that—in addition to perceptual, conceptual, and motor systems—the brain also contains an action system. The action units in this system correspond to or control such general operations as hammering. There must be at least one of these action units for each elementary action to be performed. Shallice (1978:150) holds that at the very least, there would have to be one action unit for each of the actions that can be described by a verb referring to an intentional act (for example, eating, walking, throwing, handing, and so on). We shall argue later that there must also be action units coding purely mental acts (for example, deciding, rehearsing). Input to action units is hypothetically from cognitive units in gnostic and conceptual analyzers. The hammering unit will not be activated unless a hammer, nails, and a board are actually present. Inputs from semantic units coding the knowledge that hammering is appropriate in the situation at hand will also be necessary. An action unit along with its inputs may be seen as coding a proposition. The action unit defines the action itself (for example, hammering) while the inputs define the cases or components of the action, such as instrument (for example, hammer), recipient (for example, nail), location (for example, board), and so on.

Executive ignorance

Output from action units goes to the motor system, which controls the exact details of the action in question. These details include the specific muscular contractions necessary in order to execute the action. Shallice (1978) holds that the action system follows a principle of executive ignorance; that is, the action unit does not control the details of an action. Subjectively, we are conscious of deciding to execute an action, but we are not conscious of the details. The idea of executive ignorance corresponds well with conscious experience. Look at some small object in front of you. Decide to pick it up. You are conscious of the decision. Presumably, this corresponds to activation of an action unit. Then, the next thing you know, you have picked up the object. You were not conscious of whatever processes intervened between activation of the action unit and the motor behavior that was brought about by this activation. We consciously decide to pick something up but we do not consciously ask ourselves questions such as "ARE MY BICEPS CONTRACTING? IS THE VELOCITY OF MY HAND DECELERATING AT THE PROPER RATE?" These fine points are taken care of by the motor system outside of conscious awareness.

Necessity of the action system

Why postulate an action system? We just saw that we can decide to execute general actions, not specific motor responses. In Chapter 7 we saw that it is general actions rather than specific motor responses that are learned even by rats in mazes. Thus, the existence of action units is consistent with both introspective and behavioral data. Furthermore, as Wickelgren (1979a) has pointed out, direct connections between stimulus units (for example, units in the semantic analyzer) and response units (for example, units in the motor system) are not theoretically plausible. Rather, it is necessary to postulate intermediate chunking units in order to explain all but the most primitive stimulus-response pairings. Action units may be seen as chunking units of this sort.

Shallice (1978) notes that it is often necessary that one and only one action be dominant at any one time. This is because actions are often incompatible; for example, talking and eating. If you try to do both at the same time, you may choke. If you choke, you may die. That is to be avoided. Shallice argues that lateral inhibition among action units assures that, when one action unit is active, other action units—especially those coding similar and/or incompatible actions—will be inhibited. As in the case of other analyzers, the idea is that an activated action unit laterally inhibits other surrounding units.

Structure of the action system

Shallice's contention that the action system is hierarchically arranged suggests that perhaps the action system is a multilayered system like the other analyzers we have discussed. At the top level would be action units such as those we have discussed. These hypothetically receive input from perceptual or conceptual units and send output to motor units. They are also connected in an excitatory fashion with units at the next lower level of the action system. These deeper-level units code more general categories or plans of action. The hypothetical arrangement is shown in Figure 12–2. Various units—such as hammering, painting, sanding, and so on—are connected to a deeper unit labeled REPAIRING. Other units at this deeper level might code other general categories of action, such as MAKING FRIENDS, READING, LOSING WEIGHT, GOING TO A RESTAURANT, and so on. Schank and Abelson (1977) refer to such sequences of actions as *scripts*. We could apply Estes' (1972a) asymmetrical lateral inhibition model (see Chapter 9) to explain how the action units get activated by a script unit in the correct serial order.

In my elaboration of Shallice's theory of the action system, I postulate several deeper levels (Martindale, 1980). Below the level of script units is hypothetically a stratum of disposition units. Each disposition unit is connected to or collates

FIGURE 12–2   The structure of the action system

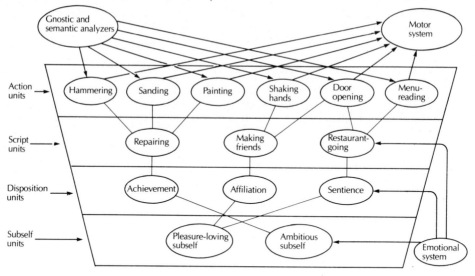

many script units. Murray's list of 20 or so basic motives (1938) might be seen as an approximation of the alphabet of dispositions. An example of a disposition unit would be what Murray called the need for achievement. Hypothetically, the disposition unit coding achievement would be strongly connected to scripts focally involving achievement (for example, repairing) and less strongly connected or not at all connected to scripts not involving achievement (for example, going to a restaurant).

At the deepest level of the action system are hypothetically subself units. These are essentially the distinctive features of the action system. Each is connected to a set of dispositional units. The reason for postulating such units has to do with observations pertinent to social psychology (people often exhibit quite different selves in different situations), personality psychology (people sometimes exhibit sudden conversions from one coherent self to another), and abnormal psychology (patients are sometimes found who exhibit multiple personalities). On a more mundane level, you have probably noticed that one part of you sometimes carries on a covert running commentary on what another part of you is doing. This is especially likely when you get into an unusual and uncomfortable situation where your usual subself has to turn over control of behavior to an unpracticed and rather alien subself. Thus, as you politely carry on about your rich uncle George's prize rose bushes, a partially inhibited subself gives you its comments on your obsequious, self-serving hypocrisy. All of these phenomena are consistent with the postulation of a set of subselves existing in a lateral inhibitory network. It would seem that the subjective sense of "I-ness" accompanies activation of most subself units.

Metaphorically, we might see the action system as a bureaucracy for controlling behavior. In computer terms, the action system might be likened to an executive monitor which oversees or controls processing in the analyzers and the motor system. The currently active subself primes a set of disposition units. These prime a set of plan or script units which, in turn, prime a set of action units.

Presumably, this vertical activation is subjectively felt as intention, volition, or will. Objectively, it makes sense to speculate that—unless stimuli are very strong or the actions involved are very habitual and automatic—action units need both vertical priming from deeper level units in the action system as well as stimulus input from other analyzers before they become activated enough to unleash the behavior that they control. The function of the vertical priming is to assure that one does not do anything out of character. If it were not there, our behavior would be more or less completely under the control of external stimuli. That is, perception or understanding of a stimulus would activate an action unit and this unit would unleash the behavior it controlled. The vertical structure of the action system gives the self—or selves—some say in things. It gives the currently activated subself and disposition units at least as much power over action as the external stimuli.

Connections to other analyzers

We have already mentioned that action units receive inputs from cognitive units in gnostic and conceptual analyzers and send outputs to the motor system. Figure 12–2 shows some units on deeper levels of the action system receiving inputs from the emotional system. Why? Because very often these units correspond to things we take distinct pleasure—or displeasure—in doing. For example, many people like to go out with members of the opposite sex. However, they are rather neutral about many of the specific actions involved, such as knocking on doors, buying movie tickets, walking, and so on. The deeper-level units code what we speak of as dispositions or motives. Thus, the deeper-level units are the ones that tend to be connected to the emotional system.

As well as sending output to the motor system, the action system must also send outputs back to gnostic and conceptual analyzers. As the TOTE model suggests, action units must be intimately connected with test or goal units. As shown in Figure 12–3, an action unit must prime gnostic units coding its expected outcome. This priming serves to keep attention centered on the relevant perceptual

FIGURE 12–3   Relationships among action units, stimulus units, and goal-image units

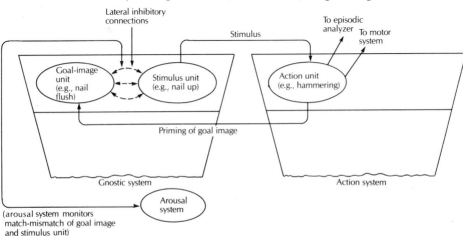

inputs. That is, the partial activation makes it likely that these units will be more activated by incoming stimuli than units coding stimuli not relevant to the task at hand. Without such priming, we would be continually distracted from the task at hand. Any stimulus more intense than the one involved in the ongoing activity would seize attention. Very often an action is intended to transform a perceptual state (for example, NAIL UP) into its opposite (for example, NAIL FLUSH). Thus, the percept (NAIL UP) that initiates an act is the inverse of the percept coding the goal state (NAIL DOWN). It is not unreasonable to suppose that full achievement of a goal state causes full excitation of the unit coding it (NAIL DOWN). This unit, in turn, laterally inhibits whatever unit (NAIL UP) initiated action in the first place. On the other hand, failure to achieve the goal leads to a mismatch and the mismatch leads to attention, reactivation of the unit initiating the action (NAIL UP), and consequent reactivation of the action unit. Klein (1967) suggests a similar possibility. In this view, a sort of opponent-process relation connects units coding the stimuli eliciting actions and the stimuli coding the expected effects of these actions. Lateral inhibition between these opposing units may be important in perceiving the incongruity that leads to thought and action. When we conceive of a goal, we tend to have images of the desired state of affairs. This is consistent with the idea that there must be excitatory connections from action units to gnostic units coding the goal of the action.

THOUGHT, ACTION, AND PERCEPTION

Thought as mental action

How are thought and action related? We have already mentioned Lashley's contention (1958) that thought is the same process as action except that the motor system is not activated in thinking. This seems quite reasonable. We might go so far as to speculate that action units have two thresholds. If activation of the unit passes the higher threshold, a motor act results. If activation of the unit passes the lower threshold, a mental act (that is, a thought) occurs. In other words, a *thought* is mental act corresponding to a moderate degree of activation of an action unit. Thinking, in this view, is a series of such mental acts. Action units are connected in an excitatory fashion to units in gnostic and conceptual analyzers so as to form propositions. We might thus expect thought to be accompanied by images and concepts brought to consciousness because of spillover of activation into gnostic and conceptual analyzers. These images and thoughts might be said to be the objects of thought rather than thought itself.

While the two-threshold hypothesis may hold for the majority of thoughts, it cannot be generally true. The two-threshold view leads to the prediction that thought should always precede action since the activation of an action unit would obviously have to cross the lower threshold before it crossed the higher one. However, this is not the case with highly practiced or habitual behaviors. Thus, a smoker lights a cigarette without thinking. The driver of a car or the rider of a bicycle execute all sorts of actions without conscious awareness. Perhaps the more habitual an action becomes, the lower its action-threshold becomes so that eventually the action-threshold may be lower than the thought-threshold. In this case, thought would follow rather than precede action if it occurred at all. This is consistent with the observation that thinking about automatic behaviors interferes with their execution. The reason for this would be that, in order to think about such actions, the units coding them have to be overactivated.

There must be a large set of action units that code purely mental acts or operations rather than motor behaviors. Examples of such operations might be deciding, rehearsing, comparing, adding, subtracting, and so on. It hardly makes sense to think of such units as having two thresholds since there is no motor behavior to be unleashed. Of course, we sometimes scribble some notes or speak aloud when we engage in such mental acts, but these behaviors are the materials used by the operation rather than being the operation itself.

Delegated thought and autonomous thought

It makes sense to think that action units controlling mental operations could delegate thinking to conceptual and gnostic analyzers. An example of delegated thinking would occur in a psychological experiment. The action system maintains the mental set of where to find the stimulus, what decision has to be made, how to make the response indicating the decision, and so on. However, when the stimulus (for example, DOES A CANARY HAVE INERTIA?) is perceived, the thinking necessary to come up with the answer is delegated to the semantic analyzer. It also makes sense that autonomous thought not really under the control of the action system can occur. Such thought is likely when a person has nothing much to do. In such cases, the action system often seems to delegate some trivial make-work problem to a conceptual analyzer (for example, HOW MANY STATES HAVE I VISITED?) Generally, the analyzer persists for a few moments at the problem and then thought wanders to other topics. Such autonomous thoughts can equally well be cued off by some percept that happens to catch our attention rather than being initiated by the action system.

It is thus probably too restrictive to define thinking as a series of mental acts centered in or controlled by the action system. It might be better to define thinking as serial activation of any cognitive units coding propositions. Episodic units are structurally similar to action units in that they, too, may be seen as coding propositions. For that matter, semantic units may also be seen as coding propositions—for example, FLIES (ROBIN, SOUTH, WINTER). Even gnostic units could be seen as coding propositions. For example, the unit coding the image of a bird is connected to units coding the component features of a bird, to the semantic unit coding the meaning of a bird, and so on. We could see these associations as defining a proposition of sorts.

Necessary conditions for thought

Despite the clear exceptions we have just noted, much thought does seem to consist of imagined or mental action. This raises the question of how to keep the degree of activation of action units high enough so that thought can occur but not so high that action will occur. The structure of the action system suggests several conditions where thought rather than action should be found. One possibility involves insufficient vertical facilitation. For example, if you do not have a very high need for achievement, you may only think about repairing a broken chair rather than actually repairing it. Another possibility involves lateral inhibition: an activated script unit for studying may inhibit the less strongly activated script unit for chair repairing. Again, you will think about repairing the chair but not act upon these thoughts. It is hardly worth mentioning that if the stimuli for an act are weak (you only imagine the broken chair), the relevant action unit is not likely to become strongly activated. A more general possibility concerns the amount of nonspecific input the action system is receiving from the arousal system.

In the case of delegated and autonomous thinking, the cognitive units involved may be the same ones that are involved in perception. A variant of the two-threshold theory also makes sense in this case. Perhaps if the activation of such units crosses a lower threshold, thought results; but if activation crosses a higher threshold, perception results. This perception can be either veridical or hallucinatory. The same things keep activation of such units in a moderate range: weak vertical facilitation (the stimulus is not physically present), lateral inhibition by neighboring units, and low arousal. As noted in Chapter 4, thought may become hallucinatory when arousal is high or when cognitive units are disinhibited because of low levels of lateral inhibition.

TYPES OF THINKING

A-thinking versus R-thinking

Now that we have some idea of what thinking may be, I have to complicate matters by telling you that there seems to be a whole family of different types of thinking. It is conventional to divide thought into at least two types. McKellar (1957) differentiates what he calls A-thinking and R-thinking. R-thinking, the logical, realistic thought of "sane, adult wakefulness," rests upon two foundations—taking relevant, external evidence into account and making correct logical inferences. On the other hand, A-thinking is not corrected by taking reality into account, and it does not follow the rules of conventional logic. Examples of A-thinking include fantasy, dreaming, and hallucination. It is only R-thinking that clearly connects stimuli with responses. In the case of A-thinking, the linkage is certainly looser. McKellar notes that A-thinking is not closely linked with reality (perception). It is equally true that it tends not to result directly in motor action. When it does result in such action, we often wish that it had not, since the resultant actions are not very adaptive.

Primary process thinking versus secondary process thinking

A-thinking and R-thinking have generally been treated as poles of a continuum rather than as two discrete types of thought. The best-known theory is Freud's (1900) concept of the primary process versus secondary process continuum.[1] The basic idea is that thinking can range anywhere between the two ends of the dimension. For example, the thought involved in solving a logical problem would be very secondary process, the thought exhibited during dreaming would be very primary process, while the type of thinking found in fantasy or reverie

[1] It should be noted that I have borrowed Freud's terms *primary process* and *secondary process* as general labels for the two polar types of thinking that we are discussing. Freud (1900) had a theory about the ultimate causes of these types of thought that is very different from the one presented here. Use of Freud's labels does not imply an acceptance of his theory.

would be somewhere in between the two poles. As we shall see in Chapter 13, thought toward the primary process end of the continuum is hypothetically found in a variety of contexts ranging from the thought of children and psychotics to the thought involved in creative and religious inspiration. Thus, it is important to find out how it works.

Freud held that a number of psychological processes change in a systematic manner with movement along the continuum of types of thought. Secondary process thought is purposeful, while primary process thought is associative, undirected, and freely wandering. Secondary process thought is oriented toward reality and follows the laws of conventional logic, while primary process thinking is autistic (not oriented toward reality) and takes no account of time or logical contradiction. The units of secondary process thinking tend to be abstract symbols of one sort or another. Those of primary process thinking tend to be concrete images. Secondary process states are affectively rather neutral, but in primary process states, our thoughts seem to be driven by motives, emotions, and wishes.

Eros versus logos

Carl Jung (1963) gives us a more poetic description of what Freud called the primary process-secondary process continuum. What Freud called primary process thinking, Jung said follows the principle of *eros*. Here, merging, synthesis, relationship, and intuition dominate. Everywhere similarities and analogies are seen and differences are ignored. On the other hand, Jung says that *logos* dominates what Freud called secondary process states. Logos separates, divides, and grasps things in terms of their differences rather than their similarities. In summary, eros synthesizes and sees similarities, while logos analyzes and sees differences.

Dedifferentiated versus differentiated thinking

Heinz Werner (1948) has given the most general and satisfactory answer to the question of what in general is supposed to change as we move from primary process to secondary process thinking. According to Werner (1948), organismic development in general and the development of mind in particular consists of an "increasing differentiation of parts and an increasing subordination, or hierarchization" of these parts. According to Werner, primary process thought is dedifferentiated, while secondary process thought is differentiated and hierarchically organized. Hypothetically, in primary process states, mental contents and functions that we normally think of as separate and distinct are merged and undifferentiated. For example, we conceive of hearing and seeing as being completely different mental functions carried out by separate analyzers. However, for the primary process mind, they may be the same global and undifferentiated process, as we shall see in Chapter 13 when we discuss the experience of synaesthesia. By the same token, concepts—such as MAN and WOMAN—that are distinct for secondary process cognition become merged and confused for primary process cognition.

Werner argues that the differentiated mental functions found in secondary process states operate in a hierarchical fashion. To use our terms, the motor system or the semantic system is controlled by the action system in such states.

The action system organizes, modulates, inhibits, or uses these lower systems. For example, it can delegate thinking to the semantic analyzer. In primary process states, on the other hand, this hierarchical subordination breaks down. The lower systems are disinhibited and break free of control by the higher system. Autonomous thought may result. In secondary process states, thought is reflective; that is, it is guided by the plans and intentions coded by the action system. In primary process states, thought becomes reflexive and undirected, since the guidance provided by the action system is not present.

The geography of thought

In earlier chapters, we argued that the set of currently activated cognitive units constitutes the contents of consciousness. We divided consciousness into two parts. Attention consists of the most activated units, while short-term memory or the fringe of consciousness consists of the remaining, less activated units. If thinking consists of activation of a series of cognitive units, then by definition it must occur in consciousness. But where? It could occur either in focal attention or in the fringe regions. It makes sense to argue that secondary process thought refers to the series of units occupying the focus of attention, while primary process thought may be seen as referring to the series of units occupying the fringe of consciousness; that is, both types of thought can go on simultaneously. Secondary process thought refers to what transpires in focal attention, while primary process thought refers to the sequence of activity in short-term memory. This idea has been suggested by Ehrenzweig (1953) and Neisser (1967), among others. The hypothetical locations of primary process and secondary process thinking are illustrated in Figure 12–4A.

Attention merely means fairly complete or full activation of a cognitive unit. On the other hand, when we say that a unit is in short-term memory we mean that it is less fully activated. If it were even more activated, it would capture attention. It must be the case, then, that a fairly high level of activation of cognitive units is necessary for secondary process thinking. A high level of activation of a cognitive unit implies that the unit will activate other units with which it is connected and laterally inhibit surrounding units. The subjective aspect of this is that we will be conscious of what the unit codes, what its attributes are, and what it is not. In other words, we will be aware of the implications and meaning of the proposition that the unit codes. Less than complete activation will lead to primary process thinking. A partially activated cognitive unit will not be able to activate other units with which it is connected or to laterally inhibit surrounding units to any great extent. The subjective aspect of this is that we will be only very vaguely aware of whatever the unit codes.

This line of reasoning would also apply to states, such as reverie and dreaming, where secondary process thinking is diminished or absent. In such states, attention is defocused or diffused. Nothing is focused upon clearly and more things seem to share the dim focus. Conceptually, the distinction between relevant and irrelevant gradually disappears with movement toward primary process thought. Waking thought picks and chooses its contents according to the problem at hand. Primary process thought is more egalitarian. The most trivial detail

FIGURE 12–4   The geography of thought. When attention is focused, secondary process thought occurs in the focus of attention and primary process thought occurs in short-term memory (A). When attention is not focused, all thought has a primary process character (B).

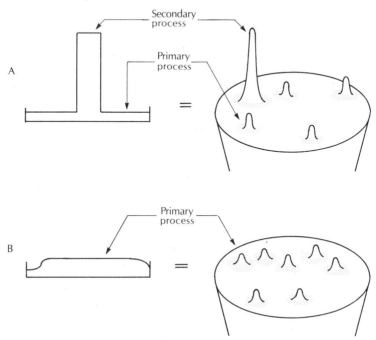

or experience is as likely as our profoundest concerns to occupy the center stage of our dreams. Cognitive units are more equally activated, and none can completely capture attention. Thought as a consequence has a more primary process character in such states. Shallice (1978) explicitly identified primary process thought with a situation where large numbers of cognitive units are weakly and about equally activated (see Figure 12–4B). Of course, we may imagine a whole continuum of possibilities between the states illustrated in A and B.

Thought, arousal, and lateral inhibition

When are we likely to encounter a situation where many cognitive units are about equally activated? You may recall that we discussed this question in Chapters 10 and 11. One cause of such a state would be the case where arousal is low. Inputs from the arousal system hypothetically serve to exacerbate the differences in activation among cognitive units by increasing lateral inhibition. Thus, primary process thought must occur in the presence of low arousal and weak lateral inhibition. It does indeed occur in low-arousal states, such as drowsiness. In Chapter 11, we argued that right-hemisphere analyzers may operate in a primary process fashion. This may be because they receive a relatively small amount of input from the arousal system. However, primary process thought also occurs in very high-arousal states, such as panic (see Chapter 13). With very high arousal, large numbers of cognitive units can also be equally activated. Again, lateral inhibition is weak, and no one unit can inhibit others. As we saw in Chapter 10, the general principle is that increases in arousal will exacerbate differences in the activation of cognitive units only up to a point. Beyond that point, more and more cognitive units will start to reach maximal activation. The implication is that the degree to which thought has a secondary process character should be an inverted-U function of level of arousal (see Figure 12–5). This hypothesis has been suggested by Blum (1961), Bruner (1957), and Martindale (1971) among others.

FIGURE 12–5   The relationship between type of thinking and level of arousal. Secondary process thinking is hypothetically found only with medium levels of arousal. Primary process thinking is found with either high or low levels of arousal.

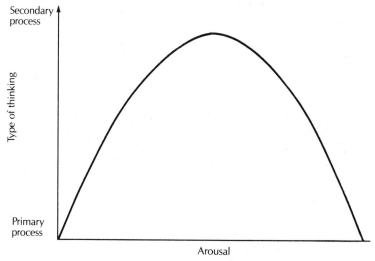

Since in high-arousal states the activation of cognitive units hypothetically oscillates in an unstable manner (see Chapter 10), we shall concentrate our attention in this chapter on the more tractable case of primary process thought accompanied by low arousal.

Hypothetically, relatively equal activation of cognitive units and low levels of lateral inhibition account for the characteristics of primary process thinking. An example of this is the lack of purpose in such thought. Freud (1900) argued that primary process thinking is wish fulfilling; that is, in primary process thought motives or goals are satisfied by hallucinatory activation of goal images. In a secondary process state, action units activate units coding their goals, but these goal units are also inhibited by neighboring units which code the perceptual reality that these goals are not met (see Figure 12–3). In a primary process state, lateral inhibition is hypothetically lessened. The goal units and their neighboring units now operate together. They excite each other rather than inhibiting each other. Primary process thought literally cannot be goal directed since the lateral inhibitory mechanisms for coding goals have disappeared.

THE GRAMMAR OF THOUGHT

If thinking involves chains or strings of symbolic responses, then it may be fruitful to compare it with language, which also involves chains of symbolic responses (words). According to Jakobson (1956), three basic questions of interest are found in regard to any language: (1) What are the possible elements or words? (2) How are they pronounced? (3) What are the rules for sequencing them? The first is the question of *selection:* What is the lexicon or dictionary of words in a given language? What does each one mean? To what general classes do they belong? The second question concerns *realization rules:* How are the words translated into the perceptual media of speech sounds, gestures, or written words? The third question concerns *combination* or *syntax:* By what rules can the words be strung together? The answers to these questions will constitute a grammar of the language in question. Similar questions may be asked in regard to thought. Since we have postulated a continuum of types of thought, we theoretically need a whole set of grammars of thought. That is a rather tall order. Fortunately, it seems to be that the grammar of primary process thinking is a degenerate case of the grammar of secondary process thinking. In any event, a grammar of thought must answer the questions of selection, combination, and realization. What are the elements of thought? By what rules are these elements sequenced? How are the elements apprehended?

MENTAL REALIZATION

Levels of realization

We argued above that the basic elements of thought are mental acts that correspond to (1) the partial activation of action units that would, if further activated, unleash behavior, to (2) the activation of action units controlling mental operations, or to (3) the activation of conceptual or gnostic units coding propositions. When we speak, abstract propositions are realized as speech sounds. It makes sense to speak of mental realization, but the situation is more complex with thought than it is with speech. In the case of thinking, we can envision multiple levels of realization (see Figure 12–6). Activity in the action system can

FIGURE 12–6   Levels of realization involved in thinking

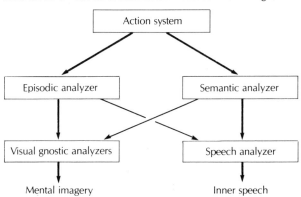

be realized by activity in the episodic analyzer or the semantic analyzer. Units in these analyzers may, in turn, be realized by activation of units in visual analyzers (mental images) or in the speech analyzer (inner speech).

It makes some sense to argue that the mental acts of secondary process thought represent activation of units in the action system. The immediate constituents of the propositions coded by these units may be units in conceptual analyzers which themselves code abstract propositions. On the other hand, as thought becomes more primary process in character, the mental acts are more likely to represent activation of units in conceptual or gnostic systems. This is consistent with the hypothesis that these systems may come to operate in an autonomous fashion in primary process states. Mental acts of this sort would not have the direction or goal-oriented quality found in secondary process thinking. Furthermore, such mental acts would be more likely to be accompanied by ideas of a perceptual nature. This is because the constituent elements of the propositions coded by conceptual and gnostic units are more likely to be perceptual in nature than is the case with action units. Regardless of the origin of the proposition involved in a mental act, if mental realization reaches the gnostic level, it would seem that secondary process thought prefers to express itself via the speech analyzer while primary process thought prefers to express itself via the image system.

Realization of propositions

SECONDARY PROCESS REALIZATION

Hypothetically, units in the action system code abstract propositions. Recall Fillmore's description of a proposition (1968) in which he says that it consists of an action represented by a verb and a series of case categories, such as agent, instrument, recipient, time, location, and object. A proposition can also have values on various modalities, such as tense (for example, present, past, future), negation (affirmation or negation), and mode (for example, conditional, intentional). There is no difficulty in realizing or expressing either the cases or the modalities of propositions in secondary process thought. (If there were, we would not be able to understand what a proposition was in the first place.) Presumably, this realization can be on the purely abstract, conceptual level or the conceptual realization can be expressed in either overt or covert speech.

PRIMARY PROCESS REALIZATION

Loss of modality. Absence of modality is one aspect of primary process thinking: It takes no account of time (tense) or contradiction (negation). It involves an inability to conceive the merely possible (conditional mode), and it confuses wish with reality (intentional mode). There are several possible reasons for this, one of which has to do with the tendency of primary process propositions to be realized via the image system. If we want to realize a proposition as a scene or series of visual images, it is apparent that it will be very difficult to represent modality. For example, consider tense. What is the difference between an image representing something that will happen as opposed to something that has happened? In speech, we can say I AM GOING TO TOWN, I SHALL GO TO TOWN, or I WENT TO TOWN, but in the language of images, the representations of past, present, and future actions are the same. The same problem arises with negation. In speech, there are different forms for I AM GOING TO TOWN versus I AM *NOT* GOING TO TOWN. How can we express negation in visual images? I suppose that we could have an image of going to town with an X drawn over the image. But have you ever had an image like that? In short, it is difficult or impossible to express all aspects of modality when thoughts are realized as images.

As you can see, the mere fact that a proposition is realized via the image system can give it many of the characteristics of primary process thinking. Is this the only cause of these characteristics? Do dreams, for example, have these characteristics only because they tend to be realized as visual images? It is fairly clear that the image system cannot read or execute codes specifying the modality of propositions. However, it is not altogether clear that these codes would be passed to any system in the first place in a primary process state; that is, maybe the codes are unreadable in primary process propositions. This possibility is made more plausible when we consider what happens to information about cases in primary process propositions.

Loss of case information. Both the speech system and the image system can realize the cases of propositions so long as they refer to concrete actions and events. For example, consider the cases of agent and recipient. The propositions KILL (JOHN, MARY) and KILL (MARY, JOHN) yield quite different visual images and also quite different linguistic utterances (JOHN KILLS MARY versus MARY KILLS JOHN). The proposition can be realized about equally well in words or in visual images. However, the imagery system has difficulty realizing a proposition involving abstract terms, such as DEVALUES (INFLATION, MONEY)—INFLATION DEVALUES MONEY. If we insist upon realizing such a proposition in images, we will have to concretize it. This, too, is an attribute of primary process thinking.

However, no matter how it is realized, primary process thinking seems to involve a loss of case information (Martindale, 1976a). This is illustrated by the retaliating fears that are found in primary process thought (Fenichel, 1945). In fact, the propositions KILL (JOHN, MARY) and KILL (MARY, JOHN) are equivalent for the primary process thinker. If John is thinking in a primary process manner and takes it into his mind to kill Mary, this thought brings with it the fear that Mary wants to kill him. Why? Because primary process thought does not differentiate between the agent and the recipient of a proposition. Evidently, the labels of relations coding the cases and modalities of propositions become smudged with movement toward a primary process state. Matte-Blanco (1959) makes a similar point using different terms.

MENTAL CONTENT

Types of mental content

MENTAL ACTS

Thinking could possibly procede without any palpable ideas or images. This would be the case if it consisted solely of a series of mental acts not realized via activation of any units in gnostic analyzers. Külpe (1912) and others at the University of Würzberg were the first to call attention to imageless thoughts. Besides operations such as comparison and decision, there are a number of more or less imageless thoughts. Examples would be intentions, expectations, and mental sets. However, thinking almost always seems to involve some sort of mental content. This is reasonable, since action units and conceptual units may be seen as chunking units coding propositions. The components of these propositions are ultimately units in gnostic analyzers.

IDEAS

We might use the term *idea* to refer to the components of the propositions coded by action units or conceptual units. Wundt (1896) held that ideas are psychical compounds and that "all psychic compounds may be resolved into psychical elements." Psychical elements were seen as discrete sensory qualities or features, such as redness, warmth, and so on. In our terms, they would correspond to units on lower levels of gnostic analyzers. There are, Wundt said, two types of ideas. A *complex idea* is "the image of some external object" (Wundt, 1896). Complex ideas are what we would call mental images or unitary percepts (for example, the idea of a red house). In our terms, complex ideas would correspond to activation of units at the highest level of gnostic analyzers. An *aggregate idea* is what we would call a concept. Examples of aggregate ideas would be the concepts of justice, time, or democracy. In our terms, aggregate ideas would correspond to the activation of units in semantic memory.

If Wundt had used the terms, *primary process* and *secondary process,* he would readily have agreed that there is a tendency for aggregate ideas (concepts) to predominate in secondary process states and complex ideas (images) in primary process states. In fact Wundt (1896) held that intellectual thought operates with aggregate ideas, while what he called associative thought operates with complex ideas. Freud, Werner, and Jung would also agree with this hypothesis. Two possible explanations exist for this. One would be that the two types of ideas are indigenous to the two types of thought. Perhaps the two types of thought draw from different lexicons; that is, perhaps primary process tends to consist of activation of units in gnostic or perceptual analyzers while secondary process thinking tends to consist of activation of units in conceptual analyzers. This cannot be completely right, though. Secondary process thinking involves taking account of reality. Ultimately, reality is coded by activity of units in gnostic analyzers. It must be the case, then, that secondary process thought is accompanied by activity in both conceptual and gnostic analyzers. On the other hand, primary process thought tends to be accompanied by activity in gnostic analyzers in the comparative absence of activity in conceptual analyzers.

MOTIVES

For Wundt (1896), motives are a special subclass of ideas: "Every motive is a particular idea with an affective tone attaching to it." At least in theory, any idea can become a motive if affect becomes attached to it. In our model, a motive would be a cognitive unit or set of cognitive units that is connected with the emotional system. Secondary process thinking deals with ideas that are affectively neutral as compared with the ideas that dominate primary process thinking. Psychoanalytic theorists (for example, Fenichel, 1945) would say that primitive oral, anal, and sexual motives are prominent in primary process thinking. These would be ideas connected to oral, anal, and sexual centers in the emotional system. The units likely to be activated in secondary process thought are not connected to such primitive emotional centers. However, secondary process thought is even more clearly motivated than is primary process thought; that is, it is directed by goals, intentions, and dispositions. We have argued that these are motives: They, too, are cognitive units connected to the emotional system. However, the emotions or drives in this case are not so strong or primitive as those connected to the units that are apt to be activated in primary process states.

Differentiated versus dedifferentiated mental contents

DEDIFFERENTIATION OF CONCEPTS

In Werner's view, secondary process thought operates on differentiated mental contents, while primary process thought operates on dedifferentiated mental contents. We can translate this into our model as follows: with movement toward a primary process state, cognitive units that normally operate in a differing manner (code different concepts) come to operate together (code dedifferentiated or global concepts). In previous chapters, we have described the contents and structure of some of the gnostic and conceptual analyzers. What we said in these chapters must be true only for secondary process states. In primary process states, we would expect cognitive units to code less differentiated percepts and concepts. How could this occur? Figure 12–7 illustrates a fragment of semantic memory. In Figure 12–7A is shown the pattern of activation and inhibition that might be expected in a secondary process thought about a CANARY. The CANARY unit is connected via token nodes to units coding information about it (for example, CANARY isa BIRD and CANARY has CAGE. Activation of the CANARY unit activates these other units. This activation also sets up a pattern of lateral inhibition of units surrounding the activated units.

Primary process thought occurs in the context of low activation. There are two likely consequences of this: First, activation may be insufficient to activate fully the remote type nodes that define the token nodes through which CANARY is connected with other units. Thus, for example, the primary process thinker

FIGURE 12–7 Portions of semantic memory during secondary process thinking (A) and during primary process thinking (B). In a primary process state, activation of cognitive units is insufficient to activate remote type units or to laterally inhibit neighboring cognitive units.

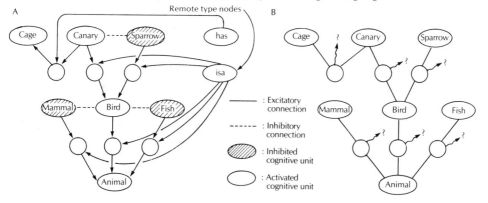

will be aware that CANARY and CAGE are related but will not be aware of *how* they are related. Similarly, the primary process thinker forgets exactly how a CANARY and a BIRD are related. As shown in the figure, loss of information about the meaning of intermediate token nodes implies that information about the directionality of relations is also lost. This is because this information is also given by the remote type node. The second consequence of lessened activation will be that lateral inhibition will be lessened. This will lead the primary process thinker to forget that a CANARY is NOT a SPARROW or that a BIRD is NOT a FISH. Figure 12–7B illustrates this state of affairs.

The loss of information occurring in primary process states allows us to explain several mechanisms of primary process thinking first described by Freud (1900) in connection with dreams. These mechanisms are condensation, displacement, symbolism, and part-for-whole thinking. Condensation refers to the fact that one dream element can simultaneously represent several different things. For example, one dream element might simultaneously be a canary, a sparrow, and even a cage. This follows from the dedifferentiated nature of primary process concepts. In our example, Figure 12–7A represents the differentiated concept, CANARY; Figure 12–B represents a condensed or undifferentiated CANARY-CAGE-SPARROW concept. In a dream, a concept can be represented by a similar concept (symbolism) or by a concept to which it is related by contiguity (displacement). Examples might be representing a bird by a fish (symbolism) or a canary by a cage (displacement). Since information about the precise way in which concepts are related has been lost, anything a concept is related to can be used to represent it. Part-for-whole thinking rests upon a similar equivalence. Because of the loss of directionality of relations in primary process states, a part (for example, a canary) can represent the whole (for example, birds in general).

MAGICAL THINKING

Werner's (1948) discussion of magical thought is illustrative of the dedifferentiation present in primary process thinking. We see a sort of homegrown magical thought in children and psychotics, but the principles of such thought are most apparent in the institutionalized magical thought of preliterate societies. Sympathetic magic involves operations on a symbol that are supposed to have effects on the thing the symbol stands for. The voodoo practice of sticking pins into effigies in order to cause pain to the person the effigy represents is an example. Sympathetic magic makes perfect sense if one does not differentiate between an object and a symbol that stands for that object. For example, in voodoo, the victim and the effigy are not differentiated. In the absence of this distinction, it is perfectly reasonable that to manipulate the symbol is to manipulate the object itself.

Contagious magic involves operations such as burning a lock of hair in order to cause pain to the person the hair came from. This sort of magic is based on a lack of differentiation between part (the hair) and whole (the person). When this distinction is not made, it follows that to manipulate the part is to manipulate the whole. Part of the reason that the magician retains faith in the efficacy of magical procedures must be that he also fails to differentiate between succession and causality; that is, he makes the logical error of *post hoc ergo propter hoc*. All people eventually suffer some misfortune or illness. The fact that this occurs *after* a magical operation implies to primary process thought that it was *caused* by the operation. The reason is that the concepts of succession and causality are not differentiated. They are treated as the same thing.

MENTAL SEQUENCING

The laws of association

The traditional laws of association were originally formulated to describe the rules of sequencing in all types of thought. Actually, they only describe sequencing in primary process states. These laws have a very long history. According to Aristotle, there are four laws of association: One idea elicits another because of similarity, contrast, prior contiguity in space, or prior contiguity in time. Later theorists have tried to reduce these four in varying combinations to two basic laws of association: association by similarity and association by contiguity. On word association tests there are, to use modern terms, two types of responses: syntagmatic (contiguity) associations, such as PRETTY–GIRL, and paradigmatic, such as PRETTY–BEAUTIFUL (similarity), or PRETTY–UGLY (contrast). Both similarity and contrast responses are paradigmatic in that they come from the same class. Interestingly enough, syntagmatic responses are relatively common in childhood but give way to paradigmatic ones in adulthood (Woodrow and Lowell, 1916). Adults given chloral hydrate (which decreases arousal) regress to giving syntagmatic associates (Luria and Vinogradova, 1959). Thus, there is some evidence that syntagmatic or contiguity sequencing predominates in primary process states and paradigmatic or similarity sequencing predominates in secondary process states.

Respondent versus operant sequencing

The associationists originally tried to explain all mental sequencing with the laws of association. However, the more secondary process thought was studied, the more clear it became that it does not follow the laws of association. Wundt (1896) pointed this out clearly, though he did not use the term *secondary process*. Titchener (1923) pointed out that even more active types of fantasy—as opposed to passive reverie—do not follow the laws of association. What laws does secondary process thinking follow, then?

Just as there are two types of mental contents, there seem to be two types of mental sequencing. As Hobbes (1642) put it:

> This Trayne of Thoughts, or Mental Discourse, is of two sorts. The first is Unguided, without Designe, and inconstant: . . . In which case the thoughts are said to wander, and seem impertinent one to another, as in a Dream . . . And yet in this wild ranging of the mind, a man may ofttimes perceive the way of it, and the dependence of one thought upon another. . . . The second is more constant; as being regulated by some desire, and designe.

These two types of sequencing correspond to primary process thinking and secondary process thinking.

Eric Klinger (1971) has discussed differences between primary process and secondary process sequencing. He sees several basic differences between these two types of thought that have implications for sequencing. In terms of concern with impact on the environment, secondary process thought is oriented toward effecting some goal or purpose in the external world. On the other hand, primary process thought is not goal oriented. Freud (1900) held that it ignores external reality or at least makes no distinction between it and internal reality. As a consequence of this, the conclusions of primary process thought are not evaluated in terms of external reality. On the other hand, secondary process thinking involves at least intermittent assessment of external reality. Since such thought is goal oriented, progress toward the goal must be evaluated. Feedback from perceptual reality guides or modifies secondary process thought. Since primary process thought has no goal, it cannot very well be modified according to whether or not it is approaching or receding from a goal. In summary, then, the sequence of secondary process ideas is governed by feedback regarding progress toward a goal. On the other hand, the sequencing of primary process ideas does not involve such feedback. What does govern it then?

Klinger says that primary process thinking follows *respondent sequencing*. Each idea is elicited by the preceding idea. This name is derived from a term initially used in behaviorist psychology. *Respondent behavior* is behavior that is automatically elicited by a stimulus. For example, touching a hot stove *elicits* a withdrawal reaction. By the same token, in a primary process state, activation of one cognitive unit simply elicits activation of another one via an associative bond. Activation wanders rather aimlessly from one unit to another. Respondent behavior may be contrasted with operant behavior. With operant behavior, the organism emits an instrumental response that may be reinforced (that is, rewarded or punished). Operant behaviors are spoken of as being emitted, since they do not have the automatic, reflexlike quality of elicited behaviors. Reinforcement governs whether an operant behavior will be emitted again. Such behaviors, then, are governed by feedback from the environment concerning their consequences. This sounds like secondary process thinking. Because of this similarity, Klinger calls the sequencing of such thought *operant sequencing*. Respondent behavior is involuntary, while operant behavior is voluntary. The same distinction applies in the mental realm. Primary process thinking, governed by respondent sequencing, is involuntary. It seems effortless and automatic. On the other hand, secondary process thinking, governed by operant sequencing, involves a subjective sense of effort.

Hierarchical versus lateral sequencing

If we combine Klinger's theory with other considerations discussed so far in this chapter, we can arrive at a formulation concerning mental sequencing in primary process and secondary process states. First, let's consider a chain of ideas (that is, activated cognitive units) in a primary process state. Such a state involves weakly activated cognitive units. Subjectively, it corresponds to effortless, unfocused attention. In such a state, we expect little vertical spreading of activation and weak lateral inhibition. Furthermore, weakly activated units are unlikely to be able to activate units in other analyzers. Thus, the activation has got to move around in a fairly lateral or horizontal direction in the same analyzer, as shown in Figure 12–8A. Now, let's consider a series of ideas in a secondary process state. Secondary process thought is effortful and goes along with focused attention. In Chapter 7 we argued that such effortful, focused attention goes with fairly strong activation of cognitive units along with a spreading of vertical excitation and strong lateral inhibition. Thus, in any one analyzer, secondary process sequencing should tend to be vertical rather than horizontal (see Figure 12–8B).

FIGURE 12–8 Primary process thinking tends to be confined to one analyzer. Within that analyzer, sequencing tends to be horizontal, as shown in A. Secondary process thinking tends to involve a movement of activation back and forth between conceptual and gnostic analyzers. Within any one analyzer, sequencing tends to be vertical, as shown in B.

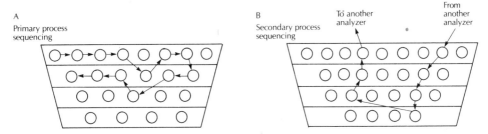

Fairly strong activation of cognitive units should enable these units to activate units in other analyzers. Consider what we mean by secondary process thought. It is abstract or conceptual. This means that it involves activation of units in the action system or conceptual analyzers. On the other hand, it takes account of reality. This means that it also involves activation of units in gnostic analyzers. External reality is, after all, a pattern of activation of sets of units in gnostic analyzers. Thus, secondary process sequencing must also involve a flow of activation back and forth between conceptual and gnostic analyzers.

SUMMARY AND CONCLUSIONS

We saw in previous chapters that a mismatch between expectation and perception eventuates in attention, arousal, and affect. According to this chapter, such a mismatch also results in action. This action can be overt (motor behavior) or mental (thought). We proposed that there is an action system which generates both behavioral and mental acts. Hypothetically, this system is structurally similar to the other analyzers we have discussed. Action units at the highest level of the action system are connected with units in the motor system and in conceptual analyzers so as to code propositions describing acts. A subset of action units hypothetically codes purely mental acts or operations. Units at successively deeper levels of the action system hypothetically code scripts, dispositions, and subselves. Lateral inhibitory relations among units on each level of the action system code information about serial order and assure that units coding contradictory or incompatible actions will not become simultaneously activated.

We argued that there are several varieties of thinking. First, thought can consist of activity of action units coding purely mental operations or of moderate activity of action units that—if more fully activated—would unleash motor behavior. Second, thought can also consist of activity of units in conceptual or gnostic analyzers. Such thinking can be delegated (that is, under the general control of the action system) or autonomous (that is, spontaneous activity not guided by the action system). Theorists, such as Freud, Jung, and Werner, assert that there is a continuum of types of thinking ranging from secondary process (purposeful, reality-oriented thought) to primary process (associative, autistic thought). Presumably, all of the types of thought mentioned earlier can occupy any point on the primary process-secondary process continuum. However, autonomous thinking is most likely to operate in a primary process fashion, and thought centered in the action system which is induced by a mismatch between goals and perceptual reality is most likely to operate in a secondary process fashion.

Hypothetically, secondary process thinking is dependent upon moderate arousal. Such moderate arousal allows one or two cognitive units in an analyzer to seize attention. Units in the focus of attention are able to activate other units to which they are connected and to laterally inhibit surrounding units. This corresponds to a subjective awareness of the meaning and implication of the propositions that the units code. Secondary process thinking may be seen as corresponding to a series of such attentional fixations. The serial order of these attentional fixations will be determined by what Klinger calls operant sequencing: The ultimate goal of the train of thoughts and the implications or outcomes of prior thoughts are taken into account in determining which cognitive unit will be activated next.

Primary process thinking is dependent upon either low or very high arousal. Either state leads activated cognitive units in an analyzer to be about equally activated. Such relatively equal activation is found in several conditions: units in short-term memory or the fringe of consciousness; units in analyzers that seem to operate in a global fashion (for example, right-hemisphere spatial analyzers); and units in any analyzer when inputs from the arousal system are uniformly low (for example, states of drowsiness). Low and relatively equal activation of cognitive units leads to weakening of lateral inhibition and to an inability of units to activate fully other units with which they are connected. High and relatively equal activation of cognitive units has similar consequences, but here the situation is more complex because of the unstable oscillation hypothetically found in such a state.

Loss of lateral inhibition leads to a breakdown of the match-mismatch system. As a consequence, goals and percepts are equated or confused, and primary process thought takes on a wish-fulfilling character. Low activation may eventuate in the inability of intermediate token nodes chunking together cognitive units to activate the remote type nodes that define them. As a consequence, the primary process thinker knows that cognitive units are related but does not know how they are related. With propositions, this leads to loss of information about modalities and even about cases. With concepts, this leads to several primary process mechanisms, such as condensation, displacement, symbolism, part-for-whole thinking, timelessness, and tolerance of logical contradiction. Loss of lateral inhibition and loss of information about the content and direction of relations in primary process states presumably explains the respondent sequencing found in such states. Activation moves from one unit to another in an associative but undirected fashion.

13

States of consciousness

CONSCIOUSNESS AND COGNITIVE UNITS

According to Wundt (1896), "Consciousness is not a particular mental process, coordinate with others; it consists entirely in the fact that we have internal experiences." Titchener (1923) defined *consciousness* as "The sum-total of mental processes occurring *now*, at any given 'present' time." These definitions are consistent with our equation of consciousness with the set of cognitive units that is activated at a given point in time. William James (1902) made the observation that our normal, waking consciousness is but one special type of consciousness. In the last chapter we saw that thought varies along a continuum from secondary process to primary process. Consciousness as a whole seems to vary along this continuum, and as thought varies, so do perception, emotion, and all other mental processes.

We shall define a primary process state of consciousness as one where all activated cognitive units are about equally activated. On the other hand, consciousness will be defined as being secondary process in nature to the degree that activated cognitive units show graded or differential degrees of activation. In previous chapters we have investigated the implications of these differences in pattern of activation for attention and thinking. In this chapter, we shall examine the circumstances in which consciousness varies and how this variation affects subjective experience, perception, and other mental processes.

THE CONTINUUM OF STATES OF CONSCIOUSNESS

Normal alterations of consciousness

FROM WAKING TO DREAMING

Consider what happens as you move from a waking, problem-oriented, secondary process state to a state of sleep and dreaming. There is a quite gradual transition through a series of other states, each with its own characteristics. Figure 13–1

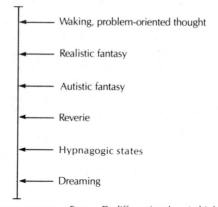

FIGURE 13–1   The continuum of types of thought

Secondary process = Logos = Differentiated = R-thinking

- Waking, problem-oriented thought
- Realistic fantasy
- Autistic fantasy
- Reverie
- Hypnagogic states
- Dreaming

Primary process = Eros = Dedifferentiated = A-thinking

presents a continuum stretching between the two points—waking and dreaming. In waking consciousness, we are often oriented toward problems—usually presented by the outside environment—that we attempt to solve in an abstract and conceptual manner. When we cease to be confronted directly with such problems, thought continues but by rather different means. We lapse into fantasy. In fantasy states, our thought is no longer structured into "if-then" units, but into "then-then" units. That is, we shift from logical propositions to inner narratives. Accompanying this shift is a replacement of abstract and conceptual mental contents by concrete and perceptual ones. A spectrum of types of fantasies ranges from more realistic ones that are problem oriented—as when we practice various possible social strategies and mentally simulate their probable outcomes—to the more autistic castles-in-the-air sort of fantasy where we flap about on golden wings from one fantastic scene to the next. The basic difference would seem to be the degree to which the fantasy is practically oriented toward a problem in reality. As we move toward the primary process end of the continuum, our fantasies become more autistic; that is, they have less relevance to reality.

At some hazy point, fantasy may be said to shade off into reverie. By reverie, I mean those states where thought has seemingly become more or less wholly undirected. One image, scene, or memory follows another, but they no longer form a coherent narrative as is the case with fantasies. Another difference is that in states of reverie we do not have a feeling of control of the sequence of thought. In fantasy, we often back up and revise the story if the way it is going does not please us. This tends not to happen in reverie, since the train of thought is not going in any particular direction in the first place.

Reverie, in turn, shades into hypnagogic states. These occur in the drowsy twilight state between sleep and waking. Hypnagogic images occur in many forms. For some people, they are intensely vivid visual images. For others, they may be equally intense auditory images. Because long-term memory for such images is very poor, you may go through the hypnagogic state every night but simply not remember it. Herbert Silberer (1912) held that many of these experiences symbolize the act of falling asleep or changing state of consciousness. For this reason he called them *autosymbolic phenomena*. In the hypnagogic state, the flow of images seems to be completely automatic, and any effort to control or focus upon the images destroys them.

Finally, we reach dreams. The dream is in some ways more like a fantasy than a reverie or string of hypnagogic images in that it often consists of a fairly coherent narrative. However, it belongs on the end of the continuum by virtue of its completely automatic character and lack of orientation toward conscious purpose and reality. Furthermore, the dream as actually dreamed is much less of a narrative than it seems to be when recalled after waking. Much of its structure is really added on in retrospect by the waking mind in the course of efforts to organize and remember the dream after waking. You may leave out the things that did not make any sense at all and rearrange those things that seemed to be dreamed out of order.

INCIDENCE OF NORMAL VARIATION IN CONSCIOUSNESS

It would be wrong to think of yourself as being in a secondary process state during the entire time you are awake. To establish this, you need only pay close attention to what passes in your mind as you read this book. You will find that you lapse again and again into fantasy and reverie. Put differently, wisps of primary process mentation intrude more or less constantly into consciousness. This contention is supported by the results of thought-sampling experiments. As the name implies, these are experiments where people are periodically asked to report what they are thinking about. This can be done in a laboratory while subjects are working at some task or—by means of a remote signaling device—while they are going about their everyday business. Even during a relatively demanding signal detection task, subjects report stimulus-independent mentation up to 40 percent of the times they are queried (Antrobus, Coleman, and Singer, 1967). Using trained subjects, Klinger (1978) found that—both inside and outside the laboratory—only about 60 percent of thought samples are operant or secondary process in character. The remaining 40 percent of thought samples are primary process or respondent to varying degrees.

Foulkes and Fleisher (1975) employed the method of thought sampling while their subjects were in an isolated cubicle with their eyes closed. Most sampled thoughts involved some mental imagery, usually of a visual nature. Surprisingly, the subjects reported that these images were hallucinatory 27 percent of the time. At the time it was occurring, the experience seemed like it was really happening and the person did not know that it was just something he or she was making up. Of all thought samples, about 40 percent were hallucinatory, regressive (that is, fragmented, distorted, or bizarre), or both. Thus, we quite often move quite far from the secondary process pole of consciousness even while we are fully awake.

The individual development of consciousness

Freud, Jung, and Werner held that movement along the primary process-secondary process continuum is found in many other contexts besides the di-

urnal rhythm of sleeping and waking. One of the most important of these contexts is ontogeny, or the development of the individual organism. As it develops
from infancy to adulthood, the child is held to move from primary process to
secondary process consciousness. In a very general sense, the newborn infant
is held always to be in the state of consciousness that the adult is in when
dreaming. Thus, not only thought but other mental processes, such as perception,
operate in a primary process manner. In this view, as the child grows older,
it becomes capable of more secondary process cognition. It passes through
states that are analogous to adult states of reverie, fantasy, and so on. It is important to note that Freud, Jung, and Werner did not say that the child's waking
consciousness is completely identical to the adult's dream thought. That would
be silly. Rather, they pointed to very general similarities.

The historical development of consciousness

Freud, Jung, and Werner held that phylogeny as well as ontogeny follows a
movement from primary process to secondary process modes of thought. That
is, the ascent of humanity from a precivilized state to a civilized one is paral-
leled by a movement from primary process to secondary process consciousness.
Hypothetically, the waking consciousness of all people at some very early stage
was dreamlike and hallucinatory. Only across the course of time did the capacity
for secondary process cognition gradually evolve. Lévy-Bruhl (1910) proposed
the same hypothesis in his discussion of primitive versus scientific mentality.
Jung and his followers have argued that traces of the journey toward secondary
process consciousness may be found in mythology; that is, myths created at a
given point in time reflect the dominant state of consciousness at that time. If
this is true, then if we arranged the myths of a given civilization into historical
order, we would have a symbolic history of the development of consciousness.

One of Jung's ideas (1963) is that female characters in myths and other
narratives tend to symbolize primary process states of consciousness while male
figures tend to symbolize more conscious, secondary process states. This may
sound like a rather sexist theory, but it is only likely to be the case if the myths
of a given society were created by men. Be that as it may, the basic hypothesis
is that the balance of power between male and female characters in a myth
symbolizes the balance of power between secondary process consciousness and
primary process consciousness. If there is any truth to this idea, then we should
expect male characters to become stronger and female characters to become
weaker in a historical series of myths. Neumann (1954) argues that just such a
trend is found in the mythology of various societies.

The hypothetical first state of the individual and of humanity in general is one
of complete lack of differentiation. Self and objects, conscious and unconscious,
are not differentiated. Hypothetically, there is no consciousness as such but only
a blissful void. Neumann calls this the uroboric state. Because consciousness is
undifferentiated, we should not really expect to find differentiated male and female characters. Archaic myths are often dominated by symbols of wholeness,
such as the uroboros (a snake eating its own tail), circles, spheres, and deep,
hollow, enveloping areas, such as valleys, abysses, caves, the underworld, and the

sea. The argument is that this set of themes symbolizes the state of original unity or dedifferentiation.

With the initial growth of consciousness, we would expect secondary process states to be weak and fleeting. The infant lapses easily into sleep and is incapable of sustained or focused attention. This is what Neumann calls the hermaphroditic stage. If the Jungian ideas about symbolism are correct, we would expect myths created during this stage to involve strong female figures (representing the dominant primary process mode of cognition) and weak males (representing secondary process consciousness). Indeed, Neumann argues that the earliest Western myths show this pattern in that they involve "great mother" figures and passive, effeminate, narcissistic sons who submit passively to them. Examples of this sort of male would be Narcissus or Hyacynthus. Great mother goddesses, such as Ishtar, Isis, or Astarte, are undifferentiated as to their attributes. They are simultaneously protective, tender, and mothering on the one hand and cruel, vicious, and evil on the other. They may be simultaneously deities of virginity and of fertility and of war and of peace. These contradictory and polyvalent characteristics are present because secondary process cognition is too weak and fleeting to be able to analyze or differentiate these symbols of the dominant primary process mode of cognition.

Further development of consciousness leads to what Neumann calls the stage of struggle. Consciousness is more powerful but still at the mercy of the unconscious. Neumann holds that the myths created during this period tend to describe a rather effeminate and impotent hero struggling against seduction by a mother figure, fleeing from the seduction and, finally, being destroyed. Thus, Phaedra tries to seduce her stepson Hippolytus, he resists and flees, and she causes his destruction in the sea. Pentheus fights against the unconscious as personified by the frenzied and drunken bacchantes but, in the end, they tear him to pieces. The destruction of the fleeing heroes hypothetically symbolizes the ability of primary process cognition to overwhelm or destroy secondary process cognition. In the myths of this period, we see a differentiation of great mother goddesses into goddesses that can be better understood from a secondary process perspective. Thus, the ambivalent Astarte may be seen as being differentiated into separate figures, such as Athena and Aphrodite. Athena is pure, good, and oriented toward action and thought. Aphrodite is sexual, passive, and lascivious. Neumann attributes this differentiation to the growth of secondary process consciousness. Greater powers of analysis lead to a compartmentalization of the otherness of primary process states.

Neumann's final stage is the heroic stage. Here, we have an essentially modern, adult consciousness: a strong capacity for secondary process consciousness whose power is manifested by a firm differentiation of self versus object, conscious versus unconscious, and good versus evil. In the myths of this period, male figures are strong and heroic. Hercules or Theseus would be examples. In one way or another, male figures have finally gained the upper hand over female figures. This hypothetically symbolizes the ascendance of secondary process consciousness over primary process consciousness. Female figures are firmly differentiated. On the one hand are anima figures who tend to be pure, good, and either helpful or in need of help. On the other hand are figures of pure evil, such as Medusa. Hypothetically, the two types of mythic females symbolize the good and bad aspects of primary process consciousness, respectively.

Regression

Freud, Jung, and Werner all saw the major types of psychopathology or mental illness as involving *regression* from secondary process consciousness back toward comparatively more archaic or primitive forms of consciousness. In this they followed the thinking of Hughlings Jackson (1884), who held that higher, more advanced processes are most susceptible to injury and that their injury or malfunctioning *disinhibits,* or allows the appearance of, genetically earlier and more primitive modes of mental functioning. As Jung graphically put it, you have only to let the dreamer rise and walk about and you have the psychotic. These theorists hold that healthy experiences, such as creative inspiration and religious ecstasy, also involve regression toward a primary process state of consciousness. It would seem that regression can also be induced in normal adults by a variety of procedures, such as hypnosis. In the next section, we shall see what these procedures are and why they induce an altered state of consciousness.

INDUCTION OF ALTERED STATES OF CONSCIOUSNESS

General principles

If we wanted to induce a primary process state of consciousness, we would need to produce a situation where all activated cognitive units were about equally active. How could we do this? One method would be to restrict the sensory environment so that there would be no salient stimuli capable of seizing attention. After awhile, we might expect that activation of cognitive units would run down or even out. We might try to speed up this process by adapting or fatiguing cognitive units. This could be accomplished by several means including prolonged stimulation, repetitive stimulation, or intense stimulation. A variant of this procedure would be simultaneously to activate incompatible cognitive units and let them inhibit each other. A more direct method would be simply to tell people not to focus their attention on anything but just to let mentation occur without attending to it. This is rather easier said than done, since attention is involuntarily drawn to certain stimuli. Finally, we could administer some sort of drug having the capability of equalizing the activity of cognitive units. All of these methods can induce altered states of consciousness.

Sensory restriction

One of the easiest ways to induce altered states of consciousness seems to be to decrease sensory input. Reports of arctic explorers and prisoners undergoing extended periods of solitary confinement have stressed the disordering of normal thought patterns consequent upon prolonged isolation. Sensory deprivation experiments have shown the same thing (see Chapter 10). Subjects in sensory deprivation experiments report an inability to think in a logical and directed manner, inability to focus their attention, and, often, vivid visual and auditory hallucinatory images. In the terms we have been using, sensory deprivation

moves people from a secondary process to a primary process state of consciousness.

One goal of psychoanalytic psychotherapy is to induce a mild regression from
a secondary process to a primary process state. The classical analytic situation
with the patient lying prone on a comfortable couch, often with his eyes closed,
with the analyst out of sight and saying very little, may be seen as constituting
a mild sort of sensory deprivation. Some forms of meditation essentially rely upon
sensory deprivation in order to alter consciousness: One is supposed to close
one's eyes and blot out thoughts and perceptions as much as possible. Eventually,
an alteration in consciousness does seem to come about. As we shall see in
Chapter 15, some creative people seem to impose a sort of voluntary sensory
restriction on themselves. This seems to facilitate the regression apparently
necessary for creative insight or inspiration.

Dreaming was the first closely examined type of primary process consciousness. Sleep, of course, involves a voluntary sensory deprivation where we cut
down on visual, auditory, and other types of input. In fact, all of the phenomena
that we described in the section on normal alterations of consciousness can be
seen as being based upon sensory deprivation. So long as the environment
presents us with interesting or important stimuli, we stay in a fairly secondary
process state of consciousness. If the environment becomes boring or if we
voluntarily turn our attention away from it, we will eventually fall asleep. On the
way to sleep, we pass through fantasy, reverie, and hypnagogic states.

Adaptation

MONOTONOUS STIMULATION

Prolonged exposure to the same stimulus configuration should lead to adaptation of the cognitive units coding the stimulus. It is really rather arbitrary where
we leave off talking about sensory restriction and where we begin talking about
monotonous stimulation. A polar explorer, for example, could be said to be
exposed to monotonous stimulation or to sensory deprivation. The difference is
clearer in what is called *concentrative meditation* (Goleman, 1978). With this sort
of meditation, a person is instructed to focus attention on a single stimulus—for
example, one's navel, a flower, or a geometric pattern—and keep it focused
there. Meditation of this sort is usually carried out in the context of a restricted
sensory environment. The result of prolonged attention should be that the cognitive units coding the stimulus should fatigue and, since no other stimuli in
the restricted sensory environment are capable of seizing attention, a primary
process state should result. This does seem to be what happens.

REPETITIVE STIMULATION

A variety of techniques for altering consciousness rely primarily on rhythmic or
repetitive stimulation in the context of a restricted sensory environment. Many
theorists (for example, Gill and Brenman, 1959) explain hypnosis as a regression
toward a primary process state of consciousness. A hypnotic state is often induced
by having the subject focus attention on a repetitive source of stimulation, such
as a swinging pendulum or the rhythmic and sonorous voice of the hypnotist. A

similar phenomenon is seen in another variant of concentrative meditation (Goleman, 1978), where one focuses attention upon a repetitive rather than an unchanging stimulus. Often this is a *mantra*—such as the syllable, OM—that one repeats over and over. Many types of prayer may be seen as variations of this technique. Farrell (1979) argues that rhythmic stimulation of the sort produced by certain types of poetry and music is capable of altering consciousness. We saw in Chapter 7 that repetitive stimulation rather quickly induces drowsiness (Gastaut and Bert, 1961) and that flashing lights can induce stroboscopic hallucinations if the subject is staring into a ganzfeld (Smythies, 1959). In all of these cases, it could be argued that repetition of the same stimulus fatigues the cognitive units involved in perceiving and attending to it.

OVERSTIMULATION

Sensory flooding can also induce alteration in consciousness. This technique is used rather systematically in brainwashing and in certain types of religious rites. Stress of one sort or another seems to be more or less uniformly implicated in inducing the sorts of neurotic and psychotic states that can be conceptualized as involving a regression to a primary process state of consciousness. While these disorders are almost certainly based upon predispositions, these predispositions are generally actualized by stress. Sensory flooding and stress may be seen as involving strong or intense stimuli. Such stimuli would be expected to lead to relatively rapid fatiguing of the cognitive units coding them.

Collative stimulation

So far we have dealt with causes which all may be seen as involving either net increases or decreases in the overall amount of sensory input. The implication is that we require a certain moderate and varied flow of sensory stimulation in order to maintain secondary process thinking. Too much or too little input induces regression to primary process states. There is evidence that the collative properties of perceptual input are also important. The frustration-regression hypothesis holds that frustration may induce a regression to genetically early modes of behavior. Conflict of one sort or another is often held to be the cause of neurosis. The basic idea behind projective tests, such as the Rorshach Inkblot Test, is that ambiguous or unrealistic stimuli induce a sort of mild regression. Since the formless inkblot cannot be dealt with on the realistic secondary process level, primary process mechanisms hypothetically come into play.

Contemplation of logical paradoxes plays a role in the induction of religious states of consciousness. The beginner of Zen meditation is given a *koan* or riddle (for example, What is the sound of one hand clapping?) to solve. Since the koan cannot be solved with secondary process logic, it seems eventually to induce a regression to a primary process state. Perhaps a similar function may be ascribed to such Christian doctrines as those concerning the immaculate conception or the trinity. In general, we might argue that if inputs are too novel, incongruous, unfamiliar, or ambiguous, then they cannot be apprehended with our standard set of secondary process schemata. We have to regress to primary process states where the schemata are looser in order to apprehend them. Neumann (1954:327–28) gives a vivid description of the effect of incongruous stimuli on the mind:

> The antithetical structure of such content makes conscious orientation impossible and eventually leads to fascination. . . . New reactions are constantly released, consciousness finds itself at a loss, and affective reactions begin to appear. All bivalent contents that simultaneously attract and repel act in like manner upon the organism as a whole and release powerful affective reactions, because consciousness gives way, regresses, and primitive mechanisms take its place.

We have argued that collative properties of stimuli serve to focus attention. How can they now be brought forth as causes of defocused attention? Indeed, collative properties, such as incongruity, do focus attention. However, if the incongruity cannot easily be resolved by building a new cognitive model, we would expect more and more attention to be devoted to it. Eventually, because of prolonged attentional activation of the cognitive units involved, these units should begin to fatigue and a primary process state should result.

Instructions to regress

In concentrative meditation, an altered state of consciousness is hypothetically induced by fatiguing of cognitive units. The other major type of meditation is what Goleman (1978) calls mindfulness meditation. Zen meditation belongs to this tradition. In large part, Zen training involves direct instructions to think in a primary process manner; that is, the initiate is told to be passively aware of everything but not to focus attention on anything. It is not terribly difficult to shut off voluntary attention, but what about involuntary attention? Interestingly, a lot of Zen training is aimed at decoupling the mechanisms of involuntary attention. We saw that Zen meditation involves the contemplation of logical paradoxes. The eventual result of this may be to get the initiate to ignore the collative properties of stimuli. Another aspect of Zen doctrine is that nothing has any meaning or that things do not really differ in their meaningfulness. This may be seen as an attempt to decouple the involuntary tendency to attend to meaningful stimuli.

Instructions to regress are also found in other contexts. The fundamental psychoanalytic rule of having the patient say everything that comes to mind, of free associating rather than discoursing logically, is essentially a direct prescription for primary process mentation. One criticism of hypnosis is that it is not really an altered state of consciousness at all. Rather, the subject is just complying with the hypnotist's instructions—namely, act in a regressed manner. Even drugs that quite clearly alter consciousness are subject to expectation effects; that is, the person's conscious experience is affected by what he or she has been led to expect will happen.

Drugs

Drugs also induce primary process states. In general, drugs of this sort may be grouped into two types: First are the central nervous system depressants, such as alcohol and chloral hydrate. On the other hand are stimulants that range from caffeine through marijuana to drugs such as LSD, psilocybin, and methamphetamine. While all of these drugs have their own specific effects, it is interesting that, just as increases or decreases in sensory input induce altered states, so drugs that excite or depress the nervous system induce such states. In general, drugs that neither excite nor depress seem not to have a consciousness altering effect.

THE TIME COURSE OF ALTERATION IN CONSCIOUSNESS

Eastern schools of meditation have formulated several theories about the stages one goes through in the induction of an altered state of consciousness (see Goleman, 1978). Our model would lead us to believe that most of the methods of induction described earlier should lead consciousness through at least three successive states: an initial period of adaptation, a period of disinhibition and oscillation, and a final period of equalization of activation. Most of the methods involve some sort of fatiguing process, the absence of environmental stimuli sufficient to drive cognitive units, or both. It seems reasonable enough to suppose that—after some period of time—no one set of cognitive units will be able to command sufficient activation to seize attention completely enough so that secondary process consciousness is present.

However, once these units have decreased in activation, other units will be disinhibited. When the activity of the latter units decays, yet other units will be disinhibited. Activation cannot fade away gradually in a network with inhibition. Rather, activation in the network oscillates. Since we have hypothesized that cognitive units exist in such an inhibitory network, it seems reasonable to expect such oscillation. In the prolonged absence of stimulation, we would expect the oscillations to damp down; that is, whatever cognitive units are activated should be more and more equally activated. This corresponds to increasing degrees of primary process consciousness. Hypothetically, the oscillation is what keeps thought going in the absence of stimulation. At about the time we might expect the oscillation to die out, what Konorski (1967) called off-units may fatigue, disinhibit cognitive units even more, and set up a pattern of oscillation strong enough to produce hallucinatory experience. All schools of meditation recognize such an hallucinatory stage. We see an analog of it in hypnagogic images and in the hallucinations resulting from prolonged sensory deprivation.

When may we expect the stage of complete equalization of activity—which Eastern religions call by such names as *nirvana* or *no-mindedness*—to set in? Unless you have practiced meditation for 20 years or so, the answer is probably "never." Consider what happens when you go to sleep. Following the hypnagogic state, there is a state of relatively quiescent sleep. Just as you are headed for nirvana, though, the arousal system gives the analyzers a booster shot of arousal and a dream ensues. We saw in Chapter 10 that there are both diurnal and ultradian arousal cycles. Among other things, these cycles presumably keep at least some oscillation of activation going on in the analyzers. Thus, we never reach a completely primary process state of absolutely equal amounts of activation in all cognitive units.

THE PHYSIOLOGICAL BASIS OF CONSCIOUSNESS

Hypothetically, the primary process-secondary process continuum is related to arousal in an inverted-U fashion (see Figure 12–5). Note that all of the methods of inducing an altered state of consciousness involve either an increase or a decrease in arousal (see Chapter 10). If either high or low arousal can induce a primary process state of consciousness, it does not necessarily follow that there is no subjective difference between states induced by either the high or low arousal. We noted in Chapter 10 that cognitive units may be approximately equally activated in either high- or low-arousal states. However, the pattern of activation is a lot more unstable in high-arousal states. Fischer (1971) describes states of consciousness as arrayed along the continuum shown in Figure 13–2. The

FIGURE 13–2   Fischer's topography of conscious states

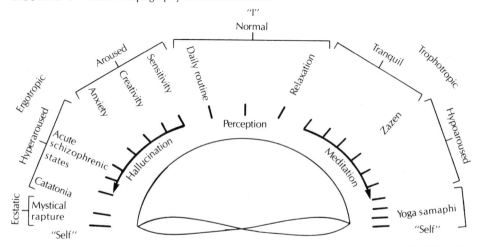

Source: R. Fischer, "A Cartography of the Ecstatic and Meditative States," *Science* 174 (1971):898. Copyright 1971 by the American Association for the Advancement of Science.

normal, waking state of consciousness and the normal level of arousal are at the top of the diagram. As arousal is decreased from this level (Fischer calls this increasing trophotropic arousal), one passes through various states of consciousness that accompany quietistic meditation techniques used by Eastern religions. As arousal is increased from this level (Fischer calls this increasing ergotropic arousal), one passes through states of consciousness ranging from creative excitement to the ecstatic delirium typical of Western mysticism. Fischer holds that the states on either side of the continuum at the same distance from the normal state have a good many similarities but are not identical. They are also different in some important respects.

Another parallel that could be drawn is that between primary process states and lower brain centers controlling visceral arousal (the limbic system) and secondary process states and higher, neocortical brain centers (the neomammalian brain). Perhaps consciousness moves toward the primary process pole as activity in the limbic system gains ascendance over activity in the cortex. This is especially likely in the case of high cortical arousal. It may be that high arousal triggers limbic-system arousal. This would be another reason why altered states of consciousness induced by high arousal are not exactly the same as those induced by low arousal. In Chapter 12 we drew a parallel between primary process thought and right-hemisphere activity and secondary process thought and left-hemisphere activity. It makes sense to speculate that consciousness may move toward the primary process pole as the right hemisphere gains ascendance over the left.

DIFFERENTIATION, INHIBITION, AND CONSCIOUSNESS

Werner (1948) identified what we have called secondary process consciousness with a state where there is differentiation of mental processes and contents and where mind functions in an hierarchically integrated fashion. On the other hand, primary process consciousness involves dedifferentiation and a breakdown of hierarchical control. Differentiation may be equated with differential activation of cognitive units. Such differential activation corresponds to a state of focused attention where some cognitive units are highly activated and others inhibited. In Chapter 12 we saw how such a pattern of activation can serve as the basis for secondary process thinking and how relative equalization of activation brings about primary process thinking. In the next section we shall see how defocusing of attention also induces many of the subjective experiences attendant upon alteration in state of consciousness.

Defocusing of attention or equalization of activation in the action system has some rather dire consequences for consciousness. Recall that we located the self in the action system and that we hypothesized that the action system controls or directs the activity of the other analyzers. We might expect that equalization of activation in the action system should have several consequences. First, it should lead to changes in the experience of the self and to a lessening of self-control. Second, it should allow the other analyzers to escape from the domination of the action system and to function in an autonomous fashion. In other words, dedifferentiation of activity in the action system should lead to the breakdown of hierarchical control that Werner said occurs in altered states of consciousness. In a later section we shall see that alteration in consciousness does seem to be accompanied both by disinhibition of normally subordinate analyzers and by profound changes in the experience of self.

DEFOCUSED ATTENTION AND ALTERED STATES OF CONSCIOUSNESS

Capacity for voluntary selective attention

We have more or less equated primary process consciousness with defocused attention. Alteration in consciousness can be induced by placing people in situations that do not allow focused attention. Thus, in the case of sensory restriction, there are no stimuli upon which to focus one's attention. Defocused attention can also be observed in naturally occurring altered states of consciousness. For example, young children are notably deficient in their capacity to focus attention for any period of time. Psychotics also exhibit a similar deficit. This deficit is quite marked in the acute stage of schizophrenia:

Everything seems to grip my attention although I am not particularly interested in anything. I am speaking to you just now but I can hear noises going on next door and in the corridor. I find it difficult to shut these out and it makes it more difficult to concentrate on what I am saying to you.

Things are coming in too fast. I lose my grip of it and get lost. I am attending to everything at once and as a result I do not really attend to anything (McGhie and Chapman, 1961).

Objectivity versus subjectivity

Mental events in the focus of attention and in the fringe of attention seem to be apprehended or experienced in completely different ways. If you will relax, close your eyes, and ask yourself what is in your consciousness, you will find two sorts of mental events. First, there are focal ideas or images. For example, you may be wondering what I'm getting at, or you may be thinking that you are tired, or you may be inspecting a mental image of one sort or another. Now you could easily give a verbal account of these events. But there is also something else there, an ineffable background sense of self, or bodily awareness, of pure existence. If you bring any of the background or fringe experiences into the focus of consciousness, you change them. To use a classic example: until you finish reading this sentence, you were not focally aware that your shoes are filled with your feet. Yet, at the same time, this awareness existed at some peripheral level before you became focally conscious of it. James compared this change to trying at catch a snowflake in one's hand. The very act of doing this changes the snowflake into a drop of water.

In apprehending a fringe experience, we turn it from subject into object. We objectify it. Just as Schactel used the term *objectification* in speaking of perception to indicate that the act of perceiving changes or structures raw sensory inputs, Goldstein (1939) uses it in speaking of consciousness. He used the term *Bewusst haben* or "having something consciously" to refer to objectified mental contents in the focus of consciousness and the term *Erleben*—which can be roughly translated as "experience"—to refer to the subjective background of consciousness. The feeling in the background and the focal awareness of it are quite different but exactly how they are different is difficult to put into words. In terms of our model of consciousness, bringing something from the fringe to the focus of attention corresponds to boosting the activation of the cognitive unit coding the fringe event. This increase in activation objectifies the event in that we become aware of the various labeled relations that define the cognitive unit. It must be that fully activated cognitive units are experienced objectively while less than fully activated units are experienced subjectively or ineffably. But in a primary process state, no cognitive units are fully activated. Such states must be more subjective or ineffable.

Ineffable meaning

When we are drunk, things seem, as William James (1902) put it, to be more utterly utter. There is a certain sense of being able to see into the very heart of things. Ludwig (1966) relates the story of an experimental subject who had been given LSD. The subject had to go to the men's room and there, written in plain English over the urinal, he was awed and amazed to see the secret of the meaning of the universe. Although this book is not about the meaning of the universe, the topic is of enough general interest to make note of what the subject saw. The sign read: "Please flush after using."

The increased sense of the ineffable meaningfulness of things is not restricted to drug-induced states. The same thing is seen in the acute phase of schizophrenia, as the following quotation makes clear:

> At the onset of panic, I was suddenly confronted with an overwhelming conviction that I had discovered the secrets of the universe, which were being rapidly made plain with incredible lucidity. The truths discovered seemed to be known immediately and directly, with absolute certainty. I had no sense of doubt or awareness of the possibility of doubt (Anonymous, 1955, p. 679).

Equalization of meaning

Another consequence of the defocusing of attention in altered states of consciousness is an equalization in the perceived meaning of things. In a secondary process state, focal attention automatically divides the perceptual world into two sets of phenomena: relevant or meaningful (that is, events in the focus of attention) and irrelevant or meaningless (that is, events in the fringe of consciousness). If the focus of attention is wider or more inclusive in altered states, it follows that phenomena normally held to be insignificant or irrelevant will become infused with meaning. As you read this book, you focus your attention on the content of what you are reading. You ignore the details of the type in which the book is set. You ignore the arrangement of pens and pencils on your desk. You may stop to wonder what some word in the text means, but you never stop to wonder what the redness of your pen—or its blueness or its blackness—means. These are meaningless in a secondary process state. But this is less so in an altered state, where meaning seems to be more equitably spread out over the field of consciousness.

The defocusing of attention and consequent equalization of meaning in altered states can have opposite consequences depending upon the person's interpretation of the experience. Castaneda (1971:82) quotes the Yaqui sorcerer Don Juan on the experience of *seeing*—his term for the mystical state—as follows: "Everything is equal and therefore unimportant. For example, there is no way for me to say that my acts are more important than yours, or that one thing is more essential than another, therefore all things are equal and by being equal they are unimportant." However, at another point Don Juan (Castaneda, 1971: 159) says, "When you *see* there are no longer familiar features in the world. Everything is new. Everything has never happened before. The world is incredible. . . . Nothing is any longer familiar."

Shallow processing

CONCRETENESS

Primary process consciousness tends to deal with concrete realities. Things have a unique and ineffable meaning but not by virtue of being subsumed under abstract concepts; that is, stimuli or events are not apprehended as mere examples of conceptual categories. Everything is unique and different. Piaget (1937) argues that children are more or less buried in the world of concrete reality until puberty. Only then do they become able to differentiate reality from possibility, what actually is from what might be. Goldstein (1939) has described how brain damage and schizophrenia result in a regression to this sort of concreteness. We have argued that relatively complete activation of cognitive units is necessary for deep processing to occur. However, such complete activation is generally lacking in primary process states. A consequence of this should be relatively shallow processing. The primary process thinker does not become aware of the conceptual meaning or significance of mental events.

MEMORABILITY

The decreased capacity for focused attention and deep processing is probably the basis for another attribute of altered states of consciousness. Based on self-observations, Rapaport (1957) holds that the more primary process the state of consciousness, the worse is subsequent memory for what transpired in the state. Thus, you can remember quite well what you had for lunch yesterday but may be quite unable to remember what you dreamed last night, even though the dream occurred more recently than the lunch. As William James (1890) noted, unless something is specifically attended to, it is not remembered. You will recall the experiments that showed that material in short-term memory (that is, the fringe of consciousness) which is not specifically rehearsed or attended to seems to be lost within only 10 to 15 seconds. But primary process consciousness is all fringe and no focus, so it cannot very well involve rehearsed or focal attention. Thus, if focal attention is very weak in altered states of consciousness, it makes sense that memory for what transpired in such states should be very poor.

Dedifferentiation of mental contents

CONCEPTUAL DEDIFFERENTIATION

In Chapter 12 we discussed at some length why primary process states should be accompanied by dedifferentiated concepts. Concepts are hypothetically coded by cognitive units and their meaning is coded by excitatory and inhibitory associations with other cognitive units. If arousal is too high or too low, the inhibitory associations cease to operate and the labels of the excitatory associations cannot be read. The result is that a set of cognitive units (which are supposed to code quite different concepts) may come to act as a diffuse unit; that is, they may become simultaneously active. The subjective experience is of a vague, global, or dedifferentiated concept. We may apply a similar line of reasoning to other mental contents.

PERCEPTUAL DEDIFFERENTIATION

A primary process state should have the same effect on percepts as it does on concepts and emotions. There is some evidence that this is the case. A good example of this is found in dreams, where two objects can simultaneously occupy the same position in space (Freud, 1900). This same phenomenon is also found in creative inspiration (Rothenberg, 1971). It could be seen as being based upon a dedifferentiation of activity in cognitive units in the analyzer dealing with spatial localization.

Intersensory dedifferentiation

Another set of phenomena found in primary process states of consciousness rather clearly involves dedifferentiation. At first glance, these phenomena may seem paradoxical, since what is merged are mental contents that are seemingly processed by completely different analyzers. All of the other phenomena involve a merging or mass action of units in the same analyzer. How could completely discrete analyzers that are hypothetically different structures in different parts of the brain get merged? I doubt that they could. I shall describe the phenomena first and then offer a possible explanation for them.

SENSE OF ONENESS

The first or most basic differentiation is that between self and world or subject and object. All of the other differentiations we have discussed are in one way or another dependent upon this one. One of the hallmarks of the altered state of consciousness sought by the mystic is the experience of oneness or unity with the external world. The boundaries between the self and external world are momentarily dissolved and self and world become one unitary thing. Thus, James (1902:310) quotes a mystic as saying of his experience, "I felt myself one with the grass, the trees, birds, insects, everything in Nature." There is every reason to believe that this sort of statement reports a subjective perceptual experience rather than being merely rhetorical; that is, it would seem that the mystic really comes to feel toward external objects the same sense of "me-ness" that the rest of us reserve for our own bodies. Thus, the mystic may feel the same sense of "me-ness" in regard to an external tree that you feel toward your hand or your leg. Bucke (1901) referred to this fusion experience as cosmic consciousness. Freud called it the oral oceanic experience, since he thought that it is the characteristic state of consciousness of the newborn infant in what he called the oral stage of development.

DEPERSONALIZATION

Sometimes, alteration in consciousness is accompanied by a change in bodily awareness that is just the reverse of the mystical sense of oneness with the world. Depersonalization may take various forms. The sense of "me-ness" may shrink so that it no longer fills the whole body. In this case, the person may have the feeling that an arm or a leg is no longer a part of the self. In out-of-body experiences, the person mislocates "me-ness." The self no longer seems to be inside the body but rather is experienced as being somewhere else. In derealization, the sense of "me-ness" vanishes altogether. All of these forms of depersonalization are experienced in a variety of altered states of consciousness ranging from psychosis to meditation (Deikman, 1966).

SYNAESTHESIA

Synaesthesia involves a lack of differentiation among inputs from the different senses. There are various forms of synaesthesia; for example, color-tone synaesthesia involves seeing colors when tones are heard or vice versa. Synaesthesia is found in many contexts where we would argue that primary process cognition is being employed. Werner (1948) presents evidence that synaesthesia is common among children and that it declines with age until it is relatively rare among adults. He gives several examples, such as a child exclaiming, "The leaf smells green."

Synaesthetic experiences tend to be induced by hallucinogenic drugs, such as LSD and mescaline. A subject described the effects of mescaline as follows: "I think that I hear noises and see faces, and yet everything is one and the same. I cannot tell whether I am seeing or hearing. I feel, taste, and smell the sound. It's all one. I, myself, am the tone" (Werner, 1948). In this account we see both multiple synaesthesias and a loss of the differentiation between self and world. Synaesthesia is also a common experience of psychotics. A psychotic patient quoted by Werner (1948) commented that "When I say red, that means a concept which can be expressed in color, music, feeling, thinking, and in nature. And when this idea is expressed in any one way, the other forms of the idea are felt to be there, too. Hence, man has not five senses, but only one."

PHYSIOGNOMIC PERCEPTION

Where synaesthesia refers to a lack of differentiation among the senses, physiognomic perception involves a lack of differentiation between the perceptual and emotional realms. As such, it leads to what John Ruskin (1844) called the *pathetic fallacy*, the attribution of emotion to inanimate objects as suggested by the phrases "gloomy sky" or "brooding mountains." Physiognomic perception is hypothetically found in many primary process states. Children, psychotics, and preliterate peoples sometimes ascribe souls to inorganic objects. For example, they may treat trees or storms as being alive and possessing a conscious will. This is referred to as *animism*. A young subject of Werner's (1948), on seeing a drinking glass lying on its side spontaneously remarked on the "poor, tired glass." A psychotic patient confronted with swinging doors started in panic and exclaimed, "The doors are devouring me."

Explanation of intersensory dedifferentiation

THE MAP AND THE MIXER

I think that we can explain all of these phenomena in terms of dedifferentiation or disturbance in two analyzers we have not yet discussed. It is clear that we have detailed knowledge about our location in the world and the location of the various objects of which we are currently aware. We know where we are in relation to these objects and where they are in relation to one another. It seems to be the case that we keep track of this knowledge quite separately from knowledge of what these objects are. As Szentágothai and Arbib (1974) put it, the *what* and the *where* of perception are taken care of by different systems.

Damage to certain areas of the right hemisphere can leave the ability to recognize unitary percepts intact but render the patient unable to recognize the spatial relations among the objects that they can still clearly perceive and recognize (Konorski, 1967). Figure 13–3 shows a schematic view from the top of two analyzers—

FIGURE 13–3 Top layers of the map and the mixer. Hypothetically, the map provides information about the spatial location of self and objects; the mixer contains chunking units that label the objects in the map.

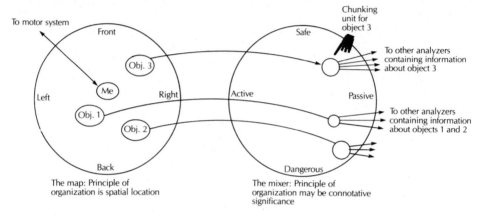

the map and the mixer. The idea is that the cognitive units on the top level of the map serve as a two-dimensional grid. Activation of a unit turns it into a pointer indicating one's own position or the position of an environmental object. Thus, the position of self and of each object in the environment is indicated by an activated unit that is rather like a blip on a radar screen. The various blips contain no information at all about what the various objects are. Deeper levels of the map might be used to compute information about the velocity or acceleration of the blips. This is only a guess, though. Presumably, the map is an evolutionarily old analyzer. Any organism that moved around much would need one. It would have to be intimately related to the motor system. If you think about what the motor system does, it may make more sense why the map does not contain explicit information about what is in any given location. The motor system dutifully executes the details of action-system commands. All it really needs to know is which blip represents the self. It would not be much use to inform it about the meaning of an object it was supposed to pick up or about the fact that the object was first detected by the auditory analyzer. The motor system would not be able to decode or understand this information anyway.

On the other hand, the action system and other conceptual analyzers would also have occasion to use or consult the map. These systems would need to be able to deduce what was where. In order to correlate the where of things with the what of things, we need the mixer. It contains intermediate chunking nodes that couple an object in the map with information about it in the various analyzers. It is possible that the principle of organization of the mixer might have to do with the connotative meaning or significance of inputs rather than having all of the visual chunking units in one area, all of the auditory ones in another area, and so on. Perhaps chunking units for dangerous objects are in one region, chunking units for attractive objects in another, and so on. Why arrange things this way? Osgood, Suci, and Tannenbaum (1957) have shown that people often agree on the connotations of concepts (for example, whether they are good versus bad or strong versus weak) regardless of the perceptual nature or denotative meaning of these concepts. The mixer would be a possible place to store information about the connotations of things. A more compelling reason is that such a principle of arrangement would allow attention to be focused on the most dangerous object among several regardless of which gnostic analyzer had processed its signals. The idea is that the unit coding the most dangerous object in the field would be the most activated and would laterally inhibit surrounding units. It would also cause the unit coding its position in the map to be highly activated so that it could laterally inhibit surrounding units coding the locations of less relevant objects. If you have not guessed, I should warn you that my hypothesis about the principle of organization of the mixer is extremely speculative.

When you perceive the world around you, this must consist of simultaneous activity of cognitive units in the map (you see where things are), the gnostic analyzers (you know what these things are), and the mixer (you know which auditory, visual, olfactory, and so on percepts go together with which object). Whichever unit codes the person's location in the field would be coupled to yet another analyzer keeping track of exactly where all the parts of the person—for example, head, arms, legs—are in relation to one another (Konorski, 1967).

SELF AND WORLD

I think you will agree that a certain sense of "me-ness" pervades your body sensations while it is definitely absent from your perception of the external world. The "me-ness" is restricted to the units marking your location in space. This is illustrated in Figure 13–4A. In the mystical sense of oneness with the world, the "me-ness" spreads to include at least parts of the external world (see Figure 13–4B). This could happen with a lowered degree of lateral inhibition so that the activation of the unit marking the mystic's position in space spread laterally. On the other hand, depersonalization can involve the case where part of the person is felt as alien (see Figure 13–4C) or an out-of-body experience where the "me-ness" is attached to a pseudo-object outside the person's body (see Figure 13–4D). Exactly what causes depersonalization, I do not know. It is rather reminiscent of the fractionation of attention hypothetically occurring with very high arousal, though (compare Figure 13–4D with Figure 10–6D).

THE PRIMORDIAL SENSORIUM

What is the psychological basis of intersensory symbolism? Werner's idea was that the primitive organism possesses an undifferentiated primordial sensorium. Inputs from the different senses all end up in the same sensorium or at least, there is considerable overlap. Perception is holistic rather than being confined to one discrete sense. Werner's idea is that in the primitive or regressed mind, physiognomic perception and synaesthesia constitute the natural state of

FIGURE 13–4   The sense of "me-ness" in a secondary process state (A), during mystical experience of oneness with the world (B), and during two types of depersonalization (C and D). Hatched lines indicate placement of the sense of me-ness.

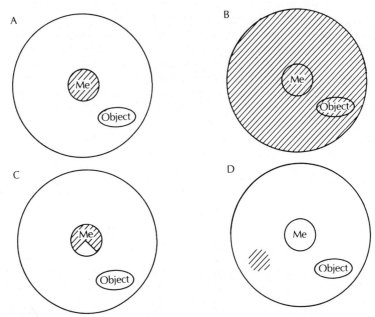

affairs. Only with development or movement toward secondary process states is there a segregation of sensory inputs to discrete sensory receiving areas. The other possible explanation is the reverse of Werner's: synaesthesia and other intersensory correlations are learned from experience rather than representing primordial conditions. The problem with this explanation is that children should get better rather than worse at synaesthesia with increasing age. But they do not.

We could identify Werner's primordial sensorium with a dedifferentiated version of what we called the mixer. In such a state, this analyzer would commingle inputs from various analyzers. This would be the case especially if—as shown in Figure 13–6—the principle of organization had something to do with the connotative significance of percepts. In such a case, a visual input might activate a unit in the mixer which would—in a low-arousal or dedifferentiated state—activate surrounding units connected to other nonvisual analyzers. The result would be synaesthesia. If the mixer were organized according to the emotional and motivational significance or connotations of percepts, we could invoke a similar explanation to account for physiognomic perception.

THE ACTION SYSTEM AND ALTERED STATES OF CONSCIOUSNESS

The action system and hierarchical control

In secondary process states, the action system hypothetically serves as an executive monitor. It uses and controls other analyzers. It delegates tasks to them. There is some reason to believe that it may exert an inhibitory control over them; that is, it may actively suppress spontaneous activity in other analyzers. One mechanism for this might be diffuse excitatory connections from the action system to off-units these systems. If this were the case, then the more activated the action system was, the more it would suppress activity in other analyzers. A state of equalized activity or of low activity in the action system should have several consequences. First, it should lead to changes in functions carried out by the action system. These include control of actions of all sorts as well as self-control, sense of self, and maintenance of enduring dispositions. Second, it should disinhibit other analyzers. This would allow these analyzers to operate in an autonomous and uncontrolled fashion.

Deactivation of the action system

DEAUTOMATIZATION

The most direct consequence of equalized levels of activation in the action system is that there is insufficient energy to drive action units coding normally automatic acts. Such acts come to require attention. Both James (1902) and Deikman (1966) comment on this "deautomatization" in mystical states. It is also common in schizophrenia. McGhie and Chapman (1961) quote one patient as saying, "I have to do everything step by step, nothing is automatic now." Another explains the feelings in more detail:

> I am not sure of my own movements any more. It's very hard to describe this but at times I am not sure about simple actions like sitting down. . . . I found recently that I was thinking of myself doing things before I would do them. If I am going to sit down, for example, I have got to think of myself and almost see myself sitting down before I do it. . . . If I could just stop noticing what I am doing, I would get things done a lot faster (McGhie and Chapman, 1961).

DECREASED SELF-CONTROL

In Chapter 12 we argued that inputs to action units from deeper levels of the action system give internal dispositions as well as external stimuli a say in behavior. The balance of power is likely to be shifted in favor of external stimuli if these deeper-level units are deactivated. One of the first theories about hypnosis was Charcot's. He held that hypnosis is due to what he called *dissociation*. In the dissociated state, the normally automatic part of the person (what we would call action units) is dissociated from, or becomes autonomous from, the waking, guiding, and controlling part (what we would call the dominant subself). This, Charcot said, leads the person automatically to accept the commands of the hypnotist. In a normal state of consciousness, the deeper centers control the shallower ones. In hypnosis, the hypnotist commands them because the person's own deeper centers have lost control of them. Ludwig (1966) holds that people in many sorts of altered states of consciousness are more suggestible than those in a normal state. Many of the effects of psychedelic drugs seem to be the effect not of the drug itself but of expectation or suggestion. Religious trance also seems to make people particularly suggestible or open to accepting the opinion of an external authority. Those who view the hypnotic state as an altered state of consciousness see this alteration as important in explaining the hypnotic subject's suggestibility.

We have equated amount of vertical activation with the subjective sense of will or volition. There seems to be a loss of subjective sense of will or control in altered states of consciousness. The mystic feels himself to be at one with God and under God's control. As James (1902) put it: "The mystic feels as if his own will were in abeyance, and indeed sometimes as if he were grasped and held by a superior power." At another extreme, certain types of schizophrenics develop the delusion that alien forces are controlling their thoughts.

DISINHIBITION OF DISPOSITIONS

Units at deeper levels of the action system coding dominant dispositions and subselves presumably tend to stay activated for long periods of time. Otherwise, we could forget who we were and what our dispositions were. These units presumably exert strong lateral inhibition on neighboring units coding incompatible subselves and dispositions. Thus, if activation of these units were decreased sufficiently, we should expect a disinhibition of the neighboring units. Alteration in state of consciousness should, then, be accompanied by rather drastic changes in personality. If you think about your own dreams and fantasies, I am sure you will agree that you do many things in them that you would not even think of doing in real life. On the other hand, the dispositions that you satisfy in action are rather less likely to appear in your dreams and fantasies. One way of accounting for this would be to argue that in a primary process state, normally inhibited dispositions are disinhibited. By the same token, the person who is under the influence of alcohol, marijuana, or hypnosis may do or say things that he or she would be embarrassed to do or say in a sober state.

DISINHIBITION OF SUBSELVES

Hidden observers. Hilgard (1977) discovered what we called hidden observers during hypnosis. A deeply hypnotized person can be rendered insensitive to pain. However, when asked if some part of the person is feeling the pain, a large percentage of subjects respond affirmitively. It could be argued that hypnosis is induced by adapting or fatiguing the dominant subself. This would disinhibit usually inhibited subselves. Strange as it may seem, Watkins and Watkins (1979) found that a given subject may have several hidden observers and that these hidden observers give themselves names (for example, The Machine, Medusa, The Evil One) and can state when they were born. The hidden-observer phenonemon seems to be a genuine one. If unhypnotized people are asked to feign a hypnotic state, they do not report hidden observers (Watkins and Watkins, 1979). This suggests that the hypnotized subjects are not just trying to comply with what they think the hypnotist wants them to say.

Multiple personality. In cases of multiple personality, consciousness loses its unity. Completely different selves seem to coexist in the same mind with consciousness being passed from one to another of them. Prince's case (1929) of Miss Beauchamp illustrates this. Her most important subselves were Sally and the Saint. Their characteristics were more or less opposite. The Saint was prim, religious, and serious while Sally was fun-loving and hated religion. Sally was coconscious; that is, she was aware of the Saint. Occasionally, she would seize complete control of consciousness. On the other hand, the Saint was not directly aware of Sally's existence. However, Sally would occasionally write letters to her taunting her about sinful or uncharitable thoughts she (the Saint) had had. While the Saint had no sensory deficits, Sally could not feel pain or temperature at all. Each of the personalities could experience only some emotions. For example, Sally never felt fear while the Saint never felt anger. Figure 13–5 illustrates how

FIGURE 13–5   Hypothetical view of Miss Beauchamp's action system

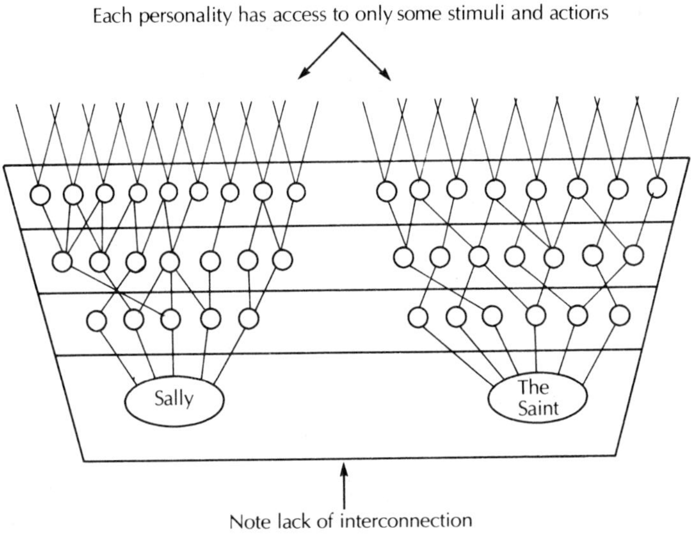

Each personality has access to only some stimuli and actions

Note lack of interconnection

such a situation might come about. Hypothetically, the action system in the normal personality is richly interconnected but is segregated in multiple personality. In this case, each subself controls only a subset of action units. Presumably, Sally controlled no action units with access to information about pain, temperature, or fear. Hypothetically, the columns of units controlled by each subself laterally inhibit each other. Emergence of secondary subselves in cases of multiple personality seems often to follow a fatiguing of the dominant subself brought about by strong, traumatic stimulation. This fatiguing could be seen as disinhibiting one of the subselves normally held in check by activation of the units coding the dominant subself.

Disinhibition of other analyzers

PERCEPTUAL AUTONOMY

Hallucinations.   Sensory impressions can arise without external stimulation in altered states of consciousness. In the secondary process state, perceptual systems are not only subordinated to the action system but are also under the control of environmental stimuli. With regression, perceptual systems seem to become autonomous from both sources of control, and the person has perceptual experiences not induced by environmental stimuli. The hallucinations of the psychotic are one clear example of this. The dreams and hypnagogic images of the normal person are another example. In comparison with the mental imagery of the waking state, the imagery of dreams is generally more vivid and always less under conscious control. Vividness of mental imagery also seems to decrease as the child develops into the more abstract adult. Some theorists, such as Galton (1907), have claimed that there is an inverse relationship in adults between degree of ability for abstraction and vividness of mental imagery.

Inner light. One concomitant of mystical experience is often the sensation of an inner light:

> All at once, without warning of any kind, I found myself wrapped in a flame-colored cloud. For an instant I thought of fire, an immense conflagration somewhere close by in that great city; the next, I knew that the fire was within myself. Directly afterward there came upon me a sense of exultation, of immense joyousness (Bucke, 1901, p. 7).

William James (1902) notes that this sensation is a frequent one in mystical experiences and recalls Saint Paul's blinding vision on the road to Damascus and the cross that the Emperor Constantine saw in the sky as examples of it.

SENSORY INTENSIFICATION

One phenomenon that is found in a wide variety of altered states of consciousness is the intensification of sensory impressions. This phenomenon is found with many psychedelic drugs. A firsthand report on the effects of marijuana runs as follows:

> The usual, most noticeable effect is intensification of sensation and increased clarity of perception. Visually, colors are brighter, scenes have more depth, patterns are more evident, and figure-ground relations are both more distinct and more easily reversible.
> . . . . Sounds become more distinct, with the user aware of sounds he otherwise might not have noticed. . . . Taste and smell are also enhanced under marijuana. The spice rack is a treasure of sensation, and food develops a rich variety of tastes (Anonymous, 1969, p. 335).

Klüver (1966) reports that similar effects are induced by mescaline. Deikman (1966) taught naive subjects an experimental meditation technique in a laboratory situation. His subjects reported a number of perceptual changes, including a tendency to see colors as more vivid and intense. In the initial stages of zen meditation, a similar phenomenon is observed (Yasutani-Roshi, 1967). Acute schizophrenics also commonly report an intensification of sensations:

> "Noises seem to be louder to me than they were before . . . I notice it most with background noises." "Colours seem to be brighter now almost as if they are luminous" (McGhie and Chapman, 1961).

> On several occasions my eyes became markedly oversensitive to light. Ordinary colors appeared to be much too bright, and sunlight seemed dazzling in intensity. When this happened, ordinary reading was impossible, and print seemed excessively black (Anonymous, 1955, p. 681)

EMOTIONAL DISINHIBITION

Going along with the disinhibition of the perceptual systems is a disinhibition of the emotions. The quotation from Bucke (1901) refers to the intense joy of the mystical experience. Rapaport (1957) holds that in all altered states of consciousness, there is a tendency for emotions to become stronger and less modulated. Freud (1900) held that primary process thought is much more under the sway of primitive drives and wishes than is the case in waking consciousness. Many altered states of consciousness are followed by feelings of rejuvenation, of being born again. This is especially true of religious and mystical states, but we can see something of the same feeling even after emerging from such mundane experience as sleep. Everyone has gone to sleep burdened down by cares and conflicts only to awake the next morning feeling refreshed and carefree. This feeling of rejuvenation and freshness is not a general consequence of all altered states of consciousness. It is notably lacking, for example, following the altered state induced by alcohol.

MEASUREMENT OF STATE OF CONSCIOUSNESS

We should be able to tell from the content of a person's speech or writing where on the primary process-secondary process continuum he or she is; that is, the content of language should reflect the content of consciousness. This is hardly a novel conclusion. The theorists who developed the notion of the continuum of states of consciousness in the first place did so largely on the basis of differences in speech and verbal reports. Had they confined themselves to direct observations of consciousness, they would have had only their own consciousness to observe. In order to infer whether a person is thinking in a primary process or a secondary process manner, we have to observe some overt behavior. Speech or writing is generally the best candidate for such observation. Unless we can develop a quantitative index of state of consciousness, we have little hope of testing the various theories about consciousness.

Actually many of the attributes of type of thought and consciousness might be expected to lead to straightforward differences in language content. Look at the list of categories in the left-hand column of the top section of Table 13–1. Each describes a hypothetical attribute of secondary process thinking. For example, such thought is theoretically supposed to deal with abstract concepts and operations. If it does, then speech based upon it should contain lots of words describing such concepts and operations. Some such words are listed in the right-hand column of the table. Secondary process consciousness is closely related to action, especially purposeful action (instrumental behavior) and social interaction (social behavior). It is supposed to involve inhibition, control, and delay (restraint, order, moral imperatives). It is also supposed to take account of time (temporal references). We can make a fairly exhaustive list of words indicating each of these attributes. It would certainly be reasonable to expect that speech generated by secondary process thought should contain a high frequency of such words as compared to speech generated by primary process thinking.

We can follow the same procedure with respect to primary process thinking. The bottom section of Table 13–1 lists some hypothetical attributes of primary process thinking, along with words that ought to indicate the presence of these attributes. We argued that primary process thought tends to occur at a more perceptual level than does secondary process thinking. While secondary process thought oscillates between abstraction and perception, primary process thought tends to stay on the perceptual level. If this is so, then speech describing it should

TABLE 13–1   Categories of words indicative of
secondary process and primary process thinking

Secondary process:
> Abstraction: know, may, thought
> Social behavior: say, tell, call
> Instrumental behavior: make, find, work
> Restraint: must, stop, bind
> Order: simple, measure, array
> Temporal references: when, now, then
> Moral imperatives: should, right, virtue

Primary process:
> Drives
>> Oral: breast, drink, lip
>> Anal: sweat, rot, dirty
>> Sex: lover, kiss, naked
>
> Regressive cognition
>> Unknown: secret, strange, unknown
>> Timelessness: eternal, forever, immortal
>> Consciousness alteration: dream, sleep, wake
>> Brink-passage: road, wall, door
>> Narcissism (body parts): eye, heart, hand
>> Concreteness (spatial references): at, where, over
>
> Perceptual disinhibition
>> Passivity: die, lie, bed
>> Voyage: wander, desert, beyond
>> Random movement: wave, roll, spread
>> Diffusion: shade, shadow, cloud
>> Chaos: wild, crowd, ruin
>
> Sensation
>> General sensation: fair, charm, beauty
>> Touch: touch, thick, stroke
>> Taste: sweet, taste, bitter
>> Odor: breath, perfume, scent
>> Sound: hear, voice, sound
>> Vision: see, light, look
>> Cold: cold, winter, snow
>> Hard: rock, stone, hard
>> Soft: soft, gentle, tender
>
> Icarian imagery
>> Ascend: rise, fly, throw
>> Height: up, sky, high
>> Descend: fall, drop, sink
>> Depth: down, deep, beneath
>> Fire: sun, fire, flame
>> Water: sea, water, stream

have more references to perceptual phenomena (sensation). Primary process thought should contain more references to primitive motives (drives). Primary process thought is supposed to be disordered, diffuse, and uncontrolled. The category, Perceptual disinhibition, gets at one aspect of this. Primary process thought is supposed to be symbolic. Murray (1955) and Ogilvie (1968) argue that Icarian imagery (references to fire, water, rising, and falling) constitutes a set of primitive, preverbal symbols for drives and emotions. Finally, the category, Regressive cognition, contains several categories referring to other aspects of primary process thinking, such as Timelessness, Narcissism or increased body awareness, and Concreteness.

I used the categories shown in Table 13–1 to construct the Regressive Imagery Dictionary (Martindale, 1975). This is a list of 2,900 words, each of which is assigned to one of the categories shown in the table. The words listed there are examples of some of these words. The basic idea behind the dictionary is that a primary process text should contain a lot of the primary process words and few of the secondary process words. Conversely, a more secondary process text should contain fewer primary process words and more secondary process words. The dictionary is actually applied to texts by a computer program, COUNT (Martindale, 1973b). The computer program has been written so as to "read" a keypunched text. It takes each word in such a text, removes suffixes to find the word's root form, and then looks the word up in the dictionary. When the program has looked up all of the words in a text, it prints out a tally telling what percentage of text words belong to each of the dictionary categories. The reason for having a computer program rather than a person do this has to do with speed. It takes the computer only a few seconds to do what it would take a person many hours to do.

The dictionary allows us to investigate several questions. The first question of interest has to do with the idea that primary process thinking and secondary process thinking are polar opposites. If they are, then texts that use a lot of primary process words should use few secondary process words and vice versa. In other words, the two types of content should correlate negatively with each other. I have analyzed well over 1 million words of texts including poetry (Martindale, 1975, 1978a), literary narratives (Martindale, 1978b, 1979b), folktales (Martindale, 1976b), fantasy stories of normal subjects (Covello and Martindale, 1978), writing of subjects given drugs (Martindale and Fischer, 1977), speech of patients in psychoanalysis (Martindale, Reynes, and Dahl, 1974), and speech of pathological groups (Martindale, 1977b). In all of these cases, there is, in fact, a strong negative correlation between primary process content and secondary process content. Texts of all sorts that use a lot of primary process words do in fact use few secondary process words and vice versa. Furthermore, the secondary process categories intercorrelate with each other as do the primary process categories. Thus, the dictionary does seem to be getting at one consistent and unitary dimension.

The second question of interest is whether we find primary process thinking where we are supposed to according to the theorists. In the cases that I have investigated, we do. In a large-scale study of poetry, it was found that the more symptoms of psychopathology reported in poets' biographies the more primary process content their poetry contains (Martindale, 1975). Texts written under the influence of both psilocybin (Martindale and Fischer, 1977) and marijuana (West et al., 1980) contain more primary process content than control texts. Another study showed that stories written by younger children contain more primary process content than those written by older children (West, Martindale, and Sutton-Smith, 1980). Folktales from more primitive societies contain more primary process content than those from more advanced societies (Martindale, 1976b). People who show greater amounts of right-hemisphere brain activity write stories containing more primary process content (Covello and Martindale 1978). There is even evidence for Neumann's hypotheses (1954): in poetry written by men, the more primary process the content, the stronger female characters are and the weaker male characters are (Martindale, 1975). Thus, in general, we do actually find more primary process content in texts produced by those groups that hypothetically engage in more primary process thinking.

SUMMARY AND CONCLUSIONS

The secondary process-primary process continuum hypothetically describes the basic dimension along which not only thinking varies but along which all aspects of consciousness vary. We identified secondary process consciousness as a state where cognitive units are activated to differing degrees. On the other hand, to the extent that cognitive units are equally activated, primary process consciousness will be found. Thus, movement from secondary process to primary process consciousness may be equated with movement from focused attention to defocused attention. A variety of methods can be used to induce a primary process state of consciousness. In one way or another, these methods have the effect of increasing or decreasing arousal from the level conducive to secondary process cognition. As we saw in earlier chapters, both increases and decreases in arousal tend to equalize the activation of cognitive units.

Equalizing the activation of cognitive units has several consequences: The vertical flow of activation is lessened so that processing is shallower and the labels of associations become illegible. Lateral inhibition is lessened so that normally inhibited cognitive units are disinhibited and antagonistic units co-exist peacefully. Taken together, decreased lateral inhibition and decreased vertical activation lead to dedifferentiation of mental contents and to a loss of distinctions that are maintained in secondary process states. For example, the distinction between relevant and irrelevant is lost; different and even contradictory concepts, emotions, and percepts become merged; distinctions between self and world, emotion and perception, and even the different sensory modalities are lost. Equalization of activation in the action system leads to a loss of will and self-control and even to the disinhibition of alien dispositions and subselves. It also unleashes other analyzers from action-system control so that hallucinations and sensory intensification occur. In short, equalizing the activation of cognitive units brings about the phenomena observed in a wide variety of altered states of consciousness.

We saw that it is a plausible undertaking to attempt to measure state of consciousness indirectly by measuring language content. When we do so, we find support for the contention that primary process and secondary process define the poles of a continuum. Further, we find support for theoretical predictions concerning where the language of a given type of person should be located on this continuum. Thus, although much that has been proposed about types of thought and consciousness may seem speculative, many of these proposals can be scientifically investigated. Such investigations are important in that one of the best ways of gaining an understanding of any phenomenon is by seeing how it changes under different circumstances. I hope that our discussion of cognition in altered states of consciousness in this chapter has given you a better perspective on the cognitive processes occurring in normal states which we discussed in earlier chapters.

14

Narratives

IMPORTANCE OF STUDYING NARRATIVES

We spend a lot of our time either processing or producing narratives. Some of these—such as fantasies, dreams, and recollections—are private mental events. Other narratives are overt and may be cultural productions, such as myths, novels, movies, television programs, and so on. They may also be individual. When we converse with other people, most of us probably spend most of our time producing and listening to narratives. One person tells a story about something, the other person responds with a related story, the first person tells yet another story, the other person responds in kind, and so it goes. Narratives may be seen as descriptions of sequences of behaviors generated by the action system. Presumably, memory for such sequences of action is stored in the episodic analyzer. As we saw in Chapter 12, the action system is really the key or pivotal system of the mind. It is here that our perceptions, goals, and behaviors are coordinated. Narratives, then, provide us with an indirect means of studying the action system. The content of overt narratives should provide us with a means of seeing what actions are interesting or important to people. Furthermore, the structure of such narratives should give us insight into the structure of both episodic memory and the action system.

TEXT GRAMMAR

What is a story?

What is a story? Most people would agree that it is a series of propositions. A proposition, you will recall, describes a single event or state of affairs: for example, WALK (JOHN, TOWN, PAST)—JOHN WALKED TO TOWN. One proposition by itself is not a story. To get a story, we need to string together a couple of propositions. An example might be: JOHN WAS BORED. HE WALKED TO TOWN. THERE, HE WAS NOT BORED. Although uninteresting, this is certainly a story.

If a narrative consists of a string of propositions, it makes sense to ask several questions. What propositions can be used in a narrative? How must these propositions be expressed? What rules govern their sequencing? These are Jakobson's questions (1956) concerning lexicon, realization rules, and syntax that must be answered by any grammar. Conventional linguistic grammar will not help us at all with these questions, since it deals only with individual sentences or propositions; that is, conventional grammar deals with how words are arranged to form sentences. What we need is a grammar that will tell us how sentences are arranged to form narratives. There has been a lot of interest recently in formulating just this sort of grammar. It is referred to as a *text grammar* or a *narrative grammar*.

Aims of text grammar

A text grammar aims to do three things. First, it must answer the question of selection. What are the ultimate units of a narrative? As we will see later, the general answer is that these units are not propositions. They are more general or abstract than propositions. A narrative is composed of a set of these more abstract units. The second question concerns realization rules. There is general agreement that the abstract units are ultimately realized as a set of propositions. These propositions are, in turn, realized as sentences, and so on. Finally, there is the question of sequencing. By what rules are the abstract units arranged to form a narrative? It is interesting that one widely accepted idea is that sequencing tends to involve a movement from a state of incongruity toward one of relative congruity. In other words, narratives seek the same ultimate end as human thought and action. I suppose that should not really be surprising. After all, narratives are descriptions of human thought and action.

CONSTITUENT UNITS OF NARRATIVES

Propositions

In Chapter 9 we argued that the proposition is the basic unit of episodic memory. A proposition can describe a single event. We just said that a narrative is a series of propositions. Why do we need to look any further than the proposition to find the basic units of narratives? One reason is that narratives can be awfully long. A novel, for example, may consist of thousands of propositions. How could we remember all of these propositions let alone remember them in the correct order? When we read or hear a sentence, we forget the exact words that it contained and remember a proposition coding its meaning. Perhaps we do something similar with the propositions that make up a narrative, such as recode them into an even more general form.

Episodes

An episode can be defined as a set of propositions that are related to one another in some way. According to Mandler and Johnson (1977), the most basic sort of episode would be one chunking together three events: a beginning event which causes a development event which in turn causes an ending event. My example about John being bored, going to town, and not being bored anymore could be seen as describing an episode. In a real story, the beginning, development, and ending events could actually subsume a good many subevents described by a number of propositions. Furthermore, a story—such as a novel or a movie—may be composed of a number of episodes. According to Mandler and Johnson (1977), the episode, not the sentence or proposition, is the basic unit of story recall. If this true, then the surface structure of a narrative—especially if it just elaborates the expression of an episode—should be poorly recalled. Mandler and Johnson (1977) constructed stories with the same number of episodes but varied the numbers of words. Some of the stories were told concisely. Others expressed the same number of episodes in a more long-winded fashion. The number of words used in a story had no effect on recall of the stories. This supports the idea that episodes are the basic units. If words or sentences were the units of recall, stories with more words should be less well remembered.

Black and Bower (1979) wrote stories composed of several episodes. Some of the episodes were realized by a lot of propositions. Others were realized by only a few. Episodes that were realized by more propositions were better recalled, but the number of propositions expressing any one episode did not affect recall of other episodes no matter how many propositions expressed these other episodes; that is, just because one episode subsumed a lot of actions did not interfere with memory for other episodes. If propositions rather than episodes were the basic units of story memory, this would not have been the case. Why? We can only remember so many chunks of information about a narrative. If these chunks are episodes, then the number of subchunks (propositions) one episode contains should have no effect on memory for other episodes. On the other hand, if these chunks were propositions, then the number of propositions should have a direct effect on memory.

Mandler (1978) constructed a story containing two episodes. However, in the surface structure, the two episodes were interleaved. One sentence concerned the first episode, the second sentence concerned the other episode, the third sentence concerned the first episode, and so on. When asked to recall the story, subjects clustered the sentences concerning the two episodes; that is, they tended to recall all of the sentences concerning one episode, then all of the sentences concerning the other one. Such clustering suggests that subjects had assimilated the propositions expressed by the sentences to deeper-level episode units.

If episodes are the basic units in which narratives are coded, it should not make too much difference exactly how they are realized. Baggett (1979) constructed parallel versions of the same narrative consisting of 14 basic episodes. One version was a printed text. The other was a motion picture without words. One group of subjects read the text, while another group watched the movie. Recall was very similar for both groups; that is, both groups recalled about the same number of episodes and the same details about them. The medium (text versus film) was relatively unimportant. This supports the idea that deep-level episodes—rather than medium-specific (verbal or visual) propositions—are important in story recall.

If people understand and recall stories by assimilating them to episode units, understanding and recall should be poor if the stories do not fit these schemata very well; that is, ungrammatical stories should be poorly recalled. Thorndyke (1977) constructed two versions of a story. One version was a normal story. In the other, the propositions were randomly reordered, and all causal and connective propositions were deleted. Thus, it was not made explicit that one component of an episode had caused or brought about the next component of the episode. As would be expected, recall for the normal, grammatical stories was much better than memory for the disordered stories. Episode units can also act like procrustean beds. That is, if a story does not fit a schema, subjects often elaborate their memories of it so that the story does fit (Glenn, 1978). For example, events or reactions that are not explicitly stated in the story (but must logically have occurred according to the episode schema) may be added to one's memory and are then recalled as if they were actually part of the original story. For example, in my story about John going to town, I did not make it explicit that John went to town *because* he was bored. However, you probably filled in or deduced this implicit causal relationship.

Functions

Many episodes can be used to make up a story. Is it possible that there could be even deeper-level units that chunk together episodes? Perhaps we understand the meaning of episodes in terms of these deeper-level units. The first text grammar was proposed by the Russian folklorist, Vladimir Propp (1928). Propp worked with a collection of 100 Russian fairy tales. He noted that these tales have a wide variety of episodes and characters but that their plots are quite similar. His contention was that the plot of a story is made up of a series of functions. He defined a *function* as "an act of a character, defined from the point of view of its significance for the course of the action." A function is, in other words, an action or episode that is significant for the development of the plot of the story.
    Propp asks us to consider the following episodes:

1.   A tsar gives an eagle to a hero. The eagle carries the hero away to another kingdom.
2.   An old man gives Sucenko a horse. The horse carries Sucenko away to another kingdom. . . . (Propp, 1928:19–20)

These episodes are clearly similar to one another, although they differ considerably in their specifics. Propp asks us to ignore these details. When we do this, we see that in each case, two events are described. First, the protagonist receives something. The surrounding context—not given in these excerpts—makes clear that this thing is a magical agent. Second, this magical agent transfers the protagonist to another location. Such general classes of action—receipt of a magical agent or transfer by a magical agent—are what Propp called functions.
    Stories, Propp argued, are composed from a limited number of functions. To be specific, Propp showed that only 31 functions (for example, departure, return, lack, liquidation of lack) are necessary to describe the plots of his entire set of 100 fairy tales. Of course, we would expect to get a somewhat different list of functions if we looked at a set of stories other than Russian fairy tales. However, the point is that we should be able to find such a list of functions no matter what type of stories we examined. Furthermore, the list would hypothetically be quite similar to the list found for the fairy tales.

Metafunctions

There are several problems with Propp's grammar. Later theorists have raised several questions about the lexicon of functions. One question has to do with whether the 31 functions are really the ultimate units of narrative. If we can equate such diverse events as getting a horse from an old man and getting an eagle from the tsar under one rubric, why do we have to stop there? How do we know that this is the right level of abstraction. Perhaps the process should be continued so that similar functions would be grouped together to form even more abstract metafunctions. Maybe Propp discovered the alphabet of narratives rather than the distinctive features.

Propp himself pointed out that many of his functions are related to one another by a principle of inversion. For example, lack is the inverse of liquidation of lack just as departure is the inverse of return. This gives us a clue that we might be able to group the functions into a smaller number of metafunctions. Indeed, Todorov (1971) says that we can group together Propp's 31 functions into 5 metafunctions. Two of these have to do with states of EQUILIBRIUM, two with states of TRANSITION and one with states of DISEQUILIBRIUM. We might see these metafunctions as being the ultimate distinctive features of any narrative. (We shall describe Todorov's theory in more detail when we take up the topic of narrative syntax or sequencing.)

NARRATIVE REALIZATION AND ASSIMILATION

The successive levels of abstraction that we have just described would fit nicely into the episodic analyzer, as illustrated in Figure 14–1. The basic idea is this: When people hear or read a narrative, they decode the sentences into propositions. This decoding corresponds to activation of proposition units at the highest level of the episodic analyzer. After several of these proposition units have been activated, a deeper level episode unit is activated. In a simple story, only a few propositions may be necessary to bring about this activation. In a longer story,

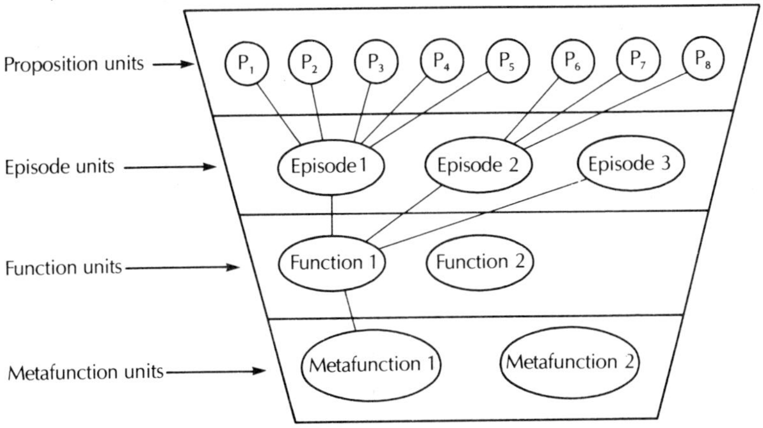

FIGURE 14–1　A hierarchical narrative grammar is a description of the structure of the episodic analyzer

the episode may be described by many propositions. This episode unit will tend to activate an even deeper-level function unit. Depending upon how long or complex the story is, only one or very many episode units may converge on the same function unit. Finally, the function unit activates the metafunction unit to which it is connected. In a long novel, thousands of propositions, hundreds of episodes, and five or ten functions may be decoded before a metafunction unit—for example, disequilibrium—is fully activated.

In this view, understanding and remembering a story involves assimilating it to a hierarchically arranged set of proposition, episode, function, and metafunction units. This hierarchy of units could be called the story schema. Although they differ in their details, this is the view accepted by most current theories of text grammar (for example, Kintsch and van Dijk, 1978; Mandler and Johnson, 1977; Thorndyke, 1977). In order to create rather than to understand a story, one operates the system in reverse. This is evidently a lot easier said than done, since it is much easier to understand a good story than to create one.

NARRATIVE SYNTAX

Propp's finite-state syntax

The syntax of Propp's text grammar (1928) is simple and straightforward: The 31 functions occur in an invariant order. Propp's narrative grammar can be called a finite-state grammar. There are a finite number of states (functions), and they have to be used in one order. Each function can be realized in two ways: it can be deleted altogether or it can be expressed as a set of one or more episodes. In turn, these episodes are expressed as a set of one or more propositions. These are, in turn, expressed as sentences. Once this is done, one goes to the next function. Finally, when one has gone through the entire list of functions, the narrative is completed. To some extent, the order of functions is dictated by the nature of reality. The hero cannot very well return until he has left in the first place. In other cases, though, the reason for the sequence is unclear. Why, for example, should reconnaissance always follow violation? There is no question that the plots of Russian fairy tales do unfold in the sequence described by Propp. The question is why this should be so. Propp does not give a satisfactory answer to this question, but a number of other theorists have tackled it.

Transformational narrative syntax

Todorov (1971) has argued that any narrative will deal with the following five metafunctions: EQUILIBRIUM$_1$ $\longrightarrow$ TRANSITION$_1$ $\longrightarrow$ DISEQUILIBRIUM $\longrightarrow$ TRANSITION$_2$ $\longrightarrow$ EQUILIBRIUM$_2$. Under each of these metafunctions could be grouped a number of Proppean functions. A full narrative would describe the full sequence: An initial state of affairs (EQUILIBRIUM$_1$) is changed in some way (TRANSITION$_1$) into a state of affairs that is opposite to it (DISEQUILIBRIUM). This state is then changed in some way (TRANSITION$_2$) so that we get back to a state that is analogous to the initial one (EQUILIBRIUM$_2$). Not all narratives trace the whole sequence, but Todorov says that any narrative must deal with a sequence of at least three metafunctions. Sad stories will deal with the first set of metafunctions: EQUILIBRIUM$_1$ $\longrightarrow$ TRANSITION$_1$ $\longrightarrow$ DISEQUI-

LIBRIUM. An example might be: ALL WAS PEACEFUL. BARBARIANS INVADED. THEN, ALL WAS RUIN AND CHAOS. Happier stories will describe the last set of metafunctions: DISEQUILIBRIUM $\longrightarrow$ TRANSITION$_2$ $\longrightarrow$ EQUILIBRI-UM$_2$. Here is an example: ALL WAS RUIN AND CHAOS. THE BARBARIANS WERE CIVILIZED. THEN, ALL WAS PEACEFUL (AGAIN). Note that Todorov's metafunctions are systematically related to one another. EQUILIBRIUM$_1$ and EQUILIBRI-UM$_2$ are at least partially identical. Both are the inverse of DISEQUILIBRIUM. TRANSITION$_1$ and TRANSITION$_2$ are also in an inverse relationship. This is because the first describes a movement from EQUILIBRIUM to DISEQUILIBRIUM while the second describes an opposite movement.

The match-mismatch principle and narration

Rather than talking about equilibrium and disequilibrium, we could talk about matches and mismatches. It strikes me that a disequilibrium will always involve some sort of mismatch. This could be a mismatch between, say, expectation and perception, wish and reality, or just about any other polarity. When we look at things in this way, we can put narration in the context of a number of other phenomena. Perception is a match-mismatch process. It involves an attempt to match an incoming stimulus with a set of preexisting cognitive units. If there is a perfect match, nothing happens other than passive recognition. A mismatch of one sort or another brings about arousal, attention, thought, and action. Depending upon how extreme the mismatch is, we will also observe pleasure or displeasure and interest or disinterest. All of this pleasure, interest, attention, thought, and action is aimed at removing the mismatch and replacing it by a perfect match. This end may be achieved by either changing internal schemata so that they fit perceptual reality or changing perceptual reality so that it fits the internal schemata. A narrative is a description of the sequence of events leading up to and/or following a mismatch. If this is so, then the ultimate text grammar is virtually the whole science of cognitive psychology. Actually cognitive psychology is, in large part, the study of the sequence of events brought about by a mismatch.

If narratives are about incongruity—about its creation, confrontation, and resolution—this has hedonic consequences. It tells us why people like stories. They like them because, as the Wundt curve tells us, they like at least medium degrees of incongruity. Mismatches, whether real or imaginary, give us pleasure so long as they are not too extreme. In the final analysis, it is difficult for the mismatches found in narratives to be too extreme. After all, a narrative is just a story. If it is too shocking, surprising, or discomforting, we can back off a bit and remind ourselves of this fact.

THE EXAMPLE OF EDGAR ALLAN POE'S NARRATIVES

Poe's master plot

As an example of how text grammar works, let's consider Edgar Allan Poe's tales. Elsewhere, I have argued that these tales fit nicely with Todorov's (1971) scheme (Martindale, 1973c). In several of Poe's stories, too much is buried. In "The Black Cat," the narrator kills his wife and inters her body in the cellar of their house. In his haste, however, he inadvertently buries a cat along with her. The police arrive, the cat yowls, and the wife's body is disinterred. In "The Tell-Tale Heart," the narrator kills an old man and hides his body under the floorboards of his room. He buries the man's watch along with him. The police arrive, the watch is heard ticking, and the man's body is disinterred. We can diagram the plot of these stories as shown in the first two rows of Figure 14–2. Each begins with an initial situation in which the two main characters are united in an unstable, un-

FIGURE 14–2   Diagrams of the plots of six of Poe's tales and of his metaphysical treatise, *Eureka,* showing similarity of structures. The elements in each column are similar for each of the narratives.

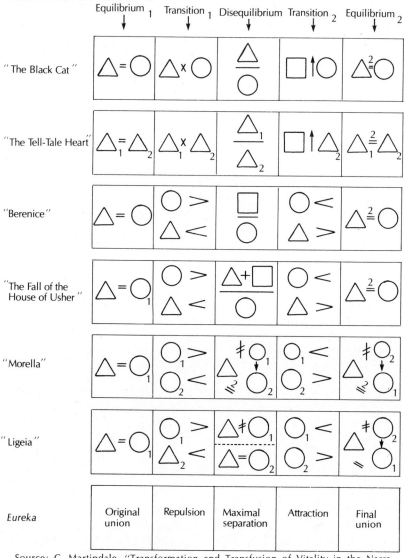

Source: C. Martindale, "Transformation and Transfusion of Vitality in the Narratives of Poe," *Semiotica* 7 (1973) pp. 47, 51–53.

clear, or ambivalent relationship (for example, $\triangle = 0$). They both love and hate each other. In the second column, we see that there is a transition in this relationship: One character is murdered (for example, $\triangle \times 0$). This is followed by burial of the secondary character, as shown in column 3 (for example, $\frac{\square}{0}$). The next major event, shown in column 4, is the exhumation of the buried character (for example, $\square \uparrow 0$). Each of the tales ends with some sort of reunion (for example, $\triangle \overset{2}{=} 0$). The hero is confronted with the transformed (that is, dead) body of the secondary character. The metafunctions diagrammed in Figure 14–2 are related as Todorov (1971) hypothesizes. Metafunctions 1 and 5 are analogous and both are the inverse of metafunction 3: There is union in columns 1 and 5 but maximal separation in column 3. Furthermore, columns 2 and 4 are in some senses opposites of each other. Column 2 concerns separation, while column 4 concerns reunion.

Although its surface structure is quite different, the deep structure of "Berenice" is quite similar to that of the two tales we have just discussed (see row 3 of Figure 14–2). Initially Berenice and Egaeus are united in an ambiguous relationship. Poe is rather mysterious as to exactly what is going on between the two. Gradually, Berenice loses energy and falls into a trance $(0 >)$. At the same time, Egaeus gains energy $(\triangle <)$—he becomes more and more oversensitive. Finally, Berenice seems to die and is buried. Egaeus falls into a trance $(\triangle >)$, exhumes Berenice's body, and extracts her teeth. Unfortunately, it is later discovered that Berenice was not actually dead. She has revived from her trance by the next morning $(0 <)$. We may presume that there is a final union $(\triangle \overset{2}{=} 0)$ that is different from the original one (if for no other reason than that Berenice no longer has any teeth).

The deep structure of "The Fall of the House of Usher" is exactly analogous (see row 4 of Figure 14–2). Roderick and Madelaine Usher are united in an ambivalent and ambiguous way. Madelaine weakens and falls into a trance while Roderick gains in nervous energy. Believing Madelaine to be dead, the narrator and Roderick place her body in the cellar. As soon as this is done, Roderick begins to lose energy. We learn later that Madelaine is at the same time gaining energy. In the end, she returns, clasps Roderick in her arms, and they die.

In another type of tale, there is a different sort of energy interchange. In "Morella," for example, we begin with the usual ambiguous relationship (see row 5 of Figure 14–2). Morella becomes pregnant. As the child grows in her womb, she weakens. At the moment of her daughter's birth, Morella dies. As the child grows up, she also grows sicker. Moreover, she comes to resemble Morella more and more. When she is ten years of age, she is baptized and given the name Morella. As soon as this is done, she dies and the ghostly words, "I am here," are heard. Morella has gradually possessed the child's body, and this possession becomes complete at the moment of baptism. "Ligeia" has a similar plot. It is diagrammed in row 6 of Figure 14–2. The major difference is that Ligeia dies in square 3 and the narrator marries someone else. This detail does not faze the plot or Ligeia's spirit. Ligeia gradually possesses the new wife until, at the climax, she is transmuted into Ligeia.

We can summarize the structure of all of these stories as shown in the bottom row of Figure 14–2. The first metafunction is an original ambiguous and/or ambivalent union between two characters. I have labeled the second metafunction repulsion. This metafunction can be realized as either murder or a transfer of energy. The third metafunction is one of maximal separation. This can be realized in several ways. A burial may or may not be explicitly described. If there is a burial, it does not seem to be crucial exactly who does the burying. At this point in the plot, the original union described by the first metafunction is inverted: there is now disjunction rather than conjunction. The fourth metafunction is the inverse of the second one. That is, whatever was done in the second part of the plot is undone in this part. If a character was buried, the character is dug up; if a character lost energy, this energy is regained. Finally, the fifth metafunction is in one sense identical to the first function. The original union is reestablished. The difference is that it is reestablished in a way that is unpleasant, destructive, and (probably the crucial thing) permanent.

Poe wrote a book titled *Eureka* in which he set forth a speculative theory of cosmology about the origin of the universe and its eventual end. The basis of the theory is the postulation of two opposing forces: repulsion (identified with electricity, light, heat, vitality, and consciousness) and attraction (identified with gravitation, darkness, coldness, death, and unconsciousness). The universe was at first, Poe held, in a state of original unity. The force of repulsion propelled everything away from the original center. At some time, this dispersion will reach a state of maximal expansion. Then, the force of attraction will become predominant, and everything will collapse back into a final unity. This sequence of events clearly follows the text grammar we have formulated to describe Poe's tales.

Poe's narrative world

The five metafunctions are related to one another in the way that Todorov's theory (1971) says that they should be. Theoretically, Todorov's general principles apply to any narratives, not just to Poe's stories. It is the content that Poe fits into the metafunctions that differentiate his stories from someone else's. The general rules of narration are particularized to deal with this content. This results in a narrative world that is markedly different from the real world. Some of the features of this world are rather peculiar. For one thing, the quantity of vitality seems to be constant in Poe's world. One character can become more energetic only at the expense of another, only by appropriating that character's energy. Worse still, this process does not equilibrate; that is, the quantity of vitality does not finally get evenly distributed among all of the characters. Rather, one character sucks up all of the energy until the other one seems to be dead. Then, the energy starts to flow in the other direction, and that tide cannot be stemmed either. What accounts for the creation of such a strange world? We shall deal with this question after considering some necessary background.

NARRATIVES AND THE EMOTIONAL SYSTEM

Motives as the constituents of narratives

We have said that narratives are composed of descriptions of actions. When we process a narrative, these actions are assimilated to hierarchical story schemas.

These schemas seem ultimately to have to do with classes of acts aimed at re-solving conflicts, incongruities, and the like. Of course, these deep structures can be realized in many different ways. The question arises, however, as to whether they can be realized in any way at all; that is, does it make any difference what specific actions are used in a narrative? Can a narrative be about any resolution of any incongruity or only about certain types of resolutions. A moment's thought reveals that some actions are a lot better candidates for a narrative than others.

We can construct any number of narratives that are perfectly grammatical and follow all of the rules discussed so far. But many of these narratives will be devoid of any interest. Here is an example: ON A DARK NIGHT IN OCTOBER, I WAS WRITING IN MY STUDY. SUDDENLY, MY PEN RAN OUT OF INK. I ROSE. I REFILLED THE PEN. I RESUMED MY DREARY TASK. I doubt that you would want to read an expanded version of this story. Yet, it is certainly a grammatical narra-tive. Disequilibrium sets in and is resolved. However, running out of ink is simply not good story material. Let's try another story: ON A DARK NIGHT IN OCTO-BER, I WAS WRITING IN MY STUDY. SUDDENLY, THE BLACK INK TURNED BLOOD RED. I DROPPED THE PEN AND ROSE IN TERROR. BUT THE PEN, HELD NOW BY SOME UNSEEN HAND, WROTE ON. THESE WERE THE WORDS THE GHOSTLY HAND INSCRIBED: UNLESS NARRATIVE UNITS ARE CONNECTED TO THE EMOTIONAL SYSTEM, A NARRATIVE WILL BE OF NO INTEREST. Thanks to the unseen hand, we have a hypothesis about our question. The units that tend to find their way into narratives are those connected to the emotional system. Recall that in Chapter 12 we defined cognitive units connected to the emotional system as motives. Narratives could in principle be composed of any episodic units at all, but in practice they are not. Why? Unless narratives concern motives, they will not be of interest. If they are not of interest, narrators will not use them. Even if they did, whoever was exposed to the narrative would not process it if there was any way to avoid doing so.

Murray's motivational narrative grammar

THEMAS

Henry Murray (1938) developed a theory that in many ways anticipated Shal-lice's theory of the action system (1978). While Murray was essentially interested in constructing a theory of personality, in so doing he more or less inadvertently constructed a narrative grammar. In order to test his personality theory, Murray (1943) developed the Thematic Apperception Test (TAT). This test consists of a series of somewhat ambiguous pictures. The subject's task is to make up an imaginative story about each of these pictures. Murray's idea is that the basic unit of a narrative is the *thema*. A thema has three components: *press* (a stim-ulus), *actone* (an action), and *need* (a motive). Note that a thema is rather like an event except that it also contains a need. Actually, a thema is exactly analogous to a primed action unit in the action system (see Figure 14–3). This figure shows two types of action units. The one on the left gets input from a stimulus unit and sends output to a response unit. However, it has no input from deeper-level units in the action system. Such a unit would correspond to a trivial or automatic action. The action unit on the right corresponds to what Murray calls a thema.

FIGURE 14–3   Murray's themas consist of combinations of press, actone, and motive. As shown, themas can be related to the action system.

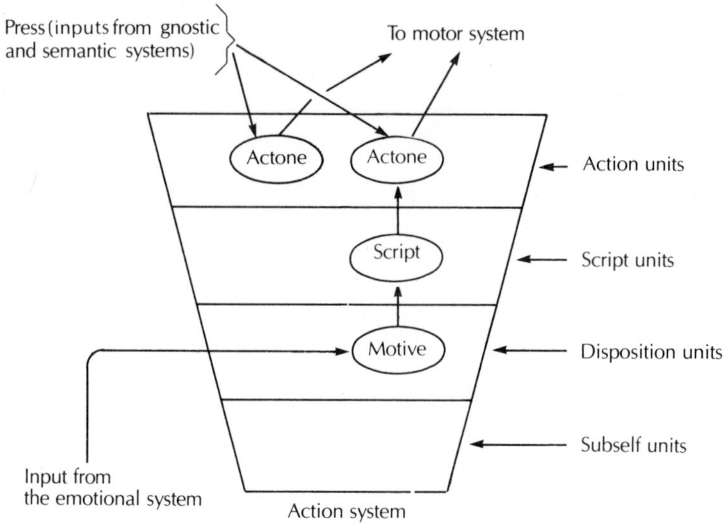

It gets input from both a stimulus unit (press) and a deeper-level unit (need), and it sends output to a response unit. Murray says that only events controlled by this sort of action unit turn up in a narrative. This considerably restricts the lexicon of units that can be used in narratives. The narrative grammars we have considered to this point do not make this restriction.

MOTIVES

While Murray says that the thema is the basic unit of narration, he argues that themas can be classified as expressions of a relatively small number of needs or motives. As illustrated in Figure 14–3, Murray's actones correspond to what we have called action units, while his motives may be seen as corresponding to what we have called dispositions. In a general sense, Murray's motives correspond to Propp's functions. Propp says that a narrative is a set of propositions that express a series of functions. Murray says that a narrative is a set of themas (motivationally relevant propositions) that expresses at least one motive. If Murray's theory is correct, then it is important to know what sorts of needs and presses there are. This would give us a specification of what sorts of things stories can be about. Murray (1938) did attempt to do just this, although he made no claim that his lists of needs and presses was the last word on the subject. Aside from visceral needs, such as hunger and thirst, Murray lists the 20 needs shown in Table 14–1. These, he says, can be grouped into four main categories: ascendance motivation (for example, *n* Dominance, *n* Autonomy), deference motivation (for example, *n* Deference, *n* Abasement), orderliness motivation (for example, *n* Order), and sensuousness motivation (for example, *n* Sex, *n* Sentience). Murray also attempted to enumerate the set of possible presses, but he was a good deal more tentative in this regard.

TABLE 14–1 Murray's needs

Need	Brief Definition
n Abasement	To submit passively to external force. To accept injury, blame, criticism, punishment. To surrender. To become resigned to fate. To admit inferiority, error, wrongdoing, or defeat. To confess and atone. To blame, belittle, or mutilate the self. To seek and enjoy pain, punishment, illness, and misfortune.
n Achievement	To accomplish something difficult. To master, manipulate, or organize physical objects, human beings, or ideas. To do this as rapidly and as independently as possible. To overcome obstacles and attain a high standard. To excel one's self. To rival and surpass others. To increase self-regard by the successful exercise of talent.
n Affiliation	To draw near and enjoyably co-operate or reciprocate with an allied other (an other who resembles the subject or who likes the subject). To please and win affection of a cathected object. To adhere and remain loyal to a friend.
n Aggression	To overcome opposition forcefully. To fight. To revenge an injury. To attack, injure, or kill another. To oppose forcefully or punish another.
n Autonomy	To get free, shake off restraint, break out of confinement. To resist coercion and restriction. To avoid or quit activities prescribed by domineering authorities. To be independent and free to act according to impulse. To be unattached, unconditioned, irresponsible. To defy conventions.
n Counteraction	To master or make up for a failure by restriving. To obliterate a humiliation by resumed action. To overcome weaknesses, to repress fear. To efface a dishonor by action. To search for obstacles and difficulties to overcome. To maintain self-respect and pride on a high level.
n Defendance	To defend the self against assault, criticism, and blame. To conceal or justify a misdeed, failure, or humiliation. To vindicate the ego.
n Deference	To admire and support a superior. To praise, honor, or eulogize. To yield eagerly to the influence of an allied other. To emulate an exemplar. To conform to custom.
n Dominance	To control one's human environment. To influence or direct the behavior of others by suggestion, seduction, persuasion, or command. To dissuade, restrain, or prohibit.
n Exhibition	To make an impression. To be seen and heard. To excite, amaze, fascinate, entertain, shock, intrigue, amuse, or entice others.
n Harmavoidance	To avoid pain, physical injury, illness, and death. To escape from a dangerous situation. To take precautionary measures.
n Infavoidance	To avoid humiliation. To quit embarrassing situations or to avoid conditions which may lead to belittlement: the scorn, derision, or indifference of others. To refrain from action because of the fear of failure.
n Nurturance	To give sympathy and gratify the needs of a helpless object: an infant or any object that is weak, disabled, tired, inexperienced, infirm, defeated, humiliated, lonely, dejected, sick, mentally confused. To assist an object in danger. To feed, help, support, console, protect, comfort, nurse, heal.
n Order	To put things in order. To achieve cleanliness, arrangement, organization, balance, neatness, tidiness, and precision.
n Play	To act for "fun" without further purpose. To like to laugh and make

TABLE 14–1 *(Continued)*

Need	Brief Definition
	jokes. To seek enjoyable relaxation of stress. To participate in games, sports, dancing, drinking parties, cards.
n Rejection	To separate oneself from a negatively cathected object. To exclude, abandon, expel, or remain indifferent to an inferior object. To snub or jilt an object.
n Sentience	To seek and enjoy sensuous impressions.
n Sex	To form and further an erotic relationship. To have sexual intercourse.
n Succorance	To have one's needs gratified by the sympathetic aid of an allied object. To be nursed, supported, sustained, surrounded, protected, loved, advised, guided, indulged, forgiven, consoled. To remain close to a devoted protector. To have always a supporter.
n Understanding	To ask or answer general questions. To be interested in theory. To speculate, formulate, analyze, and generalize.

Source: Extracted from *Explorations in Personality: A Clinical and Experimental Study of Fifty Men of College Age*, edited by Henry A. Murray (New York: Oxford University Press, 1938), pp. 152–226. Copyright 1938 by Oxford University Press, Inc. Renewed 1966 by Henry A. Murray. Reprinted by permission of the publisher.

CURRENT CONCERNS

It may be a hopeless enterprise to try to enumerate a fixed number of motives. Klinger (1971) suggests that a better concept is what he calls the *current concern*. A current concern is, in terms of our model, a deep-level unit in the action system that is at least temporarily activated, generally by the emotional system. It is activated when a goal is selected, and it remains activated until the goal is reached or the quest for it is abandoned. There are many more possible current concerns than there are needs in Murray's list. The best way of looking at Murray's list of needs is as a list of things that are most likely to become important current concerns. By the same token, his list of presses is simply a list of stimuli most likely to elicit or be linked with important current concerns.

THE NEED FOR ACHIEVEMENT PLOT

David McClelland and his colleagues have done extensive research concerned with scoring narratives for motivational content. Most of these narratives have been stories produced in response to Thematic Apperception Test stimuli, but similar scoring systems have also been applied to a variety of other narratives ranging from literary texts and children's readers to presidential addresses and popular ballads. The most extensively investigated need has been the need for achievement (n Achievement). McClelland et al. (1958) developed an objective system for assessing whether a narrative concerns n Achievement and, if so, to what extent it does so. The first decision in scoring a story for n Achievement concerns whether it contains any reference to an achievement goal. An achievement goal is "success in competition with some standard of excellence." Such a goal may be indicated by (1) overt reference to such a goal, (2) a character in a story accomplishing something unique, or (3) a character in a story being involved in long-term pursuit of a goal for its own sake.

If any of these themes is present, the story is then scored for how much of the complete *n* Achievement plot the story contains. This plot is diagrammed in Figure 14–4. A story receives one point for each of the components of the plot that is present:

FIGURE 14–4   The *n* Achievement plot

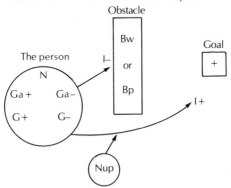

Source: D. C. McClelland, J. W. Atkinson, R. A. Clark, and E. L. Lowell, "A Scoring Manual for the Achievement Motive," in *Motives in Fantasy, Action, and Society,* ed. J. W. Atkinson (Princeton, N.J.: Van Nostrand, 1958), p. 180.

1. Stated need for achievement (*N*). A character in the story explicitly states a desire to reach an achievement goal.
2. Instrumental activity in pursuit of an achievement goal. This activity can be successful (I+), unsuccessful (I–), or doubtful as to its outcome (I?). The crucial thing is trying, not what happens.
3. Anticipatory goal states. A character anticipates goal attainment (Ga+) or failure (Ga–). Again, the emotion, not whether it is positive or negative, is the crucial factor.
4. Obstacles or blocks hindering achievement of the goal. These can be caused by a person (Bp) or by the world in general (Bw).
5. Nurturant Press (Nup). Another character helps the character in pursuit of the achievement goal.
6. Affective states associated with goal attainment (G+) or failure to reach the goal (G–).
7. Achievement Thema (Ach Th). The story gets an extra point if the achievement plot is the central or only plot in the story.

Heyns, Veroff, and Atkinson (1958) constructed a scoring scheme for *n* Affiliation. It is almost identical to the one for *n* Achievement except, of course, the goal is affiliation rather than achievement. Similarly, Veroff (1958) constructed another analogous system to measure *n* Power. Here the goal is power—control or influence over another person. The basic idea behind all of these scoring schemes or text grammars is that a narrative is generated by a mismatch (discrepancy between an imagined state of affairs and a goal). However, not just any mismatch will do. It has to concern an important motive. These measures of n Achievement, n Affiliation, and n Power are reliable; that is, different scorers agree in their ratings of stories. They are also valid in the sense that people who might reasonably be expected to have high levels of a given need tend to write stories that express that need (see Atkinson, 1958).

Archetypes

We said that functions are expressions or realizations of deeper-level metafunction units. Could motives or dispositions be connected to such deeper-level units? In Chapter 12, we argued that dispositions are connected to subself units. Closely related to the notion of the subself is Jung's concept of the *archetype* (1953). Archetypes are, according to Jung, universal forms that collate certain classes of dispositions. Examples of archetypes would include the wise old man, God, and the great mother. The ego in Jung's terms corresponds to our concept of the dominant subself. Another archetype, the shadow, hypothetically collects together and represents all of the dispositions that a person finds personally distasteful, bad, or evil. These thoughts, feelings, and actions are part of the person's action system, but the person does not approve of or identify with them. On the other hand, the persona subsumes or collates the actions representing a person's public personality. The animus and the anima are especially important archetypes. They represent the dispositions a person has that are generally felt to be appropriate to the opposite sex. In a woman, the animus represents her masculine traits. In a man, the anima represents his feminine traits.

Archetypes are not images but deep-level chunking nodes. Confusion arises because these units tend to become connected with image units. The specific image that they become connected with will vary from person to person. More confusion arises, Jung says, because we tend to project these images; that is, we think of archetypes as external objects or people rather than as parts of ourselves. The most common example of this is falling in love. When a man falls in love, he projects his anima archetype onto a specific woman. When a woman falls in love, it is her animus archetype that is projected. Think of what happens when you are in love. The loved person has a strange and wonderful power. His or her presence arouses profound emotions. This is a general characteristic of archetypes. When they enter consciousness, they are accompanied by strong emotions. These emotions may be positive, as when we fall in love. They may also be strong feelings of the numinous or holy, the uncanny, or the ineffable and otherworldly in the case of other archetypes. The reason for this is presumably that the archetype units are connected with very deep levels of the emotional system.

In Jung's view, the characters in narratives should tend to be representations of archetypes. The action or plot of a narrative should describe the resolution of some sort of opposition between archetypes. Archetypal representations are ubiquitous in narratives. Jung would say that all narratives are about archetypes. It could not be otherwise. Narratives are about actions and motives that are ultimately subsumed by some archetype (subself) or the other. To the extent that a narrative approaches a description of the thoughts, emotions, and actions that are most prototypical of archetypes, it will be of interest. It will survive. Jung says that this is the case with myths and great works of literature.

INTERPRETING NARRATIVES

Allegory and symbolism

How do we know what a narrative is about? Any story has a literal meaning. It is simply about the actions and events that it describes. However, we know that narratives can also symbolize actions and events that they do not literally describe. In some cases, we know this because the narrator explicitly tells us. This is the case with fables and allegories. Consider the fable about the ant and the grasshopper. The ant stores food for winter and the grasshopper does not. Winter comes and the grasshopper is in trouble. This story is not really about ants and grasshoppers at all. Rather, everyone agrees that it is about lazy and industrious people. In the case of fables, the author often attaches a moral at the end just in case the reader has missed the point. Allegories are also about something other than the literal story that they tell. Remember John Bunyan's *Pilgrim's Progress*. In case the reader is so naive as to be tempted to understand the story literally, Bunyan gives hints by naming the characters so as to suggest what they represent—Christian, Mr. Goodheart, and so on.

Freudian interpretation

GENERAL THEORY

What about narratives where the narrator provides no hints as to the symbolic meaning of the narrative? Why should we assume that a narrative necessarily has such a symbolic meaning? The general reason is that we like or dislike it more than seems reasonable on the basis of the literal meaning. Some stories are fascinating, but we cannot say why. They do not seem to be about any motive or goal that is of concern to us. This leads us to suspect that there is more to them than meets the eye. How are we to proceed in such cases? Freud (1900) suggests one method in his book on *The Interpretation of Dreams*. His idea was that dreams are wish fulfillments—often of a symbolic nature. Although he first worked out his theory to apply to dreams, Freud himself generalized this idea to the hypothesis that all narratives (for example, fantasies, literary stories, and myths as well as dreams) are symbolic wish fulfillments and that this is the reason that they give us pleasure. The dream as told is a narrative. Freud called it the manifest content. It gives the literal meaning of the dream. His desire was to infer what he called the latent content. This is the symbolic meaning of the dream. Since Freud thought that dreams are wish fulfillments, he said that the latent content would be a straightforward statement of what the wish behind a particular dream was. Freud said that the reason it is not always obvious that a narrative is a wish fulfillment is that this fact is often disguised. That is, the hypothesis is that a narrative is a disguised wish fulfillment. The disguising features are especially likely to be present when the wish being fulfilled is one that would arouse anxiety, guilt, or shame if the narrator knew it was being expressed.

We might cast Freud's idea into the form of an equation:

$$\text{Narrative} = K_1 \times (\text{Wish}) + K_2 \times (\text{Defense})$$

In this equation, K_1 and K_2 would be weights expressing how strong the wish and the defenses against the wish were. Consider first a case where K_2 is 0. Such a case might arise if the wish concerned a motive, such as thirst. Most of us have no guilt about taking a drink of water when we are thirsty. Let's say that one becomes thirsty while sleeping. Freud says that a dream about drinking would be likely in this case. Why not just get up and get a drink? Because the sleeper wants to remain sleeping. It is easier to dream. In this case, the dream should be a straightforward wish fulfillment.

We can integrate Freud's hypothesis with the model of the action system developed in Chapter 12 (see Figure 14–5A). The thirst motive excites an action

FIGURE 14–5   Freudian wishes can be seen as motive units in the action system (A). Displacement and symbolism could be due to the activity of off-units in the action system (B).

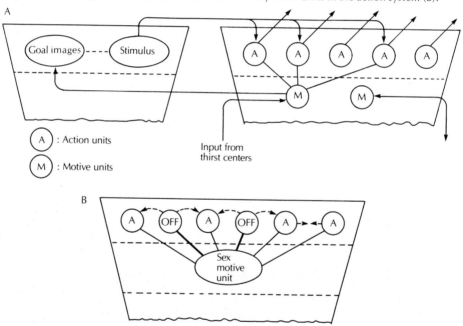

unit connected with drinking. In turn, this action unit excites its goal image (water). Since dreaming occurs in a primary process state, the goal image is not inhibited by the unit coding its opposite (lack of water). Thus, in a primary process state, the wish activates the unit coding the wished for object. This activation constitutes satisfaction of the wish. There is no need to resort to real action.

THE DREAM WORK

What about cases where the motive would arouse anxiety? In such cases, Freud argued that latent and manifest content are related by five distorting

transformations: displacement, symbolization, condensation, secondary elaboration, and concretization. Together, these transformations perform what Freud
called the dream work (see Figure 14–6). These transformations tell us in general

FIGURE 14–6   Freud's theory of the dream work

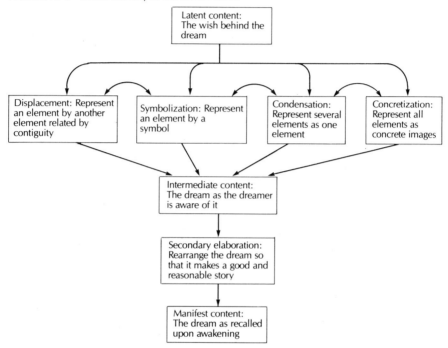

how manifest and latent content are related to one another. As we saw in Chapter 12, these transformations are likely in any primary process state regardless
of whether or not an anxiety arousing motive is activated or not. However, Freud
did not see things this way. In Figure 14–5B, I show how we could wire up an
analyzer to work in a Freudian manner. Consider a wish where the motive involved is sex, and the problem is that the action units of highest typicality (that
is, those most strongly connected with the motive unit) will arouse anxiety if
they are activated. They may be repressed by off-units so that this situation will
not arise. The idea is that the motive unit is connected in an excitatory fashion
with the off-unit. Thus, when the motive unit is activated, it activates the off-unit,
and the off-unit laterally inhibits surrounding units coding specific sexual thoughts
or acts. The result should be that the motive unit now activates only action units
of low typicality; that is, it activates units that are only weakly or remotely connected to the motive unit. This is what is involved in symbolization and displacement. Consider two people with the same amount of sexual drive. The person
with low guilt or anxiety may dream directly about sexual intercourse. The person
with high guilt may dream about an action—such as kissing or having a conversation with a member of the opposite sex—that is less directly connected with
the motive unit. Actually, the more the motive was activated, the more indirectly
we might expect to see it expressed in a defensive person. Why? Because activa-

tion of the motive unit also activates the off-units. The more the motive is activated, the more the off-units are activated and the more they laterally inhibit on-units coding sexual actions. Freud did make this prediction, but he did not express it in these terms.

FREE ASSOCIATION

The Freudian rules concerning transformations give us a hint about how manifest and latent content are related, but they do not give us the specific meaning of dream elements. Freud's approach was to have the dreamer free associate to each dream element. Say that the dream concerned reading a book in a library when, all of a sudden, a snake emerged from the book. Freud's approach would be to have the dreamer say everything that came to mind about reading, books, snakes, and libraries. The rationale is essentially that the associations would provide context that will allow one to infer the meaning of each dream element. This is essentially the way that one infers the meaning of anything when this meaning cannot be directly determined. Consider these associations:

A LIBRARY is dark.

A LIBRARY is warm.

A LIBRARY is peaceful.

All of my needs are met in a LIBRARY.

I feel like a child when I am in a LIBRARY.

My mother has a LIBRARY.

Now, a Freudian might be tempted to say that LIBRARY symbolizes WOMB. Why? Because we could substitute WOMB for LIBRARY in each sentence and all of the sentences would still make sense. In interpreting the library dream, the Freudian would also want to get associations to the other dream elements and translate them also. The whole translation would have to be internally coherent. Also, it would have to be a translation without remainder; that is, all of the details would have to be accounted for. It would hardly do to say that the dream symbolized a return to the womb, but the book and snake were just extra and had no meaning. Much of psychoanalytic theory is speculative and unscientific. However, in some of his earlier work, Freud made quite testable hypotheses about what would today be called narrative grammar. We see an example of this in his analysis of the case of Schreber.

CONTEXTUAL ASSOCIATES AND THE CASE OF SCHREBER

There is nothing in Freud's method that absolutely requires that the narrator be present to give free associations. The point is to find the context of the narrative elements. In a long narrative, the narrative itself provides this context. Freud (1911) himself used this method in his analysis of the autobiography of Daniel Paul Schreber (1903). Schreber was a judge who got it into his head that God had changed him into a woman so that he could give (re)birth to Christ. In fact, God had done nothing of the sort. Schreber was quite deluded in his beliefs, and this is why Freud was interested in his autobiography. In the autobiography,

Schreber talked a lot about God and/or the sun impregnating him. Freud (1911) argued that the sun and God really symbolized Schreber's father; that is, the real root of his psychosis was a homosexual attraction toward his own father. Rather than being stated directly, this attraction was represented in a symbolic fashion. Ultimately, Freud's reason for this hypothesis was that the delusions made sense—or at least made more sense—if FATHER was substituted for SUN and GOD.

Laffal (1965) did a statistical analysis of Schreber's autobiography that supports Freud's hypothesis. There are almost no direct references to Schreber's father in his autobiography. However, there are lots of references to various other males. Laffal reasoned that if SUN and GOD symbolize Schreber's father, they could be considered male symbols. If this were the case, then SUN, GOD, and MALE should occur in similar contexts; that is, the sentences containing these key words should tend to contain other words that are the same. On the other hand, sentences concerning FEMALES should contain a very different set of words. SUN, GOD, and MALE should be mutually substitutable for each other, but they should not be substitutable for FEMALE. Laffal went through Schreber's autobiography and selected all of the sentences containing a reference to one of the four categories: SUN, GOD, MALE, or FEMALE. Then he tabulated the other words in each type of sentence. In fact, the sentences referring to SUN and GOD were more similar in their content to the sentences referring to MALES than to those referring to FEMALES.

ARE NARRATIVES WISH FULFILLMENTS?

Is it true that narratives are wish fulfillments? Only partially. A lot of research has been done on the topic. The general procedure has been to deprive people of something so as to arouse a motive and then have them write narratives. For example, we could make people hungry and then have them write narratives. Would they write stories about eating? The general result of such studies is that arousal of a motive leads people to write narratives *about* that motive but these stories are not necessarily about fulfillment of the motive (Klinger, 1971; McClelland et al., 1953). Thus, arousal of a motive leads people to compose narratives about the actions connected with the motive. Hungry people write stories about food but these stories do not necessarily describe successful quests for food.

DRIVE AND DEFENSE IN NARRATIVES

There is a good bit of support for Freud's idea that narratives are the product of a compromise between drive and defense. For example, Clark and Sensibar (1955) showed male subjects slides of nude females and then had them write fantasy stories. These stories contained less sexual content than stories written by subjects who had not seen the slides. However, the stories of sexually aroused subjects contained more content that raters agreed indirectly symbolized sexual activity. Why? Perhaps because the formal setting made the sexually aroused subjects guilty about expressing their sexual motivation. This seems to have been the case. The experiment was repeated, but this time it was conducted by an attractive female experimenter rather than by a male experimenter as before. Now the sexually aroused subjects' stories had even less sexual content than before. On the other hand, when the experiment was repeated in the context of a fraternity beer party, the stories of sexually aroused subjects (those who had seen the slides) contained more sexual content than the stories of control subjects. Leiman and Epstein (1961) gave their subjects questionnaires to find out two things: how guilty they felt about sex and how deprived they were of sex. They also had these subjects compose fantasy narratives. For low-guilt subjects, the more deprived of sex they had recently been, the more sexual content their stories contained. Just the opposite was found for high-guilt people. The more sexually deprived they were, the less sexual content their stories contained.

The monomyth

THE GRAMMAR OF THE MONOMYTH

The type of narrative that deals with a quest for some valuable object or power has many variations. A lot of myths deal with this plot. In fact, it is so common in myth and literature in general that Campbell (1949) calls it the *monomyth*. Campbell provides us with a grammar of this type of quest narrative (see Figure 14–7). The basic plot is as follows: The hero sets out from the everyday world.

FIGURE 14–7   Narrative grammar for the monomyth

Source: Joseph Campbell, *The Hero with a Thousand Faces*, Bollingen Series XVII. Copyright 1949 by Princeton University Press. Copyright © renewed 1976 by Princeton University Press. Diagram from p. 245 reprinted by permission of Princeton University Press.

He reaches what Campbell calls the *threshold of adventure*. This can be realized in a variety of ways. Generally, the basic plot involves descent into some sort of underworld, the destruction or overcoming of a dragon, and the saving of an anima figure whom the hero often marries. Often, too, the hero obtains some treasure or elixir that had been guarded by the dragon. After this, the hero returns to the everyday world. Often, this return involves a rebirth of some sort. The hero has been changed into a more powerful person. He is now in a position to benefit mankind or himself in some way.

JUNGIAN INTERPRETATION OF THE MONOMYTH

The Jungian translation of the monomyth would be that consciousness (the hero) regresses (goes on the journey to the underworld), eludes or binds the negative or dangerous aspects of primary process thought (kills the dragon), and returns to a secondary process state united with the beneficent qualities of primary process thought (treasure or power). Such regression-and-return is the hypothetical basis of all creative or original ideas (see Chapter 15). Indeed in quest myths, the impetus for the descent often has to do with a situation or difficulty that cannot be met by conventional thought and action. It is interesting that, in most of these myths, there is a detail that lends credibility to the Jungian interpretation. The hero usually overpowers the evil forces of the underworld not by brute force but by thought, cunning, or trickery. Perseus gets around the fact that he cannot look directly at Medusa by using his shield as a mirror; Odysseus has himself tied to a mast so that he may hear the sirens' songs without being overwhelmed; Theseus unwinds a ball of string so that he may find his way out of the labyrinth. In each case, it is the secondary process qualities of foresight, planning, and analysis that assure victory.

TRENDS IN THE CONTENT OF MONOMYTHS

The Jungian interpretation of the monomyth says that it symbolizes a movement from a secondary process state of consciousness to a primary process state and then a return to a secondary process state. If this is true, then we can make a prediction about the types of words used throughout such narratives. The prediction is quite straightforward: If we segmented a monomyth narrative, we should find relatively few primary process words in the initial segments. Then, the percentage of primary process words should gradually rise to a peak, after which they should decline. Why? If the narrative is about moving to a primary process state and then returning from it, then this should show up in word usage. Otherwise, how would anyone ever have gotten the idea that this was what the narrative was about in the first place?

I tested this prediction with five monomyth narratives (Martindale, 1979b). Three of the narratives described a journey to and a return from hell: Book 6 of Virgil's *Aeneid*, the first 60 cantos of Dante's *Divine Comedy*, and the *Tibetan Book of the Dead*. Two of the narratives were alchemical narratives describing a journey to and return from a region analogous to hell or the underworld: *Aurora Consurgens* (von Franz, 1966), and the parable given in Silberer (1917). Each of these narratives was keypunched and divided into short segments. Then, these segments were analyzed with the Regressive Imagery Dictionary (Martindale, 1975), which was described in Chapter 13. The results of this analysis are shown in Figure 14–8. As you can see, primary process content does increase and then decrease as predicted. Statistical tests showed that this pattern was significant for all five of the narratives.

WHAT WERE POE'S TALES REALLY ABOUT?

All of the narratives analyzed in the previous section describe successful journeys. The hero returns alive and well. Moreover, he is in some sense reborn.

FIGURE 14–8   Amount of primary process content in successive segments of five monomyth narratives

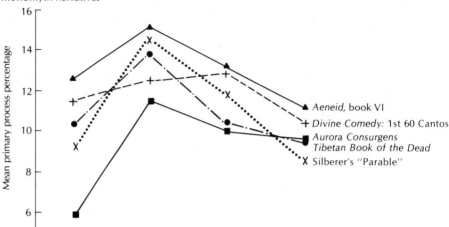

Source: C. Martindale, "The Night Journey: Trends in the Content of Narratives Describing Transformation of Conciousness," *Journal of Altered States of Consciousness* 4 (1979):329.

What about the opposite case, where there may be a journey of some sort but it ends in death and defeat rather than in victory. Most of Edgar Allan Poe's tales are of this type. The burial tales can be interpreted as follows. The hero (secondary process consciousness) tries to bury (repress) the secondary character (the unconscious). But this attempt fails. The unconscious wells up and overwhelms the conscious mind. According to psychoanalytic theory, such an attempt at repression is always unsuccessful (Fenichel, 1945). The unconscious has all of the energy in the psyche. If the conscious mind attempts to wall it off, then consciousness will necessarily run out of energy. When it does so, the repression will collapse and whatever was buried (repressed) will return.

In terms of our model, we might want to put this as follows: if one tries to keep one set of cognitive units continually activated, they will eventually fatigue (sink into the unconscious). Whatever units they were laterally inhibiting (repressing) will then be disinhibited and will seize or overwhelm consciousness. If we place this activity in the action system, it does make some sense: if a subself unit and its component dispositions are kept very activated so as to laterally inhibit (repress) surrounding units, eventually the activated units will fatigue and consciousness will be seized by a disinhibited alien subself and its component dispositions. Regardless of exactly how we express the idea, note that this line of reasoning explains what happens in Poe's tales. The reason that the hero (secondary process consciousness or the set of activated cognitive units) runs out of energy is that he has sealed off the source of his energy. Because of this, the buried character gets more and more energy. Eventually the hero's energy is exhausted and the buried character bursts forth. If this is the case, then we can make a prediction about the trend of primary process content. It should decline as the secondary character weakens and is buried. Since the burial hypothetically represents a triumph of the dominant subself or of secondary process consciousness, primary process content should be low at the point of burial. However, primary process content should begin to increase as the hero loses energy and the buried character revives and returns from the grave. We would expect this pattern in narratives such as "Ligeia," "The Fall of the House of Usher," and "Berenice," all of which describe unsuccessful burial attempts. On the other hand, Poe did write several narratives about successful burial, such as "Eleonora" and "The Cask of Amontillado," which are variants of the typical monomyth. In these cases, we would expect the pattern of increasing and then decreasing primary process content. I analyzed these five narratives using the Regressive Imagery Dictionary (Martindale, 1978b). The results, shown in Figure 14–9, were as predicted. Statistical tests showed that the difference in trend between the two types of narrative was significant.

FIGURE 14–9 Amount of primary process content in successive segments of Edgar Allan Poe's narratives about successful burial and about unsuccessful burial

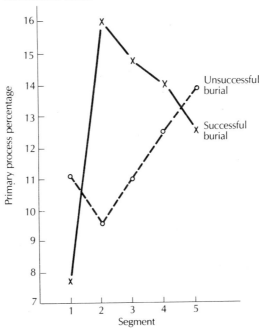

Source: C. Martindale, "A Quantitative Analysis of Diachronic Patterns in Some Narratives of Poe," *Semiotica* 22 (1978):300.

SUMMARY AND CONCLUSIONS

Regardless of how it is presented, a story is initially understood as a series of propositions. The units coding these propositions hypothetically activate deeper-level units coding episodes, functions, and metafunctions. Thus, a story is ultimately understood by assimilating it to a hierarchical story schema defined by these units. Narratives seem to describe the transformation of a state of equilibrium into a state of disequilibrium and/or the transformation of a state of disequilibrium into a state of equilibrium. In general, then, they describe either the creation or the resolution of a mismatch between a goal and a state of affairs. Usually, they deal with the resolution of such a mismatch. We noted that this coincides with the fact that mismatches generate attention, thought, and action and that narratives describe these processes.

Many potential stories would be perfectly grammatical but will never be produced. It would seem that the material that can be used in a narrative is severely constrained. Unless a narrative is about a mismatch involving a fairly important and universal motive, no one will take much interest in it. Given the effort involved in producing and processing all but the simplest stories, this means that virtually all narratives will concern a rather small number of motives. This is because there are not very many important motives. It would also seem to follow that there would not be very many basic plots either. Long before the current interest in text grammars, psychologists, such as Murray, Freud, and Jung, more or less unwittingly proposed such grammars based on the assumption that narratives are about motives.

Some narratives seem to grasp our interest to an extent that seems surprising given their manifest content. This suggests that they are symbolic, that they are about something other than they seem to be on the surface. We described Freud's ideas about how symbolic narratives can be encoded and decoded and saw that there is empirical evidence supportive of at least some of his assertions. The monomyth or quest plot is perhaps the most widespread plot in myth and literature. Although stories based upon it often have a good deal of intrinsic interest and excitement, the fascination this theme exerts suggests that it may have a deeper symbolic meaning. Jung hypothesized that the plot symbolizes alteration in consciousness—a descent into the unconscious and a successful or profitable return. Quantitative studies of trends in primary process content across the course of monomyth narratives are supportive of this idea. We saw that part of the horror in horror stories, such as some of Edgar Allan Poe's narratives, may arise from their symbolization of pathological alteration in consciousness—an unsuccessful attempt to escape from the unconscious.

15

Creativity

DEFINITION OF CREATIVITY

Originality and appropriateness

A creative idea is one that is original and useful or appropriate for the situation in which it occurs. By original, I mean that the idea is novel. No one has had it before. To say that an idea must be useful or appropriate as well as unusual in order to be creative allows us to differentiate between what is creative on the one hand and what is bizarre, odd, or ridiculous on the other. The notion that the activation of cognitive units is maintained by combustion of gasoline is, so far as I know, an original one. I am pretty sure that it is also a stupid idea. It does not fit with anything we know about cognition, biology, or drinking habits. We would hardly want to label it as creative. Insane people often have ideas that are deviant and unusual, but these ideas are not, in general, creative ones since they are inappropriate and unrealistic.

Remote associations

Creative productions are always novel combinations of preexisting elements. As the French mathematician, Henri Poincaré (1913) put it, "To create consists of making new combinations of associative elements which are useful." Creative ideas, he went on to say, "reveal to us unsuspected kinships between other facts well known but wrongly believed to be strangers to one another. Among chosen combinations the most fertile will often be those formed of elements drawn from domains which are far apart." The poet André Breton (quoted by Mednick, 1962) said much the same about creative productions: they show a "capacity to grasp two mutually distant realities without going beyond the field of our experience and to draw a spark from the juxtaposition." Mednick (1962) defines *creativity* as the "forming of associative elements into new combinations which either meet specified requirements or are in some way useful." He goes on to

365

say that the more mutually remote the elements are, the more creative the resultant new combination.

A poet creates by putting together old words in new ways, while a painter does so by combining familiar visual features or images in new ways. A scientist creates by putting together old concepts in new ways. Creative ideas can almost always be traced back to a novel analogy or simile. This is easy to see in poetry. Consider this simile by John Donne,

> and your bodies print
> like to a grave, the yielding downe doth dint.

The reason that this image is generally held to be creative is the analogy drawn between remote associates—a grave and the depression in a bed left by a living person's body. These things are, of course, unlike in many ways and like in only a few. But the rules for writing poetry have never said that things compared must be exactly alike in all respects. If they did, it would be impossible to write poetry.

Science and poetry

The basic difference between poetic creativity and scientific creativity really has to do with what is concluded from the newly perceived analogy. McCormick invented the grain reaper on the basis of an analogy between grain and hair (Weber, 1969). It occurred to him that grain is like the hair on a person's head. Mechanical clippers are used to cut hair, *therefore* something like hair clippers could be used to cut grain. Again, the core of the creative idea was an analogy— in this case, the perception that grain is like hair. Had McCormick been a poet rather than the practical person he was, he might have worked the analogy into a poem. For example,

> Your hair is like the golden grain,
> And the dandruff thereupon is but the chaff.

Another example of a creative scientific idea is the concept of cortical or cognitive lateral inhibition. This idea was independently formulated by von Békésy (1967), Crowder (1978), Deutsch (1969), and Konorski (1967). In all of these cases, the basic analogy was that between cells in the retina and cells in a single layer of cortex: If there is lateral inhibition among retinal cells, then there may be lateral inhibition among cortical cells or cognitive units. This analogy was then, as we have seen, used as the basis for explaining many empirical findings that previously had been attributed to a variety of quite unrelated causes.

CREATIVITY AND CLASSIFICATION

Attending to analogies

In general, creativity involves the perception of an analogy between two or more elements. What is done with this analogy varies according to the creative person's field of endeavor. The poet may simply state the analogy as a simile or use it as the basis for a metaphor. The scientist will tend to conclude something from it. To perceive an analogy between two things means to categorize them both as members of the same class. In other words, it involves the connection of two cognitive units to the same deeper-level superordinate or chunking unit. Consider an uncreative analogy: A DUCK IS LIKE A CHICKEN. In everyone's memory, DUCK and CHICKEN are rather strongly connected to common superordinates (for example, FOWL, BIRD, ANIMAL). Thus, they are close associates. It strikes us that the analogy is obvious. Why? Probably because the two elements have simultaneously occupied the focus of everyone's attention at some time or another. Now consider this analogy: A DUCK IS LIKE A METEOR. Although it hardly occupies the pinnacle of creativity, it is certainly more creative than my DUCK-and-CHICKEN analogy. Even though both elements must be at least weakly and indirectly connected to a common superordinate (for example, THINGS THAT MOVE THROUGH THE ATMOSPHERE), they have probably not simultaneously occupied the focus of attention for most people. They are, thus, *remote associates*. Even though two elements may be connected to a common superordinate, unless they simultaneously occupy the focus of attention, one will not be aware of the connection. To have a creative idea, it is obviously necessary to be conscious of it (that is, to have both elements of the analogy simultaneously activated.)

To summarize, a creative idea is one wherein two or more remotely associated elements (cognitive units) are seen to be similar or analogous (connected to the same superordinate unit). Ideas vary as to how creative they are. If many people have noted the connection to the common superordinate, the idea is not creative at all. More creative would be an idea where the connection is implicit in other's minds but has not been attended to. Even more creative, of course, would be the case where the creator is the first one to construct the common superordinate.

Structural basis of creativity

How do creative ideas originate? How can one simultaneously activate two cognitive units that satisfy the two criteria of creativity? They have not been simultaneously activated in others' minds (originality), and they share some meaningful superordinate (appropriateness). In order to answer this question, it may help to recall how cognitive units are hypothetically arranged. In Figure 15-1,

FIGURE 15-1   Example of a superordinate category unit and subordinate instance units

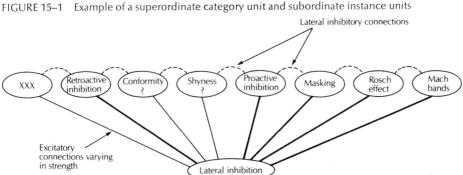

we show a set of cognitive units all connected to a common superordinate. In the example, the subordinate units are all connected to a superordinate unit coding the concept of LATERAL INHIBITION. We have discussed some of them—for example, MACH BANDS, THE ROSCH EFFECT, PROACTIVE INHIBITION, and so on—as being due to lateral inhibition. Others—for example, SHYNESS, CONFORMITY—have not been attributed to lateral inhibition and may, in fact, have nothing to do with it. As with other conceptual domains, the units are shown as differing in the strength with which they are connected to the superordinate unit. In terms of this example, having a creative idea would consist of (1) simultaneously activating two of the lower-order units (that is, becoming aware of their similarity or mutual connection to a common superordinate) and (2) concluding something from this awareness (for example, borrowing methods used to study one unit to study the other). How can we do this?

CAN WE SYSTEMATICALLY GENERATE CREATIVE IDEAS?

Activation via superordinate units

The most obvious way to generate a creative idea might seem to be to access the superordinate unit. This would, of course, activate all of the subordinate units. However, there are several problems with this method. First, in a real-life situation, we usually would not know what the superordinate unit was. The task would be to discover it. Konorski did not have Figure 15–1 in front of him when he first conceived that proactive inhibition and masking are similar (in that both are hypothetically due to lateral inhibition). For you to come up with a really creative idea, you would need to find some phenomenon to place in the blank unit marked XXX in Figure 15–1.

An even greater difficulty is that having a creative idea often corresponds to establishing a new association between a cognitive unit and a superordinate. It is not that the unit coding XXX is already directly connected to the LATERAL INHIBITION unit and that you just have to remember this connection. Rather, it must be that creativity has to do with making a new connection. However, given the rich interconnections among units in an analyzer, every cognitive unit must be at least indirectly connected to every other cognitive unit. The connection may be circuitous, but it must be there. Activation of a superordinate unit is unlikely to activate such indirectly connected units. If it could do this, it would end up activating nearly every cognitive unit in the brain.

How about this procedure: Access an even higher-level superordinate unit coding INHIBITION in general. Certainly, this should produce activation of subordinate units coding instances of inhibition, whether or not these were coded as instance of LATERAL INHIBITION. However, there is a problem with this strategy. Activation of the superordinate unit—if known—would strongly activate the units that were most strongly bonded to it. These, in turn, might be expected to laterally inhibit less strongly bonded units. Thus, activating the superordinate unit would most likely lead to thinking only of the most obvious subordinates. It might actually make your discovery of the XXX phenomenon more difficult. Remember that we have to activate whatever unit codes XXX strongly enough to get it into the focus of attention. It looks as if the method of trying to deduce creative ideas should actually backfire.

Serial searching

Perhaps a better method would be to reverse our procedure; that is, we could activate a series of subordinate units (other than those shown in Figure 15–1). To be thorough, we would want to activate the units coding all of the other concepts which we have stored in semantic memory. First, each unit could be activated. Then, in turn, we would activate each of the units shown in Figure 15–1 and see if a fruitful analogy occurred to us. The problem with this proposal is that we cannot systematically access cognitive units. Human beings have no ability to perform this type of serial progression through all of the contents of semantic memory. We could conceivably do this with a dictionary if we wanted to, but we cannot do it with the subjective lexicon coded in our brains. As we have seen, the subjective lexicon is organized so as to be accessed not serially but in a parallel manner. But what is accessed is determined by the external stimulus configuration and/or whatever units were activated at the prior moment of time. How, then, do creative ideas arise?

THE CREATIVE PROCESS

Stages of the creative process

How do obviously creative people come up with creative ideas? One way of approaching this question is to look at the recollections of such people. There is general agreement that several different stages are involved. Wallas (1926) has suggested that four successive stages commonly occur in the creative process: preparation, incubation, illumination, and verification. Helmholtz (1896) was the first to discuss the first three stages in the context of a discussion of the origin of his own creative scientific ideas. He stated that, at first, he worked intensively on a problem but often came up with no solution. This is the stage of preparation. During this stage, the elements known or presumed to be relevant to the problem are thought about or learned. When progress was not forthcoming, he set the problem aside for a period of time. This is the period of incubation. Then, often with no apparent cause, a solution occurred to him. This is the stage of illumination. It is in the illumination or inspiration stage that the creative analogy occurs to the thinker. This consists of the simultaneous juxtaposition of two or more elements in the focus of attention. These elements may be ones entered into memory during the preparation stage. As often as not, though, some seemingly irrelevant element provides the key to the creative solution. Following inspiration is the verification or elaboration stage. During this stage, the creative idea is subjected to logical and critical scrutiny. Does it make sense? Is it useful? The elaboration stage also involves expressing the idea or taking some action on the basis of it. For the scientist, this will often involve the design and execution of an experiment or other empirical investigation to test the idea. The poet or writer will have to fit the idea into a form that follows the rules of the genre in which he or she is working.

The effortlessness of creative inspiration

It seems to be the case that some period of incubation followed by effortless illumination or inspiration is very common in creative production. Creative ideas do not arise from purely logical, intellectual thought for either scientists or artists. Ghiselin (1952) concluded from a study of self-reports by creative people that "production by a process of purely conscious calculation seems never to occur." This is a strong statement, but investigators have concluded the same thing for quite a while. Plato held that "it is not by wisdom that poets create their works but by a certain natural power and inspiration, like soothsayers and prophets, who say many fine things but who understand nothing of what they say." Poets and other writers are particularly explicit about the effortless, non-intellectual nature of creative inspiration. Nietzsche (1908) described the composition of *Thus Spake Zarathustra* as follows: "Everything occurs quite without volition, as if in an eruption of freedom, independence, power and divinity. The spontaneity of the images and similes is most remarkable." Blake's (1803) comment about the composition of his poem on Milton is even more extreme: "I have written this poem from immediate dictation, 12 or sometimes 20 or 30 lines at a time without premeditation, and even against my will." Even the seemingly conventional English novelist, Thackeray (1899), describes a similar possession: "I have been surprised at the observations made by some of my characters. It seems as if an occult power was moving the pen. The personage does or says something, and I ask, how the dickens did he come to think of that?"

It is surprising to many lay people that scientists and mathematicians give very similar descriptions of their own experiences. An example comes from the French mathematician, Henri Poincaré (1913):

> One evening contrary to my custom, I drank black coffee and could not sleep. Ideas rose in crowds; I felt them collide until pairs interlocked, so to speak, making a stable combination. By the next morning I had established the existence of a class of Fuchsian functions, those which come from the hypergeometric series; I had only to write out the results, which took but a few hours.

EXPLANATIONS OF CREATIVE INSPIRATION

Random searches

BLIND VARIATION

Since we have such limited ability to search our minds in a systematic fashion, perhaps creative ideas arise more or less at random. D. T. Campbell (1960) proposes just this when he argues that creativity can be accounted for by a process of *blind variation and selective retention*. By blind variation, he means not purely random combination of mental elements but a process that is closely akin to randomness. Mental elements co-occur in the focus of attention in large part because of the stimuli that confront us. These stimuli are not random, but they are not very systematic either. Certainly, with respect to whatever problem we are trying to solve at a given moment, most of our experience can be considered to be random; that is, each action or experience may be purposeful, but the relation of these purposes to the problem is likely to be random.

Campbell's point about the importance of blind variation in creative production makes most sense when we think about combinations of mental elements brought about by external stimulation. Let's say that you are still trying to think of the XXX phenomenon. As you go about your daily business, almost everything that occurs to you will be random with respect to this problem. It is certainly reasonable to think that these random events could activate cognitive units that might suggest an answer to your problem. According to Campbell, people go through life combining various pairs of mental elements. Most quickly pass from thought and are forgotten. However, some that are seen as useful are remembered and, perhaps, acted upon. This is *selective retention.*

CHANCE AS A FACTOR IN CREATIVITY

There is some evidence for the importance of random factors in creative production. The poet, Dylan Thomas, used to leave blanks in his poems. Then, he would eavesdrop on conversations in hotel lobbies and other places and use words that he overheard to fill in these blanks. Computers have been programmed to write quite creditable poems by a similar method. The program is provided with lists of nouns, verbs, and adjectives. It then draws at random from these lists to fill in blanks in sentences provided to it. As might be imagined, this produces some outrageous gibberish. But the surprising thing is that some things that sound like modern poetry are also produced.

In science, there are numerous examples of *serendipity.* These are cases where an important discovery is made quite by accident. This is the way Roentgen discovered x-rays and the Curies discovered radium. ·B. F. Skinner discovered the importance of reinforcement schedules by chance. He was doing studies of the effects of food rewards on animals' performance. One day he ran short of the food being used as a reward. To conserve it, he stopped rewarding every response and began rewarding only every other response. To his surprise, the animals' rate of responding went up rather than down.

Unfocused attention

Campbell's theory does a fairly good job of explaining creative insights that are occasioned by perceptual inputs. However, it does not provide an adequate explanation of experiences such as Poincaré's where "ideas rose in crowds." A lot of creative ideas seem to occur not so much as a result of a specific external stimulus, but as a consequence of a particular way of thinking in the creative person. What is really important in creativity may not be so much a random external stimulus but the way in which the person responds to the stimulus. After all, everyone is subjected to random stimuli, but only a few people have creative ideas.

A necessary prerequisite for having a creative idea is having both of the elements to be combined in the focus of attention at once. Recall that we discussed the question of how many things we can attend to at once in Chapter 7. The answer given today is the same as the estimate William James made in 1890: Generally, only one thing can be attended to at once. If this were always the case, no one would ever have any creative ideas. Indeed, no one would have any ideas of any sort. If only one thing could ever be attended to at any one time, we would never be able to realize any similarities at all since, to do so, several items need to be attended to simultaneously.

Perhaps the reason that creative ideas are so rare is simply the fact that most people at most times attend to only one mental element at a time. On the other hand, since everyone has some ideas and some people have creative ideas, the focus of attention must sometimes be able to accommodate at least two elements. Furthermore, the more elements that a person can focus on simultaneously, the more likely that a creative idea will result. Why? Because the more elements that can be focused upon, the more candidates there are for combination. Thus, with two elements—A and B—in the focus of attention, only one relationship—AB—can be discovered. With three elements—A, B, and C—there are three potential relationships—AB, AC, and BC—to be discovered. With four elements, there are six potential relationships, and so on. Thus, a person who could focus simultaneously upon four elements would be able to come up with creative ideas six times as fast as someone who could focus on only two elements at a time.

Mendelsohn (1976) has advanced the theory that individual differences in attentional capacity are in fact the key to differences in creativity. "The greater the attentional capacity," he writes, "the more likely the combinational leap which is generally described as the hallmark of creativity." Dewing and Battye (1971), Mendelsohn and Griswold (1966), and Ward (1969), carried out studies on the relationship between the range of cue utilization and creativity. Recall that the range of cue utilization refers to how many stimuli fall within the focus of attention. A person with a narrow range of cue utilization has narrowly focused attention. Only the most focally relevant stimuli are attended to. On the other hand, a person with a wide range of cue utilization has less focused attention. Both relevant and irrelevant stimuli are focused upon. As would be predicted, all of these studies consistently produced evidence that more creative people do, in fact, display a wider range of cue utilization than do less creative people.

Dykes and McGhie (1976) studied the performance of creative and uncreative subjects on shadowing tasks. In one part of the experiment, the words coming to the shadowed ear consisted of a meaningful prose passage. Random words were presented to the unshadowed ear. After the experiment, a recognition-memory test was given for words presented in both the shadowed and the unshadowed channels. Creative subjects recalled more of the words from the unshadowed channel than did the uncreative subjects. Since these words found their way into long-term memory, they must have been attended to. In another part of the experiment, both channels contained random lists of words. Sometimes words that were close associates occurred simultaneously in both the shadowed and the unshadowed channels. At other times, the words in the two channels were unrelated. As compared to less creative people, creative subjects switched (that is, mistakenly repeated the word from the channel they were supposed to disregard) more often when highly associated word pairs were presented. Both of these results—better memory for the unshadowed message and more intrusions from the unshadowed channel—support the contention that creative people have less focused attention.

Primary memory and creativity

Earlier, we talked about someone who could hypothetically focus simultaneously on four elements. Can anyone do this? It seems doubtful. In previous chapters, we divided consciousness or primary memory into two parts: attention (the most activated cognitive units) and short-term memory (cognitive units that are activated but less so than those in the focus of attention). Maybe, creativity has to do with the total number of elements in consciousness; that is, maybe more units can be simultaneously active in creative people, regardless of whether these elements are in the focus of attention per se or only in short-term memory. A number of theorists have indeed said that what we have called short-term memory is, in fact, the crucial locus for creativity. Rugg (1963) comments on this:

> It is my thesis that the illuminating flash of insight occurs at a critical threshold of the conscious-nonconscious continuum on which all of life is lived. The true locus of the creative imagination is the border state that marks off the conscious from the nonconscious. . . . I have never succeeded in finding an adequate name for it. I have tried many: intuitive, autistic, quiet, relaxed, permissive, accessible, hospitable. The state is certainly permissive, yet it is more than that. It is actively magnetic, attracting materials out of the nonconscious into the vestibule of the conscious mind (pp. 39–40).

I would argue that the most adequate name for what Rugg refers to is simply short-term memory. Here is what may happen in the mind of creative people during creative inspiration: Stimuli activate cognitive units, but these units are less strongly activated than in uncreative people. Further, in creative people, more units are simultaneously activated—perhaps either because units are more inter-connected or because they laterally inhibit each other less. When two simultaneously activated units are related in a particular way (for example, they provide an answer to a problem), they emerge into the focus of attention. Thus, the creative person is essentially continually combining elements outside the focus of attention. This is consistent with Poincaré's (1913) comment that only useful or potentially useful combinations present themselves to attention:

> The sterile combinations do not even present themselves to the mind of the inventor. Never in the field of consciousness [that is, attention] do combinations appear that are not really useful, except some he rejects, but which have to some extent the characteristics of useful combinations. All goes on as if the inventor were an examiner for the second degree who would only have to question the candidate who had passed a previous examination (pp. 386–87).

This line of reasoning would explain how random perceptual inputs could trigger creative ideas. Perhaps, the units coding the problem being worked on stay in a primed state during the period of incubation. They are in a more or less permanent state of partial activation. Dissimilar stimuli will not resonate with them, and they will stay in the fringe of consciousness. However, if a stimulus is somehow similar to these units, it will fully activate them. Then they leap into the focus of attention and combine with the stimulus that elicited them to form a creative idea. An analogy would be a mother who hears her child cry out in the night. Although she may sleep through all sorts of other noises, the child's crying immediately awakens her. Presumably, this is because the units coding this cry remain in a permanent state of partial activation. In spite of the fact that several theorists have implicated what we now call short-term memory in the creative process, there are no experimental studies in this area. However, Mednick (1962) has proposed a theory essentially the same as this— though stated in quite different terms—that has generated a good deal of research.

Flat associative hierarchies

ASSOCIATIVE HIERARCHIES

Before presenting Mednick's theory, we need to review some background material that we first discussed in Chapter 10. Consider a word-association test. The examiner says a word, which hypothetically activates its representation in morphemic and semantic analyzers. Via direct and indirect associations, it also activates other units coding other words. This is the habit family hierarchy or associative hierarchy elicited by the word. The subject's task is to respond with the first word that comes to mind. This response is presumably the most activated unit in the associative hierarchy. In a variant of this procedure, called *continuous association,* the subject must give the first word that comes to mind, then the second, and so on. Presumably, the subject responds first with the unit (other than the one coding the stimulus) that is most activated, then with one that is coded by the next most activated unit, and so on. On the basis of responses by many subjects, it is possible to construct norms that specify the probability of various responses to a given stimulus word. Actually the *associative hierarchies* elicited by any given stimulus word are quite consistent across subjects; that is, a stimulus word tends to elicit the same words in the same order from all subjects.

However, people do differ in the steepness of their associative hierarchies. A person with steep hierarchies has just a few responses to the stimulus word (see Figure 15–2A). Note that the first several responses are closely bonded to

FIGURE 15–2   Examples of steep (A) and flat (B) associative hierarchies. The hierarchy of possible responses to the stimulus-word, TABLE, is shown.

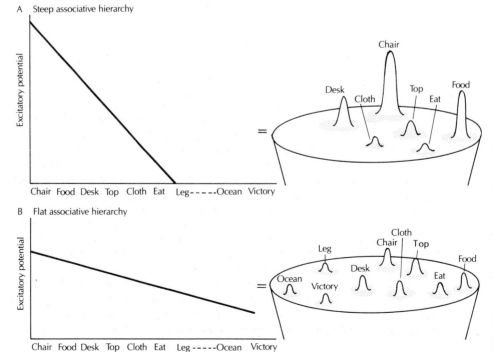

the stimulus; that is, the probability that they will be given is very high. The stimulus tends regularly and consistently to elicit these responses. On the other hand, some people tend to have flatter associative hierarchies (see Figure 15–2B). The stimulus activates more cognitive units. The more probable responses (that is, the most activated cognitive units) are less strongly bonded to the stimulus (that is, the units are less activated) than is the case for the person with steep gradients. On the other hand, the remote associates in the hierarchy have much higher probability than they do for a person with steep gradients. That is, the cognitive units coding them are more activated.

PRIMARY MEMORY AND ASSOCIATIVE HIERARCHIES

The associative hierarchies shown in Figure 15–2 can be seen as specifying the degree of activation in a set of cognitive units. The greater the activation of a unit, the higher the probability that the word it codes will be given as a response. Note that the same units are activated regardless of whether the associative hierarchy is steep or flat. What is different is how activation is distributed across these units. The diagrams in Figure 15–2 are essentially the same ones used to illustrate states of focused attention (Figure 15–2A) and defocused attention (Figure 15–2B). Degree of focus of attention and steepness of associative gradient are two terms for the same phenomenon. It is also of interest to note that attention and short-term memory are reciprocally related to one another. In a state of focused attention, the attended units are a lot more activated than the units in short-term memory. In a state of defocused attention, they are not much more activated. Thus, in a state of defocused attention, units in short-term memory are more activated—relative to units in the focus of attention—than is the case in a state of focused attention. It is rather arbitrary whether we talk about underactivation of some units (those in the focus of attention) or over-activation of other units (those in short-term memory). To say that less is going on in the focus of attention is equivalent to saying that more is going on in the fringe of consciousness. Thus, to say that creative people have less focused attention implies that they have relatively more activation of units in the fringe of consciousness or short-term memory. Mednick (1962) puts this in terms of the steepness of associative gradients.

MEDNICK'S THEORY

The person with steep gradients responds in a stereotyped fashion—the same responses tend always to be given to the same stimulus—while the person with flat gradients responds in a more variable fashion. In other words, the person with steep associative gradients should be uncreative while the person with flat associative gradients should be creative. This is Mednick's theory of creativity (1962). Mednick's argument is that creativity is the capacity to combine remote associates. For example, the poet's task is essentially one of taking a word-association test. Say that the intention is to make up a simile about a table. The poet must generate responses to the stimulus, TABLE, until a usable response that fits into the frame, A TABLE IS LIKE _____, is found. This response is hardly likely to be a close associate of TABLE. Otherwise, some other poet would have thought of it centuries ago. Thus, a unit coding a remote associate must be activated. This is, of course, much more likely for a person with relatively flat associative gradients. For a person with steep gradients, the probability of activating a unit coding a remote associate is virtually zero. Figure 15–2 thus illustrates the hypothetical difference between creative and uncreative people in terms of how activated a set of cognitive units in an analyzer might be in response to the same stimulus. Several of the units in the uncreative person's analyzer are highly activated, and others, not very activated (Figure 15–2A). On the other hand, the units are more equally activated in the creative person's mind (Figure 15–2B). The crucial difference has to do with the pattern of activation.

REMOTE ASSOCIATIONS AND CREATIVITY

Mednick (1962) devised a clever test of creativity based upon his theory. In the Remote Associates Test, the subject is confronted with 30 sets of three items. For each set, the task is to find a fourth word that is related to all three of the stimulus words. The trick is that the fourth word is associatively rather than logically related to the stimulus word. Here is an example of the sorts of items that the test contains:

| Railroad | Girl | Class | _____ |
| Surprise | Line | Birthday | _____ |

(The answers are working and party.) People who are creative (as defined by their having produced work that is judged to be creative) do in fact score higher on this test than do uncreative people. As would be predicted from the hypothesis that they have flatter associative gradients, high scorers on the Remote Associates Test produce more associations and continue associating longer on word association tests than do low scorers (Mednick, 1962). As would be predicted from our equation of flat associative gradients and defocused attention, high scorers on the Remote Associates Test do show a wider range of cue utilization than low scorers (Mendelsohn and Griswold, 1966).

For most people, it is a lot easier to learn paired associates composed of close associates (for example, TABLE–CHAIR) than to learn those composed of remote associates (for example, TABLE–OCEAN). This should be especially true for uncreative people if they have steep associative hierarchies. Having such hierarchies means that the strength of CHAIR given the stimulus TABLE is quite high whereas the strength of OCEAN given the stimulus TABLE is quite low. On the other hand, if creative people tend to have flat associative hierarchies, there should be less difference in the strength of close and remote associates. Creative people should thus show less of a difference in their ability to learn paired-associate lists composed of close as opposed to remote associates. Brown (1973) conducted an experiment that confirmed this prediction.

According to Mednick's theory, the content and relative ordering of associative hierarchies is the same in creative and uncreative people. What differs is the relative response strengths of the elements. In our terms, the units coding remote associates are relatively more activated in creative people while the units coding close associates are relatively less activated. Evidence from continuous word association tasks supports this hypothesis. At first, creative and uncreative people give the same responses in the same order (Mednick, 1962). Research by

Christensen, Guilford, and Wilson (1957) with the Alternate Uses Test and related tasks also provides evidence for this contention. On the Alternate Uses Test, subjects have to think of unusual uses for common objects. Most people think of pretty much the same uses first. Original or unusual uses are thought of later. The probability of thinking of an original use for an object goes up over trials. The basic difference between creative and uncreative people is that the uncreative people think of the obvious uses and then stop. The creative people also think of these obvious uses first, but then go on to think of unusual uses.

PROBLEM-SOLVING SET

There are several classic demonstrations of how having a single dominant response to a situation can interfere with creative problem solving. Luchins (1942) presented his subjects with a series of water-jar problems. The task was to figure out how to obtain a given amount of water using three jars of differing capacity. For example, the first problem was to obtain exactly 100 quarts of water from three jars of different capacities: A (21 quarts), B (127 quarts), and C (3 quarts). The way to do this is to fill jar B, fill jar A from jar B, and then fill jar C twice from jar B; 100 quarts will remain in jar B. The first six problems could all be solved in exactly this way—that is, the correct quantity was equal to B − A − 2C. In the course of solving the first few problems, most subjects realized this. They developed a set to solve the problems in this way. In other words, this solution became their dominant response to the experimental situation. Problem 7 and all later problems could be solved in this way or in a far simpler way using only two of the jars. For example, problem 7 calls for getting 20 quarts from three jars: A (23 quarts), B (49 quarts), and C (3 quarts). The easiest solution is simply to fill jar A and pour off 3 quarts by filling jar C. This will leave 20 quarts in jar A. However, one can also use the more circuitous method that worked on the first few problems. This is exactly what most subjects did. They tended to persist with the earlier solution. It had become the dominant response to the problem and prevented their seeing the simpler solution.

FUNCTIONAL FIXITY

A related phenomenon is called *functional fixity* (Dunker, 1945): If an object has a dominant function or use, this tends to prevent us from thinking of using it in another way. In order to study functional fixity, Dunker presented subjects with several problems. In one of the problems, the task was to fix a candle to a wall. The materials at hand consisted of the candle, three kitchen matches, and a matchbox filled with thumbtacks. The most obvious solution—tacking the candle to the wall with the thumbtacks—would not work. The solution was to tack the matchbox to the wall (that is, use it as a platform) and set the candle on it. Surprisingly, it took people a rather long time to think of this if they ever did. The reason would seem to be that they perceived the matchbox only in terms of its dominant function—as a container—and this prevented their thinking of other uses for it. Glucksberg and Danks (1968) presented subjects with a functional fixity problem that required the use of a wrench to complete an electrical circuit. More subjects solved the problem when they had to refer to the stimuli—

including the wrench—with nonsense names than when they simply called each by its usual name. Hypothetically, calling the wrench a wrench also led subjects to think of the wrench as only a wrench; that is, it led them to think of it only in terms of its dominant function.

Primary process thinking

KRIS'S THEORY

The psychoanalytic theorist, Ernst Kris (1952), has proposed that creativity involves the use of primary process thinking. He argued that the inspirational phase of the creative process involves a temporary regression to a primary process state of consciousness. This primary process state facilitates creative inspiration in that it involves free-associative thought. Whereas the psychotic or the dreamer generally uses primary process cognition to deal with personally relevant, emotion-laden material, the creative person can hypothetically use this type of thought to deal with neutral cognitive elements. Creative people have compared creative inspiration with the thought that occurs in dreams. Weber (1969) cites several examples: Hebbel said that "The state of poetic enthusiasm is a dreamlike state." Schopenhauer, in a formulation closer to Kris's, held that "A great poet . . . is a man who, in his waking state, is able to do what the rest of us do in our dreams."

Recall that in earlier chapters we said that primary process states of consciousness are characterized by defocused attention, flat associative gradients, and equally activated cognitive units. Thus, this part of Kris's theory essentially says exactly what Mednick's and Mendelsohn's theories say, although Kris originally expressed it with a quite different vocabulary. Kris goes on to say that the elaboration or verification stage of the creative process involves a return to a secondary process state of consciousness. In this state, logical, analytic, reality-oriented thought is used to assess the validity of the creative inspiration and to put it into final form. We can extrapolate this hypothesis to Mednick's and Mendelsohn's theories as well. Presumably, creative people only have flat associative hierarchies or defocused attention during the inspirational stage of the creative process. It would not do to carry out the hard work of elaboration with defocused attention.

What really characterizes the creative person, according to Kris, is the ability to shift back and forth between primary and secondary process states. In contrast, less creative people are less variable. They are locked at one point on the primary process-secondary process continuum, at least during their waking hours. This place may be anywhere along the continuum.

EMPIRICAL EVIDENCE

Several lines of empirical evidence support Kris's contention that creative people have more access to primary process states of consciousness. They report a higher frequency of daydreaming (Singer and McCraven, 1961) and remember their nighttime dreams better (Hudson, 1975) than do less creative people. Several studies suggest that dreaming may actually be important to the creative process (Lewin and Glaubman, 1975; Glaubman, et al., 1978). In these studies, subjects were given a problem they would have to solve in a creative fashion the next morning. Then, they went to sleep in the laboratory. One group of subjects was awakened every time they began to show the rapid eye movements that accompany dreaming. They were thus systematically deprived of any chance to dream. A control group was awakened an equal number of times but during nonrapid-eye-movement sleep. The dream-deprived subjects did significantly worse on the creativity tasks in both studies. Dreaming is a period of primary process mentation. If primary process thinking is necessary for creativity, it makes sense that dream deprivation could lessen creativity. Creative people also turn out to be more susceptible to hypnosis (Bowers and van der Meulen, 1970; Bowers, 1979). They can be hypnotized more easily than can uncreative people. Daydreaming, dreaming, and hypnosis are all primary process states of consciousness.

Studies of verbal responses to the Rorschach and the Thematic Apperception Tests suggest that creative people exhibit more primary process content in their fantasies, but that this material is adaptively integrated rather than being pathological (Myden, 1959; Pine, 1959; Pine and Holt, 1960). Wild (1965) tested creative and uncreative people for their ability to shift between regulated (secondary process) and unregulated (primary process) thought on word-association and object-sorting tests. She asked subjects to take these tests in a normal state, while they were pretending to be a very conventional person, and while they were pretending to be an unconventional person. As would be expected, the creative subjects could shift between the two states better than the less creative subjects.

Creative people tend to show the disinhibition characteristic of primary process states on a number of levels. In fact, Anderson and Cropley (1966) have proposed the hypothesis that creativity is altogether due to an inability or an unwillingness to internalize the stop rules that the average person has learned. Creative people tend not to use the defense mechanism of repression (Barron, 1955; Fitzgerald, 1966; Myden, 1959). Rather, they freely admit to all sorts of pathological and negative things about themselves (Barron, 1968). They also tend to be less inhibited or compliant in laboratory situations designed to measure conformity (Barron, 1968). When creative people are asked to check adjectives that describe their personalities, the common factor seems to be one of disinhibition. Here are examples of adjectives picked by creative people of various types: gloomy, loud, unstable, bitter, dissatisfied, pessimistic, irritable (Barron, 1952); original, envious, enthusiastic, impulsive (van Zelst and Kerr, 1954); inventive, enthusiastic, determined, industrious (MacKinnon, 1962). On the other hand, here is how uncreative subjects see themselves: contented, gentle, conservative, patient, peaceable (Barron, 1952); contented, conventional (van Zelst and Kerr, 1954); virtuous, good, rational, concerned with others (MacKinnon, 1962). The greater willingness of creative people to engage in risk-taking behavior (Anderson and Cropley, 1966; Pankove and Kogan, 1968) is also consistent with the disinhibition hypothesis.

CREATIVITY AND AROUSAL

Equivalence of theories of creativity

Creativity must be related to level of arousal. Why? Because the determinants of creative behavior—whether described in terms of flat associative gradients, defocused attention, or primary process state of consciousness—are all systematically related to level of arousal. The relationship between these constructs and level of arousal is diagrammed in Figure 15–3. Flat associative hierarchies are

FIGURE 15–3   Relationship between arousal and steepness of associative hierarchies, focus of attention, and secondary process versus primary process quality of thinking

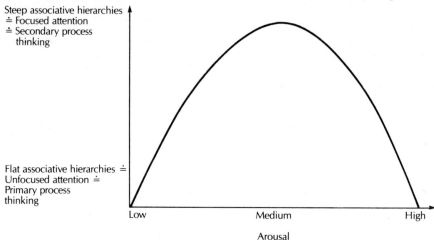

found when arousal is either high or low, whereas steep gradients are found with medium levels of arousal. Similarly, defocused attention and primary process thought are found under conditions of either high or low arousal, but focused attention, secondary process thinking, and steep associative hierarchies are found with medium levels of arousal. If creativity involves flattening of associative hierarchies, defocusing of attention, and use of primary process thinking, then creative people must be in comparatively low or high states of arousal, at least during creative inspiration. We can, then, translate Kris's hypothesis from the psychological to the physiological level: If creative people are more variable along the secondary process-primary process continuum, then they must also be more variable along the arousal continuum (Martindale, 1977a).

Induced arousal and creativity

The origin of the idea that there is a relationship between creativity and arousal goes back at least to Hull (1943). Recall his behavioral law: increases in drive make the dominant response to a stimulus even more dominant. That is, increases in what would now be called arousal (drive) make behavior more stereotyped and predictable. Conversely, decreases in arousal increase the variability of behavior. (As discussed in Chapter 10, this is only true up to a point. Under extremely high levels of arousal, behavior becomes disorganized and, hence, more variable and less predictable.)

Studies of both word-association tasks (Coren and Schulman, 1971; Horton, Marlowe, and Crowne, 1963) and creativity tests (Dentler and Mackler, 1964; Krop, Alegre, and Williams, 1969) have shown that stress produces decrements in originality. If people are placed under stress, they will give more stereotyped word associations and will do worse on paper and pencil tests of creativity. Martindale and Greenough (1973) have shown that even loud noise, which hypothetically increases cortical arousal, produces decrements on tests of creativity.

Creativity and individual difference in arousal

BASAL LEVEL OF AROUSAL

The findings about the effects of induced arousal on creative performance suggest that perhaps creative people could simply be less aroused in general. However, this does not seem to be the case. It turns out that people who are more original on word-association tests (Trapp and Kausler, 1960; Worrell and Worrell, 1965) as well as on direct measures of creativity (Maddi and Andrews, 1966) tend to score *higher* on tests of anxiety than those who are less original. Tortarella (1968) found that stress causes more interference on problem-solving tasks for high scorers on the Remote Associates Test than for low scorers. This suggests that these more creative subjects have higher basal levels of arousal— or are closer to their optimal level of arousal—than less creative subjects. In a series of eight studies, my colleagues and I (Martindale and Armstrong, 1974; Martindale and Hines, 1975; Martindale and Hasenfus, 1978; Martindale, Covello, Hines and Mitchell, 1980) have found no consistent relationship between basal cortical arousal as measured by amount of EEG alpha waves and creativity. It must be arousal during creative inspiration rather than arousal in general that differentiates more and less creative people.

AROUSAL DURING CREATIVE INSPIRATION AND ELABORATION

Martindale and Hines (1975) measured amount of alpha-wave activity while people took two tests of creativity (the Alternate Uses Test and the Remote Associates Test) and a test of intelligence (the IPAT Culture Fair Test). Results for subjects obtaining high, medium, and low scores on the creativity tests are shown in Figure 15–4. As you can see, the highly creative group of subjects exhibited differential amounts of alpha-wave activity while they took the three tests. On the other hand, the other two groups showed no evidence of this pattern. Recall that more alpha-wave activity means *less* cortical arousal.

The Alternate Uses Test is a fairly pure measure of creativity in that it does not correlate with tests of intelligence. On the other hand, the Remote Associates Test shows some correlation with intelligence tests. The IPAT is a pure measure of intelligence in that it is unrelated to creative ability. If creativity requires unfocused attention, least focusing should be necessary to do well on the Alternate Uses Test, most on the IPAT, and an intermediate amount on the Remote Associates Test. If we assume that the more alpha activity there is, the less focused attention is, this is exactly the pattern shown by the highly creative group. They show the lowest arousal while taking the Alternate Uses Test, more arousal while taking the Remote Associates Test, and even more arousal while taking the intelligence test. On the other hand, the less creative groups showed about equal levels of arousal while taking all three tests.

Perhaps when a task calls for creative performance, creative people defocus

FIGURE 15–4   Alpha-wave presence in high-, me-
dium-, and low-creative people while taking the Alternate Uses Test (USES), the Remote Associates Test
(RAT), and an intelligence test (IPAT)

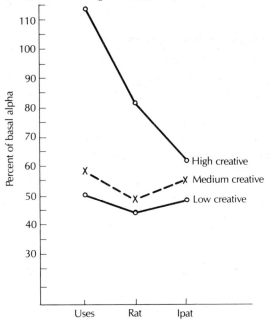

Source: C. Martindale, "Creativity, Consciousness,
and Cortical Arousal," *Journal of Altered States of Consciousness* 3 (1977):78.

their attention or at least show no increase in focusing from basal levels. This
unfocused attention is accompanied by a decrease in cortical arousal or at least
by no increase in arousal from basal levels. On the other hand, less creative
people focus their attention too much. This prevents them from being creative.
It also shows up as a sharp increase in cortical arousal. These differences should
be seen during creative inspiration, since this is the stage where defocused attention is helpful. On the other hand, they should not be found during the
elaboration stage, since defocused attention is not useful there. Martindale
and Hasenfus (1978) tested this hypothesis. In one study, EEG activity was monitored while subjects thought about a story they would write (the inspirational
phase) and while they actually wrote the story (the elaboration phase). All of
the subjects were urged to be as creative as they could. No EEG differences were
found between more and less creative people during the elaboration phase.
However, as predicted, more creative subjects exhibited less cortical arousal
during the inspirational phase than did the less creative subjects. Similar results
were found in a second study in which people were asked to free associate (the
analogue of the inspirational phase) and to make up stories (the analogue of the
elaboration phase). The importance of creativity was emphasized for half of the
subjects, but nothing about creativity was mentioned for the other half. The

results were quite specific: creative people showed lower cortical arousal than did uncreative people during the inspirational phase *if* they were told to be creative but not otherwise.

CREATIVITY AND SELF-CONTROL

The findings in regard to the relationship between creativity and cortical arousal during creative performance are in line with predictions. Creative people are less cortically aroused during inspiration than are uncreative people. But it is somewhat surprising that this difference is only found when subjects are explicitly told to be creative. One possible explanation for this might be that creative people are capable of controlling their own level of cortical arousal. Perhaps, when they are told to be creative, they exert self-control and maintain a low level of arousal. The reason for doing this might be that they have learned from experience that such a state is more conducive to creativity. Kamiya (1969) introduced the technique of *biofeedback*. His procedure was as follows. Some electronic circuits were built that would automatically detect the presence of alpha waves. The output from these circuits caused a tone to come on. Then, electrodes were attached to a subject's scalp and EEG was recorded. Whenever a subject produced alpha waves, the tone sounded. Kamiya instructed subjects to keep the tone on (or off) as much as possible. It turned out that people were able to do both of these things and that they tended to get better with practice.

If creative people had better control over their own level of cortical arousal, they should perform better on a biofeedback task than uncreative people. Two studies (Martindale and Armstrong, 1974; Martindale and Hines, 1975) were conducted to investigate this question. Both used methods similar to those described earlier, and both yielded the same results. The results were quite clear. Creative subjects did better than uncreative subjects at control of their brainwaves at first. However, this advantage disappeared after only a few minutes. Uncreative people were not very good at this task initially, but they improved markedly over trials; that is, they got better at both alpha suppression and alpha enhancement. On the other hand, creative people did not improve their performance over trials. They actually got worse. The amount of alpha that they produced drifted upwards over trials regardless of whether they were supposed to be producing alpha or suppressing it.

CREATIVITY AND REACTIVITY

Respondent control of arousal. Creative people are not very good at biofeedback tasks. Thus, the reason that they show differential degrees of arousal in response to different task demands must not have to do with self-control. It must be an automatic reaction of some sort. Exactly what brings about the reaction is not clear. The poor self-control of arousal on the part of creative people should really have been expected in the first place. Recall that creative people describe themselves with words that stress lack of inhibition and control. The retrospective accounts of creative inspiration quoted above all emphasize the effortless and automatic character of such thought. Creative people have used several methods in order to facilitate their own creativity. It is interesting that none of these methods are operant ones; that is, none involve self-control. Rather, they are respondent. They involve placing oneself in the presence of some stimulus and letting that stimulus *elicit* a response. The methods used are often ones that would elicit a change in level of arousal.

Although there is no evidence that they actually do enhance creativity, some creators have used drugs and alcohol in the belief that they do. Clearly, this is a respondent method: drugs automatically elicit changes in arousal. Other respondent methods are more bizarre. For example, the German poet Schiller felt that he could not write unless his desk drawers were filled with rotting apples. Other methods that would seem at first glance to be rather silly superstitions, in fact, do have a physiological effect. These include Schiller's practice of writing with his feet plunged in ice water; Bossuet's of composing with his head wrapped in furs; Byron's writing with his head near the fireplace and his feet in a cold draft; and the habit of Milton, Descartes, and Leibnitz of doing their creative thinking while lying prone in bed. Ribot (1906) points out that all of these methods would have the effect of increasing blood flow to the brain. (A reciprocal relationship exists between peripheral blood flow and that to the brain. For example, making one's feet colder will constrict blood vessels in the feet and this will automatically dilate blood vessels going to the brain.) One very common practice resorted to by creative people is withdrawal that is often so extreme that it may result in self-imposed sensory deprivation. Think of the ubiquity of the image of the withdrawn artist—Vigny in his tower of ivory, Proust in his cork-lined room, Hölderlin in his tower at Tübingen, and Flaubert at Croisset. We have seen that sensory deprivation does induce alteration in arousal and a primary process state of consciousness.

Oversensitivity. Why do artists withdraw in the first place? According to their own reports, they do not generally do this because they know that it will enhance their creativity. Rather, they often say that they do it in order to escape excessive stimulation. The stereotype is that artists are oversensitive. This does really seem to be the case for many of them. Proust withdrew to his cork-lined room because normal levels of light and noise were painful. When he did go out—always at night—he kept the shades of his carriage drawn because he claimed that the streetlights hurt his eyes. The Belgian poet, Emile Verhaeren, had his doorbell disconnected because its ringing caused him physical pain. A lot of creative people do, in fact, seem to amplify the intensity of stimuli to the extent that stimuli most of us do not even notice become almost unbearably intense. This suggests that they are more arousable.

There is evidence based on self-reports of creative people that does not quite fit with the idea that creative people are simply oversensitive. Sometimes they seek out extremely strong stimuli. Even more paradoxically, it is sometimes the very same people who complain of oversensitivity who do this. The English poet Swinburne, for example, complained of oversensitivity but also apparently enjoyed quite strong stimulation of a masochistic sort (for example, being whipped). When poets leave their ivory towers, it is often in order to seek strong stimulation. They go traveling to exotic places, seek out riots and revolutions, and so on. We shall try to make sense of this seeming anomaly a little later.

Preference for novelty. Creative people exhibit another trait that—at first glance—seems to be at odds with their oversensitivity. They love novelty, complexity, and incongruity. The French poet, Charles Baudelaire, summed up what seems to be the attitude of many creative people when he said that "the beautiful is always bizarre." Several empirical studies bear out the contention that creative people like novelty, ambiguity, and related collative properties. Barron and Welsh (1952) constructed a test of design preference. In this test, subjects are shown several paired designs. In each case, one of the designs is complex and asymmetric, while the other is simple and symmetrical. The task is simply to say which member of each pair is preferred. Creative people uniformly tend to prefer the more complex, asymmetric, ambiguous designs, while uncreative people tend to like the simpler, more symmetric ones. This has been shown for creative artists (Barron, 1953) and architects (MacKinnon, 1962) to mention only several studies.

It strikes me that one of the quickest ways to get an idea of a person's creativity is to watch that person's reaction to a novel idea. Creative people tend to become excited and enthusiastic when they are presented with a new idea. They exhibit positive affect. Often, the idea suggests other new ideas to them. On the other hand, flaws in the idea are often overlooked. Thus, the reaction seems to be one of positive affect and unfocused attention. These phenomena suggest low or medium arousal. Uncreative people react quite differently. They immediately begin to pick the idea apart and tell you what is wrong with it. Often, they seem even to become angry. In other words, the reaction seems to be one of negative affect and focused attention. It is as if the new idea had too much arousal potential.

Creative people seem not merely to like novelty. They also actively dislike things that are not novel or unusual. The English writer, George Moore (1886) illustrates this with his rather extreme self-description: "I am feminine, morbid, perverse. But above all perverse, almost everything perverse fascinates me . . . the commonplace, the natural, is constitutionally abhorrent." In speaking of scientific geniuses, Koestler (1964) remarks that they share "on the one hand skepticism, often carried to the point of iconoclasm, in their attitude toward traditional ideas, and dogmas" as opposed to "an open-mindedness that verges on naive credulity towards new concepts." In general, creative people seem often to react to conventional ideas in the way that uncreative people react to novel ideas: They focus their attention, get angry, and look for defects.

Creativity, reactivity, and arousal. How can we put all of this together? One is tempted to think that creative people do not obey the Wundt curve (see Figure 15–5). As shown, uncreative people conform their preferences to the Wundt curve. They like stimuli with medium arousal potential (for example, conventional ideas or stimuli of medium intensity) and dislike stimuli with higher arousal potential (for example, novel ideas or very intense stimuli). On the other hand, creative people actually dislike stimuli with medium arousal potential (for example, conventional ideas or stimuli of medium intensity). But, rather paradoxically, they like stimuli with even higher arousal potential (for example, unconventional ideas or intense stimuli). I assume that both creative and uncreative people are neutral toward stimuli with very little arousal potential (for example, the assertion that $2 + 2 = 4$) or with a great deal of arousal potential (for example, extremely bizarre ideas or extremely intense stimuli).

How can we account for the rather odd preference curves of creative people?

FIGURE 15–5 Hypothetical preference curves for creative and uncreative people

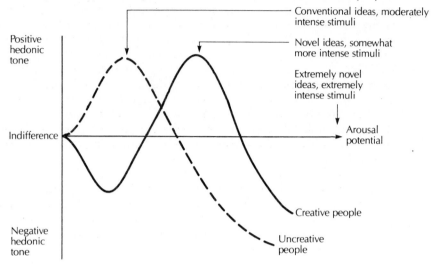

Rather than saying that the Wundt curve is wrong, I would prefer to postulate that there is something wrong with the arousal system of creative people (see Figure 15–6). In uncreative people, the more arousal potential a stimulus has, the more arousal it induces. However, in the case of creative people, the relationship is not so simple. Increasing arousal potential increases arousal up to a point. Then, there is a "paradoxical" dip in arousal. This dip hypothetically corresponds

FIGURE 15–6 Hypothetical arousal reactions of creative and uncreative people

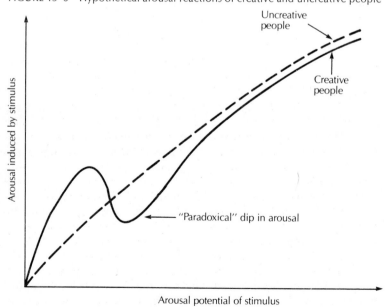

to the pleasure and defocused attention induced by stimuli with fairly high arousal potential. Hypothetically, it could explain why telling creative people to be creative induces a decrease in their arousal. This particular task demand has sufficient arousal potential to induce the paradoxical decline in arousal.

It would be idle to speculate too much as to the cause of the dip in arousal. This sort of paradoxical relaxation response to stimulation has often been observed but not related specifically to creativity (see Morrell, 1966). It could be due to quick fatiguing of what we have called *cognitive units* or to what Pavlov (1927) called *transmarginal inhibition*. More important are the cognitive consequences of the dip. Hypothetically, stimuli of moderately high arousal potential produce declines in arousal in creative people. The consequences of this would be a defocusing of attention, a flattening of associative gradients, or a primary process state of consciousness. Regardless of what we call this state, it should facilitate the assimilation of ordinarily incongruous stimuli to global or dedifferentiated categories; that is, it should lead the person to equate or see as similar a wider range of stimuli (see Chapters 12 and 13). Why? Among other things, because of decreased lateral inhibition. Creativity itself may be the *XXX* phenomenon we began looking for at the beginning of this chapter.

SUMMARY AND CONCLUSIONS

We defined a creative idea as one that is original and also useful or appropriate for the situation in which it occurs. Creative ideas are always based upon new combinations of preexisting elements; that is, the basis of creativity is the perception of an analogy or of the fact that two cognitive units can be connected to a common superordinate category. We saw that it is difficult to discover creative ideas by systematic processes, such as deduction or serial comparison of ideas. Indeed, creative inspiration or insight seems never to involve such systematic procedures. Rather, it occurs in an effortless and automatic fashion.

There are several explanations of creative inspiration, but we saw that they are all really the same theory stated in different words. Campbell argues that creativity could be the product of quasi-random combination of ideas. We argued that this makes sense if cognitive units coding the problem one is working on remain partially activated in short-term memory. A random percept or idea could then activate or combine with these units to give the solution. Rugg and others have suggested that creativity does involve relatively high activation of cognitive units in short-term memory. Mendelsohn argues that creativity involves unfocused attention. But we saw that unfocused attention logically implies relatively high activation of units in short-term memory. Thus, Rugg's and Mendelsohn's theories can be combined into one theory that creative inspiration involves relatively equal activation of cognitive units in primary memory (which consists of focal attention plus short-term memory). However, this is precisely Mednick's theory—although he expressed it in terms of associative hierarchies. In fact, it is also Kris's theory—though he expressed it in terms of primary process thinking. Kris notes that creative elaboration must involve secondary process thinking rather than primary process thinking. Thus, creative people must have an above average ability to shift from unfocused attention or primary process thought to focused attention or secondary process thought.

Creativity must be related to cortical arousal. This is because the hypothetical cause of creativity—whether it is referred to as defocused attention, primary process thought, flat associative gradients, or equally activated cognitive units—is a unitary phenomenon crucially dependent upon level of arousal. Induced increases in arousal lead to decrements in creativity. While individual differences in creativity are not related to basal or resting differences in arousal, they are related to differences during creative task performance. Creative people are relatively less aroused during creative inspiration and more aroused during creative elaboration, whereas this difference is not found in uncreative people. This difference is apparently not due to self-control of arousal level since creative people cannot exert such self-control except for very brief intervals. It must be due to differences in reactivity.

We saw that creative and uncreative people do differ in their reactivity to stimulation. Uncreative people seem to prefer stimuli of medium arousal potential. Their preferences are predicted by the Wundt curve. However, creative people seem actively to dislike stimuli of medium arousal potential as well as stimuli of high arousal potential. They seem to show maximal preference for stimuli with somewhat higher arousal potential than is the case with uncreative people. We speculated that this could be because stimuli in a certain range induce a "paradoxical" decrease in arousal in creative people. This decline in arousal is accompanied by defocused attention, pleasure, and primary process thinking.

16

Cognitive evolution

CAMPBELL'S THEORY OF COGNITIVE EVOLUTION

Requirements for evolution

The Danish philosopher Soren Kierkegaard (1841) remarked that "Concepts, like individuals, have their histories and are just as incapable of withstanding the ravages of time as are individuals." Not only ideas or concepts but everything related to them shows historical change. Language, which is used to express concepts, changes continually. So do more complex results of cognitive processes, such as art and science. Are these changes capricious and random or do they have a direction? Do later ideas evolve from earlier ones, as is the case with individuals? This is the question of *cognitive evolution.* D. T. Campbell (1974, 1975) argues that historical change in cognitive products, such as language, art, and science, is determined by an evolutionary process analogous to Darwinian natural selection. The principle involved is one of "blind variation and selective retention."

There are three requirements for evolution according to Campbell. First, there must be *variation.* In the case of biological evolution, variation is supplied by such factors as mutation. Random mutation of a gene produces an organism with a new trait. In the case of cognitive evolution, variation can, as we shall see, be either random or purposeful. The second necessary factor is *selection.* Some consistent process must operate to favor one sort of trait over another. In biological evolution, the selection mechanism has to do with adaptation. A more adaptive trait increases the probability that its possessor will survive and reproduce. The selection mechanism in cognitive evolution is probably reinforcement. Ideas that are reinforced (because they are useful, interesting, or pleasurable) tend to survive. Finally, for evolution to occur, there must be methods of *retention;* that is, the traits selected must be retained and passed on to others. In biological evolution, this is taken care of by sexual reproduction. In cognitive evolution, the retention system is based upon the fact that our language, beliefs, and ideas are learned from other people. We do not make up our own language but learn the one we hear others speaking. By the same token, we do not make up our concepts from scratch. Rather, for the most part, we take them over from other people. But, you may argue, each of us does come up with some new concepts. This is indeed true, and it is this innovation that provides the variation upon which selection processes operate.

Replication

To survive, a cognitive product must be transferred to other people. Child-rearing, education, and imitation account for this. To take an example close at hand, I am attempting to replicate my ideas by writing this book. As you read it, ideas that once existed only in my mind come to exist in your mind as well. Replication is not confined to formal education. We continually imitate other people's ideas and behaviors. We do so at least in part because we believe that doing so will be beneficial to us; that is, we believe that it will lead to rein-forcement, profit, or happiness.

Variation

RANDOM VARIATION

Everyone learns a set of ideas and behaviors. These may come directly from other people or they may come from them indirectly, in the form of books or other cultural artifacts. Some of these ideas and behaviors will be reproduced by the individual. If all learned behaviors were reproduced exactly, there would be no variability. Evolution could not occur. However, it is very difficult to pro-duce an exact replica or copy of anything. Even if we wanted to reproduce exactly things we have learned, we would not be able to do so. As we saw when we considered memory, one remembers the gist of material rather than exact in-formation about it. For example, you could not repeat Chapter 14 of this book verbatim. You assimilated a few basic points which you could express in your own words. Thus, if you had to replicate Chapter 14 by telling someone else about it, you would certainly change it a great deal. The words would be differ-ent. Some of the points would be left out because you had forgotten them. Other points might be added because you thought of them as you read and added them to your memory schema.

CREATIVE VARIATION

Variation is also introduced by creativity. In the last chapter, we said that creativity involves novel combinations of old elements. Such combinations are of two types. On one level, all thought and language is creative in that it strings together sequences of ideas or words that have seldom if ever been strung together in exactly that fashion before. Probably no one has ever written the previous sentence before. Thus, mere use of learned elements induces variability. Even if we could exactly reproduce the elements we have learned, we would not combine them in the same order as other people. On another level, some thought and language is creative in another sense. A poet more or less consciously sets out to produce novel combinations of words. So, too, a scientist consciously tries to produce new combinations of ideas. Thus creativity can be either spontaneous, as in the production of normal speech, or purposeful, as in the production of poetry. Both types of creativity will produce variation upon which selection mechanisms can work.

SERIAL REPRODUCTION EXPERIMENTS

Even rather simple stimuli cannot be transferred from one person to another without some change. This is demonstrated by serial reproduction experiments. In such experiments, people are instructed to make exact copies of things they are shown. The first subject is shown a stimulus. Then, when the stimulus is no longer present, the subject has to produce a copy of it. This copy is shown to another subject, who attempts to reproduce it, and so on. The procedure is the same as the parlor game where a group of people sit in a row, a message is started at one end, and each person whispers the message to the next person. What generally happens in such experiments is that the original stimulus is gradually transmuted into a quite different thing. For example, in Figure 16–1 the original stimulus is a stylized bird seen from the front. After 18 successive reproductions, it has been transformed into a naturalistic cat seen from the back.

Allport and Postman (1947) reviewed the results of several studies on serial reproduction. They concluded that three types of effects are found in such experiments. The most important of these effects is *assimilation*. Stimuli are assimilated to preexisting memory schemata. We can see the process of assimilation in the series of designs illustrated in Figure 16–1. What began as the outline of a bird degenerates into a rather amorphous blob. Then, the blob is apparently assimilated to the cat-schema. Going along with assimilation may be secondary elaboration. Once subjects have decided that they are dealing with a cat, they add whiskers and a tail even though these were not present at first. Another tendency is *leveling* or simplification. In serial reproduction experiments, details tend to drop out over time. Stories get shorter, and drawings become simpler. Simplification may be seen as a consequence of assimilation to memory schemas. As we have seen, such schemas resemble ideal prototypes rather than complete photographs. *Sharpening* or exaggeration, Allport and Postman's third general characteristic, involves accentuation of some details at the expense of others. Allport and Postman see this as a corollary of leveling. If some details are omitted, others will of necessity be accentuated. In some cases, there can be a movement toward complexity rather than toward simplicity in serial reproduction, but this is rare (Haddon, 1907).

It would seem that the results of serial reproduction are best explained as follows: Each subject assimilates the stimulus to a memory schema. This involves simplification or loss of detail. A memory will always tend to be simpler than the percept it codes. Bear in mind that no selection pressure—other than the need for exact copying—is present in serial reproduction experiments. They are important, however, in illustrating that variability is present even when people do not want it to be. Even if human beings aimed to do nothing but exactly reproduce what they had learned, the variation necessary for cognitive evolution would still be present.

FIGURE 16–1   Serial reproductions of a drawing of a stylized bird

Original drawing   Reproduction 1   Reproduction 2

Reproduction 3   Reproduction 4   Reproduction 5   Reproduction 6

Reproduction 7   Reproduction 8   Reproduction 9   Reproduction 10

Reproduction 11   Reproduction 12   Reproduction 13   Reproduction 14

Reproduction 15   Reproduction 16   Reproduction 17   Reproduction 18

Source: F. C. Bartlett, *Remembering* (Cambridge, Eng.: Cambridge University Press, 1932), pp. 180–81.

Selection

We see that cognitive performance is variable. We learn cognitive elements but could not reproduce them exactly even if we wanted to. Further, these cognitive elements are used by combining them, and these combinations are novel and variable rather than stereotyped regardless of whether they are found in routine behavior—such as everyday thought and speech—or in purposeful creativity. What selection pressures operate on these behaviors? In general, any behavior that is emitted is subject to reinforcement; that is, it may be rewarded or punished. The well-established law of effect says that behaviors that are rewarded will tend to be repeated. If behaviors of a certain type always tend to be rewarded, then this would certainly be a basis for systematic selection. It would seem that this must be the case. Behaviors can be rewarded by other people. They can, of course, also be covertly rewarded by the person who emits the behavior.

AROUSAL POTENTIAL AND COGNITIVE EVOLUTION
Arousal potential and the dispensation of reinforcement

Which behaviors are most likely to be rewarded? Presumably, those that bring most pleasure to whomever is dispensing the rewards. And which behaviors would these be? The Wundt curve tells us that behaviors that induce medium arousal potential should induce most pleasure. It must be, then, that behaviors with medium arousal potential are most likely to be rewarded. Behaviors with very little arousal potential induce no affective response. They should be ignored. On the other hand, behaviors with a lot of arousal potential induce displeasure. They should meet with punishment.

Recall that arousal potential is a function of psychophysical, ecological, and collative properties. Let us consider the latter. Collative properties include things such as novelty, incongruity, and surprisingness. Other things being equal, a behavior with a medium degree of novelty is more likely to be reinforced than either an extremely novel or a very predictable behavior. The same considerations apply to other collative variables, such as complexity. So far as we know, the Wundt curve has governed hedonic tone at all places and at all times. Thus, there would seem to be a selection pressure for novelty, incongruity, and complexity that has operated consistently since the dawn of time. Across time, behaviors with medium amounts of collative properties have been more likely to be rewarded. Hence, their chance of survival has been greater.

Arousal potential tends to habituate. Each time that a behavior is repeated, it will lose an increment of arousal potential. Thus, a behavior that had medium arousal potential at time$_1$ will eventually come to have lower arousal potential at time$_2$. As arousal potential falls, probability of reward should also fall. Now, slightly more novel or complex behaviors should be rewarded. This should set up an historical pressure for more and more novelty; that is, a given behavior should be gradually changed in the direction of greater complexity or variability in order to maintain its pleasure-inducing capacities. An historical series of such behaviors should give evidence of having more and more arousal potential.

The historical fate of behaviors

The historical fate of a class of behaviors should be determined by the amount of arousal potential that these behaviors elicit. Behaviors that elicit very little arousal potential will be ignored. They will neither be rewarded nor punished. If such behaviors are transferred from one person to another across long stretches of time, they should become simpler and simpler. Why? They are neither rewarded nor punished, but each time they are relearned, they are subjected to the simplifying effects of memory. Some of the aspects of language might exemplify this sort of trend. Most of us react negatively if we hear speech that is grammatically incorrect. But we do not notice many aspects of speech. No one is likely to notice if you avoid the subjunctive, for example. We also ignore minor variations in pronunciation. The point is that many of the details of speech are ignored since we tend to focus our attention on the meaning of what is said rather than on exactly how it is said. The details of speech do indeed seem to drift toward simplicity (Martinet, 1962, 1964). After a few hundred years of drifting, pronunciation and even syntax have changed radically. For example, English as it was spoken in 1200, say, is virtually unintelligible to a speaker of modern English.

On the other hand, behaviors that elicit a lot of arousal potential are likely to be punished. Thus, they are likely to decrease in frequency or—in anticipation of punishment—not to be emitted at all. However, if they are not extinguished altogether, their arousal potential may decline to the medium range. This is because repetition of a stimulus leads to habituation. With each repetition, the stimulus loses a quantum of arousal potential. We see examples of this in clothing fashions. Newly introduced fashions (see-through blouses for example) often elicit shock and outrage. After awhile, though, this shock lessens, and the new fashion may be adopted by those who formerly disapproved of it.

Behaviors in the midrange of arousal potential offer the most interesting evolutionary possibilities. They induce pleasure and should be rewarded. However, in order to avoid loss of these rewards because of habituation, such behaviors should tend gradually to move in the direction of greater arousal potential. Later in this chapter, we shall explore in detail how this works in the case of art. The basic idea is that successive artists have to produce works of art with more and more arousal potential in order to compensate for habituation. This is not to say that they are always able to do this. If they cannot do it, the art form will gradually become extinct because people will pay less and less attention to it over time. On the other hand, art forms that have survived must have become more complex, novel, or striking over time. It is precisely this gradual increase in arousal potential that has allowed their survival.

Pressures for simplification and complication

If this line of reasoning is at all correct, then there has been a consistent pressure for novelty in virtually all significant lines of human endeavour. However, the tendency toward simplification because of assimilation to preexisting memory schemata must also be seen as a consistent selection pressure. If a behavior is to survive, it must be learned by someone else. This learning will invariably involve some degree of simplification. Thus, while the arousal system presses for novelty and increasing complexity, the memory system presses in the opposite direction. Which of these systems exerts more pressure will determine whether a series of cognitive products becomes simpler or more complex over time. The fact that human life has apparently become more complex over the course of time suggests that the pressure for novelty must generally have been greater than the pressure for simplification.

AESTHETIC EVOLUTION

Why study art?

In order to see if the ideas advanced in the first part of this chapter are correct, we could examine the history of just about any sort of cognitive product. Why should we look at the history of art forms? Aside from the intrinsic interest and importance of art, there are several reasons. First, the pressure for novelty seems to be quite high in the case of art. Second, we can find artistic traditions where a relatively few people have produced a reasonably small number of art works (that can be located, dated and measured) over a very long period of time. Thus, it is more feasible to study art than to study belief systems or cultural practices. Third, as compared with other cultural products, such as law for example, art seems generally to be rather insulated from outside social and cultural pressures. It is perhaps the best place to observe cognitive evolution undisturbed by external forces. Although we shall concentrate on historical trends in poetry in this section, the principles can be generalized to other forms of art as well.

Intrinsic pressure for novelty

In the past several hundred years there has emerged a consensus among aestheticians that "multaneity in unity," "ordered disorder," or "contradictory unity" is central to art (see Gilbert and Kuhn, 1939). Art is characterized by incongruity, surprise, and deformation within the context of some overall unity. There is a consensus on this point on the part of almost all current approaches to art and literature—French structuralism (for example, Lévi-Strauss, 1958), American-English "new criticism" (for example, Empson, 1930), Russian semiotics (for example, Lotman, 1970), psychoanalytic theory (for example, Kris, 1952), and the psychobiological approach (for example, Berlyne, 1971).

According to Berlyne (1971), liking or preference for a stimulus is based upon the arousal potential of that stimulus. The arousal potential of any stimulus is hypothetically determined by collative properties (for example, novelty, complexity, surprisingness, unpredictability), ecological properties (signal value or meaning), and psychophysical characteristics (for example, stimulus intensity). In Chapter 10, we reviewed evidence supporting the contention that people prefer stimuli with a medium degree of arousal potential and that they do not like stimuli with either very high or very low arousal. Kamann (1963) and Evans (1969) have found this effect with literary stimuli, and Day (1967) has found it with visual designs.

Evidence is also available to show that reaction to most of the components of arousal potential tends to habituate; that is, repeated presentation of a given work decreases that work's arousal potential or impact value, so that a work of art—or any stimulus for that matter—gradually loses its arousal potential. The consequence is that a work with medium arousal potential will not keep on having medium arousal potential forever but will gradually lose its capacity to elicit interest, liking, and attention. Several studies have shown that repeated presentation of the same aesthetic stimulus eventually leads to a decline in liking for that stimulus (Berlyne, 1970; Skaife, 1967).

It follows, then, that if a series of artists were to keep on producing the same work of art—or similar works of art—liking for their productions would decrease over time. In order to compensate for this tendency toward habituation, it would be necessary for successive works of art to have more and more arousal potential. In principle, this could be accomplished by manipulating any of the components of arousal potential. For example, successive composers could create louder and louder musical compositions or successive painters could paint larger and larger paintings. However, there are practical limits to how loud a piece of music can be or how large a painting can be. In a medium such as poetry, it would be essentially impossible to compensate for habituation of arousal potential by increasing stimulus intensity, since poetry consists of printed words. On the other hand, collative properties, such as novelty or unpredictability, are much freer to vary in all of the arts. Thus, the necessity to increase the arousal potential of aesthetic products over time must eventually come down to a pressure to increase novelty, incongruity, and other collative variables.

Consider a successive series of poets trying to think of a simile or metaphor concerning the same thing. In composing a simile, a poet hypothetically begins with the stimulus word and then produces word associates until an associate is found that (1) makes sense when used in the simile and (2) has not been used before. The poet cannot very well use an associate that makes no sense (for example, Your lips are like your nose) because the simile would have too much arousal potential and would induce displeasure. On the other hand, if an associate has been used before (for example, Your lips are like red wine) the simile would have too little arousal potential and readers would be bored. Presumably, the poet will tend to use the first word associate that both makes sense and has not been used before. Thus, earlier poets will use the obvious word associates. Over time, then, poets would have to move further and further out on the associative hierarchies surrounding the words they dealt with in order to find usable words; that is, an avoidance gradient is set up which travels outwards over time. This is shown in Figure 16–2. Does this sort of process actually occur? Let's examine some examples.

FIGURE 16–2   In order to compose similes, a poet must draw responses from associative hierarchies. Avoidance gradients prevent the use of responses already used by previous poets.

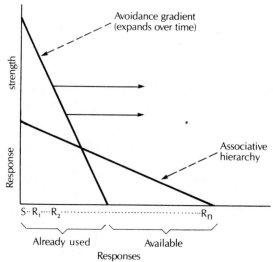

Source: C. Martindale, *Romantic Progression: The Psychology of Literary History* (Washington, D.C.: Hemisphere, 1975), p. 38.

Historical trends in arousal potential

EXAMPLES

Here are some examples of poetic images from a successive series of 18th-through 20th-century French poets. As you can see, incongruity does tend to increase from the earlier to the later images.

> Beneath your fair head, a white delicate neck
> Inclines and would outshine the brightness of snow.
> Chénier, "Les Colombes"

> Waterloo! Waterloo! Waterloo! bleak plain!
> Like a wave which boils in an urn too full,
> In your arena of woods, of hills, of valleys,
> Pale death mingled the dark battalions.
> Hugo, "L'Expiation"

> The violin quivers like an afflicted heart;
> Melancholy waltz and languid vertigo!
> Baudelaire, "Harmonie du soir"

> This evening a done-for sun lies on the top of the hill.
> Lies on its side, in the straw, on its overcoat.
> A sun white as a gob of spit in a tavern
> On a litter of yellow straw.
> Laforgue, "L'Hiver qui vient"

> I love you opposite the seas
> Red like the egg when it is green
> You move me into a clearing
> Gentle with hands like a quail.
> Breton, "Tiki"

EMPIRICAL STUDIES

Is this increase in the incongruity of similes and metaphors used in French poetry a general trend? In order to find out, I studied samples of the poetry of a representative series of 21 19th- and 20th-century French poets (Martindale, 1975). The measure of arousal potential was an index of the tendency for words with four types of opposite connotations (strong versus weak, active versus passive, good versus bad, and approach versus attack) to co-occur in the same sentence. This index did exhibit a significant linear increase over the time span covered by the study.

Cohen (1966) studied several forms of incongruity in a historical series of French classical, romantic, and symbolist poetry. Texts by three poets in each of these successive periods were examined. First, Cohen looked at the number of times nouns were modified by adjectives that were, in strict grammatical terms, inappropriate. An example would be the use of an animate adjective (for example, BITTER) to modify an inanimate noun (for example, STAIRS) as in Victor Hugo's metaphor, "I climbed the bitter stairs." Such incongrous modifications occurred at a rate of 3.6 percent in the classical texts. The rate rose to 23.6 percent in romantic texts, and to 46.3 percent in symbolist poetry. Cohen also examined the incongruity between sound and sense occasioned by enjambment. *Enjambment* is the lack of a punctuation mark at the end of a poetic line. When there is no punctuation at the end of a line of poetry, the pause at the end of a line will not coincide with pauses occasioned by the grammatical sense of sentences, as it would if there were punctuation at the end of the line. Over time, French poets came more and more to disregard Alexander Pope's maxim that sound should echo sense: Enjambment was found in 11 percent of classical lines, 19 percent of romantic lines, and 39 percent of symbolist lines.

In order to test some parts of the theory of aesthetic evolution more extensively, I have gathered samples from the poetry of a series of English poets (Martindale, 1978a, 1979a). The samples consist of over 325,000 words from a series of 109 poets born in 23 successive 20-year periods from 1490–1949. Thus, the samples contain poetry written across a span of about 470 years from around 1510 to the present. For all except the first several periods, five poets represent each of these periods. I constructed a Composite Variability Index to measure the collative properties of texts (Martindale, 1978a). The goal was to create a general index of the degree of complexity, surprisingness, incongruity, ambiguity, and variability of a text. The index is composed of the following measures: mean polarity of words (the degree to which a word receives extreme ratings on scales measuring activity, potency, and evaluation—hypothetically a measure of semantic intensity or strikingness), mean meaningfulness of words (the number of word associations given to a word in a one-minute period of time—hypothetically a measure of use of words with multiple meanings and, hence, more potential ambiguity), hapax legomena percentage (percentage of words occurring only once in a document—an index of complexity or difficulty), coefficient of variation of word frequency, coefficient of variation of word length, and coefficient of variation of phrase length (hypothetically measures of variability). These measures are computed by several computer programs and then added together in ways that need not concern us. This index of variability increases over time. In fact, it goes straight up across the entire 470-year time span. The linear trend is highly statistically significant, and the small deviations from this trend are insignificant. Thus, the arousal potential of English poetry seems to have been increasing at a constant rate for the last 470 years. The fact that the rate of change has remained constant suggests that the increase in arousal potential was brought about by evolutionary forces internal to the poetic system rather than reacting to or reflecting external social or cultural pressures.

The direction of aesthetic evolution

TRENDS IN PRIMARY PROCESS CONTENT

How could successive poets produce poetry that became more and more novel, original, or incongruous over time? In order to answer this question, it is necessary to ask how novel responses or works of art are produced in the first place. According to Kris (1952), novel or original responses are produced by a biphasic process. An initial inspirational stage involving regression to a primary process state of consciousness is followed by a subsequent stage of elaboration with (usually) a relatively less regressed mode of thought. By regression, recall that we mean a movement from secondary process thinking toward primary process thought. As we saw in Chapters 12 and 13, the secondary process-primary process continuum may be seen as the fundamental axis along which states of consciousness and types of thought vary. Recall that secondary process cognition is abstract, logical, and reality-oriented; while primary process cognition is concrete, irrational, and autistic. It is the thought of dreams and reveries.

Novel responses could emerge in two ways from the regression-elaboration process: (1) Holding the amount of elaboration constant, deeper regression should lead to more free-associative thought and thus increase the probability of original combinations of elements. In other words, to produce a more novel response one could regress to a more primary process level. (2) Holding the amount of regression constant, decreasing the degree of elaboration should lead to statements that were original by virtue of being nonsensical or nonsyntactic in varying degrees. Utterances of the second type should generally be more improbable than those of the first type. For example, a statement composed of close associates but with a low degree of elaboration (such as, chairs the fooding tables) is probably less probable than even the most farfetched metaphor concerning a table that is elaborated into a syntactically and semantically meaningful form.

Since increasing the novelty of utterances by elaborating less is more drastic than increasing novelty by regressing more during inspiration, we would expect poets to favor the method of increasing depth of regression rather than the method of decreasing level of elaboration. If possible, successive poets should engage in deeper and deeper regression while maintaining the same level of elaboration. Each poet would then have to regress further in search of usable combinations of words not already used by his or her predecessors. This is illustrated schematically in the left-hand side of Figure 16–3A. We should expect the increasing remoteness of similes and metaphors to be accompanied by content indicating the increasingly deeper regression toward primary process cognition required to produce them.

We can also express this in terms of the analogy of successive poets moving

FIGURE 16–3   (A) Amount of regression and elaboration in a hypothetical series of poets under continual pressure for novelty. (B) The flatness of associative gradients corresponding to the degree of regression illustrated in A.

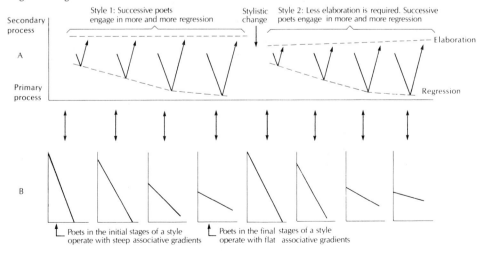

out along associative hierarchies in order to find usable word associates. The best way to move out on an associative hierarchy is to flatten out the hierarchy. This will increase the probability of the remote associates. Thus, we could say that successive poets need to operate with flatter and flatter associative hierarchies. This is illustrated on the left-hand side of Figure 16–3B. Recall that we have equated flattening of associative hierarchies with movement toward a primary process state of consciousness (see Chapters 12, 13, and 15). To say that successive poets need to operate with flatter associative hierarchies is just another way of saying that they need to regress to more primary process states.

STYLISTIC CHANGE

Eventually a turning point—caused by audience pressures or the difficulty of deeper regression—should be reached. At that time, increases in novelty would be much easier by decreasing the level of elaboration, by loosening the rules governing the production of poetry. This corresponds to a period of major stylistic change. Hypothetically, stylistic change allows poets to return to word combinations composed of relatively close associates. Stylistic change is accomplished by (1) changes in the poetic lexicon such that entirely new stimulus words are dealt with or (2) loosening the stringency of poetic rules so that previously forbidden word combinations are allowed. Accordingly, at least a partial return from deep to shallow regression should accompany stylistic change. Poets can once more move back toward steeper associative gradients (secondary process cognition) to find the previously discarded close associates that are now usable. Once such stylistic change had occurred, the process of increasing regression would be expected to begin anew (see Figure 16–3).

Perhaps the clearest example of this process can be seen in French poetry. Virtually all 19th-century French poets accepted the stylistic rule that the word *like* had to join like words. That is, if a poet wanted to compose a simile, A is like B., then A and B had in fact to be alike at least in some arcane manner. By the end of the 19th century, this had become quite a difficult task. Previous poets had used up all of the obvious analogies. Around 1900, the stylistic rule was explicitly abrogated. It became acceptable poetic practice to combine unlike words with the word *like*. Thus, the surreal image, "The earth is blue like an orange," was perfectly acceptable. Surreal images tend to be composed of easily accessible word associates such as *blue* and *orange*. No great regression is needed think of *orange* given the word *blue*, since the two are close associates. The surrealists merely used close associates that previous poets had been unable to use because of the stylistic rules under which they operated.

LONG-TERM TRENDS

It may be useful to summarize what we have said up to this point. The theoretical predictions are illustrated in Figure 16–4. Successive poets must produce poetry having more and more arousal potential. We have already seen that there is evidence that they did so in the cases we examined. In order to do so, successive poets hypothetically engaged in more and more primary process thinking. However, this trend was periodically interrupted by stylistic changes that

FIGURE 16–4   Summary of theoretical predictions concerning historical trends in poetry and other arts

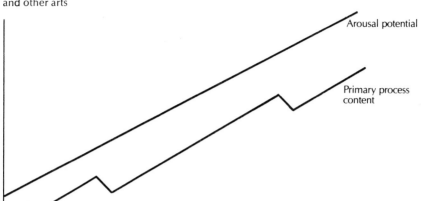

allowed poets to keep on increasing arousal potential at the expense of some-what less regression. If this is true, then primary process content in poetry should increase over time as shown in Figure 16–4. Indexes of stylistic change should coincide with the periodic declines in primary process content as illustrated in the figure. Let's take a look at the evidence.

EMPIRICAL STUDIES

If the theory is correct, we should expect that subsequent 19th-century French poets should have engaged in deeper and deeper regression in their search for usable analogies. The amount of primary process content should increase across the course of the century. However, it should decline with the adoption of the new style that permitted virtually any words at all to be combined to form metaphors and similes. There is quantitative evidence that successive 19th-century French poets did in fact regress more and more up to about 1900, when the process was reversed and depth of regression decreased, presumably be-cause of the loosened stylistic rules (Martindale, 1975). The Regressive Imagery Dictionary (see Chapter 13) was applied to the series of French poetic texts de-scribed earlier. As can be seen in Figure 16–5, the amount of primary process content rises until period 5 (about 1900) and then declines.

The Regressive Imagery Dictionary was also applied to the longer series of English poetic texts described earlier. The results, as shown in Figure 16–6, are quite straightforward. Primary process not only rises over time, but it also ex-hibits the predicted oscillations, which coincide with generally recognized

FIGURE 16–5   Primary process content in 19th and early 20th-century French poetry

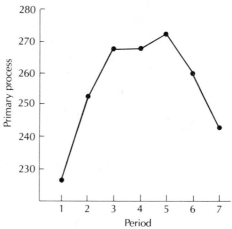

Source: C. Martindale, *Romantic Progression: The Psychology of Literary History* (Washington, D.C.: Hemisphere, 1975), p. 150.

FIGURE 16–6   Primary process content in English poetry from the 16th century to the present

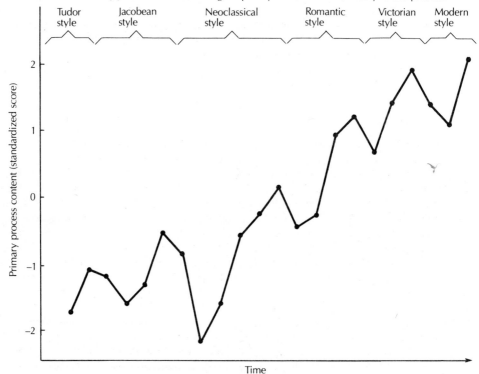

stylistic changes (see Figure 16–4). Primary process content falls when a new style is introduced, increases while the style is in fashion, and declines again when the next style is introduced. Both the linear trend and the oscillatory trend are statistically significant (Martindale, 1979a).

THE EVOLUTION OF SCIENCE

Selection pressures on scientific ideas

PRESSURE FOR SECONDARY PROCESS THINKING

The task of a scientist is to produce ideas. There are several constraints on this process. One of the most severe and unyielding of these is that the ideas have to be true. More precisely, the ideas cannot be contradicted by the evidence of reality. Furthermore, this constraint cannot be evaded by producing ideas that cannot in principle be tested against reality. Scientific ideas have to be falsifiable; that is, they have to be susceptible to being shown to be incorrect. This is one selection pressure that is common to all scientific disciplines.[1]

Many ideas are not contradicted by reality but only a few of them qualify as scientific ones. For example, if I see John talking with Mary, I can assert that JOHN AND MARY ARE TALKING. This is certainly a falsifiable idea, but it is not a scientific idea. Why? One reason is that scientific ideas are also supposed to be conceptually general or abstract; that is, there is a selection pressure for generality. This simply means that my idea about John and Mary would not survive in scientific circles. If I myself did not reject it, other scientists certainly would and it would be ignored. Being ignored, it would die. Thus, scientific ideas are subject to two seemingly contradictory selection pressures. On the one hand, they have to be concrete and perceptual (related to and not contradicted by reality). On the other hand, they have to be abstract, general, and conceptual. These two selection pressures are not really contradictory at all. Recall that we defined secondary process thinking as a cognitive activity involving both perceptual and conceptual analysis. Thus, there are not two contradictory pressures operating on science at all. There is one consistent pressure for secondary process thinking.

THE STRUCTURE OF SCIENTIFIC EXPLANATION

The dual demands for abstraction and concreteness in science are clear if we examine the structure of a scientific explanation. According to Hempel and Oppenheim (1948), a scientific explanation has the form of a logical syllogism:

Major premise: Statement of a general law.
Minor premise: Statement of empirical conditions.

---

[1] It may occur to you that scientists are in the position of poets before the 20th century, who had to produce realistic similes. Why don't scientists discard this constraint and produce surrealistic science? In fact, this is exactly what mathematics has done. In its early stages, mathematics was an empirical science. The constraint for realism has long since been abandoned so that mathematicians produce theories that do not necessarily correspond to empirical reality. As in the case of Riemann's non-Euclidean geometry, it may later turn out that the theory does describe some aspect of reality, but this is not the initial concern or goal of the pure mathematician.

Deduction: Statement of empirical observation predicted by the general
                  law.

An example might be:

Major premise: A behavior that is rewarded will be performed more fre-
                  quently
Minor premise: Keypecking (an example of a behavior) was followed by food
                  (an example of a reward)
Deduction: Therefore, keypecking increased in frequency (an example
                  of performance)

The point of a scientific experiment is to see whether the deduction is, in fact, correct. In this case, the experimenter would be interested in whether keypecking really did increase in frequency.

Scientific laws cannot be tested directly because they refer to classes of phenomena. We could never do one single experiment in which we could test the law that rewarding a behavior leads to its being performed. Why? Because the units of the law—BEHAVIOR, REWARD, AND PERFORMANCE—refer to a whole host of things. A behavior can be anything from writing a novel to a knee jerk. A reward can be anything from water to being elected president. This is why we can never prove scientific laws. Simply too many ways exist that each of the component units can be realized.

SCIENTIFIC IDEAS AND THE WUNDT CURVE

Not every secondary process idea qualifies as a scientific one. Rather than asserting that John and Mary are talking, I could propose a more secondary process formulation or law: PEOPLE SOMETIMES TALK TO ONE ANOTHER. This idea will not win me any acclaim in scientific circles either. Everyone knows this already. The idea is not novel. In order to be accepted, a scientific idea has to be novel. More precisely, in order to generate any excitement, interest, or liking on the part of other scientists, an idea has to be novel. A moment's thought, though, reveals that not just any novel secondary process idea will do.

It seems reasonable to say that the reaction of a scientist to an idea must fol- low the Wundt curve; that is, liking for a scientific idea should be determined by the same sorts of factors that determine liking for anything else. Ideas of medium arousal potential should be preferred. Let's consider what determines the arousal potential of a scientific idea. One factor is certainly novelty. In science, just as in art, ideas must be novel or they count for nothing. Thus, one way an idea could have essentially no arousal potential would be if it was exactly the same as a previously proposed idea. The Wundt curve would lead us to expect that scientists should prefer ideas with a medium degree of novelty or incongruity. These would be ideas that were novel but not so novel that they clashed with other currently held ideas. When first suggested, the idea that the earth is in orbit around the sun rather than vice versa was quite novel. As a consequence, it engendered a good deal of displeasure. Scientists take particular pleasure in theories that produce counterintuitive predictions—that is, predictions that are not obvious on the basis of common sense. Generally, such predictions do not fly in the face of common sense either. They have a medium degree of novelty or incongruity.

At any point in time, one might assume that ideas that were secondary process to a medium degree should be preferred. These would be ideas with a medium degree of abstractness and/or a medium degree of fit with reality. Hypothetically, scientists would prefer ideas with a medium degree of fit with reality. Clearly, ideas that are extremely incongrous with reality are disliked. Why should a perfect fit not be preferred most? This is, after all, the ultimate goal of science. There are several reasons. Most important is that if an idea completely explained whatever it was supposed to explain, it would die. There would be nothing left to do. Researchers would have no further problems to solve. Other researchers would not refer to or cite the idea—since they would turn their efforts toward ideas still offering problems. In evolutionary terms, this means that the idea would become an extinct museum piece. On the other hand, scientists should also prefer ideas with medium levels of conceptual complexity. A very simple concept would be trivial while an extremely complex one would require too much effort and arousal to think about.

TRENDS IN ART AND SCIENCE

We traced change in art to habituation of arousal potential. Since stimuli lose their arousal potential with repeated exposure, successive artists have to produce art with more and more arousal potential. In order to do this, they have to engage in more and more primary process thinking. Can we make an analogous argument for science? I think that we can, but the pressure to increase arousal potential in the case of science must lead in an opposite direction: toward less rather than more primary process thought. Broadly speaking, a poet's task is to create ideas of the form "X is like Y" where X and Y are coordinates on the same level. They are horizontally related. Habituation of arousal potential forces successive poets to draw X and Y from more and more distant domains. We said that they do this by engaging in more and more *primary process* thought over time. Scientists have to do something quite different. They have to produce statements of the form, "X is related to Y," where X and Y are on different levels. X is conceptual while Y is an observable percept. They are vertically rather than horizontally related. The pressure on a scientist should, then, be to expand the distance between X and Y in a vertical direction. That is, scientists should engage in more and more *secondary process* thought over time.

In the case of poetry, we said that the amount of primary process thought does not go straight up over time. Rather, it increases in an oscillating fashion. This is because there are two ways of increasing the arousal potential of poetry: regressing more or elaborating less. When further regression becomes difficult, poets elaborate less; that is, they may engage in stylistic change. It would seem that an analogous oscillating *decrease* in primary process thought is found in science. In general, successive scientists increase the arousal potential of their ideas by engaging in more and more secondary process cognition. When this becomes particularly difficult, they may bring about what Kuhn (1962) calls a paradigm change. This allows arousal potential to keep on increasing while degree of secondary process thinking declines temporarily. This idea is illustrated in

Figure 16–7, where I show the opposite sorts of trends we might expect to find in scientific thought and poetic thought.

FIGURE 16–7   Hypothetical trends in the amount of primary process thought necessary in art and in science. The periodic oscillations are probably not synchronized.

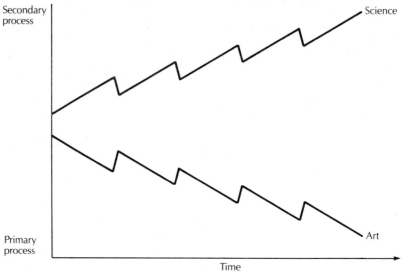

Although they are almost always intermingled, there are really two types of scientific thought: thinking of general laws and making deductions from these laws. The deductive aspect of scientific thought is clearly secondary process in nature. As we saw in Chapter 15, scientists often seem to conceive of general laws by means of primary process thought; that is, the inspiration or insight upon which the general law is based occurs in a primary process state. The final formulation, of course, requires a good bit of secondary process thought. In general, scientific thought is deductive. During periods of paradigm change, there tends to be more theorizing than deducing. This is the reason for postulating that the amount of primary process thought increases during periods of paradigm change. In the following sections, we shall see why this sort of historical trend should be found.

Kuhn's theory of scientific change

PARADIGMS

Scientific ideas tend to be clustered into whole sets of propositions (theories) rather than being isolated propositions such as the one used in our example about people talking to one another. These theories are further organized into what Kuhn (1962) calls paradigms. A paradigm is a general way of attacking the problems of a scientific discipline. It consists of a set of theories, methods, and beliefs or goals. Kuhn stresses that paradigms tend to be rather amorphous. Often, they are best defined as consisting of a prototypical set of model problems and solutions to them. In this, they are rather like natural categories in Rosch's view; that is, they are fuzzy sets defined by prototypes rather than by a rigid set of features or rules. Examples of successive paradigms would be Newtonian physics versus Einsteinian physics and Ptolemaic astronomy versus Copernican astronomy. Closer to home, we might say that cognitive psychology is a paradigm that is in the process of replacing behaviorist psychology.

TYPES OF SCIENCE

Normal science. Kuhn (1962) says that there are two types of science. Normal science operates within the confines of a universally accepted paradigm that defines its problems and provides its methods. It consists of routine testing of hypotheses derived from established theories. These hypotheses are logically deduced from theories, and the scientist has every reason to expect that experiments based upon them will yield positive results. Kuhn likens normal science to puzzle solving. Its primary interests are increased precision of measurement, testing of obvious theoretical predictions, and minor elaboration of the paradigmatic theory. "Normal science does not aim at novelties of fact or theory and, when successful, finds none" (Kuhn, 1962:52) Note that the scientists likely to be engaged in such an enterprise do not sound like the creative personality type that we described in Chapter 15. They logically deduce hypotheses and do not seek novelty.

Over the course of time, normal science produces more and more confirmations of theoretical hypotheses and more and more precise measurements. When unsuccessful, normal science produces *anomalies*—results not in conformity with theoretical predictions. What happens then? Usually nothing, Kuhn says. Many anomalies must be accumulated before any change is likely. Any single anomaly can be attributed to a variety of causes—for example, the experiment was performed incorrectly, the theory was not interpreted correctly in selecting measurements, and so on. The most likely reaction to anomaly is a minor revision in the theory.

Revolutionary science. Revolutionary science is fundamentally different from normal science, Kuhn says. It consists of thinking of a completely new paradigm. The new paradigm is often initially looser or more intuitive than the old paradigm it replaces. It is worth noting that new paradigms are often proposed by people who do resemble the creative personality type described in Chapter 15. If the new paradigm is accepted by other scientists, normal science resumes under its umbrella. Kuhn calls the replacement of one paradigm by another a *paradigm shift.* The distinction between normal and revolutionary science is never really quite as extreme as this summary suggests. We saw earlier that normal science itself involves activities that sound somewhat like revolutionary science (modifying the general laws). Kuhn (1970) himself admits this. Revolutionary science might be redefined to mean modifying general laws that are crucial for a variety of theories within a paradigm; that is, it involves changing the laws upon which the whole paradigm rests.

The Copernican revolution in astronomy is a good example of what Kuhn means by a paradigm shift. The Ptolemaic system of astronomy held that the sun and planets revolve in a circular fashion around the Earth. If this were the case, then the path of a given planet across the sky should be a smooth arc. In fact, at some times, planets appear to stop in their tracks, move backwards for a while, and then resume their forward course. This is an anomaly for the model. The reaction was to revise the model by adding epicycles; the heavenly bodies not only rotate around the Earth, but they do so in a spirallike fashion. More precise observations revealed that this model was still not completely satisfactory. A planet does not always appear to move at exactly the same speed. One way to handle this would be to add epicycles to the epicycles. Still, the model did not exactly fit the observations. More epicycles were called for.

A confusing variety of further modifications were suggested. It is clear that, as Kuhn (1962) puts it, "Astronomy's complexity was increasing far more rapidly than its accuracy and that a discrepancy corrected in one place was likely to show up in another." In terms of the Wundt curve, the arousal potential of Ptolemaic astronomy was increasingly rapidly. It was becoming too complex and too contradictory. Copernicus proposed a fundamentally different theory in his book, *De Revolutionibus*. The theory was, of course, that all of the planets—including the Earth—follow circular orbits around the sun. With hindsight, this seems to be a reasonable simplification. The theory easily explains why planets sometimes seem to move backwards in their orbits: The Earth catches up with them and then passes them. However, at the time, things were quite otherwise. The most obvious difficulty was that the theory was wildly implausible. Immediate experience suggests that the earth is quite stationary. Otherwise we should feel ourselves moving. Furthermore, Copernicus' model actually fit the observational data more poorly than did the Ptolemaic model. Only with Kepler's modification of the Copernican model (that is, ascribing elliptical rather than circular orbits to the planets) almost 100 years later did the new model outperform the predictions from Ptolemaic theory.

THE HISTORY OF SCIENCE

Kuhn's basic idea is that the history of science is not a process of accumulation of more and more knowledge. Rather, it consists of a series of paradigms. Within any one paradigm, normal science is carried out. Then, a period of revolutionary science occurs and brings about a paradigm change. Normal science resumes under the guidance of the new paradigm. This sounds rather like the history of poetry with its series of styles: Within any one style, one could say that normal poetry is carried out. Then a period of revolutionary poetry brings about a new style. Kuhn himself has remarked that the resemblance is not coincidental. He patterned his theory after theories of artistic change. Another similarity concerns the cumulation of knowledge. The general belief is that scientific knowledge cumulates or progresses while artistic knowledge does neither. Kuhn, though, argues that scientific knowledge does not cumulate as much as is commonly believed. The history of science is not cumulative because the new paradigm generally destroys many of the facts produced by the old paradigm. For example, modern chemistry defines things in terms of compounds and elements. From the viewpoint of this paradigm, earlier experiments that used not pure compounds or elements but naturally occurring substances—for example, wood or mud—are completely meaningless. In other cases, the facts and laws of the old paradigm are severely restricted in their range or rendered only approximately valid. From the perspective of modern physics, the laws of classical Newtonian physics are mere approximations that hold only in medium ranges of space and time. From the perspective of cognitive psychology, many of the laws of behavioristic psychology apply not to organisms in general but only to certain lower animals.

Exhaustion in normal science

SCIENCE AND GOLD MINING

What goes wrong with normal science so that it is overthrown by revolutionary science? We can get an idea of what happens to normal science by looking at the life cycle of scientific specialty areas. Examples of scientific specialty areas would be the study of semantic memory or the study of text grammars. Holton (1973) compares a scientific specialty area to exploring for gold. The task is to discover all of the gold in a given area. The gold corresponds to interesting scientific ideas. A prospector confronted with the task knows that gold is discovered by walking around looking for it, which takes time. The expectation would be that over time more and more gold will be discovered. Conversely, the more time that has passed, the less gold that will be left to discover. To make matters worse, once gold is discovered, lots of people will rush in to help find it. The result will be that most of the gold will be discovered quickly. The amount left to be discovered will drop off quickly with time. Holton argues that this happens with specialized areas in science. They are very soon mined out.

Holton (1973) points out that the gold-mining analogy has to be complicated in one important respect. Ideas are not simply removed from the pool of possible ideas waiting to be discovered. Already discovered ideas can be recombined to form new ideas. Thus, discovery of a given idea can potentially add to, rather than subtracting from, the pool of ideas waiting to be discovered. It would seem that this tendency of ideas to propagate other ideas expands the range of possibilities for a specialty area but does not open up an infinite range of possibilities. It merely postpones the inevitable time when there are no longer any useful ideas left to be discovered.

TRENDS IN SECONDARY PROCESS CONTENT OF NORMAL-SCIENCE PUBLICATIONS

Later workers in a specialty area should have to engage in more secondary process thought than earlier ones. Less deduction should be required to retrieve earlier ideas than later ones. This is only another way of saying that the earlier ideas are more obvious. If more deduction is required over time, this means that more secondary process thought will be required. Data from a study in progress support this hypothesis. I analyzed samples from the *Journal of the Experimental Analysis of Behavior* from 1958 to 1976 with the same measures used in my studies of poetry. This journal is the chief outlet of scientists doing work in operant psychology. Over the time span studied, the percentage of primary process content declined monotonically. This is consistent with the hypothesis that later workers had to engage in more secondary process thought than earlier ones.

The life cycle of scientific paradigms

Crane (1972) has argued that the considerations raised by Holton apply to whole paradigms as well as to individual specialty areas. Her theory of the life cycle of a paradigm is shown in Figure 16–8. When a paradigm first appears, it

FIGURE 16–8   Crane's model of the stages in the life of a scientific paradigm

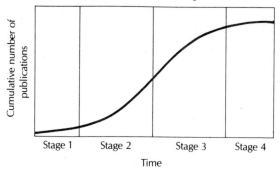

	Stage 1	Stage 2	Stage 3	Stage 4
Characteristics of knowledge	Paradigm appears	Normal science	Solution of major problems	Exhaustion
			Anomalies appear	Crisis
Characteristics of scientific communities	Little or no social organization	Groups of collaborators and an invisible college	Increasing specialization	Decline in membership
			Increasing controversy	Decline in membership

Source: D. Crane, *Invisible Colleges: Diffusion of Knowledge in Scientific Communities* (Chicago: University of Chicago Press, 1972), p. 173.

is espoused by a small, unorganized group of scientists. Presumably these people formulate the general laws and develop the basic methods that define the paradigm. Once a paradigm is established, normal science begins. Normal science is carried out by the members of what she calls an invisible college—a group of people who interact with each other and share the same goals and values. In the late stages of a paradigm, most major problems have been solved. This leads scientists to specialize on increasingly specific problems. This is necessary in order to extract the remaining ideas. In this stage, anomalies may also appear. In the final stage, there is exhaustion and/or crisis. The paradigm offers few possibilities and many problems or anomalies. As a consequence of this, members defect and are not replaced by new adherants.

Paradigms can hypothetically die for two reasons. There can be exhaustion without anomaly; that is, the paradigm has succeeded too well and there are no problems left to be solved. This is essentially what happened to Euclidean geometry. After the time of Euclid, there was nothing left to be done. The fit with reality had become perfect. Although Crane does not put it in these terms, we could say that arousal potential was zero and the field elicited no further interest (in the sense of scientists wanting to work in the area). In the case of exhaustion with anomaly a rather different set of affairs exists. The exhaustion is not perceived as such. What is perceived is that fit with reality can be obtained only with very complex theories. Further, new ideas can be generated only with considerable effort. In addition, there are undeniable anomalies or incongruities. Complexity, effort, and incongruity add up to high arousal potential, and high arousal potential means negative affect. In contrast, a new paradigm—if it is to be successful—will have somewhat lower arousal potential: The fit with reality is not perfect, but neither are anomalies present as is the case for an old paradigm. Anticipated payoff in relation to effort is also higher.

It would seem that the new paradigm finally wins by default. The old paradigm does not die. Rather, its adherents die. Since they have not been able to recruit new disciples, the paradigm dies with them. As the physicist, Max Planck (1950) observed, "A new scientific truth does not triumph by convincing its opponents and making them see the light, but rather because its opponents eventually die, and a new generation grows up that is familiar with it." Once this happens, the new paradigm becomes dominant and the process begins anew. There is no reason to expect that cognitive psychology will escape this fortune or this fate.

SUMMARY AND CONCLUSIONS

Campbell argues that ideas, beliefs, and behaviors of all sorts are subject to evolutionary change. The three requirements for evolution are (1) mechanisms for replication or reproduction, (2) variation in whatever is reproduced, and (3) mechanisms for selection that consistently favor one type of variation over other types. In the case of cognitive evolution, learning provides the mechanism for replication. Our ideas, beliefs, and behaviors are learned from other people. In this learning process, variation is introduced. Learning consists of assimilating material to memory schemata. In general, this involves simplification of the assimilated material. However, it can also produce creativity in cases where the material is assimilated to an unusual or unintended schema. Serial reproduction experiments demonstrate that, even when people attempt to produce exact copies of things, variation is introduced. When copying is done by a series of people, this variability cumulates, and quite radical deviations from the original stimulus are observed. A group of people all attempting to produce an exact copy of the same thing would produce a set of variants. Most of these variants would probably be simpler than the original, but some would be more complex or novel. The Wundt curve suggests that there should be a consistent selection pressure operating against the simpler variants and in favor of those with slightly higher arousal potential. Thus, the process of replication or assimilation to memory schemata tends to simplify while selection pressures based upon hedonic considerations operate in favor of increased complexity. Whether a series of ideas, behaviors, or cognitive products will become simpler or more complex over time will depend upon the balance between these two forces.

In both art and science, there seems to have been long-standing and consistent selection pressures for increases in arousal potential. We saw that the history of poetry seems to have been largely determined by this pressure. Poetry consists of arranging words according to certain rules. For example, words have to be combined in order to form metaphors and similes. In order to increase arousal potential, successive poets need to combine more and more remote associates in their metaphors. In order to think of these increasingly remote associates, successive poets have to regress more and more toward primary process states of consciousness. The history of poetry is punctuated by stylistic changes. Essentially, these increase the population of words that can be used in poetry or loosen the rules governing their combination. The result is that poets writing in the new style can keep on increasing the arousal potential of their poetry without the necessity for such deep regression. However, the longer the new style has been in existence, the more regression that will be necessary to think of word combinations with sufficient arousal potential. There is quantitative evidence for this general formulation. For series of poems produced by a given poetic tradition, indexes of arousal potential increase monotonically over time. The primary process content of these poems increases also but in an oscillating fashion; such content rises while a given style is in fashion, declines somewhat with the introduction of a new style, rises again, and so on.

While poetry combines words in a horizontal fashion (for example, A is like B), science combines ideas in a vertical fashion (for example, A is a consequence of B). In poetry, pressure for novelty operates to make successive word combinations more distant, remote, or farfetched. The best way of producing such remote combinations is primary process thinking. In science, pressure for novelty operates to make successive combinations of ideas more remote in a vertical direction; that is, more and more abstract concepts are combined with more and more concrete and precise observations. The best way of producing remote combinations of this sort is secondary process thinking. Thus, successive scientists should have to engage in thought that is increasingly secondary process in nature. However, just as poetry exhibits periodic stylistic changes, science exhibits periodic paradigm shifts. We saw that such paradigm shifts do not always occur for purely rational reasons. In fact, Kuhn and others have argued that they are never brought about by completely rational considerations. Scientific paradigm shifts may be seen as being accompanied by a movement toward a more primary process manner of thinking than was necessary in the last stages of the preceding paradigm. However, once the new paradigm is established, successive scientists must engage in more and more secondary process thinking. Thus, the degree of secondary process thought in a scientific discipline should increase over time in an oscillating pattern. Of course, this is just the opposite of what seems to happen in poetry and the other arts. Thus, art and science may in many respects be seen as mirror images of one another. This must be a consequence of the fact that they are organized endeavors aimed at expanding human knowledge by use of the two basic modes of cognition—primary process and secondary process—at our disposal.

References

Abbs, J. H., and Sussman, H. M. (1971) Neurophysiological feature detectors and speech perception: A discussion of theoretical implications. *Journal of Speech and Hearing Research* 14:23–36.

Abelson, R. P., and Rosenberg, M. J. (1958) Symbolic psycho-logic: A model of attitudinal consistency. *Behavioral Science* 3:1–13.

Aderman, D., and Smith, E. E. (1971) Expectancy as a determinant of functional units of perceptual recognition. *Cognitive Psychology* 2:117–29.

Alajouanine, T.; Lhermitte, F.; and de Ribaucourt-Ducarne, B. (1960) Les alexies agnosiques et aphasiques. In T. Alajouanine, ed., *Les grandes activités du lobe occipital*. Paris: Masson.

Allport, G. W., and Postman, L. (1947) *The psychology of rumor*. New York: Henry Holt.

Alpert, R. (1953) Perceptual determinants of affect. M.A. thesis, Wesleyan University.

Anderson, C. C., and Cropley, A. J. (1966) Some correlates of originality. *Australian Journal of Psychology* 18:218–27.

Anderson, J. R., and Bower, G. H. (1972) Recognition and retrieval processes in free recall. *Psychological Review* 79:97–123.

_____. (1973) *Human associative memory*. Hillsdale, N.J.: Erlbaum.

Anonymous (1955) The autobiography of a schizophrenic experience. *Journal of Abnormal and Social Psychology* 51:677–89.

Anonymous (1969) The effects of marijuana on consciousness. In C. T. Tart, ed., *Altered states of consciousness*. New York: Wiley.

Antrobus, J. S.; Coleman, R.; and Singer, J. L. (1967) Signal detection performance by subjects differing in predisposition to daydreaming. *Journal of Consulting Psychology* 31:487–91.

Arbib, M. A. (1972) *The metaphorical brain: An introduction to cybernetics as artificial intelligence and brain theory*. New York: Wiley.

Arieti, S. (1955) *Interpretation of schizophrenia*. New York: Robert Brunner.

Ashby, W. R.; von Foerster, H.; and Walker, C. C. (1962) Instability of pulse activity in a net with threshold. *Nature* 196:561–62.

Atkinson, J. W., ed. (1958) *Motives in fantasy, action, and society*. Princeton, N.J.: Van Nostrand.

Averbach, E., and Coriell, A. S. (1961) Short-term memory in vision. *The Bell System Technical Journal* 40:309–28.

Baddeley, A. D. (1966a) Short-term memory for word sequences as a function of acoustic, semantic, and formal similarity. *Quarterly Journal of Experimental Psychology* 18:362–65.

_____. (1966b) The influence of acoustic and semantic similarity on long-term memory for word sequences. *Quarterly Journal of Experimental Psychology* 18:302–9.

_____. (1978) The trouble with levels: A reexamination of Craik and Lockhart's framework for memory research. *Psychological Review* 85:139–52.

Baddeley, A. D., and Ecob, J. R. (1973) Reaction time and short-term memory: Implications of repetition effects for the high speed exhaustive scan hypothesis. *Quarterly Journal of Experimental Psychology* 25:229–40.

413

Baggett, P. (1979) Structurally equivalent stories in movie and text and the effect of the medium on recall. *Journal of Verbal Learning and Verbal Behavior* 18:333–56.

Bahrick, H. P.; Fitts, P. M.; and Rankin, R. E. (1952) Effects of incentives upon reactions to peripheral stimuli. *Journal of Experimental Psychology* 44:400–406.

Bakan, P. (1971) The eyes have it. *Psychology Today* 4:64–67.

Bard, P., and Mountcastle, V. B. (1948) Some forebrain mechanisms involved in expression of rage with special reference to suppression of angry behavior. *Research Publications of the Association for Nervous and Mental Disease* 27:362–404.

Barnes, J. M., and Underwood, B. J. (1959) 'Fate' of first-list associations in transfer theory. *Journal of Experimental Psychology* 58:97–105.

Baron, J. (1973) Phonemic stage not necessary for reading. *Quarterly Journal of Experimental Psychology* 25:241–46.

Baron, J., and Thurston, I. (1973) An analysis of the word superiority effect. *Cognitive Psychology* 4:207–28.

Barron, F. (1952) Personality style and perceptual choice. *Journal of Personality* 20:385–401.

————. (1953) Complexity-simplicity as a personality dimension. *Journal of Abnormal and Social Psychology* 68:163–72.

————. (1955) The disposition toward originality. *Journal of Abnormal and Social Psychology* 51:478–85.

————. (1968) *Creativity and personal freedom.* Princeton, N.J.: Van Nostrand.

Barron, F., and Welsh, G. (1952) Artistic perception as a possible factor in personality style: Its measurement by a figure preference test. *Journal of Psychology* 33:199–203.

Bartlett, F. C. (1932) *Remembering.* Cambridge, Eng.: Cambridge University Press.

Battig, W. F., and Montague, W. E. (1969) Category norms for verbal items in 56 categories: A replication and extension of the Connecticut category norms. *Journal of Experimental Psychology Monograph* 80 (3, Pt. 2).

Baudelaire, C. (1851) *Les paradis artificiels.* In *Oeuvres complètes.* Paris: Editions Gallimard, 1961.

Békésy, G. von. (1967) *Sensory inhibition.* Princeton, N.J.: Princeton University Press.

Berkeley, G. (1710) *A treatise concerning the principle of human knowledge.* In *Works of Berkeley.* Oxford, Eng.: Clarenden Press, 1871.

Berlin, B., and Kay, P. (1969) *Basic color terms: Their universality and evolution.* Berkeley: University of California Press.

Berlyne, D. E. (1965) *Structure and direction in thinking.* New York: Wiley.

————. (1967) Arousal and reinforcement. In D. Levine, ed., *Nebraska symposium on motivation,* vol. 15. Lincoln: University of Nebraska Press.

————. (1970) Novelty, complexity and hedonic value. *Perception and Psychophysics* 8:279–86.

————. (1971) *Aesthetics and psychobiology.* New York: Appleton-Century-Crofts.

Berlyne, D. E., and Slater, J. (1957) Perceptual curiosity, exploratory behavior and maze learning. *Journal of Comparative and Physiological Psychology* 50:228–32.

Berlyne, D. E.; McDonnell, P.; Nicki, R. M..; and Parham, L. C. C. (1967) Effects of auditory pitch and complexity on EEG desynchronization and on verbally expressed judgments. *Canadian Journal of Psychology* 21:346–67.

Berscheid, E., and Walster, E. (1974) A little bit about love. In T. L. Huston, ed., *Foundations of interpersonal attraction.* New York: Academic Press.

Bessel, F. W. (1823) *Astronomische Beobachtungen.* Königsberg: Academia Albertina.

Beurle, R. L. (1956) Properties of a mass of cells capable of regenerating pulses. *Philosophical Transactions of the Royal Society, B* 240:55–94.

Bever, T. G., and Chiarello, R. J. (1974) Cerebral dominance in musicians and nonmusicians. *Science* 185:537–39.

Bexton, W. H.; Heron, W.; and Scott, T. H. (1954) Effects of decreased variation in the sensory environment. *Canadian Journal of Psychology* 8:70–76.

Bjork, E. L., and Murray, J. T. (1977) On the nature of input channels in visual processing. *Psychological Review* 84:472–84.

Black, J. B., and Bower, G. H. (1979) Episodes as chunks in narrative memory. *Journal of Verbal Learning and Verbal Behavior* 18:309–18.

Blackwell, H. R., and Schlosberg, H. (1943) Octave generalization, pitch discrimination, and loudness thresholds in the white rat. *Journal of Experimental Psychology* 33:407–19.

Blake, W. (1803) Letter to Thomas Butts. In A. G. B. Russell, ed., *The letters of William Blake.* London: Methuen, 1906.

Blakemore, C. (1975) Central visual processing. In M. S. Gazzaniga and C. Blakemore eds., *Handbook of psychobiology.* New York: Academic Press.

Bloch, A. M. (1885) Expériences sur la vision. *Comtes Rendues, Société Biologique* 2:493.

Blum, G. (1961) *A model of the mind.* New York: Wiley.

Blumenthal, A. L. (1977) *The process of cognition.* Englewood Cliffs, N.J.: Prentice-Hall.

Bogen, J. E. (1969) The other side of the brain II: An appositional mind. *Bulletin of the Los Angeles Neurological Society* 34:135–62.

Bolles, R. C. (1975) Learning, motivation, and cognition. In W. K. Estes, ed., *Handbook of learning and cognitive processes,* vol. 1. Hillsdale, N.J.: Erlbaum.

Bouma, H. (1970) Interaction effects in parafoveal letter recognition. *Nature* 226:177–78.

Bousfield, W. A. (1953) The occurrence of clustering and the recall of randomly arranged associates. *Journal of General Psychology* 49:229–40.

Bousfield, W. A., and Barclay, W. D. (1950) The relationship between order and frequency of occurrence of restricted associative responses. *Journal of Experimental Psychology* 40:643–47.

Bousfield, W. A.; Cohen, B. H.; and Whitmarsh, G. A. (1958) Associative clustering in the recall of words of different taxonomic frequencies of occurrence. *Psychological Reports* 4:39–44.

Bower, G. H. (1972) Mental imagery and associative learning. In L. Gregg, ed., *Cognition in learning and memory.* New York: Wiley.

Bower, G. H., and Clark, M. C. (1969) Narrative stories as mediators for serial learning. *Psychonomic Science* 14:181–82.

Bowers, K. S., and van der Meulen, S. (1970) The effect of hypnotic susceptibility on creativity test performance. *Journal of Personality and Social Psychology* 14:247–56.

Bowers, P. (1979) Hypnosis and creativity: The search for the missing link. *Journal of Abnormal Psychology* 88:564–72.

Bransford, J. D., and Franks, J. J. (1971) The abstraction of linguistic ideas. *Cognitive Psychology* 2:331–50.

Briggs, G. E. (1954) Acquisition, extinction, and recovery functions in retroactive inhibition. *Journal of Experimental Psychology* 47:285–93.

Broadbent, D. E. (1958) *Perception and communication.* New York: Pergamon.

––––––. (1971) *Decision and stress.* New York: Academic Press.

Broadhurst, P. L. (1959) The interaction of task difficulty and motivation: The Yerkes-Dodson Law revived. *Acta Psychologica* 16:321–38.

Broca, P. (1861) Remarques sur la siége de la faculté du langage articulé suivies d'une observation d'aphémie. *Bulletin de la Société Anatomique de Paris* 36:330–57.

Brown, A. S. (1973) An empirical verification of Mednick's associative theory of creativity. *Bulletin of the Psychonomic Society* 2:429–30.

Brown, C. R., and Rubinstein, H. (1961) Test of response bias explanation of word-frequency effect. *Science* 133:280–81.

Brown, J. (1958) Some tests of the decay theory of immediate memory. *Quarterly Journal of Experimental Psychology* 10:12–21.

Brown, R., and McNeill, D. (1966) The "tip of the tongue" phenomenon. *Journal of Verbal Learning and Verbal Behavior* 5:325–37.

Bruner, J. S. (1957) Going beyond the information given. In J. Bruner et al., *Contemporary approaches to cognition.* Cambridge, Mass.: Harvard University Press.

Bruner, J. S., and Postman, L. (1949) On the perception of incongruity: A paradigm. *Journal of Personality* 18:206–23.

Bruner, J. S., and Potter, M. C. (1964) Interference in visual recognition. *Science* 144:424–25.

Bruner, J. S.; Goodnow, J. J.; and Austin, G. A. (1956) *A study of thinking.* New York: Wiley.

Bucke, R. M. (1901) *Cosmic consciousness: A study in the evolution of the human mind.* New York: Dutton, 1926.

Bursill, A. E. (1958) The restriction of peripheral vision during exposure to hot and humid conditions. *Quarterly Journal of Experimental Psychology* 10:113–29.

Butler, R. A. (1957) The effect of deprivation of visual incentives on visual exploration motivation in monkeys. *Journal of Comparative and Physiological Psychology* 50:177–79.

Butler, R. A., and Harlow, H. F. (1954) Persistence of visual exploration in monkeys. *Journal of Comparative and Physiological Psychology* 47:258–63.

Butler, S. R. (1971) Organization of cerebral cortex for perception. *British Medical Journal* 27:544–47.

Callaway, E. (1959) The influence of amobarbital (amylobarbitone) and methamphetamine on the focus of attention. *Journal of Mental Science* 105:382–92.

Callaway, E., and Dembo, D. (1958) Narrowed attention: A psychological phenomenon that accompanies a certain physiological change. *Archives of Neurological Psychiatry* 79:74–90.

Callaway, E., and Thompson, S. V. (1953) Sympathetic activity and perception. *Psychosomatic Medicine* 15:443–55.

Campbell, D. T. (1960) Blind variation and selective retention in creative thought as in other knowledge processes. *Psychological Review* 67:380–400.

––––––––. (1974) Evolutionary epistemology. In P. A. Schilpp, ed., *The philosophy of Karl Popper.* LaSalle, Illinois: Open Court.

––––––––. (1975) On the conflicts between biological and social evolution and between psychology and moral tradition. *American Psychologist* 30:1103–26.

Campbell, J. (1949) *The hero with a thousand faces.* Princeton, N.J.: Princeton University Press.

Carmichael, L.; Hogan, H. P.; and Walter, A. A. (1932) An experimental study of the effect of language on the reproduction of visually perceived forms. *Journal of Experimental Psychology* 15: 73–86.

Carmon, A., and Nachson, I. (1973) Ear asymmetry in perception of emotional non-verbal stimuli. *Acta Psychologica* 37:351–57.

Carpenter, R. H. S., and Blakemore, C. (1973) Interactions between orientations in human vision. *Experimental Brain Research* 18:287–303.

Cartwright, D., and Harary, F. (1956) Structural balance: A generalization of Heider's theory. *Psychological Review* 63:277–93.

Castaneda, C. (1971) *A separate reality: Further conversations with Don Juan.* New York: Simon & Schuster.

Cavanaugh, J. P. (1976) Holographic and trace-strength models of rehearsal effects in the item recognition task. *Memory and Cognition* 4:186–99.

Chapman, L. J., and Chapman, J. P. (1959) Atmosphere effect re-examined. *Journal of Experimental Psychology* 58:220–26.

Cherry, E. C. (1953) Some experiments on the recognition of speech with one and with two ears. *Journal of the Acoustical Society of America* 25:975–79.

Chomsky, N. (1957) Review of B. F. Skinner, *Verbal behavior. Language* 35:26–58.

Christensen, P. R.; Guilford, J. P.; and Wilson, R. C. (1957) Relations of creative responses to working time and instructions. *Journal of Experimental Psychology* 53:82–88.

Clark, R. A., and Sensibar, M. R. (1955) The relationship between symbolic and manifest projections of sexuality with some incidental correlates. *Journal of Abnormal and Social Psychology* 50:327–34.

Clement, D. E., and Carpenter, J. S. (1970) Relative discriminability of visually presented letter pairs using a same-different choice reaction time task. *Psychonomic Science* 20:363–64.

Cofer, C. N.; Bruce, D. R.; and Reicher, G. M. (1966) Clustering in free recall as a function of certain methodological variations. *Journal of Experimental Psychology* 71:858–66.

Cohen, J. (1966) *Structure du langage poétique.* Paris: Flammarion.

Cole, M., and Perez-Cruet, J. (1964) Prosopagnosia. *Neuropsychologia* 2:237–46.

Cole, R. A.; Coltheart, M.; and Allard, F. (1974) Memory of a speaker's voice: Reaction time to same or different voiced letter. *Quarterly Journal of Experimental Psychology* 26:1–7.

Collins, A. M., and Loftus, E. F. (1975) A spreading activation theory of semantic processing. *Psychological Review* 82:407–28.

Collins, A. M., and Quillian, M. R. (1969) Retrieval time from semantic memory. *Journal
of Verbal Learning and Verbal Behavior* 8:240–47.

_____. (1972) How to make a language user. In E. Tulving and W. Donaldson, eds.,
Organization of memory. New York: Academic Press.

_____. (1973) Experiments on semantic memory and language comprehension. In
L. W. Gregg, ed., *Cognition in learning and memory.* New York: Wiley.

Conrad, C. (1972) Cognitive economy in semantic memory. *Journal of Experimental Psychology* 92:149–54.

Conrad, R. (1963) Acoustic confusions and memory span for words. *Nature* 197:1029–30.

_____. (1964) Acoustic confusions in immediate memory. *British Journal of Psychol-
ogy* 55:75–84.

Cooper, W. E. (1975) Selective adaptation to speech. In F. Restle; R. M. Shiffrin; N. J.
Castellan; H. R. Lindman; and D. B. Pisoni, eds., *Cognitive theory,* vol. 1. Hillsdale,
N.J.: Erlbaum.

Coren, S., and Schulman, M. (1971) Effects of an external stress on commonality of verbal
associates. *Psychological Reports* 28:328–30.

Corteen, R. S., and Wood, B. (1972) Autonomic responses to shock-associated words in
an unattended channel. *Journal of Experimental Psychology* 94:308–13.

Covello, E., and Martindale, C. (1978) Creativity, hemispheric asymmetry, and primary
process content in narratives. Paper presented at American Psychological Association
convention, Toronto.

Craik, F. I. M. (1970) The fate of primary memory items in free recall. *Journal of Verbal
Learning and Verbal Behavior* 9:143–48.

_____. (1973) A 'levels of analysis' view of memory. In P. Pliner; L. Krames; and T.
Alloway, eds., *Communication and affect.* London: Academic Press.

Craik, F. I. M., and Levy, B. A. (1970) Semantic and acoustic information in primary
memory. *Journal of Experimental Psychology* 86:77–82.

Craik, F. I. M., and Lockhart, R. S. (1972) Levels of processing: A framework for memory
research. *Journal of Verbal Learning and Verbal Behavior* 11:671–84.

Craik, F. I. M., and Tulving, E. (1975) Depth of processing and the retention of words in
episodic memory. *Journal of Experimental Psychology: General* 104:268–94.

Craik, F. I. M., and Watkins, M. J. (1973) The role of rehearsal in short-term memory.
Journal of Verbal Learning and Verbal Behavior 12:599–607.

Crane, D. (1972) *Invisible colleges: Diffusion of knowledge in scientific communities.*
Chicago: University of Chicago Press.

Cronin, D.; Bodley, P.; Potts, L.; Mather, M. D.; Gardner, R. K.; and Tobin, J. C. (1970)
Unilateral and bilateral ECT: A study of memory disturbance and relief from depression.
Journal of Neurology, Neurosurgery and Psychiatry 33:705–13.

Crowder, R. G. (1978) Mechanisms of auditory backward masking in the stimulus suffix
effect. *Psychological Review* 85:502–24.

Crowder, R. G., and Morton, J. (1969) Precategorical acoustic storage (PAS). *Perception
and Psychophysics* 5:365–73.

Dallett, K. M. (1965) 'Primary memory': The effects of redundancy upon digit repetition.
Psychonomic Science 3:237–38.

Davidson, R. J., and Schwartz, G. E. (1977) The influence of musical training on patterns
of EEG asymmetry during musical and non-musical self-generated tasks. *Psychophysiology* 14:58–63.

Day, H. I. (1967) Evaluations of subjective complexity, pleasingness and interestingness
for a series of random polygons varying in complexity. *Perception and Psychophysics*
2:281–86.

_____. (1968) The importance of symmetry and complexity in the evaluation of com-
plexity, interest and pleasingness. *Psychonomic Science* 10:339–40.

Day, M. E. (1964) An eye-movement phenomenon related to attention, thought and
anxiety. *Perceptual and Motor Skills* 19:443–46.

Deci, E. L. (1971) Effects of externally mediated rewards on intrinsic motivation. *Journal
of Personality and Social Psychology* 18:105–15.

Dee, H. L., and Fontenot, D. J. (1973) Cerebral dominance and lateral differences in perception and memory. *Neuropsychologia* 11:167–73.

Deikman, A. J. (1966) Deautomatization and the mystic experience. *Psychiatry* 29: 324–38.

Dentler, R. A., and Mackler, B. (1964) Originality: Some social and personal determinants. *Behavioral Science* 9:1–7.

Dermer, M., and Berscheid, E. (1972) Self-report of arousal as an indicant of activation level. *Behavioral Science* 17:420–29.

Descartes, R. (1662) *Traité de l'homme.* In *Oeuvres de Descartes.* Paris: Léopold Cerf, 1897–1913.

Deutsch, D. (1969) Music recognition. *Psychological Review* 76:300–7.

————. (1970) Tones and numbers: Specificity of interference in short-term memory. *Science* 168:1604–5.

————. (1972) Mapping of interactions in the pitch memory store. *Science* 175: 1020–22.

Deutsch, D., and Feroe, J. (1975) Disinhibition in pitch memory. *Perception and Psychophysics* 17:320–24.

Deutsch, J. A., and Deutsch, D. (1963) Attention: Some theoretical considerations. *Psychological Review* 70:80–90.

DeValois, R. (1958) Discussion. In S. H. Bartley. Some facts and concepts regarding the neurophysiology of the optic pathway. *A.M.A. Archives of Ophthalmology* 60: 784–85.

De Vito, J. (1970) *The psychology of speech and language.* New York: Random House.

Dewing, K., and Battye, G. (1971) Attention deployment and nonverbal fluency. *Journal of Personality and Social Psychology* 17:214–18.

Di Lollo, V. (1977) Temporal characteristics of iconic memory. *Nature* 267:241–43.

Dobelle, W. H.; Mladejovsky, M. G.; and Girvin, J. P. (1974) Artificial vision for the blind: Electrical stimulation of visual cortex offers hope for a functional prosthesis. *Science* 183:440–44.

Domarus, E. von (1944) The specific laws of logic in schizophrenia. In J. Kasanin, ed. *Language and thought in schizophrenia.* Berkeley: University of California Press.

Dorman, M.; Studdert-Kennedy, M.; and Raphael, L. (1977) Stop consonant recognition: Release bursts and formant transitions as functionally equivalent context-dependent cues. *Perception and Psychophysics* 22:109–22.

Dumas, R., and Morgan, A. (1975) EEG asymmetry as a function of occupation, task, and task difficulty. *Neuropsychologia* 13:219–28.

Dunker, K. (1945) On problem solving. *Psychological Monographs* 58, no. 270.

Dunn-Rankin, P. (1968) The similarity of lower-case letters of the English alphabet. *Journal of Verbal Learning and Verbal Behavior* 7:990–95.

Dykes, M., and McGhie, A. (1976) A comparative study of attentional strategies of schizophrenic and highly creative normal subjects. *British Journal of Psychiatry* 128:50–56.

Eason, R. G., and Dudley, L. M. (1971) Physiological and behavioral indicants of activation. *Psychophysiology* 7:223–32.

Easterbrook, J. A. (1959) The effect of emotion on cue utilization and the organization of behavior. *Psychological Review* 66:183–201.

Ebbinghaus, H. (1885) *Über das Gedächtnis.* Leipzig: Dunker & Humbolt.

Eccles, J. C. (1969) Excitatory and inhibitory mechanisms in brain. In H. H. Jasper; A. A. Ward; and A. Pope, eds., *Basic mechanisms of the epilepsies.* Boston: Little, Brown.

Egan, J. P.; Carterette, E. C.; and Thwing, E. J. (1954) Some factors affecting multi-channel listening. *Journal of the Acoustical Society of America* 26:774–82.

Ehrenzweig, A. (1953) *The psycho-analysis of artistic vision and hearing.* New York: Braziller, 1965.

Eimas, P. D.; Cooper, W. E.; and Corbit, J. D. (1973) Some properties of linguistic feature detectors. *Perception and Psychophysics* 13:247–52.

Eimas, P. D., and Corbit, J. D. (1973) Selective adaptation of linguistic feature detectors. *Cognitive Psychology* 4:99–109.

Empson, W. (1930) *Seven types of ambiguity.* London: New Directions.

Engel, R. (1928) Experimentelle Untersuchungen über die Abhängigkeit der Lust and Unlust von der Reizstärke beim Geschmacksinn. *Archiv für die gesamte Psychologie* 64:1–36.

Erdmann, B., and Dodge, R. (1898) *Psychologische Untersuchungen über das Lesen auf experimenteller Grundlage.* Halle, Germany: M. Niemeyer.

Eriksen, B. A., and Eriksen, C. W. (1974) Effects of noise letters upon identification of target in nonsearch task. *Perception and Psychophysics* 16:143–49.

Esposito, N. J., and Pelton, L. H. (1971) Review of the measurement of semantic satiation. *Psychological Bulletin* 75:330–46.

Estes, W. K. (1972a) An associative basis for coding and organization in memory. In A. W. Melton and E. Martin, eds., *Coding processes in human memory.* Washington, D.C.: Winston.

_____. (1972b) Interactions of signal and background variables in visual processing. *Perception and Psychophysics* 12:278–86.

Estes, W. K., and Taylor, H. A. (1964) A detection method and probabilistic models for assessing information processing from brief visual displays. *Proceedings of the National Academy of Sciences* 52:446–54.

Evans, D. R. (1969) Conceptual complexity, arousal and epistemic behaviour. Ph.D. dissertation, University of Toronto.

Evans, E. F., and Whitfield, I. C. (1964) Classification of unit responses in the auditory cortex of the unanesthetized and unrestrained cat. *Journal of Physiology* 171:476–93.

Evey, R. J., (1959) Use of a computer to design character recognition logic. *Proceedings of the Eastern Joint Computer Conference.* Boston.

Eysenck, H. J. (1967) *The biological basis of personality.* Springfield, Ill.: Charles C Thomas.

Eysenck, M. W. (1977) *Human memory: Theory, research and individual differences.* Oxford, Eng.: Pergamon.

Fant, G. (1973) *Speech sounds and features.* Cambridge, Mass.: MIT Press.

Farrell, J. P. (1979) Poetry and altered states of consciousness. *Journal of Altered States of Consciousness* 5:123–45.

Fenichel, O. (1945) *The psychoanalytic theory of neurosis.* New York: Norton.

Fillmore, C. J. (1968) The case for case. E. Bach and R. G. Harms, eds., *Universals in linguistic theory.* New York: Holt, Rinehart & Winston.

_____. (1969) Toward a modern theory of case. In D. A. Reibel and S. A. Schane, eds., *Modern studies in English.* Englewood-Cliffs, N.J.: Prentice-Hall.

Fischer, R. (1971) A cartography of the ecstatic and meditative states. *Science* 174: 897–904.

Fischler, I. (1977) Associative facilitation without expectancy in a lexical decision task. *Journal of Experimental Psychology: Human Perception and Performance* 3:18–26.

Fischler, I., and Goodman, G. O. (1978) Latency of associative activation in memory. *Journal of Experimental Psychology: Human Perception and Performance* 4:455–70.

Fitzgerald, E. T. (1966) Measurement of openness to experience. *Journal of Personality and Social Psychology* 4:655–63.

Flexner, A. J., and Tulving, E. (1978) Retrieval independence in recognition and recall. *Psychological Review* 85:153–71.

Flom, M. C.; Heath, G. G.; and Takahashi, E. (1963) Contour interaction and visual resolution: Contralateral effects. *Science* 142:979–80.

Fontenot, D. J. (1973) Visual field differences in the recognition of verbal and non-verbal stimuli in man. *Journal of Comparative and Physiological Psychology* 85:564–69.

Foulkes, D., and Fleisher, S. (1975) Mental activity in relaxed wakefulness. *Journal of Abnormal Psychology* 84:66–75.

Franz, M. L. von (1966) *Aurora consurgens: A document attributed to Thomas Aquinas on the problem of opposites in alchemy.* Princeton: Princeton University Press.

Freedman, J. L., and Loftus, E. F. (1971) Retrieval of words from long-term memory. *Journal of Verbal Learning and Verbal Behavior* 10:107–15.

Freeman, G. L. (1940) The relationship between performance level and bodily activity. *Journal of Experimental Psychology* 26:602–8.

_____. (1948) *The energetics of human behavior.* Ithaca, N.Y.: Cornell University Press.

Freud, S. (1900) *The interpretation of dreams.* New York: Modern Library, 1938.

————. (1911) Psycho-analytic notes upon an autobiographical account of a case of paranoia (dementia paranoides.) In *Collected papers,* vol. 3. New York: Basic Books, 1959.

Friedman, M. J., and Reynolds, J. H. (1967) Retroactive inhibition as a function of response-class similarity. *Journal of Experimental Psychology* 74:351–55.

Fry, D. B. (1974) Right ear advantage for speech presented monaurally. *Language and Speech* 17:142–51.

Fry, D. B.; Abramson, A. S.; Eimas, P. D.; and Liberman, A. M. (1962) The identification and discrimination of synthetic vowels. *Language and Speech* 5:171–89.

Fujisaka, H., and Kawashima, T. (1970) Some experiments on speech perception and a model for the perceptual mechanism. *Annual report of the Engineering Research Institute, University of Tokyo* 29:207–14.

Gainotti, G. (1972) Emotional behavior and hemispheric side of the lesion. *Cortex* 8:41–55.

Galin, D. (1974) Implications for psychiatry of left and right cerebral specialization: A neurophysiological context for unconscious processes. *Archives of General Psychiatry* 31:572–83.

Galin, D., and Ellis, R. R. (1975) Asymmetry in evoked potentials as an index of lateralized cognitive processes: Relation to EEG alpha asymmetry. *Neuropsychologia* 13:45–50.

Galin, D., and Ornstein, R. (1972) Lateral specialization of cognitive mode: An EEG study. *Psychophysiology* 9:412–18.

Galton, F. (1907) *Inquiries into human faculty and its development.* London: J. M. Dent.

Gampbel, D. H. (1966) Temporal factors in verbal satiation. *Journal of Experimental Psychology* 72:201–6.

Gardner, G. T. (1973) Evidence for independent parallel channels in tachistoscopic perception. *Cognitive Psychology* 4:130–55.

Gastaut, H., and Bert, J. (1961) Electroencephalographic detection of sleep induced by repetitive sensory stimuli. In G. E. W. Wolstenholme and M. O'Connor, eds., *The nature of sleep.* London: Churchill.

Gazzaniga, M. S. (1970) *The bisected brain.* New York: Appleton-Century-Crofts.

Gazzaniga, M. S. and Hillyard, S. A. (1971) Language and speech capacity of the right hemisphere. *Neuropsychologia* 9:273–80.

Gershuni, G. V.; Kozhevnikov, V. A.; Maruseva, A. M.; Avakyan, R. V.; Radionova, E. A.; Altman, J. A.; and Soroko, V. I. (1960) Modifications in electrical responses of the auditory system in different states of higher nervous activity. *Electroencephalography and Clinical Neurophysiology,* supplement 13.

Geschwind, N. (1972) Language and the brain. *Scientific American* 226(4):76–83.

————. (1979) Specialization of the human brain. *Scientific American* 241(3):180–99.

Ghiselin, B., ed. (1952) *The creative process.* Berkeley: University of California Press.

Gibson, E. J. (1969) *Principles of perceptual learning and development.* New York: Appleton-Century-Crofts.

Gibson, E. J.; Gibson, J. J.; Pick, A. D.; and Osser, H. (1962) A developmental study of the discrimination of letter-like forms. *Journal of Comparative and Physiological Psychology* 55:897–906.

Gibson, E. J.; Osser, H.; Schiff, W.; Smith, J. (1963) An analysis of critical features of letters, tested by a confusion matrix. Final report on Cooperative Research Project No. 639, Office of Education, Department of Health, Education, and Welfare.

Gibson, J. J., and Radner, M. (1937) Adaptation, aftereffect and contrast in the perception of tilted lines. I. Quantitative studies. *Journal of Experimental Psychology* 20: 453–67.

Gilbert, K. E. and Kuhn, H. (1939) *A history of esthetics.* Bloomington: Indiana University Press.

Gill, M., and Brenman, M. (1959) *Hypnosis and related states.* New York: International Universities Press.

Glanzer, M., and Cunitz, A. R. (1966) Two storage mechanisms in free recall. *Journal of Verbal Learning and Verbal Behavior* 5:351–60.

Glass, A. L., and Holyoak, K. J. (1975) Alternative conceptions of semantic memory. *Cognition* 3:313–39.

Glass, A. L.; Holyoak, K. J.; and O'Dell, C. (1974) Production frequency and the verification of quantified statements. *Journal of Verbal Learning and Verbal Behavior* 13:237–54.

Glaubman, H.; Orbach, I.; Aviram, O.; Frieder, I.; Frieman, M.; Pelled, O.; and Glaubman, R. (1978) REM deprivation and divergent thinking. *Psychophysiology* 15:75–79.

Gleitman, H. (1955) Place learning without prior performance. *Journal of Comparative and Physiological Psychology* 48:77–79.

Glenberg, A.; Smith, S. M.; and Green, C. (1977) Type I rehearsal: Maintenance and more. *Journal of Verbal Learning and Verbal Behavior* 16:339–52.

Glenn, G. C. (1978) The role of episodic structure and of story length in children's recall of simple stories. *Journal of Verbal Learning and Verbal Behavior* 17:229–47.

Glucksberg, S. (1962) The influence of strength of drive on functional fixedness and perceptual recognition. *Journal of Experimental Psychology* 63:36–41.

Glucksberg, S., and Danks, J. (1968) Effects of discriminative labels and of nonsense labels upon availability of novel function. *Journal of Verbal Learning and Verbal Behavior* 7:72–76.

Godfrey, J. J. (1974) Perceptual difficulty and the right-ear advantage for vowels. *Brain and Language* 1:323–36.

Goldstein, A. G. (1957) Judgments of visual velocity as a function of length of observation time. *Journal of Experimental Psychology* 54:457–61.

Goldstein, K. (1939) *The organism.* Boston: Beacon Press.

Goldstein, L., and Stoltzfus, N. W. (1973) Psychoactive drug-induced changes of interhemispheric EEG amplitude relationships. *Agents and Actions* 3:124–32.

Goldstein, L.; Stoltzfus, N. W.; and Gardocki, J. F. (1972) Changes in interhemispheric amplitude relationships in the EEG during sleep. *Physiology and Behavior* 8:811–15.

Goleman, D. (1978) A taxonomy of meditation-specific altered states. *Journal of Altered States of Consciousness* 4:203–13.

Goodglass, H., and Calderon, M. (1977) Parallel processing of verbal and musical stimuli in right and left hemispheres. *Neuropsychologia* 15:397–407.

Gordon, H. W. (1978) Left-hemisphere dominance for rhythmic elements in dichotically-presented melodies. *Cortex* 14:58–70.

Gottesman, L., and Chapman, L. J. (1960) Syllogistic reasoning errors in schizophrenia. *Journal of Consulting Psychology* 24:250–55.

Gray, J. A., ed. (1964) *Pavlov's typology: Recent theoretical and experimental developments from the laboratory of B. M. Teplov.* New York: Macmillan.

Greenberg, J. H., and Jenkins, J. J. (1964) Studies in the psychological correlates of the sound system of American English. *Word* 20:157–77.

Griffith, J. S. (1963) On the stability of brain-like structures *Biophysical Journal* 3:299–308.

Gross, C. G. (1973) Inferotemporal cortex and vision. *Progress in physiological psychology,* vol. 5, New York: Academic Press.

Grossberg, S. (1980) How does the brain build a cognitive code? *Psychological Review* 87:1–51.

Haber, R. N. (1958) Discrepancy from adaptation level as a source of affect. *Journal of Experimental Psychology* 56:370–75.

Haber, R. N., and Standing, L. G. (1970) Direct estimates of apparent duration of a flash followed by visual noise. *Canadian Journal of Psychology* 24:216–29.

Haddon, A. C. (1907) *Evolution in art: As illustrated by the life-histories of designs.* London: W. Scott.

Halliday, A. M.; Davison, K.; Browne, M. W.; and Kreeger, L. C. (1968) A comparison of the effect on depression and memory of bilateral and unilateral ECT to the dominant and non-dominant hemispheres. *British Journal of Psychiatry* 114:997–1012.

Hamilton, W. (1859) *Lectures on metaphysics and logic.* Edinburgh: Blackwood.

Haney, G. W. (1931) The effect of familiarity on maze performance of albino rats. *University of California Publishings in Psychology* 4:319–33.

Harnad, S. (1972) Creativity, lateral saccades and the nondominant hemisphere. *Perceptual and Motor Skills* 34:653–54.

Harter, M. R. (1967) Excitability cycles and cortical scanning: A review of two hypotheses of central intermittency in perception. *Psychological Bulletin* 68:47–58.

Hebb, D. O. (1949) *The organization of behavior.* New York: Wiley.

————. (1955) Drives and the C. N. S. (Conceptual Nervous System). *Psychological Review* 62:243–53.

Hécaen, H. (1967) Brain mechanisms suggested by studies of parietal lobes. In C. H. Millikan and F. L. Darley, eds., *Brain mechanisms underlying speech and language.* New York: Grune & Stratton.

Hécaen, H., and Ajuriaguerra, J. de (1956) Agnosie visuelle pour les objets inanimés par lésion unilatéral gauche. *Revue Neurologique* 94:222–33.

Hefferline, R. F., and Perera, T. B. (1963) Proprioceptive discrimination of a covert operant without its observation by the subject. *Science* 139:834–35.

Heider, E. R. (1972) Universals in color naming and memory. *Journal of Experimental Psychology* 93:10–20.

Heider, E. R., and Olivier, D. C. (1972) The structure of the color space in naming and memory for two languages. *Cognitive Psychology* 3:337–54.

Heider, F. (1946) Attitudes and cognitive organization. *Journal of Psychology* 21:107–12.

Heilman, K. M.; Scholer, R.; and Watson, R. T. (1975) Auditory affective agnosia. *Journal of Neurology, Neurosurgery and Psychiatry* 38:69–72.

Hellyer, S. (1962) Supplementary report: Frequency of stimulus presentation and short-term decrement in recall. *Journal of Experimental Psychology* 64:650.

Helmholtz, H. von (1896) *Vorträge und Reden.* Brunswick, Germany: Friedrich Vieweg und Sohn.

Hempel, C. G., and Oppenheim, P. (1948) Studies in the logic of explanation." *Philosophy of Science* 15:135–75.

Hernández-Péon, R.; Scherrer, H.; Jouvet, M. (1956) Modification of electrical activity in cochlear nucleus during "attention" in unanesthetized cats. *Science* 123:331–32.

Hess, E. H. (1975) *The tell-tale eye.* New York: Van Nostrand.

Heyns, R. W.; Veroff, J.; and Atkinson, J. W. (1958) A scoring manual for the affiliation motive. In J. W. Atkinson, ed., *Motives in fantasy, action, and society.* Princeton, N.J.: Van Nostrand.

Hilgard, E. R. (1977) *Divided consciousness: Multiple controls in human thought and action.* New York: Wiley.

Hines, D., and Martindale, C. (1973) Functional brain asymmetry, primary process thinking and natural language. *Electroencephalography and Clincial Neurophysiology* 34:773.

————. (1974) Induced lateral eye movements and creative and intellectual performance. *Perceptual and Motor Skills* 39:153–54.

Hirsch, H. V. B., and Spinelli, D. N. (1970) Visual experience modifies distribution of horizontally and vertically oriented receptive fields in cats. *Science* 168:869–71.

Hobbes, T. (1642) *Leviathan.* New York: Liberal Arts Press, 1958.

Hochberg, J. (1972) The representation of things and people. In E. H. Gombrich; J. Hochberg; and M. Black, eds., *Art, perception, and reality.* Baltimore: Johns Hopkins University Press.

Hockey, G. R. J. (1970) Signal probability and spatial location as possible bases for increased selectivity in noise. *Quarterly Journal of Experimental Psychology* 22:37–42.

Hodgkin, A. L. (1964) The ionic basis of nervous conduction. *Science* 145:1148–54.

Hoffman, H. S., and Ison, J. R. (1980) Reflex modification in the domain of startle: I. Some empirical findings and their implications for how the nervous system processes sensory input. *Psychological Review* 87:175–89.

Holton, G. (1973) *Thematic origins of scientific thought: Kepler to Einstein.* Cambridge, Mass.: Harvard University Press.

Holyoak, K. J., and Glass, A. L. (1975) The role of contradictions and counter-examples in the rejection of false sentences. *Journal of Verbal Learning and Verbal Behavior* 14:215–39.

Hommes, O. R., and Panhuysen, L. H. H. M.   (1971)   Depression and cerebral dominance. *Psychiatria, Neurologia, Neurochirurgia* 74:259–70.

Hoppe, K. D.   (1977)   Split brains and psychoanalysis. *Psychoanalytic Quarterly* 46:220–44.

Horton, D. L.; Marlowe, D.; and Crowne, D.   (1963)   The effect of instructional set and need for social approval on commonality of word association responses. *Journal of Abnormal and Social Psychology* 66:67–72.

Houston, J. P.   (1967)   Unlearning of specific associations in the AB-AC paradigm. *Journal of Experimental Psychology* 74:254–58.

Houston, J. P., and Mednick, S. A.   (1963)   Creativity and the need for novelty. *Journal of Abnormal and Social Psychology* 66:137–41.

Howarth, C. F., and Ellis, K.   (1961)   The relative intelligibility threshold for one's own and other people's names. *Quarterly Journal of Experimental Psychology* 13:236–240.

Howes, D. H., and Solomon, R. L.   (1951)   Visual duration threshold as a function of word-probability. *Journal of Experimental Psychology* 41:401–10.

Hubel, D. H., and Wiesel, T. N.   (1963)   Receptive fields of cells in striate cortex of very young, visually inexperienced kittens. *Journal of Neurophysiology* 26:994–1002.

_____.   (1965)   Receptive fields and functional architecture in two nonstriate visual areas (18 and 19) of the cat. *Journal of Neurophysiology* 28:229–89.

Hudson, L.   (1975)   *Human beings: The psychology of human experience.* New York: Anchor Press.

Hugelin, A.; Dumont, S.; and Paillas, N.   (1960)   Formation réticulaire et transmission des informations auditives au niveau de l'oreille moyenne et des voies acoustiques centrales. *Electroencephalography and Clinical Neurophysiology* 12:797–818.

Hull, C. L.   (1943)   *Principles of behavior.* New York: Appleton-Century-Crofts.

Humphreys, L. F.   (1939)   Generalization as a function of method of reinforcement. *Journal of Experimental Psychology* 25:361–72.

Huxley, A. F.   (1964)   Excitation and conduction in nerve: Quantitative analysis. *Science* 145:1154–59.

Jackson, J. H.   (1884)   Evolution and dissolution of the nervous system. In J. Taylor, ed., *Selected writings of John Hughlings Jackson,* vol. 2. London: Hodder & Stoughton, 1932.

Jacobson, J. Z.   (1973)   Effects of association upon masking and reading latency. *Canadian Journal of Psychology* 27:58–69.

Jacobson, J. Z., and Rhinelander, G.   (1978)   Geometric and semantic similarity in visual masking. *Journal of Experimental Psychology: Human Perception and Performance* 4:224–31.

Jakobson, R.   (1956)   Two aspects of language and two types of aphasic disturbances. In R. Jakobson and M. Halle, *Fundamentals of language.* The Hague: Mouton.

Jakobson, R.; Fant, G.; and Halle, M.   (1963)   *Preliminaries to speech analysis.* Cambridge, Mass.: MIT Press.

James, W.   (1890)   *The principles of psychology.* New York: Holt, Rinehart & Winston.

_____.   (1902)   *The varieties of religious experience.* New York: Collier, 1961.

Jaynes, J.   (1977)   *The origins and history of consciousness in the breakdown of the bicameral mind.* Boston: Houghton Mifflin.

Jenkins, J. G., and Dallenbach, K. M.   (1924)   Oblivescence during sleep and waking. *American Journal of Psychology* 35:605–12.

Jevons, W. S.   (1871)   The power of numerical discrimination. *Nature* 3:281–82.

Johnston, J. C., and McClelland, J. L.   (1974)   Perception of letters in words: Seek not and ye shall find. *Science* 184:1192–94.

Jung, C. G.   (1953)   *Two essays on analytical psychology.* New York: Bollingen.

_____.   (1963)   *Mysterium coniunctionis: An inquiry into the separation and synthesis of psychic opposites in alchemy.* New York: Bolligen.

Kahler, E.   (1968)   *The disintegration of form in the arts.* New York: Braziller.

Kahneman, D.   (1973)   *Attention and effort.* Englewood Cliffs, N.J.: Prentice-Hall.

Kaltsounis, B.   (1973)   Effect of sound on creative performance. *Psychological Reports* 33:737–38.

Kamann, R.   (1963)   Verbal complexity and preferences in poetry. *Journal of Verbal Learning and Verbal Behavior* 5:536–40.

Kamiya, J.   (1969)   Operant control of EEG alpha rhythm and some of its reported effects on consciousness. In C. Tart, ed., *Altered states of consciousness*. New York: Wiley.

Kant, I.   (1781)   *Critique of pure reason*. London: Macmillan & Co., 1963.

Katz, A. N.   (1980)   Relating creativity to individual differences in asymmetric hemispheric functioning. Paper presented at American Psychological Association convention, Montreal.

Katz, J. J., and Fodor, J. A.   (1963)   The structure of a semantic theory. *Language* 39: 170–210.

Keppel, G., and Underwood, B. J.   (1962)   Proactive inhibition in short-term retention of single items. *Journal of Verbal Learning and Verbal Behavior* 1:153–61.

Kierkegaard, S.   (1841)   *The concept of irony*. New York: Harper and Row, 1965.

Kiesler, C. A. and Pallak, M. S.   (1976)   Arousal properties of dissonance manipulations. *Psychological Bulletin* 83:1014–25.

Kimura, D.   (1961)   Cerebral dominance and the perception of verbal stimuli. *Canadian Journal of Psychology* 15:166–71.

————.   (1966)   Dual functional asymmetry of the brain in visual perception. *Neuropsychologia* 4:275–85.

————.   (1967)   Functional asymmetry of the brain in dichotic listening. *Cortex* 3:163–78.

Kinsbourne, M.   (1972)   Eye and head turning indicates cerebral lateralization. *Science* 176:539–41.

Kintsch, W.   (1968)   Recognition and free recall of organized lists. *Journal of Experimental Psychology* 78:481–87.

————.   (1972)   Notes on the structure of semantic memory. In E. Tulving and W. Donaldson, eds., *Organization of memory*. New York: Academic Press.

Kintsch, W., and van Dijk, T. A.   (1978)   Toward a model of text comprehension and production. *Psychological Review* 85:363–94.

Klein, G. S.   (1967)   Peremptory ideation: Structure and force in motivated ideas. In R. R. Holt, ed., *Motives and thought: Essays in honor of David Rapaport*. New York: International Universities Press.

Klein, W.; Plomp, R.; and Pols, L. C. W.   (1970)   Vowel spectra, vowel spaces, and vowel identification. *Journal of the Acoustical Society of America* 48:999–1009.

Klemmer, E. T., and Muller, P. F.   (1969)   The rate of handling information: Key pressing responses to light patterns. *Journal of Motor Behavior* 1:135–47.

Klinger, E.   (1971)   *Structure and function of fantasy*. New York: Wiley.

————.   (1978)   Dimensions of thought and imagery in normal waking states. *Journal of Altered States of Consciousness* 4:97–113.

Klüver, H.   (1928)   *Mescal and the mechanisms of hallucinations*. Chicago: University of Chicago Press, 1966.

Koestler, A.   (1964)   *The act of creation*. New York: Macmillan.

Koffka, K.   (1935)   *Principles of gestalt psychology*. New York: Harcourt, Brace & World.

Kohler, I.   (1962)   Experiments with goggles. *Scientific American* 206(5): 62–72.

Kolers, P. A.; Eden, M.; and Boyer, A.   (1964)   Reading as a perceptual skill. *MIT Research Laboratory of Electronics, Quarterly Progress Report* 74:214–17.

Konorski, J.   (1967)   *Integrative activity of the brain*. Chicago: University of Chicago Press.

Kosslyn, S. M.   (1976)   Can imagery be distinguished from other forms of internal represenation? Evidence from studies of information retrieval times. *Memory and Cognition* 4:291–97.

Kripke, D. F., and Sonnenschein, D.   (1978)   A biologic rhythm in waking fantasy. In K. S. Pope and J. L. Singer, eds., *The stream of consciousness: Scientific investigations into the flow of human experience*. New York: Plenum.

Kris, E.   (1952)   *Psychoanalytic explorations in art*. New York: International Universities Press.

Kroll, N.; Parks, T.; Parkinson, S.; Bieber, S.; and Johnson, A.   (1970)   Short-term memory while shadowing: Recall of visually and of aurally presented letters. *Journal of Experimental Psychology* 85:220–24.

Krop, H. D.; Alegre, C. E.; and Williams, C. D. (1969) Effects of induced stress on convergent and divergent thinking. *Psychological Reports* 24:895–98.

Kuennapas, T., and Janson, A. J. (1969) Multi-dimensional similarity of letters. *Perceptual and Motor Skills* 28:3–12.

Kuhn, T. S. (1962) *The structure of scientific revolutions*. Chicago: University of Chicago Press.

————. (1970) Logic of discovery or psychology of research. In I. Lakatos and A. Musgrave, eds., *Criticism and the growth of knowledge*. Cambridge: Cambridge University Press.

Külpe, O. (1912) The modern psychology of thinking. In J. M. Mandler and G. Mandler, eds., *Thinking: From association to gestalt*. New York: Wiley, 1964.

LaBerge, D., and Samuels, S. J. (1974) Toward a theory of automatic information processing in reading. *Cognitive Psychology* 6:293–323.

Lacey, J. I. (1967) Somatic response patterning and stress: Some revisions of activation theory. In M. H. Appley and R. Trumbull, eds., *Psychological stress*. New York: Appleton-Century-Crofts.

Laffal, J. (1965) *Pathological and normal language*. New York: Atherton.

Lamb, S. M. (1966) Linguistic structure and the production and decoding of discourse. In E. C. Carterette, ed., *Brain function*, vol. 3. Berkeley: University of California Press.

Lane, H. L. (1965) The motor theory of speech perception: A critical review. *Psychological Review* 72:275–309.

Lashley, K. (1958) Cerebral organization and behavior. In F. A. Beach et al., eds., *The neuropsychology of Lashley: Selected papers of K. S. Lashley*. New York: McGraw-Hill, 1960.

Leiman, A. H., and Epstein, S. (1961) Thematic sexual responses as related to sexual drive and guilt. *Journal of Abnormal and Social Psychology* 63:169–75.

Lettvin, J. Y.; Maturana, H. R.; McCulloch, W. S.; and Pitts, W. H. (1959) What the frog's eye tells the frog's brain. *Proceedings of the Institute of Radio Engineers* 47:1940–51.

Lévi-Strauss, C. (1958) *Structural anthropology*. Garden City, N.Y.: Anchor Press, 1967.

Levy, J. (1974) Psychobiological implications of bilateral asymmetry. In S. J. Dimond and J. G. Beaumont, eds., *Hemispheric function in the human brain*. New York: Wiley.

————. (1979) Human cognition and lateralization of cerebral function. *Trends in Neurosciences* 2:222–25.

Levy, J.; Trevarthen, C.; and Sperry, R. W. (1972) Perception of bilateral chimeric figures following hemispheric deconnexion. *Brain* 95:61–78.

Lévy-Bruhl, L. (1910) *How natives think*. New York: Washington Square Press, 1966.

Lewin, I., and Glaubman, H. (1975) The effect of REM deprivation: Is it detrimental, beneficial, or neutral. *Psychophysiology* 12:349–53.

Lewis, J. L. (1970) Semantic processing of unattended messages using dichotic listening. *Journal of Experimental Psychology* 85:225–28.

Liberman, A. M. (1970) The grammars of speech and language. *Cognitive Psychology* 1:301–23.

Liberman, A. M.; Harris, K. S.; Hoffman, H. S.; and Griffith, B. C. (1957) The discrimination of speech sounds within and across phoneme boundaries. *Journal of Experimental Psychology* 54:358–68.

Lindsay, P. H., and Norman, D. A. (1977) *Human information processing: An Introduction to psychology*. New York: Academic Press.

Lindsley, D. B. (1957) Psychophysiology and motivation. In M. R. Jones, ed., *Nebraska symposium on motivation*, vol. 5. Lincoln: University of Nebraska Press.

Lindsley, D. B.; Bowden, J.; and Magoun, H. W. (1949) Effect upon EEG of acute injury to the brain stem activating system. *Electroencephalography and Clinical Neurophysiology* 1:475–86.

Lisker, L., and Abramson, A. S. (1964) A cross-language study of voicing in initial stops: Acoustical measurements. *Word* 20:384–422.

Locke, J. (1690) *An essay concerning human understanding*. Oxford: Clarenden. 1894.

Loftus, E. F. (1975) Spreading activation within semantic categories: Comments on Rosch's "Cognitive representations of semantic categories." *Journal of Experimental Psychology: General* 104:234–40.

Lotman, Y. M.   (1970)   *Struktura xudozestvennogo teksta.* Moskow: Iskusstvo.

Luchins, A.   (1942)   Mechanization in problem solving. *Psychological Monographs* 54, no. 248.

Ludwig, A. M.   (1966)   Altered states of consciousness. *Archives of General Psychiatry* 15:225–34.

Luria, A. R., and Vinogradova, O. S.   (1959)   An objective investigation of the dynamics of semantic systems. *British Journal of Psychology* 50:89–105.

Lynn, R.   (1966)   *Attention, arousal and the orienting reaction.* Oxford: Pergamon.

MacFarlane, D. W.   (1930)   The role of kinaesthesis in maze learning. *University of California Publishings in Psychology* 4:277–305.

Mach, E.   (1865)   Über die Wirkung der räumlichen Vertheilung des Lichtreizes auf die Netzhaut. *Sitzungsberichte mathematisch-naturwissenschaftlichen der Kaiserlichen Akademie der Wissenschaft* 52:303–22.

MacKinnon, D. W.   (1962)   The personality correlates of creativity. A study of American architects. In G. S. Nielson, ed., *Proceedings of the 14th International Congress of Psychology.* Copenhagen: Munksgaard.

MacLean, P.   (1958)   Contrasting functions of limbic and neocortical systems of the brain and their relevance to psychophysiological aspects of medicine. *American Journal of Medicine* 25:611–26.

————————.   (1979)   Paul MacLean and the triune brain. *Science* 204:1066–68.

Maddi, S. R., and Andrews, S.   (1966)   The need for variety in fantasy and self description. *Journal of Personality* 34:610–25.

Magnussen, S., and Kurtenbach, W.   (1980)   Adapting to two orientations: Disinhibition in a visual aftereffect. *Science* 207: 908–9.

Malmo, R. B.   (1959)   Activation: A neuropsychological dimension. *Psychological Review* 66:367–86.

Mandler, J. M.   (1978)   A code in the node: The use of a story schema in retrieval. *Discourse Processes* 1:14–35.

Mandler, J. M., and Johnson, N. S.   (1977)   Remembrance of things parsed: Story structure and recall. *Cognitive Psychology* 9:111–51.

Maritain, J.   (1953)   *Creative intuition in art and poetry.* Cleveland: Meridian Press, 1965.

Martin, L. J.   (1906)   An experimental study of Fechner's principles of aesthetics. *Psychological Review* 13:142–219.

Martindale, C.   (1971)   Degeneration, disinhibition, and genius. *Journal of the History of the Behavioral Sciences* 7:177–82.

————————.   (1973a)   An experimental simulation of literary change. *Journal of Personality and Social Psychology* 25:319–26.

————————.   (1973b)   COUNT: A PL/I program for content analysis of natural language. *Behavioral Science* 18:148.

————————.   (1973c)   Transformation and transfusion of vitality in the narratives of Poe. *Semiotica* 7:46–59.

————————.   (1975)   *Romantic progression: The psychology of literary history.* Washington, D.C.: Hemisphere.

————————.   (1976a)   The grammar of altered states of consciousness: A semiotic reinterpretation of aspects of psychoanalytic theory. In D. Spence, ed., *Psychoanalysis and contemporary science,* vol. 4. New York: Macmillan.

————————.   (1976b)   Primitive mentality and the relationship between art and society. *Scientific Aesthetics* 1:5–18.

————————.   (1976c)   Structural balance and the rules of narrative in *Les liaisons dangereuses. Poetics* 5:57–73.

————————.   (1977a)   Creativity, consciousness, and cortical arousal. *Journal of Altered States of Consciousness* 3:69–87.

————————.   (1977b)   Syntactic and semantic correlates of verbal tics in Gilles de la Tourette's syndrome: A quantitative case study. *Brain and Language* 4:231–47.

————————.   (1978a)   The evolution of English poetry. *Poetics* 7:231–48.

————————.   (1978b)   A quantitative analysis of diachronic patterns in some narratives of Poe. *Semiotica* 22:287–308.

————————.   (1979a)   Historical trends in the style and content of English poetry. Paper presented at Fourth International Conference on Computing in the Humanities, Hanover, N.H.

————. (1979b) The night journey: Trends in the content of narratives describing transformation of consciousness. *Journal of Altered States of Consciousness* 4:321–43.

————. (1980) Subselves: The internal representation of situational and personal dispositions. In L. Wheeler, ed., *Annual review of personality and social psychology*, vol. 1. Beverly Hills: Sage Publications.

Martindale, C., and Armstrong, J. (1974) The relationship of creativity to cortical activation and its operant control. *Journal of Genetic Psychology* 124:311–20.

Martindale, C., and Fischer, R. (1977) The effects of psilocybin on primary process content in language. *Confinia Psychiatrica* 20: 195–202.

Martindale, C., and Greenough, J. (1973) The differential effect of increased arousal on creative and intellectual performance. *Journal of Genetic Psychology* 123:329–35.

Martindale, C., and Hasenfus, N. (1978) EEG differences as a function of creativity, stage of the creative process, and effort to be original. *Biological Psychology* 6:157–67.

Martindale, C., and Hines, D. (1975) Creativity and cortical activation during creative, intellectual, and EEG feedback tasks. *Biological Psychology* 3:71–80.

Martindale, C.; Covello, E.; Hines, D.; and Mitchell, L. (1980) Hemispheric asymmetry, arousal, and creativity. Unpublished paper.

Martindale, C.; Reynes, R.; and Dahl, H. (1974) Lexical differences between working and resistance sessions in psychoanalytic therapy. Paper presented at Society for Psychotherapy Research Meeting, Denver.

Martinet, A. (1962) *A functional view of language*. Oxford: Oxford University Press.

————. (1964) *Elements of general linguistics*. Chicago: University of Chicago Press.

Massaro, D. (1970) Preperceptual auditory images. *Journal of Experimental Psychology* 85:411–17.

Massaro, D., and Schmuller, J. (1975) Visual features, preperceptual storage, and processing time in reading. In D. Massaro, ed., *Understanding language*. New York: Academic Press.

Matte-Blanco, I. (1959) Expression in symbolic logic of the characteristics of the system ucs. or the logic of the system ucs. *International Journal of Psycho-Analysis* 40:1–5.

McClelland, D. C. (1958) Risk-taking in children with high and low need for achievement. In J. W. Atkinson, ed., *Motives in fantasy, action, and society*. Princeton, N.J.: Van Nostrand.

————. (1961) *The achieving society*. Princeton, N.J.: Van Nostrand.

McClelland, D. C.; Atkinson, J. W.; Clark, R. A.; and Lowell, E. L. (1953) *The achievement motive*. New York: Appleton-Century-Crofts.

————. (1958) A scoring manual for the achievement motive. In J. W. Atkinson, ed., *Motives in fantasy, action, and society*. Princeton, N.J.: Van Nostrand.

McClelland, J. L. (1979) On the time relations of mental processes: An examination of systems of processes in cascade. *Psychological Review* 86:287–330.

McGeoch, J. A. (1932) Forgetting and the law of disuse. *Psychological Review* 93:352–70.

————. (1942) *The psychology of human learning*. New York: Longmans, Green.

McGhie, A., and Chapman, J. (1961) Disorders of attention and perception in early schizophrenia. *British Journal of Medical Psychology* 34:103–16.

McGuire, W. J. (1960) A syllogistic analysis of cognitive relationships. In M. J. Rosenberg, and C. I. Hovland, eds., *Attitude organization and change*. New Haven: Yale University Press.

McKay, D. G. (1973) Aspects of the theory of comprehension, memory and attention. *Quarterly Journal of Experimental Psychology* 25:22–40.

McKee, G.; Humphrey, B.; and McAdam, D. W. (1973) Scaled lateralization of alpha activity during linguistic and musical tasks. *Psychophysiology* 10:441–43.

McKellar, P. (1957) *Imagination and thinking*. New York: Basic Books.

McKinney, J. P. (1966) Verbal meaning and perceptual stability. *Canadian Journal of Psychology* 20:237–42.

McNamara, H. J.; Long, J. B.; and Wike, E. L. (1956) Learning without response under two conditions of external cues. *Journal of Comparative and Physiological Psychology* 49:477–80.

McNichol, D., and Howes, P. M. (1971) The effects of context on the perception of speech. *Australian Journal of Psychology* 23:305–10.

Mednick, S. A. (1962) The associative basis of the creative process. *Psychological Review* 69:220–32.

Meier, R. L. (1965) Information input overload: Features of growth in communication-oriented institutions. In F. Massarik and P. Ratoosh, eds., *Mathematical explorations in behavioral science.* Homewood, Ill.: Dorsey Press.

Melton, A. W., and Irwin, J. M. (1940) The influence of degrees of interpolated learning on retroactive inhibition and overt transfer of specific responses. *American Journal of Psychology* 53:175–203.

Mendelsohn, G. A. (1976) Associative and attentional processes in creative performance. *Journal of Personality* 44:341–69.

Mendelsohn, G. A., and Griswold, B. B. (1966) Assessed creativity potential, vocabulary level, and sex as predictors of the use of incidental cues in verbal problem solving. *Journal of Personality and Social Psychology* 4:423–31.

————. (1967) Anxiety and repression as predictors of the use of incidental cues in problem solving. *Journal of Personality and Social Psychology* 6:353–59.

Meyer, D. E.; Schvaneveldt, R. W.; and Ruddy, M. G. (1975) Loci of contextual effects in visual word recognition. In P. M. A. Rabbitt and S. Dornic, eds., *Attention and performance V.* New York: Academic Press.

Milgram, S. (1970) The experience of living in cities. *Science* 167:1461–68.

Miller, G. A. (1956) The magical number seven, plus or minus two: Some limits on our capacity to process information. *Psychological Review* 63:81–97.

Miller, G. A., and Isard, S. (1963) Some perceptual consequences of linguistic rules. *Journal of Verbal Learning and Verbal Behavior* 2:217–28.

Miller, G. A., and Nicely, P. E. (1955) An analysis of perceptual confusions among some English consonants. *Journal of the Acoustical Society of America* 27:338–52.

Miller, G. A.; Galanter, E.; and Pribram, K. H. (1960) *Plans and the structure of behavior.* New York: Holt, Rinehart & Winston.

Miller, G. A.; Heise, G. A.; and Lichten, W. (1951) The intelligibility of speech as a function of the context of the test materials. *Journal of Experimental Psychology* 41:329–35.

Miller, J. G. (1978) *Living systems.* New York: McGraw-Hill.

Milner, B. (1966) Amnesia following operation on the temporal lobes. In C. W. M. Whitty and O. L. Zangwill, eds., *Amnesia.* London: Butterworths.

————. (1968) Visual recognition and recall after right temporal-lobe excision in man. *Neuropsychologia* 6:191–209.

Milner, B.; Branch, C.; and Rasmussen, T. (1966) Evidence for bilateral speech representation in some non-right-handers. *Transactions of the American Neurological Association* 91:306–8.

Mishkin, M., and Forgays, D. G. (1952) Word recognition as a function of retinal locus. *Journal of Experimental Psychology* 43:43–48.

Monsell, S. (1978) Recency, immediate recognition memory, and reaction time. *Cognitive Psychology* 10:465–501.

Montague, W. E.; Adams, J. A.; and Kiess, H. O. (1966) Forgetting and natural language mediation. *Journal of Experimental Psychology* 72:829–33.

Montgomery, K. C. (1954) The role of exploratory drive in learning. *Journal of Comparative and Physiological Psychology* 47:60–64.

Moore, G. (1886) *Confessions of a young man.* New York: Capricorn Books, 1959.

Moray, N. (1959) Attention in dichotic listening: Affective cues and the influence of instructions. *Quarterly Journal of Experimental Psychology* 11:56–60.

Morgan, A. H.; McDonald, P. J.; and MacDonald, H. (1971) Differences in bilateral alpha activity as a function of experimental task with a note on lateral eye movements and hypnotizability. *Neuropsychologia* 9:459–69.

Morrell, L. K. (1966) Some characteristics of stimulus-provoked alpha activity. *Electroencephalography and Clinical Neurophysiology* 21:552–61.

Morton, J. (1969) Interaction of information in word recognition. *Psychological Review* 76:165–78.

Moruzzi, G., and Magoun, H. W. (1949) Brain stem reticular formation and activation of the EEG. *Electroencephalography and Clinical Neurophysiology* 1:455–73.

Moyer, R. S. (1973) Comparing objects in memory: Evidence suggesting an internal psychophysics. *Perception and Psychophysics* 13:180–84.

Mulkay, M. J. (1975) Three models of scientific development. *The Sociological Review* 23:509–26.

Munsinger, H. L., and Kessen, W. (1964) Uncertainty, structure and preference. *Psychological Monographs* 78 (9, whole no. 586).

Murdock, B. B. (1961) The retention of individual items. *Journal of Experimental Psychology* 62:618–25.

––––––––. (1962) The serial position effect of free recall. *Journal of Experimental Psychology* 64:482–88.

Murray, H. A. (1938) *Explorations in personality: A clinical and experimental study of fifty men of college age.* New York: Oxford University Press.

––––––––. (1943) *Thematic apperception test.* Cambridge, Mass.: Harvard University Press.

––––––––. (1955) American Icarus. In A. Burton and R. E. Harris, eds., *Clinical studies of personality,* vol. 2. New York: Harper and Row.

Myden, W. (1959) Interpretation and evaluation of certain personality characteristics involved in creative production. *Perceptual and Motor Skills* 9:139–58.

Neisser, U. (1964) Visual search. *Scientific American* 210:94–102.

––––––––. (1967) *Cognitive psychology.* New York: Appleton-Century-Crofts.

Nelson, J. I., and Frost, B. J. (1978) Orientation-selective inhibition from beyond the classic visual receptive field. *Brain Research* 139:359–65.

Nelson, P. G.; Erulkar, S. D.; and Bryan, S. S. (1966) Responses of units of the inferior colliculus to time-varying acoustic stimuli. *Journal of Neurophysiology* 29:834–60.

Nelson, T. O. (1977) Repetition and depth of processing. *Journal of Verbal Learning and Verbal Behavior* 16:151–72.

Nemiah, J., and Sifneos, P. (1970) Affect and fantasy in patients with psychosomatic disorders. In O. W. Hill, ed., *Modern trends in psychosomatic medicine.* New York: Appleton-Century-Crofts.

Neumann, E. (1954) *The origins and history of consciousness.* New York: Bollingen.

Nietzsche, F. (1908) *Ecce Homo.* In *Complete works of Friedrich Nietzsche.* New York: Macmillan, 1924.

Norman, D. A. (1968) Toward a theory of memory and attention. *Psychological Review* 75:522–36.

––––––––. (1969) Memory while shadowing. *Quarterly Journal of Experimental Psychology* 21:85–93.

Norman, D. A., and Bobrow, D. G. (1976) On the role of active memory processes in perception and cognition. In C. N. Cofer, ed., *The structure of human memory.* San Francisco: Freeman.

Norman, D. A., and Rumelhart, D. G. (1975) *Explorations in cognition.* San Francisco: Freeman.

Ogilvie, D. (1968) The Icarus complex. *Psychology Today* 3(7): 30–34, 67.

Olds, J., and Milner, P. (1954) Positive reinforcement produced by electrical stimulation of septal area and other regions of rat brain. *Journal of Comparative Physiology* 47: 419–27.

Ornstein, R. (1972) *The psychology of consciousness.* San Francisco: Freeman.

Ortega y Gasset, J. (1948) *The dehumanization of art.* Garden City, N.Y.: Doubleday, 1956.

Osborn, A. F. (1957) *Applied imagination.* New York: Scribner.

Osgood, C. E. (1960) Some effects of motivation on style of encoding. In T. A. Sebeok, ed., *Style in language.* Cambridge, Mass.: MIT Press.

Osgood, C. E.; Suci, G. J.; and Tannenbaum, P. H. (1957) *The measurement of meaning.* Urbana: University of Illinois Press.

Paivio, A. (1975) Neomentalism. *Canadian Journal of Psychology* 29:263–91.

————. (1978) The relationship between verbal and perceptual codes. In E. C. Carterette and M. P. Friedman, eds., *Handbook of perception,* vol. 8. New York: Academic Press.

Palermo, D. S., and Jenkins, J. J. (1964) *Word association norms.* Minneapolis: University of Minnesota Press.

Pankove, E., and Kogan, N. (1968) Creative ability and risk-taking in elementary school children. *Journal of Personality* 36:420–39.

Pavlov, I. (1927) *Conditional reflexes.* London: Oxford University Press.

Penfield, W., and Roberts, L. (1959) *Speech and brain mechanisms.* Princeton, N.J.: Princeton University Press.

Peterson, L. R., and Peterson, M. J. (1959) Short-term retention of individual verbal items. *Journal of Experimental Psychology* 58:193–98.

Peterson, L. R.; Rawlings, L.; and Cohen, C. (1977) The internal construction of spatial patterns. In G. H. Bower, ed., *The psychology of learning and motivation.* New York: Academic Press.

Pfaffman, C. (1960) The pleasures of sensation. *Psychological Review* 67:253–68.

Piaget, J. (1937) *The origins of intelligence in children.* New York: Norton, 1952.

————. (1950) *The psychology of intelligence.* New York: Harcourt, Brace & World.

Pillsbury, W. B. (1897) A study in apperception. *American Journal of Psychology* 8:315–93.

Pine, F. (1959) Thematic drive content and creativity. *Journal of Personality* 27:136–51.

Pine, F., and Holt, R. R. (1960) Creativity and primary process: A study of adaptive regression. *Journal of Abnormal and Social Psychology* 61:370–79.

Pisoni, D. B. (1973) Auditory and phonetic memory codes in the discrimination of consonants and vowels. *Perception and Psychophysics* 13:253–60.

————. (1975) Auditory short-term memory and vowel perception. *Memory and Cognition* 3:7–18.

————. (1978) Speech perception. In W. K. Estes, ed., *Handbook of learning and cognitive processes,* vol. 6. Hillsdale, N.J.: Erlbaum.

Pisoni, D. B., and McNabb, S. D. (1974) Dichotic interactions and phonetic feature processing. *Brain and Language* 1:351–62.

Planck, M. (1950) *Scientific autobiography.* London: Williams & Norgate.

Podgorny, P., and Shepard, R. N. (1978) Functional representations common to visual perception and imagination. *Journal of Experimental Psychology: Human Perception and Performance* 4:21–35.

Poincaré, H. (1913) *The foundations of science.* Lancaster, Pa.: Science Press.

Pollack, I., and Pickett, J. M. (1964) Intelligibility of excerpts from fluent speech: Auditory vs. structural context. *Journal of Verbal Learning and Verbal Behavior* 3:79–84.

Posner, M. I. (1969) Abstraction and the process of recognition. In G. Bower, ed., *Advances in learning.* New York: Academic Press.

Posner, M. I., and Boies, S. J. (1971) Components of attention. *Psychological Review* 78:391–408.

Posner, M. I., and Keele, S. W. (1968) On the genesis of abstract ideas. *Journal of Experimental Psychology* 77:353–63.

Posner, M. I., and Rogers, M. G. K. (1978) Chronometric analysis of abstraction and recognition. In W. K. Estes, ed., *Handbook of learning and cognitive processes,* vol. 5. Hillsdale, N.J.: Erlbaum.

Posner, M. I., and Snyder, C. R. R. (1975) Attention and cognitive control. In R. Solso, ed., *Cognition and information processing: Third Loyola symposium.* New York: Winston.

Posner, M. I.; Goldsmith, R.; and Welton, K. E. (1967) Perceived distance and the classification of distorted patterns. *Journal of Experimental Psychology* 73:28–38.

Postman, L., and Stark, K. (1969) Role of response availability in transfer and interference. *Journal of Experimental Psychology* 79:168–77.

Postman, L.; Jenkins, W. O.; and Postman, D. L. (1948) An experimental comparison of active recall and recognition. *American Journal of Psychology* 61:511.

Postman, L.; Stark, K.; and Fraser, J. (1968) Temporal changes in interference. *Journal of Verbal Learning and Verbal Behavior* 7:672–94.

Preston, M. S. (1971) Some comments on the developmental aspects of voicing in stop consonants. In D. L. Horton and J. J. Jenkins, eds., *Perception of language.* Columbus, Ohio: Merrill.

Prince, M. (1929) *Clinical and experimental studies in personality.* Cambridge, Mass.: Sci-Art.

Pritchard, R. M. (1961) Stabilized images on the retina. *Scientific American* 204(6):72–78.

Pritchard, R. M.; Heron, W.; and Hebb, D. O. (1960) Visual perception approached by the method of stabilized images. *Canadian Journal of Psychology* 14:67–77.

Prohovnik, I. (1978) Cerebral lateralization of psychological processes: A literature review. *Archiv für Psychologie* 130:161–211.

Propp, V. (1928) *Morphology of the folktale.* Austin: University of Texas Press, 1968.

Quastler, H., and Wulff, V. J. (1955) Human performance in information transmission. *Technical report R–62.* Urbana: Control Systems Laboratory, University of Illinois.

Quillian, M. R. (1962) A revised design for an understanding machine. *Mechanical Translation* 7:17–29.

_____. (1967) Word concepts: A theory and simulation of some basic semantic capabilities. *Behavioral Science* 12:410–30.

Rapaport, D. (1957) Cognitive structures. In J. E. Bruner et al., *Contemporary approaches to cognition.* Cambridge, Mass.: Harvard University Press.

Rasmussen, T., and Milner, B. (1977) The role of early left-brain injury in determining lateralization of cerebral speech functions. *Annals of the New York Academy of Sciences* 299:355–69.

Ratliff, F. (1965) *Mach bands: Quantitative studies on neural networks in the retina.* San Francisco: Holden-Day.

Reicher, G. M. (1969) Perceptual recognition as a function of meaningfulness of stimulus material. *Journal of Experimental Psychology* 81:274–80.

Reitman, J. S. (1971) Mechanisms of forgetting in short-term memory. *Cognitive Psychology* 2:185–95.

Restle, F. (1957) Discrimination of cues in mazes: A resolution of the "place-vs.-response" question. *Psychological Review* 64:217–28.

Restorff, H. von (1933) Über die Wirkung von Bereichsbildungen im Spurenfeld. *Psychologie Forschung* 18:299–42.

Ribot, T. (1906) *Essay on the creative imagination.* London: Kegan Paul.

_____. (1911) *The psychology of the emotions.* New York: Walter Scott.

Riegl, A. (1901) *Spätrömische Kunstindustrie nach den Funden in Österreich-Ungarn.* Vienna: Staatstruckerei, 1927.

Riggs, L. A.; Ratliff, F.; Cornsweet, J. C.; and Cornsweet, T. N. (1953) The disappearance of steadily-fixated objects. *Journal of the Optical Society of America* 43:495–501.

Rips, L. J.; Shoben, E. J.; and Smith, E. L. (1973) Semantic distance and the verification of semantic relations. *Journal of Verbal Learning and Verbal Behavior* 12:1–20.

Rizzolatti, G.; Umilta, C.; and Berlucchi, G. (1971) Opposite superiorities of the right and left cerebral hemispheres in discriminative reaction time to physiognomical and alphabetical material. *Brain* 94:431–42.

Robbins, K. I., and McAdam, D. W. (1974) Interhemispheric alpha asymmetry and imagery mode. *Brain and Language* 1:189–93.

Robson, J. G. (1975) Receptive fields: Neural representation of the spatial and intensive attributes of the visual image. In E. C. Carterette and M. P. Friedman, eds., *Handbook of perception,* vol. 5. New York: Academic Press.

Roediger, H. L. (1973) Inhibition in recall from cueing with recall targets. *Journal of Verbal Learning and Verbal Behavior* 12:644–57.

Roediger, H. L.; Stellon, C. C.; and Tulving, E. (1977) Inhibition from part-list cues and rate of recall. *Journal of Experimental Psychology: Human Learning and Memory* 3:174–88.

Rohwer, W. D. (1966) Constraint, syntax and meaning in paired-associate learning. *Journal of Verbal Learning and Verbal Behavior* 5:541–47.

Rosch, E. (1973a) Natural categories. *Cognitive Psychology* 4:328–50.

_____. (1973b) On the internal structure of perceptual and semantic categories. In T. E. Moore, ed., *Cognitive development and the acquisition of language.* New York: Academic Press.

————. (1975) Cognitive representations of semantic categories. *Journal of Experimental Psychology* 104:192–233.

Rosch, E., and Mervis, C. B. (1975) Family resemblances: Studies in the internal structure of categories. *Cognitive Psychology* 7:573–605.

Rosch, E.; Simpson, C.; and Miller, R. S. (1976) Structural bases of typicality effects. *Journal of Experimental Psychology: Human Perception and Performance* 2:491–502.

Rossi, G. F., and Rosadini, G. (1967) Experimental analysis of cerebral dominance in man. In C. H. Millikan and F. L. Darley, eds., *Brain mechanisms underlying speech and language.* New York: Grune & Stratton.

Rothenberg, A. (1971) The process of Janusian thinking in creativity. *Archives of General Psychiatry* 24:195–205.

Rubenstein, H.; Lewis, S. S.; and Rubenstein, M. A. (1971) Evidence of phonemic recording in visual word recognition. *Journal of Verbal Learning and Verbal Behavior* 10:645–57.

Rudnicky, A. I., and Cole, R. A. (1977) Adaptation produced by connected speech. *Journal of Experimental Psychology: Human Perception and Performance* 3:51–61.

Rugg, H. (1963) *Imagination.* New York: Harper & Row.

Rumelhart, D. E., and Siple, P. (1974) Processes of recognizing tachistoscopically presented words. *Psychological Review* 81:99–118.

Rumelhart, D. E.; Lindsay, P. H.; and Norman, D. A. (1972) A process model for long-term memory. In E. Tulving and W. Donaldson, eds., *Organization of memory.* New York: Academic Press.

Rundus, D. (1971) Analysis of rehearsal processes in free recall. *Journal of Experimental Psychology* 89:63–77.

Ruskin, J. (1844) *Modern painters.* London: Smith, Elder.

Sachs, J. S. (1967) Recognition memory for syntactic and semantic aspects of connected discourse. *Perception and Psychophysics* 2:437–44.

Sakitt, B. (1976) Iconic memory. *Psychological Review* 83:257–76.

Samuels, S. J. (1970) Recognition of flashed words by children. *Child Development* 41:1089–94.

Scarborough, D. L.; Cortese, C.; and Scarborough, H. S. (1977) Frequency and repetition effects in lexical memory. *Journal of Experimental Psychology: Human Perception and Performance* 3:1–17.

Schachtel, E. (1959) *Metamorphosis.* New York: Basic Books.

Schachter, S. (1964) The interaction of cognitive and physiological determinants of emotional state. In L. Berkowitz, ed., *Advances in experimental social psychology,* vol. 1. New York: Academic Press.

Schachter, S., and Singer, J. E. (1962) Cognitive, social, and physiological determinants of emotional state. *Psychological Review* 69: 379–99.

Schachter, S., and Wheeler, L. (1962) Epinephrine, chlorpromazine and amusement. *Journal of Abnormal and Social Psychology* 65:121–28.

Schank, R., and Abelson, R. (1977) *Scripts, plans, goals and understanding.* Hillsdale, N.J.: Erlbaum.

Schlosberg, H. A. (1954) Three dimensions of emotion. *Psychological Review* 61:81–88.

Schopenhauer, A. (1818) *Die Welt als Wille und Vorstellung.* In *Arthur Schopenhauer's Sämmtliche Werke.* Leipzig: F. A. Brockhaus, 1891.

Schreber, D. P. (1903) *Memoirs of my nervous illness.* Cambridge, Mass.: Robert Bentley, 1955.

Schuberth, R. E., and Eimas, P. D. (1977) Effects of context on the classification of words and nonwords. *Journal of Experimental Psychology: Human Perception and Performance* 3:27–36.

Schultz, D. P. (1965) *Sensory restriction: Effects on behavior.* New York: Academic Press.

Schwartz, G. E.; Davidson, R. J.; and Maer, F. (1975) Right hemisphere lateralization for emotion in the human brain: Interactions with cognition. *Science* 190:286–88.

Seamon, J. G., and Gazzaniga, M. S. (1973) Coding strategies and cerebral laterality effects. *Cognitive Psychology* 5:249–56.

Sekuler, R. (1975) Visual motion perception. In E. C. Carterette and M. P. Friedman, eds., *Handbook of perception,* vol. 5. New York: Academic Press.

Sekuler, R., and Ganz, L. (1963) A new aftereffect of seen movement with a stabilized visual image. *Science* 139:419–20.

Selfridge, O. G. (1959) Pandemonium: A paradigm for learning. In D. V. Blake and A. M. Uttley, eds., *Proceedings of the symposium on the mechanization of thought processes.* London: H. M. Stationary Office.

Selfridge, O. G., and Neisser, U. (1960) Pattern recognition by machine. *Scientific American* 203:60–68.

Severance, E., and Washburn, M. F. (1907) The loss of associative power in words after long fixation. *American Journal of Psychology* 18:182–86.

Shallice, T. (1972) Dual functions of consciousness. *Psychological Review* 79:383–93.

————. (1978) The dominant action system: An information-processing approach to consciousness. In K. S. Pope and J. L. Singer, eds., *The stream of consciousness: Scientific investigations into the flow of human experience.* New York: Plenum.

Sharpless, S., and Jasper, H. (1956) Habituation of the arousal reaction. *Brain* 79:655–80.

Shepard, R. N. (1967) Recognition memory for words, sentences, and pictures. *Journal of Verbal Learning and Verbal Behavior* 6:156–63.

Shepard, R. N., and Metzler, J. (1971) Mental rotation of three-dimensional objects. *Science* 171:701–3.

Shiffrin, R. M., and Atkinson, R. C. (1969) Storage and retrieval processing in long-term memory. *Psychological Review* 76:179–93.

Shiffrin, R. M., and Gardner, G. T. (1972) Visual processing capacity and attentional control. *Journal of Experimental Psychology* 93:72–82.

Shiffrin, R. M., and Geisler, W. S. (1973) Visual recognition in a theory of information processing. In R. L. Solso, ed., *Contemporary issues in cognitive psychology: The Loyola symposium.* Washington, D.C.: Winston.

Shiffrin, R. M., and Schneider, W. (1977) Controlled and automatic human information processing: II. Perceptual learning, automatic attending and a general theory. *Psychological Review* 84:127–90.

Shockey, L., and Reddy, R. (1974) Quantitative analysis of speech perception: Results from transcription of connected speech from unfamiliar languages. Paper presented at the Speech Communication Seminar, Stockholm, Sweden.

Shucard, D. W.; Shucard, J. L.; and Thomas, D. G. (1977) Auditory evoked potentials as probes of hemispheric differences in cognitive processing. *Science* 197:1295–98.

Shulman, H. G. (1972) Semantic confusion errors in short-term memory. *Journal of Verbal Learning and Verbal Behavior* 11:221–27.

Silberer, H. (1912) Report on a method of eliciting and observing certain symbolic hallucination phenomena. In D. Rapaport, ed., *Organization and pathology of thought.* New York: Columbia University Press, 1951.

————. (1917) *Problems of mysticism and its symbolism.* New York: Moffat, Yard.

Sillito, A. M. (1979) Inhibitory mechanisms influencing complex cell orientation selectivity and their modification at high resting discharge levels. *Journal of Physiology* 289: 33–53.

Simon, H. A. (1974) How big is a chunk? *Science* 183:482–88.

Singer, J. L., and McCraven, V. G. (1961) Some characteristics of adult daydreaming. *Journal of Psychology* 51:151–64.

Skaife, A. M. (1967) The role of complexity and deviation in changing taste. Ph.D. dissertation, University of Oregon.

Skinner, B. F. (1953) *Science and human behavior.* New York: Macmillan.

————. (1975) The steep and thorny way to a science of behavior. *American Psychologist* 30:42–49.

Slamecka, N. J. (1968) An examination of trace storage in free recall. *Journal of Experimental Psychology* 76:504–13.

————. (1969) Testing for associative storage in multitrial free recall. *Journal of Experimental Psychology* 81:557–60.

Smith, E. E., and Spoehr, K. T. (1974) The perception of printed English: A theoretical perspective. In B. Kantowitz, ed., *Human information processing: Tutorials in performance and cognition.* Hillsdale, N.J.: Erlbaum.

Smith, E. E.; Shoben, E. J.; and Rips, L. J. (1974) Structure and process in semantic memory: A featural model for semantic decisions. *Psychological Review* 81:214–41.

Smith, S., and Lewty, W. (1959) Perceptual isolation using a silent room. *Lancet* 1:342–45.

Smythies, J. R. (1959) The stroboscopic patterns. II. The phenomenology of the bright
phase and after images. *British Journal of Psychology* 50:305–24.

Sokolov, E. N. (1960) Neuronal models and the orienting reflex. In M. A. Brazier, ed.,
The central nervous system and behaviour. New York: J. Macy.

————. (1963) *Perception and the conditioned reflex.* New York: Macmillan.

Solomon, P.; Kubzansky, P. E.; Leiderman, P. H.; Mendelson, J. H.; Trumbull, R.; and Wex-
ler, D., eds. (1961) *Sensory deprivation.* Cambridge, Mass.: Harvard University Press.

Spence, K. W. (1956) *Behavior theory and conditioning.* New Haven: Yale University
Press.

Sperling, G. (1960) The information available in brief visual presentations. *Psychological
Monographs* 74:(whole no. 11).

Sperry, R. W., and Gazzaniga, M. S. (1967) Language following surgical disconnection of
the hemispheres. In C. H. Millikan and F. L. Darley, eds., *Brain mechanisms underlying
speech and language.* New York: Grune and Stratton.

Spieth, W.; Curtis, J. F.; and Webster, J. C. (1954) Responding to one of two simultaneous messages. *Journal of the Acoustical Society of America* 26:391–96.

Standing, L. (1973) Learning 10,000 pictures. *Quarterly Journal of Experimental Psychology* 25:207–22.

Steck, L., and Machotka, P. (1975) Preference for musical complexity: Effects of context.
Journal of Experimental Psychology: Human Perception and Performance 104:170–74.

Steinheiser, F. H., and Barroas, D. J. (1973) Chronometric analysis of speech perception.
Perception and Psychophysics 13:426–30.

Stennett, R. G. (1957) The relationship of performance level to level of arousal. *Journal
of Experimental Psychology* 54:54–61.

Sternberg, S. (1966) High-speed scanning in human memory. *Science* 153:652–54.

Stevens, K. N. (1968) On the relations between speech movements and speech perception. *Zeitschrift für Phonetik Sprachwissenschaft und Kommunikationforschung* 21:
102–6.

————. (1975) The potential role of property detectors in the perception of consonants. In G. Fant and M. A. A. Tatham, eds., *Auditory analysis and perception of
speech.* New York: Academic Press.

Stevens, K. N., and House, A. S. (1972) Speech perception. In J. Tobias, ed., *Foundations
of modern auditory theory.* New York: Academic Press.

Stevens, S. S. (1961) The psychophysics of sensory function. In W. A. Rosenblith, ed.,
Sensory communication. Cambridge, Mass.: MIT Press.

————. (1966) Matching functions between loudness and ten other continua. *Perception and Psychophysics* 1:5–8.

Stratton, G. M. (1897) Vision without inversion of the retinal image. *Psychological Review* 4:341–60.

Streufert, S. (1969) Increasing failure and response rate in complex decision making.
Journal of Experimental Social Psychology 5:310–23.

Studdert-Kennedy, M. (1975) Dichotic studies II: Two questions, *Brain and Language*
2:123–30.

Szentágothai, J., and Arbib, M. A. (1974) Conceptual models of neural organization.
Neurosciences Research Program Bulletin 12:307–510.

Tanner, W. P., and Swets, J. A. (1954) A decision-making theory of visual detection.
Psychological Review 61:401–9.

Thackeray, W. M. (1899) *The works of W. M. Thackeray,* vol. 12. London: John Murray.

Thayer, R. E. (1967) Measurement of activation through self-report. *Psychological Reports* 20:663–78.

Thompson, R. F. (1973) *Introduction to biopsychology.* San Francisco: Albion.

Thomson, D. M., and Tulving, E. (1970) Associative encoding retrieval: Weak and
strong cues. *Journal of Experimental Psychology* 86:255–62.

Thorndyke, P. W. (1977) Cognitive structures in comprehension and memory of narrative discourse. *Cognitive Psychology* 9:77–110.

Tinbergen, N. (1951) *The study of instinct.* Oxford, Eng.: Clarenden.

Titchener, E. B. (1923) *A text-book of psychology.* New York: Macmillan.

Todorov, T. (1971) The two principles of narrative. *Diacritics* 1:37–44.

Toffler, A. (1970) *Future shock.* New York: Random House.

Tolman, E. C. (1932) *Purposive behavior in animals and men.* New York: Holt, Rinehart & Winston.

Tolman, E. C. and Honzik, C. H. (1930) Introduction and removal of reward, and maze performance in rats. *University of California Publishings in Psychology* 4:257–75.

Tortarella, W. (1968) The effects of a stressful situation on a creative task. *Dissertation Abstracts* 28:1214.

Toulmin, S. (1972) *Human understanding: The collective use and evolution of concepts.* Princeton, N.J.: Princeton University Press.

Townsend, J. T. (1971) Alphabetic confusion: A test of models for individuals. *Perception and Psychophysics* 9:449–54.

_____. (1972) Some results on the identifiability of parallel and serial processes. *British Journal of Mathematical and Statistical Psychology* 25:168–99.

Trapp, E., and Kausler, D. (1960) Relationship between MAS scores and association values of nonsense syllables. *Journal of Experimental Psychology* 59:233–38.

Treisman, A. M. (1969) Strategies and models of selective attention. *Psychological Review* 76:282–99.

Treisman, A. M., and Riley, J. G. A. (1969) Is selective attention selective perception or selective response? A further test. *Journal of Experimental Psychology* 79:27–34.

Tulving, E. (1972) Episodic and semantic memory. In E. Tulving and W. Donaldson, eds., *Organization of memory.* New York: Academic Press.

Tulving, E., and Gold, C. (1963) Stimulus information and contextual information as determinants of tachistoscopic recognition of words. *Journal of Experimental Psychology* 66:319–327.

Tulving, E., and Pearlstone, Z. (1966) Availability vs. accessibility of information in memory for words. *Journal of Verbal Learning and Verbal Behavior* 5:381–91.

Tulving, E., and Thomson, D. M. (1973) Encoding specificity and retrieval processes in episodic memory. *Psychological Review* 80:352–373.

Tulving, E., and Watkins, M. J. (1975) Structure of memory traces. *Psychological Review* 82:261–75.

Turnbull, C. M. (1961) Some observations regarding the experiences and behavior of the BaMbuti pygmies. *American Journal of Psychology* 74:304–8.

Turvey, M. T. (1973) On peripheral and central processes in vision: Inferences from an information processing analysis of masking with patterned stimuli. *Psychological Review* 80:1–52.

Uexküll, J. J. von (1934) *Streifzüge durch die Umwelten von Tieren und Menschen.* Berlin: J. Springer.

Underwood, B. J. (1948a) Retroactive and proactive inhibition after five and forty-eight hours. *Journal of Experimental Psychology* 38:29–38.

_____. (1948b) 'Spontaneous recovery' of verbal associations. *Journal of Experimental Psychology* 38:429–39.

_____. (1949) Proactive inhibition as a function of time and degree of prior learning. *Journal of Experimental Psychology* 39:24–34.

_____. (1957) Interference and forgetting. *Psychological Review* 64:49–60.

_____. (1965) False recognition produced by implicit verbal responses. *Journal of Experimental Psychology* 70:122–29.

Underwood, G. (1976) *Attention and memory.* Oxford: Pergamon.

Van Zelst, R. H., and Kerr, W. A. (1954) Personality self-assessment of scientific and technical personnel. *Journal of Applied Psychology* 38:145–47.

Vella, E. J.; Butler, S. R.; and Glass, A. (1972) Electrical correlates of right hemisphere function. *Nature* 236:125–26.

Venables, P. H. (1964) Input dysfunction in schizophrenia. In B. A. Maher, ed., *Progress in experimental personality research,* vol. 1. New York: Academic Press.

Veroff, J. A. (1958) A scoring manual for the power motive. In J. W. Atkinson, ed., *Motives in fantasy, action, and society.* Princeton, N.J.: Van Nostrand.

Vitz, P. (1966) Affect as a function of stimulus variation. *Journal of Experimental Psychology* 71:74–79.

————. (1972) Preference for tones as a function of frequency (hertz) and intensity (decibels). *Perception and Psychophysics* 11:84–88.

Wada, J. A. (1949) A new method for the determination of the side of cerebral speech dominance. A preliminary report on the intracarotid injection of sodium amytal in man. *Medicine and Biology* 14:221–22.

Wallas, G. (1926) *The art of thought.* New York: Harcourt, Brace & World.

Walley, R. E., and Weiden, T. D. (1973) Lateral inhibition and cognitive masking: A neuropsychological theory of attention. *Psychological Review* 80:284–302.

Wanner, E. (1968) On remembering, forgetting, and understanding sentences: A study of the deep structure hypothesis. Ph.D. dissertation, Harvard University.

Ward, W. C. (1969) Creativity and environmental cues in nursery school children. *Developmental Psychology* 1:543–47.

Warren, R. M. (1970) Perceptual restoration of missing speech sounds. *Science* 167: 392–93.

Warren, R. M., and Warren, R. P. (1970) Auditory illusions and confusions. *Scientific American* 223:30–36.

Watkins, J. G., and Watkins, H. H. (1979) Ego states and hidden observers. *Journal of Altered States of Consciousness* 5:3–18.

Watkins, M. J. (1975) Inhibition in recall with extralist 'cues.' *Journal of Verbal Learning and Verbal Behavior* 14:294–303.

Watkins, M. J., and Tulving, E. (1975) Episodic memory: When recognition fails. *Journal of Experimental Psychology: General* 104:5–29.

Watson, J. B. (1913) Psychology as the behaviorist views it. *Psychological Review* 20: 158–77.

Waugh, N. C., and Norman, D. A. (1965) Primary memory. *Psychological Review* 72:89–104.

Weber, J. P. (1969) *The psychology of art.* New York: Delacorte.

Weimer, W. B. (1973) Psycholinguistics and Plato's paradoxes of the *Meno. American Psychologist* 28:15–33.

Werblin, F. S., and Dowling, J. E. (1969) Organization of the retina of the mudpuppy, *Necturus maculosus,* II. Intracellular recording. *Journal of Neurophysiology* 32:339–55.

Werner, H. (1948) *Comparative psychology of mental development.* New York: International Universities Press.

Wernicke, C. (1874) *Der aphasische Symptomen-complex.* Breslau: Franck & Weigert.

Wertheimer, M. (1912) Experimentelle Untersuchungen über das Sehen von Bewegung. *Zeitschrift für Psychologie* 61:161–265.

————. (1923) Untersuchungen zur Lehr von der Gestalt, II. *Psychologische Forschung* 4:301–50.

West, A.; Martindale, C.; and Sutton-Smith, B. (1980) Age trends in content and lexical characteristics of children's fantasy narrative productions. Paper presented at Eastern Psychological Association convention, Hartford, Connecticut.

West, A.; Martindale, C.; Hines, D.; and Roth, W. (1980) Marijuana-induced primary process content on the Thematic Apperception Test. Unpublished paper.

Wheeler, D. (1970) Processes in word recognition. *Cognitive Psychology* 1:59–85.

White, C. T. (1963) Temporal numerosity and the psychological unit of duration. *Psychological Monographs* 77:no. 12.

Whorf, B. L. (1956) *Language, thought, and reality.* New York: Wiley.

Wickelgren, W. A. (1976) Memory storage dynamics. In W. K. Estes, ed., *Handbook of learning and cognitive processes,* vol. 4. Hillsdale, N.J.: Erlbaum.

————. (1977) *Learning and memory.* Englewood Cliffs, N.J.: Prentice-Hall.

————. (1979a) Chunking and consolidation: A theoretical synthesis of semantic networks, configuring in conditioning, S-R versus cognitive learning, normal forgetting, the amnesic syndrome, and the hippocampal arousal system. *Psychological Review* 86:44–60.

————. (1979b) *Cognitive psychology.* Englewood Cliffs, N.J.: Prentice-Hall.

Wickelgren, W. A., and Corbett, A. T. (1977) Associative interference and retrieval dynamics in yes-no recall and recognition. *Journal of Experimental Psychology: Human Learning and Memory* 3:189–202.

Wickelgren, W. A., and Norman, D. A. (1966) Strength models and serial position in short-term recognition memory. *Journal of Mathematical Psychology* 3:316–47.

Wickens, D. D. (1973) Some characteristics of word encoding. *Memory and Cognition* 1:485–90.

Wild, C. (1965) Creativity and adaptive regression. *Journal of Personality and Social Psychology* 2:161–69.

Williams, P. J. (1964) Deductive reasoning in schizophrenia. *Journal of Abnormal and Social Psychology* 69:47–61.

Wilson, H. R., and Cowan, J. D. (1972) Excitatory and inhibitory interactions in localized populations of model neurons. *Biophysical Journal* 12:1–24.

Wood, C. C. (1975) Auditory and phonetic levels of processing in speech perception: Neurophysiological and information processing analysis. *Journal of Experimental Psychology: Human Perception and Performance* 1:3–21.

Wood, C. C.; Goff, W. R.; and Day, R. E. (1971) Auditory evoked potentials during speech perception. *Science* 173:1248–51.

Woodrow, H., and Lowell, F. (1916) Children's association frequency tables. *Psychological Monographs* 22:no. 5 (whole no. 97).

Worden, F. (1967) Attention and auditory electrophysiology. In E. Stellar and J. M. Sprague, eds., *Progress in physiological psychology*. London: Academic Press.

Worrell, J., and Worrell, L. (1965) Personality conflict, originality of response, and recall. *Journal of Consulting Psychology* 29:55–62.

Wundt, W. (1874) *Grundzüge der physiologischen Psychologie*. Leipzig: Engelmann.

_____. (1896) *Lectures on human and animal psychology*. New York: Macmillan.

Wyatt, D. F., and Campbell, D. T. (1951) On the liability of stereotype or hypothesis. *Journal of Abnormal and Social Psychology* 46:496–500.

Yarbus, A. L. (1967) *Eye movements and vision*. New York: Plenum.

Yaroush, R.; Sullivan, M. J.; and Ekstrand, B. R. (1971) The effect of sleep on memory. II: Differential effects of the first and second half of the night. *Journal of Experimental Psychology* 88:361–66.

Yasutani-Roshi (1967) Introductory lectures on Zen training. In P. Kapleau, ed., *The three pillars of zen: Teaching, practice, and enlightenment*. Boston: Beacon Press.

Yerkes, R. M., and Dodson, J. D. (1908) The relation of strength of stimulus to rapidity of habit formation. *Journal of Comparative and Neurological Psychology* 18:459–82.

Yund, E. W., and Efron, R. (1976) Dichotic competition of simultaneous tone bursts of different frequency: IV. Correlation with dichotic competition of speech signals. *Brain and Language* 3:246–54.

Zubek, J. P., ed. (1969) *Sensory deprivation: Fifteen years of research*. New York: Appleton-Century-Crofts.

Name index

Subject index

Free recall, 137, 139, 194
  modified, 232
  modified-modified, 233
  modified-modified-modified, 235
Frustration-regression hypothesis, 318
Function, 83, 342, 344, 350, 354
Function unit, 214, 344, 364
Functional fixity, 377–78

G

Galvanic skin conductance, 239–40
Galvanic skin response, 161
Ganglion cell, 40, 51–53, 55–56, 61–65
Gestalt principles, 18–20
Gnostic analyzers; *see also each analyzer*
  action system, 290, 293, 304
  auditory, 77–78
  emotional, 78
  function of, 75
  inputs to, 73, 75
  lateralization of, 271–72, 287
  level of processing, 79
  location of, 75, 269–71
  primary process thinking, 304
  selective attention, 164
  short-term memory, 135, 149, 154
  structure of, 73–74
  visual, 75–77
Gnostic area, 74
Gnostic unit, 73–74
  hallucination, 98–99
  proposition, 295, 301
  psychical element, 304
  thinking, 309
  unitary percept, 73, 99, 304
Goal
  and the action system, 293–94, 356
  and primary process thinking, 310
  and secondary process thinking, 305, 308
Goal unit, 293–94, 300
Grandmother cell, 39–40
Great mother goddesses, 315
Guilt, 242
Gustatory analyzer, 79

H

H.M., 94
Habit family hierarchy; *see also* Associative
    hierarchy
  and arousal, 252
  definition, 250
Habit strength, 250
Habituation, 166–69, 243, 261, 394–96, 405
Hallucination
  A-thinking, 296
  causes, 98–99
  disinhibition, 333
  lateral inhibition, 296
  neurotransmitters, 38–39
  off-units, 320
  in primary process states, 314, 333
  in psychosis, 333
  during sensory deprivation, 25, 316
  stroboscopic, 174–75, 318
  in thought-sampling experiments, 313
Hallucinogenic drugs, 39, 327
Hapax legomena percentage, 398

Heart rate, 239–40
Hedonic tone, 293
  adaptation level, 259–61
  arousal, 388
  arousal potential, 256–61, 385–88, 393–95
  the arousal system, 257, 263
  attention, 257, 385
  collative properties, 258–59
  ecological properties, 259
  mismatch, 250, 309
  psychophysical properties, 258
  the Wundt curve, 256–59, 393, 411
Hercules, 315
Hermaphroditic stage, 315
Heroic stage, 315
Heroin, 246
Hidden observer, 332
Hierarchical feature analysis
  in letter recognition, 50
  level of processing, 128
  in pandemonium system, 48–50
  in perception, 72
  in speech recognition, 77–78
Hippocampus
  connection to cognitive units, 89, 91, 94
  learning, 94
Hippolytus, 315
Horizontal association, 221
Horizontal cell, 55
Horseshoe crab, 57–59, 198
Hyacynthus, 315
Hypercomplex cell, 66
Hypnagogic state, 312–13, 317, 320, 333
Hypnosis, 319
  creativity, 379
  disinhibition, 332
  dissociation, 331
  hidden observers in, 332
  regression, 316–17
Hypothalamus, 265

I–J

Icarian imagery, 336
Iconic memory, 282
  duration of, 131–32
  locus of, 132
  masking, 131
  partial-report method, 130–31
Idea, 304
Illumination; *see* Creative inspiration
Image system, 302
Image unit
  archetype, 354
  semantic unit, 182
Imageless thought, 96, 303
Impact value; *see* Arousal potential
Incidental learning, 173, 216
Incongruity, 242, 385, 393, 395–96, 411
  and action, 289–90
  in narrative, 340, 345, 349
  in poetry, 397–98
  in scientific ideas, 404–5
Incubation
  definition, 369
  primed cognitive units, 373
I-ness; *see* Me-ness
Information processing, 3–4, 72–73, 84–86

*This book has been set linotype, 9 and 8 point
Optima, leaded 2 points. Chapter numbers are 30
point Benquiat Book and chapter titles are 18 point
Benquiat Book. The size of the type page is 30 picas
by 46½ picas.*